The UN
Security Council

FROM THE COLD WAR TO THE 21ST CENTURY

EDITED BY
DAVID M. MALONE

LYNNE
RIENNER
PUBLISHERS

BOULDER
LONDON

Published in the United States of America in 2004 by
Lynne Rienner Publishers, Inc.
1800 30th Street, Boulder, Colorado 80301
www.rienner.com

and in the United Kingdom by
Lynne Rienner Publishers, Inc.
3 Henrietta Street, Covent Garden, London WC2E 8LU

Library of Congress Cataloging-in-Publication Data
The UN Security Council : from the Cold War to the 21st century / David M. Malone, editor
  p. cm.—(A project of the International Peace Academy)
  Includes bibliographical references and index.
  ISBN 1-58826-215-4 (hc : alk. paper)
  ISBN 1-58826-240-5 (pb : alk. paper)
  1. United Nations. Security Council. I. Malone, David, 1954– II. Series.
JZ5006.5.U545 2004
341.23'23—dc22

                                                              2003058572

British Cataloguing in Publication Data
A Cataloguing in Publication record for this book
is available from the British Library.

Printed and bound in the United States of America

The paper used in this publication meets the requirements
of the American National Standard for Permanence of
Paper for Printed Library Materials Z39.48-1992.

  5 4 3 2 1

For Thomas M. Franck
Judge, scholar, teacher extraordinaire
Friend and mentor to many of those involved in this volume
With much admiration and affection

CONTENTS

ACKNOWLEDGMENTS

A volume of this scope could not have been undertaken without extensive collaboration and assistance. First and foremost, my thanks go to Sebastian von Einsiedel, my coauthor on this volume's chapter relating to Haiti and my associate in editing the volume. He has been tireless throughout. The other authors and I have benefited greatly from his incisive comments on our texts. He proved exemplary in keeping us all on track, meeting deadlines, and covering the main bases set out for each chapter. In the process, he has become exceptionally knowledgeable about the UN Security Council. It has been a privilege to work with him.

Beyond providing an excellent chapter, my colleague Simon Chesterman supported Sebastian and me throughout with excellent editorial advice. Further welcome editorial advice was provided by Dr. Nicholas Wheeler of the University of Wales at Aberystwyth. I am most grateful to both.

Next, I would like to thank all of the authors for contributing, within a tight time frame, to this venture. They were good-humored in addressing comments on their drafts and welcomed the multiple, sometimes clashing perspectives offered to them at our authors' meeting. They also provided me with valuable suggestions on the aims, shape, and ultimate contents of the volume as a whole.

During our authors' meeting, we were joined by a number of extremely helpful friends of this project, including Sir Brian Urquhart; Sir Jeremy Greenstock, permanent representative of the UK to the UN; Ambassador Adolfo Aguilar Zinser, permanent representative of Mexico to the UN; Ambassador Wegger Strømmen of Norway; Professor Thomas M. Franck of New York University and of the International Court of Justice in The Hague; Professor Lori Damrosch of Columbia University; Ambassador Nancy Soderberg of the International Crisis Group; and Nicole Lannegrace, Joseph Stephanides, and Sam Daws of the UN Secretariat. Their contributions helped shape our approach to the volume and were greatly valued by us all. Kishore Mahbubani, Paul Heinbecker, and Hubert Wurth, the permanent representatives respectively of Singapore, Canada, and Luxembourg to the UN (the first two are contributors to the volume), hosted the authors' meeting; I am most grateful to them.

This project could not have been planned or completed without generous research funding from the Ford Foundation, the U.S. Institute of Peace, the government of Sweden, and the core support the International Peace Academy (IPA) receives from the governments of Denmark and Norway.

Much of my own work on the volume was undertaken during a residency at the Diplomatic Academy in Vienna, Austria, the oldest such institution in the world, and surely the most distinguished. I am deeply grateful to its director, Ernst Sucharipa, and to his colleagues for this honor and pleasure.

My writing on the Security Council started at the time of my doctoral studies under the supervision of Sir Adam Roberts at Oxford University. I remain deeply grateful to him and to his colleagues at the university's outstanding Centre of International Studies for their encouragement and active help. My reflection on the Council's evolution has continued during my years at the IPA, particularly through the teaching Professor Franck invited me to share with him at New York University Law School, a genuinely exciting environment. To him and to our students, I am much indebted for great wisdom on the one hand, and probing questioning on the other. Professor Michael Doyle of Princeton University, recently a senior adviser to the UN Secretary-General, has for the past ten years in his written work and in many other ways shed light on the work of the Council on Cambodia and elsewhere. I and all of the authors are indebted to him.

I am grateful to the board of the IPA and to its chair, Rita Hauser, Esq., herself a keen observer of the Council, for allowing me to undertake this time-consuming project. Of all nongovernmental entities, the IPA probably enjoys the closest continuous association with the Security Council, but this only made clear to us how much work would be involved in trying to distill in these pages its essence over the past fifteen years. UN Secretary-General Kofi Annan, honorary chair of the IPA board, offered strong support for this project from its outset. To him and his Secretariat colleagues, my warm thanks.

Finally, my IPA colleagues have been very patient while this project absorbed much of my attention. They have all contributed to whatever success it achieves by making it possible for me to devote significant time to it. I have never worked with a more able or dedicated team. Their perspectives are reflected in myriad ways throughout the volume and daily enrich my understanding of the many crosscutting themes and the multilateral institutions on which they work.

—*David M. Malone*

The UN
Security Council

1

Introduction

DAVID M. MALONE

Why this volume now? Much has changed for the United Nations Security Council since the end of the Cold War. Its decisions—largely improvised and inconsistent though they may be—have, for good and ill, profoundly affected international relations. Among other things, the Council's decisions have eroded conceptions of state sovereignty firmly held during the Cold War years, altering the way in which many of us see the relationship between state and citizen the world over.

Two crises in international relations centered on Iraq, in 1990–1991 and in 2002–2003, have led to two totally different views of the UN in general and the Council in particular. Following the first, marked by the mobilization of many countries to eject Iraqi occupation forces from Kuwait under a strong Council mandate, extraordinary and unjustified euphoria took hold among practitioners and some scholars about the potential of the UN to serve as the agent for the "new world order" advertised by President George H. W. Bush in 1990. At the time of the second crisis, obituaries were written for the UN, as well as for the idea of international order that it represents. In both cases, these extreme views of the UN suggested that international practitioner, media, and scholarly opinion was not rooted in a sound understanding of what the Security Council is good at and what it is bad at. Moreover, there was a general failure to understand how the Council continues to coexist with an older form of international relations still based on sovereign states pursuing their various national interests. This volume seeks to give a rounded assessment of the strengths and weaknesses of the Council as an institution. It also seeks to identify what is novel and what may be enduring in its approaches to a widening agenda of international security issues since the end of the Cold War.

Given the centrality of individual state interests at the UN, however unpalatable to some, the question arises as to whether the Council, in terms of the perceived legitimacy of its decisions, can be more than the sum of its parts. Perhaps the key driver in Council decisions today, both actively and passively, is the agenda of the United States. This has raised questions about the extent to which the Council can resist (beyond the Iraq issue) the "pull" of U.S. policy preferences. As of mid-2003, there is also concern that the Council could find itself confined to mandating UN humanitarian, peacekeeping, and transitional government mop-up operations after U.S.-led military interventions. This tension—between military and political power and the power of legitimacy—runs through this volume.

Aim and Scope

It is hard enough to take a snapshot of the Council, with its long agenda, opaque proceedings, and uncertain impact on international relations, at any given time. Perhaps for this reason, the Council has not been addressed often other than through the lens of international law, a particular crisis, or one individual's memoirs. Sidney Bailey and Sam Daws's magisterial volume on the Council's procedures, which also covers with great acuity a number of substantive issues, is the principal reference tool for students of the Council.[1] Other brief but incisive overviews were offered by Sir Brian Urquhart and the late Sir Anthony Parsons in the early 1990s, but they are now mostly of historical interest.[2] The Council today displays elements of continuity with the Council described so admirably by Andrew Boyd in *Fifteen Men on a Powder Keg* more than thirty years ago, not least with respect to the salience of national interest within it.[3] However, with the geopolitical setting completely altered by the end of the Cold War, the issues addressed by the Council and the way in which they are addressed have evolved radically. Furthermore, the Council occasionally today features female ambassadors, most recently including Madeleine Albright of the United States and Patricia Durant of Jamaica.

By slicing and dicing in many different ways the Council's decisions and activities, the substantive themes of its work, and the institutional developments in its life, this volume attempts to assess its objectives and performance during the turbulent, frequently hyperactive years it has experienced in the post–Cold War era. The contributors represent a mix of practitioners, many of whom have served on the Council or sought to implement its mandates; knowledgeable academics, a number of whom have published extensively on related topics; and members of the community of nongovernmental organizations (NGOs) interacting frequently with the Council.

As in any endeavor of this type, even an ambitious and long one such as this, choices were required. The reader might wonder why we address certain trends and not others—for example, why we do not offer a chapter on developments in peacekeeping. As topics like this one are addressed in a number of chapters from a variety of perspectives, we decided that offering a synthesis chapter covering them risked repetition. In other instances, we thought that a particular phenomenon or case, no matter how important or interesting in its own right, shed little more light on the workings and aims of the Council than did some other case offered in the volume. Accordingly, while we do present in Chapter 7 a thoughtful exploration by Elizabeth Cousens of the Council's tentative and unconvincing approach to conflict prevention, we do not devote a chapter to peacebuilding (or "nation-building" as U.S. government officials sometimes refer to it) because a number of our case chapters deal with the inadequacies of the Council's strategies to date for sustaining the peace it sometimes helps to establish. As for Iraq, its importance has been such within the Council that it is addressed in many of the chapters, centrally so in those on the use of force, weapons of mass destruction, and sanctions.

Our Approach

Our approach is not theoretically driven. When the contributors met in January 2003, they debated key issues pertaining to the Council, joined by a number of Council ambassadors. Helpfully urged on by Thomas M. Franck, we did consider a number of possible models for the Council's role in international relations: an Athenian model, essentially consultative; a Congress of Vienna conclave model under which the Council is devoted to norm-development, as many in Washington would have us believe is the Council's most characteristic trait today; and a Roman model allowing for mobilizational governance—under this scheme, the Council serves as a senate constraining the emperor. In the post–Cold War era the Roman model may apply best, with the U.S. president cast as emperor, but contemporary history is proving sufficiently fluid that we were not persuaded that any such theoretical approach would be profitable for this venture. We are content to let our research and conclusions serve as theory fodder for others.

One snare for any writer on the Security Council relates to its identity. As a matter of convenience, authors sometimes refer to the Council when they mean its members, a majority of its members, or only some of its members. Another relates to assessments of UN "success" and "relevance." Differences of appreciation will be clear throughout the volume and in its conclusions, being defined largely in the eye of individual beholders.

The table of contents makes clear our approach to the story. The first section focuses on factors in Council decisionmaking that are new in the post–Cold War era, often drivers of decisionmaking such as the humanitarian impulse or terrorism. We move on to focus for several chapters on one key change: the greater resort to the provisions of Chapter VII of the UN

Charter allowing for the enforcement measures of sanctions and the use of force. We then offer ten chapters covering evolving institutional factors affecting the Council, from the role of NGOs to pressures for Council reform. In order to illustrate a number of these themes, we offer eleven brief case studies that we believe shed particular light on new approaches by the Council. In the final section, we seek to offer an interpretation and an integration of points raised in all these chapters, doing justice to none of the contributors singly, but aiming to offer one possible synthesis of their views. In neither this introduction nor in the final section do we follow the order of the table of contents; rather, we seek to isolate key crosscutting themes.

The End of the Cold War at the UN

How did the changes in the Council in the post–Cold War era come about? The Council initially viewed its role as preventing a third world war. As the Cold War came to define global politics, the Council moved to tackle prevention of regional conflicts (often between client states or proxies of the superpowers) from spilling into a global conflagration. In this, the Council made a helpful contribution on several occasions.

One important signal of the decisive thaw in the Cold War was a noticeable improvement in the climate among the permanent five (P-5) members of the UN Security Council as of 1986. The first evidence of the relaxation in East-West tensions within the Council was the cooperative manner in which these countries discussed options for the position of UN Secretary-General as Javier Pérez de Cuéllar's first term drew to a close in 1986.

In late 1986, Sir John Thomson, the UK permanent representative to the UN, took the initiative to call together the P-5 ambassadors, at his residence away from UN headquarters and delegation offices, for an informal discussion on how they could contribute to an early end of the murderous Iran-Iraq War.[4] The others welcomed this initiative, although China apparently remained reserved over P-5 activism for some time. A system of regular P-5 informal meetings soon took hold. These meetings helped anticipate and defuse conflicts among the five and allowed them to exchange notes on their national positions respecting various crises of the hour, if not formally to coordinate their positions.

As it turned out, the P-5 agreed without much difficulty to a second term for the incumbent, who in January 1987 challenged them publicly to tackle resolution of the Iran-Iraq War.[5] As of mid-1987, Security Council proposals for a cease-fire, monitored by a small UN observer mission, were making serious headway. The post–Cold War era, initially such a hopeful one, had started at the UN.

Soviet president Mikhail Gorbachev's celebrated *Pravda* and *Izvestia* article of September 17, 1987, seeking "wider use of . . . the institution of UN military observers and UN peacekeeping forces in disengaging the troops of warring sides, observing cease-fires and armistice agreements," called for the P-5 to become "guarantors" of international security.[6] However, P-5 cooperation required some time to take root.[7]

Converging perspectives among the P-5 on a number of international crises, particularly on the need to disentangle the superpowers from them, allowed the Council to initiate action toward settlements. Between 1988 and late 1989 it established five peacekeeping operations to assist the settlement of conflicts in Afghanistan (UNGOMAP) and between Iran and Iraq (UNIIMOG), to implement linked agreements on the withdrawal of Cuban troops in Angola (UNAVEM I) and independence for Namibia (UNTAG), and to help the resolution of three conflicts in Central America (ONUCA).

While the end of the Cold War had to some extent already unlocked the Council's potential to contribute to the resolution of serious problems of international peace and security, drawing on newfound cooperation between the superpowers, the Council's approach to conflicts remained relatively cautious until the Iraqi invasion of Kuwait in August 1990.

Operation Desert Storm and Its Immediate Aftermath

This event, and Iraq's formal annexation of Kuwait only days later, led the Council to adopt a mandate authorizing the use of force by a coalition of member states.[8] Council decisions on Iraq, including measures adopted following the March 1991 end of hostilities to bring about the partial disarmament of Iraq, to encourage protection of Iraqi minorities, and to provide humanitarian assistance to the Kurdish population, were important not only in their own right but also because they proved precedential in many respects.[9]

The success of the coalition's military campaign against the Baghdad regime, in retrospect, appears to have induced an era of euphoria in the Council, an era that could not have arisen during the Cold War.[10] Having successfully tackled a conceptually straightforward challenge to international peace and security in the form of Saddam Hussein's attack on Kuwait, the Council now waded into the murkier waters of civil wars and intercommunal strife, with which it had little experience. The Council seemed to believe that because enforcement of its decisions against Iraq had been successfully carried out, the constraints on and limitations of UN peacekeeping had fallen away. This era of euphoria can be described as lasting roughly between March 6, 1991, the date of Resolution 686, on the end of hostilities in the Gulf region, and October 13, 1993, when the

Council adopted Resolution 873 following the failure to deploy successfully the UN Mission in Haiti (UNMIH)—this only a week after the deaths of
eighteen U.S. Army Rangers in Somalia had seriously undermined
prospects for the sustainability there of UNOSOM II.[11] The unique circumstances of the Gulf crisis, notably the threat that supplies of petroleum, the
lifeblood of the major Western economies, could be cut off, did not recur.
Consequently, neither did the unity of purpose that characterized international response to Iraq's attack on Kuwait. During this period of barely thirty-one months, the Council accelerated the pace of its work, adopting 185
resolutions, versus 685 in the preceding forty-six years of UN history, and
launching fifteen new peacekeeping operations as compared to seventeen in
the previous forty-six years.[12]

Building on an emerging view in much of the world that the UN
Security Council was at last coming into its own, the first ever Security
Council summit was convened January 31, 1992, to discuss new orienta-
tions and activities for the Council. The summit's statement, the high-water
mark of enthusiasm over a purported new international order, noted (optimistically) that "the Security Council has begun to fulfill more effectively
its primary responsibility for the maintenance of international peace and
security."[13]

Recently elected Secretary-General Boutros Boutros-Ghali responded with a wide-ranging, thoughtful, and ambitious document, *An Agenda
for Peace*. This report advocated, inter alia, consideration in certain circumstances of a "preventive deployment" of UN peacekeepers to forestall hostilities known to be looming; and, when circumstances warranted, the use of force by the UN itself rather than by coalitions of member
states.[14] *An Agenda for Peace* noted that peacekeeping had been carried
out "hitherto" with the consent of all parties, hinting that this might not
be necessary in the future. It seemed to assume a quantum leap in the
willingness by member states to support UN action in the peace and
security field.

By January 1995, following serious setbacks in Bosnia and the inability to stop the genocide in Rwanda, the UN's most disastrous failure in
decades, Boutros-Ghali, in the *Supplement to an Agenda for Peace* (more
of a reassessment than an addendum), was sounding a more "realistic"
note, drawing lessons from the UN's experience on the ground over previous years: "Neither the Security Council nor the Secretary-General at present has the capacity to deploy, direct, command or control [enforcement]
operations except perhaps on a very limited scale. . . . It would be folly to
attempt to do so at the present time when the Organization is resource-
starved and hard pressed to handle the less demanding peacemaking and
peacekeeping responsibilities entrusted to it."[15]

Major Trends

Emergence of the Permanent Five

The much improved climate among the P-5 in the post–Cold War era can be gauged by the sharp decline in the use of the veto: only 12 substantive vetoes were invoked from January 1990 to June 2003, compared to 193 during the first forty-five years of the UN's history.[16] Veto threats remained highly relevant, as the Council's dealings on Kosovo in 1999 and Iraq in early 2003 make clear, but very few issues seriously divided the P-5 after 1987 (the Arab-Israeli conflict remaining one of them). The ability and disposition of the five permanent members—those holding veto power—to cooperate with each other seriously diminished the margin for maneuver of other Council members, as several chapters in this volume make clear (such as Chapter 16, on Council working methods, by Susan Hulton, and several case studies by a variety of contributors). Some of them, including Finland and Canada, had in earlier times developed skills and occupied political space as "helpful fixers"; or, in the case of some developing nations, had learned how to play the permanent members against each other, greatly amplifying the voice and enhancing the apparent influence of the nonaligned movement within the Council.[17]

Soon, however, elected members were grumbling that they were systematically marginalized, a complaint given more weight by a tendency of the Secretariat to consult privately with some or all of the P-5 before advancing recommendations to the Council as a whole. Chapter 17, on relations between permanent and elected members of the Council, by Kishore Mahbubani, an ambassador representing a nonpermanent member of the Council, makes clear why this dynamic is grating and may have proved counterproductive over time. Tacit collusion between the P-5 and the Secretariat was aggravated, from the perspective of other members, by the growing resort to "informal consultations" for decisionmaking purposes rather than the open Council meetings that had served as the principal forum for Council decisionmaking in earlier decades.[18] High-handed behavior by the P-5 reached a zenith in December 2002, when the United States forced the Council presidency to reverse a Council decision on access to a report by UNMOVIC and inspectors of the International Atomic Energy Agency, insisting on differentiated arrangements for permanent and elected members, a highly undignified (and unusually public) process widely denounced, not least by Kofi Annan.[19]

The P-5 do not "manage" the Council, although they do dominate it, not least by monopolizing most of the drafting. Scheduling is coordinated by the presidency, and individual agenda items have increasingly been managed by limited-membership steering groups, often "Groups of

Friends" (generally but not always composed of Council and recent past Council members), who along with the Secretary-General propose options and preferred courses of action to the Council as a whole. Teresa Whitfield examines this important, often controversial, recent development in Chapter 21.

The Permanent One

It would be misleading to suggest that the P-5 are not only often cohesive but also equal. It has been clear for some years, perhaps mostly strikingly so since the Dayton Accords of late 1995, that the United States has emerged not only as the sole remaining superpower but also as the principal driver of the Council's agenda and decisions, passively and actively. This development introduced new challenges into management of the Council's goals, work, and decisions, for both good and ill, as discussed by Nathan Miller and Frederick Rawski in Chapter 24, on the U.S. relationship with the Security Council, sometimes described elsewhere as an effort at dual containment.[20]

An Expanding Agenda: Substantive Innovation

The post–Cold War period has been marked by the Council's disposition to tackle many more conflicts than it had been able to earlier, when it was stymied by East-West animosities and the plethora of vetoes (cast and threatened) by the permanent members. The end of the Cold War unlocked implementation of the Council's earlier decisions on Namibia, as documented in Chapter 27 in Cedric Thornberry's gripping account of this early episode of UN-controlled transitional arrangements. Since 1990 there have been momentous shifts in the Council's approach to conflict and its resolution. Factors held by the Council as constituting a threat to international peace expanded to include a coup against a democratically elected regime (documented in Chapter 31, on Haiti, coauthored by Sebastian von Einsiedel and myself, and in Chapter 5, on democratization, by Gregory Fox); a range of humanitarian catastrophes (discussed in Chapter 30, on Bosnia, by Mats Berdal, and in Chapter 35, on East Timor, by Stewart Eldon), particularly those generating large outflows of displaced persons and refugees, internally and internationally (as discussed in Chapter 3 by Thomas Weiss); and acts of terrorism (as cataloged in Chapter 6 by Edward Luck).[21] Steven Ratner, in Chapter 37, on the role of the Council in international law, explores some of the relevant issues.

This, in turn, allowed the Council to act on a range of conflicts, mostly internal in nature, which it most likely would have avoided in the past, when the Cold War antagonists often played out their hostility through regional proxies and were prepared to frustrate Council involvement. These included conflicts in El Salvador (discussed in Chapter 28 by Blanca Antonini); Sierra Leone (detailed in Chapter 33 by John Hirsch); the former Yugoslavia (dealt with in this volume most directly by Mats Berdal in Chapter 30, and Paul Heinbecker in Chapter 34); Mozambique (dissected in Chapter 29 by Aldo Ajello and Patrick Wittmann); and Rwanda (discussed in Chapter 32 by Howard Adelman and Astri Suhrke, and enriched by separate insider accounts from Colin Keating and Ibrahim Gambari in Chapters 32.1 and 32.2). In many of these conflicts, the Security Council found itself contending with armed nonstate actors, a new phenomenon addressed here in Chapter 8 by Andrés Franco. The Council's decisions in the 1990s proved highly innovative in shaping the normative framework for international relations and stimulated several radical legal developments at the international level, notably the creation of international criminal tribunals for the former Yugoslavia and Rwanda in 1993 and 1994 respectively. This greatly intensified pressure for a more universal International Criminal Court (ICC), a statute for which was adopted at a diplomatic conference in Rome in 1998. These developments are covered in this volume by ICC judge Philippe Kirsch, John Holmes, and Mora Johnson in Chapter 19. As Cameron Hume argues in Chapter 38, the Council will have to continue to be creative in adapting to new challenges posed by failing states and transnational threats.

Interstate conflicts did not altogether cease to break out, as Chapter 36 by Adekeye Adebajo, on the Ethiopia-Eritrea conflict of the late 1990s, demonstrates. However, with very few exceptions, the wreckage of the Cold War was successfully addressed once the superpower confrontation came to an end. Certain conflicts of an earlier era, such as the Israeli-Arab dispute, addressed by Bruce Jones in Chapter 26, and the worrying tensions over Kashmir, still bedevil the international agenda, but they are rare. Peter Wallensteen and Patrik Johansson, in Chapter 2, make clear that, contrary to media and public perceptions, conflict is on the decline and there are few reasons to harbor nostalgia for the nuclear terror–induced "stability" of the Cold War.

An intriguing trend relates to the Council's role in mandating UN roles in the oversight of territories. This occurred not only in Namibia and Eastern Slavonia but also, in a less comprehensive form, in Cambodia and Bosnia. It reached its zenith in Kosovo, touched upon in Chapter 34 by Paul Heinbecker, and East Timor, covered in Chapter 35 by Stewart Eldon and supplemented in Chapter 35.1 with a separate view from the field by Ian Martin. The Council's role in mandating such "virtual trusteeships" is discussed in Chapter 15 in a crosscutting manner by Simon Chesterman.

Nevertheless, in the late 1990s, serious tensions resurfaced in the Council over issues relating to state sovereignty, legitimacy of the use of force, and the growing incidence of unilateralism by some major UN members. Differences crystallized in 1998 and 1999 over conflicting objectives and approaches among the P-5 to Iraq and Kosovo. While discord over Kosovo was contained by agreement on the parameters of a UN-administered transitional regime in this territory, the agreement was achieved at the price of lack of clarity over future constitutional arrangements and could hold the seeds of future problems. Iraq remained highly nettlesome, with the P-5 coming together on key resolutions such as 1284 and 1441, but ultimately deadlocked by mid-March 2003, when military action against Iraq was initiated by the United States and several of its allies.

The ebb and flow of Council business has tended to obscure the extent to which its decisions cumulatively since 1990 have undermined rigid conceptions of state sovereignty and eroded the position of governments claiming the sovereign right to conduct themselves at home free of international interference, even on matters that could undermine domestic security and the stability not only of their own countries but eventually of neighboring ones (for example, by massively abusing human rights or engaging in ethnic engineering or cleansing).

Chapter VII of the UN Charter
Prior to 1990 there was little resort to those provisions in the UN Charter relating to the coercive measures the Council can invoke. Mandatory sanctions were imposed by the Council in only two instances: Southern Rhodesia in 1966 and South Africa in 1977. A naval blockade to enforce the Rhodesia sanctions regime was authorized but rapidly failed once it became clear that force would not be used to back it up. The use of force itself was explicitly authorized only in the case of Korea in the early 1950s (in the absence from the Council of the Soviet Union), and in a much more tentative and limited way in the Congo in the early 1960s. The latter episode was not widely considered a success, confirming in many the view that the use of force should be avoided by the Council in its decisionmaking.

With the new mood among the P-5, the Council, with several intractable conflicts on its agenda, moved rapidly in the post–Cold War era to impose its will on a range of international actors through a dizzying array of sanctions regimes (occasionally backed up by naval blockades) discussed in Chapter 11 by David Cortright and George Lopez and through the frequent authorization of force, both by troops under UN command and by coalitions of member states. In Chapter 13, David Angell adds a personal comment on Canada's efforts to ensure a degree of enforcement of the sanctions regime against UNITA in Angola. New issues, such as internal disarmament, became subject to enforcement, notably in Iraq as discussed in admirably dispassionate fashion by Pascal Teixeira da Silva in Chapter

14. Adam Roberts discusses in Chapter 9 the links between the use of force, international law, and the authority of the security council, while Frank Berman dissects in Chapter 10 perhaps the most famous of the enforcement resolutions, 678 of November 1990, on Iraq. Chapter VII decisions occasionally gave rise to significant tensions among the permanent five, as documented in Chapter 12 by Peter van Walsum in a personal account of his two years as chair of the Council's Iraq sanctions committee. Much of this struggle unfolded privately, although insightful reporting by Colum Lynch of the *Washington Post* and Carola Hoyos of the *Financial Times* occasionally revealed it through the media.

While the Council's assertive exploration of the Chapter VII provisions initially seemed to hold out the hope that a new world order could be constructed with the UN at its center, many of the coercive strategies of the Council failed because of the application of insufficient or inappropriate resources, wishful thinking, and a flight from reality that seemed to overtake the Council in the years 1992–1995. Doubtless a sense of individual responsibility of member states was seriously undermined by the mechanics and compromises of committee decisionmaking, but several instances of spectacular Council failure seem no less lurid years later than they did in the headlines of the day, notably those arising from the UN's involvement in Bosnia, Somalia, and Rwanda.

Because of a greater resort to the Council to authorize the use of force internationally, but also because of a noticeable tendency to avoid doing so in certain cases, arguments have grown that, even beyond narrowly constructed cases of self-defense, explicit Council authorization for the use of force may no longer be required, however politically useful it can prove.

Institutional Factors
During its early decades, the Council had few institutional partners. This has changed radically since the early 1990s. Today, due to limited resources and for reasons of substantive burden-sharing, the Council's decisions often foresee cooperation with regional organizations (broadly defined to include such institutions as NATO as well as more classic regional organizations as originally envisaged in Chapter VIII of the UN Charter). This trend is discussed in Chapter 20 by Shepard Forman and Andrew Grene. NGOs have also come to play an important role, although a largely unheralded one, in the Council's life. James Paul discusses aspects of this development in Chapter 25, as does Joanna Weschler in Chapter 4, on human rights in the life of the Council.

The relationship between the Secretary-General and the Security Council is explored in Chapter 18 by Marrack Goulding, the UN's premier negotiator for many years, who contrasts the tenure of Secretary-General

Boutros Boutros-Ghali (1992–1996) with that of Secretary-General Javier Pérez de Cuéllar (1982–1991). He (and Mahbubani) make clear that the Secretariat's relationship with the Council is often intermediated by the P-5. In Chapter 22, Connie Peck offers an account of that increasingly ubiquitous figure in international relations, the special representative of the UN Secretary-General, mostly responsible for overseeing complex peace operations or mediation efforts in the field. The Council's relationship with these individuals has varied in form and substance but is increasingly recognized as important. In a Council retreat during December 2002, extensive discussion occurred on the function and importance of appropriate incumbents.[22]

With the more active role played by the Council in international relations has come pressure for Council reform under several headings: its working methods, composition, and the veto all came under heavy criticism as of the early 1990s. However, pressure for reform has achieved little change beyond the Council's increasingly open working methods, as discussed by Bardo Fassbender in Chapter 23, and there is little prospect of early agreement among the membership on significant change in years to come, not least because it is widely accepted that there is a tradeoff between expansion of the Council, to achieve a more representative composition, and effectiveness of the body, which continues to be much prized by a number of powerful governments. While most countries have developed a scheme for Council reform perfectly tailored to maximizing their own situation with respect to a reformed Council, their preferred fallback is not some other country's scheme but the status quo.

The Media

The media play an important role in the life of the Council, often producing international pressure for action to address man-made disasters or to head off cataclysms, including those concerning North Korea and Iraq and potentially involving weapons of mass destruction. The Cable News Network (CNN) has often been described as the Council's "sixteenth member," and its UN bureau has done much through its weekly program "Diplomatic License" to make the Council and its decisions better understood. The British Broadcasting Corporation (BBC) has consistently sought to interpret insightfully iconic images of Council ambassadors meeting in the fabled Council chamber and then delivering themselves of competitive but often misleading (and soon forgotten) pronouncements on the proceedings.

The media influence the Council most strongly through its member states. Governments react to public pressure, largely shaped by the media. Governments mostly like to tax and spend. By and large, they are averse to risk. Thus, when international crises develop and public pressure to address them builds through the media, a default option for governments is to delegate to multilateral organizations such as the UN the responsibility to respond.

That said, media reporting of the Council itself is mostly reactive and event-driven. The Council's "home" broadsheet, the *New York Times,* has given it considerable attention, often in commendable depth through the writing of Barbara Crossette and James Traub. The Paris daily *Le Monde* has also done an excellent job of looking beyond the wire service headlines, and the *Financial Times* has fielded talented correspondents at the UN.[23] However, there may not be much more to be said, and we consequently do not offer a chapter specifically covering this topic.

Envoi

In order to set the stage, Peter Wallensteen, one of the world's foremost thinkers on both the nature and the pattern of violent conflicts today, together with Patrik Johansson, discusses in Chapter 2 the trends in Council decisions in recent years. Thereafter, as outlined above, we address a number of individual factors and cases relevant to the Council's performance in the post–Cold War era. Our conclusions aim to offer a range of broader thematic observations.

Notes

1. Sydney D. Bailey and Sam Daws, *The Procedure of the Security Council,* 3rd ed. (Oxford: Clarendon, 1998).

2. Brian Urquhart, "The UN and International Security after the Cold War," and Anthony Parsons, "The UN and the National Interests of States," in Adam Roberts and Benedict Kingsbury, eds., *United Nations, Divided World: The UN's Roles in International Relations,* 2nd ed. (Oxford: Clarendon, 1993), pp. 81–124.

3. Andrew Boyd, *Fifteen Men on a Powder Keg: A History of the UN Security Council* (New York: Stein and Day, 1971).

4. For an account of evolving dynamics within the UN Security Council, particularly among the P-5, 1986–1990, see Cameron Hume, *The United Nations, Iran, and Iraq: How Peacemaking Changed* (Bloomington: University of Indiana Press, 1994), esp. pp. 81–82, 88–102.

5. SG/SM/3956, January 13, 1987, p. 5.

6. Mikhail S. Gorbachev, "Reality and the Guarantees of a Secure World," *FBIS Daily Report: Soviet Union,* September 17, 1987, pp. 23–28.

7. Interviews with Alexander M. Belonogov, permanent representative of the USSR to the UN, 1986–1990, and John Thomson, permanent representative of the UK to the UN, 1982–1987, conducted respectively in Ottawa on March 20, 1996, and in Princeton on April 15, 1996.

8. Resolution 678, November 29, 1990. Operation Desert Storm originally was confined to aerial attacks on Iraq. The broader military campaign was designated as Operation Desert Saber, but the moniker Desert Storm eventually displaced it.

9. A number of the measures adopted by France, the UK, the United States, and their allies, particularly in northern Iraq (to protect, through a no-fly zone, and provide assistance to the Kurds), were initiated without explicit Council authorization. These measures were, however, not then seriously challenged within the Council. Some of the humanitarian activities of Operation Provide Comfort were eventually taken over by the UN.

10. Contributing importantly to the unity of the international community in confronting Saddam Hussein in 1990 was an impressive diplomatic campaign by President George H. W. Bush, his secretary of state, James Baker, and their skilled U.S. ambassador at the UN, Thomas Pickering, to assemble a formidable diplomatic coalition to this end. These conditions were not reproduced in 2002 when the United States sought to increase pressure on the Baghdad regime.

11. Resolution 873 reimposed sanctions on Haiti.

12. During this period, the UN launched the following new peacekeeping operations: UNIKOM in Kuwait (1991), MINURSO for Western Sahara (1991), ONUSAL in El Salvador (1991), UNAVEM II in Angola (1991), UNAMIC in Cambodia (1991), UNPROFOR in the former Yugoslavia (1992), UNTAC in Cambodia (1992), UNOSOM in Somalia (1992), ONUMOZ in Mozambique (1992), UNOSOM II (1993), UNOMUR in Uganda-Rwanda (1993), UNOMIG in Georgia (1993), UNOMIL in Liberia (1993), UNMIH in Haiti (1993), and UNAMIR in Rwanda (1993). In addition, the Council authorized the U.S.-led Unified Task Force in Somalia (UNITAF, 1992), and a UNPROFOR presence, in effect a preventive deployment, in Macedonia (1992).

13. S/23500, January 31, 1992, p. 2.

14. A/47/277, June 17, 1992.

15. A/50/60, January 3, 1995, p. 18.

16. All vetoes since May 1990 were by the United States (mostly on the Israeli-Palestinian struggle), except for two by Russia (one over the financing of UNFICYP in Cyprus and another over sanctions against Serbia), and two by China (both on peacekeeping operations, one in Guatemala, the other in the former Yugoslav Republic of Macedonia, although each was motivated by a Taiwan connection). This count does not include vetoes on the selection of the UN Secretary-General, mostly registered during nonpublic sessions of the Council.

17. During periods when seven members of the nonaligned movement sit in the Council, they theoretically possess a "sixth veto." By all withholding consent simultaneously, they can block resolutions. However, the cohesion of the movement has proved weak within the Council in recent years (although it was displayed to a degree in March 2003 on Iraq).

18. For an account of the evolving dynamics within the Security Council, see Hume, *The United Nations, Iran, and Iraq;* and C. S. R. Murthy, "Change and Continuity in the Functioning of the Security Council Since the End of the Cold War," *International Studies* 32, no. 4 (October–December 1995): 423.

19. Julia Preston, "U.S. Is First to Get a Copy of Report on Iraqi Weapons," *New York Times,* December 10, 2002.

20. See Simon Chesterman and David M. Malone, "High Stakes: The Fate of the Security Council," *International Herald Tribune,* January 27, 2003.

21. How far the Council's agenda has opened up to nontraditional issues can be gauged from its refusal in 1989 to accede to UK pressure for discussion of international narcotrafficking and environmental issues as potential threats to peace, while on January 10, 2000, under a U.S. presidency (in the person of Vice President Al Gore), it engaged in a debate on the implications of the AIDS pandemic in Africa for stability and peace on that continent in the twenty-first century.

22. S/2002/1388, December 20, 2002.

23. In fact, all three of the major wire services, Agence France Presse, the Associated Press, and Reuters, report very well on the UN through insightful and sharp correspondents, but the nature of their clientele discourages extensive analysis. The Inter-Press Service, an agency favoring developing-country perspectives, has done well at the UN on this latter score.

2

Security Council
Decisions in Perspective

PETER WALLENSTEEN AND PATRIK JOHANSSON

The United Nations Security Council was created in an atmosphere of major power cooperation. Its design assumed that the leading actors in world affairs would have to cooperate with each other and, with the introduction of the veto, even be induced to do so. However, from the very beginning of its practical operation in 1946 the Council came to operate in an entirely different atmosphere. The slow but seemingly irrevocable drift into the Cold War had a paralyzing effect on the Council. Major changes in the international system, such as liberation wars, peaceful decolonization, and increasing North-South divides, did not change the way the Cold War impacted on the Council. Only during the détente of the late 1980s did the Council return to its original operation: to be an organ that would function when the major powers cooperated. This means that the Council's single most formative experience since its inception is the end of the Cold War. In this chapter we set out to demonstrate this. It amounts to the emergence of a new Security Council, which for the first time is functioning as was originally intended under the United Nations Charter. It means that the role of the Council, its conflict agenda, its actions, and its approaches to new security threats have changed. These four aspects will be scrutinized in the following pages. The conclusion is that the Council has become an important organ in international affairs. As long as there are cooperative relations between the major powers, it is likely to remain this way. The structure of the Council, however, remains the same, which raises some issues with respect to Council reform.

A New Role

It will be no surprise to those that follow UN affairs that the end of the Cold War has been the single most formative experience in the existence of the Security Council. There are many ways to demonstrate this in a systematic way. The simplest one is to count the absolute number of all Council resolutions and those taken under Chapter VII (providing for enforcement measures), as well as those tabled resolutions that were blocked through vetoes by permanent Council members. The statistics for all resolutions in the period 1946–2002 are presented in Figure 2.1, which shows clearly the activation of the Council. For the period 1946–1989 the annual average number of passed resolutions was fifteen; since then the average has been more than sixty. The Council has moved from roughly one decision per month to one per week. This is indeed a dramatic change.

At the end of the 1980s the Cold War was in a phase of détente. For the two superpowers, however, it remained to decide how all Cold War–related hot wars around the world were to be handled. The speech by Soviet president Mikhail Gorbachev to the UN General Assembly in December 1988, in which he made clear that the Soviet Union was planning to use the Security Council as a way of handling international conflicts, was crucial in engaging the UN in peace settlements. In reality, it meant that the overextended Soviet empire would use the UN as a way of extracting itself from a set of commitments.

Thus, while the two blocs of East and West still were intact, the UN began to take on a new role. This could be seen already in 1987 in the efforts to end the Iran-Iraq War. In his memoirs, UN Secretary-General Javier Pérez de Cuéllar states that informal consultations between the Security Council's permanent members began in 1987 in efforts to deal with this war. It was followed by the agreement on Soviet withdrawal from

Figure 2.1   Security Council Resolutions, 1946–2002

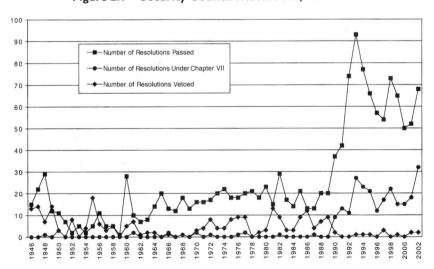

Afghanistan in 1988. In the years 1988–1990 there was considerable peace-making activity, showing that this new Soviet strategy was met with sympathy and support on the opposite side. Cooperation became the norm on matters as varied as the conflicts in Angola, Namibia, Cambodia, and Central America. The relations between the most significant major powers changed, and the UN became a vehicle for that change, even helping to reinforce it by being an arena where viable solutions could be worked out.

Groundwork was laid before, but the catapulting experience was Iraq's invasion of Kuwait on August 2, 1990, and the immediate Council reaction to undo this breach of international peace and security. Certainly, during the Cold War some countries had managed to get away with occupation of neighboring territories, as exemplified by Turkey (northern parts of Cyprus), Indonesia (East Timor), and Israel (the West Bank, the Gaza Strip, and the Golan Heights), but none of these moves had been awarded international recognition. When Iraq tried to annex Kuwait, it may have expected protection from at least one permanent member and thus committed a monumental misreading of the new global conditions. Since then, furthermore, the conflicts and crises surrounding Iraq have continued to be a top priority on the Council's agenda. From 1990 to 2002 matters relating to Iraq have resulted in sixty-three Council resolutions, of which fifty-eight were adopted under Chapter VII. This is close to 8 percent of all resolutions and almost 25 percent of all Chapter VII resolutions for this period.

Crises over Yugoslavia also became a major concern for the Security Council. The failure of the European Union (and its earlier incarnation) to deal with the crisis soon made it an issue for the UN Security Council and, later, for the North Atlantic Treaty Organization (NATO). In fact, since 1946 more than 50 percent of all Chapter VII resolutions have concerned the post–Cold War conflicts in Iraq and Yugoslavia. Whether this is a reasonable proportion of Council attention or not, it is testimony to the international significance of these two situations for the post–Cold War order.

The dramatic rise in Chapter VII resolutions since the end of the Cold War can be seen in Figure 2.1.[1] Ninety-three percent of all Chapter VII resolutions passed from 1946 to 2002 have been adopted since the end of the Cold War. The Council, when acting under Chapter VII, can order enforcement measures and wield a unique authority in the international system, becoming an important actor in itself. The continuous media attention to the discussions in the Security Council in the past decade contrasts with the more sporadic coverage seen before. Chapter VII resolutions underscore the significance of a particular issue, and media attention will naturally follow. Dividing Council history into four-year periods, we can observe that until 1989 only once did Chapter VII resolutions constitute slightly more than one-tenth of all Council resolutions in a single period. They usually made up 5 percent or less. Since 1990, however, around 25 percent of all resolutions have been adopted under Chapter VII. In 2001 and 2002 the shares were 35 and 47 percent respectively.[2]

Figure 2.1 also shows that the permanent members have cast 294 vetoes in the period 1946–2002. Forty-four of these have concerned the election of a new Secretary-General and thus did not directly deal with conflict management. The remaining 250 vetoes are distributed as follows: the Soviet Union and Russia 119, the United States seventy-six, the United Kingdom thirty-two, France eighteen, and China five. This can be further refined. For instance, forty-eight of the Soviet vetoes and six of the U.S. vetoes concerned the election of new members to the organization and belonged to the first two decades of UN history. Subtracting such vetoes, the United States and the Soviet Union have cast a nearly equal number of vetoes—seventy and seventy-one respectively. While until 1970 the Soviet Union was the most frequent user of the veto, since 1970 it has been the United States. However, the veto has not been in frequent use since the end of the Cold War. For the decade 1991–2000 there were only seven vetoes, the lowest for any decade in UN history.[3]

The changed use of the veto is one more indication of the shift in the working atmosphere of the Council. Many of the vetoes in the earlier period were predictable. Typically, a majority would put forward a draft resolution that it expected to be rejected by a permanent member. There was, in other words, a propagandistic use of the Council, making both sides equally responsible, even if the attention was directed on the one casting the negative vote. In many cases, the majority hoped to score a political point or win approval for its perspective in this way. Since the end of the Cold War, however, there has been less of this maneuvering among the major powers. A spirit of cooperation has prevailed, and a new set of rules has dominated the agenda. Increasingly, it has been seen as irresponsible to force other members of the Council to veto a proposed resolution. The vetoes that have been cast have concerned issues that were considered by at least one of the permanent members as touching upon its vital interests, such as Israel (in the U.S. case) and Taiwan (in the Chinese case).

In this context it is interesting to note that there are some earlier examples in which Council members have refrained from tabling resolutions that would have drawn a veto in all likelihood. From this perspective it is no surprise that the Council did not adopt a resolution in relation to the U.S. involvement in the Vietnam War; nor was there a single veto against a draft resolution in relation to that war. For instance, in 1966 the United States brought the issue to the Council but was repelled by France and the Soviet Union with the argument that North Vietnam was not represented in the UN. Similarly, during the 1979–1988 Soviet war in Afghanistan, no Council resolution was adopted on that conflict. After the Soviet Union vetoed a draft resolution in 1980 calling for the immediate and unconditional withdrawal of all foreign troops from Afghanistan, no more drafts were brought to a vote.

Furthermore, of all the resolutions that have been adopted on the Arab-Israeli conflict, only one has been adopted under Chapter VII—Resolution 54 (1948), which established a threat to the peace in accordance with Article 39 and ordered the parties concerned to issue cease-fire orders.[4] Also, there has only been one instance in which a Chapter VII resolution regarding the Arab-Israeli conflict has been vetoed—in 1982, when the United States vetoed (while five other members abstained) a draft resolution referring to the Israeli annexation of the Syrian Golan Heights as an act of aggression.

This means on the one hand that members of the Council have increasingly refrained from provocative behavior, and on the other hand that some acute conflicts have not come to the table of the Council. In that case, other parts of the UN system have been activated, as exemplified by the Secretary-General (on Afghanistan) and the General Assembly (on the Arab-Israel conflict).

This analysis of the voting records tells us that a new Security Council emerged since the end of the Cold War. It is more cooperative, it is making serious decisions, and it is more deeply involved in the issues on its agenda. This has enhanced the standing of the Security Council, making it the key organ of the UN on issues relating to peace and security. The General Assembly is now overshadowed by the Council. During much of the Cold War it was the other way around. The "Uniting for Peace" resolution (1950), for instance, gave the Assembly an instrument for being involved in security affairs when the Council was blocked.[5] The remarkable role played by Secretary-General Dag Hammarskjöld in the midst of the Cold War in the 1950s rested on support in the General Assembly and on the skillful use of the responsibilities given to the Secretary-General by Article 99 of the Charter. The position of the Secretary-General in the post–Cold War period is entirely different, as the Council today is highly active in formulating its own decisions. It still needs the Secretariat for implementation, however. At the same time, there has not been the same willingness to grant increased resources to the Secretariat. On the contrary, it has suffered from a strongly enforced ceiling on its budget. This in turn has forced the Council itself to take a more active role in implementation, as has been noted in sanctions implementation and in counterterrorism work.[6]

A New Conflict Agenda

In order to determine whether the Council's new activism also translated into a readiness to live up to its responsibility for a wider set of conflicts, one should look at the Council's agenda and at the conflicts on which it takes explicit decisions. In reporting on armed conflicts in the world, the Uppsala Conflict Data Project has recently published information on the period 1946–2001.[7] Figure 2.2 shows the number of such conflicts in categories of varying intensity. A visual inspection and a comparison to Figure 2.1 show some of the differences. Much of the rising conflict material from the early 1960s until the late 1980s was not handled by the Council. It is only from the time of the Council's activation around 1988 that the curves start to take similar shapes. This suggests that not only did the Council become more active after the end of the Cold War, but also that it began to handle the more pertinent conflicts of its time. Today, the Council reflects, more than ever, the concerns that the international community shares.

Still, there are important observations to be made. We would, for instance, expect the Council to deal with the most severe conflicts, no matter their location and no matter the parties involved. Unfortunately, that does not seem to be the case. There are very serious conflicts in the post–Cold War period that have not been attended to by the Council, for instance those in Algeria, Burma/Myanmar, Colombia, Kashmir, Northern Ireland, Sri Lanka, and the Sudan.[8] This means that there is selectivity with respect to the conflicts that enter the agenda of the Council.[9] An example is the Kurdish issue, which concerns the demands of an ethnic group for statehood. There have been wars around this issue in Turkey, Iran, and Iraq, and conflicts in Syria and Azerbaijan. Still, there is not one Council resolution

Figure 2.2   Number of Armed Conflicts by Level of Intensity, 1946–2001

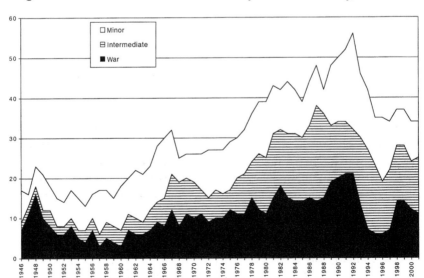

explicitly mentioning this issue. It can only be inferred from references to humanitarian concerns (e.g., in Resolution 688 [1990]).

This can be subjected to more systematic scrutiny. Using data from the Uppsala project, we can identify the thirty longest wars since 1946—that is, the thirty armed conflicts with the longest unbroken sequences of years of war-level intensity (at least 1,000 battle-related deaths during one year). Examples are the conflict in Chad, which was fought at war-level intensity every year from 1965 to 1988. So was the conflict in Guatemala, from 1969 to 1987. Regarding the thirty conflicts since 1946 registered as wars for the highest consecutive number of years, the Security Council has adopted Chapter VII resolutions only in four. Mandatory sanctions have been introduced in three cases, and eight different peacekeeping missions have been deployed to these conflicts. This means that twenty-six of the thirty longest wars since 1946 have not been defined by the Security Council as threats to international peace and security (Article 39). We need to ask why this is so.

The pattern that can be discerned is the following. States that are somewhat powerful in the international system, be they permanent members or other member states, and that have an interest in preventing international attention to a particular issue, are often capable of doing so. Through diplomatic and political means they may be able to block Council deliberations on these issues. That this applies to the permanent members is no surprise. Their strong constitutional and real-world position gives them a choice of whether to use the UN or other fora. Clearly, direct confrontations between the major powers have been handled outside the Security Council. This was true for the Cold War period, but it remains a valid observation also later. For instance, the dispute between the United States and China over a U.S. military aircraft that was forced to make an emergency landing in China in 2001 was taken up only between the two. Whether conflicts directly involving permanent members will come onto the Council's agenda is determined by the calculations made by these members. It is likely, for instance, that regional issues that are of interest to several of them are more likely to come onto the agenda, as exemplified by the crises of Yugoslavia and Iraq. In case the Council cannot make the decisions that one or the other permanent member prefer, they have the possibility of acting militarily on their own. In that case, it is likely to spark a debate on the legality of the action, as evidenced in the crises over Kosovo in 1999 and Iraq in early 2003.

It is more interesting to study other states and their significance for agenda-setting. Their relative influence in the international system seems to be an important aspect. For instance, a leading state such as India has a strong international position, and thus we can see that none of the conflicts that concerned this country has been handled by the Council since the early 1950s. Similarly, Sri Lanka, a smaller but respected member state, has prevented any mentioning of the Tamil question. However, these countries are exposed to changes in their relative significance. The dynamics are discernible in the case of Indonesia, which was a strong member of the nonaligned movement, maintained close ties with the Western world, and over years had record economic growth figures. Thus the East Timor question, which emerged in 1975, did not come to the Council's agenda until 1999. At that time, Indonesia's international position had weakened, not least by the Asian economic crisis. Almost simultaneously the standing of the opposition in East Timor had improved, not least through the awarding of the Nobel Peace Prize to Bishop Belo and resistance leader José Ramos-Horta in 1996. Thus it was finally possible for the Council to attend to the situation. Perhaps there is a rule here. For the weaker party it is important to get the Council and the UN Secretariat to attend to its questions, while strong parties often will prefer to deal with the matters on their own. The weaker is likely to gain from the attention, as it forces foreign ministries around the world to attend to the issue, public opinion awareness increases, and the media have stronger incentives to take up the questions. In 1999 the East Timor issue became one of international concern and a priority agenda item for the Council.

Furthermore, once an issue has been added to the Council's agenda it might be difficult to remove it. The way an issue has been formulated in the UN is also likely to be the way member states will react to it. That dynamic could be seen in the treatment of the Iraq issue in 2002–2003, when Resolution 1441 (2002) built on previous decisions relating to preventing Iraq from producing weapons of mass destruction. In reality, the United States also raised questions of potential future terrorism and the nature of the regime. This reformulation of the question did not get the Council's endorsement. There is, in other words, inertia with respect to how a particular conflict is seen, in spite of what may happen on the ground.[10]

There is also a geographical dimension. Clearly, conflicts in Africa, Europe, and the Middle East are more likely than others to end up on the Council's agenda. Of the 1,400 resolutions, more than 400 have dealt with conflicts in Europe, with a similar number for conflicts in the Middle East/North Africa. More than 350 have concerned conflicts in Africa proper. In contrast, there are fewer than 100 resolutions each on Asia (including the Pacific) and the Americas. The pattern is similar concerning action taken. For instance, with respect to mandatory sanctions, Haiti is the only one out of sixteen sanctions regimes that has not concerned Europe, the Middle East, or Africa. There have been more than ten peacekeeping missions each in Europe and the Middle East/North Africa, and nearly twenty in Africa. There are only seven in Asia, and eight in the Americas (four of which were in Haiti). This means that conflicts in Asia come more seldom onto the Council's agenda. It may require exceptional development, as just described in the case of East Timor. Matters pertaining to the Americas are in the same category. The conflicts in Central America remained outside the UN agenda for most of their duration, coming onto it only during the late phase of peacemaking and peacekeeping.

The relative neglect of some parts of the world contrasts with the attention accorded to conflicts located north, east, and south of the Mediterranean. These areas have a particular legacy in UN affairs: Yugoslavia, Iraq, and issues in sub-Saharan Africa. The geographical patterns may reflect the asymmetric integration that exists between Western Europe and conflict regions in Africa, southeastern Europe, and the Middle East. They are all economically dependent on Europe, linked through colonial and cultural heritage, and geographically close. This closeness combines with the fact that Europe is strongly represented on the Council. Three permanent members are European countries, and one, the United States, is dominated by similar perspectives. There are two elected seats for Western Europeans and there is one for Eastern Europe. This means that six or seven of the Council's fifteen members are directly drawn from European roots. It might not be surprising that the Council is particularly attentive to matters of concern to Europe.

The contrast to Asia is marked. It is less connected to Europe and has many strong states within its confines. Classical realpolitik is more typical of East, South, and Southeast Asia than present-day Europe, as is the reluctance to resort to international organizations.

In a similar vein, we can see the Americas as a separate security system, where U.S. dominance, military interference, internal democratization, local guerrilla movements, and economic interests mold political actions in a different way. The study of the Security Council agenda suggests that international peace and security after the end of the Cold War is approached in different ways in different geographical regions. In some, the UN has become more significant than ever. A general observation still remains true, however: the stronger position of the permanent members in determining the agenda and the importance of the relative influence of other states in blocking some issues of their particular concern.

New Measures

Among the major categories of actions available to the Council, two of the most significant are sanctions and peacekeeping operations. Figures 2.3 and 2.4 compare the number of conflicts with different types of UN action for the period 1946–2001. For reasons of clarity, we have chosen to use separate figures for Council resolutions and for Council actions. Thus in Figure 2.3 we present armed conflicts (which are usually the reason for Council

Figure 2.3 Armed Conflict and Resolutions, Four-Year Periods, 1946–2001

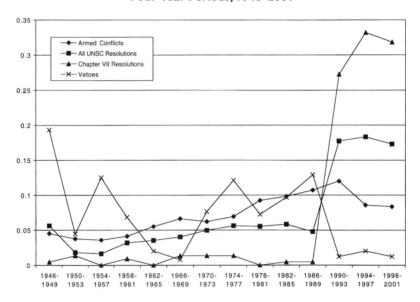

Figure 2.4 Conflicts and UN Actions, Four-Year Periods, 1946–2001

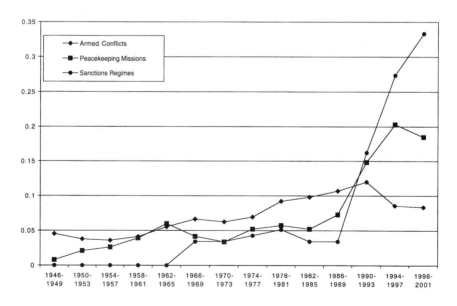

action), all Council resolutions, Chapter VII resolutions, and vetoes. In Figure 2.4 we present armed conflicts, peacekeeping missions, and sanctions regimes, according to the same principle.

The period 1946–2001 is again divided into fourteen four-year periods (see note 2). For each four-year period we have calculated its share of the total number for the variable in question (resolutions, conflicts, measures). For example, from 1946–2001 the Security Council adopted a total of 1,386 resolutions. Seventy-eight of those were adopted during the four-year period 1946–1949, which thus constitutes 5.6 percent of all 1,386 resolutions, as indicated in Figure 2.3. This way the relative changes that have taken place in the Council's mode of operation are easier to depict.[11]

Figure 2.3 shows the distribution of the 225 armed conflicts that were active in 1946–2001. As we saw earlier, they increase continuously until the early 1990s, with a slight decline in the following years. The curves for all resolutions, Chapter VII resolutions, and vetoes illustrate again the difference between the Cold War and post–Cold War periods: the increase in the number of resolutions adopted, particularly of those under Chapter VII, is very marked, as is the decrease of the number of vetoes cast. Turning to Figure 2.4, we see that the different types of action show a similar dramatic pattern, strongly pronounced for the three most recent periods: most sanctions regimes and peacekeeping operations have been set up since the end of the Cold War. This is especially marked for sanctions, where a third of all regimes initiated by the Council were actually active in the latest four-year period, at a time when peacekeeping operations appeared to have peaked. Still, this is not enough evidence for suggesting that the Council has a clear preference for any particular type of activity. Rather, we can say that the Council began using *all* instruments available to it. As there is a reduction in armed conflict, one might even venture to argue that there was some success in achieving international peace and security, although this is not the occasion for making a full evaluation.

This means that the Council in the first decade of the twenty-first century should have empirically grounded experiences for formulating strategies of peacemaking. In the case of sanctions there is an international process where lessons from sanctions failures have been systematically turned into refining the instrument. This means that there is now more knowledge on how to make targeted sanctions—as opposed to comprehensive sanctions—appropriate and potentially successful.[12] It could be of interest to evaluate also other Council instruments in the same light. It is obvious as well that other actors have increased their peace activities since the end of the Cold War. In a study of non-UN peacekeeping missions, the same patterns that are discerned in Figure 2.4 can be observed: such missions have become more frequent and, in fact, are as numerous as UN-led missions. There are also some distinct differences, where, for instance, non-

UN missions are more often used in internal affairs.[13] NATO now has its own peacekeeping missions, as do the Organization for Security and Cooperation in Europe (OSCE), the African Union, the Economic Community of West African States (ECOWAS), and others. The European Union has developed a strategy for peace operations and has instituted its own sanctions on some countries (Burma/Myanmar, Zimbabwe, Belarus). Thus the activation of international organizations in matters of peace and security is a typical trait of the post–Cold War period. The instruments used are similar. Their separate contribution to the reduction in the number of armed conflicts needs to be established more closely, however.

The purpose of many of these measures is to contribute to the peaceful settlement of disputes. The post–Cold War period has been one of unusual peacemaking. There is an unprecedented record of peace agreements. We can observe that the Council often is involved in the peacemaking phases of a conflict. It appears that there is an understanding among conflict parties to turn to the UN at a moment in time when they are interested in a negotiated settlement. Thus the UN has come to be connected with a number of peace agreements. Some of its peacekeeping missions are part and parcel of such settlements. This means that the UN is likely to be involved in conflicts when they are in a period that is "ripe for resolution."[14] The common understanding of the UN as a force for peace, rather than an institution that enforces compliance or even authorizes the use of force, has solid support in the record of Council action.

Judging from the actions that have been taken, we can conclude that most of them aim at stopping a particular war, contributing to mutual settlement, or inducing the parties to move in that direction by imposing sanctions on one or more sides in a conflict. From being an arena of conflict and tension during the Cold War, the Council has become an organ for concerted action to reduce war, using all means at its disposal. Some of these measures, however, do require further refinement to become more efficient.

New Threats to Security

The security agenda after the Cold War clearly has enlarged. That can be seen in the proliferation of new concepts of security: environmental security, human security, and democratic security. Also conflict prevention has achieved new urgency. The Council has been challenged to follow the paths or even take the lead. Some of these new concerns are reflected in significant Council decisions.

Most recently, of course, matters relating to international terrorism have come to the fore (see Chapter 6). Prior to September 11, 2001, the Security Council had adopted more than ten resolutions dealing with international terrorism. An equally large number of resolutions on international terrorism have been adopted since September 11. Libya, Sudan, and the Taliban regime in Afghanistan all became targets of Council-mandated sanctions for their involvement in international terrorism.

At the same time there has been a move to see security in a broader perspective, prompting the Council to adopt resolutions on thematic issues rather than specific conflicts. Thus the Council adopted resolutions on the role of women in the prevention and resolution of conflicts and in peace-building,[15] on children in armed conflict,[16] and on the issue of HIV/AIDS.[17] Further, the Council has introduced a broader analysis of international peace and security, for example in Resolutions 1170 (1998), 1318 (2000), and 1327 (2000). In these decisions the need to address root causes of conflict was emphasized, including the economic and social dimensions and the link between sustainable development and international peace and security. Resolution 1327 highlights the importance of democracy and all human rights—civil, political, economic, social, and cultural. Special attention has been given to Africa in this context.

It is possible that the concern with terrorism has negatively affected the attention to the broader security agenda. Most resolutions concerning women, children, and a wider security concept were adopted prior to September 11. The pattern is not entirely obvious, however. For instance, an important resolution (1460) concerning child soldiers and the protection of women and children in humanitarian crises was adopted in early 2003. It is noteworthy, however, that about a third of the resolutions regarding terrorism have been taken under Chapter VII, both before and after September 11. In contrast, none of the decisions concerning women, children, conflict prevention, and sustainable development were adopted under Chapter VII.

The Council in this way may have made clear that its primary concern is the management of crisis and armed conflict. Broader concerns are seen in relation to that. Matters that have received considerable attention in public debate and in scholarly discussions, such as possible links between environmental degradation and security, have not had explicit support in Council deliberation. The same is true for religion and security, or population development and security. There is a tendency of a broadening agenda, no doubt, but urgent world events may prevent the Council from taking up other challenges.

This means that the Council remains a preeminent organ for handling international crises. The experiences since the Cold War have given it a special role in formulating global policy in these matters. Although there are other organizations venturing into the same field, all would probably subscribe to the notion that the Council is unique and the lead organ. Thus it remains important that the Council uses considered arguments and aims for impartiality and consistency in its treatment of international conflicts, wherever they arise.

Conclusion

The Security Council has clearly moved far away from its form of operation during the Cold War. We can justifiably describe it as a *new* Council: it has a higher level of activity, it has taken up crucial issues that are threatening regional or global peace, its decisions are now binding the membership to enforce its action, it has activated the means at its disposal, and it has been receptive to new challenges. This means that the Council is a new forum for formulating policies. This all contributes to give the Council an important role in doing what the Charter and the membership expect it to do: maintain international peace and security.

It is important, however, to recall that the Council is not entirely a new body. Some elements are old and entrenched in the UN Charter. For instance, the Council is not an independent body that by itself selects which concerns it will attend to. It acts under the joint authorization of the capitals of member states. This means, as we have seen, that certain conflicts receive more attention than others. Some threats to regional or international peace are not brought onto the agenda of the Council or do not receive serious consideration. This gives rise to the fear that the Council will apply double standards to conflicts and that it is governed by the strength of particular member states. This affects its credibility and heightens the urgency to consider ways in which other issues can be brought to the Council. The way in which it has been able to respond to the threat of terrorism may be instructive: in that case the Council is taking a global, comprehensive approach. There are other issues that may require similar methodologies. This could be particularly relevant for some old and lingering conflicts where no consistent approach appears to have developed, as in Palestine, Kashmir, and Korea, although the UN was a party to those conflicts in their early stages. The authority of the Council could in these situations be used to break ingrained stalemates.

The Security Council is an organ for dealing with *immediate* and serious crisis. We have seen that it responded more effectively than most other international organizations in taking action on the new post–Cold War crises, rather than by taking action on old, protracted conflicts. In the future the Council may need to formulate sustained strategies for maintaining the peace. For instance, a surprising element for the Council in the early 1990s was the ferocity of some ethnic conflicts. It might be necessary for the Council to consider long-term preventive strategies for promoting constitutional change and international insight into multicultural situations, building on principles of democracy, human rights, and self-determination. Other international organizations have been more innovative in this regard, for instance the creation of the OSCE's high commissioner on national minorities.

The Security Council is an organ that, as we have outlined, builds on the will of the membership to cooperate. This means that the Council is dependent on its composition and on the policies of the capitals in a few countries. The matter of reforming the Council with respect to its composition should also be part of the agenda for the future. For instance, the short two-year terms for elected members put them at a serious disadvantage vis-à-vis the permanent members when new crises emerge (see Chapter 17). In order to ensure new ideas, one might also consider whether the states that naturally became permanent members in 1945 today may need to yield to others or be supplemented. Permanency should not extend to eternity.

We have seen that the resort to the veto has declined, but it remains an important consideration in the diplomacy that surrounds many decisions. In the new cooperative conditions after the Cold War it might be appropriate also to raise issues of voting rules. In early 2003 a new discussion emerged on the rules of decisions. For instance, should a negative vote by one permanent member (what has been a veto) be overturned if the other fourteen members (or a large fraction of the Council, say, two-thirds) have the opposite view? Should this apply to decisions under Chapter VII? In this way, it may be possible to bring Council attention to more conflicts than is now the case.

The broader security agenda also illustrates the importance of the Council's links to other organs of significance for the maintenance of international peace and security, in particular the international financial institutions. Many issues interconnect, and more determined strategies could be built if there were closer relations with such institutions. There could be regular meetings, even a representation in the Council of such institutions (as is the case for the Secretariat today), perhaps also the other way around.

If it is true that the world after the Cold War is different, as we have sought to demonstrate in this chapter, it requires new ways of conducting Council affairs. It may, for instance, need a stronger Secretariat that can prepare, implement, and evaluate Council decisions more effectively and feed back new information quicker. The complexity of the new issues, where economy links with politics, diplomacy, and lifestyles, may require closer connection between the Secretariat, other global centers, and representative popular movements.

Notes

1. A resolution is counted as being adopted under Chapter VII if it either contains an explicit mentioning of Chapter VII or makes an explicit determination that there is a threat to or breach of the peace, or an act of aggression. See Global Issues Research Group, Foreign and Commonwealth Office, *Research Analysts Memorandum: Table of Vetoed Draft Resolutions in the United Nations Security Council, 1946–1998* (London: Global Issues Research Group, September 1999).

2. The annual fluctuations have been wide. In the first years of the Council

the total number of resolutions was low, and thus a few Chapter VII resolutions would constitute a large share. For instance, of eleven Security Council resolutions adopted in 1950, three were under Chapter VII (i.e., 27 percent, all of which dealt with the war in Korea). After this there were no Chapter VII resolutions for a full decade. To make trends more easily identifiable, we have used four-year averages here, and also in Figures 2.3 and 2.4. Note that the numbers for 2001 and 2002 in the text refer to individual years and are not strictly comparable to the others. The trend is marked, however.

3. United States three, Russia two, China two. In addition, there was one veto by the United States in the election of the Secretary-General in 1996.

4. The resolution did not refer to any action under Articles 41 and 42—that is, peaceful or forceful action in case of violations.

5. This was the reason why the UN could be involved in Afghanistan, through the special representative of the Secretary-General, in spite of the Soviet veto. Also, the Assembly could attend to the Palestinian issue when the Council did not.

6. On sanctions implementation, see Peter Wallensteen, Carina Staibano, and Mikael Eriksson, eds., *Making Targeted Sanctions Effective: Guidelines for the Implementation of UN Policy Options* (Uppsala, Sweden: Uppsala University, Department of Peace and Conflict Research, 2003); and www.smartsanctions.se.

7. Definitions, delimitation, and data are available through the website www.peace.uu.se and the Uppsala Conflict Data Project. For some of the theoretical underpinnings, see Peter Wallensteen, *Understanding Conflict Resolution: War, Peace, and the Global System* (London: Sage, 2002).

8. The UN Military Observer Group in India and Pakistan (UNMOGIP) operates on the borders separating the two countries, but this does not mean that the internal dynamics and roots of the Kashmir conflict are attended to. On the Sudan there was a sanctions decision, but it did not concern the war in southern Sudan.

9. Wallensteen, *Understanding Conflict Resolution,* pp. 231–261.

10. An extreme and unfortunate case was the Council's definition of the conflict in Rwanda as a civil war in early 1994, thus focusing on cease-fire efforts rather than on preventing genocide.

11. Some activities continue for a longer period, requiring special procedures to achieve comparability. Thus the curve for armed conflicts is based on the number of conflicts active in a given year, not on the number of conflicts initiated. In this case the base is the number of conflict years. For example, 17 armed conflicts were active in 1946, 16 in 1947, 23 in 1948, and 21 in 1949 (see Figure 2.2), which sums to 77 conflict years. In Figure 2.3, the value 4.5 for "armed conflicts" for the four-year period 1946–1949 means that the 77 conflict years of that period constitute 4.5 percent of the 1,701 conflict years of the whole period 1946–2001. The same principle is used for sanctions regimes and peacekeeping missions in Figure 2.4: the number of active regimes and missions during a given year.

12. For more on this, see www.smartsanctions.se, www.smartsanctions.ch, and www.smartsanctions.de.

13. Birger Heldt and Peter Wallensteen, "Peacekeeping Operations by the UN and Non-UN Actors, 1948–2000: Two Separate Processes?" paper presented to the International Studies Association annual convention, Portland, Oreg., February 25–March 1, 2003.

14. The phrase was coined by I. William Zartman, *Ripe for Resolution: Conflict and Intervention in Africa,* 2nd ed. (New York: Oxford University Press, 1989).

15. Resolution 1325 (2000), reaffirmed in Resolution 1327 (2000). See also Louise Olsson, *Gendering UN Peacekeeping: Mainstreaming a Gender Perspective in Multidimensional Peacekeeping* (Uppsala, Sweden: Uppsala University, Department of Peace and Conflict Research 1999).

16. Resolutions 1261 (1999), 1314 (2000), and 1379 (2001), the last of which also highlights the special needs of girls affected by armed conflict.

17. Resolution 1308 (2000).

PART I

Security Council Decisionmaking: New Concerns

3

The Humanitarian Impulse

Thomas G. Weiss

Humanitarian values have become central to foreign and military policies since the outset of the 1990s. Humanitarians often lament that national interests are obstacles to realizing their objectives. In truth, calculations about vital interests by governmental decisionmakers explain intervention, which is unlikely to succeed unless there is a demonstrated willingness to take casualties and stay the course. This chapter focuses on the trends that have emerged since the 1990s that may circumscribe the chances for a more consistent respect for humanitarian values over the next ten years.

The end of the Cold War made possible UN decisions about international security that had not been feasible for some forty years. A key explanation for the sheer expansion in activity by the Security Council in the 1990s was the humanitarian "impulse," the understandable human desire to help those in life-threatening distress resulting from armed conflict.[1] Invariably, this urge translates into a limited political momentum and a sliding scale of commitments. This impulse does not necessarily imply efforts that are "impulsive," which are more likely to be "emotionally-charged and based on incomplete or biased media coverage."[2] Rather it reflects the stark reality of international politics that permits action to come to the rescue of some, but not all, war victims. This momentum, for instance, has made coalitions of the willing an episodic phenomenon in world politics. When humanitarian and strategic interests coincide, a window of opportunity opens for those seeking to act on the humanitarian impulse in the Security Council.

The title of this chapter is not slanted to the humanitarian "imperative," the preference of those who believe that humanitarian values must be universal to be meaningful and who are dismayed by the uneven quality of Security Council decisions. The humanitarian imperative entails an obligation to treat victims similarly and react to crises consistently—in effect, to deny the relevance of politics, which consists of drawing lines and weighing effectiveness and available resources. Humanitarian action is desirable but not obligatory. The humanitarian impulse is permissive. The humanitarian imperative would be peremptory.

The humanitarian impulse is the maximum to which the community of states can aspire. It was respected more often in the 1990s than earlier, and it may be respected more systematically still. Lest the ideal become the enemy of the good, international action in some cases is better than in none.

The dramatic evolution in attitudes toward the limits of sovereignty affects the ability of humanitarian organizations to come to the rescue. The post–Cold War years underscore the expectations to respect fundamental human rights placed on sovereign political authorities. The growth in the weight of humanitarian values to sustain diplomatic and military action is clear to seasoned observers—although David Rieff would now contest whether this development has been productive.[3] "In the 1990s," summarizes Adam Roberts, "humanitarian issues . . . played a historically unprecedented role in international politics."[4]

S. Neil MacFarlane notes that "normatively based challenges to the sovereign rights of states are hardly new in international history," but still the Security Council was largely missing in action regarding humanitarian matters during the Cold War.[5] There was virtually a humanitarian tabula rasa at the outset of the 1990s. No resolution mentioned the humanitarian aspects of any conflict from 1945 until the Six Day War of 1967, and the first mention of the International Committee of the Red Cross (ICRC) was not until 1978.[6] In the 1970s and 1980s, "the Security Council gave humanitarian aspects of armed conflict limited priority . . . but the early nineteen-nineties can be seen as a watershed."[7] During the first half of the decade, twice as many resolutions were passed as during the first forty-five years of UN history. They contained repeated references to humanitarian crises amounting to threats to international peace and security, and they repeated demands for parties to respect international humanitarian law.

Whether one takes issue with Edward Luttwak's disparaging remarks about "Kofi's rule . . . whereby human rights outrank sovereignty," humanitarian intervention undoubtedly was among the most controversial topics within UN circles in the 1990s.[8] The Secretary-General's own speeches were widely debated.[9] "The age of humanitarian emergencies" led to policies of "saving strangers."[10] An academic cottage industry grew,[11] and governments sponsored a host of policy initiatives and published reports on the topic: the Canadian-inspired International Commission on Intervention and State Sovereignty (ICISS) published *The Responsibility to Protect;*[12] a Swedish initiative, the Independent International Commission on Kosovo, published the *Kosovo Report;*[13] the U.S. government published an overview of humanitarian programs and a report on humanitarian intervention;[14] and the Dutch and Danish governments published major inquiries into the legal authority for intervention.[15]

"Intervention" here only refers to three categories of threatened or actual coercion against the expressed wishes (or without the genuine consent) of a target state or group of political authorities: sanctions and embargoes, international criminal prosecution, and military force. The Security Council approved all varieties of coercion in unprecedented numbers during the 1990s. Sanctions are a vast and heated topic; much has already been written about their negative humanitarian impact, particularly in reference to Iraq.[16] International criminal prosecution, even of heads of state, assumed new vitality with the arrest of Manuel Noriega in 1989 but assumed even greater importance with legal actions against Slobodan Milosevic and Biljana Plavsic at The Hague.[17] The Council's decisions in the 1990s proved highly innovative in shaping norms and stimulated legal developments, including the international tribunals for the former Yugoslavia in 1993 and Rwanda in 1994 and the creation of the International Criminal Court in 1998. And the most severe and intense kind of intervention, the use of deadly force by outside militaries, constituted a most notable story of the 1990s.

This chapter focuses on the Security Council's demonstrated concerns with the plight of the civilian victims of armed conflicts, particularly of internal wars. Extreme suffering consistently led to intense scrutiny but selective responses, especially with respect to Chapter VII military operations. A minority of international lawyers suggested that there was emerging customary law on humanitarian intervention.[18] Others disputed the extent to which custom could actually take precedence over treaty and viewed Kosovo as an unfortunate departure that threatened the Charter regime.[19]

Legal interpretations notwithstanding, state behavior and expectations certainly changed over the decade. Exceptions to the principle of nonintervention became less exceptional. Post-1991 practice demonstrates support or tolerance for respecting the humanitarian impulse, often against the will of local authorities. UN-authorized actions with an expressed humanitarian purpose were manifest (northern Iraq, Somalia, Haiti, the former Yugoslavia, Rwanda, Albania, and East Timor) along with non-UN authorized actions that were seen by many states as legitimate (the North Atlantic Treaty Organization [NATO] in Kosovo) or that were endorsed ex post facto (the Economic Community of West African States [ECOWAS] in Liberia).

Significant institutional innovations in the international handling of humanitarian challenges usually occur after wars have ended, when new kinds of horrors shock consciences and expose the inadequacies of existing organizations and their standard operating procedures. The founding of the modern humanitarian system is usually dated to 1864, when Henri Dunant, appalled by the slaughter wrought by a fierce battle between French and Austrian forces in Solferino, Italy, in the wake of the War of Italian Unification, established the ICRC. Immediately after World War I and the Russian Revolution, two sisters, Eglantyne Jebb and Dorothy Buxton, founded Save the Children. Albert Einstein and other refugees founded the International Rescue Committee (IRC) during the 1930s as Nazism reared its ugly head. World War II and its immediate aftermath led to the founding of a host of agencies—Oxfam, Catholic Relief Services (CRS), World Vision, and CARE along with the United Nations family, including the UN Children's Fund (UNICEF) and the UN High Commissioner for Refugees (UNHCR). The French Doctors Movement—beginning with Médecins sans Frontières—emerged when dissident staff within the ICRC revolted against institutional orthodoxy in the Biafran War.

The sea changes in world politics in the 1990s led to no next generation of humanitarian institutions, nor to a transformation of existing institutional machinery—except the establishment of the largely powerless Department of Humanitarian Affairs (DHA) in 1992 (and its successor, the Office for the Coordination of Humanitarian Affairs [OCHA], in 1997).[20] Whether September 11, 2001, has altered the terrain sufficiently to foster more significant change is a proposition worth examining, but it appears unlikely.

The end of the Cold War led to new conflicts and crises, along with the eruption of long-simmering ones held in check by East-West tensions. Moreover, the budgets of humanitarian organizations expanded from U.S.$2 billion at the beginning of the decade to U.S.$6 billion in 2000.[21] In an unprecedented fashion the numbers and activities of intergovernmental and nongovernmental organizations grew, and "humanitarian" became a household word.

The implications of changes in the nature and scope of Security Council decisions resulting from the humanitarian impulse since 1991 are examined here from three angles: ethical, rhetorical, and military. The different perspectives applied to recent humanitarian trends nonetheless overlap. The difficulties in separating them mirrors the increased connections between the formerly more discrete members of the international humanitarian enterprise.[22]

Ethical Landscape

In the 1990s, lively debates unfolded about the right of the community of states to intervene in internal affairs to protect civilians, with some observers contending that there even exists a duty to do so.[23] The proper conduct of military and civilian personnel in humanitarian operations also was the subject of controversy. The ICISS's reframing of the central moral issue is noteworthy—replacing the rights of outsiders to intervene with the rights of affected populations to assistance and protection and the obligations of outsiders to come to the rescue. Moving away from the picturesque vocabulary of the French Doctors Movement alters the debate in fundamental ways. The new framework not only requires an evaluation from the perspective of intervening capitals, but it also means emphasizing those in need and the duty of others to aid and protect them.

Whatever one's views on the feasibility, desirability, or likely impact of vigorous military efforts on behalf of war-affected populations, the dominant moral discourse about humanitarian action has changed. This can be illustrated by reviewing a scholarly journal devoted to the study of the impact of values on international politics, *Ethics & International Affairs*. At the outset of the post–Cold War era, humanitarian action was central in only about 10 percent of articles, whereas in the mid-1990s it reached almost a third and, by the end of the decade, comprised nearly half of the journal's main articles.

Greater moral attention from policy- and decisionmakers will not bring peace on earth, but it can help protect and improve the fragile character of norms that protect the vulnerable. In the United States and elsewhere, some cynics even claim that there was no policy in the 1990s except this softhearted and soft-headed approach, which was distracting attention from more central security threats.

Since September 11, there has been an adjustment between narrowly defined national interests and moral impulses. Washington's response in Afghanistan resembles interventions in the 1970s undertaken by India, Tanzania, and Vietnam (see below). Self-defense and regime change were immediate justifications, but humanitarian benefits were an important byproduct of what Michael Walzer calls "the most successful interventions in the last thirty years."[24]

They generated substantial humanitarian benefits but were not even partially justified by the interveners in such terms. At the time, international order was grounded unquestionably on the inviolability of state sovereignty, and states were far less attuned to humanitarianism than vital interests. India's invasion of East Pakistan in 1971 and, later in the decade, Tanzania's invasion of Uganda and Vietnam's invasion of Kampuchea were unilateral efforts geared to overthrow menacing and destabilizing regimes in contiguous countries, and all were explicitly justified as self-defense. None was approved by the Security Council—and Vietnam's was actually condemned. Yet they now are frequently cited as evidence of an emerging right to humanitarian intervention.

The U.S. intervention in Afghanistan is a mixture of the 1970s and

1990s. What began as essentially a U.S. operation, albeit in concert with other nations and the Northern Alliance, was recognized by the Security Council as a legitimate act of self-defense, thereby making moot Article 51's call for possible ongoing scrutiny by the Council. Operation Enduring Freedom is unique to date, but it is perhaps a harbinger by combining legitimate self-defense and the humanitarian impulse. The casus belli in Afghanistan was an attack on U.S. soil. However, a humanitarian rationale and rhetorical flourishes accompanied defense of U.S. territory. Ex post facto, Washington pointed to favorable and indisputable humanitarian consequences—liberation of women and girls, an end to malnutrition, and reconstruction. That the military baton has been partially passed to NATO strengthens this argument.

To return to the 1990s, many Security Council decisions had an ethical grounding. Resolution 794, which approved the U.S.-led military effort in Somalia in December 1992, set a new standard for "humanitarian" hype—the word was mentioned no fewer than eighteen times. The debate in October 1993 led to the publication of Presidential Decision Directive 25 and reticence about the desirability of humanitarian intervention in the midst of the Rwandan genocide.[25] Nonetheless, humanitarian concerns remained central to U.S. and Western responses. Joseph Nye's remark about Kosovo merits repeating: "Policy experts may deplore such sympathies, but they are a democratic reality."[26]

What happens to the centrality of national interests and power maximization at the beginning of a new century? If the distance between ethical and interest perspectives has shrunk since September 11, is the way open for new thinking about the intersection of values and interests?

Michael Ignatieff has noted that places leading to moral pleas for humanitarian intervention are "bad neighborhoods" in which groups such as Al-Qaida can flourish. This argument seemed far-fetched when attacks took place against U.S. embassies in East Africa and the USS *Cole*. It is less so now. "Our current debate about humanitarian intervention continues to construe intervening as an act of conscience," Ignatieff writes, "when in fact, since the 1990s began, intervening has also become an urgent state interest: to rebuild failed states so that they cease to be national security threats."[27]

Newly discovered "harder" interests join the "softer" line of argument from those who state that vital interests should also include wider international stability, respect for multilateral decisions, and compliance with such norms as international human rights and humanitarian law. Hence, humanitarian intervention not only can be morally legitimate but also can be justified on security grounds.

The humanitarian impulse has permeated foreign and defense policy establishments as well as transformed conceptions of interests and parameters of policy. The belief that democratic states have a long-term national interest as well as moral responsibility to promote human rights was dubbed "good international citizenship" by Australian foreign minister Gareth Evans.[28] Lloyd Axworthy's conviction about the link between basic rights and international security sustained Canada's human security agenda, which was continued by Sadako Ogata and Amartya Sen as chairs of the Commission on Human Security.[29]

The wake of the war on terrorism represents clear dangers for humanitarians and civil libertarians. Less obvious is the possibility that appropriately framed vital interests can also coincide with the humanitarian impulse. In a less interconnected world, collapsing states and humanitarian disasters could be isolated and kept at arm's length. Responses, if any, were mainly driven by moral imperatives because there were few genuine implications for security. Now failed states and human catastrophes pose problems not only to the denizens of war zones and their immediate neighbors but also to peoples worldwide. Robust responses, including military ones, "are thus strategic and moral imperatives."[30]

An accurate scorecard for intervention is required. Keeping the "humanitarian" in "humanitarian intervention" requires a just war focus on means and ends. This is not a trivial semantic distinction designed to score debating points but rather to ensure that informed discussions occur about the reality of the humanitarian impulse when vital interests are present. Even when there is a requirement to address extreme cases of suffering, one can never set aside the possibility of abuse or selective application. After September 11 the temptation to "take off the gloves" and set aside the laws of war in the pursuit against terrorism must be resisted.[31]

The dynamics of state failure and the challenge of nonstate actors enter into this discussion. States are not created equal—neither strong nor failed ones. With 191 UN member states and growing, it is hardly surprising that some are crumbling or have collapsed. But not all weak states actually fail (Chad), and some failed states make a comeback (Lebanon). Viable indicators are required for thresholds that could justify both humanitarian and strategic responses, either reactive or preventive, in weak states. The rise of nonstate actors presents still other problems for fulfilling the promise of the humanitarian impulse in contemporary wars. Despite the predilection to exercise the humanitarian option, the UN's capacity to respond adequately remains a question mark.[32]

Rhetorical Landscape

At the beginning of the 1990s, many observers resented the Security Council's powers of self-definition about what constituted a "threat to international peace and security," which supposedly reflected mainly the diabolical wishes of the great powers. In the middle of the decade the Commission on Global Governance supported decisions motivated by the humanitarian impulse but found the stretched definition ill-advised. It recommended "an appropriate Charter amendment permitting such intervention but restricting it to cases that constitute a violation of the security of people so gross and extreme that it requires an international response on humanitarian grounds."[33]

Factors seen as legitimate by the Security Council included a range of humanitarian disasters, especially those involving large exoduses by internally and internationally displaced persons. Civil wars became the standard bill of fare, but rights trumped sovereignty in enough decisions that it was no longer fatuous to hope for what Francis M. Deng, the special representative of the Secretary-General for internally displaced persons, had dared to call "sovereignty as responsibility."[34]

Endorsed by the ICISS in its opening sentence, state sovereignty is not challenged but reinforced. However, if a state is unwilling or unable to protect the rights of its own citizens, it temporarily forfeits a moral claim to be treated as legitimate. Its sovereignty, as well as its right to nonintervention, are suspended, and a residual responsibility necessitates vigorous action by outsiders to protect populations at risk. In brief, the three traditional characteristics of a state in the Westphalian system—territory, authority, and population—are supplemented by a fourth: respect for human rights.

Vituperative reactions to Kofi Annan's speeches sought to parse the issue as pitting a North enthusiastic about humanitarian intervention against a reluctant South. Historically, the invocation by powerful states against weaker ones made that caricature politically attractive, at least on the surface. In addition, diplomats as well as officials of the UN and nongovernmental organizations (NGOs) seem unable to imagine organizing discussions except across a North-South divide.

However, regional consultations by the ICISS and by the Fund for Peace and the Council on Foreign Relations suggest that such simplistic generalizations—if they ever made sense—no longer apply.[35] For example, many Africans tend to see the necessity for more, not less, humanitarian intervention. Rwanda was a sufficient enough trauma that the founding document of the newly christened African Union contains objectives that are diametrically opposed to those of its predecessor, the Organization of African Unity. Article 4 of the Constitutive Act stipulates "the right of the Union to intervene in a Member State pursuant to a decision of the Assembly in respect of grave circumstances, namely: war crimes, genocide and crimes against humanity."[36] Although the motivations are anything except humanitarian, powerful states that routinely spouted anti-intervention stances (China, India, and Russia) have become more openly supportive—in their cases, against armed fundamentalists with separatist agendas in Muslim areas.[37]

Recent initiatives reflect changes in the moral and strategic landscape. Humanitarian intervention becomes more plausible while motives become more clouded. When there is sufficient operational capacity and political will, legal objections have little consequence. Article 2 of the UN Charter, stipulating the principle of nonintervention, is one thing. But sovereignty is "organized hypocrisy," as Stephen Krasner reminds us.[38]

Moreover, humanitarian issues are only the tip of the increasingly visible iceberg of human security. By the end of the decade, AIDS was recognized in Security Council Resolution 1308 as a threat to international peace and security. A Charter amendment for humanitarian intervention was hardly necessary when, increasingly, states accept the legitimate purview of the Security Council to define "threats to international peace and *human* security."

The broadening of the acceptable basis for Security Council decisions, as well as an opening of minds and perspectives about North-South divisions, has implications for multilateral diplomacy. The energy spent and the ink spilled on Security Council reform have been poor investments. Rather than any official constitutional changes, the broadened scope of activities and the gradual evolution in working procedures hold more potential for substantial change than proposals for altering the Council's composition, eliminating the veto, or using emergency sessions of the General Assembly.[39]

The resilience of long-standing shibboleths among many nonpermanent members of the Council suggests a need for more pragmatic and less predictable positions. Is rapid and complete localization the best strategy (i.e., the Afghan model), or a more massive external presence with longer-term trusteeship (i.e., the model in the Balkans and East Timor)? Are the recommendations to strengthen the UN's military oversight as recommended by the Brahimi Report not better seen as desperately needed by countries torn by conflict rather than as a possible invasion of sovereignty and a drain on development funds? What would be the operational and resource implications of implementing the doctrine of responsible sovereignty?

Political correctness has long been the bane of the UN's existence. It does not serve the individual or collective interests of the vulnerable and weak states in the global South.

Military Landscape

The extent to which the Security Council has adopted decisions under Chapter VII was without precedent, but so too was the UN's demonstrated inability to conduct enforcement operations. The unwillingness by major powers to spend money was matched by an unwillingness to run risks. Whether or not the Council adequately anticipated and appreciated the difficulties is open to question, but too many UN-mandated or UN-controlled military activities encountered significant resistance and loss of life. Decisions were not matched by resources (e.g., in the so-called safe areas in Bosnia, probably the least safe havens in the Balkans). And after forces were deployed, they failed to generate consent in the field. Worst of all, in the face of casualties, the world organization cut and ran in Somalia and Rwanda and thereby made a mockery of the humanitarian impulse.

Moreover, moral and realpolitik consequentialists alike argued that the unintended negative effects (rewards for ethnic cleansers in Bosnia, mass flight from Kosovo once bombing began) meant that bad consequences often outweighed good intentions.[40] Others saw the use of force as undermining international order or obfuscating neocolonial projects.[41]

By the end of the 1990s, the United Nations itself was effectively out of the business of serious military action. The ambitions of Secretary-General Boutros Boutros-Ghali in his 1992 *Agenda for Peace* were considerably subdued by 1995 in his *Supplement to an Agenda for Peace*.[42] The world organization's comparative advantage was in peacekeeping. Acting on the humanitarian impulse, let alone peace enforcement, required not consent and impartiality but the personnel of a major-league military.

The dominant military trend over the 1990s was "subcontracting" by the Security Council.[43] The devolution of responsibility for the enforcement of Chapter VII decisions, virtually all of which had a substantial humanitarian rationale, went to "coalitions of the willing." Instead of being the "doer" envisaged by the Charter, the Security Council often became the "approver" of operations conducted by others. What began as an experiment in the Gulf War and northern Iraq ended up being the standard operating procedure in Somalia, the Balkans, Haiti, and East Timor. The disparity between demand and supply—along with inadequate financing and diminished confidence—meant that the world organization increasingly relied on regional organizations and ad hoc coalitions to ensure compliance with enforcement decisions.

In brief, not everyone can act on the humanitarian impulse. The nature of violence in contemporary war zones means that only the militaries of major powers, and not neutrals or smaller powers, need apply. Military clout is far more important than moral clout, as evidenced by "humanitarian bombing." Furthermore, certain kinds of heavy airlift capacity are absolutely essential for many humanitarian efforts. Yet such technology and airlift capacity are available only from NATO and the United States.

Over the course of the 1990s, the Security Council adopted new roles in acting upon the humanitarian impulse. Sometimes the world organization handed over responsibilities entirely, sometimes it was in the backseat (instead of the driver's seat), and sometimes it worked in tandem with an array of regional institutions. For these eventualities, there are at least three conceptual challenges to military doctrine.

The most critical is to fill a doctrinal void in operationalizing the humanitarian impulse. A number of specific challenges are distinct from those of either peacekeeping or war-fighting, the well-understood endpoints on a spectrum of international military action. What about challenges in-between? How can protection be afforded to populations at risk? How can those who prey upon them be deterred?

Over the course of the 1990s, operations in the middle of the spectrum were common. Two related but distinct sets of objectives exist within the category of enforcement decisions—namely, compelling compliance and providing protection.[44] The former, commonly referred to as "peace enforcement," requires vast military resources and political will. It involves the search for comprehensive political settlements leading to sustainable peace. It contains traditional peacekeeping tasks such as monitoring cease-fires, but it also encompasses complex tasks whose ultimate success requires deadly force. Examples include the Implementation Force (IFOR) and the Stabilization Force (SFOR) organized by NATO in Bosnia, the U.S.-led Multinational Force (MNF) in Haiti, and the UN Mission in Sierra Leone (UNAMSIL). A variant is the application of deadly force to compel parties to the negotiating table. NATO air strikes preceding the signing of the Dayton Accords are one example. Another is the early phase of intervention in Liberia where ECOWAS deployed its monitoring group (ECO-MOG).

Another form of enforcement action, "coercive protection," is directly pertinent for the humanitarian impulse, but it has a variety of forms that are rarely specified. The most common are maintaining humanitarian corridors, disarming refugees, protecting aid convoys, and creating safe havens or protected areas. Prominent examples include the no-fly zone in northern Iraq and the so-called safe areas in Bosnia.

A particularly important dimension of this kind of operation is the force posture of intervening troops. Coercive protection is distinct from other operations, which have military forces oriented in relation to other military forces. Peacekeeping involves the monitoring of military cease-fires or the interposition of forces between armed parties to the conflict; compelling compliance involves the potential use of force against conflict-ing parties or spoilers; and war-fighting involves combat against designated opponents. In contrast, the provision of coercive protection requires the interposition of forces between potential attackers (armies, militias, and gangs) and civilians.

Buried in the "gray area" of the responsibility to protect civilians are numerous tasks that are not favored by militaries around the world: the forcible disarmament of belligerents (especially in refugee camps like those in the mid-1990s in eastern Zaire); the meaningful protection of safe areas (the gruesome counterexample of Srebrenica comes immediately to mind); and the protection of humanitarian workers (as expatriates like Fred Cuny and local officials alike would testify, if they were alive).

There has been little success in meeting the challenges of coercive protection since the end of the Cold War. There seems to be a lack of institutional adjustment, at least as is indicated by military doctrines that, to date, have failed to specify ways to meet the needs for coercive protection of civilians, the challenge of the responsibility to protect.[45]

The second challenge results from the necessity to ensure more than a modicum of international accountability for operations that are approved by the United Nations but fall totally under another institution's operational control. In only a few conflicts—Georgia and West Africa—has the world organization monitored the activities of the regional organizations acting as subcontractors for an internationally approved operation. If the UN's imprimatur for a coalition of the willing is to be meaningful, more accountability and transparency are necessary for future subcontractors. What kinds of monitors in which situations with which types of mandates would be helpful? What kinds of independent reports should go back to the Security Council before an ongoing mandate is renewed? Can international finance be used to secure, as a quid pro quo, independent international monitoring?

Finally, military establishments have become interested in humanitarian tasks that were until recently seen as peripheral. No longer are politicians and humanitarians chasing a uniformly reluctant military and pleading for help. Military budgets, operational training, and officers' career paths are benefiting from humanitarian tasks. "Military humanitarianism" was once viewed as an oxymoron—indeed, some humanitarians still refuse to put the two words together—but it is an accurate depiction of a central aspect of contemporary preparations by armed forces. What was once feared as "mission creep" is not necessarily unwelcome. Although National Security Adviser Condoleezza Rice quipped that the Eighty-second Airborne Division's comparative advantage was not in escorting schoolchildren, there are other tasks in operations motivated by humanitarianism that require first-rate militaries.

Conclusion

The prominence of the humanitarian impulse altered the ethical, rhetorical, and military landscapes of Security Council decisionmaking in the 1990s. The nature and scope of enforcement decisions have amounted, on occasion, to a fundamental increase in the relevance of humanitarian values in relationship to narrowly defined vital interests. After September 11, the distinction between the moral and the self-interested has become less pronounced—or, perhaps better stated, the threat of terrorism has added salience to issues that transcend previously humanitarian dimensions. The beat of war drums for Iraq and the war itself had nothing to do with humanitarian action, but that justification eventually emerged after others fell flat. Indeed, the initial aftermath had all the makings of a major humanitarian crisis. In any event, the experience of the 1990s is clear: potential victims and perpetrators of genocide and ethnic cleansing may find that neighbors, ad hoc coalitions, or even single states have two reasons, moral and geostrategic, to intervene.

At the end of the day, however, predictions are not sensible. As any military historian anxious to avoid fighting the last war knows, lessons are difficult enough to identify in the first place because political, temporal, military, strategic, and geographic translations from one situation to another are methodologically arduous and operationally problematic. Everything is not sui generis, but there are severe limits to comparisons across cases. In thinking merely of temporal dimensions, for instance, making use of cases of intervention during the Cold War has little contemporary significance. And trying to apply lessons from cases between 1990 and the events in October 1993 in Mogadishu is of limited utility when attempting to gauge the willingness of Washington and others to run risks in the Congo even after Rwanda's genocide. The ultimate impact of wars in Afghanistan and Iraq is anyone's guess.

Three stages of individual and organizational learning are commonplace in the business literature but too rarely penetrate analyses of humanitarian intervention: identification, when problems are observed and data are collected; diagnosis, when information is analyzed and underlying beliefs are questioned; *and* implementation, when revised policies and procedures are actually institutionalized and public and bureaucratic support is mobilized on behalf of changes. Scholars and practitioners who are members of the international conference circuit frequently employ the conventional vocabulary of "lessons learned," but decisionmakers and bureaucrats rarely take steps to correct their courses. Have governments and agencies really learned from efforts in Bosnia that halfhearted or symbolic military action may be as bad as or worse than no action at all? Have they actually learned that humanitarian gestures cannot replace substantial commitments?

Why is there a gap between lessons compiled and lessons actually learned, between rhetoric and reality? Some suggest that evaluations defuse pressure for change rather than stimulate it. Cynics simply point to hypocrisy and leave it at that. Sometimes they are right, but often there are other reasons. Governments and agencies are not monoliths. Those who conduct evaluations, draft resolutions, and make statements have not always secured political backing. Competing interests dominate bureaucratic decisionmaking. Even when lessons appear to have been agreed in headquarters, it can prove extremely difficult to translate them into practice on the ground.

To the extent that lessons remain relegated to file drawers, coffee tables, or book jackets, the concept of learning is perverted. It would be more accurate to speak of "lessons spurned." Alex de Waal points to a puzzling contemporary paradox—the international system "appears to have an extraordinary capacity to absorb criticism, not reform itself, and yet emerge strengthened."[46] Academic and policy analysts should be struck about how little the international humanitarian system has changed over the 1990s.[47] A greater-than-usual degree of modesty is in order.

Policy analysis tends to extrapolate from recent headlines—an acute version of Andrew Hurrell's criticism of social scientists as being mired in a "relentless presentism."[48] In the aftermath of the intervention on behalf of the Kurds, there was nothing that humanitarians could not do; the end of the Cold War signaled not only a UN renaissance but also the birth of a new world order. Virtually to the day only three years later, in April 1994, apparently nothing could be done in the face of Rwanda's genocide. In 1999, depending on one's point of view, the humanitarian intervention vintage was either an annus mirabilis or an annus horribilis because of Kosovo and East Timor.

The tragic attacks of September 11 riveted the world's attention upon an international response to terrorism, and a war in Iraq then became the obsession. But in spite of the distractions, diplomats and scholars are forced to revisit thorny humanitarian issues. In the wake of military action against the Taliban and a spreading war on terrorism, dilemmas of humanitarian intervention once again found the spotlight, and the aftermath of the war in Iraq brought back to center stage the familiar challenges of access to, as well as assistance and protection of, civilians trapped in hapless countries. So too is the cast of characters, humanitarian agencies, and outside military forces. Furthermore, "it is only a matter of time before reports emerge again from somewhere of massacres, mass starvation, rape, and ethnic cleansing," write Gareth Evans and Mohamed Sahnoun. "And then the question will arise again in the Security Council, in political capitals, and in the media: What do we do?"[49]

Undoubtedly the attacks against New York and Washington, and the Bush administration's vendetta against Saddam Hussein, have increased pressures on the armed forces, especially in the United States, to focus on fighting wars and avoid the "distractions" of humanitarian work. However, there have been substantial humanitarian dimensions to the effort—including the liberation of the female half of the Afghan population. Indeed, the effort has partially been sold in such terms, and satisfying humanitarian needs is crucial to the mission's ultimate success. One analyst somewhat optimistically speculates that "it may be that mobilization on this scale, although its first aim is self-defense, will galvanize the Western allies to a more activist concern for misery across the globe."[50] Another argues in a more instrumental way that "if America and the West are to achieve safety for themselves in the coming years, they will have to show that they care about more than just their own suffering."[51]

Even when conscience-shocking events occur in faraway places that do not directly threaten vital interests, publics often clamor that "something be done." If interests and humanitarian concerns overlap—if there is sufficient symmetry between the humanitarian impulse and strategic stakes—perhaps publics will demand more robust action to protect civilians from the ravages of war and thugs posing as political leaders. If previous experience in Afghanistan and the ongoing efforts on the ground in Iraq are any indication, and as the ever-widening war against terrorism in such places as Indonesia makes clear, the challenges of fragmentation and humanitarian action are certainly not unique to the 1990s. The humanitarian impulse remains vital.

Notes

I am grateful to Peter J. Hoffman and Larry Minear for comments on earlier drafts of this chapter.

1. Such an impulse also appears in the face of natural disasters, but the politics of helping are totally different when acting upon request rather than against the will or stated wishes of local political authorities.

2. Matthew S. Parry, "Pyrrhic Victories and the Collapse of Humanitarian Principles," *Journal of Humanitarian Assistance* (October 2002): 4, www.jha.ac/articles/a094.htm.

3. David Rieff, *A Bed for the Night: Humanitarianism in Crisis* (New York: Simon and Schuster, 2002).

4. Adam Roberts, "The Role of Humanitarian Issues in International Politics in the 1990s," *International Review of the Red Cross* 81, no. 833 (March 1999): 19. See also, Michael Ignatieff, "Human Rights: The Midlife Crisis," *New York Review of Books* 46, no. 9 (May 20, 1999): 58–62.

5. See S. Neil MacFarlane, *Intervention in Contemporary World Politics,* Adelphi Paper no. 350 (Oxford: Oxford University Press, 2002), p. 79. He cites, among others, the struggles between Protestants and Catholics in fifteenth- and sixteenth-century Europe, the interventionist tendencies of the French Revolution, and the position of the Holy Alliance in the nineteenth century; humanitarian intervention is also a theme.

6. Christine Bourloyannis, "The Security Council of the United Nations and the Implementation of International Humanitarian Law," *Denver Journal of International Law and Policy* 20, no. 3 (1993): 43.

7. Th. A. van Baarda, "The Involvement of the Security Council in Maintaining International Law," *Netherlands Quarterly of Human Rights* 12, no. 1 (1994): 140.

8. Edward Luttwak, "Kofi's Rule: Humanitarian Intervention and Neocolonialism," *The National Interest* no. 58 (Winter 1999–2000): 60.

9. Kofi A. Annan, *The Question of Intervention* (New York: United Nations, 1999).

10. See Raimo Väyrynen, *The Age of Humanitarian Emergencies,* Research for Action no. 25 (Helsinki: World Institute for Development Economics Research, 1996); and Nicholas J. Wheeler, *Saving Strangers: Humanitarian Intervention in International Society* (Oxford: Oxford University Press, 2000).

11. For example, see the 2,200 entries essentially in English from the 1990s in the key-worded bibliography of Thomas G. Weiss and Don Hubert, *The Responsibility to Protect: Research, Bibliography, and Background,* supplementary volume of the International Commission on Intervention and State Sovereignty (Ottawa: International Development Research Center, 2001), pp. 225–336, www.iciss-ciise.gc.ca.

12. International Commission on Intervention and State Sovereignty, *The Responsibility to Protect* (Ottawa: International Development Research Center, 2001).

13. Independent International Commission on Kosovo, *Kosovo Report* (Oxford: Oxford University Press, 2000).

14. *Interagency Review of U.S. Government Civilian Humanitarian and Transition Programs,* document dated July 12, 2000; and Alton Frye, ed., *Humanitarian Intervention: Crafting a Workable Doctrine* (New York: Council on Foreign Relations, 2000).

15. Advisory Council on International Affairs and Advisory Committee on Issues of Public International Law, *Humanitarian Intervention* (The Hague: AIV and CAVV, 2000); and Danish Institute of International Affairs, *Humanitarian Intervention: Legal and Political Aspects* (Copenhagen: Danish Institute of International Affairs, 1999).

16. For overviews, see David Cortright and George A. Lopez, eds., *The Sanctions Decade: Assessing UN Strategies in the 1990s* (Boulder: Lynne Rienner, 2000); and Thomas G. Weiss, David Cortright, George A. Lopez, and Larry Minear, eds., *Political Gain and Civilian Pain: Humanitarian Impacts of Economic Sanctions* (Lanham, Md.: Rowman & Littlefield, 1997).

17. For overviews, see Michael J. Perry, *The Idea of Human Rights: Four Inquiries* (New York: Oxford University Press, 1998); and Thomas Risse, Stephen C. Ropp, and Kathryn Sikkink, eds., *The Power of Human Rights: International Norms and Domestic Change* (Cambridge: Cambridge University Press, 1999).

18. Christopher Greenwood, *Humanitarian Intervention: Law and Policy* (Oxford: Oxford University Press, 2001).

19. See Simon Chesterman, *Just War or Just Peace? Humanitarian Intervention and International Law* (Oxford: Oxford University Press, 2001); and Michael Byers and Simon Chesterman, "Changing Rules About Rules? Unilateral Humanitarian Intervention and the Future of International Law," in J. F. Holzgrefe and Robert O. Keohane, eds., *Humanitarian Intervention: Ethical, Legal, and Political Dilemmas* (Cambridge: Cambridge University Press, 2003), pp. 177–203.

20. For a discussion, see Thomas G. Weiss, "Humanitarian Shell Games: Whither UN Reform?" *Security Dialogue* 29, no. 1 (March 1998): 9–24.

21. See Joanna Macrae, ed., *The New Humanitarianisms: A Review of Trends in Global Humanitarian Action,* HPG Report no. 11 (London: Overseas Development Institute, 2002).

22. See, for example, Larry Minear, *The Humanitarian Enterprise: Dilemmas*

and Discoveries (Bloomfield, Conn.: Kumarian, 2002); Marc Lindenberg and Coralie Bryant, *Going Global: Transforming Relief and Development NGOs* (Bloomfield, Conn.: Kumarian, 2001), esp. pp. 65–99; and Thomas G. Weiss, *Military-Civilian Interactions,* 2nd ed. (Lanham, MD: Rowman & Littlefield, 2004).

23. See Mario Bettati and Bernard Kouchner, *Le devoir d'ingérence* (Paris: Denoël, 1987); and Mario Bettati, *Le droit d'ingérence: Mutation de l'ordre international* (Paris: Odile Jacob, 1996).

24. Michael Walzer, "The Argument About Humanitarian Intervention," *Dissent* (Winter 2002): 29.

25. See Samantha Powers, *"A Problem from Hell": America and the Age of Genocide* (New York: Basic Books, 2002).

26. Joseph P. Nye Jr., "Redefining the National Interest," *Foreign Affairs* 78, no. 4 (July–August 1999): 30.

27. Michael Ignatieff, "Intervention and State Failure," *Dissent* (Winter 2002): 115.

28. See Nicholas J. Wheeler and Tim Dunne, "Good International Citizenship: A Third Way for British Foreign Policy," *International Affairs* 74, no. 4 (1998): 847–870.

29. Lloyd Axworthy, "Human Security and Global Governance: Putting People First," *Global Governance* 7, no. 1 (2001): 19–23; and Rob McRae and Don Hubert, eds., *Human Security and the New Diplomacy* (Montreal: McGill-Queen's University Press, 2001).

30. See Robert I. Rotberg, "Failed States in a World of Terror," *Foreign Affairs* 81, no. 4 (July–August 2002): 127.

31. See Michael Ignatieff, "Human Rights, the Laws of War, and Terrorism," Dankwart Rustow Memorial Lecture, CUNY Graduate Center, October 10, 2002.

32. The role of nonstate actors is discussed in Thomas G. Weiss and Peter J. Hoffman, "Comprehending and Coping with Non-State Actors: Making Humanitarianism Work," in Simon Chesterman, Michael Ignatieff, and Ramesh Thakur, eds., *The Failure and the Crisis of Governance: Making States Work,* forthcoming.

33. Commission on Global Governance, *Our Global Neighbourhood* (Oxford: Oxford University Press, 1995), p. 90.

34. Francis M. Deng, "Frontiers of Sovereignty," *Leiden Journal of International Law* 8, no. 2 (1995): 249–286; and Francis M. Deng et al., *Sovereignty as Responsibility* (Washington, D.C.: Brookings Institution, 1995).

35. For a summary of ICISS consultations, see Weiss and Hubert, *The Responsibility to Protect,* pp. 349–398. See the Fund for Peace website, www.fundforpeace.org, regarding perspectives from Africa and the Americas.

36. See www.sudmer.com/cen-sad/constitutive.

37. Giandomenico Picco, "New Entente After September 11th? U.S., Russia, China, and India," *Global Governance* 9, no. 1 (January–March 2003), pp. 15–21.

38. Stephen D. Krasner, *Sovereignty: Organized Hypocrisy* (Princeton: Princeton University Press, 1999).

39. Thomas G. Weiss, "The Illusion of UN Security Council Reform," *Washington Quarterly* 26, no. 4 (Autumn 2003): 141–167.

40. A vast array of humanitarian agencies supported this stance, joining forces with Henry Kissinger following his book *Does America Need a Foreign Policy? Toward a Diplomacy for the Twenty-First Century* (New York: Simon and Schuster, 2001).

41. See Robert Jackson, *The Global Covenant: Human Conduct in a World of States* (Oxford: Oxford University Press, 2000); and Mohammed Ayoob, "Humanitarian Intervention and State Sovereignty," *International Journal of Human Rights* 6, no. 1 (Spring 2002): 81–202.

42. Boutros Boutros-Ghali, *An Agenda for Peace* (New York: United Nations, 1995).

43. See Thomas G. Weiss, ed., *Beyond UN Subcontracting: Task-Sharing with Regional Security Arrangements and Service-Providing NGOs* (London: Macmillan, 1998).

44. This is spelled out in detail in Weiss and Hubert, *The Responsibility to Protect*, chap. 8.

45. John Mackinlay has analyzed the doctrinal need to define accurately types of insurgents in order to avoid a "one fix approach and craft different force postures and counter-strategies." The same argument applies to the protection of civilians. See John Mackinlay, *Globalisation and Insurgency,* Adelphi Paper no. 352 (Oxford: Oxford University Press, 2002), p. 12.

46. Alex de Waal, *Famine Crimes: Politics and the Disaster Relief Industry in Africa* (Oxford: James Currey, 1997), p. vi.

47. For a discussion of the failures to change as a result of analyses, see Nicola Reindorp and Peter Wiles, *Humanitarian Coordination: Lessons from Recent Experience* (London: Overseas Development Institute, 2001); and A. Wood, R. Apthorpe, and J. Borton, eds., *Evaluating International Humanitarian Action: Reflections from Practitioners* (London: Zed Books, 2001).

48. Andrew Hurrell, foreword to Hedley Bull, *The Anarchical Society: A Study of Order in World Politics,* 3rd ed. (New York: Columbia University Press, 2002), p. xiii.

49. Gareth Evans and Mohamed Sahnoun, "The Responsibility to Protect," *Foreign Affairs* 81, no. 6 (November–December 2002): 100.

50. Dana H. Allin, *NATO's Balkan Interventions,* Adelphi Paper no. 347 (Oxford: Oxford University Press, 2002), p. 98.

51. Nicolaus Mills and Kira Brunner, preface to Nicolaus Mills and Kira Brunner, eds., *The New Killing Fields: Massacre and the Politics of Intervention* (New York: Basic Books, 2002), pp. ix–x.

4

Human Rights

Joanna Weschler

For decades, human rights were considered strictly internal matters of the state and hence outside the scope of the Security Council. That view was held particularly strongly by the communist bloc, but almost all governments were ambivalent at best about the Council's entering an area so widely perceived as a matter of state sovereignty. Diplomats as well as politicians insisted that human rights and security were wholly separate and should be kept that way.

Today, nobody any longer seriously questions the relevance of human rights to the Council's work and the need for human rights information and analysis at every stage of the Council's action. However, this acceptance has come gradually and haltingly. Only since the end of the Cold War has the Council established that it—and the world at large—has any say in the human rights situation inside sovereign countries. Perhaps most important for the gradual acceptance of the relevance of human rights to the work of the Security Council has been the realization that in order to achieve lasting peace agreements human rights need to be addressed. But to this day, human rights remain among the most sensitive matters, and they are often trumped by other considerations.

This chapter examines the process in which the Security Council went from considering human rights to be nearly taboo, to accepting, at least on the rhetorical level, the need to include human rights in the scope of its work. It looks at the evolution of the approach to human rights over the years and analyzes some key developments.

Human Rights in the Security
Council's Peacemaking and Peacekeeping

While the end of the Cold War created the first opportunity for a more systematic inclusion of human rights in the Security Council's outlook, they were not entirely absent from the Council's work even in its early years. Several resolutions contained human rights language, for instance with respect to the situation in Hungary in 1956 (Resolution 120), in the Congo in 1961 (Resolution 161), and in the Dominican Republic in 1965 (Resolution 203). In the late 1960s and 1970s several Council resolutions, mostly in the context of the decolonization of Africa, evoked the Universal Declaration of Human Rights and other human rights instruments. Through the early 1990s, several resolutions related to South Africa contained strong human rights language, including calls for the release of prisoners, stays of executions and clemency, and the condemnation of massacres.[1]

However, it was only with respect to El Salvador in the early 1990s that the Council adopted for the first time a comprehensive approach to human rights as part of a peace process. This episode showed both the potential and the feasibility of a broad human rights agenda in the practice of the Security Council. In Resolution 693 (1990), the Council for the first time created a human rights component within a mission it authorized, the UN Observer Mission in El Salvador (ONUSAL). Its mandate can serve as a model human rights directive even today.[2] The tasks of the mission included, inter alia, the active monitoring of the human rights situation, the investigation of specific cases of alleged violations of human rights, the promotion of human rights, the making of recommendations to eliminate violations of human rights, and a reporting requirement to the Secretary-General and, through him, to the Security Council and the General Assembly.

The early deployment of a sophisticated human rights mission by the Council deterred abuses and thus helped create a climate of confidence needed by both sides to make compromises necessary for the signing of the final peace accords. Later, the human rights component of ONUSAL, through its work on both past and ongoing human rights abuses, was instrumental in ensuring a relatively peaceful and smooth transition.[3]

Unfortunately, the El Salvadoran model was not consistently adopted in later peacekeeping operations. This may be related to the fact that the final stages of the El Salvador peace negotiations took place in a truly matchless moment of history.[4] The collapse of the Soviet Union opened a unique window of opportunity in terms of what suddenly became politically possible within the Council. That window, however, soon narrowed once again with the escalating conflict in the Balkans, where the main actors expressed great reluctance to make human rights an inherent part of any package.

When the Council in early 1992 established the UN Transitional Authority in Cambodia (UNTAC), human rights were part of the mandate.[5] Yet there were never more than twenty-one human rights officers among the 22,000 personnel deployed. Furthermore, the entire UN effort in

Cambodia was focused on keeping the timetable for the elections, and as a result the mission was reluctant to respond effectively and in a timely fashion to human rights violations in order not to jeopardize those elections. In subsequent Council resolutions on Cambodia, human rights were rarely mentioned.

Human rights violations were at the core of concerns in Haiti following the September 1991 coup that landed democratically elected president Jean-Bertrand Aristide in exile. Initially, the Council considered the developments in Haiti an internal matter of the state. In February 1993, however, a joint UN–Organization of American States human rights observer mission was deployed. Nevertheless, the Council largely left human rights outside the scope of its subsequent decisions and statements on Haiti. Thus, for example, there was no mention of human rights in the Governor's Island Agreement, negotiated with the help of Council members in summer 1993.

Still, by 1995 the Security Council was increasingly making the connection between peacekeeping and human rights. Operations in Angola, Liberia, and Georgia, among others, all had a human rights component, and the Council was receiving regular updates on human rights developments in the periodic reports of the Secretary-General on those operations.

Human Rights Violations
as a Threat to Peace and Security

A key moment for the Council's acceptance of human rights as a legitimate factor in its work came with the passage in April 1991 of Resolution 688 on Iraq. It condemned "the repression of the Iraqi civilian population in many parts of Iraq . . . the consequences of which threaten international peace and security in the region." Even though this condemnation was not backed by any specific action (the Council took no further steps to compel the regime to change its treatment of the civilian population), Resolution 688 was groundbreaking, for it represents the first instance in which the Council explicitly states that such repression leads to threats against international peace and security. China abstained, as did India, while Cuba, Yemen, and Zimbabwe voted against.

Soon afterward, in January 1992 at the first ever Security Council summit, several heads of state talked about human rights as being an integral part of peace and security, and the statement adopted by the summit noted that human rights verification had become one of the tasks of UN peacekeeping.[6] What had been already happening for a few years now received a political blessing from at least some of the key Council actors.

In August 1992 the Council for the first time ever decided to invite a special rapporteur of the UN Commission on Human Rights (CHR), Max Van der Stoel, to address the body. Despite the political pronouncements during that earlier summit, the very fact of allowing a human rights expert to address the Council was extremely controversial, and four countries—India, China, Ecuador, and Zimbabwe—had their reservations noted in the record. India's ambassador was particularly passionate about the issue: "Deviation from the Charter, in which the nations of the world have reposed their faith and support, could erode that confidence and have grave consequences for the future of the Organization as a whole. . . . The Council . . . cannot discuss human rights situations per se or make recommendations on matters outside its competence."[7] These words reflected well the still prevalent attitude of many governments toward the Council's involvement with human rights.

Neither this and a subsequent presentation Van der Stoel made to the Council, nor his recommendation that human rights monitors be placed on the ground in Iraq,[8] were supported or acted upon by the Council. Furthermore, the seminal Resolution 688, which had been referred to in some of the subsequent resolutions on Iraq in 1991 and 1992, was for a decade thenceforth dropped from the long litany of resolutions always recalled when new resolutions on Iraq were passed.[9] And while humanitarian issues have since played a role in the Council's approach to Iraq, human rights violations have never proved among its key concerns.

By 1992 the conflict in the Balkans was in full rage, and the attention of the Council was increasingly turning to that part of the world. Its resolutions made frequent references to the humanitarian aspects of the conflict and slightly less frequently to human rights.[10] In a new approach, the Council in Resolution 771 of August 13 asked states and international humanitarian organizations to provide information on violations of humanitarian law and the Secretary-General to make recommendations regarding specific measures to be taken. Furthermore, a special session of the CHR held in Geneva decided to appoint a special rapporteur on human rights in the former Yugoslavia and, in a move unusual for the CHR, asked the Secretary-General to make the rapporteur's reports available to the Security Council. The former prime minister of Poland, Tadeusz Mazowiecki, was appointed to the post in August 1992, and for the first time the Council was regularly receiving human rights information from a specialized human rights mechanism.

However, the main actors involved in the peacemaking efforts in the Balkans—of which the Council was only one—continued to display uneasiness about addressing human rights issues, largely on the grounds that this would only complicate matters further and delay any settlement, not least because of the fact that they were negotiating with individuals directly responsible for massive human rights violations.

The extent of grave breaches of the Geneva Conventions prompted the Council to eventually create a separate track for addressing them: its

Resolution 780 established a commission of experts to investigate such breaches and suggest further steps. The commission was underfunded and largely moribund, but eventually it paved the way for the establishment under Chapter VII of the Ad Hoc Criminal Tribunal for the Former Yugoslavia in October 1993 (Resolution 877). It was a groundbreaking move, the first explicit acknowledgment that accountability for the most egregious war crimes and crimes against humanity was key to the maintenance of peace and security and that individual responsibility for such crimes was of concern to the Council.

Yet it took nearly a year for the prosecutor to be appointed and significantly longer for the tribunal itself to become operational. These early difficulties were clearly a reflection of the great ambivalence the main political actors felt about mixing human rights and justice with security issues. In fact, many in the human rights community suspected at the time that the establishment of the tribunal was primarily a gesture aimed at public opinion and that various bureaucratic stumbling blocks would prevent the court from ever performing its stated functions. That this did not prove the case may be related to a massive advocacy effort undertaken by human rights organizations that put significant pressure on the UN Secretariat and key member states—in particular the Western permanent members of the Council—to allow the tribunal to get off the ground.

The Security Council and Human Rights Catastrophes

Only a day before the presidents of Burundi and Rwanda were killed when their airplane was shot down on April 6, 1994, the Council had renewed the mandate of the UN Assistance Mission in Rwanda (UNAMIR). This peacekeeping mission was originally mandated in October 1993 to implement the Arusha Peace Accords. Rwanda had been plagued by ethnic violence, with hundreds of civilians killed in a series of massacres and incidents since 1990 for the sole reason of being Tutsi. These abuses were well documented, including by the UN system itself. As subsequent investigations—notably the 1999 report by the Carlsson Commission[11]—would reveal, the Secretariat and some of the members of the Council had known of numerous warning signs of the looming threat of genocide in Rwanda, and plenty of information about the atrocities was available throughout the weeks of carnage. An August 1993 report by the CHR special rapporteur on extrajudicial executions recommended that any transitional arrangements introduced in Rwanda should have human rights at their heart.[12] However, the mandate of UNAMIR, in what was perhaps one of the most serious human rights mistakes on the part of the Council, did not include any human rights component.

Furthermore, the Council not only did not take steps to prevent genocide before its onset; it also failed to act once the slaughter started and even reduced the UN presence on the ground.[13] The Council studiously avoided the use of the word "genocide," and for months it did not take any actions to address the human rights disaster. The first references to specific human rights activities appeared in June 1994 when in Resolution 925 the Council welcomed the visit of the newly appointed high commissioner for human rights to Rwanda, noted the appointment of the special rapporteur by a special session of the CHR, and requested the Secretary-General to ensure that UNAMIR extend close cooperation to the special rapporteur. Resolution 935, passed in July, asked the Secretary-General to establish a commission of experts to collect all available information, including that gathered by the special rapporteur, and to report to the Council on possible appropriate next steps. As a result, through its Resolution 955 later in the year, the Council established the Ad Hoc International Criminal Tribunal for Rwanda. Still, with hundreds of thousands of lives lost despite the advance warnings and despite the UN presence on the ground, Rwanda remains one of the darkest episodes in UN history, and several of the Council members shoulder a large share of the blame.

In 1995 another human rights disaster occurred under close UN watch. Council-created "safe areas" in Bosnia were overrun by the Serb forces, and thousands of male inhabitants were forcefully removed and then slaughtered. Particularly appalling were the events in Srebrenica, where the Dutch UN peacekeeping battalion not only did not attempt to protect the local population but also forced the civilians who had sought refuge in the UN compound in Potocari out of the compound and straight into the hands of the awaiting Serbs. Several thousand men and boys were subsequently taken away by the Serbs and never seen again. To have created the so-called safe areas without providing them with adequate military protection was probably one of the most serious and fatal mistakes in the history of the Council. The big powers, under pressure from public opinion, had wanted to appear resolute in addressing the massive human rights violations. But unwilling to put their troops at risk, they had not been resolute enough to back their words with soldiers and resources. In essence, they used Security Council resolutions as fig leaves to cover their inaction.

The Council condemned the offensive and expressed its concern about the missing men and boys in presidential statements issued in July 1995, in the immediate aftermath of the events. Mazowiecki, the human rights rapporteur, visited the area within days and in an almost unprecedented move—by UN standards—resigned from his post upon his return, explaining that he no longer could be associated with the UN after it had failed so horribly the people it was supposed to protect.[14] But the Council waited until December 1995, after the signing of the Dayton Peace Accords, to pass a resolution in which it explicitly condemned the human rights violations committed and stressed the need to fully investigate the events. However, as of late 2003 the Council has not taken any active steps to pursue the matter, and the fate of the thousands of men and boys removed from the UN "safe area" has remained officially unsolved.

Soul-Searching by the UN

In the late 1990s the United Nations subjected itself to a thorough analysis of its own role in the tragedies of Rwanda and Srebrenica.[15] The report on Rwanda by former Swedish prime minister Ingvar Carlsson in particular focused on the need to incorporate human rights information in the work of the Council. It recommended an improvement in "the flow of information on human rights issues. Information about human rights must be a natural part of the basis for decision-making on peacekeeping operations, within the Secretariat and by the Security Council."

The Report of the Panel on United Nations Peace Operations, commonly known as the Brahimi Report, followed this critically important analysis.[16] In particular, it offered concrete recommendations on steps to prevent human rights disasters from occurring. The report criticized in particular the UN's concept of impartiality and the Secretariat's tendency to be overly optimistic in its reports to the Council, and it highlighted the need for the United Nations and the Council to be prepared to effectively deal with "spoilers" of peace accords. The report correctly emphasized the need to improve the gathering and flow of information and the importance of the human rights components of peacekeeping and peacebuilding operations. The report also stressed that consistency with "prevailing human rights standards and humanitarian law" needed to be a basic condition of any peace agreement to be implemented with the participation of the United Nations.

The Security Council and Human Rights Information

One symptom of the Council's unease about human rights was its reluctance to even hear information on the subject. The three occasions on which the Council heard UN special rapporteurs on human rights in formal debates in 1992 remained the three sole such examples for the next decade.

The elected ten often experienced frustration and felt that while the permanent five had their own channels, they were not receiving enough information about key events. Such was the backdrop when, in March 1992, that month's president of the Council, Venezuelan ambassador Diego Arria, was contacted by a Croat priest who had just come out of the Balkan conflict zone. Ambassador Arria wanted the priest to convey his eyewitness account to other members of the Council. Not being able to find a formal way, Arria simply invited his fellow ambassadors to meet with the priest in the delegates' lounge. Some ten or eleven ambassadors attended, and clearly they were stunned by what they heard and were able to appreciate the critical importance of firsthand information.[17] That meeting was the first of what later came to be known as "Arria Formula" briefings.

There proved an even stronger resistance, however, to receiving information from human rights sources independent of the UN, notably nongovernmental organizations (NGOs). For many years, the Security Council was considered off-limits to NGOs and vice versa. In March 1992, during his Council presidency, Ambassador Arria felt that the Secretariat was not providing sufficient information on the situation in Somalia. He decided to invite the head of Africa Watch (now the Africa Division of Human Rights Watch) to brief him in the presidency office. He recalled how a Secretariat official was flabbergasted by this fact and insisted that meeting with NGOs in Security Council rooms was unacceptable.[18]

In the early weeks of genocide in Rwanda, some members of the Council strove to obtain human rights information independently. The Czech ambassador, Karel Kovanda, sought out a Rwanda expert from Human Rights Watch, to whom he conveyed his concern that the Council was not being fully informed about what was happening on the ground. On April 18, 1992, he hosted an informal briefing by the NGO expert in his residence, which all the elected members of the Council attended.[19] For months afterward, several nonpermanent delegations on the Council took pains to keep themselves informed through independent sources.

After the first Arria Formula briefing, that format was used by the Council to obtain human rights information, but only in extremely rare situations. In late 1996 the Council, alluding to the political sensitivity of having a human rights briefing,[20] declined to hear the human rights rapporteur on Burundi, in spite of the growing emergency in the Great Lakes region. It was not until November 1999 that French ambassador Jean-David Levitte organized an Arria Formula briefing with a human rights rapporteur on another Great Lakes country, the Democratic Republic of Congo. Subsequently, several other such briefings were held,[21] and by 2001 informal briefings by a UN human rights investigator had become more or less acceptable. Since the late 1990s, human rights NGOs have also occasionally briefed the Council, mainly through the Arria Formula.

The Turn of the Millennium: A Mixed Bag

By the late 1990s, the Council was increasingly including human rights in its mandates and statements. It appeared to be increasingly concerned with the implementation of its resolutions, yet it still showed a degree of inconsistency.

When the Council established the mandate in Sierra Leone in July 1998, it demanded full respect for human rights by all parties; and among the tasks of the civilian staff of the UN Mission in Sierra Leone (UNAMSIL) was providing regular reports on violations of international human rights and humanitarian law to the Council. But when in 1999 a peace accord signed in Lomé granted amnesty to the worst violators of human rights[22]—something that prompted the Secretary-General to instruct his envoy to add a disclaimer next to his signature explicitly stating that for the UN the amnesty could not cover international crimes of genocide, crimes against humanity, war crimes, and other serious violations of international humanitarian law—the Council essentially ignored this caveat and did not address the issue of impunity when establishing the post-Lomé operation. It took the subsequent reignition of conflict, many lives lost or destroyed, and a nearly total collapse of the peace process for the Council to start addressing the most pressing human rights issues through, among other things, the establishment of a special court, insistence on strengthening the human rights unit of UNAMSIL, and efforts meant to deprive the worst violators of their financial base, the diamond trade.[23]

When dealing with Taliban-ruled Afghanistan, the Council repeatedly expressed its deep concern about the human rights situation there. Of special concern were the rights of women and girls. Resolutions 1267 (1999) and 1333 (2000), which established sanctions designed to force the Taliban to turn over Osama bin Laden, expressed the Council's concern with respect to human rights violations. The aftermath of the removal of the Taliban by U.S. forces, the signing of the Bonn Agreement, which established a transitional government, and the deployment of a UN peacebuilding mission, the UN Assistance Mission in Afghanistan (UNAMA), raised the prospect of greater freedom for the Afghan people. Yet UNAMA, despite all lessons previously learned (and even with Lakhdar Brahimi himself in charge), took a minimalist approach to human rights. A year later, in many parts of the country other than Kabul, life looked not much different from life under the Taliban, with dissent being suppressed (including by torture), the press muzzled, and women back in their burqas.[24]

The Role of the Secretary-General

An Agenda for Peace, Boutros Boutros-Ghali's optimistic manifesto written in early 1992 at the invitation of the Security Council summit in the heady aftermath of the collapse of communism, envisioned a wide-ranging role for the UN in confronting armed conflict and humanitarian disaster. The document listed human rights violations among the causes of conflict and stressed the need for human rights expertise in peacekeeping and postconflict activities.[25] However, Boutros-Ghali rarely spoke about human rights and often insisted that they were an internal matter of the state.

When Kofi Annan took over as Secretary-General in 1997, the tragedies of Rwanda and Srebrenica were still very fresh in memory. And perhaps because of that Annan, a UN insider who had been intimately involved in these events as the head of UN peacekeeping at the time, made human rights an important element of his early agenda.

Time and again, especially during his first year in office, he emphasized that human rights were integral to all UN activities, including security and development. On the institutional front, he made the High Commissioner for Human Rights part of his cabinet-style Policy Coordination Group (subsequently renamed the Senior Management Group) and had him participate in the four executive committees covering the four main areas of UN activities.[26] After years of institutional exile suffered by human rights and the respective part of the Secretariat, this was nothing short of revolutionary. On numerous occasions, Annan emphasized the relevance of human rights issues to security even at the risk of provoking those among the permanent five, notably China, most reluctant to embrace the relevance of human rights in the security context.[27]

Perhaps the most important moment in which Annan made human rights concerns a key factor for unfolding events came in September 1999, at the height of the postreferendum violence in East Timor. He stated publicly that senior Indonesian officials risked prosecution for crimes against humanity if they did not consent to the deployment of an available multinational force[28] and insisted that sovereignty must give way to the imperative of stopping crimes against humanity. For Annan, overcoming the lack of political will and inappropriate mandates from the Security Council was key if the Council was to respond to gross and systematic violations of human rights.[29]

Although he did not start the trend, Annan has certainly been instrumental in establishing human rights firmly on the Council radar screen. This has been particularly visible since September 11, 2001. Annan has been the strongest public voice in trying to prevent human rights from becoming another casualty of terrorism. He has consistently emphasized that there must be no tradeoff between addressing human rights and fighting terrorism.

The Security Council's Relationship
with the High Commissioner for Human Rights

After decades of calls to establish the post of a high-level official responsible for all UN human rights activities, in 1993 the General Assembly created the post of the high commissioner for human rights. The original proposals had called for the official to be based in New York, close to the political center of the organization. This part of the proposal, however, met insurmountable resistance from many governments, and thus the high commissioner joined the rest of the UN human rights machinery in the Geneva exile, to which the Human Rights Division had already been sent from New York in 1974.

Ecuadorian ambassador José Ayala Lasso, who less than two years earlier had argued before the Council that "human rights per se do not fall within the competence of the Security Council,"[30] was named the first UN high commissioner for human rights. Lacking any human rights background, combined with his deep aversion to outspokenness, Lasso was ill-suited for the job. Not surprisingly, he shied away from trying to press human rights issues onto the Council's agenda.

His successor, however, former Ireland president Mary Robinson, who served as high commissioner from September 1997 until September 2002, early on in her tenure launched an effort to establish direct contacts with the Council and, despite initial resistance, achieved a degree of success. Since mid-1999, either she or her New York representative held monthly briefings with the president of the Security Council to provide information on key human rights developments. Robinson also undertook efforts to address the Council formally. In spite of some reluctance on the side of certain Council members—notably China because of a previous meeting between the high commissioner and the Dalai Lama—Robinson was able to address the Council on September 16, 1999, at the invitation of the Secretary-General. Other meetings and consultations followed, including most recently also on country-specific rather than generic issues.

Chipping Away at the Supremacy of State Sovereignty

One of the key factors in making human rights acceptable to most governments as an inherent element of the Council's outlook was the gradual abandonment—over a decade or so—of the absolutist approach to state sovereignty. That process culminated in the wake of the violence in East Timor with the Secretary-General's address to the General Assembly on September 20, 1999, in which he counterposed the concepts of state sovereignty and individual sovereignty, describing the latter in terms of human rights and fundamental freedoms.[31] He pointed out the challenge of forging international unity behind the principle that massive and systematic violations of human rights should not be allowed to stand, and he raised the issue of so-called humanitarian intervention.

That speech produced a heated debate and led to the creation of an international commission headed by Gareth Evans and Mohamed Sahnoun, which produced an important report, *The Responsibility to Protect*.[32] In its conclusions, the commission argued that state sovereignty implied responsibility and that in cases where the population was suffering serious harm as a result of internal war, insurgency, repression, or state failure and where the state in question was unwilling or unable to provide protection, the principle of nonintervention needed to yield to the international responsibility to protect.

The commission concluded that the Council was the most appropriate body to authorize intervention in the face of massive human rights and humanitarian law violations, but it also pointed out, citing the example of Kosovo, that in cases where the Council could not agree, it should not be seen as the last resort. Among the recommendations, the commission included a call on the permanent members of the Council to agree not to exercise their veto power to obstruct the passage of resolutions authorizing military intervention for human protection purposes for which there was otherwise majority support. As of late 2003, just one of the permanent five, France, was known to be willing to apply this principle.

Conclusion

The attitude of the Security Council toward human rights has been convulsive: a series of starts and stops, with interspersed progress and setbacks. Overall, however, the attitude has been evolving toward a general acceptance of the responsibility to take steps, whenever possible, to prevent massive human rights violations and to protect those most vulnerable. Council insiders vividly describe how the very mention of the words "human rights" would "wake certain members up" or cause major "body language changes."[33] By all accounts, however, this phenomenon belongs to the past, and while the Council is still far from consistency and full resolve in its approach to human rights, important steps have been taken.

In the early to mid-1990s, each time the Council addressed matters related to the impact of armed conflict on civilians, including massive flows of displaced persons and refugees, it acted as if it needed to justify its concern by making the case that each such case posed a threat to peace and security. By issuing the February 1999 presidential statement and then passing Resolution 1265 in September on civilians in armed conflict, however, it took a huge leap, condemning the deliberate targeting of civilians by combatants as a violation of humanitarian and human rights law. In Resolution 1296 (2000) it went on to request that the Secretary-General bring to its attention situations in which civilians are particularly vulnerable and address issues related to the protection of civilians in his reports on matters with which the Council was already seized. It followed with resolutions addressing other groups vulnerable in conflict, such as women and children.

Between 1994 and 1999 the Council went from failing to act in the face of genocide in Rwanda, and abdicating its responsibility to see its own resolutions implemented in the case of Srebrenica, to hands-on engagement, including an emergency visit aimed at mitigating violence and preventing further violations in East Timor. But with the Kosovo crisis in 1999, the Council also learned that it risked becoming irrelevant when, due to the veto system, it was unable to react to severe human rights violations and, given enough public pressure to act, there was another actor ready to step in.

With each crisis and each new intervention, in places such as Iraq, Bosnia, Somalia, and East Timor, the concept of state sovereignty has continued to erode. As of 2003, the Council appears to have firmly accepted the link between security and human rights and the relevance of human rights information for its decisionmaking. One Council ambassador attributed the decreasing overall reluctance to deal with human rights issues to the Council's growing interest in seeing its resolutions implemented and in particular its increased focus on achieving concrete results on the ground.[34]

With its two Chapter VII ad hoc tribunals now fully operational, the Council has also helped to firmly establish the concept of international justice. The tribunals, as well as the mixed national/international special court for Sierra Leone, which the Council was instrumental in creating, show that—at least in certain situations—the Council now accepts the link between accountability and peacemaking, peacekeeping, and peacebuilding.

For the time being, the issue remains open on how effective the Council can or wants to be in decreasing or preventing suffering caused by human rights violations, but it appears that human rights are no longer likely to disappear from the Council's radar screen anytime soon.

Notes

1. See Sydney D. Bailey, *The UN Security Council and Human Rights* (New York: St. Martin's, 1994).

2. For details of the mandate, see Secretary-General's report S/22494, April 16, 1991, para. 8a–8e.

3. Human Rights Watch, *The Lost Agenda: Human Rights and UN Field Operations* (New York: Human Rights Watch, 1993).

4. One of the participants, former Venezuelan ambassador Diego Arria, recalled a symbolic moment: a December 25, 1991, meeting during which final details of the peace accord were being polished in the apartment of Secretary-General Javier Pérez de Cuéllar. A few other key ambassadors participated. At some point the Secretary-General had to step out of the room because the Soviet ambassador urgently needed to talk to him. Pérez de Cuéllar returned after a few minutes and informed his guests that he had just been notified that the Soviet Union ceased to exist. Interview with Diego Arria, November 13, 2002.

5. Resolution 745 (1992).

6. S/PV.3046 and S/23500, both January 31, 1992.

7. S/PV.3105, August 11, 1992.

8. For details, see Max Van der Stoel's interim report to the General Assembly, A/47/367, sec. 3.

9. A reference to Resolution 688 reappeared in Resolution 1441, which was passed on November 8, 2002, and paved the way to resumed Iraq inspections.

10. From late 1992 the Council presidency has been regularly briefed by the UN delegate of the International Committee of the Red Cross, which acquired observer status at the UN in October 1990.

11. S/1999/1257, December 16, 1999.

12. E/CN.4/1994/7/Add.1, August 11, 1993, para. 61.

13. Resolution 912 (1994).

14. Tadeusz Mazowiecki's press conference in Geneva, July 27, 1995. Also his letter dated July 27, 1995, to the Secretary-General.

15. S/1999/1257, December 16, 1999 and A/54/549, November 15, 1999.

16. S/2000/809, August 21, 2000.

17. Interview with Diego Arria, November 13, 2002.

18. Ibid.

19. Interview with Alison Des Forges, October 24, 2002.

20. Phone interview with Paulo Sergio Pinheiro, October 20, 2002.

21. Phone interview with Roberto Garreton, October 27, 2002.

22. S/1999/777, July 7, 1999.

23. Resolutions 1306 (2000), 1315 (2000), 1346 (2001).

24. Human Rights Watch, *All Our Hopes Are Crushed: Violence and Repression in Western Afghanistan* (New York: Human Rights Watch, 2002).

25. S/24111, June 17, 1992.

26. Secretary-General's press conference, Headquarters New York, February 13, 1997.

27. Kofi A. Annan, "Address to the Academy of Social Sciences and the Institute of International Relations," Shanghai, May 1997.

28. Secretary-General's press conference, Headquarters New York, September 10, 1999.

29. A/55/1, August 30, 2000.

30. S/PV.3105, August 11, 1992.

31. SG/SM/7136, September 20, 1999.

32. International Commission on Intervention and State Sovereignty, *The Responsibility to Protect* (Ottawa: International Development Research Center, 2001).

33. Confidential interviews.

34. Interview with Jeremy Greenstock, New York: November 15, 2002.

5

Democratization

Gregory H. Fox

In 1993 the Security Council for the first time urged a member state other than South Africa or Rhodesia to organize itself as a "democracy."[1] The occasion was the still-hopeful effort to bring peace and stability to Somalia.[2] Thereafter the floodgates opened. From 1993 through 2000, the Council referred to "democracy" in fifty-three resolutions, all of them favorable.[3] The Council has praised democratic governance for reasons ranging from its role in fostering national reconciliation, to ensuring security in states recently emerging from civil war, to assisting in the reconstruction of governing infrastructures. It has dispatched missions to a broad variety of states to organize, monitor, and adjudicate elections. And based on the outcome of two monitored elections—in Haiti and Sierra Leone—the Council not only refused to recognize regimes that overthrew the elected leaders as legitimate but also authorized the use of armed force to depose the usurpers and return the elected leaders to office.[4] Democracy has become so integrated into the policy objectives regularly pursued by the Council that in a July 2002 resolution the Council could urge Bosnia-Herzegovina to "make progress towards fully meeting the standards of a modern democracy" without any debate among its members on this passage and without pausing to elaborate on what was meant by such a broadly phrased exhortation.[5]

This chapter examines the Council's recent and growing engagement with issues of democratic governance. The primary question it addresses is how a body charged by the UN Charter with primary responsibility for "maintaining international peace and security" has come to address this most domestic of issues of how nations select their leaders. What links does it perceive between its mandate to maintain stable relations *among* states and the nature and quality of governance *within* states? Is democratic governance seen as an end in itself, or does the Council view its advocacy as instrumental, potentially enhancing other more traditional objectives? And

69

having "internationalized" the question of national governance by urging states to pursue democratic agendas, what role exists for the international community in the process of reform?

I will argue that despite the seeming polarity between international conflict and domestic governance, the Security Council has consistently found strong links between the two. Democracy, in the Council's repertoire of practice, is above all a means of ending, preventing, sublimating, and diverting violent internal conflict. In part, this view is premised on the theory that repressive and exclusionary political practices are a significant contributing cause of many civil wars. It is also premised on the rejection—now well supported in international law—of solutions to civil wars involving either permanent domination of one party over another, or the partition of a state between two or more of the warring factions.[6] Finally, the preference for democracy is a reflection of the limited resources available to the Council (and the international community generally) to supervise postconflict societies. Democratic institutions are seen as mechanisms of self-policing that, if functioning properly, create incentives for domestic actors to avoid a return to conflict, thereby relieving international actors such as the United Nations from assuming the burden.

Most of the conflicts in which the Council has promoted some form of democratic politics have been internal civil wars, suggesting only a weak link to its Charter mandate to address *international* peace and security. But in this respect the Council's concern with democracy is hardly unique. Virtually all of the large-scale conflicts of the post–Cold War era have been civil wars, and the Council has not hesitated to expand the reach of the remedial devices at its disposal to address wars that in scale and intensity rival (and even surpass) the interstate wars of the same period. In an era when "domestic" issues such as human rights, environmental degradation, corruption, and nontariff barriers to trade have all become the legitimate subjects of international legal scrutiny, the Council's concern with domestic warfare seems hardly controversial. Indeed, the Council has been criticized more for its failure to address certain internal conflicts than for being too aggressive in taking on the problem as a category of action. The Council's advocacy of democratic institutions can be seen as but one more aspect of its newfound concern with internal conflict. Yet suggesting the lack of democracy as a cause of civil war and the establishment of democratic institutions as a means of preventing such war is a substantial leap forward.

Early Action: Antiapartheid Initiatives

Before the Security Council's embrace of democratic values in the 1990s, Cold War divisions precluded it from addressing virtually any aspect of national governance. The relative merits of socialism and democratic capitalism were the putative center of divisions between East and West, making consensus on even a minimum set of "democratic" institutions impossible. Even provisions of human rights treaties guaranteeing an individual right to political participation did not use the world "democracy," focusing instead on the details of electoral procedures and associated rights of political contestation.[7]

There was one significant exception to the Council's early abstention from issues of democracy: its condemnation of apartheid in South Africa and Southern Rhodesia.[8] The central issue of racial discrimination certainly dominated discussion of apartheid in the Council and other UN organs. But at bottom, South Africa's systematic exclusion of black and colored citizens from participation in government was a question of majority rule, the central feature of any democratic system. At first, the Council's condemnations were extremely general, describing apartheid in a 1963 resolution as "inconsistent with the principles contained in the Charter of the United Nations."[9] In April 1964, however, a group of experts established by the Council phrased its proposed solution to race-based exclusions in democratic terms: "It is only on the road of free and democratic consultation and cooperation and conciliation that a way can be found towards a peaceful and constructive settlement."[10] The Council endorsed the group's report and specifically its conclusion that "all of the people of South Africa should be brought into consultation and should thus be enabled to decide the future of their country at the national level."[11]

This tentative reconceptualization of the problem stalled along with all other Council initiatives toward South Africa until the late 1970s, when increasing public pressure and the intransigence of the white leadership finally led the Council to impose a mandatory arms embargo in 1977. Thereafter, the Council's prescriptions for acceptable reform in South Africa began explicitly to invoke democratic principles and mechanisms. In 1980 the Council recognized "the legitimacy of the struggle of the South African people for the elimination of apartheid and for the establishment of a democratic society in which all the people of South Africa as a whole, irrespective of race, colour, or creed, will enjoy equal and full political and other rights and participate freely in the determination of their destiny."[12] A prescription of majority rule and free elections was clearly implicit in this language, which the Council repeated in several subsequent resolutions.[13]

In 1983 the South African government announced plans for a new constitution, which was approved by an exclusively white referendum in November. The constitution provided for segregated chambers of parliament for colored persons and Indians, but none at all for black South Africans. The Council declared the constitution "null and void" and urged all governments and organizations not to recognize the results of elections held under the constitution and to continue "to assist the oppressed people of South African in their legitimate struggle for a non-racial, democratic society."[14] When the transition to majority rule finally occurred in 1994, the Council welcomed "the first all-race multiparty election and the establishment of a united, democratic, non-racial government of South Africa."[15]

Democracy and Conflict Resolution

The end of the Cold War brought democratic transitions—real, nascent, and illusory—to states in every region of the world. This revolution in governance at the national level had an immediate effect on discussion of governance issues within the Council. Political democracy no longer demarcated the fault line between East and West. The ideological barrier that had kept democratization off the table for discussion in the Council was suddenly broken. As a result, the Council was able to include the promotion of democratic transitions in the mix of solutions to its most challenging security problem of the 1990s: destructive civil wars.

The collective security provisions of the Charter were ill-equipped to address the seeming epidemic of civil wars that marked the end of the Cold War. The states in which these conflicts occurred often lacked the strong political infrastructures needed to resolve the disputes. As one report observed in 2001:

> The main threat to the security of the international community is the weakness of states owing to a lack of democratic structures and an inability to manage and combat such phenomena as organized crimes, international and domestic terrorism, corruption, lack of political liberties, human rights abuses, religious and ethnic conflicts, and aggressive nationalism. In many states, institutional mechanisms are unable to resolve these problems with norms and the tenets of the rule of law.[16]

Any meaningful attempt to resolve these conflicts thus fell to external actors. The Security Council quickly became the forum for discussing proposed solutions. Yet the UN Charter was drafted in the long shadow of World War II and assumed that the principal threats the organization would address would be threatened or actual *interstate* conflicts. These conflicts were assumed to threaten the international order by definition, and Chapter VII of the Charter set out mechanisms by which states would pledge material and political support for their suppression. The Charter makes no mention of internal conflicts.

The realities of the early 1990s demanded that the Council revisit this interstate orientation. As a jurisdictional matter it did so in short order, finding a series of internal conflicts and their consequences to constitute "threats to the peace," triggering its Chapter VII authority.[17] Human rights violations, mass starvation, ethnic cleansing, and other "domestic" events were held to constitute "threats to the peace." Various types of interventions in civil war followed. These developments in turn left the Council with the difficult task of finding Charter-based solutions to conflicts its architects had never envisioned it would address in the first place. Nothing in the Charter suggested how the Council should seek to resolve civil wars: how to reintegrate the most hateful of belligerents into single political societies, and which institutional reforms to prescribe so that the chances of conflict recurring were minimized.

The Secretary-General early on declared that the UN would become involved in assisting postconflict societies. In *An Agenda for Peace,* UN Secretary-General Boutros Boutros-Ghali declared the organization would engage in "rebuilding the institutions and infrastructures of nations torn by civil war and strife."[18] The Secretary-General made clear that those institutions would be built according to democratic models, asserting: "There is an obvious connection between democratic practices—such as the rule of law and transparency in decision-making—and the achievement of true peace and security in any new and stable political order. These elements of good governance need to be promoted at all levels of international and national political communities."[19]

Beginning with the second UN Angola Verification Mission (UNAVEM II) in June 1991 and continuing through the end of 2002, the Council authorized seventeen missions to postconflict states, virtually all with a mandate to oversee some aspect of a transition to democratic governance.[20] The most common task has been monitoring elections, though in keeping with the widely accepted view that democracy is not defined by elections alone, the missions have performed many other tasks as well (discussed below). In establishing an observer mission to Tajikistan in 1994, for example, the Council stated that "the international assistance provided by this resolution must be linked to the process of national reconciliation, including *inter alia* free and fair elections."[21] In the same year, the Council called on the parties in Mozambique—which had just held its first postconflict election—to base national reconciliation "on a system of multi-party democracy and the observance of democratic principles which will ensure lasting peace and political stability."[22] And in reviewing the factors contributing to ongoing conflict in Africa, the Council in 1997 identified democracy promotion as one of the ways the UN contributes to conflict resolution on the continent.[23] Many developing states resisted the formal adoption of democracy as an objective of the organization, fearing it would serve as a "guise for intervention or for attempts to destabilize their regimes."[24] Yet in 2001, reviewing the UN's democracy promotion activities in the ten years after publication of *An Agenda for Peace,* Secretary-General Kofi Annan reaffirmed the link between democratic governance and conflict prevention:

> The work undertaken by the United Nations to support democracy in its
> Member States contributes significantly to conflict prevention. Such
> assistance encompasses the provision of comprehensive support in the
> area of governance and the rule of law, including electoral assistance. It
> has been proven to play an important role in preventing the breakdown of
> democratic institutions and processes, particularly in societies in transi-
> tion, or in new or restored democracies.[25]

The Secretary-General's views reflect much recent scholarship in finding internal political dynamics at the root of contemporary conflict, rather
than the realist pursuit of state interest. This is obviously true of internal
conflict, which is by definition rooted in the inability of domestic political
institutions to accommodate satisfactorily the conflicting demands of
national groups. In the Secretary-General's words: "At the center of virtually every civil war is the issue of the state and its power—who controls it,
and how it is used. No armed conflict can be resolved without responding
to these questions. Nowadays, the answers almost always have to be democratic ones, at least in form."[26]

Recent scholarship has also suggested that in the short term democratic
openings in fragile, postconflict societies may actually increase instability
by encouraging open competition between extreme nationalist and ethnic
factions.[27] A vigorous debate has ensued as to whether international actors
should act on this data by curbing their enthusiasm for immediate postconflict elections. While this may well occur, a tactical retreat from immediate
democratic transitions is unlikely to alter the Council's now well-established view that long-term solutions to internal conflict must include democratic governance.

Means of Democracy Promotion

How has the Security Council operationalized the view that democratic
institutions may contribute to preventing the recurrence of civil conflict? A
regular set of practices has come to typify UN missions to postconflict
states. The missions are generally divided into separate units or components, each responsible for a different aspect of assisting the transition from
conflict-ridden and usually nondemocratic government to a stable, elected
government. Some units assume tasks only tangentially related to democracy promotion: supervising cease-fires, overseeing the disarmament of combatants and the demobilization of fighters, demining, repatriating refugees,
initiating economic recovery plans, and the like. Others, such as electoral
units, are at the heart of democratic institution-building. Many missions
also have separate human rights components. Still other units assist local
courts in judicial training programs, anticorruption initiatives, and law
reform efforts.

These traditional democratic institutions present useful building blocks for the infrastructure of a democratic society. But their promotion is predicated on the existence of a minimum level of centralized state authority that is capable of both overseeing their functioning and compelling adherence to their rulings. A wholly failed state, with no governing institutions commanding adherence from more than a fraction of the population, cannot be approached as a mere project of "reform." A more fundamental reconstitution of legitimate authority must occur first.

Facing this predicament in Somalia, the Security Council endorsed the innovative approach of a conference on national reconciliation. After the Council authorized intervention in December 1992, it recognized that distributing humanitarian aid to needy Somalis, however successful in the short term, would be quickly nullified if nothing were done to address the anarchy then reigning throughout the country. The Council thus authorized the Secretary-General to offer "assistance to the people of Somalia in rehabilitating their political institutions and economy and promoting political settlement and national reconciliation."[28] As the UN later noted, the organization "had not previously attempted to help build governmental structures from the ground up."[29] On March 27, 1993, a broad range of Somali parties assembled in Addis Ababa for a conference on national reconciliation, largely through the Secretary-General's efforts. The conference adopted an agreement setting out transitional mechanisms designed to "prepare the country for a stable and democratic future."[30] A Transitional National Council (TNC), functioning as the "repository of Somali sovereignty," would guide the country through a transitional phrase. That process would "prepare the country to enter a constitutional phase in which the institutions of democratic governance, rule of law, decentralization of power, protection of human rights and individual liberties, and the safeguarding of the Somali Republic are all in place."[31] But those holding real power in Somalia were unwilling to cede authority to the TNC, and the well-known collapse of the Somalia mission put an end to Council efforts to promote that body as the center of a democratic nation-building enterprise.

Virtually all of these tasks could be described as contributing to "democratization" broadly understood. Theories of democracy that emphasize distributive equality as well as an equality of political participation would support such a holistic conception, emphasizing actual attainment of "the good" over the simple provision of "the right." While the postconflict missions authorized by the Council have, as described, been multifaceted—more so as the 1990s progressed and the UN came to understand that instability could arise from any number of sources in postconflict states—the Council's understanding of "democracy" has been much narrower. Democracy in its view can roughly be described as the set of institutions, rights, and norms that enable citizens to choose their leaders and influence (or in some circumstances directly *make*) policy. It is a view that focuses primarily on the political arena and within that on competitive elections. No "official" Council definition exists, though other UN organs and divisions (the Secretary-General, the Human Rights Commission, and the Electoral Assistance Division of the Department of Political Affairs) have expounded at length on the nature of the "democracy" in their work. Yet this essentially procedural conception of democracy is evident in the context of Council references to democracy, which in its resolutions occur almost solely in relation to the holding of elections. It is also evident in the consistent separation between divisions of postconflict missions that address electoral matters—as to whose work the term "democracy" is consistently applied—and other divisions in relation to which it is not. This is true even for divisions working on issues of human rights.

At the same time, one cannot abstract from Council practice a view of democracy that begins and ends with elections. Certainly the Secretary-General has pointedly rejected this view.[32] The most important evidence of a "participatory" understanding of democracy is the Council's approval of missions assuming plenary control over all governmental functions in Kosovo and East Timor. This international administration of territory allowed the Council to design, in essence, a blueprint for governing institutions that reflects both its accumulated practice and human rights norms bearing on the appropriate relation between government and citizen. In both cases, the Council described the structures it was creating as democratic in nature.

In Kosovo, the Council in Resolution 1244 (1999) established an "interim administration" for Kosovo that had as one of its central goals "organizing and overseeing the development of provisional institutions for democratic and autonomous self-government pending a political settlement, including the holding of elections."[33] Elaborating on this formula, the Secretary-General described the interim administration as involving multi-ethnic governmental structures, the application of international instruments on human rights, pluralistic party structures, administrative procedures of democratic governance, and elections.[34]

The Goals of Council Democracy Promotion
The preceding discussion suggests that the Security Council has viewed democracy as a means of responding to internal conflicts and the attendant tasks of national reconstruction they engender. This section explores the specific ways in which democracy is perceived to address internal conflict.

National Reconciliation

The Council most frequently justifies its democracy promotion efforts as a way of fostering reconciliation among warring or recently warring parties. Democracy is often identified as the means by which parties negotiating an end to internal conflicts may ultimately channel differences that at the time appear insurmountable. In expressing concern over the deteriorating situation in Burundi in 1996, for example, the Council gave support to outside efforts "to facilitate a comprehensive political dialogue with the objective of promoting national reconciliation, democracy, security and the rule of law in Burundi."[35] And as the European Union representative told the Council shortly after the Dayton Accords ended fighting in Bosnia, "Reconciliation is one of the vital ingredients in any process of building a society. The holding of free, fair and democratic elections throughout the territory is crucial in this respect."[36]

That democratic institutions may sublimate ethnic or other hostilities is also evident in statements by the target states themselves. Speaking on the UN mission authorized after the Dayton Accords, the Bosnian ambassador told the Council that his government was "committed to furthering existing democratic institutions and establishing new ones . . . which will guarantee safety, justice and respect for all citizens of Bosnia and Herzegovina, regardless of their ethnic or religious background."[37] Similarly, the Tajik ambassador told the Council in 1994 that his government was "convinced that only political dialogue, in combination with the measures we are undertaking to democratize the country's political life . . . will pave the way towards national reconciliation in Tajikistan."[38] These comments came after the Council had approved an observer mission to the country.

Council members have thus described democratization as a civilizing influence, an effort to address root causes of conflict through institutionalized processes, and in so doing to confront directly the view that *only* violent conflict can secure each side's political aims. In this view, democratic institutions capable of responding to the parties' fundamental grievances would substantially reduce the security dilemma many theorists identify as the origin of recourse to force in states with deep ethnic cleavages and lacking political institutions with greater legitimacy and coercive capacities than the warring parties themselves.[39]

Internal Security

Closely related to fostering national reconciliation is the goal of maintaining internal security. Indeed, the two may be seen as the diplomatic and military sides of the same postconflict coin. Often democracy and internal security appear in Council discussions as intertwined objectives, with one asserted as an essential prerequisite to achieving the other. Reduction of violence and insecurity is seen as necessary for democratic institutions to function, while democratic institutions are promoted as a means of preventing the recurrence of conflict. The former question often emerges in discussions of security measures needed at election time, when animosities between previously warring parties are at their most pointed and violence often flares.[40] The latter rests on the (some would say overly) optimistic view that Clausewitz's maxim can be reversed and politics can become the continuation of war by other means. In this view, a "postsettlement election succeeds or fails relative to war termination to the extent that it contributes to ending the fighting."[41] Given the destructive nature of civil conflicts and their prominence on the Council's agenda in the post–Cold War period, it is clearly the second relation between democracy and conflict that is the most important for the Council's work.

Thus, given the Council's now uniform practice of authorizing an electoral component in its postconflict missions, one can legitimately impute a palliative conception of democratization efforts to the Council. But like most theorists addressing the causes of civil conflict and effective strategies for their termination, the Council has not articulated a simplistic cause-and-effect relation between democracy and the prevention of civil wars. Its views on causation are complex and multifaceted. In a 1999 resolution, for example, the Council highlighted "the need to address the causes of armed conflict in a comprehensive manner . . . including by promoting economic growth, poverty eradication, sustainable development, national reconciliation, good governance, democracy, the rule of law and respect for and protection of human rights."[42] Moreover, its various initiatives in postconflict states have been launched simultaneously and are described as symbiotic. In addressing the Secretary-General's proposal to create a mission to Tajikistan, for example, the British ambassador argued that it was essential that the Secretary-General report soon "not only that the cease-fire has been extended but also that progress is continuing with national reconciliation and the promotion of democracy."[43] He concluded that "a new United Nations Mission of this sort needs to be linked to a clear political process resulting in a negotiated settlement and a representative and sustainable national government."[44]

Building Governmental Infrastructure

Many of the democracy promotion missions involve substantial constitutional reforms in the target states. Prior governing structures, often unacceptable to at least one party to the recently ended conflict, are changed with a view to creating national consensus and greater inclusiveness. Democratic principles are often integral to this reform process, serving as the building blocks for electoral laws, separation-of-power schemes, human rights regimes, and judicial institutions. Where the Council's mandate includes law reform, democratic principles are often explicitly derived from international law sources. The reform process in Kosovo took this internationalization of domestic institutions a step further and incorporated international human rights institutions directly into the domestic judicial structure.[45]

The influence of democratic principles on the task of institution-building is again clearest in missions where the Council has not built on existing governing structures but worked from an effective blank slate. In East Timor, the Secretary-General reported to the Council on October 4, 1999, that "local institutions, including the court system, have for all practical purposes cased to function."[46] As a result, the UN transitional administration would be "entrusted with the task of rebuilding a structure of governance."[47] This, the Secretary-General stated, would be guided by the principles of "participation and capacity-building."[48] Accepting these recommendations, the Council in Resolution 1272 mandated the UN Mission in East Timor (UNTAET) "to support capacity-building for self-government" in East Timor and to "carry out its mandate effectively with a view to the development of local democratic institutions."[49]

Regional Stability

The conflicts serving as the impetus for many of the Council's democracy promotion efforts often have important regional consequences.[50] The war in Bosnia profoundly destabilized the entire Balkan region in the early 1990s; the Central American civil wars of the 1980s involved many of the states in the region; the ongoing conflict in Cambodia prior to the 1991 Paris Accords had consequences for neighboring Vietnam and Thailand; and the civil war in the Democratic Republic of Congo has involved not only virtually all its neighbors but other states in southern and eastern Africa as well.

Democracy promotion's contribution to regional stability is a further consequence of its perceived role in reducing conflict within the target state. In part this may be attributable to regional states seeing a substantial reduction in threats to their own interests once a peace accord is brokered in the target state. But it may also be ascribed to the view, articulated most prominently by Anne-Marie Slaughter, that democratic states develop dense networks of intergovernmental ties, which have the effect of further reinforcing the values underlying institutions in each state.[51] Slaughter argues that while international efforts to legislate democratic procedures will take time and may "afford easy targets for nationalist and cultural opposition," governmental networks established between liberal democratic states can "help build and even establish specific governmental institutions, as well as strengthening and occasionally legitimating their existing members."[52] This horizontal approach provides a better prospect for creating embedded, legitimate governing institutions, Slaughter claims, because it substitutes "national for supranational bureaucrats" in the process of transmitting democratic values and processes.[53] In this view, a regional community of democratic states would be particularly fertile ground for the development of such networks.

Economic and Financial Recovery

At best, postconflict states experience economic stagnation; at worst, their economies lie in ruins. Economic reconstruction is thus a central goal of Council-authorized reconstruction missions. Democratic institutions are seen as linked to the economic recovery project in two ways. The first involves matters of process: democratic institutions are perceived as more effective in assessing needs fairly, making decisions in a transparent manner, and utilizing aid money honestly and efficiently. If parties are guided by "the principles of democracy," the president of the Council said in a statement concerning postconflict elections in Mozambique, that will enable "the international community to continue to support Mozambique as it pursues rehabilitation and reconstruction."[54]

The second involves the politics of perception: democratic transitions create rising popular expectations that along with political reform will come economic reform, resulting in tangible benefits to ordinary citizens. New leaders thus find themselves in a dilemma. Their democratic ascendancy has driven popular expectations to often unrealistic levels, yet the principles of transparency and accountability to which they are putatively committed require them to report to their constituents that economic change will come slowly and often unevenly. The results can be destabilizing. As the Secretary-General reported to the Council in the aftermath of 1995 elections in Haiti:

> There is a growing demand for social services and infrastructure, such as medical and educational facilities, roads, electricity, and improved living conditions. These unmet demands and heightened expectations, generated by the installation of a democratically elected government, have led to frequent demonstrations in the capital and throughout the country. These events have been generally peaceful. However, the potential for violence has increased.[55]

Conclusion: Democracy Promotion by the Security Council as a Transitional Measure

The review of Council practice suggests that each of its justifications for democracy promotion has been linked, in one way or another, to its broader efforts at national reconciliation and reconstruction. One may therefore describe the Council's view of democratization as instrumental in character. Viewing democracy as a means to a collective end for these societies is surely not an unexpected conclusion. Democratic political theory is overwhelmingly instrumental, only occasionally describing popular political participation as actualizing some essential human characteristic, or in some other way viewing the right as deontological. More frequently, democracy is correlated with a variety of consequential social goods: legitimate governing institutions, a more enlightened public debate on policy issues, a more active and engaged citizenry, greater protection of private property, and so on.[56] As with these goals of a single society, the Security Council has found democratic governance to further the general welfare of the society of states on whose behalf it acts in matters of peace and security. Only in the case of apartheid have the Council and its members spoken of democracy as compelled by self-justifying notions of justice and equality.[57]

But the assembly of a more efficient set of peacemaking tools cannot, in itself, be the ultimate objective of the Council's democratization efforts. The Council is not designed to be an ongoing presence in the political lives of member states. Its role set out in the Charter is essentially reactive, responding to acts against the peace by taking measures designed to "maintain or restore international peace and security." Democratization has served the Council as a way of refashioning the internal politics of states so that conflict prevention and management functions are *self-sustaining,* thereby rendering intervention by the international community unnecessary. This is indeed a momentous change for an organization built on universal membership in a highly diverse world. The view that a particular form of government is more likely to prevent conflict among citizens by creating outlets for grievances that might otherwise turn violent seems more exclusionary than universal. The theory rests on a specific vision of the state that invests much faith in liberal theories of governance.

The consequences for international law of a liberal democratic conception of the state have been discussed elsewhere.[58] For purposes of understanding the specific role of the Security Council, the relevant point is that the Council views democracy promotion as a decidedly temporary measure. If the democratic values promoted by the Council make their expected contribution to national reconciliation, then the Council's role will come to an end. The Dutch ambassador aptly described this dynamic to the Council in a debate over East Timor: "The United Nations, which in the current stage is the indispensable Organization, should, of course, endeavour to make itself superfluous."[59] And as the Council declared in a resolution adopted that same day, the mission to East Timor would "consult and cooperate closely with the East Timorese people in order to carry out its mandate effectively with a view to the development of *local democratic institutions*."[60]

As a result, the reconstructed state will cease to be a ward of the international community and function autonomously and effectively. As the Kenyan ambassador told the Council in commenting on a mission to the Central African Republic, "A new dependency on United Nations peacekeeping operations to hold our countries together is not one that we would cherish or want to see nurtured."[61] The link between autonomy and effectiveness is crucial, for the Council's involvement begins only when citizens lose faith in the capacity of national institutions to redress their grievances. Once national institutions regain legitimacy as problem-solvers and mediators, the Council's reason for intervention ends; the state has demonstrated a capacity to avoid externalizing its problems. In the Council's view, the state has become stronger, despite external intervention to promote democratic reforms.[62] Its strength does not involve an assertion of exclusive sovereign authority often seen as antithetical to individual rights. Rather, its strength comes in areas that coincide precisely with the Council's stated interest in promoting values such as human rights and conflict resolution.

Notes

I am grateful to Sita Doddamani, Deirdre Golden, Carol Parker, and Nancy Shafer for their outstanding research assistance.

1. Many resolutions had urged South Africa and Southern Rhodesia to abandon apartheid practices and create nonracial "democratic" institutions. For a discussion, see text accompanying notes 7 and 8. In 1949 the Council urged Indonesia to adhere to a previously negotiated agreement with the Netherlands and hold "democratic elections." Resolution 67, January 28, 1949. The Council also called on India to hold a "democratic plebiscite" on the future of Jammu and Kashmir. Resolutions 126, December 2, 1957; 122, January 24, 1957; 98, December 23, 1952; 91, March 30, 1951; 80, March 14, 1950; 47, April 21, 1948.

2. The Council declared itself convinced "of the need for broad-based consultations and deliberations to achieve reconciliation, agreement on the setting up of transitional government institutions and consensus on basic principles and steps leading to the establishment of representative democratic institutions." Resolution 814, March 26, 1993.

3. The resolutions addressed a variety of states, virtually all of them in transition from conflict or nondemocratic governance, or having experienced an interruption of democratic government: Albania, Bosnia and Herzegovina, Burundi, Cambodia, the Central African Republic, the Democratic Republic of Congo, El Salvador, Haiti, Sierra Leone, and Somalia. Two topical resolutions addressed the protection of civilians during armed conflict and peacekeeping operations.

4. See Resolution 940 (1994), on Haiti; and S/PRST/1998/5, February 26, 1998, welcoming removing of junta in Sierra Leone by force dispatched by the Economic Community of West African States.

5. Resolution 1423, July 12, 2002.

6. See Gregory H. Fox, "Strengthening the State," *Indiana Journal of Global Legal Studies* 7, no. 1 (1999).

7. For example, Article 21 of the Universal Declaration, Article 25 of the International Covenant on Civil and Political Rights, Article 3 of the First Protocol to the European Convention on Human Rights, and Article 23 of the American Convention on Human Rights.

8. Space limitations permit discussion only of the South Africa case. The Council's condemnation of Southern Rhodesia was equally premised on opposition to race-based minority rule.

9. Resolution 181, August 7, 1963.

10. *Report of the Group of Experts Established in Pursuance of the Security Council Resolution 182 (1963)*, S/5658, 1964, para. 8.

11. Resolution 191, June 18, 1964, para. 5.

12. Resolution 473, June 13, 1980.

13. See Resolutions 569, July 26, 1985; 765, July 16, 1992; 772, August 17, 1992; 894, January 14, 1994.

14. Resolution 554, August 17, 1984, paras. 2, 5.

15. Resolution 919, May 26, 1994.

16. Adam Daniel Rotfeld, "The Organizing Principles of Global Society," in *Stockholm International Peace Research Institute Yearbook 2001* (Oxford: Oxford University Press, 2001), p. 3.

17. This is the only trigger in crucial Article 39 of the Charter that could conceivably cover events occurring wholly within national territory. The two other triggers for Chapter VII—a "breach of the peace" and an "act of aggression"—have not been invoked in these circumstances.

18. UN Secretary-General, *An Agenda for Peace: Preventive Diplomacy, Peacemaking, and Peacekeeping (Report of the Secretary-General pursuant to the statement adopted by the Summit Meeting of the Security Council on 31 January 1992)*, A/47/277-S/24111, June 17, 1992, para. 15.

19. Ibid., para. 59.

20. See Gregory H. Fox, "International Law and the Entitlement to Democracy After War," *Global Governance* 9, no. 2 (2003): p. 179.

21. Resolution 994, December 16, 1994.

22. Resolution 957, November 15, 1994.

23. S/PRST/1997/46, September 25, 1997.

24. Caroline E. Lombardo, "The Making of an Agenda for Democratization," *Chicago Journal of International Law* 2, no. 1 (2001): 253, 259.

25. *Prevention of Armed Conflict,* A/55/985-S/2001/574, June 7, 2001, para. 79.

26. Kofi A. Annan, "Democracy as an International Issue," *Global Governance* 8, no. 2 (2002): 135, 137.

27. See Jack Snyder, *From Voting to Violence* (New York: Norton, 2000).

28. Resolution 814, March 26, 1993.

29. United Nations, Department of Public Information, *The United Nations and Somalia* (New York: United Nations, 1996), p. 45.

30. Addis Ababa Agreement, concluded at the first session of the Conference on National Reconciliation in Somalia, reprinted in ibid., p. 264.

31. Ibid., p. 265.

32. See UN Secretary-General, *An Agenda for Democratization,* A/51/761, 1996.

33. Resolution 1244, June 10, 1999, para. 11(c).

34. *Report of the Secretary-General on the United Nations Interim Administration in Kosovo,* S/1999/779, July 12, 1999, paras. 69, 80–81, 84.

35. Resolution 1040, January 29, 1996, para. 2.

36. S/PV.3607, December 15, 1995, p. 32 (statement of Juan Antonio Yañez-Barnuevo).

37. Ibid., p. 4 (statement of Ivan Misic).

38. S/PV.3482, December 16, 1994, p. 2.

39. See Jack Snyder, ed., *Civil Wars, Insecurity, and Intervention* (New York: Columbia University Press, 1999).

40. In Mozambique, for example, the president of the Council stated that "the post-election period will be an important and delicate time" and expressed the Council's support for deployment of UN observers "over a wider area of the country, keeping in mind the need to assist the Government in maintaining security, particularly in the crucial period before, during and immediately after the elections." S/PRST/1994/51, September 7, 1994.

41. Terrence Lyons, "The Role of Postsettlement Elections," in Stephen John Stedman, Donald Rothchild, and Elizabeth M. Cousens, eds., *Ending Civil Wars: The Implementation of Peace Agreements* (Boulder: Lynne Rienner, 2002), pp. 215–216.

42. Resolution 1265, September 17, 1999.

43. S/PV.3482, December 16, 1994, p. 9 (statement of Sir David Hannay).

44. Ibid.

45. See William G. O'Neill, *Kosovo: An Unfinished Peace* (Boulder: Lynne Rienner, 2002).

46. *Report of the Secretary-General on the Situation in East Timor,* S/1999/1024, October 4, 1999, para. 33.

47. Ibid.

48. Ibid., para. 47.

49. Resolution 1272, October 25, 1999.

50. In Resolution 1201, on the Central African Republic, the Council noted "the importance of regional stability and the need to consolidate the progress achieved so far, and in particular to assist the people of the Central African Republic to consolidate the process of national reconciliation and to help sustain a secure and stable environment conducive to the holding of free and fair elections." Resolution 1201, October 15, 1998.

51. See, for example, Anne-Marie Slaughter, "Government Networks: The Heart of the Liberal Democratic Order," in Gregory H. Fox and Brad R. Roth, eds., *Democratic Governance and International Law* (Cambridge: Cambridge University Press, 2000), p. 199.

52. Ibid., pp. 203, 227.

53. Ibid., p. 235.

54. S/PRST/1994/61, October 21, 1994, p. 2.

55. *Report of the Secretary-General on the United Nations Mission in Haiti,* S/1996/416, June 5, 1996, para. 6.

56. This is the view, for example, of John Stuart Mill in *On Representative Government.*

57. See, for example, Resolution 894, January 14, 1994, on South African elections; and S/PV.2087, September 29, 1978, pp. 21, 32, on Namibia.

58. See Gregory H. Fox and Brad R. Roth, "Democracy and International Law," *Review of International Studies* 27, no. 3 (2001): 327.

59. S/PV.4057, October 25, 1999, p. 15 (statement of Peter van Walsum).

60. Resolution 1272, October 25, 1999, para. 8 (emphasis added).

61. S/PV.3867, March 27, 1998, p. 5 (statement of Thomas Amolo).

62. See Fox, "Strengthening the State."

6

Tackling Terrorism

EDWARD C. LUCK

The rapidity, unanimity, and decisiveness with which the Security Council responded to the September 11, 2001, terrorist assault on the United States were without precedent. The next day, Resolution 1368 condemned the attacks and recognized "the inherent right of individual or collective self-defense in accordance with the Charter." Sixteen days later, another unanimous resolution, 1373, required all member states to deny terrorists—regardless of place, time, or cause—the means to carry on their work. These bold moves stand in stark contrast to the Council's previous history of ambivalence and hesitation in the face of terrorism.

Why the metamorphosis? The primacy of U.S. power is no doubt part of the answer. But Washington had long pressed for a more assertive counterterrorism stance for the Security Council, with mixed results. This chapter asks why the UN has been so reluctant to grasp the challenge of terrorism and whether—for the Security Council at least—all this has changed. It identifies three clusters of obstacles—each with deep political roots—that have inhibited the Council's response:

- *Cluster One:* Disagreements on the definition, scope, and priority that should be accorded terrorism as a threat to international peace and security.
- *Cluster Two:* Divergent views on the legitimacy, effectiveness, and legality of counterterrorist measures carried out by member states singly or in ad hoc coalitions, particularly when they involve the seemingly irresolvable problems of the Middle East.
- *Cluster Three:* Uncertainties about the UN's capacities and whether a viable multilateral alternative exists for dealing with terrorism.

Nevertheless, this chapter finds some grounds for guarded optimism. Addressing developments in these three clusters, it concludes that both geopolitical events and growing worries over the scale and reach of the terrorist threat have facilitated the Council's increasing activism. Whether the Council can be transformed into an unambiguous political force against terrorism—completing its metamorphosis—remains to be seen. This chapter cautions that the progress toward acceptance of the legitimacy of counterterrorist measures outside of the UN remains vulnerable to worries both about U.S. unilateralism and about the situation in the Middle East. The advances that the Council has made since September 11, including the unprecedented work of its Counter-Terrorism Committee (CTC), therefore, rest on a worryingly thin and uneven political foundation.

Cluster One: Definition, Scope, and Priority

The Security Council's first reference to terrorists, naturally, stemmed from an incident in the Middle East. In 1948, the Council called the assassination of Count Folke Bernadotte, the UN mediator in Palestine, a "cowardly act" that appeared "to have been committed by a criminal group of terrorists."[1] Before 1970, however, the Council treated such incidents as isolated and localized events, rather than as part of a pattern that needed to be addressed frontally.[2] Western capitals—in the midst of the Cold War struggle—were understandably less attuned to such seemingly distant developments.

Few of the hundreds of terrorist incidents each year are referred to the Council. Capitals doubt that the Council can be a real asset in their counterterrorism repertoire, fear the politicization of the underlying issues, and claim that these are just domestic matters. Neither the precursors nor the results of the terrorism related to Kashmir, Northern Ireland, Kurdistan, Colombia, Sri Lanka, the Basque region, North Korea, the Philippines, Central America, Chechnya, and Indonesia have respected borders. Yet they have largely escaped the Council's attention. The Council has focused instead on the exasperating problems of the Middle East, where it has been able to do relatively little to break the cycle of terrorism and counterterrorism.

In 1968 and 1969, Secretary-General U Thant first used his good offices to address cases of airplane hijackings.[3] Media attention grew in the 1970s as subnational groups began to bomb or hijack foreign aircraft, kidnap foreign officials and businessmen, and stage cross-border raids to forward their still largely localized causes.[4] During that decade, the number of identifiable groups involved in international terrorism began to grow substantially and the first groups with a religious identification began to appear.[5] In September 1970, following a series of aircraft hijackings by the Popular Front for the Liberation of Palestine, the Security Council adopted—without a vote—its first resolution on terrorism. Resolution 286 called on "states to take all possible legal steps to prevent further hijackings or any other interference with international civil air travel."

The growing place of terrorism in the international consciousness, however, did not ensure a ready consensus on its root causes, on how it should be addressed by the world body, or even on how the term "terrorism" should be defined. The tumultuous events of 1972—including a surge in hijackings, bombings, and hostage-taking from Sweden to Belfast to Czechoslovakia to Israel, as well as the massacre of Israeli athletes at the Summer Olympics in Munich—underscored both the global dimensions of terror and the world body's political incapacity to deal with them. Divided over how to respond to an assault on Lod airport in Israel in which twenty-six passengers and three terrorists were killed, the Council was only able to produce a consensus statement of concern by its president.[6]

The killings of the Israeli athletes in Munich further polarized the Council. A nonaligned draft failed to refer either to terrorism or to the Munich events, leading the United States to cast its second veto (and first lonely one) in the Council. The U.S. permanent representative, George H. W. Bush, lashing out at Syria as a harborer of terrorists, declared: "Each of us has a responsibility to make clear that those who practice such acts, or aid or abet them in any way, are the ones deserving a censure and condemnation. Only then will we begin to eliminate this scourge from the earth, and with it the acts of counterviolence to which history inevitably proves it gives rise." [7] A U.S. draft, focused on Munich and on those states suspected of harboring or supporting terrorists, was not put to a vote. Instead, a weaker Western European draft, with an oblique reference to the Munich events and a generic condemnation of terrorism, was vetoed by both China and the Soviet Union. It received negative votes as well from Guinea, Somalia, Sudan, and Yugoslavia.[8]

With the Security Council deadlocked, the General Assembly became the locus for action. Two days after the fruitless Council votes, Secretary-General Kurt Waldheim warned that the UN could no longer remain "a mute spectator" and called on the General Assembly to take up the issue of terrorism.[9] The nonaligned, Arab, and Soviet-bloc countries responded with an agenda item that sounded more like an apologia for than a condemnation of terrorism:

> Measures to prevent international terrorism which endangers or takes innocent human lives or jeopardizes fundamental freedoms, and study of the underlying causes of those forms of terrorism and acts of violence which lie in misery, frustration, grievance and despair and which cause some people to sacrifice human lives, including their own, in an attempt to effect radical changes. (A/C.6/418, November 2, 1972)

The United States, with a more ambitious proposal, achieved even less. Presenting the Assembly with a draft convention on the prosecution and extradition of terrorist suspects, Secretary of State William P. Rogers urged the convening of a world conference to address "these totally unacceptable attacks against the very fabric of international order." These actions, he asserted, "must be universally condemned, whether we consider the cause the terrorists invoke noble or ignoble, legitimate or illegitimate."[10] Yet neither the U.S.-sponsored resolution nor a compromise draft proposed by Italy, Austria, Canada, and the United Kingdom was even put to a vote. Instead the Assembly adopted an Algerian alternative that condemned not the terrorist strikes but "the continuation of repressive and terrorist acts by colonial racist and alien regimes in denying peoples their legitimate right to self-determination and independence and other human rights and fundamental freedoms."[11]

These sterile debates continued intermittently until the late 1980s. The failure of a 1987 Syrian initiative to convene a UN conference "on the difference between terrorism and legitimate acts carried out by oppressed people struggling to overcome colonial oppression" to gain support from either the Arab bloc or the Soviet Union showed that times were changing.[12] In 1989 the Council passed Resolution 635, condemning all acts of unlawful interference with the security of civil aviation and calling on the International Civil Aviation Organization and member states to develop a means of marking sheet and plastic explosives for detection, and Resolution 638, condemning "unequivocally all acts of hostage-taking and abduction" and labeling such acts "serious violations of international humanitarian law" that would have "severe adverse consequences for the human rights of the victims and their families." Terrorism, in other words, could no longer be considered just another means of legitimate political struggle.

Even with the end of the Cold War, however, neither the Council nor the Assembly has been able to agree on a working definition of terrorism or on a comprehensive convention on its elimination.[13] With a dozen global and seven regional conventions proscribing a wide range of terrorist acts,[14] the Secretary-General and the Security Council have nevertheless had ample authority to deal with the manifestations of terrorism—that is, violence against civilians designed to instill fear and terror. Such pragmatism is beginning to produce tangible results.

Cluster Two:
Counterterrorism and Politics of the Middle East

One of the more troubling issues before the Council has been how to address counterterrorist actions by member states, whether anticipatory or retaliatory. How should the Council view preemptive, preventive, or retaliatory uses of force by member states that have been targeted by terrorists? Should attacks on terrorists be treated as threats or net contributors to international peace and security?

During the Cold War, the answers came easily to most Council members. Most of the cases reaching the Council involved, directly or indirectly, the struggles in the Middle East. Counterterrorist actions by Israel and the United States were most often brought into question, for they were the states most apt to use force against what they believed, with good reason, was a clear and present danger. For example, in August 1973, Israeli fighters intercepted an Iraqi Airlines aircraft, mistakenly thought to be carrying George Habash, head of the Popular Front for the Liberation of Palestine, in Lebanese airspace and forced it to land at a military air base in Israel. The Council unanimously condemned the Israeli action as compounding the dangers faced by civilian aircraft.[15]

The Council enjoyed no such unanimity in responding to the daring 1976 Israeli raid on the airport at Entebbe, Uganda, where more than 100 Jewish hostages and the crew of a hijacked Air France aircraft were rescued. Though the Israelis believed that Ugandan president Idi Amin was collaborating with the terrorists from the Popular Front for the Liberation of Palestine, the Organization of African Unity and its forty-seven UN member states urged the Council to condemn Israel for its "flagrant violation" of Uganda's sovereignty and to demand compensation for the losses suffered as a result.[16] In contrast, the U.S. permanent representative, William W. Scranton, praising the "combination of guts and brains" displayed in the raid, asserted "a well-established right to use limited force for the protection of one's own nationals from an imminent threat of injury or death in a situation where the state in whose territory they are located either is unwilling or unable to protect them."[17] The Africans withdrew their draft, but a U.S.-UK alternative—condemning hijacking, deploring the loss of life, and urging respect for sovereignty and territorial integrity—was defeated by an unusual 6-0-9 vote.[18]

The Council's continuing ambivalence about counterterrorism was evident in its reactions to the taking of hostages at the U.S. embassy in Tehran on November 4, 1979. Though not labeling the embassy takeover as terrorism, the Council issued a presidential statement five days later and then a unanimous resolution in early December, both calling for the release of the hostages.[19] A tougher resolution later that month threatening the use of coercive measures under Chapter VII, however, passed only by an 11-0-4 margin, with the Soviet Union abstaining.[20] When a decision by the International Court of Justice and various mediation efforts failed to budge the militants, the United States proposed comprehensive nonmilitary sanctions on Iran. This proposal was vetoed by the Soviet Union and received a second negative vote from the German Democratic Republic and abstentions from Bangladesh and Mexico (China did not vote).[21] Though the Secretary-General continued his mediation efforts, this confirmation of the Council's unwillingness to invoke its Chapter VII powers against terrorism effectively sidelined the Council for the remainder of the crisis. The Carter administration, running out of options, then resorted to an unsuccessful effort to free the hostages through unilateral military means.

Twice in 1986, vetoes were required to block Council condemnation of military actions by Israel and the United States aimed at countering terrorism. On February 4, Israeli fighters intercepted a Libyan executive jet en route from Tripoli to Damascus and forced it to land at an Israeli air base, again in the mistaken belief that there were terrorists among the passengers. Though the aircraft, which carried an official Syrian delegation, was allowed to continue its journey after being searched, Libya accused "Zionist air pirates" of having conducted a "low and ugly crime."[22] A draft resolution condemning the forcible interception, diversion, and detention of the Libyan aircraft was quickly submitted to the Council by five developing countries. In this case, however, unlike that of August 1983, the United States vetoed the draft resolution, and Australia, Denmark, France, and the United Kingdom abstained.[23]

The more tolerant attitude of the Western members of the Council toward coercive counterterrorist measures reflected a growing recognition that terrorists could, and would, strike anywhere. The year 1985 had been a particularly active and cruel one for terrorism. Among the more visible incidents were the hijacking of a TWA flight from Athens to Rome, the bombing and destruction of an Air India flight over the Atlantic, the hijacking of the Italian cruise ship the *Achille Lauro,* the kidnapping of Soviet diplomats in Beirut, the hijacking of an Egypt Air flight, the murder of eleven Supreme Court justices in Bogotá, and bloody assaults on El Al counters at the Rome and Vienna airports.[24] With terrorism having clearly assumed global proportions, and even Soviet diplomats murdered, in December the Assembly unanimously adopted a broad resolution condemning terrorism in all its forms as criminal.[25] To the U.S. permanent representative, Vernon A. Walters, the vote was "a symbol of new times."[26]

Meanwhile, the Secretary-General and the president of the Security Council had issued statements condemning terrorism following the widely publicized hijacking of the *Achille Lauro* in October 1985.[27] The Security Council, for its part, capped the year with Resolution 579, which condemned "unequivocally all acts of hostage-taking and abduction" and affirmed the obligation of states on whose territory these acts occur to secure the safe release of hostages, to prevent future incidents, and "in accordance with the rules of international law to facilitate the prevention, prosecution and punishment of all acts of hostage-taking and abduction as manifestations of international terrorism."[28] According to the president of the Council that month, Léandre Bassole of Burkina Faso, "Never have I attended a Council meeting where unanimous agreement was reached in such a short time. It proves how urgently we need to solve the problem."[29]

There was far less convergence, however, on what constituted legal and legitimate means to prevent and punish such acts. In laying out the administration's approach to "the war against terrorism" under President Ronald Reagan, Secretary of State George P. Shultz—like President George W. Bush almost two decades later—stressed the need for military action, preemption, unpredictability, and surprise:

> The public must understand before the fact that some will seek to cast any pre-emptive or retaliatory action by us in the worst possible light and will attempt to make our military and our policy makers—rather than the terrorists—appear to be the culprits. . . . I can assure you that in this Administration our actions will be governed by the rule of law; and the rule of law is congenial to action against terrorism. We will need the flexibility to respond to terrorist attacks in a variety of ways, at times and places of our own choosing.[30]

He also called for international sanctions "to isolate, weaken, or punish states that sponsor terrorism against us," a technique that did not garner favor in the Council until the 1990s. Other member states, particularly from the nonaligned movement, still had to be convinced that international law was as "congenial" for counterterrorism as Shultz asserted.

Abba Eban, then chairman of the Knesset's Foreign Affairs and Defense Committee, acknowledged that Israel's February 1986 interception of the Libyan aircraft would be criticized as a departure from international legal standards. Indeed, the vetoed draft Council resolution labeled it an "act of aerial hijacking and piracy."[31] To Eban, however, the relationship among law, terrorism, and counterterrorism formed a "paradox": "There is nothing that stands in more contradiction to the law than terrorism. But terrorism hides behind the wings of the law. What determines the international reaction is the success or lack of success."[32]

Likewise, Ambassador Walters criticized the Israeli interception on the grounds that it did not meet the standard of having the "strongest and clearest evidence that terrorists are on board." While deploring the action undertaken by Israel, the United States vetoed the February 6 resolution because it did not uphold the right of nations to intercept aircraft under "exceptional circumstances." According to Walters: "My government cannot accept a resolution which implies that interception of an aircraft is wrongful per se, without regard to the possibility that the action may be justified. . . . We must be clear that terrorist violence—and not the response to terrorist violence—is the cause of the cycle of violence which tragically mars the

Middle East and the entire world."[33] The previous October, after all, the United States had intercepted an Egyptian airliner carrying suspects from the *Achille Lauro* hijacking. Such actions, Washington claimed, could be justified only in "very narrow counterterrorism cases."[34]

The Council was also divided on how to respond to the December 1985 attacks on the El Al counters at the Rome and Vienna airports. While the nonaligned members reportedly pushed for language cautioning against Israeli retaliation, the United States sought to avoid any phrasing that would single out Israel or discourage steps to capture and punish the perpetrators. Ultimately, the president of the Council issued a statement that strongly condemned "the unjustifiable and criminal terrorist attacks," urged that those responsible be brought to justice, and, regarding retaliation, called on "all concerned to exercise restraint."[35]

A few months later, nine members of the Council were prepared to condemn the United States for not exercising sufficient restraint in response to a terrorist provocation. On April 5, 1986, a Berlin discotheque frequented by U.S. servicemen was bombed by terrorists, killing two and wounding about eighty U.S. soldiers. Claiming evidence of "direct Libyan involvement," the United States launched retaliatory air strikes against targets in Tripoli and Benghazi. Following nine meetings of the Council, a resolution sponsored by five developing countries was put to a vote. Condemning both the U.S. raid and "all terrorist activities whether perpetrated by individuals, groups, or States," the draft resolution was vetoed by France and the United Kingdom, in addition to the United States, and received negative votes from Australia, Venezuela, and Denmark (the latter for one operational paragraph).[36]

Over the next dozen years, the United States was to use its military power to strike back at terrorists or their suspected sponsors two more times. On neither occasion, however, did others seek Council censure of the U.S. actions. In 1993 the Clinton administration authorized a cruise missile strike on the headquarters of the Iraqi intelligence service in response to an attempted assassination of former president George H. W. Bush by Iraqi agents. Only after the retaliatory strikes did the United States request a meeting of the Council, wherein it asserted that Article 51 of the UN Charter "provides for the exercise of self-defense in such cases."[37] The Council members were content with holding an expeditious debate and then moving on to other business.[38]

Five years later, the UN was further marginalized when the United States launched cruise missile strikes against suspected terrorist targets in Afghanistan and the Sudan two weeks after the bloody bombings of the U.S. embassies in Kenya and Tanzania. Hitting back at Osama bin Laden's terrorist training camps in largely lawless Afghanistan caused hardly a political ripple, but the destruction of a pharmaceutical factory in

Khartoum thought to be involved in the production of chemical weapons was more controversial, both because the choice of target was questionable and because Sudan was a member of the Arab League.[39] Neither the United States nor its critics, however, chose to bring the issue to the Council. President Clinton, moreover, made no reference to Article 51 or to international law in his statement announcing the U.S. strikes.[40]

In his speech on terrorism to the Assembly the following month, President Clinton omitted any reference to the Council or even to a political or security role for the UN in the campaign against this "clear and present danger to tolerant and open societies and innocent people everywhere."[41] Surely this was not an oversight, for Clinton administration officials had complained to reporters that the Security Council had been irresolute on Iraq and the Saudi government had been uncooperative in investigating the bombing of the U.S. barracks at Khobar Towers two years before, leaving the United States with little choice but to respond unilaterally to the embassy bombings. "We're in the deterrence business," commented one official, while another underlined that the threat "was directed to us, not to the U.N."[42]

Coming from an administration that had trumpeted the doctrine of "assertive multilateralism," these comments were telling. They reflected a long-standing preference for unilateral over multilateral options in U.S. counterterrorism policy. Whatever the unilateralist impulses of the George W. Bush administration, its efforts to link multilateral diplomacy through the UN and regional institutions with the unilateral exercise of U.S. power since the events of September 11, 2001, represent, if anything, one of Washington's more vigorous attempts to involve the Security Council in counterterrorism.[43] This melding strategy can be seen in a series of generic antiterrorist resolutions, beginning with 1368 and 1373 of September 2001, in the division of labor worked out in Afghanistan, and in the tactics being pursued on weapons of mass destruction in Iraq and North Korea. The wariness that officials and publics in other countries, including allied ones, nevertheless continue to express about U.S. counterterrorism strategies underscores the depth of worries about how U.S. military dominance will be employed. These, in turn, suggest the need for caution in weighing the durability of the global antiterrorism coalition.

Cluster Three:
The Role and Capacities of the Security Council

Clearly the Council's embrace of counterterrorism as an integral part of its responsibilities for international peace and security has been slow and hesitant. During the Cold War years, the Council proffered words of support for the growing body of norms proscribing certain kinds of terrorist acts, but consensus proved elusive when it came to addressing specific events or those countries known to aid and abet terrorism. In the 1990s the Council rediscovered its enforcement powers under Chapter VII, but these were applied more readily to regional conflict than to terrorism. At the first summit-level meeting of the Council, on January 31, 1992, the fifteen heads of state and government declared "their deep concern over acts of international terrorism" and emphasized "the need for the international community to deal effectively with all such acts" as part of their "commitment to collective security."[44] They made no mention of a UN role in this quest; nor did they include terrorism among the topics the Secretary-General was asked to address in his report *An Agenda for Peace*. Nevertheless, this unanimous high-level endorsement gave some impetus to the notion that the UN should not be left behind as the bandwagon against state sponsorship of terrorism began to gain momentum.

Over the course of the 1990s the Council imposed diplomatic, arms, and economic sanctions on Libya, Sudan, and Afghanistan for their support of terrorist activities.[45] As in earlier years, the United States led the drive to get the sanctions adopted in each case. Unlike the earlier efforts, however, these succeeded. This was possible both because Russia and China were no longer prepared to block giving the Council a role in counterterrorism and because key allies came to share Washington's goal of isolating those states still supporting terrorist groups. On one level, the series of sanctions were aimed at discouraging the target states from aiding, breeding, or sheltering terrorists by raising the costs of such behavior. Yet as has been the case with sanctions related to regional conflict, it was widely recognized that economic or diplomatic sanctions alone would not necessarily compel the target state to abandon goals that were important to it. The expectation, rather, was that such unprecedented steps by the Council would help to further delegitimize state sponsorship of terrorist groups and activities. The sanctions were seen, moreover, as a deterrent, as a means of signaling the Council's newfound determination to take a firm stand against terrorism. It would do so by naming specific countries that had violated the growing body of antiterrorist norms, as well as by taking some form of Chapter VII action in especially egregious cases.

As with other applications of Council sanctions, their record as a tool to discourage support for terrorism has been uneven. They appeared to make the most difference in the case of Libya. When Libyan authorities refused to cooperate in the investigation or to turn over suspects in the bombings of Pan Am flight 103 (1998) and UTA flight 772 (1999), as called for in Resolution 731 of January 21, 1992, the Council imposed a series of aviation, arms, and diplomatic sanctions in Resolution 748 (March 31, 1992). Twenty months later, these measures were strengthened and Libyan assets frozen by Resolution 883 (November 11, 1993). Five years later, after much negotiation and various bilateral pressures, Libya did indeed turn the suspects over to the UN for an international trial.

When Sudan likewise failed to heed the Council's call (Resolution 1044 of January 31, 1996) for it to extradite suspects in an assassination attempt on President Hosni Mubarak of Egypt, the Council voted a series of restrictions on Sudanese diplomatic representatives (Resolution 1054 of August 26, 1996).[46] While Khartoum failed to produce anyone connected to the assassination plot, it did inform the Council the next month that it would no longer provide a haven for Osama bin Laden, perhaps meeting the spirit, if not the letter, of the Council's demands. The Taliban leadership in Afghanistan, bin Laden's new base of operations, however, could not be persuaded to give him up or to close his training camps despite an escalating series of Council sanctions imposed in 1999 and 2000, including an aviation ban, a freeze on financial assets, an arms embargo, and diplomatic restrictions.[47]

There are a number of reasons for the mixed results. The leaders of Libya and Sudan were not asked to give up anything really integral to their power base, whereas the Taliban depended on bin Laden and his legions for military, financial, and political support in the ongoing civil war in Afghanistan. The prospect of further isolation in the international community, moreover, apparently mattered a good deal more to the better established leaderships in Tripoli and Khartoum than to the radical clerics of the Taliban, who had little to lose either materially or diplomatically. All three targets were also subject to U.S. bombing or cruise missile attacks. The strikes on Libya and Afghanistan preceded the Council's sanctions, suggesting that Washington hoped the Council could accomplish what the unilateral use of force could not.[48] The strike on the pharmaceutical plant in Khartoum, by contrast, came more than two years later, implying that, in U.S. eyes, the sanctions had failed to budge Sudan from its support of terrorism. Finally, while none of these sanctions resolutions garnered any negative votes, the Council members were hardly unanimous in their enthusiasm for such measures. China and one or more developing countries—and Russia in one case—abstained on these votes.

Post–September 11 Prospects

Seen against this historical backdrop, the Council's counterterrorism activism after September 11, 2001, looks like a great leap forward. Resolution 1368 and others, by acknowledging the right of individual and collective self-defense under the Charter, do leave considerable discretion to affected member states. Likewise, the Council's silence on the U.S. military intervention in Afghanistan, while elaborating the humanitarian, administrative, political, human rights, and security arrangements that should complement it, echoed the tacit division of labor developed in the Gulf War and elsewhere during the previous decade.[49] The one coercive measure adopted by the Council was to tighten the already extensive sanctions on the Taliban and Osama bin Laden's Al-Qaida organization.[50] From the Council's perspective, the crisis in Iraq has largely been about the proliferation of weapons of mass destruction and Baghdad's defiance of a decade-plus of related Chapter VII demands by the Council, rather than about its support of terrorism.[51]

The one major innovation has been the work of the Council's Counter-Terrorism Committee in monitoring implementation of Resolution 1373, which requires member states to "refrain from providing any form of support, active or passive, to entities or persons involved in terrorist acts." This includes freezing assets, prohibiting the raising or transferring of funds, and denying safe haven, passage, arms, or other material support. Governments, moreover, are to share information about possible terrorist activities and to report to the CTC on steps they are taking to implement these sweeping and unprecedented obligations. This process, however, does not involve any sanctions, coercion, or even censure by the CTC or the Council. The obligations, moreover, are generic rather than aimed at any particular group, state, or incident. These features have made it much easier for member states, including some with a history of complicity in terrorist activities, to accept the work of the CTC.

The CTC has operated, under the leadership of Jeremy Greenstock of the United Kingdom, with laudable transparency and patience toward those handful of member states—sixteen as of December 2002—yet to file any report with the CTC.[52] Working with a half-dozen technical experts, the CTC has sought to identify ways in which particular member states might be helped, such as through model legislation, training, or promising administrative practices elsewhere, to meet their 1373 obligations. While the CTC is not a direct provider of such capacity-building assistance, it does act as a sort of broker between those states or groups that have relevant capacities and those in need of assistance.

Though the CTC has opened a promising new front in the struggle against terrorism, its approach has significant limitations. First, neither its funding nor its staffing is firmly integrated in the UN's regular budget or Secretariat. In bureaucratic terms, having never been authorized by the General Assembly, the CTC remains an experiment with an uncertain lifespan. Second, the CTC is designed to make greater headway with those states that are sympathetic to the counterterrorism agenda but lack legislative or executive capacity than with those problem countries that persist in providing assistance to selected terrorist groups, such as those regularly targeting Israel. Third, while its lack of teeth is consonant with the UN's current preference for a soft approach to conflict and is popular with most member states, this begs the question of who is to undertake the military enforcement of antiterrorist norms.

In facing the terrorist challenge, the Council today is hampered by two liabilities—reliance on powerful member states for military enforcement and deep divisions on the Middle East—that are as disabling now as at any point over the past thirty years. The gap in military capacity between the United States and other countries has widened substantially, as has the latter's resentment of U.S. power and allegedly unilateralist tendencies. The more others seek to use the Council to constrain Washington's pursuit of terrorists, the less certain will be either U.S. support for the world body or U.S. readiness to entrust such critical matters to the Council. On this, Washington is hardly alone. Russia, India, Israel, China, and various European countries, when confronted by cross-border terrorism, have been far from enthusiastic about involving the Council.

The divisive politics of the Middle East continue to infect the Council's efforts to address terrorism. In seeking to condemn the December 2002 attacks on an Israeli resort and aircraft in Kenya, the Security Council took a step forward that illustrated, at the same time, how difficult it has been for the Council to be balanced on these issues. According to Ambassador Aaron Jacob of Israel, this was "the first time that the Security Council has adopted a resolution without any reservations condemning terrorist attacks against Israeli civilians and Israeli targets."[53] While there have been a number of presidential statements expressing sympathy for Israeli victims in the past,[54] a statement expressing concern about a series of 1994 bombings of Jewish centers in Buenos Aires and London expressed condolences only to Argentina and the United Kingdom.[55] A line in an earlier draft mentioning the actual targets of the attacks reportedly was deleted at the insistence of Pakistan and other nonaligned countries.[56] While the December 2002 resolution overcame this obstacle, it was at the price of unanimity. Ambassador Mikhail Wehbe of Syria, casting the sole negative vote, complained that the resolution "was against the values and Charter of the United Nations" because it ignored "the terrorism Israel committed daily and the massacres committed against the Palestinian people."[57]

The Security Council must avoid becoming a prisoner of animosities and geopolitical dynamics largely beyond its control. It can neither correct the global imbalances in military assets nor resolve the underlying tensions of the Middle East. But it can make a conscious effort to act as a constructive and reliable broker in both equations. And it can build on its good work since September 11 as a political bulwark against terrorism. The extent to which it succeeds in these tasks could well determine whether the Council can break free of its troubled history in dealing with—or more often failing to deal with—terrorism. Otherwise, there could be more trouble ahead if the Council allows itself to be sidetracked and marginalized in confronting the twenty-first century's most visible and pervasive threat to international peace and security.

Notes

1. Resolution 57, September 18, 1948.
2. The State Department identified more than 150 international terrorist incidents in 1968 in 1969. These annual totals rose to more than 600 for the period 1985–1988 and have ebbed somewhat since. U.S. Department of State, Office of the Coordinator for Counterterrorism, *Patterns of Global Terrorism, 1992, 1995, and 2001* (Washington, D.C.).
3. Sydney D. Bailey, "The UN Security Council and Terrorism," *International Relations* 11, no. 6 (December 1993): 536; and U Thant, *View from the UN* (Garden City, N.Y.: Doubleday, 1978), pp. 302–308, 317–318.
4. Martha Crenshaw, "Current Research on Terrorism: The Academic Perspective," *Studies in Conflict and Terrorism* 15, no. 1 (January–March 1992): 3–4.
5. Bruce Hoffman, "Terrorism Trends and Prospects," in Ian O. Lesser, Bruce Hoffman, John Arquilla, David F. Ronfeldt, Michele Zanini, and Brian Michael Jenkins, *Countering the New Terrorism* (Santa Monica, Calif.: RAND, 1999), pp. 16–17; and Walter Enders and Todd Sandler, "Transnational Terrorism in the Post–Cold War Era," *International Studies Quarterly* 43, no. 1 (1999): 152, fig. 1.
6. S/10705, June 20, 1972; and Bailey, "The UN Security Council and Terrorism," pp. 537–538.
7. Robert Alden, "U.S. Casts a Veto in U.N. on Mideast, Citing Terrorism," *New York Times,* September 11, 1972.
8. Global Issues Research Group, Foreign and Commonwealth Office, *Research Analysts Memorandum: Table of Vetoed Draft Resolutions in the United Nations Security Council, 1946–1998,* RA Memorandum no. 2-1999 (London: Global Issues Research Group, September 1999), p. 26; S/10784 and S/10786, September 10, 1972.
9. A/8791, September 20, 1972; and Robert Alden, "Waldheim Bids U.N. Act on Terrorism," *New York Times,* September 13, 1972.
10. Robert Alden, "Rogers Asks U.N. to Set 1973 Parley on World Terror," *New York Times,* September 27, 1972. The U.S. initiative may have been spurred, in part, by a letter by thirty members of Congress to George Bush, the U.S. representative to the UN, calling for the United States to take steps in the Security Council to punish countries aiding airline hijackers. "Thirty in Congress Urge U.N. to Act in Hijacking," *New York Times,* July 24, 1972.
11. The 76-34-16 vote in the Assembly's Sixth Committee reflected the depth of the divisions in the UN on terrorism. Robert Alden, "Strong Legal Action to Combat Terrorism Is Rebuffed at U.N.," *New York Times,* December 12, 1972.
12. Paul Lewis, "Syria, Isolated at the U.N., Drops Terrorism Plan," *New York Times,* December 2, 1987.
13. For a review of General Assembly efforts to deal with terrorism, see M. J. Peterson, "Using the General Assembly," in Jane Boulden and Thomas G. Weiss, eds., *Terrorism and the UN: Before and After September 11th* (Bloomington: Indiana University Press, 2003).
14. Note to United Nations Correspondents, "United Nations Treaties Against International Terrorism," Note no. 5679, September 19, 2001, www.un.org/news/

press/docs/2001/note5679.doc.htm; and M. Cherif Bassiouni, *International Terrorism: Multilateral Conventions (1937–2001)* (Ardsley, N.Y.: Transnational, 2001).

15. Resolution 377; Bailey, "The UN Security Council and Terrorism," p. 538.

16. Kathleen Teltsch, "African Nations Bid U.N. Council Meet on Israeli Raid," *New York Times,* July 7, 1976; and Kathleen Teltsch, "Uganda Bids U.N. Condemn Israel for Airport Raid," *New York Times,* July 10, 1976.

17. Kathleen Teltsch, "Rescue by Israel Acclaimed by U.S. at Debate in U.N.," *New York Times,* July 13, 1976. Just two weeks earlier, the United States vetoed a Middle East resolution it thought to be unbalanced, S/12119, June 29, 1976. Kathleen Teltsch, "U.S. Vetoes Resolution Asking Pullout of Israel," *New York Times,* June 30, 1976.

18. Kathleen Teltsch, "Africans Abandon Anti-Israel Move in U.N.'s Council," *New York Times,* July 15, 1976; and Bailey, "The UN Security Council and Terrorism," pp. 538–540.

19. S/13616, November 9, 1979, and Resolution 457, December 4, 1979, respectively.

20. Resolution 461, December 31, 1979.

21. S/13735, January 13, 1980.

22. Judith Miller, "Libya Accuses U.S. of Role in Seizure," *New York Times,* February 5, 1986.

23. S/17796/Rev. 1, February 6, 1986; and Bailey, "The UN Security Council and Terrorism," p. 548.

24. Robert C. McFadden, "Terror in 1985: Brutal Attacks, Tough Responses," *New York Times,* December 30, 1985.

25. A/RES/40/61, December 9, 1985.

26. Elaine Sciolino, "U.N. Adopts Resolution on Terror," *New York Times,* December 10, 1985.

27. S/17554, October 9, 1985.

28. Resolution 579 of December 18, 1985, which followed a letter from the U.S. permanent representative, S/17685.

29. Elaine Sciolino, "U.N. Unanimously Condemns Hostage-Taking," *New York Times,* December 19, 1985.

30. *New York Times,* October 26, 1984.

31. "U.S. Vetoes Anti-Israel Move," *New York Times,* February 7, 1986.

32. Thomas L. Friedman, "Israelis Intercept a Libyan Civil Jet and Then Let It Go," *New York Times,* February 5, 1986.

33. "U.S. Vetoes Anti-Israel Move."

34. Milt Freudenheim, James F. Clarity, and Richard Levine, "Israel Stops the Wrong Jet," *New York Times,* February 9, 1986.

35. A/17702, December 30, 1985; and "U.N. Council Condemns Attacks," *New York Times,* December 31, 1985.

36. S/18016/Rev. 1, April 21, 1986, and Bailey, "The UN Security Council and Terrorism," pp. 548–549.

37. Excerpts from speech of U.S. permanent representative Madeleine K. Albright to the Security Council, *New York Times,* June 28, 1993.

38. In contrast, the U.S. intervention in Panama three and a half years earlier sparked wide consternation in the UN community and produced two draft resolutions that the United States was compelled to veto (one as sole vetoer and one with the United Kingdom and France), S/21048, December 23, 1989, and S/21084, January 17, 1990.

39. Steven Erlanger, "After the Attacks: The Diplomacy," *New York Times,* August 23, 1998.

40. *Washington Post,* August 21, 1998.

41. "Remarks by the President to the Opening Session of the Fifty-third United Nations General Assembly," September 21, 1998, http://clinton6.nara.gov/1998/09/1998-09-21-remarks-by-the-president-to-53rd-un.html.

42. Erlanger, "After the Attacks."

43. Edward C. Luck, "The United States, Counter-Terrorism, and the Prospects for a Multilateral Alternative," in Boulden and Weiss, eds., *Terrorism and the UN.*

44. S/23500.

45. David Cortright and George A. Lopez, *The Sanctions Decade: Assessing UN Strategies in the 1990s* (Boulder: Lynne Rienner, 2000), pp. 107–133; and Chantal de Jonge Oudraat, "The UN and Terrorism: The Role of the UN Security Council," draft chapter for Boulden and Weiss, eds., *The UN and Terrorism,* forthcoming.

46. Though the Council followed up by declaring a ban on Sudanese aircraft (Resolution 1070, August 16, 1996), it never took the additional step of setting a date for it to take effect. The vote on Resolution 1070 was 13-0-2, with China and Russia abstaining.

47. The chief sanctions resolutions were 1267, October 15, 1999, and 1333, December 19, 2000, but also see 1214, December 8, 1998, and 1363, July 30, 2001, as well as presidential statements S/PRST/1999/29, October 25, 1999, and S/PRST/2000/12, April 7, 2000.

48. Although some Washington-based pundits have credited the 1986 air strikes on Libya with persuading Muammar Qaddafi to give up his support of terrorism, others suspect that the bombing of Pan Am flight 103 two years later not only refutes that theory but actually was undertaken as an act of revenge, since his adopted daughter was apparently killed in the U.S. bombing of one of his residences. In any case, he clearly preferred to be seen to give in to UN rather than U.S. pressure.

49. See Resolutions 1378, November 14, 2001; 1383, December 6, 2001; 1386, December 20, 2001; 1401, March 28, 2002; 1413, May 23, 2002; and 1444, November 27, 2002.

50. Resolution 1390, January 16, 2002.

51. In Resolution 1441, November 8, 2002, the Council deplores, among other things, Iraq's failure "to comply with its commitments pursuant to resolution 687 (1991) with regard to terrorism."

52. Jeremy Greenstock, *Report to Security Council of Counter-Terrorism Committee,* October 4, 2002.

53. Edith M. Lederer, "U.N. Condemns Mombassa Terrorist Attacks," *Toronto Star,* December 14, 2002.

54. For example, S/PRST/1995/3, January 24, 1995, and S/PRST/1996/10, March 4, 1996.

55. S/PRST/1994/40, July 29, 1994.

56. Louis Meixler, "U.N. Condemns Blasts in Argentina, London, but Doesn't Mention Targets," Associated Press, July 29, 1994.

57. Julia Preston, "In a First, U.N. Notes Israeli Dead in Terror Attack in Mombasa," *New York Times,* December 14, 2002.

7

Conflict Prevention

ELIZABETH M. COUSENS

The question of the UN Security Council's role in conflict prevention is potentially enormous. Conflict prevention can conceivably be pursued through the full array of instruments at the Council's disposal—from various forms of peacemaking through peacekeeping to sanctions and other enforcement measures. It also potentially relates to nearly the full range of goods pursued by the UN system—including good governance, socioeconomic development, respect for human rights, and the rule of law—whose respective causal relationships to armed conflict remain contested.

This chapter does not address these broader issues. Instead, it focuses more narrowly on the UN Security Council's role in preventing conflict by doing the following: reviewing the evolution of conflict prevention as a term of art in the UN; conceptualizing the relationship between the Council and different forms of prevention; cataloging relevant instruments at the Council's disposal, and exploring their use in key cases; and identifying a set of constraints on Council action that argues for modest expectations about the Council's systematic or long-term capacity to prevent armed conflict.

The Evolution of "Conflict Prevention" as a Term of Art at the UN

The concept of conflict prevention is now prevalent and relatively uncontested within the United Nations system.[1] Its acceptance as a term of art comes after more than a decade of debate after the end of the Cold War within the UN Secretariat and among UN member states over appropriate international responses to civil wars and internal conflict. The general result of this debate in the 1990s has been to shift conflict prevention from an association with outside intervention (of the developed North in the global South) to an emphasis on the responsibility of member states to manage potential conflict within their own borders.[2]

At the same time, this period also saw rising expectations for the UN Security Council, as the body assigned primary responsibility for maintaining international peace and security, to take action to deal with potential or actual armed conflicts. This prompted a proliferation of resolutions and missions, if not always well conceived or resourced, as well as experimentation with new instruments for the Council's direct engagement. Alongside heightened expectations, indeed partly driving them, was disappointment over what were perceived to be Council failures of tragic proportion (notably in the former Yugoslavia and Rwanda) as well as growing skepticism about the Council's credibility when member states could act unilaterally outside of its purview (as in the unauthorized air campaign of the North Atlantic Treaty Organization [NATO] against Serbia or the 2003 U.S.-led coalition against Iraq).

Though contemporary analysts are accustomed to treating conflict prevention as an artifact of the post–Cold War era, the prevention of armed conflict has arguably been central to the UN from the outset, given the organization's foundational mission to "protect future generations from the scourge of war." During the Cold War, this concern principally meant an interest in—if not always a capacity for—preventing situations of instability that could lead to interstate confrontations, especially between the superpowers.

Conflict Prevention During the Cold War

A central theme of the Cold War UN was deadlock between the superpowers in the Security Council and the frequent use (and threat) of the veto. In this climate, diplomatic concert in pursuit of conflict prevention was destined to be elusive. However, a few contextual observations are worth making that bear on the current potential for and limits upon Council action to prevent conflict.

First, many of the Cold War conflicts that we would now see as ripe for well-meaning efforts to prevent them occurred in the context of decolonization, in which there was not by any means a normative consensus about the relative desirability of war prevention as opposed to national liberation. Moreover, there are too many examples of major power intervention in civil wars that, especially in the case of Council permanent members, were unlikely to be subject to Council scrutiny or action (discussed more broadly below). Second, however, under certain conditions the UN was not completely hamstrung, as its ambitious operation in the Congo between 1960 and 1963—essentially to avert state failure and further destabilization— attests. Third, the Council at times provided an instrument for the superpowers to manage their engagement in regional theaters in a way that plausibly contributed to reducing the risk of direct confrontation between them (e.g., in the deployment of the UN Observer Group in Lebanon [UNOGIL] in 1958). Finally, while an exploration of the Council's supporting role in this outcome is beyond the scope of this chapter, the central preventive challenge of the Cold War—that of averting conflict between nuclear-armed superpowers—was clearly met.

Conflict Prevention After the Cold War:
High Hopes, Visible Failures, Modest Acceptance

The real prominence of "conflict prevention" as a term of art, however, came with the end of the Cold War. Initially, UN Secretary-General Boutros Boutros-Ghali gave the concept a high profile in *An Agenda for Peace* (1992), his optimistic vision for an expanded UN role in managing conflict, as did an eminent international commission established by the Carnegie Corporation of New York in 1994.[3] These and related initiatives signaled two expectations: first, that freed of Cold War rivalries, member states might find themselves both interested in and capable of cooperation to resolve conflicts before they started; and second, that the terrain of concern could now expand beyond interstate conflict to the civil wars or regionalized conflicts that had steadily risen throughout the Cold War but that had largely been off the UN's agenda.

As conceptualized in *An Agenda for Peace,* the UN was expected to pay greater attention to internal wars as well as to the humanitarian crises that they provoked. After a first flush of successful UN efforts in resolving protracted internal conflicts in the late 1980s and early 1990s (e.g., Namibia, El Salvador, Mozambique, Guatemala and, initially, Cambodia), however, the UN was implicated in a series of horrendous failures (Bosnia, Angola, Somalia, Rwanda). Paradoxically, these failures tended to lead to calls for the UN to do more rather than to recognition that the UN might be fundamentally limited in acting in these contexts. The Bosnian, Rwandan, and Somalian episodes were particularly salient, each spurring calls for greater UN action, contributing to—among other things—a proliferation of Council resolutions and peacekeeping mandates even in the absence of a coherent strategy or sufficient resources to pursue one.

With respect to conflict prevention, the first failure of the 1990s—reiterated throughout the decade—was arguably the former Yugoslavia at each stage of its dissolution from the outbreak of the first war over Croatia and Slovenia through the second war inside Bosnia to the third war over Kosovo. The outbreak of a sequence of wars in the former Yugoslavia amounted to a tragic failure of concerned international actors to avert war given a Yugoslav state on the verge of disintegration in 1991, popular mobilization and arming within internal boundaries, warnings aplenty about the possibility of armed conflict on a large scale, and a relatively

high degree of attention from the international community—principally, the
UN and the European Community. The failure was arguably less the UN's
than that of major member states, especially key states in Europe as well as
the United States and Russia. Analyses of the wars' origins also powerfully
showed that armed conflict could be anticipated, making prevention possible, provided that it could be rendered in the interest of major powers. The
costs of both the war and subsequent peace implementation further
strengthened the case that prevention was heavily in the international community's interests.

Somalia also loomed large in shaping the conflict prevention agenda.
Here the Council was initially more effective when it acted under Chapter
VII of the Charter by authorizing a U.S.-led Unified Task Force (UNITAF)
in 1992 to contain a humanitarian crisis whose proportions were rapidly
mounting. The Somalia experience left an ambivalent legacy for conflict
prevention, however. While thousands of Somalis received desperately
needed food assistance, there was rising criticism that a solely humanitarian approach failed to deal with the underlying political conflict that generated famine in the first place. The UN, with strong U.S. support at the time,
embarked on a more ambitious strategy to resolve the conflict and support
broader "nation-building" in Somalia through deployment of a more com-
prehensively mandated mission in 1993—the second UN Operation in
Somalia (UNOSOM II), which unraveled rapidly only a few months after it
was established when it encountered armed opposition from Somali factions, first when a group of Pakistani peacekeepers were ambushed and
killed, then when a team of U.S. forces pursuing the warlord responsible
ended up in a firefight that led to nearly 1,000 Somali and 18 U.S. deaths.
The upshot was a rejection—certainly from Washington—of what was then
seen as the fool's errand of nation-building and, more broadly, a chill on
engagement in internal conflict.

While the Bosnian war was still raging and only shortly after the withdrawal of forces from Somalia, the single case of failure that most dramatically elevated the profile of the concept of conflict prevention—including
turning a spotlight on the UN and the Council's culpability—occurred in
Rwanda in 1994, when a civil war of relatively low intensity turned quickly
into a genocide of unimaginable proportions. Here the Security Council had
in fact undertaken multiple actions designed to manage and contain the
Rwandan civil war.[4] The Council's failure in 1994, then, was not precisely
to prevent conflict—which had been under way, if on a modest scale, for
four years—but to prevent its exponential escalation into genocide, especially in a context where there was already a UN mission (the UN
Assistance Mission in Rwanda [UNAMIR]) on the ground.

All three episodes led to an outpouring of studies, evaluations, lessons
learned, and articles and books whose central conclusion was that more

concrete, timely action by the Security Council—provided sufficient resources and stamina—could have saved hundreds of thousands of lives.

Over the course of the 1990s, conflict prevention was thus both promoted and contested. Some scholars argued that normative aspirations to prevent conflict, while worthy, outstripped evidence that conflict prevention was either politically possible or analytically demonstrable.[5] Different segments of the UN and donor community tended to approach the prevention of conflict based on their own likely contribution to it, most notably in debate over the relative importance of developmental and political interventions. And politically, especially among the countries of the global south, there was tension between, on the one hand, criticism that Western governments would not expend resources or troops to save third world lives, and, on the other hand, suspicion that conflict prevention was just the latest cover for new forms of intervention.[6]

After nearly a decade of argument over its content and merits, however, conflict prevention appears to have acquired a relatively uncontested status within the UN community. The current UN Secretary-General, Kofi Annan, issued a major report on conflict prevention in 2001. The consultative process surrounding it also produced General Assembly and Security Council resolutions, indicating broad support for the concept.[7] The development community, in turn, also describes conflict prevention as central to its efforts, with prevention now "mainstreamed" into standard UN development methodologies such as Common Country Assessments and the UN Development Assistance Framework. Significantly, over the course of this debate, conflict prevention advocates increasingly emphasized prevention strategies centered on the capacities of member states to manage conflict within their own borders. Though not off the table, more interventionist prevention strategies, particularly ones requiring outside troops, took a distinct backseat. This turn from more interventionist strategies was reinforced by one of the guiding precepts of conflict prevention: namely, "early" prevention—when there is rarely much scope for external military engagement—is better than late intervention. This undoubtedly helped build a broader constituency for conflict prevention. It also reflected the political reality that troop-based interventions for the sake of conflict prevention were unlikely to attract sufficient support from major member states.

Conflict Prevention: Forms and Instruments

Forms of Conflict Prevention
It may be helpful to distinguish four forms of conflict prevention. First, there is the archetype of prevention: namely, preventing conflict before it

has broken out in any serious way. Every armed conflict, in this sense, counts as a case of failure, whereas cases of success are extremely difficult to document. When armed conflict is incipient but has yet to break out, the types of interventions deployed are likely to be discreet, diplomatic, and hard to track. When there is a longer time horizon, interventions are likely to be more broadly developmental, in which case causality is much harder to establish. For the Council, incentives to act are also likely to be fairly low in the absence of violence—which, for example, Kosovar Albanians learned all too well from years of international involvement in Bosnia. Nor is it necessarily helpful to draw Council—and therefore public—attention to crises that may be receptive to quieter means of resolution.

Second, there are efforts to prevent escalation after conflict has started. Prevention of escalation can be seen in two forms, one of which more closely resembles pure conflict prevention. This first form pertains to UN actions taken at the very onset of conflict. When the Council acts speedily in order to "put the genie back in the bottle" and contain escalation, it can reasonably have been said to have prevented conflict and crisis. In the Central African Republic, for instance, the Council sanctioned an Organization of African Unity (OAU) monitoring mission to prevent a series of riots from escalating into a broader conflict, and it subsequently authorized the UN Verification Mission in the Central African Republic (MINURCA) as a follow-on force. A second illustration might be East Timor, where the Council was already engaged through having authorized the UN mission there (UNAMET). When an acute crisis broke out in late 1999 following the Timorese referendum, the UN authorized a multinational force—the International Force for East Timor (INTERFET)—and it deserves praise for timely, energetic action to prevent wider conflict and mass violence. The Council was particularly visible in this instance because of its direct role in brokering Indonesian acceptance of the international force when it sent a mission to the country; days after the mission's return, the Council authorized INTERFET.

The second form of preventing escalation relates to UN actions within an ongoing conflict, especially where there is already a UN political or military presence. Here the Council can be seen to have a significant responsibility as well as potential for effective action through its role in establishing mission mandates and the level and nature of resources it authorizes to the UN Secretariat to implement them. Again, East Timor is an example of effective Council response. In Sierra Leone, too, the UN helped roll back an escalation by rebel forces in 1999 to 2000, helped by vital reinforcement from UK forces. By contrast, UN missions in Rwanda, Angola, and Bosnia were neither appropriately designed nor sufficiently resourced to deter or respond to dramatic escalation of conflict. While this aspect of prevention fully overlaps with effective conflict management, it is worth highlighting in order to underscore that the Council will be more likely and able to take action in contexts where some violence has already occurred.

The third form of conflict prevention consists of actions taken to prevent humanitarian crisis. Somalia was conceived this way, and though UN engagement there is generally viewed as a failure after the UNOSOM II debacle, UNOSOM I and UNITAF helped save the lives of nearly 200,000 people. A further example of Council action to prevent humanitarian crisis as well as state failure—long before the concepts were en vogue—was UN action in the Congo, which sought to prevent the collapse of the nascent Congolese state following insurrection and rebellion in its eastern provinces. The UN Operation in the Congo (ONUC) in 1960 was one of the largest and most robust in UN history, helped prevent the collapse of the Congolese state, and at least created the possibility for future state-building (that the Congo was subsequently plundered by years of the Mobutu Sese Seko regime is a separate issue, related more to Cold War dynamics than to the legacy of UN intervention).

Finally, there are actions taken to prevent the recurrence of conflict, especially after negotiated settlements. Most academic studies show that internal wars tend to recur and that previous experience of war is a strong indicator of the possibility of new war. Thus the effective implementation of peace agreements becomes a critical instrument for reducing the risk of future violence. The Council's commitment to designing good mandates and mobilizing sufficient resources to implement peace agreements can be, in this way, conceptualized as part of its broader responsibility for conflict prevention.

The Council's record here is mixed. Most conflict data show a decline in the number and intensity of internal wars since the mid-1990s, which is generally attributed by researchers, at least partly, to UN peacemaking and peace implementation efforts (see Chapter 2). Yet there have been major failures. Nearly 300,000 Angolans died in their country's ensuing return to war after a UN-brokered peace agreement collapsed in 1993—and in the presence of a woefully underresourced peacekeeping operation. The genocide in Rwanda, which cost between 800,000 and 1 million lives, occurred in the context of failure to implement what is now widely recognized as a flawed accord.

More modestly, when an armistice or truce is reached at the end of an interstate conflict, stabilization or force separation arrangements can prevent the recurrence of conflict. For thirty years, the UN Disengagement Observer Force (UNDOF) has helped ensure stability between Israel and Syria (as has a non-UN multinational force in the Sinai, with respect to the Israeli-Egyptian peace). In similar fashion, the UN Mission in Ethiopia and Eritrea (UNMEE) has helped stabilize relations between the countries and prevent renewal of hostilities.

Ultimately, however, the principal challenge remains the prevention of armed conflict before it occurs in any magnitude. The section below explores existing instruments and methods at the UN's disposal for this task.

Instruments for Conflict Prevention

The Council has a variety of instruments and measures that it can deploy to help prevent the outbreak or escalation of armed conflict, including agenda-setting, fact-finding missions, diplomatic initiatives, sanctions, peace operations, and peace enforcement. This chapter focuses on just of few of these.

Normative and symbolic tools. First, the Council through its deliberations can raise the visibility of a potential conflict in order to concentrate diplomatic attention and mobilize relevant resources. Throughout the 1990s, the Council increasingly engaged in forms of public diplomacy, especially through its rotating presidencies, including greater interaction with the media (postmeeting press "stakeouts" are a recent development), encounters with key nongovernmental organizations (NGOs) (through "Arria Formula" meetings), and more frequent field missions.

Second, especially in situations that are already on the Council's agenda, the language of presidential statements, press releases, and—of course—resolutions can signal to parties to a conflict the boundaries of legitimate and illegitimate behavior. Especially when language reflects diplomatic unity, this kind of signaling can contribute to defusing tensions and discouraging aggressive behavior. An interesting case is southern Lebanon, where the Council's reports, statements, and press releases consistently defined as illegal Syrian/Lebanese/Hezbollah strikes at Israel across the UN-monitored "blue line" that has separated Israel and Lebanon since the Israeli withdrawal in early 2000. By taking a firm and consistent line against violations, the Council has signaled that major Hezbollah actions across the line would be seen as illegitimate, a position that observers in the region believe has helped to restrain Hezbollah and thereby also exerted a preventive influence on relations between Israel and Lebanon and Syria.

Both of these tools have limits, however. First, signaling to parties will be effective when it clearly emanates from Council unity *and* when signaling is not seen as a substitute for more concrete action. The latter syndrome only invites cynicism and risks diminishing the Council's overall credibility. Second, visibility can in some cases be counterproductive. It can induce parties to a conflict to play to extreme constituencies, thereby polarizing their positions and locking them into stances that have been publicly articulated. It can also prematurely expose diplomatic efforts that require discretion for their success. Moreover, bringing situations formally to the

Council's attention can force Council members to take tough positions, adding a layer of third-party involvement that may not be constructive.[8]

Diplomatic and noncoercive tools. The Council has multiple diplomatic tools to facilitate the resolution of disputes before they erupt into violence, three principle types of which stand out. First, it can authorize fact-finding missions and other types of investigations that support various mediation efforts, whether those of special envoys (appointed by the Council or the Secretary-General), the Secretary-General himself, or regional organizations. The Council here serves as an arena for mobilizing diplomatic cohesion and support for the diplomatic efforts of others. An example includes the sending of Canadian diplomat Raymond Chrétien to the Democratic Republic of Congo (DRC) in 1992 to help find ways to stem regional escalation in the Congolese civil war.

Second, the Council can send its own members on visiting missions. Since the UN's founding there have been more than thirty missions, but more than half of these have taken place since the early 1990s.[9] There are multiple examples in the 1990s, from the first mission that traveled to Bosnia at the height of the war (1993) to assess the status of "safe areas," through fact-finding missions to Burundi (1994, 1995) and the Great Lakes (2001, 2002), to critical negotiating missions to Indonesia and East Timor (1999, 2000).

Council missions have several potential preventive purposes. The first is simply to better inform Council members about facts on the ground in order to improve the quality and outcome of their own deliberations. This was especially critical in earlier years when the Council was reputedly frustrated by insufficient reporting from the Secretariat. Today there is much better information flow between the Secretariat and the Council as well as between the Council and other sources (e.g., NGOs and humanitarian agencies). In principle, even today, Council missions to trouble spots that are not high on the radar and therefore undercovered within the Secretariat could have a useful purpose. The likelihood of this being politically feasible is, however, fairly low.

The second preventive purpose of Council missions is to raise the visibility of a situation. They also create an opportunity for signaling and more direct communication of a Council position to conflicting parties. The U.S.-led, all-member mission to the DRC in 2001 arguably had this in mind.

The third type of diplomatic tool, perhaps the Council's most interesting, consists of missions to directly negotiate outcomes. A particularly compelling example is that of East Timor, where a mission sent in September 1999 galvanized regional and Council action, leading within days of the mission's return to authorization of a multinational force (INTERFET) and a broader transitional peace operation (the UN

Transitional Administration in East Timor [UNTAET]). The trip reportedly also helped bring critical U.S. policymakers on board the policy, suggesting that missions can also serve to build cohesion among Council members

The Council also serves as an arena for aligning diplomatic strategies of key member states, which is a critical condition for making practically effective any tools nominally available to it.

Semicoercive tools. The most visible action the Council can take to prevent conflict is to deploy troops or observers to a potential conflict zone. Most traditional peacekeeping operations, in some sense, have a preventive function in serving to reduce the risk of return to war. In some cases, this is about confidence-building (as in UNMEE or, arguably, UNDOF); in some, it may be about tripwires (as in the UN Iraq-Kuwait Observation Mission [UNIKOM]); in others, it is more about deterrence (as in the UN-mandated, U.S.-led presence between North and South Korea).

Worth particular mention are preventive deployment missions. The only "pure" such mission was deployed along Macedonia's border in 1992 to prevent spillover from war in the rest of the former Yugoslavia (and in 1997, also from instability in Albania when the government there collapsed).[10] Keen to avoid a new front in the multifaceted—and deadly and expensive—Balkan wars, the UN Preventive Deployment Force (UNPRE-DEP) was authorized as a deterrent, a function that was enhanced by the inclusion of U.S. troops (at that stage, the first in the Balkan theater), which served to amplify UNPREDEP as a tripwire. The force was eventually pulled out in 1999 when China vetoed its extension in response to warming Macedonian relations with Taiwan.

Two other missions can be seen in a preventive deployment vein: the above-mentioned OAU mission in the Central African Republic and, to an extent, the sequence of UN operations in Haiti—especially the first, designed to stem a potential exodus of refugees in response to increasing instability and violence.

However promising the concept, there are grounds for modest expectations that preventive deployments have broad utility. First, there remains considerable debate over whether the relative stability of Macedonia during this period was due to the presence of UNPREDEP. Second, the UNPRE-DEP model is unlikely to be replicable outside of rare occasions where great power interests are judged heavily at stake. Importantly, in the Macedonia case, major states were already heavily invested in the Balkans, which created an incentive to reinforce international presence in the broader theater. Finally, in both the Central African Republic and Haiti cases, the lasting effect of UN deployments were arguably marginal given that a major underlying source of conflict in both—internal security vacuums—was likely to persist beyond the UN engagement.

Coercive tools. The Security Council also has coercive tools at its disposal, including arms embargoes, disarmament efforts, broader sanctions, and international criminal mechanisms. Each of these is discussed fully elsewhere in this volume. For the purposes of this chapter, just a few observations are in order.

Regarding arms embargoes, these arguably can have a deescalating effect in ongoing conflicts. When imposed on one or more parties at the end of a conflict, they also can form part of a stabilization strategy to prevent recurrent conflict. Arms embargoes have a mixed record, however. In the former Yugoslavia, for instance, the chosen strategy for ultimately ending the war involved precisely the opposite: namely, rearming two of the parties (Bosniacs and Bosnian Croats) in order to create an effective ground force that could roll back Bosnian Serbs alongside a NATO-led air campaign. What this suggests is that judgments about the utility of arms embargoes in either preventing or deescalating conflict should flow from a well-designed and informed strategy for managing a given conflict.

Conceivably, the Council could also throw its weight behind efforts to coerce or heavily encourage disarmament in countries or regions at risk of conflict. However, the likelihood of deep and lasting diplomatic support for such policies is not high, even if one were to speculate beyond the Council's polarization over Iraq during the second U.S.-led coalition invasion of that country. The Council might embark instead on more concerted *non*coercive disarmament strategies, but this implies a commitment to more aggressive multilateralism from the permanent five (P-5), especially the United States, which does not appear likely at present.

Though usually deployed to contain an existing conflict, economic and other sanctions could also be part of a broader effort to forestall conflict through inducing more pacific behavior from war-inclined regimes. Sanctions on Iraq between the 1991 Gulf War and the 2003 invasion can roughly be seen in this way. There is now a vast literature on sanctions and their efficacy, much of which points to the importance of targeting these instruments in order to avoid both collateral and perverse effects. Apart from this ongoing challenge, in cases where one or more parties are nonstate actors, the operational promise of sanctions to prevent conflict diminishes considerably.

Constraints on Council Action

If the Security Council has a number of preventive instruments at its disposal, it also faces significant constraints on their use. These break down into four main categories: normative, strategic, operational, and political.

Normative Limitations

Due partly to the outcome of early debates over prevention and humanitarian intervention, the conflict prevention agenda within the UN has noticeably shifted toward an emphasis on the capacity of member states to engage in their own preventive efforts. This move suggests that there is still a relatively low comfort level within UN circles for more robust prevention strategies either where states lose any meaningful capacity to prevent internal armed violence or where elements of the state are part of the problem.

One need only try to imagine a UN response to several current situations at risk of destabilization and internal conflict. As provocative as these illustrations may be, consider Nigeria or Pakistan. Both are major UN member states (one a regional hegemon that dominates conflict management efforts in West Africa and has been a UN partner in those efforts; the other a nuclear state whose stability is critical to South and Central Asia, which also is a major troop contributor to peace operations). Both show signs of major internal strain, including sporadic (and at times quite brutal) outbreaks of civil violence to which the states in question have responded often with a heavy hand. However, the notion that the Security Council might act preventively through more than rhetorical measures to forestall conflict or deepening instability in either case is inconceivable, revealing how far the UN remains from a systematic commitment to conflict prevention.

Strategic Uncertainty

Both cases also suggest a second constraint, which is simply the difficulty of assessing what kinds of engagement might be effective. Should the Council somehow find the will and resources to undertake a range of preventive measures in, say, Pakistan, what would they be? What kind of interventions that fall within the remit of the Council might bolster the state, ease regional and other tensions, promote genuine democratic reforms, *and* do so in ways that did not risk further inflaming potential conflict with India? It is far from clear that any of the instruments mentioned above would play a constructive role in inducing positive political stabilization in Pakistan. There still remain important limits on our collective understanding of conflict prevention in specific cases and, importantly, on the availability of relevant tools or methods for Council action.

Operational Capacity

Another set of limits is practical—in particular, the absence of rapid deployment forces or any similar Council capacity for swift operational action. Here the constraint is less the South's suspicions of UN intervention than the *North's* suspicions of the UN itself and unwillingness to entrust such capacities to a collective body. This is a critical gap given the rare window for Council action when conflict has erupted but not yet escalated beyond low levels. Where one can deploy more slowly—for example, Macedonia—speed is less of an issue. But to respond to incipient escalation, speed is of the essence. In such contexts, the UN will remain dependent on the proximity of a willing regional hegemon with force projection capacity, such as Australia in East Timor, the United States in Haiti, and France in parts of Africa.

Political Limitations

The boundaries of the Council's preventive capacity, ultimately, will be set by the political interests of major member states, especially the P-5. The UN is clearly constrained in addressing conflicts that occur within the territory of one of the P-5, or in any area in which the P-5 have key interests. Thus the Council is highly unlikely to address Chechnya, the situation of Uigurs in western China, let alone Taiwan, among others. Nor, it is worth pointing out, was the conflict in Northern Ireland ever likely to involve the UN, even though the United Kingdom is generally a major supporter of UN roles elsewhere and even though there were functional areas—for example, demobilization and disarmament—where the UN has expertise and where Britain and Ireland sought third-party help. Major states are unlikely to seek UN support to resolve an internal challenge, as it signals weakness and appears to open the door to diminished control.

The Council is not significantly less constrained in addressing conflicts that implicate other powerful member states, whether this involves putting a situation on the Council agenda or shaping how it is handled once there. Prominent here is the case of Burma/Myanmar, where only recently the Secretary-General has been able to deploy an envoy even while the issue remains off the agenda. Another example is India-Pakistan relations, where, beyond a meager UN presence in Kashmir, the Council is unlikely to find entry points for engagement on the broader—and extremely volatile—issue of strategic relations. If ever there were a situation that risked jeopardizing international peace and security, it is this one, yet proactive Council action to resolve this decades-old antagonism is unimaginable absent a major shock to the international system.

Next, there are limits to the willingness of key states to deploy troops in cases where they do not perceive their primary interests to be at stake. The numbers reveal this brutally. If one calculates the costs of peace operations on a per capita basis, one has a crude but compelling indication of where the Council will commit resources.[11] Over the course of peacekeeping operations in various countries, the UN spent, for example, U.S.$5,214.06 per Bosniac, U.S.$1,840.16 per Kosovar, U.S.$132.73 per

Cambodian, U.S.$17.25 per Angolan, and U.S.$4.84 per Rwandan. The strength of the UN-mandated and U.S.-led military presence between North and South Korea is a powerful counterexample.

Even where there is strong international interest in seeing a crisis resolved, there are upper limits on what is practicable without real commitment by major powers. Consider the Israeli-Palestinian conflict. It has been on the UN's agenda for decades and the subject of multiple resolutions and statements. But the Council has been marginal in recent years as a stalled peace process slid from the fall of 2000 into a deep and prolonged crisis in which, to date, thousands have died. In the absence of the parties being interested in resolution, and given polarization within the Council, almost nothing can be done through the Council.

Conclusion

The cardinal failures of the 1990s in preventing violent conflict are largely seen as a failure of the UN and powerful member states to take effective action. The generally held view about the Council, in particular, is that it needs to be cajoled, resourced, and pressured to take more action rather than less.

Despite these expectations the record is only modestly promising. The desirability of conflict prevention, including in internal conflicts, is broadly accepted, as is the need to marshal a wide range of resources—diplomatic, military, developmental—in its pursuit. Moreover, there have been important innovations—for example, preventive deployments—as well as increasing and high-quality use of established techniques—for example, use of special envoys and direct diplomacy through Security Council missions.

Bringing such resources and tools to bear more reliably in situations at risk is, however, a tall order. In cases where powerful member states are directly involved—especially though not only the P-5—the Council is unlikely to be able to act, except minimally as an arena coordinating bilateral positions. In cases where there are no major powers directly implicated, Council unity may be more likely. But experience indicates that it will then face real challenges in mustering sufficient resources—especially troops. The most amenable cases for constructive Council action are thus likely to be those either where there is a high shared strategic interest but where the instruments required allow for mobilizing resources more slowly—for example, Macedonia—or where a strong regional power takes an interest in a relatively tractable conflict—for example, Australia in East Timor.

One need only survey the long list of crises and conflicts that have been unaddressed in any significant measure—Algeria, Burundi,

Chechnya, Colombia, Nepal, Sudan, and, curiously, even the Israeli-Palestinian conflict, which despite being an object of Council consideration has not seen the Council contribute productively to its resolution—to be reminded that the UN and its member states have far to go in matching outcome to normative aspiration.

Notes

1. UN Secretary-General, *Prevention of Armed Conflict,* S/2001/574, June 7, 2001.

2. See ibid., Resolution 55/281, August 13, 2001, and the work of the International Commission on Intervention and State Sovereignty.

3. Carnegie Commission on Preventing Deadly Conflict.

4. See Chapter 32.1 in this volume and Bruce D. Jones, *Peacemaking in Rwanda: The Dynamics of Failure* (Boulder: Lynne Rienner, 2001).

5. See Stephen John Stedman, "Alchemy for a New World Order," *Foreign Affairs* 74, no 3. (May–June 1995); and Thomas G. Weiss, "The UN's Prevention Pipe-Dream," *Berkeley Journal of International Law* 14, no. 2 (1997): 501–515.

6. Nuanced accounts of these episodes point more to flawed strategies of response than to a simple failure to respond in the first place. In the case of Rwanda, for example, international actors facilitated a peace accord that incited hard-liners toward extremity rather than moderation. See Jones, *Peacemaking in Rwanda.*

7. UN Secretary-General, *Prevention of Armed Conflict;* Resolution 1366, August 30, 2001; and Resolution 55/281, August 13, 2001.

8. It is interesting to note that two recent episodes of successful peacemaking did not involve the UN at all: namely, the accord reached between Indonesia and the Acehnese, facilitated by an independent NGO, and the agreement reached in Sri Lanka, brokered by Norway.

9. A more systematic evaluation of the uses and impact of Security Council missions would make an interesting study.

10. Initially the Macedonia mission was an extension of the UN Protection Force in Yugoslavia but was later rechristened the UN Preventive Deployment Force.

11. Figures from Stephen John Stedman, Presentation of Findings, *Ending Civil Wars: The Implementation of Peace Agreements,* Policy Forum of the International Peace Academy in New York, November 15, 2002.

8

Armed Nonstate Actors

Andrés Franco

In this chapter I discuss how Security Council decisionmaking is affected by the presence of armed nonstate actors (ANSAs) in intrastate conflicts. Finding ways to deal with ANSAs has become a fundamental challenge in the Council's task of maintaining international peace and security, especially after the dramatic changes to the international structure that came with the end of the Cold War. Before this moment, the Security Council maintained a cautious attitude toward ANSAs, among other reasons because many of them acted as proxies of either the Soviet Union or the United States. Since the early 1990s, however, the Security Council has been more flexible in its dealings with ANSAs and, in fact, has adopted a considerably more active role toward them.

A renewed consensus among the permanent members with respect to many intrastate conflicts, the changing nature of norms of sovereignty in the face of humanitarian imperatives, and the abiding limitations of state sovereignty have made intrastate conflicts more salient in the agenda of the Security Council, including the visibility and political importance of ANSAs. Most intrastate conflicts under consideration in the Council involve an individual state and at least one ANSA with specific interests that must be factored into the Security Council's actions and policy responses.

The agenda with ANSAs is complex and diverse. It is important, therefore, to understand the framework in which the Security Council is operating with respect to these actors, which are difficult to identify as subjects of Council decisions; operate nationally, regionally, and in some instances globally; act as erratic political partners in negotiations; and enjoy decentralized military, political, and economic support. Against this background I assess the importance of ANSAs for the Security Council, then create a general framework to analyze the political dynamics of Security Council–ANSA interaction.

This chapter is divided into four sections. The first section analyzes the particular challenges that the Council faces with respect to ANSAs and briefly looks at various policy responses it has adopted in the past to meet those challenges. The second section explores particular characteristics of ANSAs that contribute to shape their political standing before the Council—that is, whether they are accepted or not as partners for conflict management with the Council or against it. The third section proposes a framework of analysis to understand Security Council–ANSA interaction and attempts to identify the conditions under which the Council's efforts to influence ANSA behavior promise to be successful. Finally, the conclusion discusses some policy recommendations and their implications for day-to-day Council activity.

Challenges and Responses

The presence of ANSAs in intrastate conflicts has repeatedly confronted the Security Council with a number of difficult challenges. Examples abound: in sub-Saharan Africa, the União Nacional para a Independência Total de Angola (UNITA), the Revolutionary United Front (RUF) in Sierra Leone, and the Rassemblement Congolais pour la Démocratie (RCD) in the Democratic Republic of Congo (DRC) have acted as spoilers and have undermined UN efforts to broker lasting peace accords or dramatically complicated UN peacekeeping operations. In the Balkans, the Kosovo Liberation Army (KLA) has challenged the Security Council on many occasions not only with respect to the final status of Kosovo but also in Macedonia, where it conducted cross-border attacks in the summer of 2001. On a global level, Al-Qaida has created a colossal threat to peace and security to which the Council has not been able to structure a proportionate response.

When confronted with these challenges, the Council may engage or isolate politically an ANSA; make specific demands or express support through press statements, presidential statements, or resolutions; impose, implement, or lift targeted sanctions against it; and eventually resort to the use of force. In all cases, the Council wishes to influence ANSA behavior and produce results (e.g., protect UN staff in the field, boost a peacemaking effort, support a disarmament, demobilization, and reintegration effort, and avert the illegal exploitation of natural resources).

Through engagement or political isolation, the Council, for example, has contributed to a cease-fire in Angola; has supported the efforts of South African president Nelson Mandela as a peace broker, and later of Vice President Jacob Zuma, in Burundi in incorporating many ANSAs into a political process; has conceived and implemented the UN Organization

Mission in the DRC (MONUC); and has promoted elections in Sierra Leone with the RUF as a political party. In addition, the Council, through its statements and declarations, has made countless calls and demands to ANSAs on security, humanitarian, and political matters.

Since the early 1990s the Council has resorted to the imposition of targeted sanctions under Chapter VII against ANSAs. These measures have been quite effective with respect to UNITA and the RUF,[1] which drew most of their resources from trade in conflict diamonds. In both cases the sanctions regimes weakened the ANSAs and played an important part in pressuring them to accept peace agreements. The record has been less successful with the sanctions regimes imposed against the Taliban/Al-Qaida and the Rwandan génocidaires who took refuge in eastern Congo.[2]. In the case of Al-Qaida there have been evident political and operational difficulties in implementing sanctions against an ANSA whose actions are not limited to a particular territory and that has "officially" been classified as a terrorist group. All four cases suggest, however, that more innovative mechanisms may be needed if the Council really wishes to ensure that imposition will be followed by implementation. As Chapter 11 illuminates, there is ample room for improvement, for example in the areas of freezing financial assets and targeting arms embargoes at ANSAs.

Finally, many interpret that the Council authorized the use of force against Al-Qaida and the Taliban through Resolution 1368 (2001). There are other cases in which there has been an implicit authorization to use force against certain ANSAs when peacekeeping operations are created. Even those adopted under Chapter VII often operate under the myth of impartiality, and ANSAs have never been explicitly identified as targets of such enforcement measures in any resolution. However, "peacekeeping operations tend to favor, when it is ambiguous as to who is the spoiler, the interests of that group controlling the central state apparatus."[3] This was evident in Sierra Leone and may also happen in the Great Lakes if ANSAs in the DRC continues to spoil peace prospects.

In sum, the Council has a mixed record of success in its dealings with ANSAs. There are structural difficulties that must be considered in any analysis. First, inflexible interpretations by many UN member states of the principles of sovereign equality and nonintervention into internal matters make extremely difficult Council action against or in support of substate actors. Second, Council members are understandably concerned that action targeted at these groups could potentially enhance or worsen their legitimacy (not always in line with Council wishes). Finally, ANSAs lack representation in New York, which forces the Council to rely entirely on special representatives of the Secretary-General (SRSGs) or on diplomatic representations of the permanent members.

ANSA Factors That
Determine Security Council Perspectives

ANSAs exhibit particular characteristics that contribute to strengthening or weakening their standing before the Security Council. In international politics, and hence in the Security Council, perceptions matter. The Council develops views with respect to actors involved in a particular situation, then shapes its thinking and decisions accordingly without consideration as to whether its views are fair or unfair, true or false. There are characteristics in ANSAs, all of which are mutually influencing, that define perceptions and have a definite effect on their legitimacy and political standing before the Council. Once these come into play, the Council may throw its weight behind an ANSA's aim (it could support the KLA in its quest for an independent Kosovo); may find it difficult to go along entirely with an ANSA (Morocco's influence has impeded the Frente Polisario in being completely successful in pursuing its aims in the Council through consensual solutions); or may simply reject the political aspirations of an ANSA (as it did with UNITA after the end of the Cold War).

The aspirations of ANSAs are not always easy to interpret or identify, and on many occasions the Council determines the legitimacy of these aspirations based on judgments of an ANSA's behavior rather than on its stated objectives. This assessment frequently derives from the respect (or lack of respect) for international humanitarian law and human rights law, the level of popular support in the country, the illicit procurement of financial resources, and the level of international exposure.[4]

The level of popular support any ANSA enjoys is not easily determined, but it may be sensed by members of the Council when they face specific political conditions. If the members of the Council get the impression that an ANSA has a constituency and strong political support in the country, there may be more flexibility to accommodate its interests in the Security Council's statements and decisions. In the case of the KLA in Kosovo, for example, the support received from the population of Albanian origin was always taken into account by the Security Council. Similarly, the strong support of the Saharawis to the Frente Polisario translates into political strength in negotiations with Morocco that the Council takes into account. Of course, the ultimate test of popular support comes when an ANSA participates in a political negotiation, transforms itself into a political party, and faces the electorate. This was the case of the RUF in Sierra Leone in 2002—obtaining poor electoral results, as will probably be the case of UNITA in Angola as a fragile democracy consolidates in the coming years in that country.

The illicit/illegal procurement of financial resources is a fundamental aspect influencing the Council's perception of any ANSA.[5] In general, when ANSAs are seen as predatory and criminal, the perceived legitimacy of their putative political goals is negatively affected, regardless of whether those goals otherwise may have some merit. The October 2002 report of the panel of experts in charge of investigating the illegal exploitation of natural resources in the Democratic Republic of Congo (S/2002/1146) is a forceful reminder to members of the Council that strong links exist between the conflict in the DRC and the exploitation of resources in the eastern part of the country.

International exposure also contributes to shape perceptions in the Security Council. Some ANSAs are more sophisticated than others in managing their international relations. This sophistication depends to a large extent on the use of politically correct language in their statements, high levels of education among its leaders, extent of international exposure, and technological endowment. One positive extreme in this respect is exemplified by Polisario, which has successfully developed methods of interaction with the Security Council and its individual members. The other extreme is illustrated by the Mayi-Mayi in the DRC, a group with very limited international exposure and a fragmented and unsophisticated leadership that makes any political dialogue with the Security Council virtually impossible.

Factors Shaping the Security Council's
Ability to Influence ANSA Behavior

The Security Council is most likely to be confronted with the challenge of ANSAs in the context of intrastate conflict. Intrastate conflicts may be classified according to the degree to which the state plagued by conflict exists as a functioning institution, as well as by their international ramifications. From the perspective of the former category, an intrastate conflict may take place in the territory of a functional and legally constituted state or a weak, failing, or failed state. From the perspective of international ramifications, there are three categories of intrastate conflicts: those with no visible international ramifications, those with international ramifications (both humanitarian and security), and those with active international involvement. In the first category, the affected state maintains control of the political situation, controls or restricts the participation of the international community, including the Security Council, and attempts to close political space to ANSAs at the international level. In the second category, the state also maintains political control of the situation and controls or restricts the participation of the international community, including the Security Council. Finally, the third category represents an internationalized conflict with third states providing support to ANSAs.

Table 8.1 combines these criteria to create six types of intrastate conflicts within a simple matrix and provides examples of each case. Clearly, the Security Council has more political space to engage in situations where there is a weak, failing, or failed state, and where the conflict is character-

Table 8.1   ANSAs, Intrastate Conflicts, and the Security Council

Type of Intrastate Conflict/ Stateness	Functional and Legally Constituted States	Weak or Failed States[a]
Domestic	Council involvement highly improbable unless accepted by the affected state (e.g., Chechnya).	Council involvement possible if there is the political will. Council possesses ample autonomy to define policies with respect to ANSAs (e.g., Somalia).
Domestic with international ramifications	Council involvement improbable unless accepted by the affected state (e.g., Sri Lanka, Colombia Indonesia-Aceh, the Philippines, Sudan, Uganda).	Security Council involvement highly probable. Council would define policy with respect to ANSAs based on perspectives of states affected by a conflict's ramifications (e.g., Burundi, Angola, Kosovo).
Domestic with international involvement[b]	Council involvement probable due to similarity with intrastate conflict (e.g., Palestine-Israel conflict).	Council involvement highly probable. Relationship with ANSAs is complex due to the diversity of national interests involved (e.g., Democratic Republic of Congo, Sierra Leone, Liberia, Afghanistan pre-September 11).

Notes: a. The weakness or plain absence of the state creates a political vacuum that favors stronger political participation of the Security Council.

b. Conditions for participation by the Security Council are more favorable since it may act as an independent actor, and relations with ANSAs may be complex due to the political, financial, or military support they receive from third states.

ized by international ramifications or involvement, which tend to coincide with situations in sub-Saharan Africa, where most items on the current Council's agenda are concentrated.

In those situations where the Security Council is seized of the matter, its ability to influence ANSA behavior is determined by its particular role, as well as by the prevalent perception within the Security Council about the ANSAs involved. On the one hand, the Security Council's role can be to provide leadership, to support a regional effort, or to ascertain when it lacks a clearly defined political role and is unable to articulate a leading or supporting role because its members disagree on either. On the other hand, the Council's perception of an ANSA may or may not be consensual among its fifteen members. Table 8.2 combines these factors and identifies six scenarios or cases with varying degrees of Council ability to influence ANSAs.

In Case 1, exemplified by the approach toward UNITA in Angola and the RUF in Sierra Leone, the Council plays a leading role and acts with respect to ANSAs with a consensual perspective among its fifteen members. This is perhaps the most propitious setting for a clear and effective

Table 8.2   Security Council Ability to Influence Behavior of ANSAs

Security Council Role/ Perspective on ANSAs	Consensus	Nonconsensus
Leadership	Case 1 (Angola, Sierra Leone)	Case 2 (Western Sahara, Democratic Republic of Congo)
Support to regional effort	Case 3 (Burundi, Macedonia)	Case 4 (Somalia)
Uncertain role	Case 5 (Afghanistan pre–September 11)	Case 6 (Palestine-Isreal, Liberia)

Security Council policy toward ANSAs, and the probabilities of success may be higher than in the other five cases identified in Table 8.2.

With respect to UNITA, the end of the Cold War contributed to articulate a common vision within the Security Council. In 1993 this organ issued an arms embargo, and complementary sanctions against UNITA were implemented in 1997 and 1998. In 1999, Canadian ambassador Robert Fowler revived the Sanctions Committee for Angola and moved it to center stage with the creation of a panel that began a new investigation of sanctions violations. Despite strong reactions from various Eastern European and southern African governments, Ambassador Fowler's initiative managed to consolidate a consensual perspective in the Council and eventually produced results that weakened UNITA substantially. The death of UNITA's leader, Jonas Savimbi, caused by the Angolan army in 2002, precipitated a cease-fire on April 4, 2002; sanctions against UNITA began immediately thereafter and were subsequently lifted.

With respect to the RUF, the hostage crisis in which 500 peacekeepers were captured in early 2000 created one of the most difficult challenges posed by an ANSA to the Security Council. The United Kingdom pushed the Council into a leadership position, made action against the RUF a central item on the Council's agenda, and created conditions to overcome the crisis. After that, the Security Council supported the disarmament programs and the demobilization of more than 43,000 RUF warriors; fostered the recovery of lands previously controlled by the RUF, including diamond-producing districts; and contributed to the preparatory process of the presidential elections of 2002, in which the RUF participated as a political party.[6]

In Case 2 the Security Council plays a leading role but lacks a consensual perspective among its fifteen members with respect to ANSAs. This lack of unity hampers its effectiveness. The approaches toward the Frente Polisario in Western Sahara and, in some instances, the ANSAs involved in the Democratic Republic of Congo provide appropriate examples.

The division of the members of the Council in the case of Polisario became explicit after the Secretary-General's special envoy, James Baker, submitted on February 19, 2002, a report (S/2000/455) with four options to find a political solution to the conflict: (1) the settlement plan, which had been accepted by both parties but proved impossible to implement; (2) a framework agreement for autonomy favored by Morocco but rejected by Polisario; (3) a territorial division, of interest to Polisario but rejected by Morocco; and (4) the closure of the UN Mission for the Referendum in Western Sahara (MINURSO), an option that was rejected by both parties. The political negotiations that followed during the period up to July 2002 found France and the United States leading a small group of countries defending Morocco's interests (and hence the second option), while a dissenting group that involved, among others, Russia, Ireland, and Colombia sided with Polisario and favored the first option as an expression of the principle of self-determination. This division among the fifteen members has prevented the Security Council from delivering more tangible results in the political solution of the dispute.

With respect to the ANSAs in the Democratic Republic of Congo, the Security Council has also showed signs of division, although less pronounced than in the case of Western Sahara. The relations that the RCD and the Mouvement pour la Libération du Congo (MLC) have established with the governments of Rwanda and Uganda, respectively, coupled with the relations of these governments with some of the permanent members, have impeded the formation of a unified and cohesive perspective that would force these ANSAs to be more responsive to Council action. Although it may be impossible to assess the precise impact of this division, it has had a negative impact on the viability of the peace process. The bottom line is that the capacity of the Security Council to influence regional ANSAs has been limited.

In Case 3 the Security Council supports a regional effort and has a consensual perspective among its fifteen members with respect to ANSAs that is determined by the region's own perspective. In this case, the Security Council's effectiveness is dependent, to a large extent, on the effectiveness of the regional process in influencing the behavior of ANSAs. The approaches toward the KLA in Macedonia and the National Liberation Forces (FNL) and the Forces for Democracy and Development (FDD) in Burundi are examples of this scenario.

With respect to the KLA, the attacks in Tetovo in March 2001 came from the headquarters in Kosovo and were facilitated by a precarious security situation in the Presevo Valley in southern Serbia. Members of the North Atlantic Treaty Organization (NATO), some of which were also members of the Security Council, were particularly frustrated with the attacks since the Albanians had been their protégés since the 1999 NATO campaign over Kosovo. It was only after mediation by the European Union and NATO that in August 2001 Security Council members were able to produce a consensual perspective on this ANSA and provide political support to the signing of a framework agreement between the government of Macedonia and the KLA. This is a case of a successful regional effort supported by the Council.

The FNL and the FDD of Burundi constitute another example in which the regional effort led by South Africa has shown partial successes. The main challenge has been to attract the FNL and the FDD to the peace process, but the Security Council's capacity to achieve results has been limited by the regional mechanism's lack of capacities in spite of an existing consensus among Council members with respect to these ANSAs.

In Case 4 the Security Council supports a regional effort, but there is no consensus with respect to the ANSAs. Somalia at present is a notorious example, with a number of militia groups allegedly backed by other states in the Horn of Africa, and separatists in Puntland and Somaliland who have some political support from a permanent member of the Council. The lack of consensus within the Security Council, and the lack of political will to deal with the situation, have weakened regional efforts involving neighboring countries. Norway, as an elected member of the Council, tried hard to bring the issue back to the Council's attention, overcoming strong skepticism from some permanent members. Eventually the arms embargo against the entire nation was reinforced through the creation of a panel of experts in Resolution 1425, adopted in July 2002. And later, in mid-October 2002, the Council supported the reconciliatory conference of the Somali people, led by members of Intergovernmental Authority on Development (IGAD) (the regional organization)—especially Ethiopia, Kenya, and Djibouti. Today, however, the Council has an extremely limited capacity to influence ANSAs and other parties in Somalia.

In Case 5 the Security Council has an uncertain role in the handling of a situation even though there is consensus among the fifteen members with respect to the ANSAs involved. The Taliban in Afghanistan before September 11, 2001, is an adequate example of this scenario. Although the Security Council developed a consensual position toward this ANSA,[7] which was never a recognized government but rather a "faction," it was never effective in altering Taliban behavior. The situation was aggravated by the Council's inability to articulate a comprehensive policy for Afghanistan involving political, regional, security, humanitarian, and economic aspects. The Council was divided on the advisability of this approach and unable to define its own role vis-à-vis the situation.

Finally, in Case 6, the Security Council also has an uncertain role in the handling of a situation but lacks consensus among the fifteen members with respect to the ANSAs involved. This scenario subjects the Security

Council to considerable political pressure and weakens its effectiveness to influence ANSAs. The Palestinian-Israeli conflict and Liberians United for Reconciliation and Democracy (LURD) provide examples of this situation.

With regard to the Palestinian-Israeli conflict, the Council has been unable to define a sustained role for itself to deal with this situation, partly because the United States and Israel have considered that the Security Council has no role to play at all. In addition, there have been notorious discrepancies among Council members with respect to the ANSAs that operate in the region. The dual lack of consensus with respect to the Council's role and the nature of the ANSAs has prevented it from delivering any tangible results.

The LURD is also the object of disagreements in a Council that has been unable to define its role with respect to this situation. Decisions against Liberia have in fact been decisions against the RUF in Sierra Leone, and it has been difficult to promote sustained political discussions about the situation in Liberia in the Council. Guinea, the United Kingdom, and the United States have led the group of those who have disagreed with institutionalizing an approach of any sort. During the last months of 2002, various Security Council members insisted on the need to reexamine the sanctions to Liberia against the background of Liberia's humanitarian, political, and security needs. Nevertheless, the ineffectiveness of the Council in this case continues to be notorious. Clearly, a driving factor influencing the Security Council's attitude vis-à-vis the LURD has been the fact that Charles Taylor is regarded by many as the main destabilizing factor in the region and that those opposing him cannot be rejected and condemned absolutely.

In sum, the Security Council has a greater ability to influence ANSAs in Cases 1 and 3. In all other cases, the Council finds obstacles to maintaining international peace and security when ANSAs are involved.

Conclusion

This chapter has attempted to assess the current relationship between the Security Council and ANSAs and has arrived at two basic conclusions. First, Security Council and ANSAs influence each other more frequently in those situations where there is a weak, failing, or failed state, and where the conflict is characterized by international ramifications or involvement (e.g., in Burundi, Angola, Kosovo, the DRC, Sierra Leone, Liberia, and Afghanistan pre–September 11). Second, when the Security Council defines the ANSA as a political actor, the relation is determined by the Council's role in that particular situation (i.e., as leader, in support for a regional effort, or uncertain) and the consensus or lack of it among its members with respect to a particular ANSA.

What do these conclusions mean for day-to-day Council activity? How can the Security Council, an intergovernmental organ created to deal with state-based threats to international peace and security, confront the challenges posed to it by ANSAs? How can it make sure that its statements and decisions produce tangible results in the field where ANSAs are a dominating force?

Individual nonpermanent members discover soon in their first year on the Council that it is quite complex to connect the political discussion in New York with the political realities on the ground, especially when ANSAs are involved. This connection is possible only if all members of the Council commit to maintain the unanimity of this UN body vis-à-vis each and every ANSA in a particular situation. The messages to the ANSAs must be clear, pointed, and unambiguous. The policy toward ANSAs must be strategic, assertive, and focused. I have no doubt that ANSAs will use in their favor any hint of a lack of consensus among Council members compromising its ability to play an effective political role.

The Security Council must make explicit, clarify, or disseminate its policy and decisions. Obviously, communication with ANSAs should not go through the permanent missions to the United Nations in New York. In order to communicate with ANSAs, the Council must continue to rely on regional mechanisms (Vice President Zuma communicates with ANSAs through South Africa's mediation in Burundi); diplomatic representations of permanent members (in Angola and the DRC messages to ANSAs have been delivered by ambassadors); Security Council missions (in the DRC the Council met with the signatories of the Lusaka Agreement); and SRSGs.[8]

Security Council messages to ANSAs may or may not be effective. But what is interesting is that ANSAs, regardless of how distant they are from New York, frequently react positively to these messages if they include positive references of them, or adopt a more defensive position when the reference is critical. Some of the Congolese rebel movements, for example, pay great attention to the Security Council's press statements and other pronouncements. It is one of the rare cases where an ANSA watches, and listens to, the Security Council very carefully.[9]

Of course, matters may turn more complicated if an ANSA enjoys political support from a Security Council member. This is a tricky scenario. Support may be explicit, as with the Frente Polisario, for example, which receives backing from many members in the Council who find its political agenda legitimate, or concealed, as with LURD's fight against President Charles Taylor in Liberia (although it did not imply explicit support, it may have been handy to some members of the Council as this regime crumpled in 2003). In both cases, where political negotiations in the Council may become disruptive as the unanimity fades, the national interests of members

of the Council must concede to the collective interest of responding forcefully to situations that constitute a threat to peace and security. When this
happens, the Secretary-General and his team need to use aggressively their
capacity to influence Council perceptions and attitudes with respect to
ANSAs. The Secretary-General, via reports or briefings in informal consultations, is the institution called to set the record straight, to shape political
perceptions, and to establish the facts that will become the basis of decisions and pronouncements.

There are a number of challenges that need to be dealt with if the
Council aims at inducing behavioral changes in ANSAs, such as getting
them to enter into a political dialogue, respect international humanitarian
law and security of UN personnel, or other matters. The first challenge is to
compensate for the fact that many ANSAs are difficult to identify as targets
for Security Council action. Representatives must incorporate in their statements the fact that ANSAs are substantially different from states and that,
consequently, they operate under a different political logic and respond to
different political signals. They must struggle to come up with ideas and
instruments to target an actor that is strange, distant, and hard to compre-
hend in a New York ambiance, and the Secretariat must contribute to
induce this state of mind.

A second challenge is to act in accordance with the special geopolitical
nature of ANSAs. The agenda of the Council is state-based, which means
that decisions are normally destined for the situation in a particular state.
UN intergovernmental discussion is strongly influenced by the notion of
state sovereignty, and of course the Security Council is no exception. The
problem, however, is that most ANSAs are not confined to a specific territory but rather operate regionally or globally and hence tend to be dispersed
in a region or in the world. Council decisions that are bound for a particular
territory will be ineffectual if they target an actor that is not confined to that
specific territory. The Council's response to the Revolutionary United Front
in Sierra Leone, for example, has not been truly regional even though this
group or its branches operate mostly in West Africa. Similarly, the Council
has had to go beyond Afghanistan to attack Al-Qaida after September 11,
2001, when there was clear realization of that terrorist organization's global
ramifications. In simple words, regional approaches to conflict management make sense in dealing with ANSAs, as do global approaches to handle
global threats posed by international terrorist organizations.

The Council must also learn to strike a balance in its political judgments of ANSAs. The challenge lies in identifying when and the conditions
under which one of these actors has the capacity and willingness to act as a
unitary and responsible political partner in negotiations. Ultimately, the
Council seeks political solutions to political problems. But when a situation
involves ANSAs, it is never black and white. An attack against civilians,

involvement in drug trafficking, or simply the lack of cohesion in an ANSA's leadership are behaviors that tend to produce precipitated political judgments on the part of individual Council members (potentially jeopardizing political solutions promoted from or with the support of the Security Council). UNITA, for example, attacked civilians on many occasions just like a terrorist organization does. But in all cases, the Council was careful not to characterize this group as such, because in everyone's mind UNITA was indispensable for any political settlement in Angola.

The Security Council also needs to counterbalance the decentralized nature of military, political, and economic support to ANSAs. The Security Council, as a governing body that operates at the global level, finds it hard to halt the support ANSAs receive locally. Targeted sanctions have been an innovative mechanism to tackle this support (sanctions regimes were in place for the RUF in Sierra Leone and UNITA in Angola), but there are a number of problems in the implementation of these sanctions that play in favor of ANSAs. A number of recommendations to enhance the implementation of targeted sanctions have been prepared by the Stockholm Process on the Implementation of Targeted Sanctions. The report, introduced to the Security Council on February 25, 2003, and its numerous recommendations must be taken seriously by members of the Council.[10]

Finally, the Council must be realistic in its assessment of the security conditions for the deployment of peacekeepers in areas where ANSAs are active. Military advice must be available from an independent source that factors the risks posed by ANSAs, perhaps by putting in place some of the peacekeeping recommendations of the Brahimi Report. Currently this information is fed selectively into Council discussions through the permanent members who have diplomatic representations in places where ANSAs are active (mainly the United States, the United Kingdom, and France), or with quotations from press releases that elected members bring into the discussion. The Secretariat always brings ideas on this matter but tends to be cautious in order not to discourage potential troop contributors.

Notes

Much of the information and many of the opinions expressed in this chapter have been developed on the basis of my own experience as deputy permanent representative of Colombia on the Security Council during the period 2001–2002.

1. Resolutions 864 (1993) and 1171 (1998), respectively.

2. Resolution 997 (1995) specified that the arms embargo imposed against Rwanda in Resolution 918 (1994) applied to groups in other countries operating against Rwanda.

3. James Fearon and David Laitin, "International Institutions and Civil War," draft report, Stanford University, Department of Political Science, 2001.

4. Based on perceptions, an ANSA may be classified as a terrorist organization. It never happened before September 11, 2001, prior to which the Security

Council limited itself to links to the Taliban in Afghanistan (an "Afghan faction"). The tragic events of September 11, however, ended the traditional prudence that characterized the classification of a group as terrorist. On November 14, 2001, through Resolution 1378, the Security Council made explicit reference to Al-Qaida as a "terrorist group" with operational bases on territory controlled by the Taliban and has made similar pronouncements after terrorist attacks were carried out in Bali, Indonesia, Moscu, Russia, and Bogotá, Colombia. Other ANSAs whose actions have been condemned as "terrorist" (namely, UNITA and KLA) have never been considered "terrorist organizations" by the Council.

5. Most ANSAs obtain their resources through voluntary or forced contributions; illegal exploitation of mineral resources (gold and diamonds); looting of banks, manufacturing plants, stocks, and private property; systems of tax collection; donations from abroad; and illicit drugs.

6. Undeniably, there have been results. However, positive news about the RUF has been handled cautiously in the Security Council, especially on issues associated with its political intentions and military capacity. Its activities and presence in Liberia, full operation of its communications system, and robbery of small arms from the UN Mission in Sierra Leone in 2002 have contributed to this caution.

7. It is worth noting that this has become clear only since 1999, before which the United States, China (because of Pakistan), and some nonaligned countries were accommodating vis-à-vis the Taliban. This attitude changed when there was strong suspicion that the Taliban were harboring and supporting Al-Qaida after the 1998 attacks in Nairobi and Dar-es-Salaam.

8. This channel presents more difficulties because it involves the issue of neutrality. As they provide good offices, SRSGs have to maintain a neutral position with respect to ANSAs while at the same securing political support from the Security Council (a nonneutral body by definition). Complications intensify when the Council lacks a consensual position with respect to ANSAs.

9. A French diplomat confirmed to me that Jean-Pierre Bemba, the leader of the MLC, frequently called the Congolese permanent representative in New York to complain about certain Security Council statements.

10. The report and other relevant information may be consulted at www.smart-sanctions.se.

PART 2

Enforcing
Council Mandates

9

The Use of Force

ADAM ROBERTS

In the period since the end of the Cold War, numerous crises have given rise to demands for military action, and particularly for intervention in states without the consent of their governments. Force has been used in a wide variety of circumstances, and with a wide variety of legal justifications and authorizing bodies. The UN Security Council has played a significant role in these developments. However, it has not succeeded in ensuring that military action is restricted and managed in quite the ways that were envisaged in the Charter. Some uses of force have eluded the Council's control, often because it was divided on this issue. Furthermore, some uses of force have challenged certain aspects of the existing body of international law relating to the resort of force—the jus ad bellum. In particular, they have been seen as either violating, moving beyond, or reinterpreting the two principal accepted legal grounds for the use of force: self-defense, and authorization by the UN Security Council.

Two doctrines have been the foci of debates about a possibly expanded right of states to use force in circumstances that differ significantly from these two principal accepted legal grounds. Neither doctrine is wholly new, but their articulation has contained new elements: the doctrine of humanitarian intervention, and the doctrine reserving a right to act preemptively against emerging threats.

These events and doctrines have involved some expanded justification for intervention within states. While they create important opportunities for the UN Security Council, they also create problems. They can be seen as challenging the twin normative principles of nonintervention and the sovereign equality of states as enshrined in the UN Charter, especially in Article 2(4). Further, some of these events, and the doctrine of preemption, appear to challenge the meaning of self-defense as outlined in Article 51 of the Charter:

133

> Nothing in the present Charter shall impair the inherent right of individual
> or collective self-defence if an armed attack occurs against a Member of
> the United Nations, until the Security Council has taken measures neces-
> sary to maintain international peace and security. Measures taken by
> Members in the exercise of this right of self-defence shall be immediately
> reported to the Security Council and shall not in any way affect the
> authority and responsibility of the Security Council under the present
> Charter to take at any time such action as it deems necessary in order to
> maintain or restore international peace and security.

This wording has long been seen as raising a number of questions. Granted that the right of self-defense is "inherent," to what extent did it continue unaltered into the UN era, or was it restricted by the UN Charter? What exactly constitutes an "armed attack" or (to take a word used else- where in the Charter) "aggression"? Does Article 51 have to be interpreted narrowly as excluding any self-defense other than that in response to an actual armed attack? Why has the duty to report to the Security Council been of such little practical significance, particularly in terms of the Council exerting its authority on the situation?[1] On each of these questions there is scope for genuine disagreement, whether among lawyers or among states. These disagreements all touch on the question of the extent to which the concept of self-defense can or cannot be understood broadly and can or cannot be a basis for justifying certain acts of intervention.

Quite apart from a possible expanded interpretation of the right of self-defense, other grounds have often been advanced in justification of acts of military force. In particular, the impressive growth of international law in the UN era has contributed to such grounds. If a state persistently violates important legal norms—for example, in such fields as arms control, human rights, international humanitarian law, or environmental conservation— what should the response of other states be? There is strong acceptance in contemporary international law that forcible countermeasures are unlawful. Sometimes, however, having urged the state concerned to desist from such violations, other states and international bodies may perceive a need to use force, yet it may not always be possible to obtain Security Council authori- zation for it. If they then use force, it may be for a cause that is neither nar- rowly unilateral nor UN-approved.

I begin this chapter by noting that the doctrine of nonintervention has always suffered from certain limitations, and does so especially in today's unipolar world. I then explore the strengths and weaknesses of the UN Security Council as a means of reaching decisions regarding the use of force. I consider the issues surrounding the use of force against Iraq in vari- ous crises since 1990, with particular attention to the claim of what might be called "existing authority" or "continuing authority," as was advanced by the United States and other countries in the 2003 war. Next I consider the two distinct but similar doctrines of preemption and humanitarian intervention, and the reasons why they have failed to command general assent. Finally, I draw some conclusions from the varied practices of the post–Cold War period.

Nonintervention Versus Spheres of Influence

The nonintervention rule has long been, and remains, fundamental to international order; its observance, however, has always been imperfect. Security concerns and related considerations have often in the past led countries to intervene by force in other states, in circumstances different from self-defense against ongoing armed attack. A wide variety of states, by no means confined to great powers, have at times given a no less wide variety of reasons for intervention: self-defense against imminent threats, counterintervention to prevent a rival state from expanding its power, maintenance of peace and security, protection of nationals in other states, and protection of threatened populations within the target state.

Major powers have often made systematic efforts to impose limits on the freedom of action of other states. These efforts have always coexisted uneasily with doctrines recognizing the sovereign equality of states and the principle of nonintervention. Arguments about preventing a more dangerous situation from developing within a state frequently loomed large as justifications—as much political as legal—for placing restrictions on certain states' freedom of action. In many cases, as with the Monroe and Brezhnev doctrines, such arguments became associated with the concept of "spheres of influence."

The sphere of influence that counts now is, at last, literally a sphere: the world. If the United States can be threatened by terrorists or by what it defines as "rogue states" half a world away, then it seeks some right to intervene half a world away. If shocking abuses of citizens by their own government can be shown on television screens around the world, the demand arises for some right to intervene in distant continents. Previously, "spheres of influence" could be viewed as mere regional exceptions to the general norm of nonintervention. Now there is one sphere in which, because it is global in character, any norm justifying intervention seems to pose a more direct and general challenge to the post-1945 normative framework limiting the resort to force.

This challenge to the normative framework is further complicated by the fact that there is one preeminent military power, the United States. This fact has naturally given rise to a concern to restore balance to the international system: hence the varying degrees of French, Chinese, and Russian attachment to the idea of a multipolar world and to the idea of the UN as a central part of it. These states, and others, when opposing certain U.S.-led interventions, have generally cited the nonintervention norm as the basis for their stance. They are on firm ground in doing so. While in some instances, especially Iraq in 1991, the United States has used force for purposes that were perceived as internationally sanctioned and entirely legitimate, some subsequent U.S.-led uses of force have undoubtedly posed problems for the nonintervention norm. The U.S. doctrine of preemption adds to the litany of such problems. Thus the different power-political interests of states, and their different visions of how the world should be ordered, go hand in hand with disagreements about the legality of certain types of intervention.

Authorization by the UN Security Council

Since the end of the Cold War, the UN Security Council has played important roles both in authorizing use of force in a wide range of situations, and in contributing to certain changes in the understanding of jus ad bellum. Moreover, the Council has asserted a degree of authority over some recalcitrant states that has subsequently been important in debates concerning the use of force against those states. The idea that the Security Council can, in certain situations, require states to take certain actions inside their own borders (as with the 1998 resolutions requiring Yugoslavia to facilitate the return of displaced persons in Kosovo), and can even authorize a regime change by force (as it did with its resolution on Haiti in 1994), appears to be widely if not universally accepted. This is proof, if it is needed, that some limitations on state sovereignty may be accepted even when others are not.

The UN Security Council has authorized the use of force in a variety of situations, but has done so in ways somewhat different from those envisaged in certain provisions of the UN Charter. When confronted by situations requiring the large-scale use of force, the Security Council has not generally commanded substantial military action in the ways anticipated in many provisions of Chapter VII. Instead, its primary method for dealing with this problem has been to authorize the use of force by member states (this was compatible with certain provisions in Articles 48 and 53 of the Charter). Security Council resolutions have implicitly or explicitly authorized the use of armed forces by U.S.-led coalitions, rather than under the command of the UN as such, in the cases of Korea (1950), Iraq-Kuwait (1990), Somalia (1992), and Haiti (1994). The Security Council authorized France to lead an operation in Rwanda (1994), Italy in Albania (1997), and Australia in East Timor (1999). UN authorization of limited use of force by states has also become a common method for enforcing sanctions, air exclusion zones, and other restrictions on particular states and activities.

In Bosnia and Herzegovina in 1992–1995, the arrangements for authorization of force were particularly varied and complex. Resolution 836, adopted on June 4, 1993, included a decision that

> Member States, acting nationally or through regional organisations or arrangements, may take, under the authority of the Security Council and subject to close coordination with the Secretary-General and UNPROFOR [UN Protection Force, the peacekeeping force in the former Yugoslavia], all necessary measures, through the use of air power, in and around the safe areas in the Republic of Bosnia and Herzegovina, to support UNPROFOR in the performance of its mandate.

This was a basis for several military actions by the North Atlantic Treaty Organization (NATO) in 1994–1995. Events exposed difficulties in combining the threat or use of force with humanitarian and peacekeeping activities, and in the system of joint UN and NATO authorization of force. In August–September 1995, after the Serb conquest of the two "safe areas" of Srebrenica and Zepa, and continuing attacks on others, NATO's Operation Deliberate Force bombing campaign was followed by a cease-fire. The Dayton Accords were concluded on November 20–21, 1995. The NATO-led Implementation Force (IFOR), authorized by the Security Council and deployed in Bosnia in December 1995, had notably broad authority from the UN to use force.[2]

In addition to various forms of authorization to others, there was also a tendency in the 1990s for the Security Council to grant unusual powers to use force to certain UN peacekeeping operations. Examples included the ill-fated second UN Operation in Somalia (UNOSOM II) and the UN Mission in Sierra Leone (UNAMSIL).[3]

With respect to terrorism, the Council's general approach in the 1990s was one of firm insistence on state responsibility for stopping terrorist activities on their own territories, not a license for international military action.[4] After the events of September 11, 2001, the Security Council came closer to endorsing the use of force in response to international terrorist acts. Resolution 1368 recognized "the inherent right of individual or collective self-defence in accordance with the Charter," condemned the attacks of the previous day, and stated that the Council "regards such acts, like any act of international terrorism, as a threat to international peace and security." It also expressed the Council's "readiness to take all necessary steps to respond to the terrorist attacks of 11 September 2001, and to combat all forms of terrorism."[5] These key points were reiterated in a resolution later that month, which additionally placed numerous requirements on all states to bring the problem of terrorism under control.[6]

These resolutions were not direct authorizations of force—something not specifically required for the initiation of a self-defense action. However, by recognizing the right of self-defense in this context, they helped to clarify that there was an international legal basis for the subsequent U.S.-led intervention in Afghanistan. Further, these resolutions, and various associated statements and actions, can be seen as confirming that the law of self-defense encompassed actions by nonstate entities within the concept of "armed attack," allowed for the possibility of attacking terrorist bases operating on the soil of states unwilling or unable to prevent terrorist attacks, and recognized that a regime's responsibility was engaged for its failure to prevent and punish acts of terrorism by a movement operating on its soil, and therefore that an attack on that regime itself might be a permissible act of self-defense.[7]

Following the main phase of military hostilities in Afghanistan and the fall of the Taliban regime in December 2001, the Security Council again opted for an authorized but non-UN peacekeeping force—the International Security Assistance Force (ISAF), established in Kabul and surrounding areas in January 2002. As with the Stabilization Force (SFOR) and the NATO-led Kosovo Force (KFOR) in the Balkans, ISAF was conferred with certain powers, including to use force, that are more extensive than those of most UN peacekeeping operations.[8]

The fact that the Security Council has authorized or approved the use of force in a large number of cases, and thereby has played an important legitimizing role, cannot obscure the no less significant fact that it has frequently been unable to agree on forcible measures.[9] Sometimes, as in Rwanda in early 1994, this has been due to an unwillingness of states to supply forces. However, the failure to agree on forcible measures has more often been due to threat or use of the veto. Kosovo in 1999 was such a case, but after the war, Resolution 1244 of June 10, 1999, provided the basis for KFOR and also for a UN administration. Another case in which the Security Council could not agree on the use of force, Iraq in March 2003, is discussed in the next section.

The greatest problems regarding the legitimacy of use of force arise when it is neither authorized by the Security Council nor a straightforward case of self-defense in response to an armed attack. It would be easy to say that, apart from cases of self-defense, force should never be used except when specifically authorized by the Security Council. In virtually all crises, the argument for attempting to reach agreement in the Security Council is strong.

However, viewing formal Security Council authorization as a sine qua non of any military action other than self-defense poses a number of problems. It means that each of the five permanent members of the Security Council can veto any and every use of force other than individual or collective self-defense. Even if no veto is threatened, it means that such uses of military force depend on votes from permanent or nonpermanent members who may be remote from the crisis. Historically, because of such factors, the Security Council has been more willing to define the ends of policy than to authorize military means for attaining those ends. There have been many situations in which, at least in the view of certain key states involved, there was an overwhelming case for the use of force, but the Security Council did not, and probably could not, formally agree to authorize it. Such cases include the crises in East Pakistan in 1971, in the Kurdish areas of northern Iraq in 1991, and in Kosovo in 1999. At the same time the Council, in the latter two cases as well as in Iraq in 2003, was unable (and in some instances clearly unwilling) to condemn the use of force by intervening states or to demand an immediate cease-fire. In such instances the use of force may be legally precarious, but it is not self-evidently illegal in every case.

Sometimes the willingness of one or more member states to use force in support of proclaimed Security Council objectives may actually galvanize the other Security Council members to take action, because of concern that, otherwise, they or the Council as a whole would become irrelevant. The Iraq crisis in the months leading up to Resolution 1441 of November 8, 2002, can be read in this way. However, when in March 2003 the United States and UK spectacularly failed to secure Security Council support for a so-called second resolution on Iraq, they proved that the success of such a galvanizing strategy is by no means ensured, and may indeed incur resentment.

War in Iraq

In the period before the 2003 Iraq war, when it became apparent that a specific UN Security Council authorization was unlikely, states and international lawyers criticized the proposed U.S.-led military action in Iraq as unlawful.[10] Since this action was not a case of self-defense against an actual armed attack by Iraq, and did not have the recent and specific authorization of the UN Security Council, it could easily be viewed as having at best a doubtful basis in international law. Nevertheless, in most cases the expression of this view did not include a detailed response to the strongest part of the legal case for military action against Iraq. Such an omission is not surprising, as the debate about the reasons for, and legitimacy of, attacking Iraq lacked a clear focus.

Especially in the United States, discussion of possible action against Iraq had long encompassed many different lines of argument. In the intense debate about Iraq from summer 2002 onward, members of George W. Bush's administration variously suggested that military action was necessary and justified because of the urgent need for an end to the repression of the Iraqi people, for regime change, for preventive war to stop a possible future threat, and for anticipatory self-defense against an imminent threat.

They also spoke of Iraq as the "next phase" of the war on terrorism. Finally, they stressed the importance of securing the implementation of Security Council resolutions on Iraq. The range of rationales reflected accurately the extraordinary number of issues involved in the Iraq crisis, but meant that for a long time the debate lacked legal clarity.

 In March 2003, when the United States and the UK finally took military action against Iraq, the two governments relied on one main legal rationale: Iraq's failure to implement certain UN Security Council resolutions and the coalition's continuing authority to use force based in particular on Resolutions 678, 687, and 1441.[11]

The argument that past Security Council resolutions provide a continuing, or revived, authority to use force, in a different situation and a dozen years after they were passed, may seem tortuous, but an examination of their terms suggests that there is some substance to it. In 1990, immediately following the occupation of Kuwait, a Council resolution had affirmed "the inherent right of individual or collective self-defence, in response to the armed attack by Iraq against Kuwait."[12] Against this background, further authorization was not essential as a basis for military action to achieve the restoration of Kuwait. However, Resolution 678 of November 29, 1990, in authorizing member states to use force, specified that this was not just to secure Iraqi withdrawal from Kuwait, but also "to restore international peace and security in the area."[13] This was a prudent recognition of the need for a range of measures to ensure stability. This resolution, including its reference to restoring peace and security, was reaffirmed in Resolution 686 of March 2, 1991, concluded at the end of the campaign to expel Iraq from Kuwait. Then Resolution 687 of April 3, 1991, "the mother of all resolutions," spelled out the detailed terms of the cease-fire, as it explained in its operative paragraphs 1 and 33. The resolution covered such matters as boundary demarcation, a demilitarized zone, and renunciation of terrorism. In requiring Iraq to renounce unconditionally any biological, chemical, or nuclear weapons programs, it provided for a system of international inspection and weapons destruction by the UN Special Commission, and imposed time limits for Iraqi disarmament, much of which should have been completed by August 1991.

Thereafter, numerous Security Council resolutions found Iraq to be in breach of its cease-fire commitments. Many of them were passed unanimously. For example, Resolution 707 of August 15, 1991, condemned Iraq's violations of Resolution 687 and proclaimed it to be in "material breach" of that resolution, which had established the basis of the cease-fire. In 1998, when Iraq ceased cooperation, Resolution 1205 of November 5, 1998, condemned the country as being "in flagrant violation" of its commitments. Resolution 1441 of November 8, 2002, proclaimed Iraq to be in "material breach of its obligations under relevant resolutions," recalled the 1990 authorization of states to use force, further recalled that in its Resolution 687 "the Council declared that a ceasefire would be based on acceptance by Iraq of the provisions of that resolution," and offered Iraq "a final opportunity to comply with its disarmament obligations." Resolution 1441, taken on its own, was not a clear authorization to use force, but apart from its requirement that the Council reconvene if Iraq failed to comply fully, it did not weaken any authorization based on earlier resolutions.

The legal justification for the U.S.-led military action initiated in March 2003 would have been significantly simpler if the United States and UK had succeeded in their efforts to persuade the UN Security Council to follow up with a so-called second resolution—which would actually have been the eighteenth regarding the use of force and Iraqi compliance with disarmament terms. Such a resolution would have determined (once again) that Iraq was in breach of its obligations, and might also have specifically authorized the use of force.

However, for many members of the Security Council this was a resolution too far. France, Russia, and China, as well as several of the nonpermanent members including Germany, were plainly skeptical or totally opposed. This was not surprising, given their different interests, their different views of war, their different assessments of any threat posed by Iraq, and their stated concerns about U.S. dominance. It is asking a lot of major states that they should formally approve the initiation of a war by another power, especially when it is a hyperpower about whose policies they in any case have reservations. The effect, naturally, was to encourage a U.S. belief in the inadequacies of certain international institutions.

At the Security Council meeting on March 17, 2003, the U.S. and UK governments had to face the consequences of defeat in their efforts to obtain a second resolution. It was small consolation that they had stated on several occasions that such a resolution would be politically desirable but was not legally necessary.

In principle, can the violation of certain terms of a cease-fire constitute a justification for an eventual use of force against the violator? A provision in the chapter on armistices in the 1907 Hague Regulations on land war suggests an affirmative answer: "Any serious violation of the armistice by one of the parties gives the other party the right of denouncing it, and even, in cases of urgency, of recommencing hostilities immediately."[14] Against this, it can be argued that the post-Charter legal order creates a presumption against the use of force by states; that the decision to resume hostilities should be in the hands of the Security Council, especially in circumstances where the legitimacy of the use of force before the cease-fire depends significantly on authorization by the Council; and that, although the cease-fire was between Iraq and the coalition that had fought against it, the Security Council had defined the terms of the cease-fire, was itself a party to it, and should determine how to respond to violations.

The argument that there can be a continuity and resumption of the authority to use force contained in previous UN Security Council resolutions was asserted repeatedly in crises over Iraq in the 1990s. Thus, on January 14, 1993, in response to an attack the previous day by the United States, the UK, and France on Iraqi missile launchers, UN Secretary-General Boutros Boutros-Ghali said:

> The raid, and the forces that carried out the raid, have received a mandate from the Security Council, according to Resolution 678, and the cause of the raid was the violation by Iraq of Resolution 687 concerning the cease-fire. So, as Secretary-General of the United Nations, I can say that this action was taken and conforms to the resolutions of the Security Council and conforms to the Charter of the United Nations.[15]

The argument of continuing authority was also advanced at the time of the December 1998 crisis over inspections, when the United States and UK launched Operation Desert Fox against Iraq. It was contested in the Security Council, most notably by Russia, which asserted that the United States and UK had no right to act independently on behalf of the UN or to assume the function of "world policeman." Despite such criticisms, the strongest case for the legality of military action against Iraq in 2003 rested not on any general propositions about preventive defense, nor on Resolution 1441 taken in isolation, but upon Iraq's violations of specific UN resolutions and on the continuing authority contained in certain resolutions.

How should the nature of the claimed authorization be characterized? One critic of the concept has referred to it as "implied authorization to use force."[16] She has likened the U.S.-UK position in the Iraq crisis in late 2002 to that of the NATO countries with respect to the military action against Serbia in 1999, stating that "this doctrine of implied authority to use force is itself extremely controversial; it may involve the distortion of the words of the relevant resolutions and ignore their drafting history."[17] While this warning is important, there is a difference between the cases of Serbia and Iraq. In 1999 the UN Security Council had not specifically authorized the use of force against Serbia, whereas in November 1990 it had authorized force against Iraq. The question regarding Iraq in 2003 was whether that authority dating back to 1990 could be said to have continued or resumed. Thus, what was at issue regarding Iraq in 2003 was as much a claim of "existing authority" as a claim of "implied authority."

How much weight attaches to the past decisions of the Security

Council in authorizing force? Numerous resolutions on Iraq state that the Council has decided "to remain seized of the matter." This could be taken as implying that only the current Security Council has the right to provide authorization for the use of force. Such an implication, though attractive, would leave only a negative answer to the following key question. If the Council authorizes certain member states to undertake a task, but is then unable to agree on follow-up action, does the original authorization still stand? The simple guiding principle has to be that a resolution, once passed, remains in effect. In the absence of a new resolution repudiating earlier positions (which will always be hard to achieve, granted the existence of the veto) a presumption of continuity is plausible.

The greatest difficulty with "continuing authority" in the light of events in Iraq in 2003 concerns not so much the proposition itself, which is fundamentally strong, but its particular invocation in this crisis. Acceptance of the idea of "continuing authority" still leaves open the question of what consequences flowed from the Iraqi breaches. Furthermore, questions are raised by the lack of responsible preparation for the occupation phase, and by the doubtful quality of the evidence that Iraq still possessed weapons of mass destruction in significant quantities. Some unconvincing U.S. and UK reports and presentations before the war weakened the case. There was, inevitably, scope for disagreement as to whether the UN verification system operating under Resolution 1441 should have been set aside in favor of a use of force when the disarmament process had produced at least some results. As circumstances change after the war, it is possible that, ex post facto, other justifications for resort to force will look more convincing.

A strong argument for some concept of continuing authority is as much strategic as legal. If a major power acts on behalf of the Security Council, as the United States undoubtedly did in liberating Kuwait in 1991 and in acting in effect as a guarantor of the 1991 cease-fire terms, to what extent can its hands then be tied? The question is complicated by the fact that Iraqi compliance has almost always been the result of external military pressure. Up to a point, this has been accepted by members of the Security Council, who have at times been prepared to see the United States and its partners threaten the use of force. Many, however, have not been willing to countenance full-scale war. The result was a stalemate in which the United States found itself keeping large forces tied up in neighboring countries, its credibility called into question by the drawn-out saga of an Iraqi disarmament process. In that perspective, the issue was not so much Iraq's actual weapons of mass destruction, but rather its failure to comply fully with the verification process, and the consequent impossibility of reaching any kind of closure.

Doctrines of Preemption

Discussion of this matter is complicated by different and inconsistent uses of key terms. "Preemption," the term at the heart of recent debates, is based on the idea of preventing an attack by disabling a threatening enemy. It can encompass both anticipatory self-defense (military action against an absolutely imminent threat) and preventive military action (to nip a future threat in the bud). Any "unilateral" use by states of preventive war is particularly hard to square with existing international law.

That force may have to be used by states to address a situation before it develops into an actual attack is not a new idea. As Michael Reisman has written, "International law has been grappling with the claim of preemptive self-defense for decades."[18] In some countries, there is a long tradition of thinking about the use of force in broadly preventive terms.

For most of the post-1945 period, U.S. governments, and the international community more generally, have had ambivalent attitudes toward anticipatory self-defense and have been very skeptical about any broader concept of preemption.[19] During the Cold War, successive U.S. administrations resisted the temptation to launch preventive strikes to stop the Soviet Union and China from becoming nuclear powers. This disinclination to act preemptively is under challenge in an era of international terrorism, especially when there are concerns about weapons of mass destruction getting into terrorist hands. States now face certain dangers that cannot be deterred in any conventional sense and that may need to be tackled before they develop into an actual armed attack.

Bush's advocacy of preemption was encapsulated in the 2002 *National Security Strategy*.[20] Some of the ideas in this document represented a continuation of policies that had been evolving during the Clinton administration.[21] The document, produced annually as a legal requirement imposed by Congress, had a huge impact nationally and internationally—not because it was wholly new, but because it seemed to set certain contentious propositions in stone.[22]

The document is first and foremost a statement of national strategy. However, in redefining U.S. strategic doctrine it also necessarily addresses a number of issues that are self-evidently legal in character. In a key passage the document states:

> For centuries, international law recognized that nations need not suffer an attack before they can lawfully take action to defend themselves against forces that present an imminent danger of attack. Legal scholars and international jurists often conditioned the legitimacy of preemption on the existence of an imminent threat—most often a visible mobilization of armies, navies, and air forces preparing to attack.
>
> We must adapt the concept of imminent threat to the capabilities and objectives of today's adversaries.[23]

This passage's reference to "imminent threat" harks back to a classic exposition of the right of self-defense in the statement by U.S. Secretary of State Daniel Webster in April 1841. In response to a dispute that involved the British capture and destruction of the U.S. steamboat *Caroline* on December 29, 1837, Webster famously stated that for self-defense to be invoked there must be "a necessity of self-defence, instant, overwhelming, leaving no choice of means, and no moment for deliberation."[24] The case addressed a modern question. What is the proper response of a state to an unofficial group launching a covert attack against it across international borders? However, except at the tactical level, the *Caroline* situation was not basically about preemption, as the rebellion in Canada was actual and ongoing. Moreover, the case for preemptive action today could not possibly be confined to the *Caroline* criteria. In the Iraq crisis of 2002–2003, no one could claim that there was "no moment for deliberation": few military actions can have been the subject of more domestic and international deliberation.

The Bush doctrine suffers from a number of defects. The peremptory manner of its emergence added to the confusion surrounding it. The focus being almost entirely on the United States, it failed to consider the consequences for international relations if there were widespread claims by states of a right to act preemptively. It also failed completely to mention the nonintervention norm. By transforming the problem of how the United States might address a few hard cases into general doctrine, it appeared to undermine the nonintervention norm more directly than was necessary. Coupled with the proclamation of the "Axis of Evil" in Bush's January 2002 State of the Union speech, its effect internationally may have been to cause more anxiety and opposition than reassurance.

The impact of the doctrine on the evolution of the Iraq crisis in 2002–2003 was largely negative. The doctrine was not necessary for the war against Iraq in 2003. In the event, official justifications for the war were cast in the less abrasive terms of Security Council resolutions. It was generally critics of the United States who viewed the war as the first application of the preemption doctrine.

A fundamental question raised by the doctrine concerns whether there can be any international procedure with respect to what must always be particularly contentious decisions to use force. The UN is not ignored entirely in the *National Security Strategy:* it receives a couple of brief mentions.[25] Even after the spectacular failure of the UN Security Council in March 2003 to adopt any coherent line on Iraq, the logic of the Bush doctrine may compel the United States to take at least some problems to the UN Security Council. International legitimacy for policies toward emerging threats will not come via an improbable change in international law regarding when states may use force, but rather through agreement to specific policy goals (and ultimately action in support of them) by the Security Council and, possibly, other internationally respected bodies with legal standing with respect to particular problems or regions.

Doctrines of Humanitarian Intervention

Humanitarian intervention may be defined as "coercive action by one or more states involving the use of armed force in another state without the consent of its authorities, and with the purpose of preventing widespread suffering or death among the inhabitants." The experience of humanitarian intervention since the end of the Cold War is an object-lesson in the difficulties of turning an occasionally necessary type of action into a fixed doctrine.

Since early 1991 there have been numerous crises in which the question has arisen of whether or not external institutions should, on humanitarian grounds, organize or authorize military action within a state. Within the UN Security Council, in at least nine cases there have been resolutions citing humanitarian considerations as a basis for action, followed by multilateral military action, going well beyond traditional peacekeeping, by armed contingents from outside the country concerned.

The degree of "host-state" consent in these nine cases was varied. In four of them (northern Iraq, Somalia, Haiti, and Kosovo), military action was initiated without the approval of the government of the state. In the remaining five cases (Bosnia and Herzegovina, Rwanda, Albania, Sierra Leone, and East Timor), there was a stronger element of consent to the presence of foreign forces. However, even in the four cases of humanitarian intervention proper, elements of consent to the international presence did sooner or later play some part. In these four cases (unlike in most of the consent-based operations), U.S. forces took the lead role in the intervening coalitions. In two of these cases (northern Iraq and Kosovo), there was no explicit UN Security Council authorization of the military action. In the other two (Somalia and Haiti) there was such authorization, as there was also in the five consent-based operations, and therefore in terms of international law the initiation of these operations was uncontentious.

Despite this range of practice, all attempts since the early 1990s to reach an agreed doctrine favoring humanitarian intervention have failed. A critical test that any emerging norm or practice must pass, if it is to be accepted as part of international law, is that it be generally supported by states. Humanitarian intervention does not pass this test. Several large and powerful states (China, India, and Russia) have expressed strong opposition. Equally important, large numbers of postcolonial states, particularly in Africa and Asia, have opposed it, especially as many of them fear that they would be potential targets of intervention. Furthermore, some potential or actual interveners on humanitarian grounds, including the United States, have shown no interest in the development of a doctrine of humanitarian intervention, not least because it might tie their hands.

This does not mean that humanitarian intervention is necessarily illegal. In those cases in which it is specifically authorized by the Security Council, as in Somalia and Haiti, its lawfulness seems to be accepted by most states. In certain other cases, from East Bengal in 1971 to Kosovo in 1999, judgments about whether an action is lawful or not seem to depend heavily on how the particular crisis is viewed. Such judgments also depend on whether other issues are involved in the intervention. Such additional issues can include self-defense, rescue of nationals of the intervening country, maintenance of international peace and security, and implementation of the goals proclaimed in UN Security Council resolutions.

There are fundamental problems with the idea that states have a general "right" of humanitarian intervention.[26] It was therefore sensible of the Canadian-sponsored International Commission on Intervention and State Sovereignty, when it reported at the end of 2001, to avoid asserting such a general right. Rather, it emphasized securing an acknowledgment by states that they have a "responsibility to protect"—which is first and foremost a responsibility of all governments in relation to their own citizens.[27] This is an ingenious attempt at a reformulation of the question of humanitarian intervention, but there is so far little sign of states explicitly accepting such a responsibility. This reluctance of states is partly due to their nervousness about subscribing to any doctrine that might become a basis for intervention.

Gaullism, Super-Gaullism, and Continuing UN Roles

International divisions over the legitimacy of certain uses of force are serious. They have been damaging within the NATO alliance and also more generally. Although the East-West divide largely closed with the end of the Cold War, Russian suspicion of what is perceived as U.S. dominance and willingness to use force abroad remains, and is shared by many other states. The divide between North and South persists, and issues relating to the legitimacy of the use of force have become a major focus of contention.

The Iraq crisis of 2002–2003 exposed these divisions in dramatic form. It was a remarkable achievement of Saddam Hussein that, in a crisis over a disarmament process that was meant to have been completed more than a decade earlier, his intransigence and the U.S. response to it threatened to bring down the temples of NATO, the European Union, the UN, and international law.

Hard cases notoriously make bad law. They also make a bad basis for asserting that there is no law. The issues of humanitarian intervention and of preemption, and the prolonged crisis over Iraq, have all revolved around cases that are "hard" in the sense that they raise the question of whether force can be used in circumstances that go beyond self-defense and in which there may be no recent and specific authorization by the UN Security Council. That the answers to this question have been messy, in the sense that they have failed to command universal assent, does not mean that international law and organization are dead. There is no prospect of general agreement to a new set of black-letter rules regarding the circumstances in which the use of force may be legitimate, nor regarding new institutions that might authorize force. However, this conclusion does not mean that there has been no clear direction to the events since the end of the Cold War; nor does it mean that there are no useful guidelines to be deduced from these events.

In a series of crises since the end of the Cold War, there has been some expansion of the rationales seen as justifying the use of force. The UN Security Council has authorized force in more situations than it did in the UN's first forty-five years, and this has been largely accepted as within the Security Council's competence. An important, if more contentious, innovation has been the claim, made by the United States and others, that there can be a "continuing authority" from the Security Council to use force, and that, following the 1991 cease-fire, this provided the legal basis for major uses of force in Iraq up to and including the 2003 war. Although this argument has certain merits, the fact that it was deployed in conjunction with exaggerated statements about Iraq's prohibited weapons programs and poor preparation for the occupation and administration of the country is bound to reinforce skepticism about it.

As regards uses of force not specifically authorized by the Security Council, there has also been a degree of cautious advancement of the interlinked ideas that force may be used to implement the ends willed by the Security Council even if it could not agree on the means, and that it may on occasion be permissible to protect threatened people in urgent humanitarian crises. Regarding the law on self-defense, there has been recognition that actions by nonstate entities can fall within the concept of "armed attack," that a regime's responsibility was engaged for its failure to prevent and punish acts of terrorism by a movement operating on its soil, and therefore an attack on that regime itself might in exceptional circumstances be permissible.

This expansion of rationales has been heavily dependent on particular contexts, and attempts to turn its innovative aspects into general doctrine have been strongly contested—hence the conspicuous lack of support from states for either the doctrine of humanitarian intervention or the Bush doctrine of preemption. In both cases, these doctrinal innovations were often presented in a manner that paid insufficient attention to the continued value of the nonintervention norm. This norm remains fundamental to the conduct of international relations, and only in very exceptional combinations of circumstances may it have to yield to other norms and considerations.

The well-known weaknesses of the UN decisionmaking procedure relating to the use of force have remained serious in the post–Cold War era. They were already evident in the Kosovo crisis in March 1999, when the prospect of a Russian veto led the United States and its allies to avoid even putting a resolution authorizing force before the Security Council. The weaknesses were even more evident in March 2003, when France indicated that it would veto a resolution authorizing force against Iraq. Never before has a major power, seeking to act militarily with the claimed purpose of implementing UN Security Council resolutions, faced the openly advertised prospect of veto by an ally. The crisis confirmed the conclusion that, if the UN is valuable in many of its roles, it can fail conspicuously in others. The UN, despite the aspirations of its Charter, will continue to coexist with a system of states that is older, and is rapidly changing because of the unique U.S. role. The actual and perceived inadequacies of the UN system help to explain the U.S. role in the world as it is emerging in the post–Cold War era.

It is improbable that the causes of the UN and international law can be assisted by a simple rejection of the U.S. approach to the use of force. Indeed, the element of Gaullism in the French policy over Iraq may have encouraged a super-Gaullism in the United States: a belief that the state, at least in its U.S. incarnation, is the supreme and enduring entity in international politics, that the United States now has a unique capacity to wage war effectively, and that international law and organization are of limited importance. The absence of a plausible and appealing concept of how Europe could unite to create an effective military rival to the United States confirms that rejectionism leads into a blind alley, undermining the multilateralism it is supposed to protect.

There is no obvious workable way to reform the existing UN decisionmaking procedure as far as the use of force is concerned. Most proposed changes to the UN Charter's provisions regarding the composition or procedures of the Security Council involve increasing the number of permanent members. If they all had the veto, that would further reduce the already limited chances of obtaining agreement on controversial measures. Any proposal to reduce the existing number of states armed with the veto, or to limit the occasions on which the veto may be used, has to surmount the major procedural obstacle that, if the proposal is to be passed, each veto-wielding state will have to consent.

Institutions outside the UN may on occasion be able to act, more or less convincingly, as validating authorities for decisions on the use of force. However, no other body commands quite the same degree of international legitimacy. Any proposal for a union of democracies would run up against the objection that the Iraq crisis has exposed huge differences among them. Alliances and regional organizations such as NATO and the European Union have also been deeply divided over Iraq. Furthermore, their tradition of operating by consensus means that they are procedurally even less well equipped than the UN Security Council to take controversial decisions.

The continued significance of the UN as the preeminent vehicle for approving and coordinating international action, including certain uses of force, was indicated in the wake of the 2003 Iraq war by the passage of Resolution 1483, which resolved that the UN "should play a vital role in humanitarian relief, the reconstruction of Iraq, and the restoration and establishment of national and local institutions for representative governance," provided for the ending of sanctions, and recognized the role of the UK and the United States as occupying powers.[28] Thus, as in Kosovo in 1999, the UN, although it had earlier been unable to agree on a use of force amounting to war, could nonetheless agree on some main outlines of postwar policy, including through legitimation of current and future roles of external armed forces. In neither Kosovo nor Iraq did the postwar Security Council resolution proclaim the earlier military action to have been legal, but it did bring the consequences of such action within a clear international legal framework.

The UN therefore remains damaged but not destroyed, as one vehicle for reaching decisions on the use of force. Paradoxically, even when attempts to obtain UN authorization for force fail, the appeal to UN principles may have considerable value. In both the 1999 Kosovo crisis and the 2003 Iraq crisis, the U.S.-led coalitions presented as a key part of the legal justification for the use of force the fact that the military intervention had the purpose of ensuring implementation of UN Security Council resolutions. In the case of Iraq there was the additional claim of continuing authority from the UN Security Council to use force. These claims were more than the tribute that vice pays to virtue: they were recognition that even in the new circumstances and hard cases of the twenty-first century, force has an unavoidably close relationship to law.

Notes

I wish to thank Tony Aust, Michael Byers, Simon Chesterman, Sebastian von Einsiedel, Mary-Jane Fox, Guy Goodwin-Gill, Gur Hirshberg, Melvyn Leffler, David Malone, Thomas Pickering, Terry Taylor, and many others for their help with this chapter. Responsibility for all opinions and errors is mine alone. An earlier version of this chapter was published as "Law and the Use of Force After Iraq," *Survival* 45, no. 2 (Summer 2003): 31–55.

  1. For a discussion of these questions, see Albrecht Randelzhofer's exegesis on Article 51 in Bruno Simma et. al., eds., *The Charter of the United Nations: A*

Commentary, 2nd ed. (Oxford: Oxford University Press, 2002), pp. 788–806. He concludes, remarkably: "As regards UN members, it stands that Art. 51, including its restriction to armed attack, supersedes and replaces the traditional right to self-defence."

2. Resolution 1031, December 15, 1995, para. 14. Under Resolution 1088, December 12, 1996, IFOR was reduced in size and renamed Stabilization Force (SFOR) while retaining the same authority to use force.

3. On the extensive powers of these UN peacekeeping forces, see esp. Resolution 814, March 26, 1993 (on Somalia); and Resolutions 1270, October 22, 1999, and 1289, February 7, 2000 (on Sierra Leone).

4. See Resolution 1189, August 13, 1998.

5. Resolution 1368, September 12, 2001.

6. Resolution 1373, September 28, 2001.

7. See Yutaka Arai-Takahashi, "Shifting Boundaries of the Right of Self-Defence: Appraising the Impact of the September 11 Attacks on *Jus Ad Bellum,*" *International Lawyer* (Chicago) 36, no. 4 (Winter 2002): 1082–1083, 1101–1102.

8. Under Resolution 1386, December 20, 2001, ISAF was established in Afghanistan in January 2002. Transitions in ISAF command arrangements were noted in Resolutions 1413, May 23, 2002, and 1444, November 27, 2002. In 2003, ISAF came under NATO command.

9. I argue at greater length on this point in my article "From San Francisco to Sarajevo: The UN and the Use of Force," *Survival* 37, no. 4 (Winter 1995–1996): 7–28.

10. See, for example, the letter from sixteen international law teachers in *The Guardian* (London), March 7, 2003, p. 29.

11. See letter dated March 20, 2003, from the permanent representative of the United States to the United Nations, addressed to the president of the Security Council. See also President George W. Bush, *Address to the Nation,* March 17, 2003, www.whitehouse.gov; the five-page document titled "Iraq: Legal Basis for the Use of Force," March 17, 2003, provided to the House of Commons Foreign Affairs Committee on the same date; and *House of Lords Hansard,* written answers, March 17, 2003, col. WA1, www.fco.gov.uk.

12. Resolution 661, August 6, 1990.

13. For a detailed analysis of Resolution 678, see Chapter 10.

14. Article 30 of the 1907 Hague Regulations on land war, annexed to 1907 Hague Convention IV Respecting the Laws and Customs of War on Land.

15. Boutros Boutros-Ghali, January 14, 1993, cited in Simon Chesterman, *Just War or Just Peace? Humanitarian Intervention and International Law,* Oxford Monographs in International Law (Oxford: Oxford University Press, 2001), p. 201, where Chesterman comments that "it is unclear what status should be accorded to such a pronouncement by the Secretary-General."

16. Christine Gray, *International Law and the Use of Force* (Oxford: Oxford University Press, 2000), pp. 191–195.

17. Christine Gray, "The U.S. *National Security Strategy* and the New 'Bush Doctrine' on Preemptive Self-Defense," *Chinese Journal of International Law* (Boulder) 1, no. 2 (2002): 444. The article was completed on November 15, 2002, and is available at www.chinesejil.org/gray.pdf.

18. W. Michael Reisman, "Assessing Claims to Revise the Laws of War," *American Journal of International Law* 97, no. 1 (January 2003): 88.

19. On the long tradition of international, and U.S., ambivalence about ideas of anticipatory self-defense, see esp. Marjorie Whiteman, ed., *Digest of*

International Law, vol. 12 (Washington, D.C.: U.S. Department of State, 1971), pp. 42–77.

20. *National Security Strategy of the United States of America,* Washington, D.C., September 2002, www.whitehouse.gov/nsc/nss.html.

21. For an excellent analysis of the 2002 *National Security Strategy,* drawing particular attention to the antecedents of the policy it outlines and the limitations from which they suffered, see Robert S. Litwak, "The New Calculus of Pre-emption," *Survival* 44, no. 4 (Winter 2002–2003): 53–79.

22. The statutory requirement for the annual presidential report to Congress on national security strategy is in Title 50, U.S. Code, chap. 15, sec. 404a, enacted on October 1, 1986.

23. *National Security Strategy of the United States,* p. 15.

24. Letter from Daniel Webster to Mr. Fox, April 24, 1841, *British and Foreign State Papers,* vol. 29, pp. 1137–1138.

25. *National Security Strategy of the United States,* pp. vi, 7.

26. See the fuller exposition of this argument in my article "The So-Called 'Right' of Humanitarian Intervention," *Yearbook of International Humanitarian Law,* vol. 3, 2000 (The Hague: T. M. C. Asser, 2002), pp. 3–51.

27. International Commission on Intervention and State Sovereignty, *The Responsibility to Protect* (Ottawa: International Development Research Center, 2001). The text of this two-volume work is available at www.iciss.gc.ca and also on a CD-ROM supplied with the report volume.

28. Resolution 1483, May 22, 2003.

10

The Authorization Model: Resolution 678 and Its Effects

Frank Berman

Although the end of the Cold War predictably led to a burst of activity by the Security Council, it was not easily foreseeable that the Council would maintain such a pace, or that it would contemplate mandating the use of force under its authority. The forty-five resolutions adopted by the Council from 1990 to the end of 2002 contain, in one form or another, a mandate of this kind.

The watershed was Resolution 678 of November 29, 1990, which granted the mandate to terminate Iraq's occupation of Kuwait. Its content, and the issues that emerged in the course of its negotiation and implementation, identified and to a large extent delineated themes that have dominated the subsequent debate. This chapter is accordingly organized around a detailed analysis of the elements of that resolution. The aim will be to extract and assess the principal issues and pursue their traces through the further development of the Council's practice.[1]

Resolution 678 consists of a brief preamble and five short operative paragraphs. The preamble concludes with an invocation, in simple and generalized terms, of Chapter VII of the Charter. The first operative paragraph contains a final demand for compliance. The second operative paragraph contains the famous authorization (postponed for six and a half weeks) to "Member States co-operating with the Government of Kuwait" to "use all necessary means to uphold and implement resolution 660 (1990) and all subsequent relevant resolutions and to restore international peace and security in the area."[2] The third operative paragraph contains a request, addressed to "all States," to provide "appropriate support for the actions undertaken in pursuance of paragraph 2." And the fourth operative paragraph contains a further request, addressed now to "the States concerned," to "keep the Security Council regularly informed on the progress of actions undertaken." Finally, in the fifth operative paragraph the Council decides to remain seized of the matter. These short paragraphs conceal a range of underlying issues, many of them of cardinal importance for the Charter system of collective security.

Relationship to Self-Defense

It may be a tribute to the ingenuity of the drafters of Resolution 678 that it situated itself so close to the fulcrum between the two recognized exceptions to the prohibition on the use of force in Article 2(4) of the Charter: self-defense and the collective application of force by the UN. And the proper characterization of this resolution is still not wholly resolved. One school holds that Resolution 678 was essentially an endorsement of the right of collective self-defense with the legitimate government of Kuwait. The other holds the resolution to have been an exercise of the powers reserved to the Security Council under the Charter, albeit in an innovative form not expressly foreseen in the Charter.

The self-defense thesis depends largely on three arguments: first, the reaffirmation of the right of self-defense in the key Council resolutions; second, the identification of the authorized parties as "Member States cooperating with the Government of Kuwait"; and third (negatively), the difficulty in identifying any alternative Charter basis in the terms of Chapter VII. However, the self-defense thesis encounters a series of problems that cumulatively speak decisively against it. First, Resolution 678 contains no direct mention of the right of self-defense at all, merely a preambular invocation of the ten previous resolutions, some of which did. Next, the entire notion of "authorization," as employed in the second operative paragraph, is out of key with an "inherent" right, which Article 51 famously declares self-defense to be. Further, the purposes for which the authorization is granted, with their reference not just to Resolution 660 (which contained the call for the withdrawal of all Iraqi forces), but also to upholding and implementing "all subsequent relevant resolutions" and, even more strikingly, to "restore international peace and security in the area,"[3] seem to evince an unmistakable intention to extend the range of the authorization beyond what any normal understanding of the defense of Kuwait would cover. Finally, when the Council authorized the collective use of force under Resolution 678, this must surely be construed under Article 51 as "measures necessary to maintain international peace and security," which therefore displaced the right to use force in self-defense.

For these reasons the self-defense thesis offers a poor explanation of what the Security Council conceived itself to be doing in Resolution 678. The basis implicitly underlying the thesis is that self-defense and collective action are mutually exclusive, but is that in fact the case? Article 51 can be argued to answer the question both ways. Without doubt, in the classic case where the Council imposes a cease-fire on two contending states, whatever right either of them possessed until then to act in self-defense is extinguished.[4] However, we are becoming more than ever accustomed to complex crises that develop and reshape themselves in specific relation to the Council's sequential efforts to manage them. There is no reason in principle why, in that process, the relationship between self-defense and collective action should not also have a dynamic element—as long as the continuing claim to act in self-defense is, and remains, in support of the Council's objectives and measures. The crux is surely that, under the last sentence of Article 51,[5] the Council has the unfettered right to assume control.

The point can be well illustrated by the series of Council decisions leading up to Resolution 678. The invasion and occupation of Kuwait took place on August 2, 1990, and Resolution 660 was adopted the same day. Five days later the Council laid down the comprehensive sanctions regime in Resolution 661; by then, many member states had already adopted certain precautionary sanctions in defense of their national interests. Resolution 661 contained the usual provisions foreseeing enforcement by each member state within its jurisdiction, but nothing expressly about collective enforcement. However, inasmuch as the resolution did contain a direct and express reaffirmation of the right of individual and collective self-defense, the question immediately arose of whether states with naval forces in the area could enforce the sanctions as a measure of "collective" self-defense. The issue was eventually resolved by the adoption on August 25 of Resolution 665, which provided a Chapter VII mandate for the forceful implementation of the sanctions in respect to shipping in the Gulf.[6] However, in parallel with enforcing the naval blockade, the allies of Kuwait continued their preparations for military action against Iraq as an exercise of collective self-defense.[7] The issue of whether this course would be pursued in preference to seeking a Chapter VII mandate from the Security Council was not in the end settled until it had become clear that Resolution 678 would be adopted. The experience suggests that, subject to the Council's ultimate control, self-defense and collective measures are not regarded as wholly distinct and incompatible, especially in a case in which the Council has clearly stigmatized one state as the wrongdoer.[8]

Authorization

The whole concept of the Council "authorizing" states to use force gives rise to a number of questions.[9] What is the scope of the mandate? How is it to be interpreted? What is its duration? Who is the authorized party? What are the lines of accountability and responsibility? What residual control is retained by the Council?

The Legitimacy of Security Council Authorization
In the preamble to Resolution 678 the Council recites simply that it is "acting under Chapter VII of the Charter." This laconic form of enactment has given rise to a debate covering both whether the Council can assert powers without grounding them precisely in specific provisions of the Charter, and whether a power to "authorize" member states can be properly located within Chapter VII at all.

The first question seems largely misconceived. It derives no per contra support from the previous practice of the Council, which has virtually never found it necessary to specify a precise "legal base" for its decisions. The Council, in contrast to, say, the legislative organs of the European Union, situates itself within an international tradition in which the scope and allocation of powers are achieved with a broader brush.

Nor should the absence of an explicit "legal base" in Resolution 678 be seen as part of a flight away from specific legalism in the later practice of the Council. Resolution 678, for example, had its precursors in Resolutions 83 and 84 (1950), on Korea, and 221 (1966), on the oil embargo against Southern Rhodesia. In neither case did the Council cite a particular article as constituting the legal base for its decision. The question must now be regarded as having been put beyond dispute by the Council's practice since then.

The second question raises an issue of substance, reminiscent of the controversy that initially surrounded the creation of UN peacekeeping. Is there an implied power permitting the Council, in place of enforcing its decisions directly, to authorize member states instead to employ armed force for the purpose of bringing about their implementation? There is plainly little scope, by analogy with the case of peacekeeping, for a "Chapter VI-1/2" solution—that is to say, for cobbling together a legal rationalization out of a combination of the Council's inherent powers and the consent of states.[10] The essence of the operation is to deliver an incontestable power to the authorized member states, with a corresponding binding effect on other states.[11]

Where, though, should one locate the legal ground for doing so? Much of the argument over Resolution 678 revolved around a literal exegesis of Articles 41, 42, and 43: Did the Council have available to it military enforcement means other than UN forces put into the field by the Security Council itself—presumably on the basis of Article 43 agreements? The only argument in favor of such a rigid interpretation derives from a narrow reading of Article 39, according to which the power given to the Council to "decide what measures shall be taken" to restore international peace and security is limited by the immediately following qualification "in accordance with Articles 41 and 42." Even in relation to the most far-reaching of the Council's powers, to read Article 39 in this way is contrary to the approach toward delineation of powers adopted by the International Court of Justice.[12] Whether or not one accepts Article 24 as conferring a general power to do whatever the Council considers necessary to maintain international peace and security,[13] Article 42 does not in any case refer exclusively to the use of forces in UN uniform and under UN command. It empowers the Council to take such action "by" air, sea, or land forces as may be necessary to maintain or restore international peace and security. This, taken together with the often neglected Article 48, which expressly states that "the action required to carry out the decisions of the Security Council for the maintenance of international peace and security is to be taken by all the Members or by some of them *as the Security Council may determine*" (emphasis added), does not foreclose a mode of operation through selected groups of member states at the behest of the Council.[14]

How far does a Security Council mandate represent an *obligation,* or does it serve merely as an *empowerment* of the states addressed? In the case of a mandate conferred on a UN organ or a UN force, it represents an instruction, as the mandated body is left with no discretion whether or not to take up the mandate. Over the years, the practice of the Council has undergone a striking transformation. The Korean case, as is well known, involved a two-step process: a *recommendation* to assist the Republic of Korea,[15] followed by the creation of the Unified Command.[16] The Rhodesian case took another form, that of a specific *instruction* to the United Kingdom, reflected in the language of the operative paragraphs of Resolution 221.[17] By Resolution 678 the terminology used—which has become the most common pattern since—had expressly become that of "authorizing" groups of member states,[18] undoubtedly intended to convey an empowerment together with a sovereign *discretion* whether or not to take it up, rather than a precise obligation to act. The evidence suggests that the changed formula was chosen deliberately.[19]

Scope, Duration, and Interpretation of the Mandate

Once the Council proceeds by way of an authorization to member states, the process raises the question of the scope and extent of the mandate. Were the Council to employ armed force directly, a difference of consequential modalities becomes clear: Who determines how far the mandate extends and when it has expired or has been discharged? In the case of direct action under the Council's authority, the assumption is that the Secretary-General would return to the Council in the event that he needed further guidance or a redefinition of his authority. In the case of a mandate to member states, this does not seem to be the way in which authorizations have been conceived or have operated. The member states concerned have tended to treat the authorization as if it were closer to a *delegation*—that is, as if it opened up to them an area of autonomous decisionmaking to be exercised responsibly and subject to whatever reporting and control arrangements the Council had laid down. There is no reason why such a pattern need raise concerns about the preservation of the Council's authority under the Charter. The key authorizing phrase, which has become the standard formula since its use in Resolution 678, has been "all necessary means." It has been criticized for vagueness, but what other type of formula might the Council have employed, given the imponderables of the military confrontation with Iraq over Kuwait?[20] It retains an inherent adaptability to the circumstances of particular cases that makes it attractive, and its attractiveness resides as much in its *limiting* function as in its validating effect: action taken under the authorization has to be "necessary" for the achievement of the purpose laid down.[21] Judgments about what is "necessary" must be made by the member states acting under the authorization, but the Council's ultimate power to make or even impose its own judgment is unfettered. Something of that flavor is retained in the Council's decision, in the fifth operative paragraph, to "remain seized of the matter," which is now common form.

The problem arises in a much more troubling form, however, in relation not to the scope of the mandate but to the *purpose* for which it is given. It cannot be for the member states to determine the objective that the Council seeks to achieve in conferring the mandate. This must remain squarely within the exclusive competence of the Security Council; the "necessary means" can only be means toward an end, and the end is a matter for the Security Council collectively.

The issue becomes troublesome where the Council expresses itself in broad or open-ended terms. Resolution 678 enunciates the primary purpose to be "to uphold and implement resolution 660 (1990) and all subsequent relevant resolutions," but it surrounds this relatively precise formula with the now famous penumbra "and to restore international peace and security in the area." Although the reference to implementing earlier resolutions may at first blush seem straightforward enough, even this simple precept turns out to presuppose a series of subdecisions as to what its realization required in practice three months later. In practical terms, a process of "authorization" presupposes some form of continuing exchange between the mandated member states and the Council over both the realization of the stated objectives and, where necessary, the means granted to them to achieve them. Reporting requirements assume a key importance in this regard. To revert to Resolution 678, it is implausible that the Council believed itself to be *delegating*[22] to an undefined group of states the power to determine authoritatively what would constitute the "implementation of all subsequent relevant resolutions," or (by adding the phrase referring to the "restoration of international peace and security in the area")[23] to be resigning from its own Charter prerogatives. A continuing exchange of the kind referred to above now represents the norm and has, in various cases, led to a modification, renewal, or extension of the original mandate.[24]

The question of duration remains problematic. The Council has been torn between the desirability of a "sunset clause" approach, which is now commonplace in sanctions resolutions, and the anxiety that an authorization subjected to an explicit time limit may be treated by a recalcitrant state as a challenge to hold out against the Council's authority. The mandate in Resolution 678 contains nothing by way of a time limit beyond what may be implicit in the statement of the purpose for which the authorization was given. The *assumption* may be that mandates are adopted for limited purposes to be realized within limited times, but the Council's practice leaves the question open; only somewhat more than half of the mandates are time-limited.[25] The Council has the inherent power to impose a time limit ex post facto or to terminate or modify an authorization.[26] Similarly, a determination by the Council that a mandate had achieved its stated purpose would be conclusive and would bring any authorization under the mandate to an end.[27] But if a mandate is open-ended, can it be argued to continue in effect indefinitely, or does it lapse at some point simply by the passage of time (or does it become at some stage sufficiently stale that it requires revival by the Council)?[28] Ultimately, the question of duration may not be analytically distinct from that of the scope and purpose of the mandate the Council has conferred.

Accountability and Reporting Back

If the Council acted through UN forces it had itself deployed under Articles 42 and 43, the lines of accountability and responsibility would be clear.[29] The provisions of Articles 46 and 47, relating to the Military Staff Committee, would presumably be brought into play, possibly in some adaptation to practical circumstances. The Korean case shows that to put a UN label on a unified command assembled by a grouping of member states is a legal fiction absent mechanisms under which the UN plays a real role in strategic direction and control.

One of the most difficult problems inherent in the "authorization" model, however, is what to put in place of the "normal" reporting and accountability arrangements. Without it, the notion that the authorized parties' entitlement to resort to force is *under the authority of the Security Council* could quickly fade away.[30] Resolution 678 contains in its fourth operative paragraph, as indicated above, no more than a request to "keep the Security Council regularly informed on the progress of actions undertaken." There was a considerable lack of precision as to how reporting on the military campaign was expected to be done. The outcome seems to have been less than satisfactory to both sides of the relationship,[31] not least because there existed no mechanism by which the Council might have evaluated—and in due course discussed on a knowledgeable basis—the reports received.[32]

No regular pattern has been established since then. Sometimes the Council simply calls for regular reports; sometimes it lays down a timetable for initial and subsequent reports; sometimes it calls for reports to be made through the Secretary-General; sometimes it calls for the Secretary-General to report in parallel on his own responsibility.[33] In other words, by "deciding to remain seized of" cases in which an authorization to use force has been conferred, the Council gives itself the opportunity to develop systematic oversight, but it has failed to do so. This remains an unsatisfactory aspect of the practice of force authorizations.

To Whom Does an Authorization Apply?

In principle, one would assume that the Council would have a clear intention in mind of whom it was authorizing and that this intention would be plainly discoverable from the terms of the authorization. In the case of Southern Rhodesia, Resolution 221 named the government of the United Kingdom—only natural in circumstances in which the authorized party is procuring legal cover from the Council.[34] However, the position is not clear when the intention is that the authorization should be for the benefit of a group of states, especially if the group is one brought together ad hoc. While Resolution 83 extended its appeal for assistance to the Republic of Korea to "the Members of the United Nations," by the time of Resolution 678 such an undifferentiated call had become inconceivable. The concern was to find a formula flexible enough to encompass the coalition that the key allies of Kuwait were in the process of assembling, but also a formula that would have the effect of *excluding* states whose involvement would have been politically unacceptable.[35] The ingenious phrase "Member States co-operating with the Government of Kuwait"[36] served both purposes admirably and built on the formula already deployed in Resolution 665.[37]

The tension between a direct authorization by name, versus a collective authorization by generic description, has marked subsequent practice. A generic description need not be problematic as long as its purport is sufficiently clear.[38] No difficulty seems to have arisen in practice either in positively identifying those states intended to be included or in holding back states not included, and the generic description has become the most common pattern.[39] It has helped overcome the squeamishness evidently felt within the Council at invoking military alliances by name.[40]

Fundamental Legal Basis

Even if it is accepted that "authorization" by the Council is a necessary and legally valid development of what is inherently implicit in the Charter, a fundamental question still remains as to the essential legal basis on which a state acting under a Council authorization resorts to armed force. Put crudely, is a state furnishing a contingent to a United Nations operation (including a peace enforcement operation) in the same legal position as a state committing its own national forces under some form of national command pursuant to a Council "authorization"? Or does the essential responsibility, in the legal sense, pass to the United Nations itself in the first case, while remaining with the member state(s) in the second? And who bears the legal responsibility if a national contingent, or soldiery within a national contingent, goes beyond the proper scope of its "authorization"? As we move into an international social climate in which all acts of public power carry with them an accountability obligation of some kind, these are questions that will demand a more definite answer than they receive at present.[41]

Conclusion

This chapter suggests that the Security Council action against Iraq leading up to Resolution 678 was a fertile piece of improvisation by the Council in a particularly egregious set of circumstances. Inventive as it was, it was not wholly new; there are clear signs both of the Council drawing where possible on prior shreds of practice, thin as they were, and of exploring the potential inherent in hitherto unused Charter articles. The basic idea of Resolution 678—the authorization of member states to use force for purposes defined by the Council in respect to situations determined to be threats to the peace—has been taken up in a large number of situations in the intervening thirteen years. Nevertheless the Council has shown its strong preference for ad hoc pragmatic responses over any attempt to develop a systematic doctrine that would shape this basic idea and develop its potential, while defining the limits essential to mark out the distinction between the Council's prerogatives under the Charter and national action to serve international ends. As a result, several consequential issues either have been left unresolved or have not been dealt with very satisfactorily. This fact is becoming apparent under the harsh spotlight of the military action against Iraq. The issues, however, are ones that cannot be avoided. And in the longer term such issues will show themselves to be fundamentally important for the integrity of the regime of collective security under the United Nations Charter and for its practical viability.

Notes

1. I have derived enormous assistance from the thorough and careful analysis of successive Council mandates by Danesh Sarooshi in his admirable work *The United Nations and the Development of Collective Security: The Delegation by the UN Security Council of Its Chapter VII Powers* (Oxford: Clarendon, 2000). However, I do not share Sarooshi's analytical framework for the Council's practice in terms of the "delegation" of powers, a framework that in my view offers at one and the same time a strained account of the relationship under the Charter between the Council and the Secretary-General, and an excessive interpretation of what the Council does, and is empowered under the Charter to do, when mandating the use of force either by member states or by regional organizations. For that reason I adhere in this chapter strictly to the terminology of "authorization."

2. In Resolution 660, adopted in the immediate aftermath of the Iraqi invasion, the Council condemned the invasion and demanded the immediate and unconditional withdrawal of all Iraqi forces.

3. This phrase is drawn from Resolution 83 (1950), on the Korean case. It is not clear how wide a scope the phrase was conceived to have then, within the framework of an operation in collective self-defense.

4. Though the right itself may simply be placed in abeyance.

5. "Measures taken by Members in the exercise of this right of self-defence . . . shall not in any way affect the authority and responsibility of the Security Council under the present Charter to take at any time such action as it deems necessary in order to maintain or restore international peace and security."

6. The mandate was "to use such measures commensurate to the specific circumstances as may be necessary under the authority of the Security Council to halt all inward and outward maritime shipping, in order to inspect and verify their cargoes and destinations and to ensure strict implementation of the provisions related to such shipping laid down in resolution 661."

7. The states that were eventually to form the "coalition" that expelled Iraq from Kuwait under Resolution 678.

8. Contrast a case such as that of the Central African Republic, where it seems to have been of the essence that the "monitoring mission" (the Inter-African Mission to Monitor the Bangui Accords) should operate "in a neutral and impartial way." Resolutions 1125 and 1136 (1997) and 1152, 1155, and 1159 (1998). The use-of-force mandate was correspondingly limited to "ensur[ing] the security and freedom of movement of" the mission's personnel.

9. The term "authorizing" is used here in its legal sense of conferring a lawful power that would not otherwise exist.

10. But compare the part played by state consent in the cases of Haiti (Resolution 917 onward), Bosnia (Resolution 981 onward), Albania (Resolution 1101 onward), the Central African Republic (Resolution 1125 onward), Guinea-Bissau (Resolution 1216 onward), East Timor (Resolution 1264 onward), Sierra Leone (Resolution 1270 onward), the Democratic Republic of Congo (Resolution 291), and Afghanistan (Resolution 1386 onward). The Council was, for the most part, either acting in support of an ulterior agreement, authorizing functions actually provided for in an ulterior agreement, or basing its intervention on territorial state consent.

11. Most notably (but by no means exclusively) the state against which force was to be employed.

12. See the *Peacekeeping* and *Namibia* Advisory Opinions: I.C.J. Rep. 1962, p. 151; and I.C.J. Rep. 1971, p. 16.

13. As long as it acts in accordance with the purposes and principles of the UN. See Jean-Pierre Cot and Alain Pellet, eds., *La Charte des Nations Unies: Commentaire article par article* (Paris: Éditions Economica, 1991), pp. 458–460; and Bruno Simma et al., eds., *The Charter of the United Nations: A Commentary*, 2nd ed. (Oxford: Oxford University Press, 2002), pp. 448–452.

14. Compare, for example, the Council's express mention of unified command and control (as in Korea) in the cases of Haiti in 1994 and East Timor in 1999, but not in other cases. Article 53(1), dealing with regional agencies or arrangements, raises the question of whether Article 53 covers only "enforcement" against a fellow member of the regional arrangement (thus by deemed consent), but requires all the same the *non obstat* of the Security Council as guardian of peace and security at the *international* level.

15. Resolution 83, June 27, 1950.

16. Though again by way of a "recommendation." Resolution 84, July 7, 1950.

17. Resolution 221, April 9, 1966, operative paras. 2–3, and 4, 5. It was the United Kingdom itself that procured the resolution, and it must have taken the view that the Council could only act with dispositive legal effect through the imposition of a binding legal obligation (though the contingent subprovision at the end of the fifth paragraph to arrest and detain the *Joanna V* is put in terms of an "empowerment," it has to be taken in the context as something like an obligatory entitlement).

18. Though the Council's practice has been confusingly variable.

19. Contrast Resolution 665, which retained the "calls upon" formula for the mandate to enforce the economic sanctions against shipping in the Gulf. See note 8. The identical formula has been replicated for subsequent authorizations to intercept shipping for sanctions enforcement purposes: for example, Resolutions 787 (Bosnia), 875 and 971 (Haiti), but not 1132 (Sierra Leone).

20. The formulation has its parentage in the Korean and Rhodesian resolutions. It is intriguing that virtually an identical phrase was used by the U.S. Congress in its celebrated joint resolution on the Gulf of Tonkin incident: H.J. Res. 1145, August 7, 1964.

21. There is a close and entirely legitimate analogy with "necessity" in the law of armed conflict.

22. In the sense of "transferring," either indefinitely or for a definite period of time. Compare Sarooshi, *The United Nations and the Development of Collective Security*, p. 4.

23. See note 6 and the corresponding text.

24. The classic case being that of Bosnia. The only case that has led to a serious tension between the concept of "authorization" discussed here and an alternative concept under which the authorized party acquires a more or less autonomous power, is that of Iraq.

25. Rwanda, Haiti, Albania, the Central African Republic, Sierra Leone, East Timor, Afghanistan, the Democratic Republic of Congo, and at the very end, Bosnia. At least two of these can be explained by the reluctance of the volunteer member state(s) to be politically committed beyond a certain duration, and others are mandates conferred on UN force commands, in respect of which time-limited mandates are commonplace (though often renewed).

26. For an example, see Resolution 1031 (1995), operative para. 19.

27. A difference of view on the subject with a mandatory member state would only be of importance in the case of an *obligatory* mandate, where the mandatory state took the view that its duty had been fulfilled but the Council did not (compare the Rhodesian case: endnote 21 above).

28. The problem is particularly troubling in cases where there has been a mass of subsequent activity by the Council over a situation not yet finally resolved. This issue represents a large part of the dispute over the case of Iraq, which is the subject of such vigorous disagreement within the Council. At the level of theory, a truly perpetual authorization to resort to force at the option of the authorized party would appear to be indistinguishable from the delegation away, if only in part, of the Council's "primary responsibility" under Article 24 of the Charter. Even acceptance of the need for revival, however, would not solve the problem of how revival is brought about.

29. As they are for peacekeeping forces, including in their more recent muscular form.

30. The precise formula included in Resolution 665 and subsequently expressly in a few mandates—though presumably implied in the others. The phrase seems to have been drawn directly from Article 53(1), on enforcement action by regional arrangements or agencies.

31. For the content of the reports, see United Nations, *The United Nations and the Iraq-Kuwait Conflict, 1990–1996* (New York: United Nations, 1966), p. 159.

32. And which *might* possibly in turn have commanded the confidence of the coalition. Contrast the tentative essay three months earlier in Resolution 665 (but subsequently abandoned) to test the potentialities of the Military Staff Committee for such purposes; the concept used in the fourth operative paragraph of that resolution was in fact that of *coordination*. There is some evidence that an attempt was made to get the Military Staff Committee to meet, but under such comically strained conditions that it was not repeated. Académie du Droit International, *Colloque 1992: Le développement du rôle du Conseil de Sécurité* (Dordrecht: Martinjus Nijhoff, 1993), p. 360.

33. Compare, as examples, Bosnia (Resolutions 770, para. 4; and 816, para. 7), Rwanda (Resolution 794, para. 18), Haiti (Resolution 940, para. 13), Albania (Resolution 1114, para. 9), and the Central African Republic (Resolution 1125, para. 6).

34. Compare the statement by the UK permanent representative on April 9, 1966, S/PV. 1276. More modern instances are France in Rwanda and the United States in Somalia, but by then it had become practice to suppress the precise mention of the state by name; contrast, however, the express mention of the UK in Resolution 1413 establishing the International Security Assistance Force in Afghanistan.

35. Israel comes to mind, as much on the public relations as the policy level.

36. No definite article.

37. On the naval blockade, see note 8 above.

38. An interesting lacuna in the debate over Iraq in 2002 and 2003 was whether the descriptor used in Resolution 678 continued to fit the group of states claiming a continuing authorization to use force to procure the disarmament of Iraq's weapons of mass destruction.

39. For examples, see Resolutions 787 and 816 and subsequent resolutions on Bosnia, which coined a further ingenious periphrasis: "States, acting nationally or through regional agencies or arrangements."

40. Compare "the organization referred to in Annex 1-A of the Peace Agreement" in Resolution 1031 and subsequent resolutions on Bosnia.

41. For a first tentative essay in this direction, see the reports of the International Law Association's Committee on the Accountability of International Organizations at www/ila-hq.org. Note also the attempts to challenge before both the European Court of Human Rights and the International Court of Justice the Kosovo intervention by certain members of the North Atlantic Treaty Organization.

I I

Reforming Sanctions

DAVID CORTRIGHT AND GEORGE A. LOPEZ

When the United Nations Security Council imposed comprehensive trade sanctions on Iraq on August 6, 1990 (Resolution 661), it ushered in a new era of the use of coercive economic sanctions as a means of inducing compliance from states judged as violating international law. In the previous forty-five years of UN experience, the Security Council employed sanctions only twice, in the cases of Southern Rhodesia and South Africa. The next dozen years witnessed an active phase of Security Council decision-making, with more than seventy sanctions resolutions levied against fourteen distinct targets, including such nongovernmental entities as the Khmer Rouge in Cambodia, the União Nacional para a Independência Total de Angola (UNITA), and Al-Qaida.

The record of these Security Council sanctions is one of striking contrasts, if not contradictions. As the Council moved forcefully to use sanctions as a means for advancing the UN mandate to preserve peace and security, it found that these very same measures were undermining the second pillar of its mandate: to enhance the human condition. While sanctions provided the major powers with a powerful tool for collective action within the Council, their unpreparedness for the wide-ranging impacts of sanctions effects resulted in declining consensus on Iraq, disagreement on sanctions reforms, and missed opportunities for improving sanctions. Throughout this period, the Council—and its extended partners in the sanctions debate—learned lessons from sanctions episodes, adapted to the unanticipated consequences of sanctions impacts, and explored prospects for improving sanctions implementation. These developments are the subject of this chapter.

The Collision of Mandates

Although Security Council sanctions against Iraq, Yugoslavia, and Haiti in the early 1990s had shown signs of considerable economic impact, ironical-

ly they produced little political compliance. More dismaying was that the
Iraq sanctions produced severe humanitarian suffering among innocent and
vulnerable populations. With increased awareness of the negative health
and social impacts of these general trade sanctions, Council members felt
acutely the collision of the two central mandates of the United Nations. As
sanctions were taking hold to apply pressure for peace and security, they
were undermining the prospects for human survival.

Thus, by mid-decade the desire to avoid unintended humanitarian suffering from the imposition of economic sanctions became a dominant feature of Security Council policymaking. In 1995 the ambassadors of the five
permanent members of the Security Council wrote to the president of the
Council stating that "further collective actions in the Security Council within the context of any further sanctions regimes should be directed to minimize unintended adverse side effects of sanctions on the most vulnerable
segments of targeted countries."[1] Efforts to assess and mitigate the humanitarian impacts of sanctions became a priority concern. In 1995 the newly
created UN Department of Humanitarian Affairs commissioned a report on
the impact of sanctions on humanitarian assistance efforts.[2] In 1997 the
authors participated in a study for the Department of Humanitarian Affairs
that developed a methodology and series of specific indicators for assessing
humanitarian impacts.[3] Many of the recommendations in these studies
became the basis for an ongoing humanitarian assessment methodology
developed by the successor agency of the Department of Humanitarian
Affairs, the UN Office for the Coordination of Humanitarian Affairs
(OCHA). Efforts to assess the humanitarian impact of particular sanctions
cases became a regular feature of UN sanctions policy. Assessment reports
and missions to examine the impact of sanctions were conducted in a number of cases and provided the Security Council an opportunity to anticipate
and prevent potential humanitarian problems and respond to adverse
impacts in a timely manner.

The first humanitarian assessment report was ordered in the case of
Sudan, when the Security Council considered the imposition of aviation
sanctions. The February 1997 report predicted severe adverse humanitarian
impacts from the proposed flight ban.[4] The report coincided with indications from neighboring states that the proposed flight ban would have negative political and security impacts on them as well. As a result the Council
did not implement the sanctions. The next humanitarian impact study came
in the case of Sierra Leone. A UN interagency study found that the general
trade embargo imposed by the Economic Community of West African
States (ECOWAS) was causing serious humanitarian hardship in Sierra
Leone but that the more targeted sanctions imposed by the Security Council
had few negative side effects.[5] Humanitarian impact studies were also
ordered in the cases of Afghanistan and Liberia. The December 2000 report

on Afghanistan found that the financial sanctions and aviation ban imposed against the Taliban regime caused few adverse humanitarian consequences.[6] The October 2001 Liberia report likewise found that the targeted measures imposed against the regime of Charles Taylor—an arms embargo, financial assets freeze, travel ban, and diamond embargo—had only limited humanitarian impacts.[7]

These attempts to minimize humanitarian impacts were balanced against the Council's efforts to gain compliance with its demands. Sanctions did not produce immediate and full compliance in any of the cases examined, but in a number of cases they resulted in partial compliance or generated effective diplomatic bargaining pressure. In Yugoslavia and Libya, sanctions provided bargaining leverage that helped to produce negotiated agreements. In Cambodia, Angola, and Sierra Leone, UN sanctions combined with military pressures to weaken and isolate rebel regimes. In Iraq and Liberia, sanctions contributed to the isolation and containment of the targeted regimes. In all of these cases UN member states made at least some effort to enforce compliance with Security Council sanctions. In the five cases where the Council imposed only limited arms embargoes— Sudan, Liberia (until 2001), Rwanda, Yugoslavia (after 1998), and Ethiopia/Eritrea—UN sanctions had little or no impact. The limited measures imposed in Afghanistan prior to 2001 also had no discernible impact on the policies of the Taliban regime. In about half the cases examined, Security Council sanctions had at least some impact. In all cases the compliance of targeted regimes was limited, but the impact was sufficient in some instances to produce partial success in achieving Security Council objectives.

Adaptive Learning and Innovation

Perhaps the most important UN response to the controversies surrounding the humanitarian impact of sanctions was to alter the design of sanctions. General trade embargoes were abandoned in favor of more targeted sanctions. After the imposition of comprehensive sanctions on Haiti in 1994, following similar sanctions against Yugoslavia and Iraq, all subsequent sanctions episodes involved some form of targeted or focused sanctions. Financial sanctions, travel bans, arms embargoes, and commodity boycotts replaced general trade sanctions as the preferred instruments of UN policy. When the Security Council launched an unprecedented international counterterrorism campaign, mandated in Resolution 1373 (2001), it applied these very same tools of targeted sanctions—freezing the funds of Al-Qaida terrorists and those who support them, blocking the travel of designated individuals, and embargoing the supply of arms and recruits. In the case of sanctions against Iraq, the Security Council moved toward smart sanctions by easing pressures on Iraqi civilians while retaining tight controls over military-related imports, ultimately adopting Resolution 1409 (2002), which had a specialized list of prohibited goods.

Targeted sanctions were designed to reduce unintended humanitarian consequences by focusing coercive pressure on decisionmaking elites. By imposing costs specifically on those responsible for violations of international law, rather than on innocent bystanders, the Security Council seeks to serve its primary mission of enhancing peace and security without jeopardizing its parallel mission of improving the human condition. Targeted sanctions apply pressure on specific decisionmaking elites and the companies or entities they control. They deny access to specific products or activities that are necessary to the conduct of an objectionable policy and that are valuable to decisionmaking elites.

In each of the categories of targeted sanctions—finance, travel, arms, and commodities—the Security Council introduced important innovations. In the area of financial sanctions, the Council moved beyond freezing the assets of governments alone. In the cases of Iraq, Libya, and Yugoslavia, financial sanctions were imposed only on government assets. Beginning in 1994, with the sanctions against the military junta in Haiti, and continuing through the Angola and Afghanistan cases in the latter part of the decade, the Security Council applied financial sanctions against designated individuals and entities as well. The counterterrorism financial sanctions mandated in Resolution 1373 were also directed against entities and individuals. As the Security Council shifted toward applying sanctions on specific entities and individuals, the UN Secretariat developed the capacity, in cooperation with member states, to develop and publish lists of designated sanctions targets. These same designated entities and individuals were also subjected to targeted travel bans. In the cases of Angola, Sierra Leone, Afghanistan, and Liberia, the Security Council imposed visa bans on a list of designated targets submitted by the UN Secretariat. The Council thus adopted the practice of imposing both targeted financial sanctions and visa bans on the same list of designated entities and individuals.

The Security Council also attempted to make improvements in the design and implementation of arms embargoes. This has been the most frequently employed form of economic sanctions. Since 1990 the Security Council has imposed arms embargoes in twelve of the fourteen cases in which sanctions were applied. Arms embargoes are an ideal type of targeted sanction. They deny aggressors or human rights abusers the tools of war and repression, while avoiding harm to vulnerable and innocent populations. Although frequently employed, however, arms embargoes have suffered from numerous problems of implementation and in many cases have lacked effective enforcement. In the five instances where arms embargoes were imposed as stand-alone measures—Somalia, Liberia until 2001,

Rwanda, Ethiopia/Eritrea, and Yugoslavia in 1998–2001—the impact of these measures in reducing the supply of weapons or ending armed conflict had been minimal. Only in the case of Iraq, where the United States and other countries made a major commitment to enforcement, did the continuing restrictions on the supply of arms and dual-use technologies have an impact in constraining the target government's ability to acquire prohibited weapons and rebuild its military machine. The latter is proven by the inability of the Iraqi air force and armed forces to mount any significant resistance to U.S. forces in the 2003 war.

To overcome the problems resulting from inadequate implementation of arms embargoes, the Security Council adopted a number of policy innovations. The language and technical terms employed in the Council's arms embargo resolutions became more precise. Arms embargo resolutions regularly included prohibitions not only against the supply of arms and ammunition but also against training, military cooperation, and various support services, including air transportation. This refinement of terms and broadening of items covered helped to close loopholes and avoid ambiguities that previously impeded enforcement. More vigorous efforts also were made to monitor compliance with arms embargoes and expose those who systematically violated these measures. Efforts were made to encourage member states to criminalize violations of UN arms embargoes and to strengthen export control laws and regulations. These initiatives helped to create a firmer foundation in the domestic law of member states for penalizing companies and individuals who supply arms and military-related goods in violation of UN arms embargoes.

Commodity-specific boycotts have also become more prominent in recent years. Oil embargoes were imposed as part of the sanctions against Iraq, Yugoslavia, Khmer Rouge–controlled areas of Cambodia, Haiti, UNITA in Angola, and the military junta in Sierra Leone. An embargo on the export of timber was imposed against Khmer Rouge territory in Cambodia. Diamond embargoes were introduced more recently. As nongovernmental agencies and human rights groups documented the role of diamond smuggling in financing the armed rebellions in Angola and Sierra Leone, the Security Council took action to interdict the trade in so-called blood diamonds. The Council imposed diamond embargoes against UNITA in Angola (Resolution 1173 [1998]), the Revolutionary United Front areas of Sierra Leone (Resolution 1306 [2000]), and the government of Liberia (Resolution 1343 [2001]). As a means of enforcing these measures, the United Nations worked with diamond-exporting countries, the diamond industry, and nongovernmental organizations to establish certificate-of-origin systems designed to protect the legitimate diamond trade while screening out diamonds produced by sanctioned rebel movements. Targeted diamond sanctions thus became another tool for the Security Council to apply pressure on specific rebel movements and to curtail the lucrative financial base sustaining armed conflict in Africa.

Improving Sanctions Monitoring and Implementation

In the late 1990s the Security Council developed a number of important mechanisms for making sanctions more effective against law-violating regimes. As the situations in which sanctions were imposed—such as long-standing civil wars, or in failed economies characterized by extensive criminalization—increased in complexity, the Council recognized the need both for an expert view of the prospects for sanctions compliance in any particular case, and for more precision in fashioning the sanctions process. The creation of special investigative and expert panels dealt with the former challenge, while specially convened and nationally sponsored "processes" contributed to the latter.

Analysts have long emphasized the importance of effective monitoring to the prospects for the successful implementation of sanctions. To overcome the lack of monitoring capacity within the UN system, the Security Council began to appoint independent expert panels and monitoring mechanisms to provide support for sanctions implementation. The first panel was established in conjunction with the arms embargo against Rwandan Hutu rebels (Resolution 1013 [1995]). The Council created the UN Independent Commission of Inquiry (UNICOI), which issued six reports from 1996 through 1998 documenting the illegal supply of arms to the rebel groups in eastern Zaire. UNICOI reports provided voluminous evidence of wholesale violations of the arms embargo and contained numerous recommendations for cracking down on arms smuggling in the region.

A breakthrough toward more effective monitoring came in the case of Angola. In 1999 the Angola sanctions committee became more active in monitoring sanctions violations and encouraging greater implementation efforts. The Security Council also appointed a panel of experts and a subsequent monitoring mechanism to improve compliance with the Angola sanctions. The panel of experts and monitoring mechanism issued a series of reports that focused continuing attention on sanctions implementation efforts.[8] The development of this improved monitoring effort is described in Chapter 13.

The Angola panel of experts and the monitoring mechanism were followed by similar investigative panels for Sierra Leone, Afghanistan, and Liberia. Although the Congo was not connected with any particular sanctions case, an investigative panel was also created to examine the exploitation of mineral wealth and natural resources in that country. In each of these settings, the investigative panels produced detailed reports on sanctions violations and smuggling activities. The Sierra Leone panel of experts focused on the link between arms trafficking and diamond smuggling and found a pattern of widespread violations of UN sanctions. The panel issued numerous policy recommendations, the most important of which was that sanctions be imposed on the government of Liberia for its role in undermining sanctions implementation and providing extensive support for the rebels in Sierra Leone.[9] The Security Council created a monitoring mechanism for Afghanistan in July 2001 (Resolution 1363) and established an associated Sanctions Enforcement Support Team to strengthen the implementation of the arms embargo, travel sanctions, and targeted financial sanctions imposed against the Taliban regime. After the overthrow of the Taliban, the Council altered the mission of the monitoring group (Resolution 1390 [2002]) to investigate and provide support for the continued financial, travel, and arms sanctions on former Taliban leaders and members of Al-Qaida. The Liberia panel of experts confirmed allegations of the Monrovia government's extensive involvement with and support for the armed rebellion of the Revolutionary United Front in Sierra Leone. The panel recommended a series of measures for strengthening the enforcement of the arms embargo, diamond embargo, and travel sanctions against Liberia.[10]

Paralleling the emergence of the monitoring mechanisms and their many recommendations for improved implementation were a series of reform initiatives sponsored by the governments of Switzerland, Germany, and Sweden to increase the effectiveness of Security Council sanctions and strengthen the prospects for member-state implementation and target-state compliance. The first of these policy initiatives, the Interlaken process, was sponsored by the government of Switzerland. In 1998 and 1999 Swiss authorities convened groups of scholars, international government officials, lawyers, diplomats, and banking experts in two major seminars at Interlaken. The Interlaken initiative attempted to apply the methods utilized in combating money laundering to the challenge of implementing targeted financial sanctions. Participants in the Interlaken seminars examined the extent to which financial sanctions could achieve their goal of cutting off the financial support that is crucial to sustaining abusive regimes and the decisionmaking elites who control them. As a part of the Swiss initiative, the Thomas J. Watson Institute for International Studies at Brown University developed model legislation for governments to strengthen their capacity to implement targeted financial sanctions. The Watson Institute also produced a handbook on the implementation of targeted financial sanctions that was subsequently distributed to member states through the UN Secretariat.[11]

Building on the Interlaken process, the German Ministry of Foreign Affairs initiated a like-minded effort to refine the implementation of travel bans and arms embargoes. Managed by the Bonn International Center for

Conversion, the German initiative included meetings in Bonn in 1999 and Berlin in 2000 and considered travel bans and arms embargoes as complementary forms of targeted sanctions, identifying the links between the two and also examining the unique features of each. In the area of arms embargoes, this Bonn-Berlin process, as it was called, recommended the use of standardized lists of dual-use items drawn from the Wassenaar Arrangement to ensure common definitions of military-related technologies subject to restrictions. This recommendation would later take policy form in Resolution 1409 (2002), imposed on Iraq as part of the smart sanctions reform. The recommendations emanating from the German initiative helped to advance the capacity of the Security Council to implement travel bans and arms embargoes. The final report of the German initiative provided rich detail of the monitoring and enforcement of future travel and arms sanctions.[12]

In 2001 the government of Sweden launched a new initiative to improve sanctions policymaking at the United Nations. The Swedish program brought together the world's leading sanctions scholars, UN policymakers, and international legal experts for a series of meetings in Uppsala, Stockholm, and New York to develop recommendations for strengthening the monitoring and enforcement of Security Council sanctions. Known as the Stockholm Process on the Implementation of Targeted Sanctions, the Swedish initiative added to the work already achieved by the Swiss and German governments and helped to advance international understanding of the requirements for effectively implementing targeted sanctions.[13]

The International Peace Academy in New York played an important role in documenting the evolution of sanctions policy, hosting a number of meetings at which Security Council ambassadors and UN officials engaged in off-the-record discussions of the most pressing sanctions policy issues with experts.

Reform Opportunities and Obstacles

The enthusiasm of UN member states for improving Security Council sanctions has varied since the end of the Cold War. The "sanctions fatigue" generated by humanitarian controversies and political differences over UN policy in Iraq slowed the momentum for reform and made agreement on contentious issues more difficult. Power politics and the narrow national interests of the permanent five members of the Security Council overshadowed the concern for improving the ability of the UN system to design and implement effective sanctions. In this atmosphere of competing agendas among the permanent five, it fell to middle powers such as Canada to champion the cause of more systematic upgrading of the UN's capacity to design and execute economic sanctions. In April 2000 Canadian foreign minister Lloyd Axworthy hosted a special session of the Security Council for the purpose of initiating a working group on sanctions reform. The Canadian initiative reflected widespread agreement among UN member states that improvements in Security Council sanctions were both possible and necessary. The working group was intended to complement the Swiss and German government initiatives, with the goal of designing a new structure and road map for Security Council sanctions. The working group was constituted as a committee of the whole Security Council and was charged with developing recommendations on the structure and substance of sanctions by November 2000.

Although the Canadian initiative was greeted enthusiastically in the Security Council, differences over its anticipated results soon surfaced, especially among the permanent five. The working group's first decision, the selection of a chair, immediately aroused political differences. After considerable delay, the Council selected Ambassador Anwarul Chowdhury of Bangladesh to lead the working group, in part because Chowdhury was considered neutral on most of the controversial issues facing the Council. Looming over every issue addressed by the working group was the question of Iraq—and the sharp differences within the Council about this case. This resulted in continuing divisions over humanitarian impact, political effectiveness, and the question of what generates the lifting of sanctions.

The Chowdhury working group addressed the need for improvements in the administration, design, and monitoring of sanctions policies. The most divisive issue for the group, and the one that ultimately prevented it from reaching consensus on a final report, was the question of time limits. France and other Council members argued vigorously that all sanctions should be time-limited, with a specified date for the lifting of sanctions unless the Security Council took action to extend them. The demand for time limits using this "sunset clause" was a direct outgrowth of the experience in Iraq, where sanctions continued indefinitely and some permanent members (especially the United States) would not even consider easing them. The United States and the United Kingdom, the most vigorous advocates of maintaining indefinite pressure on Iraq, resolutely opposed any recommendation that would require time limits for Security Council sanctions. Washington and London argued that time limits would divert the attention of a targeted regime from meeting the necessary conditions for compliance to waiting until sanctions were lifted. France and other countries countered that the Security Council would always have the option of extending sanctions if a targeted regime failed to comply. They insisted on requiring an affirmative vote for the continuation of sanctions, rather than the current ability of a single member state to block the lifting of sanctions through a veto. The French argued that their proposal would empower the Security Council by requiring a consensus for the continuation of sanctions.

Although the United States and the United Kingdom opposed time limits as a general principle, in actual practice they have readily accepted time limits in several recent sanctions episodes: the arms embargo against Ethiopia and Eritrea (Resolution 1298 [2000]), the arms embargo and further sanctions imposed against Afghanistan (Resolution 1333 [2000]), and the diamond embargo and other sanctions against Liberia (Resolution 1343 [2001]). In each case, the United States and the United Kingdom voted with other member states to accept time limits of one year for the duration of the imposed measures. In the cases of Afghanistan and Liberia, members of the Security Council readily agreed that the targeted regime had failed to comply with UN demands within the designated time limit, and the sanctions were extended. In the case of Ethiopia/Eritrea, the end of the war between the two states convinced a majority of the members of the Council that the arms embargo imposed the previous year was no longer relevant, and the sanctions were lifted. Despite this practice and primarily to avoid its application in the case of Iraq, the United States and the United Kingdom nonetheless continued to oppose the concept as a general principle.

Another contentious issue for the Chowdhury working group was the question of decisionmaking procedures within sanctions committees. The United States and the United Kingdom wanted to retain the existing consensus rule, whereas France, Russia, and other countries urged a majority-vote procedure. At stake was the issue of whether a single state could impose its will on other members and block decisions that had the support of a majority of committee members. Once again the Iraq case cast a shadow over this debate. The United States and the United Kingdom did not want to lose their ability to place holds on the import of dual-use goods into Iraq, whereas France and other Council members argued that such decisions should be by majority vote, not by the will of one or two Council members alone.

Because of these and other differences, the Chowdhury group was unable to meet its November 2000 deadline for issuing a report. In the end, the members of the Security Council could not agree on a unified set of policy recommendations, and the working group quietly dissolved without issuing a report. Nonetheless, the working group reached consensus on many issues related to the administration, design, and monitoring of UN sanctions and accepted a number of important recommendations for sanctions reform. Ambassador Chowdhury did produce a paper ("Chairman's Proposed Outcome," February 14, 2001) that summarized the major agreements and proposals of the working group. Many of the working group's proposals coincided with recommendations made by the various expert panels and monitoring mechanisms. Together, these two sources—the Chowdhury working group and reports of the expert panels and monitoring mechanisms—produced a coherent agenda for reform to improve the effectiveness of Security Council sanctions. Some of the major recommendations for reform include:

- Strengthen the capacity of the UN Secretariat to administer sanctions.
- Promote greater transparency and more effective communications, to inform member states and the public about sanctions requirements and purposes.
- Develop improved guidelines and standardized reporting procedures to assist member states in the implementations of sanctions.
- Clarify the conditions that must be met for sanctions to be lifted, and consider easing sanctions partially in response to partial compliance by targeted regimes.
- Standardize and improve procedures for providing humanitarian exemptions and assistance.
- Utilize expert panels and monitoring mechanisms for the investigation of sanctions compliance.
- Take action against those who are found to be deliberately violating sanctions (the expert panels recommended imposing sanctions against such violators).
- Provide technical assistance and expert advice to states needing help in the implementation of sanctions.
- Conduct periodic assessments of humanitarian impact, third-party effects, and the progress of implementation efforts.
- Tighten the enforcement of arms embargoes through mandatory registration of arms brokers and intermediaries and the development of standardized end-use certificates for arms and military equipment.
- Improve air traffic control interdiction in zones of conflict and revoke the aircraft registrations and licenses of those who are known to be violating sanctions.
- Develop a worldwide standardized system for certificates of origin for all diamond exports.
- Improve the capacity of the UN system to maintain and update accurate lists of individuals and entities subject to travel bans and targeted financial sanctions.

Many of these policy recommendations are being implemented and practiced and have received further emphasis in the Stockholm process. The sanctions mechanism as practiced by the UN Security Council has matured significantly since the early 1990s, as UN diplomats, expert investigators, academic scholars, nongovernmental analysts, and many others have contributed to a process of learning, adaptation, and reform. The result has been a substantial transformation of sanctions policymaking. The targeted, more selective sanctions of recent years, supported by humanitarian assessment missions and the reports of expert panels, bear little resemblance to the poorly monitored, often blunt measures imposed in the early 1990s.

Many problems remain in the implementation of Security Council sanctions, but substantial progress has been made. Some of the challenges to effective sanctions policy, such as great power rivalries among the permanent five, are endemic to the international system. Other challenges, such as the development of greater member-state capacity for sanctions implementation, can be addressed through specific forms of assistance and policy improvements. The UN system has shown remarkable capacity for adaptation and learning in recent years. With continued attention to and implementation of appropriate reform recommendations, the Security Council can take further steps in the years ahead to mold the sanctions instrument into a more effective tool for preserving peace and security.

Notes

1. UN Security Council, letter dated April 12, 1995, to the president of the Security Council, S/1995/200, annex 1.

2. Claudia von Braunmühl and Manfred Kulessa, *The Impact of UN Sanctions on Humanitarian Assistance Activities,* report commissioned by the UN Department of Humanitarian Affairs (DHA) (Berlin: DHA, December 1995).

3. Larry Minear et al., *Toward More Humane and Effective Sanctions Management: Enhancing the Capacity of the United Nations System,* Occasional Paper no. 31 (Providence, R.I.: Thomas J. Watson Jr. Institute for International Studies, Brown University, 1998). This report is the published version of a study of the same title produced for the Inter-Agency Standing Committee of the UN Department of Humanitarian Affairs.

4. UN Department of Humanitarian Affairs, *Note From the Department of Humanitarian Affairs Concerning the Possible Humanitarian Impact of the International Flight Ban Decided in Security Council Resolution 1070 (1996),* New York, February 20, 1997.

5. UN, Office for the Coordination of Humanitarian Affairs, *Inter-Agency Assessment Mission to Sierra Leone: Interim Report,* New York, February 17, 1998.

6. UN, Office for the Coordination of Humanitarian Affairs, *Vulnerability and Humanitarian Implications of UN Security Council Sanctions in Afghanistan,* Islamabad, December 2000.

7. UN Security Council, *Report of the Secretary-General in Pursuance of Paragraph 13(a) of Resolution 1343 (2001) Concerning Liberia,* S/2001/939, New York, October 5, 2001.

8. UN Security Council, *Report of the Panel of Experts on Violations of Security Council Sanctions Against UNITA,* S/2000/203, New York, March 10,

2000; *Interim Report of the Monitoring Mechanism on Angola Sanctions Established by the Security Council in Resolution 1295 (2000) of April 2000,* S/2000/1026, New York, October 25, 2000; *Final Report of the Monitoring Mechanism on Angola Sanctions,* S/2000/1225, New York, December 21, 2000; *Addendum to the Final Report of the Monitoring Mechanism on Sanctions Against UNITA,* S/2001/363, New York, April 11, 2001; *Supplementary Report of the Monitoring Mechanism on Sanctions Against UNITA,* S/2001/966, New York, October 12, 2001; *Additional Report of the Monitoring Mechanism on Sanctions Against UNITA,* S/2002/486, New York, 26, April 2002; and *Additional Report of the Monitoring Mechanism on Sanctions Against UNITA,* S/2002/1119, New York, October 26, 2002.

9. UN Security Council, *Report of the Panel of Experts Appointed Pursuant to Security Resolution 1306 (2000), Paragraph 19, in Relation to Sierra Leone,* S/2000/1195, New York, December 20, 2000.

10. UN Security Council, *Report of the Panel of Experts Pursuant to Security Council Resolution 1343 (2001), Paragraph 19, Concerning Liberia,* S/2001/1015, October 26, 2001.

11. Swiss Confederation, UN Secretariat, and Watson Institute for International Studies at Brown University, *Targeted Financial Sanctions: A Manual for Design and Implementation—Contributions from the Interlaken Process* (Providence, R.I.: Thomas J. Watson Jr. Institute for International Studies, 2001).

12. Michael Brzoska, ed., *Design and Implementation of the Arms Embargoes and Travel and Aviation Related Sanctions: Results of the "Bonn-Berlin Process"* (Bonn: Bonn International Center for Conversion, 2001).

13. Peter Wallensteen, Carina Staibano, and Mikael Eriksson, eds., *Making Targeted Sanctions Effective: Guidelines for the Implementation of UN Policy Options* (Uppsala, Sweden: Uppsala University Department of Peace and Conflict Research, 2003).

12

The Iraq
Sanctions Committee

PETER VAN WALSUM

On December 11, 1998, I arrived in New York to take up my duties as
Dutch permanent representative. The Netherlands had been elected to the
Security Council for the two-year term beginning on January 1, 1999. The
instructions I had been given were mostly of a general nature, but a more
specific one concerned the chair of the Iraq sanctions committee. The
Hague had asked me to be available, should the Security Council wish to
appoint me to that office. Five days after my arrival the United States and
the United Kingdom launched their air strikes against Iraq, codenamed
Desert Fox. The immediate cause for this action was Iraqi obstruction of
the UN Special Commission (UNSCOM), but the Clinton administration
had recently also begun to speak of the desirability of a "regime change" in
Iraq. That, however, was not the acknowledged objective of the operation.
In all the official statements emanating from Washington and London it
was emphasized that the strikes were aimed at degrading Saddam Hussein's
weapons of mass destruction (WMD) program and related delivery systems. It was only after the cessation of the operation, on December 19, that
I heard President Clinton first reiterate that the United States would continue to contain and constrain Saddam Hussein and then add: "while working
toward the day Iraq has a government willing to live at peace with its people and with its neighbors." If that meant regime change, it was remote
enough. I felt there could be no doubt that at least this brief military action
had been only about weapons of mass destruction.

Some History
The sanctions against Iraq were imposed in response to that country's invasion and occupation of Kuwait on August 2, 1990 (Resolution 661).[1]
Essentially, they prohibited the import of Iraqi goods into all states, which
in practice meant oil and oil products, and the sale or supply of all products

to Iraq except for supplies strictly intended for medical purposes and, in humanitarian circumstances, foodstuffs. As a means to bring about an Iraqi withdrawal from Kuwait they were unsuccessful, but once the Gulf War (Desert Storm) had achieved that objective, the sanctions were left in place to force Iraq's full compliance with the cease-fire conditions, especially with regard to the destruction, removal, and rendering harmless of Iraq's weapons of mass destruction (Resolution 687). During the Gulf War most of Iraq's power plants, oil refineries, pumping stations, and water treatment facilities had been destroyed, and the sanctions regime had the effect of further aggravating the resulting economic hardship. Before long this led to a humanitarian crisis, which the Secretary-General brought to the attention of the Security Council in the Ahtisaari Report of March 20, 1991. In response, it was agreed that the UN should develop a plan for using Iraqi oil revenues to finance humanitarian relief. In August and September 1991 respectively, the Security Council adopted Resolutions 706 and 712 establishing the oil-for-food program. This provided for the sale of a predetermined maximum volume of Iraqi oil under the supervision of the UN; purchasers would pay directly into a UN-controlled escrow account, which would be used to pay for UN-approved purchases of foodstuffs, medicines, and materials and supplies for essential civilian needs.

Both resolutions were, however, rejected by Iraq, which claimed that the proposed procedures were a violation of its sovereignty. In April 1995 the Security Council made a concession to these Iraqi concerns by adopting Resolution 986, which gave Baghdad primary responsibility for the distribution of humanitarian goods with the exception of the Kurdish areas in the north, where distribution was kept under direct UN control. In May 1996 Iraq finally accepted the program, but preparations for its implementation were interrupted in August 1996 when Iraqi military forces marched into the Kurdish zones. This led to further delay, but in December 1996 Resolution 986 officially came into force, and food and medicine began to be delivered in the first months of 1997. Henceforth, the most comprehensive coercive economic measures ever devised by the UN were tempered by the largest humanitarian relief operation in the UN's history.

The other leg of the UN's containment policy was the inspections regime. Resolution 687 of April 3, 1991, formalized the cease-fire agreement ending the Gulf War, under which Iraq had agreed to the destruction of all its chemical and biological weapons and all its ballistic missiles with a range greater than 150 kilometers, as well as to the removal of all its nuclear-weapons-usable materials. The supervision of these operations was entrusted to UNSCOM, established by that same resolution, and the International Atomic Energy Agency (IAEA) respectively. The resolution contained a precise timetable for the successive steps to be taken in this context, according to which the entire disarmament process would be completed within four months and would then give way to a system of ongoing monitoring and verification. Had Iraq opted for compliance, it would have returned to normalcy before the end of 1991. Instead, it resorted to a practice of systematic concealment and deception, which caused the inspections and the sanctions to remain in force for much longer than had originally been envisaged. In spite of this, the inspectors scored some remarkable successes in the detection and destruction of Iraqi stocks and facilities related to its chemical, biological, ballistic missile, and nuclear weapons programs. By 1997, however, Iraq seemed so emboldened by the growing division in the Security Council—and especially among the permanent five—that it resorted to ever more active obstruction of the work of UNSCOM. In 1998 this gave rise to growing tension, finally resulting in the U.S.-British air strikes against Baghdad in December of that year. The inspectors, who had been withdrawn just before this operation, were then formally banned from returning to Iraq.

The Rules and Constraints of Sanctions Committees

Whenever the Security Council imposes sanctions it also creates a sanctions committee. The main duty of a sanctions committee is to grant or deny exemptions. A sanctions committee has the same composition as the Security Council itself—that is, it comprises the same fifteen member states, normally represented at sub–deputy permanent representative level. It is chaired by a permanent representative of a nonpermanent member, appointed by the Security Council and serving in his personal capacity. The latter provision is so strictly adhered to that the chairman of a sanctions committee cannot even ask his deputy permanent representative to stand in for him. If he is unable to chair a meeting himself, he will have to call on one of two other permanent representatives, also appointed—as deputy chairmen of equal standing—by the Security Council. The personal-capacity rule underlines the fact that the chairman receives his instructions only from the Security Council, not from his authorities as he does when he sits on the Security Council proper. The difference with the Security Council is that a sanctions committee is chaired by someone who is elected for a whole year and usually reelected for the second year that his country is a nonpermanent member of the Security Council. Another difference is that in diplomatic rank this chairman is usually senior to the other committee members. On the face of it, all this would seem to invest the chairman with some power, but the elaborate system only obscures the fact that in a sanctions committee the permanent members are even more dominant than in the Security Council.

This is partly due to the absence of a decisionmaking machinery. Nothing gives the nonpermanent members of the Security Council more

power than the rule that a resolution needs nine positive votes to be adopted. It is a very modest compensation for the blocking power held by each
permanent member, but the resulting complexity at least leaves the president of the Council some room to maneuver and encourages him to use his
skills to try and produce a broadly supported decision even in controversial
matters. In the Council, a unanimous view is often reached under the threat
of a vote. In a sanctions committee there is nothing of the sort. Decisions
are taken on the basis of consensus. If there is no consensus, there is no
decision. One might also put it this way: on a sanctions committee all fifteen members have the right of veto. A little bit of arithmetic teaches us that
a sanctions committee must be about three times as inflexible and irresolute
as the Security Council itself.

The Iraq Sanctions Committee: A Political Minefield

Iraq's preoccupation with weapons of mass destruction clearly was the key
to everything that was happening to that country. This also applied to the
weapons inspections and the sanctions regime. It occurred to me that
although these had the same objective, they were perceived quite differently. The UNSCOM weapons inspectors had in fact been rather popular with
the media. They had after all provided some entertainment with the cat-
and-mouse game they had been engaged in with the Iraqi authorities. The
sanctions regime, by contrast, was seen as a cruel and vindictive operation,
responsible for all the suffering of the Iraqi people. But then, the sanctions
had never been meant to last for more than half a year at most, and if
almost a decade later they were still there, it was only because for all these
years the weapons inspectors had been unable to give Iraq a clean bill of
health. Now UNSCOM had been withdrawn—never to return, as it turned
out—but the sanctions stayed in force. It was to be expected that henceforth
the Iraq sanctions committee would take all the flak.

These reflections did not add to my eagerness to be appointed chairman of that committee, but I consoled myself with the thought that the
weapons inspectors had been beaten by all the lies, deception, and active
obstruction they had encountered, whereas the sanctions regime, despite all
the juggling and smuggling, had been moderately successful in keeping the
big oil money out of Saddam Hussein's hands.

The Netherlands joined the Security Council on January 1, 1999. Apart
from my appointment as chairman of the Iraq sanctions committee, almost
two weeks went by without Iraq even being mentioned. When by the middle of the month the problem of Iraq was broached for the first time since
Desert Fox, the impasse appeared to be just as complete as it had been a
month earlier. It was clear that a great deal of work needed to be done

before the Council would be able to recover a modicum of consensus on how to deal with Iraq. This left me without much guidance as chairman of the sanctions committee. All I could do was faithfully implement the existing Security Council resolutions, which I did by signing piles of import authorizations, ceaselessly submitted to me by the Office of the Iraq Program at the UN Secretariat. The stalemate at the Council level gave my collaborators and me some time to reflect on the sanctions regime and ask ourselves what we were going to do with it. The sanctions regime was meant to keep Iraq's enormous potential oil revenue out of the hands of a dictator who over the years had displayed an obsession with weapons of mass destruction. The oil-for-food program, accepted by Iraq only after years of dillydallying, was meant to limit the impact of the sanctions on the civilian population, but it was clear that in spite of this, the sanctions caused a great deal of what in a military action would be termed "collateral damage." We concluded that our best course of action was to try to find new ways to reduce this unintended effect.

An immaterial form of collateral damage presented itself when I found that the sanctions regime had so far prevented most ordinary Iraqis from performing the Hajj, the pilgrimage to Mecca, which is a religious duty for every Muslim. That, at least, was the way the problem was put to me by the permanent representative of Iraq, Ambassador Saeed Hasan. Other colleagues dismissed this version and pointed out that Iraq had been offered a perfectly practicable voucher system, under which adequate oil-for-food funds would be allocated for this purpose and made available to the pilgrims in the form of vouchers or traveler's checks. Under the relevant Security Council resolutions the United Nations was not allowed to deposit the required funds with the Iraqi central bank. Hasan confirmed the existence of this proposal but added that Baghdad had never considered it a serious offer, as the proposed arrangement would have offended the dignity of Iraq. As we discussed this, it became clear to me that there was no time left to draft an alternative arrangement for the March 1999 Hajj season, but I made up my mind to start earlier the next year and then insist that the whole committee think along and actively join in the planning of an arrangement that would reconcile the Fifth Pillar of Islam, the relevant Security Council resolutions, and the dignity of Iraq.

In the context of our discussions on the Hajj problem, Ambassador Hasan expressed the wish that I visit Iraq to see things for myself. He reminded me of a provision in a Security Council document that stipulated that every chairman of a sanctions committee should at least once visit the country to which the sanctions in question applied. I replied that I would be glad to comply, and we agreed to remain in touch about a suitable date.

The Amorim Panels and Resolution 1284

Meanwhile the Security Council had begun to search for a new approach to its relationship with Iraq. At the suggestion of Canada, it established three panels to be chaired by the permanent representative of Brazil, Ambassador Celso Amorim. These panels produced three sets of recommendations regarding, respectively, disarmament, humanitarian matters (sanctions), and the issues of persons missing after the Gulf War and stolen Kuwaiti property (in particular the state archives). The recommendations of the latter two panels were mostly uncontroversial and several of them in some form or another found their way into what was to become Resolution 1284. Those of the humanitarian panel were mainly aimed at increasing the financial resources of the oil-for-food program, an objective that no delegation could object to. Regarding the recommendations of the disarmament panel, things went less smoothly. The essence of the recommendations regarding the disarmament of Iraq in the field of weapons of mass destruction was the conclusion that conditions now existed for shifting the focus of the UN effort from dismantling Iraq's WMD capacity to ensuring that Iraq would not rebuild that capacity (through a system of what was called "reinforced ongoing monitoring and verification"). Another conclusion of the panel was that any new monitoring system should be acceptable to Iraq. Russia, France, and China proposed to follow this line. Other delegations, including mine, stressed the need for preserving the original disarmament standards for Iraq and felt that the terms of reference of the weapons inspectors could not be made contingent on Iraq's approval.

In April 1999 the Netherlands joined the United Kingdom in submitting a first draft for a comprehensive ("omnibus") resolution aimed at setting the relationship between Iraq and the Security Council on a new footing. Given the politically charged nature of the issue, however, it was soon decided that the permanent five would first try to reach a consensus on the draft, with the result that for almost the entire second half of the year the elected ten had to rely on monthly briefings by the UK delegation for information on progress in the ongoing consultations (see Chapter 14). As was to be expected, it was exceedingly difficult to draft a text acceptable to all delegations. Russia and China never held out any real hope of being able to vote for the British draft unless it incorporated more of the Amorim recommendations, but France made several constructive suggestions—such as mere notification of contracts involving items related to food, health, agriculture, and education, and approval of contracts for petroleum-related spare parts by independent experts—which the UK was only too willing to take onboard. By November, after the permanent five had been in conclave for nearly six months, the elected ten began to grumble, and on December 17, 1999, the UK finally put the draft resolution to the vote. As expected, Russia, China, and Malaysia abstained, but many found it disappointing to see France abstain as well. France claimed that a consensus had been within grasp but that the United States and the United Kingdom had been unwilling to allow the talks more time. Considering that the permanent five had monopolized the drafting process for more than half a year, this did not convince many elected members. In retrospect, all there may be to say about the French abstention on Resolution 1284 is that it was consistent. On October 23, 1997, France had begun to vote with Russia and China, when it abstained on Resolution 1134 condemning Iraq for its obstruction of UNSCOM, and it has done so ever since. As a result, the divide that ran through the permanent five, separating France, Russia, and China from the United States and the United Kingdom, became a permanent feature of the Security Council's business with Iraq.

Administering the Oil-for-Food Program

All the while, the sanctions committee had been administering the oil-for-food program in accordance with Resolution 986 (1995). In the new year, that work continued on the basis of the new resolution. Due to the abstention of three of the five permanent members, Resolution 1284 did not have the intended effect of reestablishing the authority of the Security Council (Iraq had immediately rejected it), but it did introduce several practical improvements. Thanks to the new resolution, for example, there were virtually no restrictions on the import of food and medicines any longer, and the ceiling on the volume of Iraqi oil exports for humanitarian purchases had been removed. If the sanctions nevertheless continued to cause severe hardship, this was due on the one hand to the economic stagnation, dating back all the way to the Iran-Iraq War but greatly exacerbated by the Gulf War and the ensuing sanctions, and on the other hand to the intractable dual-use problem. Any delegation that suspected that goods Iraq ostensibly wished to import for peaceful purposes could also be used for the manufacture of weapons of mass destruction could place a hold on the contract in question pending further investigation. In fact, every delegation was expected to do so, but in practice only the United States, and to a lesser extent the United Kingdom, actively discharged that duty. Other delegations were either lukewarm about the sanctions regime or did not see much point in applying their limited resources to a job that would be done anyway—and so much more thoroughly—by the United States.

By far most of the criticism provoked by the sanctions regime during my two-year tenure was related to these *holds*. Due to the complexity of many contracts it often happened that suspicion raised by one product led to a hold on a large composite contract that for the greater part concerned the import of obviously harmless goods. As some of these were often of pivotal importance to the Iraqi infrastructure, the holds could have a devastating effect on the humanitarian situation. A typical example of this was Iraq's inability to import equipment for water purification on account of dual-use potential of part of that equipment. As I foresaw a progressive erosion of the public acceptance of the sanctions regime if this negative effect was not addressed, I discussed the problem first with members of the U.S. mission in New York and subsequently with experts at the State Department in Washington in an attempt at finding ways of improving the existing procedures. First, I asked whether the United States could not allocate more people to its dual-use probes so that a complex contract might be "dissected" more quickly and the hold then limited to the sensitive products. Second, I wondered whether it would not be possible to weigh the proliferation risk against the humanitarian impact in such a way that a very remote dual-use potential might be winked at if the impact of an extended hold on, for example, the public health sector would evidently be disastrous. The U.S. response to my first suggestion was positive, but the officials were not prepared to let humanitarian considerations override the principle that in the Iraqi context even the slightest risk of proliferation was unacceptable. We openly discussed the difficulty that my terms of reference did not go beyond nonproliferation and the other provisions of Resolution 687, whereas the United States was also thinking in terms of regime change. After my discussions in Washington I thought I actually saw the number of holds go down for a while, but then they went up again. I had the distinct impression that with regard to Iraq there were many schools of thought in Washington, and that U.S. policy was being pulled in different directions. The outcome of Desert Fox—Saddam Hussein firmly in the saddle, inspectors gone, and nothing left but an ever more unpopular sanctions regime—could not possibly be what the United States and the United Kingdom had bargained for. A year later, Resolution 1284 had, if anything, only emboldened the Iraqi regime, and the only consensus I could detect in Washington was that this was not the way to deal with Saddam Hussein.

Iraqi Obstruction of Humanitarian Efforts

Against this discouraging background I began the new year by actively trying to devise a new way of enabling Iraqi citizens to perform the Hajj. This involved detailed discussions on financial and legal aspects, now in the light of the brand-new Resolution 1284, as well as on the less tangible subject of the dignity of Iraq. Ambassador Hasan warned me that any arrangement that would bypass the central bank of Iraq was unlikely to be acceptable to his authorities, but I replied that this time I had engaged Iraq's friends in the discussions from the very beginning and I expected them to help me find a solution that would be acceptable to the government of Iraq. In this endeavor I received invaluable help from my Malaysian colleague,

Ambassador Hasmy Agam. The latter, himself a hajji, roundly condemned the sanctions regime (he once said that the humanitarian consequences of the sanctions regime were so unacceptable that the risk of proliferation would have to be put up with), but unlike others who played Saddam Hussein's game in insisting that only its total abolition could bring solace to the Iraqi people, he was more than ready to help me look for practical solutions. In the end, we came up with a plan that all fifteen delegations could accept. It involved neither vouchers nor cash but arranged for direct payment of the expenses to be incurred by the pilgrims outside their own country, with a small amount of pocket money for each pilgrim to be distributed jointly by UN and Iraqi government representatives. I had it formally approved by the sanctions committee—a rare event: a decision—and obtained the green light from the Security Council, after which I submitted the plan to the Iraqi delegation. The Iraqi response was twofold. The plan was, like its predecessors, dismissed as a violation of the dignity of Iraq, and the sanctions regime was once again blamed for preventing Muslims from performing their holiest religious duty. At this point the government of Saudi Arabia stepped in and offered to defray all the expenses of all the Iraqi pilgrims, but this solution was rejected by Baghdad as well.

This turned out to be a recurring theme. Whenever we tried to alleviate the humanitarian impact of the sanctions regime there was prevarication or even obstruction on the Iraqi side. At first I ascribed these incidents to the inflexibility of the Iraqi bureaucracy, which after all was a phenomenon to be expected in a country under excessively authoritarian rule. I could not really believe that a government would deliberately exacerbate the suffering of its own people in order to score a political point. Even now I would hesitate to attribute each and every incident to such a sinister motive, but I came across more and more cases where the lack of Iraqi cooperation could not easily be explained otherwise.

One of the earliest cases of this kind that I recall concerned the targeted nutrition programs for children and nursing mothers. The Office of the Iraq Program reported to the sanctions committee that although everything had been agreed and was in place to launch these programs, the Iraqi authorities continued to procrastinate. In a subsequent meeting this was reported again. Then, in August 1999, the UN Children's Fund (UNICEF) published a survey according to which Iraqi children under five were dying at more than twice the rate they were ten years ago. This was a shocking finding, and obviously everyone blamed the sanctions regime. The report's recommendations, however, were scarcely addressed to the sanctions committee but did urge the government of Iraq to "urgently expedite the implementation of targeted nutrition programmes."

There was one incident where the Iraqi authorities' bad faith could not be doubted. A Netherlands-based nongovernmental organization had offered to ship seventy-two tons of dry skimmed milk to Iraq. It was instructed by the Iraqi Ministry of Health to have the manufacturer indicate a shelf life of one year, instead of the customary two years or more. Upon the consignment's arrival in Iraq, a sample was taken for testing purposes. Six months later, the nongovernmental organization in question was informed that the consignment had been rejected. Counterchecks were made, both in the Netherlands and in a third country, which showed there was nothing wrong with the milk powder, but the Iraqi decision was declared final. Due to the arbitrarily reduced shelf life and the bulk of the consignment, reallocation was not an option. The shipment, with a value of about U.S.$300,000, was then presumably destroyed. I related this incident in a meeting of the Security Council and was never again approached about a possible visit to Iraq.

This growing suspicion that the government of Iraq felt no qualms about manipulating the misery of its own people compounded the moral dilemma that would have faced the members of the sanctions committee anyway. Naturally, none of us enjoyed playing a part in a sanctions regime that, although aimed at Saddam Hussein and his weapons programs, was hurting innocent Iraqis, who were—precisely on account of the undemocratic nature of Saddam Hussein's regime—in no way responsible for the latter's actions. It was even conceivable that the oil-for-food program, with its centralized delivery mechanism, was supplying Saddam Hussein with a welcome instrument for exercising total control over his people. All this seemed to argue against the continuance of the sanctions regime. The overriding argument for retaining it, however, was that after the withdrawal of the weapons inspectors this was the only remaining obstacle to Saddam Hussein's ambition to acquire or develop nuclear weapons. This argument was not made any less cogent by Iraqi attempts at exploiting the international community's feelings of compassion.

Challenges to the Committee's Authority

It became clearer by the day, however, that the sanctions regime alone, now based on a resolution adopted with four abstentions, simply was not potent enough to generate the pressure needed to contain Iraq. It even seemed to lack the strength to hold its own. I could not tell whether it was wishful thinking or cunning, but the Iraqi diplomats in New York began to display a serene confidence that the sanctions were becoming so untenable that their days were numbered. This view was not limited to the delegation of Iraq. Other delegations, too, showed signs of decreasing respect for the sanctions regime and, consequently, for the sanctions committee.

A special role in all this was played by the delegation of France. In the sanctions committee France would consistently outshine Russia and China in criticizing the way the United States applied the sanctions regime. It almost looked as though France was engaged in a competition with Russia to be recognized as Iraq's most devoted friend, with France simply having to work harder as a former member of the Gulf War coalition. Of course it was rumored that these two countries' policies vis-à-vis Iraq were primarily guided by economic considerations, but the claim that "it is all about oil" was—and still is—omnidirectional, so delegations took turns being suspected of having a secret oil agenda. As for France, I could not help feeling that more profoundly political considerations, involving its self-image, were at play.

Outside the committee as well, France claimed a leading role in the advocacy of Iraq's interests and the struggle against its isolation. By September 2000 a curious dispute arose about the interpretation of Resolution 670 (1990) concerning passenger flights to and from Iraq. The interpretation of this resolution had been the subject of discussion in the committee before, but it had always been impossible to reach a consensus. The resolution was unclear as to the degree of involvement of the sanctions committee. One school of thought read into the text that the committee simply needed to be notified of a proposed passenger flight, whereas the other school maintained that for such flights the committee's approval was required. The problem was that both terms—notification and approval—appeared in the text. I had at first been unwilling to resign myself to this ambiguity and had asked the UN's legal counsel, Hans Corell, to inform the committee which interpretation was the correct one, but Corell had replied that from a legal point this could not be determined. Resolutions were often drafted in haste, and unclear provisions were not uncommon. Usually in such cases, the only way out was to submit the dilemma to the Security Council, which could then cut the Gordian knot. As I did not have a high opinion of the Council's knot-cutting propensity, I had at last settled for the pragmatic procedure, which I was told had been good enough for my predecessors. This meant that I informed the committee that as chairman I had no choice but to follow the stricter interpretation, and I would therefore treat every communication, even if it was worded as a notification, as a request for approval. This was largely academic because such flights were routinely approved anyway, and all members of the committee had always gone along with this practice. It was understood by all that while there was no consensus on the interpretation of the resolution, there was agreement on the way the chair had to deal with the problem in practice.

Nevertheless, on September 21, 2000, the French delegation had a letter delivered to me notifying the committee of a civilian flight to Baghdad with French doctors, artists, and sports personalities, due to depart very early the following morning. By announcing this flight at such short notice, France was bringing things to a head, because it was technically impossible to treat this letter as a request for approval. In order to enable the committee to follow its agreed practice until agreement on a new practice could be reached, I formally requested France to delay the flight by half a day. This request was denied, and I reported the French decision to the Security Council, which, as expected, was unable to take a position on the matter.

The incident blew over, but it did not pass unnoticed that France—not Russia, China, Malaysia, or any other country—had taken it upon itself to defy the sanctions committee's chair in a way that had not been seen before. In my subsequent discussions with members of the French delegation, I detected some embarrassment, which strengthened my impression that the lengths to which France would go in its solidarity with Iraq were beginning to puzzle even its own insiders.

France risked giving the wrong signals to the Iraqi leadership, since it encouraged their noncompliance with international demands. The Iraqis themselves might be forgiven for believing that the sanctions were quietly withering away, but it was inconceivable that the authorities in Paris, Moscow, and Beijing seriously held this view. In the past, some timid sanctions had indeed become inoperative and now lay dormant, but the sanctions against Iraq were the real thing. They had been devised as a substitute for war, and once the war had taken place anyway their retention had been passionately defended by those who wanted to discourage the United States from pushing through to Baghdad. Sanctions had then been the darling of the antiwar lobby. Such sanctions would not simply go away. They were the strongest coercive measure "not involving the use of armed force," to quote Article 41 of the UN Charter, and if they were to go, they could only be replaced by war. On the one hand, I fervently wished this truth would dawn on all those who supported Saddam Hussein, for they were clearly luring him into a dead end. On the other hand, I sometimes wondered whether brief military action might not be more humane than comprehensive sanctions spun out over almost a decade.

In the end, it all seemed to boil down to the question of respect for the authority of the Security Council. My tenure as chairman of the Iraq sanctions committee ended on December 31, 2000. Eighteen days earlier, George W. Bush had been elected the forty-third president of the United States. Everyone expected his administration to come up with a new Iraq policy. The Republicans had, admittedly, always shown less respect for the United Nations than the Democrats, but they were less likely to put up with Saddam Hussein's decade-long disrespect for the authority of the Security Council.

A Postscript

After my departure from both the Security Council and the sanctions committee, the fault line between France, Russia, and China on the one hand

and the United States and Britain on the other continued to bedevil the permanent five's handling of Iraq. In the autumn of 2002 there was a brief respite, when, under the influence of the U.S. military buildup and the professed readiness of the United States to "go it alone," Resolution 1441 was adopted unanimously. For those who remembered how in 1999 the adoption of Resolution 1284 was endlessly delayed by concerns about insufficient consideration for Iraqi sensitivities, it was remarkable to see France and Russia vote for a resolution obliging Iraq to allow Iraqi officials and other persons to leave the country accompanied by their family members in order to be interviewed by IAEA and the UN Monitoring, Verification, and Inspection Commission (UNMOVIC) without the presence of observers from the Iraqi government. I felt that this was the true litmus test for Iraq's preparedness to come clean. As was to be expected, however, Iraq failed to pass this test; yet France and Russia maintained that the inspections were working.

As for the legality of the military campaign that is in progress as this postscript is being written, the debate is somewhat reminiscent of the one that followed air strikes by the North Atlantic Treaty Organization against the Federal Republic of Yugoslavia on account of Kosovo in March 1999. Some will stress the difference between the objective of averting a humanitarian disaster and that of eliminating weapons of mass destruction (let alone that of changing a regime), others will insist that both interventions were a violation of international law, but few will deny that there is a problem of legality. The United Kingdom's frantic but vain attempts at securing a "second resolution" will make it difficult for anyone to claim that the war on Iraq has an unassailable legal basis. In my opinion there is no doubt that it is not as it should be if military action is resorted to without a Security Council mandate, but it is not right either if a country consistently flouts mandatory Security Council resolutions and gets away with it because the threat of a veto by one or two permanent members prevents the Security Council from taking action against it. It is difficult to tell which of the two is the more damaging to the authority of the Security Council.

Notes

1. This section draws partly on David Cortright and George A. Lopez, "Sanctions Against Iraq," in David Cortright and George A. Lopez, eds., *The Sanctions Decade: Assessing UN Strategies in the 1990s* (Boulder: Lynne Rienner, 2000).

13

The Angola Sanctions Committee

David J. R. Angell

The adoption on December 9, 2002, of Resolution 1448 brought an end to the Security Council's sanctions against the União Nacional para a Independência Total de Angola (UNITA) rebel force in Angola. The incremental imposition of the sanctions beginning in 1993 reflected the Security Council's view that UNITA, led by Jonas Savimbi, bore primary responsibility for the continuation of Angola's civil war. The lifting of the sanctions nine years later conveyed the Council's conclusion that UNITA had ceased to pursue its objectives through military means. This chapter examines the role the sanctions played in bringing about this transformation in the behavior of UNITA and, with it, an end to three decades of armed conflict in Angola. The impact on the Security Council's ability to address economic factors in civil wars more generally is also considered.

The sanctions contained in Resolutions 864 (1993), 1127 (1997), and 1173 (1998) comprised prohibitions on the sale and supply of weapons and other forms of military assistance to UNITA, the sale or supply of petroleum and petroleum products to UNITA, representation abroad by UNITA and travel by the adult members and immediate families of the UNITA leadership, and the sale or export of diamonds by UNITA. The sanctions—the first the Council had imposed against nonstate actors—were carefully targeted but at the outset were largely without effect, having been imposed as a political gesture with insufficient attention having been given to their effective implementation. The last chairman of the Security Council committee responsible for the application of the sanctions against UNITA, Ambassador Richard Ryan of Ireland, concluded that, in the period before 1999, the sanctions had been the subject of "widespread if not total disregard."[1]

Canada assumed the chairmanship of the Security Council's Angola sanctions committee in January 1999, determined to end the violations of the sanctions, which diminished the Council's authority and undermined the credibility of sanctions as a diplomatic tool. The two Canadian chairmen, Ambassadors Robert Fowler (January 1999–August 2000) and Paul Heinbecker (August–December 2000), pursued a three-pronged strategy to reverse the culture of impunity that had arisen in the violation of the sanctions against UNITA. Their stated objective was to reduce the revenue that UNITA received from diamonds and to increase UNITA's costs in procuring weapons and petroleum, in order to help establish the conditions for a resumption of the political dialogue within Angola by diminishing UNITA's ability to wage war and to pursue its objectives through military means.[2]

Increasing Awareness

First Fowler and then Heinbecker sought to increase awareness of the scope and objectives of the sanctions against UNITA and of the fact that the Security Council was unanimous in wanting to see the sanctions applied more effectively. From May 10 to May 27, 1999, Fowler traveled to seven countries in Africa: Angola, Botswana, the Democratic Republic of Congo, Namibia, South Africa, Zambia, and Zimbabwe.[3] From July 6 to July 17, he traveled to Algeria and to four countries in Europe: Belgium, France, Ukraine, and the United Kingdom.[4] Nineteen specific recommendations were presented to the Security Council. Additional consultations were undertaken in North America.

Fowler's objectives throughout these travels were fourfold: (1) to engage governments, private companies, and opinion leaders in discussion to identify measures to improve the effectiveness of the sanctions; (2) to explore opportunities for collaboration between the Security Council and international governmental and nongovernmental organizations in improving the effectiveness of the sanctions; (3) to remind governments of their obligation, under the Charter of the United Nations, to implement the resolutions of the Security Council and to enact the necessary legislation or regulations to that end; and (4) to request member states, companies, and individuals to provide the sanctions committee with information on sanctions violations. His underlying objective was, he said, "to give teeth to hitherto ineffective sanctions and to make very clear that sanctions violations are no longer cost-free."[5]

In addition to undertaking extensive consultations with governments at the senior level (including heads of state and senior ministers) and with business sectors, diplomatic communities, and nongovernmental bodies, Fowler delivered public statements to key audiences, including the Council of Ministers of the Organization of African Unity (OAU), in Algiers, and the nineteen members of the North Atlantic Treaty Organization (NATO) and twenty-five European partners that jointly composed the Euro-Atlantic Partnership Forum, in Brussels. Fowler's message was strongly reinforced publicly by several of the organizations with which he met. For example, the OAU Council of Ministers adopted a formal decision in July 1999 reaffirming "the unwavering support of the OAU for the . . . Security Council resolutions" regarding UNITA and appealing "to all Member States to strenuously work for the implementation of all United Nations Security Council resolutions, especially those related to sanctions against UNITA." In addition, the Southern African Development Community (SADC) reaffirmed its engagement on the issue of UNITA sanctions, and the presidency of the European Union issued a statement underscoring the Union's intention "to intensify its efforts to prevent UNITA from continuing the civil war in Angola in persistent defiance of Security Council resolutions" and supporting the actions for the Council's Angola sanctions committee.[6]

In a public briefing to the Security Council following his May and July 1999 travels, Fowler indicated that he had been able "to convey the fact that many people in many places are now much more aware of both the fact and purpose of these sanctions and are taking them seriously." He concluded that the sanctions were beginning to be taken seriously.[7] Fowler and Heinbecker engaged in extensive outreach activities throughout the remainder of Canada's chairmanship of the Angola sanctions committee, including further travel to that end in Africa, Europe, and North America. Both stated clearly and repeatedly their belief that sanctions were becoming better known, that the importance the Council attached to their effective implementation was becoming better understood, and that the sanctions were at last beginning to have real impact.

Establishing Alliances

Second, Fowler sought to collaborate with international governmental and nongovernmental organizations and with the business sector in improving the impact of the sanctions against UNITA. For example, a meeting with the subregional bureau of the International Police Organization (Interpol) in Harare in May 1999 was followed by extensive consultations at Interpol's headquarters in July 1999 and by further collaboration thereafter, including the seconding of Interpol personnel to investigative bodies established by the Security Council in support of the sanctions against UNITA.

Collaboration with external bodies was most extensive with regard to the sanctions relating to diamonds, the newest, highest-profile, and perhaps most technically complex component of the sanctions regime against UNITA. UNITA's illegal diamond sales, which were estimated to have generated more than U.S.$3 billion in revenues in the 1990s, had enabled it to pursue its military campaign.

Fowler's travels in Africa and Europe in May and July 1999 included extensive consultations with the diamond sector on steps that could be taken to prevent diamonds from fueling armed conflict. In many instances these were the first detailed discussions Fowler's interlocutors had had on the issue of conflict diamonds. Fowler met repeatedly with the chairman, managing director, and board members of De Beers, with executives and their representatives from other leading diamond companies in Angola and the Democratic Republic of Congo, and with senior officers of the International Diamond Manufacturers Association (IDMA) and the World Federation of Diamond Bourses (WFDB). He met also with ministers and senior officials responsible for minerals, mines, and the economy in Angola, Belgium, Botswana, the Democratic Republic of Congo, South Africa, and Zambia; with leaders of the parastatal diamond operations in Angola, Botswana, Namibia, and South Africa; and with leaders of diamond exchanges and industry associations in Belgium and the Netherlands. Close consultation with the diamond sector by Fowler, Heinbecker, and their staff continued throughout Canada's tenure.

From the outset a carrot-and-stick approach was pursued, emphasizing determination to reduce the revenues that could be derived from conflict diamonds but also making clear the wish to avoid collateral damage to the legitimate diamond trade. By July 1999 Fowler was able to report to the Security Council that he had received evidence and assurance that the diamond industry wished to be part of the solution rather than the problem, "not just because it is the right thing to do nor because it is the law, but because to do otherwise is so manifestly not in the business interests of the industry."[8]

Proceedings at the World Diamond Congress of July 2000 reflected the swiftness with which the diamond industry, and the public, had become seized of the conflict-diamond issue. In July 1999 the IDMA had agreed to Fowler's suggestion that the issue of Angola sanctions be included on the agenda of the congress, which was to be held in Antwerp twelve months later. In fact, the World Diamond Congress was dominated by the Angola conflict-diamond issue and saw the decision by the diamond industry to create a World Diamond Council to help tackle that issue. In his keynote address to the congress, Fowler concluded that the diamond sanctions against UNITA were working and that the ongoing efforts of the diamond industry had had a significant impact in achieving these results.[9]

The formal recommendations that Fowler tabled following his travels in May and July 1999 emphasized the need for cooperation among government and industry in devising standardized diamond import and export procedures. Following his travels to Africa in May 1999, Fowler called for close interaction between the Security Council and key companies and industry councils to devise practical measures, including "a requirement that all diamond-producing countries introduce standardized and credible certificates of origin." Following his travels in Africa and Europe in July 1999, Fowler recommended that "interested Member States, including in particular those that export or import diamond, should work together to harmonize procedures and documentation for the import and export of rough diamonds . . . in consultation with the diamond industry.'"[10]

These recommendations were reinforced by an investigative panel of experts on Angola sanctions (outlined below), which in March 2000 recommended that "a conference of experts convene for the purpose of determining a system of controls that would allow for increased transparency and accountability in the control of diamonds from the source of origin to the European diamond exchanges."[11] Fowler's discussions with government and diamond industry representatives in May and July 1999 and the subsequent recommendations by Fowler and the panel of experts contributed directly to the decision of the South African government to convene in May 2000 a technical forum in Kimberley to develop more effective rough-diamond export arrangements and controls. These decisions and recommendations also contributed to the decision of the British government to convene a meeting in London the following month of representatives of countries that import rough diamonds with the objective of devising practical measures to tighten government controls and industry self-regulation on a worldwide basis. It was upon the basis of these two meetings that the Kimberley process emerged.

The Security Council's reengagement on the diamond sanctions against UNITA also led to an initiative by the British and U.S. governments at the outset to place the conflict-diamond issue on the agenda of the Group of Eight (G8) industrialized countries at the summit and foreign ministers' meeting in Japan in July 2000. The British and South African governments subsequently took the lead in placing the issue of conflict diamonds on the agenda of the UN General Assembly.

Fowler, and later Heinbecker, also worked closely with advocacy organizations and urged the diamond industry to do the same. Three nongovernmental organizations played especially important roles in generating public interest in the conflict-diamond issue: Global Witness, which published an important analysis of conflict diamonds in Angola *(A Rough Trade: The Role of Companies and Governments in the Angolan Conflict)* in December 1998; Human Rights Watch, which included detailed material on conflict diamonds within a broader report on Angola sanctions *(Angola Unravels: The Rise and Fall of the Lusaka Peace Process)* in September 1999; and Partnership Africa-Canada, which published a detailed report on conflict diamonds in Sierra Leone *(The Heart of the Matter: Sierra Leone, Diamonds, and Human Security)* in January 2000. The first of these, the Global Witness report, was published the month before Canada assumed the chairmanship of the Angola sanctions committee. The implicit threat it conveyed—that nongovernmental organizations might seek to mobilize consumer opinion against so-called conflict diamonds—served to reinforce Fowler's explicit threat of UN action against violators of the Council's diamond sanctions against UNITA.

Creating Instruments

Third, Fowler and Heinbecker sought to transform the institutional arrangements for the implementation of Council-imposed targeted sanctions through the creation of monitoring arrangements. A recommendation by the Secretary-General in February 1999 that the Security Council undertake studies "to trace violations in armed trafficking, oil supplies and the diamond trade, as well as the movement of UNITA funds" led to a more ambitious initiative: the establishment, with the adoption on May 7, 1999, of Resolution 1237, of two expert panels, later amalgamated into one. The amalgamated panel was mandated to collect information and investigate reports, including through visits to the countries concerned, relating to the violation of the measures imposed against UNITA with respect to arms and related matériel, petroleum and petroleum products, and diamonds and the movement of UNITA funds as specific in the relevant resolutions and information on military assistance, including mercenaries; to identify parties aiding and abetting the violations of the above-mentioned measures; and to recommend measures to end such violations and to improve the implementation of these measures.

The ten-member panel of experts on violations of Security Council sanctions against UNITA was chaired by Ambassador Anders Mollander of Sweden and included experts from Botswana, China, France, Namibia, the Russian Federation, South Africa, Switzerland, the United States, and Zimbabwe. The panel convened in August 1999. Panel members undertook extensive investigations in almost thirty countries. In addition, in January 2000 Fowler and two panel members conducted more than fifteen hours of interviews in Luanda with UNITA defectors, including a general formerly responsible for UNITA's logistics and a colonel formerly responsible for UNITA's communications.[12] Their testimony was among the sources of information used to corroborate information gathered by the panel of experts and also confirmed that UNITA fighters had deliberately shot down two UN aircraft in December 1998 and January 1999. In March the panel tabled a detailed report that identified sanctions violators, including at the highest level, and set out thirty-nine recommendations for action.[13] The panel's strategy of "naming and shaming" initially was strongly opposed by some UN member states, including one or two Council members who perceived their own interests to be affected indirectly, but the strategy soon came to be accepted and, later, replicated.

On April 18, 2000, the Security Council undertook, through Resolution 1295, "to consider appropriate action in accordance with the Charter of the United Nations in relation to States it determines to have violated the measures contained in [its] resolutions" regarding UNITA. This was the first time the Council had explicitly threatened to take enforcement action against a member state that had violated sanctions it had imposed. The Council's decision in this regard was to be informed by substantial bodies of information: first, the report of the panel of experts; second, any additional information that states might make available; and third, the additional findings of a new investigating body, a five-member independent monitoring mechanism established through the same resolution. In order both to ensure and to demonstrate impartiality and objectivity the members of the monitoring mechanism—Ambassador Juan Larrain of Chile as chairman and members from Senegal, Sweden, the United Kingdom, and Zimbabwe—were different from those of the panel of experts and were appointed through a different process. The objective, Fowler said, was to provide all states with an opportunity to answer the allegations of the panel, to end sanctions violations where they had occurred, and to bring their actions into conformity with the clearly articulated will of the international community.[14] The conclusions of the monitoring mechanism, tabled through seven reports over the course of a thirty-five-month period, were consistent with those of the panel of experts.[15]

In the closing weeks of Canada's two-year (1999–2000) term on the Security Council, Heinbecker pursued a further institutional innovation that remains under consideration within the Security Council: the creation of a permanent body to monitor the implementation of the Security Council's targeted sanctions instead of the ad hoc arrangements currently in place. Both the panel of experts and the monitoring mechanism had concluded that there was a very real risk that when the focus had been turned off, UNITA and its partners would go back to doing business as usual and rearm.[16] The monitoring mechanism drew a broader conclusion in asserting that "there is no doubt that, when . . . sanctions are monitored and violations investigated, and the Governments, authorities or individuals implicated in those violations receive public exposure, sanctions have an impact and become a real instrument of peace. Mere vigilance over a sanctions regime, moreover, constitutes a deterrent that also contributes to increasing its efficiency."[17] Fowler, Heinbecker, and their successor, Richard Ryan, agreed that continued vigilance was required if UNITA was to be deprived of its military capacity and if targeted sanctions were to be made to work, but this view has still to be acted upon by the Security Council.[18] Heinbecker also believed that the existing ad hoc approach was inefficient both on financial and administrative grounds and in terms of the ability to make use of the information gleaned from various investigations.

The Extension of the Angola Model

When Fowler addressed the World Diamond Congress in July 2000, he underscored the exceptional attention the Security Council had accorded to breaking the link between natural resources and armed conflict. Two sanctions regimes relating to diamonds were in place: the measures against UNITA contained in Resolution 1173 (1998), and those imposed against the Revolutionary United Front (RUF) rebel force in Sierra Leone through Resolution 1306 (2000). In addition, three investigative bodies had been established by the Council on the model of the panel of experts: the monitoring mechanism on UNITA; a panel of experts on the implementation of the Resolution 1306 sanctions against the RUF in Sierra Leone; and a panel of experts, initiated by France, on the illegal exploitation of natural resources and other forms of wealth in the Democratic Republic of Congo, established by a presidential statement on June 2, 2000[19]—the only such body that was not associated with a sanctions regime and, consequently, was unattached to any of the Council's sanctions committees.

The Council sought to ensure that its various attempts to break the links between natural resources and armed conflict were mutually reinforcing. For example, the conceptual framework for the panel of experts indicated that the two vice chairmen of the Angola sanctions committee would be associated with the panel and that "such association would have the incidental advantage of ensuring that any relevant information obtained in the course of the expert panels' work could be brought to the attention" of the two sanctions committees they chaired, on Rwanda and Sierra Leone.[20] Equally, in briefing the Council following his travels in May and July 1999, Fowler emphasized his hope that the collaborative partnerships he was putting in place—for example, with Interpol—"also might serve our collective interests in the Council with regard to other sanctions regimes in other places."[21]

Similarly, in imposing diamond sanctions against the RUF rebel force in Sierra Leone, the Security Council carefully applied the lessons that had been learned in trying to give effect to similar sanctions against UNITA. Hearings were convened in summer 2000 so that expert advice could be solicited. The diamond sanctions against the RUF were eventually introduced in two stages in order to avoid the difficulties that had initially been experienced in Angola with regard to the quality of government-issued certificates of origin. Resolution 1306 of July 5, 2000, thus "imposed a comprehensive embargo on diamond exports from Sierra Leone, with provision for the exemption of diamonds certified by the Government of Sierra Leone once the details of the certification arrangements have been agreed."

Support for the Security Council's work on the economic aspects of armed conflicts was expressed at the highest level. Resolution 1318 of September 7, 2000, adopted following a high-level debate involving heads of state and government, expressed the Council's commitment to "continue to take resolute action in areas where the illegal exploitation and trafficking of high-volume commodities contributes to the escalation or continuation of conflict." In the course of the Council's high-level Millennium debate, four heads of state and government encouraged Council action in this area.

Assessing Results

Did the sanctions against UNITA succeed in their objectives? The question cannot be answered definitively, but Fowler, Heinbecker, and Ryan and the members of the panel of experts and the monitoring mechanism were of the view that sanctions had had a real impact. Perhaps more important, the parties to the conflict in Angola were agreed that sanctions had helped to end the war. In a public statement at a meeting at the House of Lords in London in March 2002, Angola's minister of external relations, João Bernardo de Miranda, stated that the sanctions had played a direct role in bringing about the cease-fire. Statements in private by the UNITA leadership conveyed a similar view. The sanctions had curtailed UNITA's ability to pursue its objectives through military means, by choking off UNITA's access to funds and military equipment and thereby impairing its ability to resupply and recover from a series of military setbacks inflicted by the Angolan armed forces.

The Security Council's efforts to implement the sanctions may have had a broader impact as well. Fowler's initial travel took place against the backdrop of rising tensions between Angola and Zambia, in the course of which several explosions had taken place in Lusaka.[22] A senior member of President Levy Mwanawasa's government in Zambia subsequently expressed the view that the Security Council's intervention in 1999–2000, in the form of the report of the panel of experts, had played a key role in averting a war between Angola and Zambia.

Can the success of the sanctions against UNITA be replicated? Yes, provided a united Security Council strongly supports, in both word and deed, the implementation of those sanctions, and if the sanctions form part of a broad strategy of international diplomatic engagement and pressure. Ongoing monitoring of the implementation of the sanctions, through an ad hoc or permanent investigations panel mandated by the Council to identify the sources and methods of violations of the sanctions, is especially important in this regard. So, too, is a clear indication by the Council of its readiness to take action in instances where the sanctions are found to have been violated.

Notes

1. S/PV.4673, December 18, 2002.

2. See, for example, S/PV.4113, March 15, 2000; and S/PV.4027, July 29, 1999.

3. S/1999/644, June 4, 1999, annex.

4. S/1999/829, July 28, 1999, annex.

5. S/PV.4027, July 29, 1999.

6. S/1999/829, apps. 2–3.

7. S/PV.4027.

8. Ibid.

9. Address by Ambassador Robert Fowler, World Diamond Congress, Antwerp, July 18, 2000, www.un.int/canada/html/s-18july2000fowler.htm.

10. S/1999/644, annex; S/1999/829, annex; S/PV.4027.

11. S/2000/203, March 10, 2000, annex; S/PV.4113.

12. S/PV.4090, January 18, 2000.

13. S/2000/203.

14. S/PV.4129, April 18, 2000.

15. S/2000/1026, October 25, 2000; S/2000/1225, Corr.1, and Corr.2 of December 21, 2000, February 23, 2001, and March 8, 2001; S/2001/363, April 18, 2001; S/2001/966, October 12, 2001; S/2002/486, April 26, 2002; S/2002/1119, October 16, 2002; and S/2002/1339, December 10, 2002.

16. See, for example, S/2000/203, annex, para. 183.

17. S/2002/1119.

18. See, for example, S/PV.4113.

19. S/PRST/2000/20, June 2, 2000.

20. S/1999/509, May 4, 1999.

21. S/PV.4027.

22. S/1999/644, annex; S/1999/829.

14

Weapons of Mass Destruction: The Iraqi Case

PASCAL TEIXEIRA DA SILVA

From the creation of the United Nations in 1945 to 1991, the Security Council had not been involved in actual issues of disarmament, in particular with regard to weapons of mass destruction (WMD). In the context of Iraq's invasion of Kuwait and subsequent decisions taken after the Gulf War coalition had freed Kuwait and reestablished the legitimate authorities, the Security Council adopted measures that for the first time provided for the destruction of a country's WMD and their delivery systems and the establishment of an ongoing monitoring aimed at preventing the reconstitution of prohibited programs.

The uniqueness of the event—it was the first instance since the founding of the UN in which one member state sought to completely overpower and annex another—explained the uniqueness of the measures taken by the Security Council. The rationale behind the focus on WMD and ballistic missiles was due to Iraq's record with regard to the effective use of such weapons (chemical weapons against Iran and the Kurdish population, ballistic missiles against Iran, the United States, and Israel), to the potential threat they represent for the neighboring countries and the whole region (including Israel), and to the general concern on proliferation.

The purpose of this chapter is to show that the initial objectives and rules of the game established by the Security Council encountered problems due to Iraq's reluctance to cooperate, as well as deadlocks in the disarmament process. Confronted with these challenges, the Security Council tried different ways to secure Iraq's full compliance in a context of growing divergence among its members, in particular the permanent five (P-5). The use of force in December 1998 (Operation Desert Fox) complicated rather than eased the situation. Then the Council sought new approaches to achieve the same goals, but none produced definitive results. Finally, the threat to use force permitted the resumption of the disarmament process, but Council members strongly disagreed as to whether the actual use of force was the sole timely and indispensable response to Iraq's behavior, and whether it had other motivations extraneous to the Council's objectives.

Setting Out the Objectives, 1991

When Resolution 686, which brought a provisional end to the hostilities in Iraq, was being negotiated, the UK tried to introduce references to the elimination of WMD. The other permanent members discarded this proposal for different reasons. Then, as the P-5 started to consider the elements of a comprehensive resolution (later adopted as Resolution 687), the UK reintroduced the objective of destroying Iraq's stock of biological and chemical weapons and missiles and devising a mechanism to prevent it from acquiring new capabilities. The United States added the need to put Iraq's nuclear program under the control of the International Atomic Energy Agency (IAEA). The Soviet Union did not object to the latter objective but, together with France and China, underscored the regional dimension of such measures (in particular with regard to Israel's nuclear capabilities). The United States wanted to use the lifting of sanctions—in particular the oil embargo—as leverage to secure Iraq's compliance, though France, Russia, and China contended that economic sanctions should be linked only with the objectives set out in the resolutions adopted in August 1990 in the wake of Kuwait's invasion by Iraq. In the negotiation, these same three countries managed to introduce into the resolution a reference to the wider need to rid the entire Middle East of all WMD as well as to the possibility of waiving the oil embargo to purchase humanitarian goods. But the most important element of this groundbreaking resolution is that its acceptance by Iraq created the conditions for a cease-fire.

Resolution 687, together with Resolutions 707 and 715, sets out Iraq's obligations and the international community's responsibilities. Iraq must declare the locations, amounts, and types of all its prohibited weapons; agree to destroy, remove, or render them harmless under international supervision; agree to on-site inspections and allow international inspectors immediate, unconditional, and unrestricted access to areas, facilities, equipment, records, and Iraqi officials; and undertake not to use, develop, construct, or acquire these prohibited items. For its part, the UN Special Commission (UNSCOM)—the subsidiary body established by the Council to deal with biological, chemical, and missile weapons—and the IAEA had to verify Iraq's declarations; destroy or supervise the destruction of the prohibited items; and establish and run an ongoing monitoring and verification (OMV) system aimed at ensuring that Iraq does not reconstitute the prohibited programs. This OMV, which required a two-track approach—an on-site monitoring and an import-export control mechanism—was to continue for as long as the Security Council so decided.

Implementation Without Cooperation, 1991–1996

The very logic of Resolution 687 is that Iraq declares, discloses, and provides evidence, then UNSCOM and the IAEA verify. It requires not only Iraq's acceptance of the rules but also Iraq's active cooperation with these two bodies. Unfortunately Iraq never abided by its obligations in good faith, instead adopting a reverse logic: UNSCOM and the IAEA search, then Iraq explains. Thus the history of eight years of relations between Iraq and the inspection and monitoring bodies (1991–1998) was one of constant disappointments: Iraq accepted, though with reluctance, Resolution 687, then balked for several months at the OMV plans established by Resolution 715, of which Baghdad contested the legality; it produced a series of declarations that proved to be incomplete and insincere; it hid the very existence of WMD programs (biological) and many sites and much documentation; it unilaterally destroyed numerous prohibited items, thus preventing UNSCOM and the IAEA from accounting for them in a reliable way and complicating their task; it moved equipment and materials subject to monitoring and tampered with monitoring devices; and it put up innumerable obstacles to UNSCOM's and the IAEA's work and never granted full and unrestricted access as required by the Security Council. Throughout repeated crises of different magnitude and numerous negotiations with the inspection bodies, Iraq pledged cooperation and sincerity but rarely lived up to its commitments to the extent promised.

Confronted with these repeated challenges, the Security Council stuck to its objectives but had a limited number of options at its disposal to change Iraq's behavior. In a large number of press statements, presidential statements, and resolutions, the Council condemned Iraq's lack of cooperation and noncompliance, sometimes qualified as material breach of its obligations; it reiterated and strengthened the demands made to Iraq; and it reiterated, reinforced, and specified the rights and modalities of action of UNSCOM and the IAEA, expressed constant support for these two bodies, and backed their high-level missions and dialogue with the Iraqi authorities to try to resolve differences and defuse the crisis.

Beyond that, the Council had a difficult choice: accommodating Iraq's complaints that its sovereignty, territorial integrity, national security, or dignity were infringed—a move that could undermine the efficiency of the disarmament process—or using the stick of additional sanctions or military force—a solution that could lead to the breakup of the international monitoring. In June 1996, after a series of incidents during which Iraq refused UNSCOM access to designated sites, the Council accepted, though with U.S. and UK reluctance, the declaration signed by UNSCOM's executive chairman and the Iraqi first deputy prime minister recognizing Iraq's concerns with regard to its sovereignty and national security and paving the way for working out special—that is, softer—modalities for inspecting so-called sensitive sites.

On several occasions, the Council warned Iraq that failure to comply would be regarded as a "material breach" of its obligations and lead to "serious consequences." There were differences among Council members as to what it actually meant. The United States and the UK have always contended that, since the acceptance by Iraq of its obligations under Resolution 687 create the conditions for a formal cease-fire, a material breach of these obligations revives the authorization to use force given by Resolution 678 to the coalition to uphold international law.[1] France, Russia, and China hold the view that, in accordance with paragraph 34 of Resolution 687, it is for the Council to take the decision to resort to force. Between 1991 and December 1998, force was used only in one instance (January 1993) directly and explicitly linked with the failure by Iraq to cooperate with UNSCOM and the IAEA.

Deadlock: The Cumulative
Effect of Suspicion and Disincentive

From 1991 to 1997, UNSCOM's and the IAEA's achievements were impressive. They uncovered the bulk of Iraq's programs of WMD and destroyed, or verified the destruction of, many more prohibited items than during the Gulf War. But despite this unprecedented result, the disarmament process launched in 1991 found itself in a deadlock for various reasons:

• *Margin of error.* The Security Council set out two complementary goals: one retrospective, aimed at ridding Iraq of its existing WMD and ballistic missiles; the other forward-looking, aimed at ensuring that Iraq does not reconstitute these prohibited capabilities. The two goals are intertwined: the more we know about the past and remaining capabilities, the more the OMV is effective; and the OMV should be capable of shedding light on areas not uncovered by the disarmament activities. Given the dubious circumstances in which prohibited items were unilaterally destroyed and, furthermore, the very nature of WMD capabilities, in particular in biological and chemical areas where the border between civilian and military activities is blurred, it is almost impossible to determine with 100 percent certainty that Iraq has completely eliminated its WMD.[2] The mechanism established by Resolution 687 could have worked effectively had not Iraq often played hide-and-seek. So the inspection bodies and members of the Security Council became suspicious and more demanding. The more they doubted the sincerity of Iraq, the narrower was the acceptable margin of uncertainty. But this dynamic could lead to an endless process.

• *Duration of the disarmament process.* The time frame set by the Council in Resolution 687 was tight. But the process dragged on for many years. The oil embargo and the resulting impossibility for Iraq to purchase freely all goods its society required became over the years a terrible punishment more for the population than for the regime. The Security Council became aware of these practical and political drawbacks and adopted measures (Resolution 706 in 1991, Resolution 986 in 1995) to try to alleviate the harshness of this comprehensive embargo, the so-called oil-for-food mechanism, which allowed the sale of Iraqi oil to finance the purchase of humanitarian goods through a UN escrow account. The implementation of the waiver, as justified as it may be from the humanitarian point of view, paradoxically created a double disincentive. On the one hand, the leverage of economic sanctions would lose its sharpness vis-à-vis Iraq; on the other hand, it could give Iraq the impression that, though the mechanism is described as temporary, the Council was not ready to implement fully Resolution 687 (including the lifting of sanctions), and hence envisages a prolonged stalemate while trying to reduce the humanitarian effects. That is why Iraq never made use of the possibilities offered by Resolution 706, judging that it had satisfied all its disarmament obligations. Five years later, it took ten months for Iraq to accept Resolution 986.

• *Lack of flexibility.* Herein lies another vicious circle: the oil embargo could be lifted only when all disarmament obligations were fulfilled. Thus no partial progress can be rewarded, although Resolution 687 includes the possibility to "reduce or lift" the sanctions against the import of civilian goods by Iraq, "in the light of [its] policies and practices."[3] In fact, the Security Council granted exemptions to the embargo only for humanitarian purposes. The issue of using carrots in addition to sticks was nevertheless raised, for example when France proposed in 1993 to examine to what extent the fulfillment of an additional part of Iraq's obligations could lead to an easing of the sanctions regime, or in 1994 the proposal for a provisional lifting of the oil embargo six months after the beginning of the OMV system, provided that until that time Iraq continued to cooperate without incident with UNSCOM. France stressed that it was a dangerous disincentive for Iraq not to recognize its progress. These ideas were not accepted, with the United States and the UK insisting that they would unduly reduce the pressure on Iraq to comply fully with its remaining obligations.

• *Questioning UNSCOM's integrity.* This fourth problem was experienced particularly in 1997–1998. This subsidiary body of the Security Council was an institution entrusted with a technical, though complicated and often sensitive, mandate. Its personnel, recruited on criteria of competence, had to abide by the rules of international civil servants set out in Article 100 of the UN Charter. But UNSCOM, confronted with Iraq's lack of sincerity and cooperation, had to be assisted by member states able and willing to do so: intelligence information flowed between UNSCOM and member states in both directions; UNSCOM inspectors were briefed and debriefed by their governments' intelligence services; and information gathered by UNSCOM was forwarded to third countries. These practices[4] undermined UNSCOM's credibility vis-à-vis not only Iraq—which accused it of being a nest of spies[5]—but also some Council members.

Mounting Pressure: From the "Light at the End of the Tunnel" to the Use of Force, 1997–1998

All these difficulties were exacerbated in 1997–1998. Iraq increased the obstacles put to UNSCOM's work and interrupted several times the cooperation with UNSCOM, in a context of growing mutual mistrust between Iraq and the UN and of eroding consensus among the P-5, and despite efforts by the Secretary-General to help defuse the crises. Consequently UNSCOM was no longer making any progress. The Council had to find ways to achieve the objectives it had set itself in 1991.

The question of access remained a bone of contention. Again UNSCOM and the Council, while reiterating the principles, accepted to take into account Iraq's concerns. The modalities for the so-called sensitive sites were revised in December 1997–January 1998. Nevertheless a new problem arose at that time with the so-called presidential sites, and in March 1998 the Council endorsed in its Resolution 1154, despite obvious U.S. displeasure, the memorandum of understanding signed by the UN Secretary-General and Iraq's deputy prime minister, Tarek Aziz, providing again for special modalities for inspecting eight "presidential sites."

Council members were confronted with a dilemma: how to foster Iraq's cooperation and restore a minimum level of confidence without undermining the corpus of obligations established in 1991. The formula "light at the end of the tunnel," used at the time, illustrated this endeavor. Several attempts were made. On multiple occasions, the Council stressed that, if Iraq did what the resolutions required, it would then act accordingly, in particular by making the transition from investigation to monitoring and by lifting the sanctions. These reiterations were seen as a means to convince Iraq that it was worth playing by the rules.

In the same vein, in 1998 Russia, with the support of France and China, pushed hard to get a decision by the Council, on the basis of the IAEA's conclusions that it had a coherent picture of Iraq's nuclear program, to "close the nuclear file" and to ask the IAEA "to dedicate its resources to implement the OMV." But the United States and the UK opposed such a move on the grounds that not all remaining (though not essential) questions were clarified, though the Council had recognized that "within the framework of its OMV responsibilities, the IAEA will continue to exercise its right to investigate any aspect of Iraq's clandestine nuclear program." The Council's inability to take such a decision at the end of July 1998 is undoubtedly the main reason why Iraq once more suspended its cooperation with the IAEA and UNSCOM a few days later.

At the point reached by the disarmament process in 1997–1998, the need became apparent to better assess the situation in all relevant areas in order to facilitate its completion. To this effect, it was agreed in December 1997 to hold technical evaluation meetings between Iraq and UNSCOM. The same démarche inspired the concept of "comprehensive review" proposed by the Secretary-General in August 1998 and endorsed by the Council. The Council agreed to assess Iraq's compliance and agreed that "it would outline clearly in each phase remaining steps to be taken by Iraq to fulfil its obligations and would establish a likely time-frame for this purpose, assuming full Iraqi cooperation."[6] Unfortunately the Council could not implement this commitment since it linked the start of the comprehensive review with the return by Iraq to full cooperation, which was not confirmed by UNSCOM on December 15, 1998, just when Operation Desert Fox was launched.

In a situation of comprehensive economic sanctions, there are very few additional measures short of military force at the disposal of the Security Council. In June and October 1997, confronted with repeated crises and instances of lack of cooperation by Iraq, the Security Council decided, in Resolutions 1134 and 1137, to suspend the review of sanctions (see note 5) and to impose a travel ban on the Iraqi officials responsible for the noncompliance. Four Council members abstained on Resolution 1134 on the grounds that this could aggravate tensions. Indeed, Iraq reacted immediately by expelling UNSCOM's personnel.

Given the precedent of 1993, discussions among Council members—in particular the P-5—often focused on whether the terms "material breach" and "serious consequences" could be interpreted as an implicit authorization to use force. Sometimes these discussions resulted in avoiding the lethal combination of both formulas or in softening the traditional language.

Force was eventually used in December 1998 by the United States and the UK. The Council did not authorize it,[7] and some Council members expressed various degrees of disapproval. Operation Desert Fox lasted four days. Its objectives were to destroy targets linked with the WMD capabilities and to force Iraq to yield to the Council's demands. If it succeeded to some extent on the former, it definitely failed on the latter, for the immediate outcome of these air strikes was Iraq's refusal to let UNSCOM and the IAEA return,[8] as well as its decision to cut off all cooperation with the UN other than the oil-for-food program. From the point of view of Resolution 687, this resulted in a practical dead end, for the Iraqi threat did not diminish but increased with the absence of international control on the ground. Nevertheless, air strikes have continued since December 1998 in the no-fly zones as a way to exert pressure on Iraq and undermine its military capabilities.

The Search for New Approaches: From the
Suspension of Sanctions to "Smart Sanctions," 1999–2001

On January 12, 1999, France argued that nothing could replace international monitoring on the ground and that Iraq would not accept the return of monitoring if the sanctions regime remained unchanged. It proposed that a reinforced OMV should address the remaining disarmament questions in exchange for the lifting of civilian sanctions, provided that the financial transactions between Iraq and its suppliers and clients were transparent. These ideas received support from several Council members. Others (the United States, the UK, the Netherlands) had strong reservations vis-à-vis this new approach, insisting that a reinforced OMV was reliable only when there was a credible baseline of disarmament and that it would be dangerous to let Iraq be the master of its financial resources. Slovenia launched the idea of suspension of sanctions, in order to offer the kind of incentive and flexibility that had been lacking to date. The procedural solution proposed by Canada was the establishment of three panels of experts chaired by Brazilian ambassador Celso Amorim, including one on WMD issues tasked to provide the Council with an assessment of the situation and with recommendations on how to reestablish an effective disarmament/OMV regime in Iraq. This panel opened a way out of the impasse in concluding that "although important elements still have to be resolved, the bulk of Iraq's proscribed weapons programmes has been eliminated." It referred also to "a possible 'point of impasse' in the further investigation of these issues under the current procedures" and concluded that "although disarmament and monitoring address different dimensions of the broader problematique of disarmament/reacquisition of proscribed weapons, both can be implemented through the use of the same—or similar—tools . . . and the OMV is not incompatible with the continuing search for satisfactory resolution of outstanding elements from proscribed weapons programs."[9] The panel proposed to revamp the inspection and monitoring body in order to rectify past mistakes. Ambassador Amorim urged the Council to devise a bold and comprehensive approach if it considered that the status quo was not acceptable. But the Council was divided on the extent to which it should endorse the panel's suggestions—France, Russia, China, and the nonaligned being ready to subscribe to all of them, the United States, the UK, and the Netherlands being reluctant to go that far.

Resolution 1284, which was negotiated over several months in 1999 on the basis of the panel report and concrete proposals made by the UK, Russia, Canada, and France, was a compromise between diverging views. The concept of a reinforced system of OMV that addresses unresolved disarmament issues was endorsed, but the disarmament tasks set out in Resolution 687, though prioritized, remained to be completed. A new body—the UN Monitoring, Verification, and Inspection Commission (UNMOVIC)—replaced UNSCOM: the recruitment, status, training, and behavior of its personnel were to be consistent with the UN standards and rules of impartiality and professionalism; the decisionmaking process reflected more collegiality; and relations with members states were clarified (one-way traffic for intelligence information). The sanctions were not lifted, but a large part of the sanctions (oil export, and import of goods except weapons and dual-use items) might be suspended for a renewable period of six months if Iraq cooperated with UNMOVIC and the IAEA, in particular in the implementation of the reinforced system of OMV, and if progress was made in the completion of the key remaining disarmament tasks identified by the two agencies. Resolution 687 demanded the complete disarmament as a condition for lifting the oil embargo—and experience had shown how difficult it was to attain that goal; Resolution 1284 offered an intermediary stage with the suspension only when key remaining disarmament tasks were dealt with. But on this last point the formulation was ambiguous and subject to different interpretations among Council members: the United States and the UK insisted on the completion of these tasks; Russia, France, and China insisted on progress in the completion. Lack of clarity remained also on the financial and operational measures to be taken when sanctions were suspended to ensure that Iraq did not acquire prohibited items (weapons and dual-use items). Nevertheless, the United States and the UK put the text to a vote on December 17, 1999, before a consensus was reached on these two outstanding issues, thus provoking the abstention of four Council members (Russia, China, France, and Malaysia).

Iraq refused to implement Resolution 1284. It was convinced that the sanctions would not be lifted (because the United States would not allow this as long as Saddam Hussein was in power), and that the suspension of sanctions, whose conditions were not attractive enough, was seen by Baghdad as another proof of the Council's unwillingness to lift them. Therefore it was better to have sanctions without inspections than to have sanctions and inspections. Furthermore, Iraq interpreted the division of the Security Council as a sign of lack of determination in the Council to implement its own decision. In fact, UNMOVIC was established and prepared itself but until November 2002 was not allowed to go to Iraq. Attempts made by Russia and France to clarify the modalities of suspension of sanctions were not successful, with the United States insisting that Iraq should first accept the return of inspectors. Although in November 2001 the

Council reaffirmed in Resolution 1382 "its commitment to a comprehensive settlement, including any clarification necessary for the implementation of resolution 1284," it did not live up to this renewed commitment, for another approach was being pursued.

Given Iraq's refusal to implement Resolution 1284 and the absence of any international inspection and monitoring system on the ground, the new U.S. administration formulated a new strategy aimed at countering Iraq's fairly successful efforts to circumvent the sanctions regime. The proposal made in early 2001—which was referred to as "smart sanctions"—consisted of a two-track approach: focusing the sanctions regime and the oil-for-food mechanism on the dual-use items, thus responding to the criticism that sanctions have a devastating humanitarian impact; and strengthening the physical control at the borders of Iraq. Together with ongoing air strikes carried out by the United States and the UK in the no-fly zones since December 1998, these measures were considered by the United States as the appropriate tools to "keep Saddam in his box." The measures envisaged to fight smuggling were practically and politically unrealistic, and the neighboring countries of Iraq were not ready to cooperate in their implementation for reasons of economic interest or vulnerability. There only remained the revamping of the oil-for-food mechanism aimed at facilitating the import of civilian goods and reducing the huge number of contracts put on hold by the United States and the UK. The other permanent members went along with this proposal, and the Council, in Resolutions 1382 and 1409, adopted a list of the dual-use items ("goods review list"), for which the importation by Iraq remains to be authorized by the sanctions committee. Such a wobbly "smart sanctions" resolution proved insufficient to counter Iraq's "alternative strategy" and to compensate for the absence of an international presence on the ground. The status quo was serving neither the Council's objectives nor peace and security in the region.

Upholding the Resolutions or Changing the Regime: Unity and Authority of the Security Council at Stake, 2002–2003

Several approaches and means have been used since 1998 to unblock the situation. But none had been pursued by the Council with the necessary clarity of objective and steadfastness of action, in the face of an Iraqi regime that was quick to use its advantage with every disagreement among Council members. This is why none has resolved the Iraqi question.

The situation dramatically changed in early 2002 when the United States clearly put regime change in Iraq at the top of its foreign policy agenda. This was not a completely new element in U.S. policy, but the events of September 11, 2001, created a different perception of how to deal with such threats as the proliferation of WMD. Though the goal of regime change was not in keeping with the Security Council's decisions, the first effect of this assertive stance was the resumption of the dialogue between Iraq and the United Nations in March 2002. But over three rounds of talks the Iraqi authorities did not accept UNMOVIC's and the IAEA's return to their territory. On September 12, 2002, in his address to the UN General Assembly, President George W. Bush warned Iraq that, unless it accepted to be peacefully disarmed, other means (i.e., force) would be used to uphold the objectives set by the Security Council and to secure international peace and security. Immediately thereafter Baghdad accepted the immediate and unconditional return of inspectors.

Then the United States argued that the inspection regime should be strengthened to give the international community the assurances it required, and that a clear signal should be sent to Iraq that no procrastination or dishonesty would be tolerated. Resolution 1441 of November 8, 2002, indeed reinforced the inspection regime in ending the special regimes for both "sensitive" and "presidential" sites and in establishing additional rights. But the Council did not endorse some other U.S. proposals that would have changed the peaceful and multilateral nature of the inspections. Under this resolution, Iraq had to provide "a currently accurate, full and complete declaration of all aspects of its programs to develop" WMD and missiles. This was a way not only to help UNMOVIC and the IAEA to do the so-called rebaselining[10] but also to provide Iraq with a last opportunity to state the whole truth. But the most important element of this resolution was the clear warning launched by the Council that it offered Iraq a last chance to comply with Council demands. Negotiations among Council members turned on how to strike a balance between the credibility of the threat to use force and the necessity to ensure that an eventual decision in this regard was consistent with the Council's criteria and authority. The initial U.S. draft authorized member states in advance to use force against Iraq in case of noncompliance. But a majority of Council members were not ready to accept such an automatic trigger. The final compromise preserved the Council's power: lies or omissions in the declaration and the lack of cooperation by Iraq with UNMOVIC and the IAEA as reported by them were to constitute a material breach that must be reported to, and assessed by, the Council so that it could take any decision it deemed necessary.

Resolution 1441 shifted the goals and methods emphasized by Resolution 1284. The latter aimed at containing and preventing the Iraqi WMD capabilities (through a reinforced OMV) and used incentives to this end (Iraq would be rewarded with the suspension of sanctions if it cooperated), whereas the only focus of Resolution 1441 was the complete disarmament and Iraq was not induced but threatened (force would be used if it did not cooperate fully). But the unanimous adoption of Resolution 1441 concealed the fact that Council members had divergent understandings of its meaning. The first concerns the relationship between inspections and cooperation. When Resolution 1441 was being negotiated, the United States and the UK insisted that the inspection regime should be strengthened while stressing the need for full, immediate, and active cooperation by Iraq. Both elements were deemed necessary and complementary. But as UNMOVIC and the IAEA were carrying out their mandates and developing their capabilities, the United States and the UK shifted the focus to Iraq's cooperation as the sole determining element to secure compliance. Therefore they regarded as futile the proposals made by France, Russia, and Germany in February 2003 to strengthen the inspections mechanism.

The second difference concerned the assessment of Iraq's cooperation. The United States and the UK stressed that even though the Security Council had demanded full cooperation, Iraq, since the passage of Resolution 1441, had failed to demonstrate its genuine will to rid itself of its WMD and yielded to pressure by making only partial concessions. However, France, Russia, and Germany emphasized that Resolution 1441 included no deadline, although they admitted that the process could not last forever. This is why they proposed in February 2003 that the Council adopt (as provided in Resolution 1284) the list of key remaining disarmament tasks, and set a tight though realistic timetable to achieve them, as a means to provide Council members with a common basis to measure Iraq's compliance. This was discarded by the United States and UK as a delaying step.

Third, the United States and the UK regarded the handing over by Iraq of proscribed weapons and equipment (such as the Al-Samud 2 missiles) not only as proof that Iraq had not told the truth earlier but also as the tip of the iceberg of its WMD. France, Russia, and Germany saw in this the demonstration that Resolution 1441 was bearing fruits.

Finally, despite the facts that UNMOVIC and the IAEA reported that Iraq was cooperating more actively, that progress was being made in the disarmament process, and that additional time was needed to complete it, the United States and the UK concluded that using force was the only means to secure full compliance and to overcome an Iraqi pattern of dissimulation and procrastination that they said had been confirmed. Although France, Germany, Russia, and China recognized that U.S. military pressure had forced the Iraqi regime to accept the return of inspectors, cooperate with them, and comply with disarmament obligations, they held the firm view that resorting to force should be the very last option once, on the basis of the inspectors' assessment, Resolution 1441 had evidently and definitely exhausted all its potential.

The United States, the UK, and Spain prepared a draft resolution stating that, on the basis of Resolution 1441, Iraq had failed to take the final opportunity to comply with its disarmament obligations. This text aimed at closing, in a negative way, the window of opportunity offered by the Security Council in Resolution 1441 and at securing from the Council a green light to use force. Given the opposition of five Council members (including three permanent members) and the reluctance of six others, an ultimatum mechanism giving Iraq only a few days to disarm was added. But this was not sufficient to get the support of a majority and overcome possible vetoes. On March 17, 2003, the cosponsors withdrew their draft and decided to take action solely on the basis of Resolutions 1441, 687, and 678.

This raised several questions. Given the restrictive conditions attached to the use of force in the UN Charter, can an authorization to use force be implicit and unspecified? Is the principle of proportionality respected, since it is questionable that the need to secure Iraq's compliance with its disarmament obligations requires the invasion and occupation of this country by the United States without any precise mandate from the international community? Did not WMD become, if not a pretense, at least only one of the many reasons for waging war against Iraq? Indeed, President Bush said on February 26, 2003, that in the post–September 11 context the United States should preempt the potential deadly combination of terrorists and WMD, and that ridding Iraq of Saddam Hussein's dictatorship could be the starting point of a process of democratization and regeneration in the entire Middle East. Such goals are obviously extraneous to any Security Council resolution.

Conclusion

The following lessons can be drawn from the Iraqi case:

- The concept of WMD and ballistic missiles to carry them covers very different problems that require different solutions. A unique set of criteria and procedures runs the risk of creating loopholes or deadlock.
- An efficient and credible inspection regime must rely not only on the active and genuine cooperation of the country concerned but also on a professional, intrusive, and rigorous mechanism.
- It is impossible to achieve 100 percent assurance that a country has disposed of all its WMD and ballistic missiles, especially its intellectual and industrial capabilities in this area. Therefore ongoing and reliable monitoring is the indispensable complementary tool to achieve that goal.
- A good balance must be struck between carrots and sticks: both should be credible and attainable and have the support of the whole Security Council.

- Unity and cohesion of the Security Council are key to the success of such an undertaking—for the definition of the objectives, the design of the instruments, and the decisions taken at all stages of the process. Diverging goals and strategies among Council members undermine the Council's leadership and effectiveness. And it is also essential that the Council live up to its own commitments.

Notes

1. But some argue that the use of force is authorized by Resolution 678 only for the purpose of achieving the goals set out in Resolution 660 and subsequent resolutions.

2. One of the three Amorim panels concluded that "some uncertainty is inevitable in any country-wide technical verification process which aims to prove the absence of readily concealable objects or activities. The extent to which such uncertainty is acceptable is a policy judgement. Both UNSCOM and IAEA have therefore been adopting a pragmatic approach which assumes that 100% of verification may be an unattainable goal." S/1999/356, March 30, 1999, sec. 27.

3. Paragraph 21 of Resolution 687 provides that these sanctions against the import of civilian goods by Iraq are to be reviewed every sixty days, "for the purpose of determining whether to reduce or lift [them]."

4. See, for example, William Rivers Pitt and Scott Ritter, *War on Iraq* (New York: Context Books, 2002), p. 55.

5. In October 1997 the government of Iraq denied entry to its territory, or access to sites designated for inspection, of UNSCOM officials on the grounds of their nationality.

6. Letter dated October 30, 1998, from the president of the Security Council to the Secretary-General.

7. The trigger used by the United States and the UK consisted of the combination of the general warning sent by Resolution 1154 ("any violation would have severest consequences for Iraq") and of the demand made by the Council that Iraq return to full cooperation (see press statement of November 15, 1998). The Security Council had no time to make the determination prior to the launching of air strikes by the United States and the UK. These two countries just relied on the report made by the executive chairman of UNSCOM, Richard Butler, who stated that there had not been "full cooperation" by Iraq.

8. At that time Iraq did not expel the inspectors, but the executive chairman of UNSCOM took the decision to withdraw them upon request by the United States and without prior notification to the Security Council.

9. See S/1999/356, March 30, 1999, secs. 25, 32, 33.

10. That is, the assessment of the situation on the ground, including inspections of sites registered by UNSCOM and the IAEA or declared by Iraq, and the reinstallation of all monitoring equipment.

15

Virtual Trusteeship

SIMON CHESTERMAN

The power of the United Nations Security Council to administer territory is not mentioned in the United Nations Charter. Nor, however, is peacekeeping, the formula that came to define UN military action. Here, as in many other areas of the Council's activities, practice has led theory, and the Charter has been shown to be a flexible—some would say malleable—instrument.

Writing in early 1995, chastened by the failed operation in Somalia, the failing operation in Bosnia and Herzegovina, and inaction in the face of the genocide in Rwanda, Secretary-General Boutros Boutros-Ghali issued a conservative supplement to his more optimistic 1992 statement in *An Agenda for Peace*.[1] The supplement noted that a new breed of intrastate conflicts presented the UN with challenges not encountered since the Congo operation of the early 1960s. A feature of these conflicts was the collapse of state institutions, especially the police and judiciary, meaning that international intervention had to extend beyond military and humanitarian tasks to include the "promotion of national reconciliation and the reestablishment of effective government." Nevertheless, Boutros-Ghali expressed caution against the UN assuming responsibility for law and order, or attempting to impose state institutions on unwilling combatants.[2] General Michael Rose, then commander of the UN Protection Force (UNPROFOR) in Bosnia, termed this form of mission creep "crossing the Mogadishu line."

Despite such cautious words, the UN by the end of 1995 had assumed responsibility for policing in Bosnia pursuant to the Dayton Accords. The following January, a transitional administration was established with temporary civil governance functions over the last Serb-held region of Croatia in Eastern Slavonia. In June 1999 the Security Council authorized an "interim" administration in Kosovo to govern part of what remains technically Yugoslav territory for an indefinite period; four months later a transitional administration was created with effective sovereignty over East Timor until independence. These expanding mandates continued a trend begun with the operations that exercised varying degrees of civilian authority in addition to supervising elections in Namibia in 1989 and Cambodia in 1993.

This expansion was part of a larger growth in activism by the Security Council through the 1990s, which showed itself willing to interpret internal armed conflicts, humanitarian crises, and even disruption to democracy as "threats to international peace and security" within the meaning of the UN Charter—and therefore warranting a military response under its auspices. This "new interventionism," however, was constrained by the inability of the United Nations to develop an independent military capacity; as a result, Council action was generally limited to circumstances that coincided with the national interests of a state or group of states that were prepared to lead.[3]

This chapter will consider the role of the Security Council in authorizing transitional administrations within this broader political framework. First, it will consider the nature of this evolution in Council practice. The term "evolution" is used advisedly, suggesting a process of natural selection inspired by essentially unpredictable events. Second, the chapter will briefly sketch out the context for each of the major operations in this area. Analysis of these operations tends to be chronological, reflecting the transformations over time of related policy. It is instructive, however, to look instead at the discrete reasons for which the Council has authorized different forms of transitional administration. Third, the very different role accorded to the UN in Afghanistan will be considered as a possible correction to the trend toward ever-expanding mandates identified here.

An underlying question to be examined is the tension between the increased *civilian* responsibilities of UN operations and the conventional wisdom that the United Nations cannot be entrusted with *military* command outside of traditional peacekeeping. It is frequently argued that unified command of both civilian and military components increases the chances for the success of such missions and that the lack of unified command has compromised them. In the Balkans, this led to inconsistent policies on law and order, including the reluctance to pursue war crimes suspects; in Afghanistan, the military objectives of U.S. forces occasionally put them directly at odds with the political objectives of the UN civilian mission. These increased civilian responsibilities continue to be handled largely by the Department of Peacekeeping Operations (DPKO); this suggests the extent to which the organizational structure of the UN has been forced to adapt to its new role. More broadly, these developments may herald a transformation in the politics of peacebuilding: just as the Council now provides legal authorization only for those enforcement actions that coincide with the willingness of certain key states to lead the military operation, it is possible that transitional administrations will be used to consolidate the peace as those key states move on to other battles.

Security Council Administration of Territory in Theory and in Practice

A measure of the speed with which the UN Interim Administration Mission in Kosovo was established is the name itself. UN operations typically operate with an acronym, but "UNIAMIK" was dismissed as too much of a mouthful. "UNIAK" sounded like a cross between "eunuch" and "maniac"—associations judged unlikely to help the mission. "UNMIK" was the final choice, having the benefits of being short, punchy, and clear. Only in English, however. Once the operation was on the ground, it was discovered that *anmik,* in the dialect of Albanian spoken in Kosovo, means "enemy." No one within the UN was aware of the confusion until it was too late, at which time instructions went out to pronounce the acronym "oon-mik."

As this shows, Council action in the area of transitional administration has been characterized by reaction and improvisation. This, together with the highly sensitive nature of the Kosovo conflict in particular, has hampered efforts to develop best practices for such operations or plan for future contingencies. In the same year that the Kosovo mission was established, for example, the United Nations conducted the referendum on East Timor's independence from Indonesia. Though many outsiders predicted a landslide vote in favor of independence and the probable outbreak of violence, staff within the Secretariat were unable (or believed themselves unable) to prepare for postreferendum contingencies that presumed the bad faith of the Indonesian security forces. More generally, many of the elements seen as crucial to the success of past operations—notably the UN Transitional Administration for Eastern Slavonia, Baranja, and Western Sirmium (UNTAES)—concern the ultimately political questions of formulating the mandate and exercising command and control over the military component of a mission. This section will consider the legal basis for the Council's authority in this area before moving on to the political context of the recent spate of operations.

That the Security Council might be required to administer a state or territory was in fact contemplated in the drafting of the UN Charter. At the San Francisco Conference, which led to the adoption of the Charter in 1945, Norway proposed to amend the Chapter VII enforcement powers of the Council to provide that it should, in special cases, temporarily assume the administration of a territory if administration by the occupant state itself represented a threat to the peace.[4] It appears that this was withdrawn out of a concern that the inclusion of such specific powers might be interpreted as suggesting that other powers not listed were implicitly excluded.[5]

The possibility assumed practical significance swiftly in two cases in 1947 that raised the possibility of Council administration: the Free Territory of Trieste, and Jerusalem. In the event, neither proposal was implemented. As with most of the Council's powers, transitional administration remained largely an intriguing possibility until after the conclusion of the Cold War. And as with the Council's practice in other areas, the manner in which this power has subsequently been exercised departed substantially from what was envisaged when the Charter was drafted.

There is now little doubt that the Security Council possesses the power to administer territory on a temporary basis and that it may delegate that power to the Secretary-General (or his or her representative). Acceptance in practice, however, has not meant acceptance in theory. The lack of an institutional capacity to respond to the demands of transitional administration has left the UN relying on a variety of structures built around a core of DPKO personnel, with the different operations adopting idiosyncratic mission structures that reflected the varying capacities of regional organizations and UN agencies in each situation. It is occasionally argued that some form of structural change in the UN system would enable it better to respond to such challenges in the future. Reviving the Trusteeship Council, which suspended operations in 1994, is sometimes mentioned in this regard—most prominently by the International Commission on Intervention and State Sovereignty. Its report, *The Responsibility to Protect,* suggests that a "constructive adaptation" of Chapter XII of the Charter might provide useful guidelines for the behavior of administering authorities.[6] For it to provide more than guidance would require a Charter amendment, however, as Article 78 explicitly prevents the trusteeship system from applying to territories that have become members of the United Nations.[7] In any case, the direct associations with colonialism would be politically prohibitive.

More general political barriers to any such institutional changes were implicit in the Brahimi Report. Despite the "evident ambivalence" among member states and within the Secretariat, however, the report noted that the circumstances that demand such operations were likely to recur. "Thus the Secretariat faces an unpleasant dilemma: to assume that transitional administration is a transitory responsibility, not to prepare for additional missions and perform badly if once again flung into the breach, or to prepare well and be asked to undertake missions more often because they are well prepared."[8] This was not the subject of any recommendation and was not addressed in the Secretary-General's response to the report. It seems probable, then, that any institutional reforms will be incremental, driven by the exigencies of circumstance rather than doctrinal development. The next section turns, therefore, to an examination of the conditions that have led to the creation of transitional administrations in practice.

Forms of Transition

In the growing literature on transitional administration, categorization and subdivision of the powers exercised tend to predominate. Michael Doyle, for example, divides the various forms of what he terms "ad hoc semisovereign mechanisms" into four categories according to the power exercised: supervisory authority (East Timor, Kosovo, and Brcko in Bosnia), executive authority (Eastern Slavonia, Bosnia after the assertion of the Bonn powers from 1997, and Liberia under the Economic Community of West African States Monitoring Group [ECOMOG]), administrative authority (Mozambique, Cambodia, Bosnia from 1995 to 1997, Western Sahara, and Somalia under the second UN operation there—one might add the UN Relief and Works Agency), and a range of monitoring operations (this would include the formal role given to the UN in Afghanistan).[9] Other categorizations, such as the different "generations" of peacekeeping—the second and third of which were, confusingly, supposed to have been born within a matter of months—are possible.[10]

More important than the amount of power exercised, however, is its purpose and trajectory. Categorizing operations by the amount of civilian power given to the special representative of the Secretary-General (SRSG) is a useful taxonomical exercise for analyzing the capacities of the UN, but in terms of understanding the missions themselves it is comparable to categorizing peacekeeping operations by the number of troops deployed. Such an approach may help develop best practices for the logistical difficulties of large deployments, but it does not help in determining the appropriateness of such deployments for the different types of circumstances that may arise in the future. Within the limited experience of transitional administrations, this leads to an overemphasis on the administration rather than its transitional nature. Indeed, though Kosovo and East Timor are comparable in terms of the powers transferred to the SRSG in each case, the assumption of their similarity as operations was one of the major mistakes made on the ground when the UN deployed in East Timor.

In this section, the various operations will be considered by reference to the local political context within which they operated. Five categories will be used, though it would be possible to consider the missions through different lenses: (1) the final act of decolonization leading to independence; (2) temporary administration of territory pending peaceful transfer of control to an existing government; (3) temporary administration of a state pending the holding of elections; (4) interim administration as part of an ongoing peace process without an end-state; and (5) de facto administration or responsibility for basic law and order in the absence of governing authority.

Decolonization

Decolonization is perhaps the simplest context within which a transitional administration may operate. This is not to suggest that the transformation of a former colony into a functioning state is a simple task, but the clarity of the end-state and the universal acceptance of the desirability of such an outcome avoid many of the problems that have plagued other missions.

Though such comparisons are politically fraught, the role of the United Nations in such a situation may be compared to that of an administering authority under the trusteeship system. The basic goals of that system, as articulated in the Charter, were to further international peace and security; to promote the political, economic, social, and educational advancement of the inhabitants with a view to achieving self-government or independence; and to encourage respect for human rights.[11] One of the first occasions in which the United Nations was called upon to exercise quasi-governmental powers was in the course of facilitating Namibia's independence in 1990. The origins of the UN Transition Assistance Group lay in South Africa's refusal to transfer Namibia (known until 1968 as South West Africa), which it held under the mandates system of the League of Nations, to the UN trusteeship system.

Nevertheless, relative simplicity at the level of global norms has on occasion led to false assumptions of simplicity at the local level. In East Timor, for example, it was a nostrum of the expatriate expert community that the territory in late 1999 was a political and economic vacuum. Economically, this might have been true; politically, however, the situation was and remained more complex. Though the basic aim of transferring power to a broadly representative government was clear, consultation with local actors proceeded fitfully, and the lack of local capacity undermined efforts to "Timorize" the institutions of government.

The operations in West Papua (Irian Jaya) and Western Sahara also took place in the context of the withdrawal of European colonial powers. Despite commitments to respect the right of self-determination of the respective inhabitants, however, these operations are more properly considered as facilitating the transfer of territory from one power to another.

Transfer of Territory

Transfer of territory has not generally been an explicit purpose of transitional administration. Nevertheless, this is a realistic assessment of the first operation in which the United Nations undertook such powers in the field. Nominally intended to facilitate the decolonization of Dutch West New

Guinea and the realization of the population's right to self-determination, the handover to Indonesia was effectively facilitated by the United Nations. The operation, lasting from 1962 to 1963, was authorized by the General Assembly rather than the Security Council. As in the later operation in Western Sahara, it was originally intended that the people of West Papua exercise their right to self-determination through a popular consultation. In both cases, this relatively simple proposition became far more complicated as the withdrawal of a European colonial power was swiftly followed by the entry of a neighboring one—a move tacitly accepted in each case by the United Nations. West Papua's "act of free choice" resulted, remarkably, in a unanimous vote in favor of joining with Indonesia. In Western Sahara, frustration with the failure to hold a referendum called for in the decade after 1991 led to a May 2001 proposal by the Secretary-General's personal envoy that would see Morocco's claims to the territory effectively recognized for a period of up to five years, prior to a vote on Western Sahara's future. If accepted, this process will almost certainly lead to integration with Morocco.

A key element in the success of a transitional administration is the existence of political clarity. An agreement to transfer control of territory to an existing state embodies such clarity, but this is only generally possible following acceptance of this arrangement by the international community, or the defeat of the alternative regime on the battlefield. The former situation applied to West Papua and, as seems probable, Western Sahara. The latter applied UNTAES, frequently touted as one of the most successful transitional administrations to date. Croatian offensives against Serb forces had established the inevitable political outcome in the Danube region of Croatia; the UN's presence was to ensure that this outcome was attained peacefully—and on these terms the mission was indeed a success.

Elections

A third form of transition links the purpose of international administration directly to the staging of elections, with the powers to be exercised limited to the fulfillment of that end. Elections have been held in almost all of the situations in which the UN has exercised quasi-governmental authority, but for current purposes this category is limited to those situations where a transitional administration has been empowered primarily to hold an election and then withdraw. The category is therefore distinct from situations in which a referendum on the future of a territory is held (as in West Papua and Western Sahara) and where elections are part of a broader state-building project (as in Namibia and East Timor) or an ongoing peace process (as in Bosnia, Kosovo, and Afghanistan). This leaves Cambodia, where the UN Transitional Authority (UNTAC)—unprecedented at the time in both scale and mandate—was given a clearly defined role under the peace agreement signed in Paris in 1991, with the Security Council being invited to establish the mission in accordance with the wishes of the parties.

The importance of elections in this context is connected with the expansion of electoral observation missions by the UN and other actors, as well as the emerging norm of democratic governance as a "right." Nevertheless, there is now growing recognition that an election—especially a first election—can mark a highly unstable point at which to end a mission.

Evaluations of UNTAC varied considerably in the course of the mission and have continued to do so with the benefit of hindsight. Prior to the 1993 election, prophecies of doom were widespread, with questions raised about the capacity of the UN to complete such a large military and administrative operation. Immediately after the election was held with minimal violence, Cambodia was embraced as a success and a model for future such tasks. Subsequent events suggested that these initially positive evaluations were premature. Most commentators outside the UN now tend to regard UNTAC as a partial failure, pointing to the collapse of democratic structures in the 1997 coup. Within the United Nations, UNTAC continues to be regarded as a partial success.

The key question is whether success is measured according to the completion of a mandate or by reference to the state of the country left behind. In the case of Cambodia, this depends on how one views the political context of the mission. If the purpose of the mission was to transform Cambodia into a multiparty liberal democracy in eighteen months, it clearly did not succeed. If, however, one takes the view that Hun Sen (who seized power from his coalition partners in the 1997 coup) was always going to be the dominant political force in Cambodia, and that the purpose of the mission was to mollify the exercise of that power through introducing the language of human rights to Cambodian civil society, fostering the establishment of a relatively free press, and taking steps in the direction of a democratic basis for legitimate government, the mission was indeed a partial success.

Peace Process

The fourth class of transitional administrations has a rationale quite different from the previous three. Whereas the preceding categories each embody some form of political certainty in their outcome, the explicit object in some missions is to assume some or all government functions without a clear exit point—or in the hope that one will appear at a later date. The clearest examples of this are in Bosnia and Kosovo. Due to frustrations with the UN system throughout the Bosnian war, primary civilian responsibility in Sarajevo was granted to a High Representative, and military security was guaranteed by the Stabilization Force, led by the North Atlantic Treaty Organization (NATO) and operating as a multinational force under a Council mandate to be renewed every six months. In Kosovo, the dystopia of Bosnia under the High Representative and the political controversy surrounding NATO's "humanitarian intervention" led to civilian administration there being placed under a UN umbrella, though the Kosovo Force (KFOR) was also a creature of NATO.

It is in such operations that the contradiction between the means and the ends of transitional administration become most apparent, as international actors endeavor to establish the conditions for democracy through benevolent autocracy. If the circumstances in which these conditions may be met—or the processes for achieving them—are unclear, it may lock both international and local actors into a cycle of dependence. The Dayton Accords, for example, have become a de facto constitution for Bosnia.[12] They served their purpose as a peace agreement but are utterly unworkable as a constitution—any attempt to change them, however, is seen as a threat to reignite the conflict. Kosovo, by contrast, remains paralyzed by the requirement that international staff profess to have no opinion on the most crucial aspect of its political development: whether it will eventually become independent.

As will be discussed below, the UN mission in Afghanistan presents an alternative model for involving the UN in an ongoing peace process on a more limited scale. Almost certainly, however, such a confined role would have been inadequate to the task of enforcing the peace in Bosnia after Dayton, or preventing further revenge killings and attempts at secession after NATO completed its air operations in defense of the Kosovar Albanians.

State Failure

Perhaps the most complex political environment in which the UN has been called upon to exercise transitional administration-like powers is where it has not explicitly been authorized by the Security Council to do so. In Congo, Somalia, and Sierra Leone, for example, the UN and other actors found themselves in situations where a vacuum of state power demanded that some form of basic law and order functions be exercised by the only actors capable of them. Similar situations have arisen in the early stages of other operations, such as the first phase of the Kosovo and East Timor interventions. In those cases, law and order functions fell to the intervening forces—with very different results. But there is a difference between the temporary activities undertaken by KFOR and the International Force for East Timor until the deployment of a civilian administration and the activities that were thrust upon the UN by stealth or by default in the three operations mentioned here. It is no coincidence that all three took place in Africa. Somalia, in particular, highlighted the dangers of a mission's mandate going beyond the political will of troop contributors—even as it led to the implicit policy of some developed states (notably the United States) never again to contribute troops to resolving African conflicts.

The Future of UN State-Building:
Afghanistan and Beyond

During the initial stages of the U.S.-led military action against Afghanistan, there was considerable discussion about the role that the United Nations would play in postconflict Afghanistan. Some feared that the UN would be handed a poisoned chalice once the United States had completed its military objectives; others eagerly looked forward to the "next big mission" and a dominant role for the UN in rebuilding Afghanistan on the model of Kosovo and East Timor.[13] These expectations were tempered by the challenging security environment and the decision by major states contributing troops to the International Security Assistance Force (ISAF) to limit their presence to the capital city of Kabul and its immediate vicinity.[14] (Ongoing coalition actions in the east of the country continued to provide additional coercive power—referred to as the "B-52 factor"—but this was outside the control, and frequently beyond the knowledge, of the United Nations.) Expectations were also limited by the political context within which the UN was to operate: however dysfunctional, Afghanistan had been and remained a state with undisputed sovereignty. This was quite different from the ambiguous status of Kosovo and the embryonic sovereignty of East Timor.

Under the leadership of Lakhdar Brahimi, architect of the Bonn process, the UN mission adopted the guiding principle that it should first and foremost bolster Afghan capacity—both official and nongovernmental—and rely on as limited an international presence and as many Afghan staff as possible. This came to be referred to as the "light footprint" approach.[15] Such a departure from the expansive mandates in Kosovo and East Timor substantially reduced the formal political role of the UN Assistance Mission in Afghanistan (UNAMA). This was in keeping with the limited role accorded to the United Nations in the Bonn Agreement, negotiated in December 2001 after the rout of the Taliban by the United States and its foreign and local allies. But it also represented a philosophical challenge to the increasing aggregation of sovereign powers exercised in UN peace operations since the mid-1990s.[16]

On paper, UNAMA resembled earlier assistance missions that provided governance and development support to postconflict societies. In practice, however, the UN mission remained intimately involved with the Afghan transitional authority and therefore with the peace process that had put it in place. This disjunction between formal authority and practical influence posed challenges not only for the specific operation in Afghanistan but also to accepted models of UN peace operations more generally.

Senior UN staff in the mission were blunt about the reasons for the "light footprint" approach. A mission on the scale of East Timor's transitional administration was "not necessary and not possible," according to Brahimi.[17] Bolstering Afghanistan's capacity to govern itself required Afghans taking charge of their situation wherever possible, an end that would have been compromised by throwing international staff at a problem. A larger international presence would also have exacerbated the perverse effects on both politics and the economy. As another senior UN official put it, "We are protecting a peace process from the hubris of the international liberal agenda as promoted by donors."[18] Such an agenda might include setting policy (on, e.g., human rights, democracy, gender, the rule of law) in accordance with donor requirements and time lines rather than on the basis of what was locally feasible.

In any case, armchair generals' enthusiasm for the benevolent takeover of Afghanistan was cooled by its history of resistance to foreign rule. For this reason, the Security Council–mandated ISAF was reluctant to deploy outside its original sphere of operations in and around Kabul. UN senior staff argued that expansion beyond Kabul was essential to the stability of the interim authority put in place by the emergency Loya Jirga but were wary throughout to limit themselves to "endorsing" Chairman Hamid Karzai's call for a wider deployment. The United States was customarily reluctant to submit itself to a UN mandate but actively opposed any expansion of ISAF. This opposition diminished as mop-up operations in search of Osama bin Laden and Al-Qaida operatives scaled down, leaving only the reluctance of those countries that would actually supply the troops.

Most important, however, a limited role for the UN was what was politically feasible at the time of the Bonn Agreement. One should be careful about taking the passive role of the UN at face value, of course: the "procedural" decision to invite Hamid Karzai to speak at the Bonn meeting was not unconnected with his eventual appointment as chairman of the interim (and later transitional) authority. But a central element of the peace in Afghanistan established in Bonn was encouraging Afghan leaders of various stripes to see their interests as being served by buying into a political process. Asserting a lead role for the United Nations, it was argued, would have fatally undermined this aim.

This hands-off approach became central to the political strategy pursued by the UN in Afghanistan—a high-risk strategy that required two conceptual leaps from the normal mold of peace operations. The first was that it would be possible to blur the distinction that is generally assumed between negotiating a peace agreement ("peacemaking" in the UN argot) and implementing it. Thus the Bonn Agreement was seen not as a final status agreement but as a framework for further negotiations, mediated through the institutions provided for over the subsequent two-and-a-half-year period (the interim authority, the emergency Loya Jirga, the transitional authority, the constitutional Loya Jirga, and so on). The flexibility inherent in this approach may be contrasted with the peace agreements that locked the UN and other international actors into their roles in Bosnia and Kosovo. The Bonn Agreement avoided these pitfalls but presumed that the UN could continue to have a meaningful role in the ongoing negotiations. Again, on paper, there was little formal authority for the UN to do so, but through high-level diplomacy and subtle interventions in its capacity as an assistance mission, it endeavored to "cook" the political process into a sustainable outcome.

This assumed the success of the second conceptual leap, which was that the UN could make up for its small mandate and limited resources through exercising greater than normal political influence. Brahimi goes one step farther, arguing that it is *precisely* through recognizing Afghan leadership that one obtains credibility and influence.[19] Such an approach places extraordinary importance on the personalities involved. It is generally recognized that Brahimi was instrumental to the success of Bonn, but his continuing involvement and his personal relationship with Karzai and the three Panjshiri "musketeers" who largely wield power (Defense Minister and Vice President Muhammad Qassem Fahim, Foreign Affairs Minister Abdullah Abdullah, and Education Minister and Special Adviser Mohammed Yunus Qanooni) are essential to the process remaining on track.

And until the emergency Loya Jirga, things were always likely to remain on track. Indeed, the greatest achievement of the operation to the end of 2002 was that no major group had opted out of the Loya Jirga process entirely. There were cases of intimidation and pressure on the part of local commanders to have themselves or their men "elected," but this was sanguinely interpreted as a compliment to the perceived importance of the political process. Few people deluded themselves into thinking that the Loya Jirga was a meaningful popular consultation—the aim was to encourage those who wield power in Afghanistan to exercise it through politics rather than through the barrel of a gun. Mao Tse-tung's aphorism is apposite here because the most dangerous period for the UN comes after the Loya Jirga has taken place. At this point, if political methods are not seen to deliver at least some of the benefits that were promised, those commanders may revert to more traditional methods of promoting their interests.

Conclusion

It is ironic that UNAMA reached its most crucial test—the June 2002 Loya Jirga—within weeks of the conclusion of the mandate of the UN Transitional Administration in East Timor (UNTAET) and East Timor's independence celebrations on May 20, 2002. UNTAET may come to represent the high-water mark of UN transitional administrations, where the UN exercised effective sovereignty over a territory for more than two years. The UN mission in Afghanistan has a fraction of UNTAET's staff and budget and operates in a country perhaps forty times the size and thirty times the population of East Timor. Brahimi hopes that people will look back at East Timor and question whether it was necessary to assert such powers. Any such evaluation may well be colored by the fate of the UN operation in Afghanistan.

Just as generals are sometimes accused of planning to refight their last war, so too have the UN's experiments in transitional administration reflected incremental learning. Senior UN officials now acknowledge that, to some extent, Kosovo got the operation that should have been planned for Bosnia, and East Timor got the operation that should have been sent to Kosovo. Afghanistan's very different "light footprint" approach draws, in turn, upon the outlines of what Brahimi in 1999 argued would have been appropriate for East Timor.

Afghanistan therefore suggests a different, "lighter" approach to post-conflict reconstruction to the East Timor model, but East Timor is likely to be exceptional for other reasons. In particular, its small size and the uncontroversial nature of its future status made it a relatively simple case—certainly compared to the complexity of the security situation in Afghanistan or the political uncertainty of Kosovo. More generally, however, the September 11, 2001, attacks against the United States began to animate states with the idea that such reconstruction projects may involve greater national interest than had previously been recognized. Most prominently, the *National Security Strategy* adopted by President George W. Bush in September 2002 stated that "America is now threatened less by conquering states than we are by failing ones."[20] Future experimentation with the models of East Timor and Afghanistan is therefore likely to be dominated by the national interests at stake. At the same time, avoiding the appearance of imperialism or colonialism may demand a formal UN umbrella for any such operations.

The accepted wisdom within the UN community, articulated most recently in the report that bears Brahimi's name, is that a successful UN peace operation should ideally consist of three sequential stages. First, the political basis for peace must be determined. Then a suitable mandate for a UN mission should be formulated. Finally, that mission should be given all the resources necessary to complete the mandate. The accepted reality is that this usually happens in the reverse order: member states determine what resources they are prepared to commit to a problem and a mandate is cobbled together around those resources—often in the hope that a political solution will be forthcoming at some later date.

This reality means that the Council learns, if it learns at all, largely by doing. And though political resistance may prevent development of a policy or institutional framework for future transitional administrations in theory, it is unlikely to prevent the demand for such operations in practice.

Notes

I would like to thank Sebastian von Einsiedel and David M. Malone for their constructive comments on an earlier draft of this chapter.

1. UN Secretary-General, *An Agenda for Peace: Preventive Diplomacy, Peacemaking, and Peacekeeping (Report of the Secretary-General Pursuant to the Statement Adopted by the Summit Meeting of the Security Council on 31 January 1992)*, A/47/277-S/24111, June 17, 1992.

2. UN Secretary-General, *Supplement to An Agenda for Peace: Position Paper of the Secretary-General on the Occasion of the Fiftieth Anniversary of the United Nations*, A/50/60-S/1995/1, January 3, 1995, paras. 13–14.

3. See Simon Chesterman, *Just War or Just Peace? Humanitarian Intervention and International Law*, Oxford Monographs in International Law (Oxford: Oxford University Press, 2001), pp. 112–218.

4. 3 UNCIO 365, 371–372, doc. 2G/7 (n)(1).

5. 12 UNCIO 353–355, doc. 539 III/3/24.

6. International Commission on Intervention and State Sovereignty, *The Responsibility to Protect* (Ottawa: International Development Research Center, 2001), www.iciss.gc.ca, paras. 5.22–5.24.

7. *Charter of the United Nations,* art. 78.

8. *Report of the Panel on United Nations Peace Operations*, A/55/305-S/2000/809, August 21, 2000, www.un.org/peace/reports/peace_operations, para. 78.

9. Michael W. Doyle, "War-Making and Peace-Making: The United Nations' Post–Cold War Record," in Chester A. Crocker, Fen Osler Hampson, and Pamela Aall, eds., *Turbulent Peace: The Challenges of Managing International Conflict* (Washington, D.C.: U.S. Institute of Peace, 2001), pp. 529–560.

10. See, for example, Marrack Goulding, "The Evolution of UN Peacekeeping," *International Affairs* 69, no. 3 (July 1993): 451–464.

11. *Charter of the United Nations,* art. 76.

12. The accords do, in fact, include a constitution in annex 4; the reference here is to the peace agreement as a whole—especially the military aspects in annex 1A: *General Framework Agreement for Peace in Bosnia and Herzegovina,* Bosnia and Herzegovina–Croatia–Federal Republic of Yugoslavia, S/1995/999, December 14, 1995.

13. This was encouraged by the impending staff reductions in East Timor, as well as staff cuts in the office of the UN High Commissioner for Refugees.

14. See Resolution 1386, December 20, 2001, para. 1.

15. See UN Secretary-General, *The Situation in Afghanistan and Its*

Implications for International Peace and Security, A/56/875-S/2002/278, March 18, 2002, para. 98.

16. See, for example, Richard Caplan, *A New Trusteeship? The International Administration of War-Torn Territories,* Adelphi Paper no. 341 (Oxford: Oxford University Press, 2002).

17. Interview with Lakhdar Brahimi, Kabul, May 9, 2002.

18. Confidential interview, Kabul, May 2002.

19. Interview with Brahimi.

20. *National Security Strategy of the United States of America* (Washington, D.C.: U.S. Government Printing Office, September 2002), www.whitehouse.gov/nsc/nss.html, p. 1.

PART 3

Evolving
Institutional Factors

16

Council Working Methods and Procedure

Susan C. Hulton

The Security Council was recently described by one of its elected members, the permanent representative of Singapore, as "one of the most conservative institutions in the world today," particularly in its working methods and procedure. The same observer went on, however, to acknowledge that there have been "significant improvements in the Council's working methods" over the past few years.[1]

The impetus for change has come from several developments and various quarters. With the end of the Cold War, there has been greater cooperation within the Council, enabling the fifteen members to behave as a collective body. This has led to increased consensus in its decisionmaking and a greater emphasis on becoming more operational. How the Council does its work has come under increased scrutiny from within and outside its ranks as it has taken on a more active role. In response to suggestions and criticisms, it has become more open in its relationship with the wider UN membership and other actors with a role to play in maintaining international peace and security. And it has taken measures to enhance the transparency of its work. With a burgeoning workload, the Council has also sought to improve its efficiency and to adopt a more strategic approach. This chapter reviews these recent developments in the working methods and procedure of the Council, beginning with the changes in Council decisionmaking.

A Trend Toward Consensus in Council Decisionmaking?

Since the early 1990s, the habit of consensus in the Council has empirically grown, although it has not always been achieved. Resolutions are still adopted by vote, but almost all are now adopted unanimously. This is all the more noteworthy because the Council can take such decisions with less than unanimity.[2] It is recognized, however, that unity increases the authority, legitimacy, and effectiveness of the Council, and great efforts are made to achieve it whenever possible.[3] At the same time, a significant number of Council decisions—an average of fifty-three a year since 1993—take the form of presidential statements, which unlike resolutions *require* consensus. These are statements made by the president of the Council, on behalf of the Council or its members, usually read at a public meeting of the Council, each word of which has been agreed in advance by all the members of the Council.

In the light of the fissures over how to disarm Iraq, it is perhaps salutary to recall some examples of consensus having been achieved on even the most difficult issues. In relation to the Middle East, for example, after failing to reach agreement on a number of draft resolutions in 2001, the Council agreed in 2002 on four resolutions, most adopted unanimously. These included Resolution 1397 (2002), which for the first time affirmed the Council's vision of a region where two states, Israel and Palestine, exist side by side within secure and recognized borders. In the case of terrorism, there was an unprecedented coming together following the attacks of September 11, 2001. This was exemplified by Resolution 1373 (2001), imposing far-reaching binding obligations on all states to prevent and suppress terrorism and creating a Counter-Terrorism Committee to monitor implementation of the resolution. In the case of Iraq itself, with the unanimous adoption of Resolution 1441 on November 8, 2002, following eight weeks of negotiation, the Council reaffirmed its important role in dealing with Iraq's threat to international peace and security. That was an extraordinary consensus, joined by the two countries at either end of the spectrum of debate on the issue—the United States and Syria.

Such unity may be hard-won. That Council members view it as a goal worth striving for is attested to by their recourse to the device of explanations of vote (or nonvote)[4] to record their position on a draft resolution without blocking a consensus. Such statements are usually made at the time of the adoption of the resolution, either before or after the vote. Interestingly, in the case of Resolution 1441 (2002) concerning Iraq, the governments of China, France, and the Russian Federation took the unusual step of issuing a joint written statement on the interpretation of the resolution following its unanimous adoption and their individual explanations of vote.[5] On occasion, as in that instance, unity may prove short-lived. Ambiguities needed to achieve consensus may paper over differences that emerge later to prevent Council action.

A key element underpinning Council unity has been cooperation among the permanent members, which during the immediate post–Cold War period were split on only a few issues. One byproduct was the much reduced use of the veto, another striking development in Council practice in recent years. Between 1946 and 1989, some 270 vetoes were cast (on average more than six a year).[6] Since January 1990 and as of March 2003, by contrast, only thirteen have been cast in public meetings and one in a private meeting.[7] Some of the vetoes during the latter period were not of great significance in themselves and were swiftly reversed, with the states concerned subsequently agreeing to support almost identical resolutions to the ones they had vetoed. More significant have been the vetoes that blocked Security Council action or censure. Apart from one case, these vetoes have all been cast by the United States in the context of the situation in the occupied Arab territories. The other significant veto was cast by China in February 1999; that action prevented renewal of the mandate of the UN Preventive Deployment Force in the former Yugoslav Republic of Macedonia (UNPREDEP), thus bringing the first preventive peacekeeping operation to an end.

While these fourteen vetoes serve as a reminder that the veto still exists, in practice the threat, or even the mere possibility, of a veto may well be more significant than its actual use. As one Council member noted recently, although the data would show that the veto was not often used in the Council, that record "belie[d] the fact that the mere presence of the threat of the veto or its possible use more often than not determined the way the Council conduct[ed] its business."[8] A striking example was the explicit threat of a veto in the diplomatic follow-up to Resolution 1441 (2002), on Iraq.

It is too early to tell what impact the recent failure of the Council to find a collective solution to Iraq's disarmament will have on its ability to forge a consensus on other issues in the future. The need for collective action is understood by Council members themselves. However, the institutional reality is that the Council, being made up of fifteen nations at any one time, is working from national instructions; its members cannot produce unity if they do not receive instructions to do so.

Toward a More Operational Council

The Council's activity and output have both expanded enormously since the end of the Cold War. In 2002 there were 238 formal meetings of the Council, and sixty-eight resolutions were adopted. The corresponding figures for 1989 were sixty-five meetings and twenty resolutions. In the decade between January 1990 and December 1999, the Council adopted 638 resolutions, an average of sixty-four a year, compared with an average of fourteen a year over the preceding forty-four years. Not only are the resolutions more numerous, but they are often more complex. Nor do they represent the full extent of the Council's output: for example, in 2002, forty-two presidential statements were also adopted.[9] Quantity, though, is only part of the story. A striking aspect of the Council's work during this period has been its greater focus on the operational activities required to give reality to its decisions—whether in the sphere of diplomacy, peacekeeping, or enforcement.

In its diplomacy, the Council's more activist approach is discernible in several respects. First, it has engaged more directly with the parties. Its position may be conveyed to them discretely, by the president of the Council in a meeting with the permanent representative of the country concerned in New York, or by the representative of the Secretary-General on the ground. In other instances, the Council has entered into a direct dialogue with the parties in New York. It has had several meetings, for example, with the Political Committee for the Implementation of the Lusaka Cease-Fire Agreement for the Democratic Republic of Congo, as part of managing the conflict. The Council has increasingly, moreover, gone to conflict areas to convey a message or even conduct a negotiation. Of the thirty-seven missions undertaken by the Council since 1946, more than half have taken place since 1993. Since 2000 alone, the Security Council has conducted thirteen missions. Members of the Council have stressed the usefulness of such missions both in their effect on the parties on the ground and in helping members better understand the conflict concerned. The Brahimi Report, too, referred to the important role they could play:

> On the political level, many of the local parties with whom peacekeepers and peacemakers are dealing on a daily basis may neither respect nor fear verbal condemnation by the Security Council. It is therefore incumbent that Council members and the membership at large breathe life into the words that they produce, as did the Security Council delegation that flew to Jakarta and Dili in the wake of the East Timor crisis [in 1999], an example of effective Council *action* at its best: *res, non verba*.[10]

Second, the Council has been more prescriptive in promoting the settlement of an issue.[11] The limits to the Council actually "imposing" a solution on the parties, under Chapter VI of the Charter, have been demonstrated, however, in the context of its consideration of the long-standing situation in Western Sahara. Finally, the Council has resorted to a more robust form of diplomacy—diplomacy backed by force, or "coercive diplomacy"—notably in the case of Iraq, an approach endorsed by the Secretary-General in a statement made at a Council meeting on March 2, 1998.[12]

With regard to peacekeeping, the Council has established many new operations. The majority of these forces have been deployed within states involved in civil wars rather than between states, as before. This transformation in the nature of peacekeeping has given rise to new challenges, requiring more than the traditional monitoring of a cease-fire. Peacekeeping operations in such contexts have evolved into a more complex and multidimensional mechanism; in addition to military components, they may have a humanitarian relief component, as well as elements aimed at bringing about national reconciliation and reestablishing effective government. The forces established in 1999 in Kosovo and East Timor marked yet a further development, with the UN being responsible in each case for fulfilling all the functions of a government. The recommendations of the Brahimi Report seem to have had a positive impact on the Council's determination of mandates; efforts are being made to ensure that peacekeeping operations are given clear and realistic mandates and adequate means to fulfill them, though the reality since has not always matched these high standards.[13]

The Council's greater recourse to enforcement measures under Chapter VII of the Charter—through the imposition of sanctions and authorization of the use of force—is considered elsewhere in this volume. Suffice it to mention here some of the innovative mechanisms established by the Council under Chapter VII in response to new challenges: the ad hoc international criminal tribunals for the former Yugoslavia and Rwanda; the UN Special Commission (UNSCOM) and its successor, the UN Monitoring, Verification, and Inspection Commission (UNMOVIC), charged together with the International Atomic Energy Agency with overseeing the disarmament of Iraq; and the Counter-Terrorism Committee, the first committee created to oversee the implementation of a global Council resolution.

Toward a More Effective Decisionmaking Environment
How the Council conducts its business has undergone a sea change since the early 1990s, with the Council becoming more open and transparent and making efforts to adopt more efficient working methods.

Opening the Channels to Other Relevant Actors
The Council of the early 1990s could be described as hermetic. Council members had few sources of information beyond those available to their own states. And there were few opportunities to hear other voices before decisions were taken. The quality of collective decisionmaking being dependent on the inputs, the Council increasingly recognized that these must be wider than the fifteen members, which have different capacities and areas of focus in their information gathering. It has taken a number of steps to broaden and improve its information base. It has learned about crises firsthand with missions to particular trouble spots, as mentioned above. It has also opened up the consultation process to a wide range of other actors that have an ability to assist and that may be particularly impacted by the Council's decisions. Forming various concentric circles around the Council, these actors include troop-contributing countries, the wider UN membership, the Economic and Social Council (ECOSOC), the Secretariat, and nongovernmental organizations (NGOs).[14]

Troop-contributing countries.   Under pressure from those nations that provide many of the UN's peacekeeping forces, the Council has taken a number of steps to improve consultations with them. Commencing in the mid-1990s, meetings were held between members of the Council, troop-contributing countries, and the Secretariat to facilitate the exchange of information and views before the Council took decisions concerning the mandate of a particular peacekeeping operation. Cochaired by the Council presidency, these meetings allowed troop contributors to convey their views indirectly to the Council. In 2001 the Council sought to strengthen this system of consultation by providing for the holding of formal Council meetings with troop contributors to consider issues of critical importance to a specific peacekeeping operation before decisions were taken.[15] Such meetings have since been held before any change in, renewal of, or termination of a peacekeeping mandate. However, the general view of Council members and troop contributors is that the intent of the Council for these meetings to be interactive and to provide an opportunity for such countries to engage the members of the Council in a constructive dialogue has not yet been realized.[16] In January 2002 the Council accordingly established a further, complementary, consultative mechanism.[17] The new mechanism provides for joint meetings between the Council's Working Group on Peacekeeping Operations,[18] relevant troop contributors, and the Secretariat to allow maximum interactive discussion in a less formal setting of issues pertaining to specific peacekeeping operations. Early experience with the new mechanism has been favorable. The first such joint meeting was held in August 2002, with nine troop contributors to the UN Assistance Mission in Sierra Leone (UNAMSIL). The chairman reported that the smaller format and specific agenda—the adjustment and drawdown of the military component of UNAMSIL—had contributed to a more substantial debate with the troop-contributing countries. Troop contributors, while welcoming these developments, have made further proposals for enhancing cooperation with the Council, which would go beyond consultation to participation in decision-making.

The wider UN membership.   When in December 1994 the Council held a public debate on its working methods and procedure, the permanent representative of France referred to "a certain uneasiness in relations between the Security Council and Members of the United Nations." He suggested that

> this uneasiness results in large part from the fact that informal consultations have become the Council's characteristic working method, while public meetings, originally the norm, are increasingly rare and increasingly devoid of content: everyone knows that when the Council goes into

public meeting everything has been decided in advance. . . . Informal meetings are not even real Council meetings at all; they have no official existence, and are assigned no number. Yet it is in these meetings that all the Council's work is carried out.[19]

A presidential statement adopted at the conclusion of that debate declared that it was "the intention of the Council, as part of its efforts to improve the flow of information and the exchange of ideas between the members of the Council and other United Nations Member States, that there should be an increased recourse to open meetings, in particular at an early stage in its consideration of a subject."[20] Since then, there have been an increased number of open meetings, offering greater opportunities for the wider UN membership to participate in the Council's work. The figures for 2002 tell the story. The Council held a record number of formal meetings: 238—more than treble the average number of meetings (66) held annually prior to 1990. Of those meetings, 183 were public and 55 were private. Almost 80 of the public meetings consisted of open briefings and debates, with the rest predominantly devoted to adopting Council decisions.

While the high number of formal meetings was a function of the considerable increase in the Council's workload, many of the open meetings may be attributed to the efforts by Council members to promote openness and transparency in the Council's work.

ECOSOC. Because the issues before it and its decisions often involve economic and social as well as political dimensions, the Council has sought to develop a closer relationship with ECOSOC. It attempted to hold a meeting with ECOSOC members in April 2001 to discuss areas of conflict management where intergovernmental coordination needs to be enhanced, such as conflict prevention and peacebuilding. That overture was rebuffed due to the reservations of some ECOSOC members. The next year, however, saw the beginning of a new phase in cooperation between the two bodies, in relation to issues pertaining to Africa before the Council. In a presidential statement of January 31, 2002, the Council reaffirmed the importance of strengthening its cooperation with ECOSOC in the prevention of armed conflicts on the continent, including addressing economic, social, cultural, and humanitarian problems.[21] The Council has since established the Working Group on Conflict Prevention and Resolution in Africa, an ad hoc body that intends to work closely with a parallel body created by ECOSOC within its domain—an ad hoc advisory group on African countries emerging from conflict. One may thus have the beginnings of an institutional framework for ensuring a smoother transition from the responsibilities of the Council in a conflict situation to those of ECOSOC in the postconflict stage. Another concrete example of such interaction was the creation of an ECOSOC advisory group on Guinea-Bissau, which included among its members the chairman of the Security Council's Working Group on Conflict Prevention and Resolution in Africa. The latter also joined the advisory group's mission to Guinea-Bissau in November 2002. It should be noted, too, that since 2002 the president of ECOSOC has spoken at several public meetings of the Council on the situation in Africa.

Briefings by the Secretariat and other parts of the UN system. The Council receives regular briefings from the Secretary-General, his special representatives, and other senior UN officials on the political, humanitarian, and security aspects of situations before it. Since April 2001 these briefings have, at the Council's request, been more analytical and have supplemented previously circulated fact sheets containing background information. The Council has also brought in other parts of the UN system. Commencing in 1992, Sadako Ogata, the UN high commissioner for refugees, briefed the Council some twelve times over an eight-year period on developments concerning refugees and displaced persons, particularly in the former Yugoslavia and various parts of Africa. Her successor has continued to do so. In a noteworthy development, the Council has also recently invited the UN high commissioner for human rights to brief the Council on a specific situation—atrocities occurring in the Democratic Republic of Congo; one such briefing was given in a public meeting.[22] In the economic and social sphere, the Council has invited representatives of the World Bank, the International Monetary Fund, and the UN Development Programme to participate in its meetings on situations concerned with peacebuilding in, for instance, East Timor, Guinea-Bissau, and the Central African Republic.

Nongovernmental organizations. The Council's opening up to NGOs is perhaps one of the most important changes it has undergone since the end of the Cold War. "Arria Formula" meetings, introduced in 1992, created a format in which a wide range of voices—representatives of states not on the Council, nonstate parties, intergovernmental organizations, NGOs, and individuals—could be heard informally by Council members.[23] Convened and chaired by any Council member, such meetings take place away from the Council's formal and informal meeting rooms. From 1993 to 2000, Council members held more than seventy Arria Formula meetings, three of which were with representatives of NGOs. In 2001–2002, Council members held fourteen such meetings with representatives of NGOs. There is, moreover, a good deal of interaction between NGOs and Security Council members outside the Arria Formula, such as in the NGO Working Group on the Security Council.[24]

Balancing Transparency and Effectiveness

In a related and parallel development, the Council has also become more transparent, lifting the veil of secrecy that surrounded so much of its work in the past. This move was stimulated in part by the deliberations of the General Assembly, particularly its Open-Ended Working Group (OEWG) on Security Council reform. The lack of transparency was of concern to all states not members of the Council that were nonetheless affected by the Council's decisions and, in any event, wished to understand or influence developments. The Council itself, moreover, recognized that much could be done—and, learning from the lessons of modern public sector management, *should* be done—to open up its proceedings while preserving a space for informal consultations for negotiations and debate on sensitive issues.

Steps in the direction of greater transparency have been considered more deliberately and systematically since about 1993. The measures taken so far include the following:

• Many more open meetings have been held, as noted above, in line with the presidential statement of December 16, 1994, and a note by the president of the Council of December 30, 1999.[25]

• More "open briefings" have also been held, in accordance with a note by the president of the Council of October 30, 1998.[26] Such briefings have often been followed by informal consultations on the same item. The Council has thereby been able to give nonmembers the opportunity to be apprised of the latest developments in the subjects under discussion without compromising sensitive discussions and negotiations among Council members.

• A new, "hybrid" type of meeting was introduced in 2001: a private meeting open to the entire membership of the organization. It was "private" in that it was closed to the media and the public. A number of such private meetings have taken place, which non-Council members were able to attend without being invited by the Council on the basis of letters of request for participation.

• Another recent innovation has been the holding of periodic "wrap-up sessions." These have been held, at the discretion of the president of the Council, commencing in June 2001, to evaluate the procedural and substantive aspects of the Council's work during the month just ending.[27] Such sessions have been viewed by Council members and the wider membership as a useful opportunity to assess broad themes in the Council's work and to reflect on its methods and procedures.

• The Council now publishes its program of work for the month and a provisional agenda in advance of its meetings, allowing non-Council members to exert influence on specific issues. Informal consultations are now also announced in the *UN Journal* with an informal list of the subjects to be discussed.

• Information on the outcome of Council members' informal consultations of the whole has become more readily available. In October 1994, Council members agreed that the Council presidency should give informal oral briefings to nonmembers on the broad outlines of such consultations. This has invariably been done since then. The presidency also usually speaks to the news media after each session of consultations and is often authorized to make a statement to the press on behalf of Council members. Summaries of discussions held during informal consultations have also been posted on the national websites of some presidencies.

• Improvements have been made to the format and content of the annual report of the Council to the General Assembly, partly in response to criticism by member states that the report was lacking in detail and analysis and did not therefore provide a suitable basis for evaluating the work of the Council. Since July 1997 each presidency, with one exception, has prepared a brief assessment on the work of the Council for the month during which it presided, for attachment as an addendum to the Council's annual report.[28] A more recent innovation saw the addition to the latest annual report of an introduction containing an analytical overview of the Council's work.[29] This was welcomed by a number of speakers in the General Assembly debate on the report in mid-October 2002.

• In the case of the Council's subsidiary organs, the new Counter-Terrorism Committee has won accolades from Council members and nonmembers alike for its transparent, open approach. This has included frequent briefings by the chairman to inform the wider UN membership of the work under way in the committee, consultations with regional and subregional organizations, and the provision of relevant information on a dedicated website.

• With the increased targeting of sanctions against nonstate actors, the Council has had to give more thought to the manner in which it lists and delists individuals. It has recently adopted guidelines concerning its procedures for doing so in the case of the sanctions against those belonging to or associated with the Taliban or Al-Qaida.[30]

• On the technological front, a new presidential website was launched by the Secretariat in November 2001 at the request of the president of the Council.[31] It supplemented websites maintained by the individual presidencies and was designed to provide easy access to up-to-date information on the Council's work and decisions. The first live webcast of a Council meeting transmitted an open debate on the situation in Africa in January 2002. Since then, there have been more than 100 webcasts.[32]

Many of these procedural developments and others have emerged from work carried out in the Council's Working Group on Documentation and

Other Procedural Matters, an informal body that first met in June 1993 and that now meets several times a year. The main output of that group may be found in a series of notes and statements by the president of the Council, a descriptive index to which has recently been issued by the Council.[33]

Encouraging a More Focused Approach and Interactive Debate

Disputes over procedural issues—one of the hallmarks of Council meetings during the Cold War era—have all but vanished, with most such issues now being resolved in consultations. Votes on the adoption of the agenda are a thing of the past: nowadays agendas are agreed in advance (though not formally adopted) in informal consultations. With its agenda becoming overloaded, the Council has turned its attention more recently to the question of agenda management. Several members have expressed the view that a more focused approach is needed: one that would streamline the consideration of recurring, routine issues while preserving more time for substantive discussion of the main issues. There have been some useful innovations in that direction. Some presidencies have provided Council members with daily annotated agendas, indicating what needs to be done each day, with thoughts on how the items should be dealt with. Committees and working groups of the Council—such as the Working Group on Conflict Prevention and Resolution in Africa—have been used to filter and look in more depth at issues on the Council's agenda. It has been suggested, moreover, that some members might be asked to take the lead in discussions on a particular subject to ensure full and professional coverage of all items through a division of labor. Finally, in this context, greater efforts have been made to ensure continuity and cooperation between monthly presidencies of the Council, particularly when initiatives straddle two months.

In the conduct of the Council's meetings, efforts have been made to encourage more focused and interactive debates. Time limits on interventions have been called for by the presidency in a number of debates, sometimes on the understanding that longer statements could be included in the verbatim records. "Focused and operational" statements have been encouraged, with guidance being given by the presidency, particularly in the case of thematic debates and wrap-up meetings, concerning the scope of the topics under consideration. A number of meetings have been held at which there was no preestablished list of speakers, to improve the interactive nature of the debate. On occasion, Council members have departed from their customary practice of speaking before nonmembers and have either heard nonmembers first or alternated with them, again in an effort to open up the dialogue. In the case of briefings, the speaking order is now frequently interrupted by the president of the Council, who calls upon the briefer to respond to questions and comments soon after they arise, rather than at the end of the meeting, so that there can be some interaction on the points raised. Here, too, particularly where regular briefings are concerned, a premium has been put on focused interventions as opposed to a reiteration of national positions. These innovations have not all borne fruit, to the extent that points are debated more spontaneously and interactively. But there is an evolution in that direction.

Toward a More Strategic Approach

Under constant pressure to respond to events and address the details of the issues before it, the Council does not often have a chance to stand back and look at the wider picture. Increasingly, however, it has recognized the desirability of bringing more strategic thinking to its approach. The annual retreat of the Council with the Secretary-General provides one such opportunity for a strategic review of its work; these retreats have been held each spring since 1998, with the exception of 1999. Several other informal retreats of the Council have also been held, such as those organized by the International Peace Academy since 2001.[34] Council members have invariably described such gatherings, held away from the Council Chamber, as useful in providing a forum for reflection and a candid exchange of views. The monthly working lunches with the Secretary-General, too, have emerged as a valuable forum for brainstorming, as have the new "fifteen plus fifteen" lunches at which previous members of the Council join current members and share their experiences.

The Council has also begun to devote more attention to the consideration of particular thematic issues, reflecting its main concerns in dealing with current conflicts. A number of these issues relate to the humanitarian dimension of conflicts, focusing on the protection of civilians and the role of women and children in armed conflict. Others reveal the Council's efforts to address the root causes of conflicts before they erupt, as in the case of "the causes of conflict and the promotion of durable peace and sustainable development in Africa" and "Africa's food crisis as a threat to peace and security," or the factors exacerbating conflict, such as the role of small arms. Yet other issues focus on the new dimensions of peacekeeping operations, or on the need for a smooth transition from such operations to peacebuilding, as, for instance, in the item "no exit without strategy." Still others address the regional or subregional dimensions of conflicts, particularly in Africa. In taking up some of these issues, the Council has been careful to underscore their link with its role in maintaining peace and security, disclaiming any intention of aiming at a creeping extension of its jurisdiction over the business of others.

Efforts have been made to integrate the outcome of these thematic debates into the Council's work on specific situations. A few noteworthy steps in the direction of such so-called mainstreaming may be highlighted. In March 2002 the Council adopted an aide-mémoire on the protection of civilians in armed conflict, following its fourth open debate on the subject.[35] Drafted in close cooperation between the Secretariat's Office for the Coordination of Humanitarian Affairs and the members of the Council, the aide-mémoire was adopted as a practical tool to facilitate the Council's consideration of issues pertaining to the protection of civilians in the design and planning of peacekeeping mandates. In the case of Africa, recognition of the linkages between issues has been given concrete expression with the establishment by the Council of its ad hoc working group on Africa, mentioned above. This working group has been charged with, inter alia, examining "regional and cross-conflict issues" that affect the Council's work on African conflict prevention and resolution. It has done preparatory work on African issues before they come to the Council, notably in the case of a workshop on West Africa in July 2002.

Another way in which the Council seeks to move beyond simply reacting to events is through regular briefings in which it focuses on certain main themes. On Afghanistan, for instance, the Council has regularly assessed the situation on the ground and heard reports on the work of the International Security Assistance Force and the UN's role in particular. On the Middle East, Council members agreed at the beginning of 2002 to have regular monthly informal briefings on the situation. They have welcomed the opportunity this has provided to keep them up to date with developments in the region and to ensure a more regular exchange of views, including with the Secretary-General and his team.

Conclusion

As the preceding account suggests, the Council's working methods and procedures have evolved appreciably in response to the new challenges and circumstances of the post–Cold War era. The changes have been accomplished through practice and have not, thus far, been "codified" in the Council's Provisional Rules of Procedure. To some, this is a cause for concern, as it renders the achievements rather precarious: they are at the mercy of the Council at any given time and, in particular, of any given Council president. Others, however, see merit in a pragmatic approach, valuing a certain degree of flexibility in order to facilitate creative approaches suited to the challenges at hand. This debate is not new—either within or outside the Council—and is bound to continue. What is new is that the subject of how the Council does its work has a higher priority on its own agenda, and that members have expressed support for further reform that can be achieved while maintaining and improving the Council's effectiveness.

Notes

The views expressed in this chapter are mine alone and do not necessarily reflect the views of the United Nations. I gratefully acknowledge the usefulness of several internal UN sources in the preparation of this chapter: reports on aspects of Council practice prepared by colleagues in the Security Council Practices and Charter Research Branch; a paper on the Council's role and practice by the former chief of the branch, Nicole Lannegrace, delivered to the incoming members of the Council in November 2002; and a database on Council practice maintained by the Security Council Affairs Division. Among published sources on this subject, see the report on *Procedural Developments in the Security Council, 2001*, S/2002/603, June 6, 2002; Sydney D. Bailey and Sam Daws, *The Procedure of the UN Security Council,* 3rd ed. (Oxford: Clarendon, 1998); and the forthcoming eleventh and twelfth supplements to the *Repertoire of the Practice of the Security Council,* covering the years 1989–1995.

1. Ambassador Kishore Mahbubani, in the public debate on the consideration of the draft report of the Security Council to the General Assembly, September 26, 2002. S/PV.4616, p. 3.

2. A majority of nine affirmative votes is required for the adoption of a resolution, provided that, in the case of a decision on a nonprocedural matter, no permanent member has cast a negative vote (i.e., a veto). See *Charter of the United Nations,* art. 27.

3. See, for example, comments made by Council members during the wrap-up discussions on the work of the Security Council in November 2001 and December 2002 (S/PV.4432 and S/PV.4677) and during the consideration of the draft report of the Council to the General Assembly on September 26, 2002 (S/PV.4616).

4. Following the vote on Resolution 1402 (2002), on the situation in the Middle East, the representative of Syria made a statement explaining why his delegation had not participated in it. S/PV.4503, March 29, 2002, p. 36.

5. S/2002/1236, November 8, 2002.

6. See Bailey and Daws, *The Procedure of the UN Security Council,* pp. 230–239.

7. The veto cast at the private meeting was in connection with the reappointment of a Secretary-General in 1996. Bailey and Daws, *The Procedure of the UN Security Council,* p. 237. Private meetings are formal meetings of the Council, closed to the public and the media, in which participation is restricted.

8. The permanent representative of Jamaica, in the wrap-up meeting on the work of the Security Council for August 2001. S/PV.4363, p. 7.

9. These statistics provide a mere indication of the Council's workload, as much of the work takes place in informal consultations, expert groups, sanctions committees, and working groups.

10. *The Report of the Panel on United Nations Peace Operations,* A/55/305-S/2000/809, August 21, 2000, para. 276 (emphasis in original).

11. See, further, Chapter 37 in this volume, on the Council's role in shaping international law.

12. Secretary-General Kofi Annan observed that "if diplomacy is to succeed, it must be backed by force and by fairness." S/PV.3858, March 2, 1998, p. 3.

13. See, for example, the assessment in the report of the Council's informal retreat on December 11, 2002, *The Role of Mandates and the Special Representatives of the Secretary-General in the Success of UN Peacekeeping Operations,* S/2002/1388.

14. Other relevant actors include regional organizations and Groups of Friends. See Chapters 20 and 21, respectively, in this volume.

15. Resolution 1353, June 13, 2001.

16. See, for example, the assessment in the Council's 2001–2002 report to the General Assembly that the mechanism "has yet to develop its full potential." A/57/2, September 27, 2002, p. 8.

17. S/2002/56, January 14, 2002.

18. The Working Group on Peacekeeping Operations was established in 2001 to address both generic peacekeeping issues relevant to the responsibilities of the Council and technical aspects of individual peacekeeping operations.

19. S/PV.3483, December 16, 1994, p. 2.

20. S/PRST/1994/81, December 16, 1994.

21. S/PRST/2002/2, January 31, 2002.

22. S/PV.4705, February 13, 2003.

23. The Arria Formula derives its name from Diego Arria, who as permanent representative of Venezuela in 1991–1994 was the first to call such a meeting.

24. See, further, Chapter 25 in this volume, on the relationship between the Security Council and NGOs.

25. S/1999/1291, December 30, 1999.

26. S/1998/1016, October 30, 1998.

27. Four such meetings were held in 2001, in public, but with contributions restricted to the fifteen Council members. Three private wrap-up meetings were held in 2002, with participation open to non-Council members.

28. S/1997/451, June 12, 1997.

29. *Report of the Security Council: 16 June 2001–31 July 2002*, A/57/2, pp. 1–8.

30. SC/7487, August 16, 2002.

31. www.un.org/docs/sc/presidency.

32. For archived video, see www.un.org/webcast.

33. A/57/382-S/2002/1000. See also the report prepared by the Secretariat on *Procedural Developments in the Security Council, 2001,* which was circulated to the wider UN membership under a note by the president (S/2002/603, June 6, 2002) as part of the Council's efforts to promote transparency.

34. One of these, held in March 2001, focused on human rights and peacekeeping. Another, in August 2001, looked at regional approaches to conflict management in Africa. A third, held in December 2002 and cohosted by the Colombian Mission to the UN, considered the role of mandates and the special representatives of the Secretary-General in the success of UN peace operations (S/2002/1388).

35. The text of the aide-mémoire is annexed to S/PRST/2002/6, March 15, 2002.

17

The Permanent and Elected Council Members

KISHORE MAHBUBANI

On December 20, 2002, the UN Security Council held one of its occasional wrap-up sessions, at which members reflected on the achievements and failures of the Council during that year. Ambassador Martin Chungong Ayafor, deputy permanent representative of Cameroon, spoke bluntly about the perception of a fundamental problem in the relationship of the five permanent members (P-5) and the ten elected members (E-10). His comments are worth quoting at length, for he states the perceived problem clearly:

> The presence of permanent members in an institution is in itself a decisive advantage. It implies an almost perfect mastery of issues, procedures, and practices and even of what is not said. When that permanent membership is accompanied by a particularly favourable relationship of power, there is a tendency to take advantage of that position to advance one's views and interests, sometimes to the detriment of missions of general interest that led to the establishment of the institution in the first place. Despite appearances, there is a pattern of behaviour that is shared by the members of the Council, who, willingly or not, are often tempted to believe that agreement between five is the same as agreement between 15. The Security Council would benefit from returning to its initial composition. It is composed of 15 members, but little by little, it is becoming a body of five plus 10 members. That dichotomy can only affect the transparency and the legitimacy to which we all aspire.[1]

Against the backdrop of this strong public comment, which reflects a growing concern in the UN community, I will try in this chapter to develop an understanding of P-5 and E-10 relations by answering three questions. First, what is the relationship in theory between the P-5 and the E-10? Second, what in practice have been the relations between the P-5 and E-10? Third, is there a realistic solution to the problems that have emerged?

It is important to emphasize a key qualification at the outset. The great difficulty in writing about the Council is the lack of common understanding of the nature and purpose of the organ, both among analysts and among participants in the Council's deliberations. Differences in perceptions among participants in the Council also reflect varying national interests and evolving major power relationships. Also, the Council is a dynamic institution, constantly changing and adapting to new realities and demands. Hence a discussion like this on the relationship between the five veto-bearing permanent members and the ten elected members must be seen as a snapshot: it will capture some structural realities but will expose only a moment in the constantly changing geopolitical landscape, which is inevitably reflected in the world's most powerful international forum devoted to peace and security issues, the Council.

Expectations of the Council have shifted over the decades. In the early years its main function appeared to be the institutionalization of a concert of powers, legitimizing the great power status of the P-5 and ensuring that the UN did not undertake a collision course with any of them. In the 1990s, following the end of the Cold War, the Council gradually transformed itself into a problem-solving institution, living up partially to the founders' vision of providing collective security. Much of the transformation took place without careful reflection of its impact on the role and responsibilities of Council members. Hence this chapter will also suggest that it is time to begin a serious reflection on these issues.

A Theory of Relations Between the P-5 and E-10

In trying to understand what, in theory, the relationship between the P-5 and E-10 ought to be, I have not found in any academic or other literature a satisfactory analysis. Instead, most academic writings in this area focus on the main privilege of the P-5—the veto—and attempt to analyze its rationale and purpose.

In his 1973 book *The Security Council: A Study in Adolescence,* Richard Hiscocks offered a contemporaneous assessment of the veto that remains current in some senses: "The veto accurately reflected the divided world in which it was so often used. It reflected also the deliberate choice of the great powers to pursue methods of diplomacy based on national power rather than to cultivate the high principles of international cooperation and tolerance on which the United Nation's Charter is based."[2]

A deeper analysis of the privilege the P-5 awarded themselves in Article 27 of the Charter was offered by Inis Claude in his classic work *Swords into Plowshares:*

> The most celebrated of the special privileges granted to the Big Five, the right of veto in the Security Council, was not so much an instrument of great power dictatorship over small states as a factor injected into the rela-

tionships of the great powers among themselves. . . . At San Francisco the small states accepted the superiority of the mighty as a fact of life. Their first objective was to ensure that all of the great powers would accept their place in the leadership corps of the new organization; in this they were successful, and this fact was perhaps the major basis for the hope that the United Nations would prove more effective than the League. Their second objective was to constitutionalize the power of the international oligarchy; toward this end they achieved the incorporation in the Charter of a surprising array of limitations upon arbitrary behavior, including the procedural brake upon collective decisions by the great powers which was implicit in the rule of unanimity. Their third objective was to gain assurance that the most powerful members would initiate and support positive collective action within and on behalf of the organization in times of crisis; in this respect there were serious apprehensions of failure, based largely upon the fact that the veto rule foreshadowed the possible paralysis of such undertakings.[3]

In short, if Claude's analysis is correct, an implicit political compact was achieved between the mighty and not-so-mighty. In return for the veto power, the great powers committed themselves to the principles of the UN Charter and to act on behalf of collective security.

Other writers have also observed the importance of the veto in securing great power commitment. Andrew Boyd, in *Fifteen Men on a Powder Keg,* disputes British prime minister Harold Macmillan's assertion in 1962 that the frequent use of the Russian veto had undermined the Council (which Macmillan actually described as "the Cabinet of the World"). Boyd asserts: "The 'foundation on which the UN was built'—by the great powers—*was* the great-power veto."[4] And Secretary of State Cordell Hull declared in the 1940s that "our Government would not remain there a day without retaining its veto power."[5]

The record since the UN's founding in 1945 shows that the veto has accomplished the purpose of achieving great power commitment to the United Nations. No P-5 member has walked away from the UN, even the United States at the height of its disillusionment with the UN in the 1980s and 1990s. There is recognition among the P-5 that both their veto power as well as their permanency in the Council give them a privilege of significant control over a powerful global institution.

The UN Charter is a remarkable document that still appears alive and relevant although written almost sixty years ago. But the instrument of the veto and the privileges it conferred on the five victors of World War II were designed to remedy the main weakness of the first half of the twentieth century: the failure to anchor the major powers in a collective security system and to ensure that no decisions were taken against their interests. Hence it had a negative rather than positive function. As Philip C. Jessup has stated, the veto is "the safety-valve that prevents the United Nations from undertaking commitments in the political field which it presently lacks the power to fulfill."[6] What the UN Charter fails to spell out are the responsibilities associated with membership of the Council, permanent or elected. Nor has a consensus developed in practice on what those responsibilities are. The absence of a widely shared understanding of the responsibilities of both permanent and nonpermanent members of the Council has developed into a serious weakness for the organization. Indeed the actual record of the Council, especially since the early 1990s, demonstrates that this weakness has hurt the Council.

Relations Between the P-5 and E-10 in Practice

The structural weakness in the Council has resulted from a dichotomy. In the Council, the P-5 have been given power without responsibility; the E-10 have been given responsibility without power. This may appear to be an overly crude summary of the situation. But the experience of recent years shows that there has been growing unhappiness among members of the UN that the states elected to the Security Council have been excluded from the decisionmaking processes on certain issues, most prominently with respect to Iraq.

The great paradox about the Council is that this structural weakness surfaced during the phase of its history when it became more active and, often, more effective, in the 1990s. From its creation in 1945 to the end of the Cold War, the Council lay largely moribund, paralyzed by the dynamics of the Cold War. The cross-vetoes of the United States and the Soviet Union prevented any effective action, except for the deployment of a few peacekeeping operations by mutual consent. Both powers used each other's vetoes in their propaganda battles. The respective positions of the fifteen members in the Cold War would determine their role in this political theater. There was no divide between the P-5 and the E-10 then, because the P-5 were divided.

The end of the Cold War created a new dynamic in which UN Secretary-General Javier Pérez de Cuéllar sensed a great opportunity. He encouraged the P-5 to work together to find solutions to long-standing conflicts. The drafting of Resolution 598 as part of the effort to end the Iran-Iraq War has been viewed as the earliest example of a new kind of P-5 diplomacy. But the major achievement of the new P-5 cooperation related to the 1991 Gulf War. The Security Council's endorsement of the coalition's aims was a major reason for the international community's strong and united response to the Iraqi invasion of Kuwait. In the words of President George H. W. Bush, a "new world order" appeared ready to emerge.

As the 1990s evolved, the early positive fruits of P-5 cooperation in the Council gave way to many painful and bitter failures, especially in the Balkans and in Rwanda. The effete or passive responses of the Council to the killings in Bosnia and in the UN-mandated "safe areas" in Srebrenica and to the genocide in Rwanda revealed the structural weakness of the Council. Exclusive focus on the short-term national interests of the Council members without regard to the interests of the international community led to the Council's disastrous passive responses.

The institutional tragedy of these episodes was that no effort was made either by the Council members to conduct an objective inquiry into the cause of these failures or by the other UN member states to hold the Council accountable for its actions. As a consequence, a valuable opportunity was lost to learn the lessons from these disasters. The UN, the Organization of African Unity (OAU), and even the Dutch government commissioned independent reports. Both Kofi Annan and President Bill Clinton acknowledged some responsibility for the UN's failures in Rwanda. But the Council as an institution never took any responsibility; nor did it provide an account for its failures. In Chapter 32.1, Colin Keating addresses this painful episode from his vantage point as the Council's president in April 1994.

The failure of the Council to investigate these disasters was probably not an accident. Any objective inquiry would have revealed the P-5's domination of the Council and hence their heavy responsibility for this organ's failures. Edward Luck makes the following observations in *Mixed Messages:*

> Some Americans have chided the United Nations for not doing more to save lives in the Rwandan genocide, when in fact this inaction was the result of national decisions in Washington, D.C., and other key capitals that were reluctant to become too deeply involved in a situation that posed considerable risks and no easy or quick solution. In the former Yugoslavia the Security Council committed peacekeepers on the ground to implement an ever-changing mandate, subject to the disparate and wavering interests of the United States, Russia, the major Western European powers, and the Islamic states, among others.[7]

In short, the principal causes of the failures of the Council were actions or nonactions of major powers.

Apart from the formal privilege of the veto (which is rarely used in practice), one would anticipate few distinctions between the P-5 and E-10 in the day-to-day decisionmaking of the Council. Moreover, in recent years most decisions have been made by consensus. This in theory should give each of the fifteen members a veto, as their concurrence is required for a consensual decision. The increasing trend toward consensual decisionmaking might also be cited as evidence that in practice the P-5 and the E-10 work together on a level playing field in the Council.

Indeed, in the two years that I served on the Council, I could not point to a specific instance where the elected members were treated disrespectfully or as second-class citizens by the P-5. We spent most of our time in closed-door informal consultations, conducted in a small chamber that sits adjacent to the main chamber shown in most television shots of the Security Council. Even though we would have occasional sharp debates in these informal consultations, relationships at a personal level were marked by a warm sense of camaraderie, which is often generated by working together in close quarters over an extended period of time. A fly on the wall observing these proceedings could be forgiven for believing that the P-5 and E-10 representatives all contributed equally to Security Council decisions.

Structurally, however, the E-10 are at an extreme disadvantage in the Council's deliberations and decisionmaking procedures. First and most obvious, the national power of each of the P-5 countries is stronger than that of most elected members. The pecking order of states in any international organization reflects the relative national power of the states, especially their power in the area that the organization specializes in. In the field of peace and security, the P-5 remain the only five legitimate nuclear powers. Of course, within the P-5 there is also a pecking order. In UN corridors, it is often said that the Council is dominated by the P-1, as the United States is sometimes called, reflecting the unique unipolar moment that the world faces in the twenty-first century. After the United States, China and Russia are regarded as the next most important national powers. It is noteworthy, however, that even for E-10 representatives who come from states with larger economies than those of the P-5 (e.g., Japan and Germany), there is no change in the pattern of P-5 domination.

Paradoxically, however, the two most active members of the Council among the P-5 have been the UK and France. This situation could be a reflection of their traditional activist foreign policies, by which both have provided leadership on issues far from their national borders. However, many in the UN community also believe that their activism in the Council is an attempt to justify their continuing permanent membership at a time when there is increased questioning of whether permanent membership should still be conferred only on the victors of World War II nearly six decades later. Thomas Franck has noticed the tendency of these countries to refrain from using their formal veto power and notes that this "self-restraining practice, which, in effect, reduces privileges which have come to be unjustified illustrated their consciousness of the role of coherence in legitimizing the system of rules which is the UN Charter: a legitimacy in which all members have a stake."[8]

The second reason why the E-10 are disadvantaged may appear to be both obvious and questionable: the veto powers conferred by the UN Charter on the P-5. It is considered questionable only because the veto is now rarely used in the Council. However, while the formal use of the veto in the open chamber is now a rare occurrence (in 2002, for example, there were only two vetoes, both of which were exercised by the United States), its informal use in closed consultations has not diminished. For instance, despite the Charter provision stating that the veto should not be used for procedural issues, in November 2002 the U.S. delegation blocked the procedural proposal for a dialogue between the Security Council and the president of the International Court of Justice, Judge Gilbert Guillaume. Even though a majority of the Council was in favor of this dialogue, the United States exercised in effect a closed-door veto.[9]

This is only a small episode, but it reflects a reality that has become firmly entrenched in the corporate culture of the Council. The P-5 are allowed to use their veto *implicitly* in many closed-door consultations. This also explains why the Council rules of procedure remain "provisional" after nearly six decades. The P-5 have steadfastly refused all effort to remove the "provisional" label, including a valiant effort in 1997 by the representatives of Chile, Costa Rica, Egypt, Guinea-Bissau, Japan, Kenya, Poland, Portugal, the Republic of Korea, and Sweden. In the two years that I served as permanent representative of Singapore on the Council, our delegation made several procedural suggestions to improve the working methods of the Council. We expected a positive response. Instead we ran into a lot of resistance, especially from some of the P-5. We were initially puzzled until we heard the private comments of a P-5 permanent representative who expressed surprise that the "tourists" were trying to change the arrangements of the Council. This was a revealing comment. It showed that the P-5 believe that they "own" the Council. In their eyes, the E-10 should make no claim of co-ownership, even if they happen to be elected by 191 member states of the UN.

The E-10 are further hobbled by the fact that much of the agenda, procedures, and policies of the Council have been settled by the time each new elected member joins the Council. There is a delicate web of understandings reached among the previous members of the Council, especially among the P-5, on which issues should receive real attention and which should receive pro forma attention. Within the UN community, there is also a widespread belief that a complex pattern of tradeoffs has been worked out over the years. This may explain, for example, why the Council remains remarkably passive about long-standing issues on which no obvious progress has been made, despite years of resolutions and statements issued by the Council. Georgia and Cyprus are obvious examples. Indeed, the term "Cyprusization" of an issue has been added to the Council's vocabulary to describe an issue that long remains on its agenda without resolution. At the beginning of each new year, incoming elected members raise questions about these dormant issues, but few changes occur in practice.

In the spring of 2001 a few elected members (including Singapore) raised questions about the absence of a comprehensive policy by the Council on Afghanistan. Limited sanctions on the Taliban regime and statements on poppy cultivation did not amount to such a comprehensive policy. In private, some P-5 members graciously conceded that our questions were valid, but they also added that "political realities" meant that Afghanistan would remain a "strategic orphan." September 11, 2001, changed everything. Afghanistan went from being a strategic orphan to a strategic priority. The Council's position shifted with the shifting of priorities of the P-5, especially the United States.

Another impediment to the work of the E-10 is the absence of any formal institutional memory in the Council, either of the proceedings in the informal consultations (where most of the real decisions are thrashed out) or of the record of implementation or nonimplementation of the Council's decisions. The Council is serviced by a small Secretariat staff who, with limited resources, do an excellent job of managing the logistical arrangements for the many Council meetings that take place simultaneously. But the Secretariat does not provide support for the substantive deliberations or keep an institutional memory of the proceedings of the informal consultations.

This is an obvious weakness of the Council that needs to be addressed. With the current arrangements, only the P-5 members have a continuous record and memory of the Council's work over the years. As the Council often works by referring to precedents, the elected members are at an obvious disadvantage when they have either no knowledge of or background on these precedents.

Several UN Secretariat departments do attend and follow Council deliberations on issues falling under their purview. The Department of Political Affairs, for example, follows key political issues, like those concerning the Middle East; the Department of Peacekeeping Operations monitors Council deliberations on operations under its purview; and the Office for Coordination of Humanitarian Affairs follows Council discussions when a strong humanitarian dimension exists. Each is heavily burdened by its own responsibilities. Providing background briefings, guidance, and succor to the elected members would require additional resources that are not easily available in the UN system. Over the years, many officials at these departments have developed long-standing relationships with their P-5 counterparts that newly elected members cannot replicate overnight. Many of the UN Secretariat officials strive to be impartial and objective in their work, but they do face real pressures on many key issues. It is not unusual, for example, for some P-5 members to insist on seeing a draft Secretariat report before it is shared with the elected members. Episodes like this confirm that the P-5 and E-10 representatives do not operate on a level playing field in the Council.

The answer to the question of whether the Security Council is owned by all its fifteen members, by the P-5, by the 191 UN member states, or as suggested in the opening words of the UN Charter, by "We, the Peoples," remains to be answered. I do believe, however, that as the role and the influence of the Council are likely to grow in the coming years, partly as a natural consequence of globalization and the growing need for more effective global institutions, the question of the ownership of the Council will inevitably surface again.

Solutions

Any efforts to reform or improve the Council must begin with a recognition that change will not be easy. The Open-ended Working Group (OEWG) on Council Reform has been working for ten years with no tangible progress in its efforts to change the composition of the Council. The usual gridlock of competing national interests, in which each new aspirant state is strongly blocked by a jealous or threatened neighboring state, has stymied all efforts to change the composition. However, the discussions in the OEWG on what have been called Cluster II issues (i.e., the working methods of the Council) have led to tangible improvements in the Council's performance, making it, relatively speaking, more open and transparent in many of its deliberations in recent years. The P-5 have over the years become sensitized to the concerns of the other 186 member states of the UN through the discussions in the OEWG. The UK and France, in particular, have tried to take onboard some of these concerns.

Hence, any change in the Council will come only if there is a clear recognition by the P-5 that the special privileges that they enjoy in the Council are viable in the long run only if they are perceived to be legitimate in the eyes of the current membership of the United Nations. Legitimacy is an inherently fragile commodity that must be nurtured.

One key source of strength of the Council is the willingness of the 191 UN members to abide by its decisions, even when there is some unhappiness in the UN corridors with either the procedures or the policies of the Council. However, this compliance cannot be taken for granted. In June

1998 the Council faced a major crisis when the OAU collectively decided not to abide by Council-mandated flight bans on Libya. In the face of such resistance, the Council wisely suspended these sanctions.

Compliance is tied to the perception of the legitimacy of the Council's decisions. The current legitimacy of the Council is tied to the UN Charter (which has been ratified by all UN member states) and to the recognition that the Council exists as an institution within the wider UN fabric of legitimacy. If, say, the current fifteen members of the Council were to try to create their own global security council independent of the UN, their decisions would enjoy neither legitimacy nor compliance among the international community.

To preserve these assets of legitimacy and compliance the Council must try to anticipate the likely expectations of the larger UN community. One clear demand that is likely to emerge, in line with a growing global trend, is that the Council should become more accountable for its actions. Traditionally, in most constitutions and organizations, privileges come with responsibilities. The two are often seen to be opposite sides of the same coin. What is remarkable about the veto privilege accorded to the P-5 members is that it was conferred without an explicit or implicit agreement that this privilege also carried with it significant responsibilities. It is true that Article 24(1) confers "primary responsibility for the maintenance of international peace and security" to the UN Security Council (as a whole). However, the Charter does not explicitly mention the responsibilities of the P-5. Indeed the veto is not explicitly mentioned anywhere in the Charter. Instead Article 27 uses the clever euphemism "including the concurring votes of the permanent members" to simultaneously create and disguise the privilege of the veto.

Significantly, Inis Claude acknowledges that when the Charter was drafted the P-5 "were somewhat disingenuous in their preference for discussing the matter in terms of their willingness to assume special responsibility rather than their insistence upon being granted special privilege."[10] In short, the P-5 in 1945 paid lip service to the idea of assuming greater responsibilities but never intended the veto to be strictly aligned with responsibilities.

The Charter implies that the elected members should be seen as bearing some responsibility for the international system in order to get elected to the Council. Article 23 states that in the election of the "other" members, due regard should be specially paid "to the contribution of Members of the United Nations to the maintenance of international peace and security." However, here, too, no specific responsibilities are conferred on the E-10 in the Council.

The lack of clear assignment of responsibilities to either the P-5 or the E-10 members has created a structural weakness in the Council. Each member (be they P-5 or E-10) puts its national interest ahead of any collective security interests in formulating its national positions on issues before the Council. Sometimes the cumulative addition of fifteen national interests can lead to a happy result of representing the collective security interests of all 191 members of the United Nations "on whose behalf" the fifteen Council members act (Article 24[1]). Such happy results are rare because the short-term national interests of the fifteen member states can rarely reflect the long-term collective security interests of the global community. A by-product of the veto is that the collective security structure established under the Charter cannot be used against the P-5 or any state that enjoys the full and unqualified support of a P-5 member. Nor can it be used in situations, no matter how pressing, in which a particular P-5 member is opposed to taking action. In the words of Claude, "The Charter endorsed the ideal of collective security in unqualified terms, but envisaged its application in severely limited terms."[11]

A simple analogy may explain this structural weakness more clearly. In having been conferred with "primary responsibility for the maintenance of international peace and security," the Council is often compared (and often explicitly so in Council open debates) to a fire department. The fire department dispatches fire engines as soon as a fire is reported. The Council is theoretically obliged to respond each time a major conflict that threatens international peace and security breaks out. But there is a crucial difference in the nature of their responses. The fire department of, say, New York City reacts instantaneously and effectively regardless of where the fire breaks out, be it on Park Avenue, in Harlem, or in the Bronx. The Council, however, reacts only when the interests of the fifteen members, especially the P-5, are affected. Consequently conflicts that do not impinge on their national interests can be, and often are, ignored.

This is no abstract analogy. At a lunch meeting days after a Security Council visit to Burundi in May 2001, during which Council members were directly exposed to the fragility of the situation there, P-5 ambassadors made clear that if genocide were to break out in this country of little geostrategic importance, the Council would be unlikely to act much differently than it did in Rwanda in 1994. The E-10 representatives present then declared that if the P-5 did not take the lead, they had no ability to do so.

It is remarkable in some ways that the obvious failures of the Council in Bosnia, Srebrenica, and Rwanda did not make a bigger dent in the Council's standing and prestige in the international community (except perhaps in the eyes of many civil society organizations, which were appalled by these failures). Even though the Council never explicitly acknowledged its failures, it may have implicitly done so when it authorized establishment of the international criminal tribunals for the former Yugoslavia and for Rwanda. However, were the Council to remain passive again in a similar

Rwanda- or Srebrenica-type episode, it is more than likely that its credibility and effectiveness would diminish, perhaps like that of the International Monetary Fund, which was in the past perceived to be arrogant and insensitive to the concerns of the apparent beneficiaries of its actions.

Implicitly when the UN Charter conferred "the primary responsibility for the maintenance of international peace and security" to the Council, it also conveyed the expectation that the members of the Council, both permanent and elected, would balance their national interests, as well as the collective security interests of the UN family, in the decisionmaking processes of the Security Council. Now, from time to time, some permanent members may acknowledge in private that they should wear two hats in the Council, their national hat and their collective hat. However, there is still a deep reluctance to accept any specific responsibilities that are tied to membership in the Council. Jeremy Greenstock, the UK permanent representative, probably accurately captured the views of most permanent members of the Council when he said at an open debate in March 2001, "Most of the time the Security Council is dealing with decisions of policy, and not responding to an obligation under international law. Having a primary responsibility for international peace and security is not an obligation under international law; it is description of a function."[12]

It is important to stress here that when specific responsibilities are associated with membership of the Council, these responsibilities should be assigned to the permanent members *and* the elected members. When both begin to realize that they face common responsibilities through membership in the Council (and where both are held equally accountable in the public eye), there will be a built-in incentive for them to work together on a more level playing field, rather than one that is overwhelmingly tilted in favor of the P-5.

The UN Charter does state in Article 24(3) that the "Security Council shall submit annual and, when necessary, special reports to the General Assembly for its consideration." No common understanding has developed within the UN community on the meaning of the phrase "for its consideration." The annual Council reports to the General Assembly were (until 2002) pro forma exercises, in which no effort was made by the Council either to explain or to justify its actions to the General Assembly. Nor did the Council make any conscious effort to take onboard the comments made in the General Assembly debate on the Council annual reports.

This ritualistic, pro forma reporting could easily be converted into a meaningful and substantive exchange of views between the Security Council and the General Assembly. In the long run, such a substantive dialogue will be deemed necessary, as the Council and the Assembly have a symbiotic relationship with each other. Neither can exist and thrive without the other. The Council is needed to anchor the major powers within the UN system. The Assembly is needed to legitimize and implement the decisions of the Council. Healthy two-way communication will eventually be necessary between these two institutions. Curiously, no such communication now takes place.

When a productive substantive dialogue is put in place, the elected members should also see both their standing and their effectiveness increase in Council deliberations. The ten elected members can effectively convey the views and sentiments of the wider UN membership to the P-5, as well as defend the decisions of the Security Council to the other UN members. They can only do the latter effectively if they are perceived to be active partners in the decisionmaking procedures of the Council.

All this suggests that all UN members should begin a fresh round of discussions on the role and responsibilities of the Security Council, including in particular the role and responsibilities of the P-5 and the E-10. Hitherto the P-5 have been reluctant to engage in any substantive discussion in this area. Perhaps the time has come for them to recognize that it will serve their long-term interests to do so. Their permanent positions on the Council would not be threatened by such an exercise. Indeed their positions could even be enhanced if they were perceived to be effectively delivering the results that the UN community expects from them. A new partnership between the P-5 and the E-10 could therefore enhance P-5 interests as well as deliver a more effective Security Council.

Notes

I am currently serving as Singapore's permanent representative to the UN. The views expressed in this chapter, however, are my personal opinions and should not be read as reflecting the opinions of the Singaporean government.

1. S/PV.4677, December 20, 2002, New York.

2. Richard Hiscocks, *The Security Council: A Study in Adolescence* (New York: Free Press, 1973), p. 72.

3. Inis L. Claude Jr., *Swords into Plowshares: The Problems and Progress of International Organization,* 2nd ed. (New York: Random House, 1963), pp. 81–82.

4. Andrew Boyd, *Fifteen Men on a Powder Keg: A History of the U.N. Security Council* (New York: Stein and Day, 1971), pp. 62–63.

5. Edward C. Luck. *Mixed Messages: American Politics and International Organization, 1919–1999* (Washington, D.C.: Brookings Institution, 1999), p. 154.

6. Philip C. Jessup, cited in Claude, *Swords into Plowshares,* p. 147.

7. Luck, *Mixed Messages,* p. 149.

8. Thomas M. Franck, *The Power of Legitimacy Among Nations* (New York: Oxford University Press, 1990), p. 178.

9. It is also essential to mention here that there have been many academic discussions of the notion of the "double veto," a term often used to refer to the "second" veto that the P-5 can use to ascertain whether a question is procedural or not. Hence, technically, the P-5 can prevent a procedural question (on which there can be no veto) from being treated as a procedural question. See, for example, the dis-

cussion in Bruno Simma et al., eds., *The Charter of The United Nations: A Commentary,* 2nd ed., vol. 1 (Oxford: Oxford University Press, 2002), p. 489.

    10. Claude, *Swords into Plowshares,* p. 154.

    11. Inis Claude, cited in Hiscocks, *The Security Council,* p. 60.

    12. S/PV.4288 (Resumption 1), March 7, 2001, New York.

18

The UN Secretary-General

Marrack Goulding

There is a curious anomaly in the index of Adam Roberts and Benedict Kingsbury's otherwise excellent *United Nations, Divided World*. It has seventeen entries for "Secretary-General and General Assembly" and none for "Secretary-General and Security Council."[1] Yet during the eleven years (1986–1996) that I served as Undersecretary-General to Javier Pérez de Cuéllar and Boutros Boutros-Ghali, the Security Council consumed more of the Secretary-General's time, caused him more headaches, and had a greater impact on the UN's international standing than did the General Assembly; and by the time Boutros-Ghali succeeded Pérez de Cuéllar in 1992, expenditures on peace operations created by the Council were costing member states more than twice the organization's regular budget.

A full analysis of the relationship between the Secretary-General and the Security Council and its evolution during the past six decades would require a whole book. This chapter has a more modest goal. Drawing on my own experience under Pérez de Cuéllar and Boutros-Ghali, two very different Secretaries-General, I offer some conclusions about how the Security Council and the Secretary-General, two "principal organs" of the United Nations, can most effectively contribute to the achievement of the organization's first purpose: the maintenance of peace and security.[2] The terms of office of Pérez de Cuéllar (1982–1991) and Boutros-Ghali (1992–1996) embraced a period when the United Nations underwent a transformation more dramatic and visible than any since the great decolonization of the early 1960s. The consequences were not all positive. The Security Council's ability to help maintain peace and security was certainly enhanced by the end of the Cold War, and it succeeded in resolving some proxy conflicts that had been fueled by East-West competition.[3] But the meltdown of a world order that had been reasonably stable for four decades gave rise to new conflicts in both North and South, and some of these led the United Nations—member states and Secretariat alike—to overreach themselves, with disastrous results.

These turbulent events and the opportunities and dangers that accompanied them strained at times the relationship between the Council and the Secretary-General. Four aspects of that relationship are examined here: (1) the Secretary-General's perception of what the relationship should be; (2) the degree of harmony between the Secretary-General's purposes and those of the Council members; (3) the Secretary-General's ability to produce results that satisfied the Council members; and (4) the way in which the Secretary-General managed his relationship with the Council.

What Should the Relationship Be?

In 1986, the fifth year of his first term, Pérez de Cuéllar delivered the annual Cyril Foster lecture at Oxford University. It was titled "The Role of the UN Secretary-General," and its core was devoted to the political functions of the Secretary-General.[4] Pérez de Cuéllar saw these as being based on two provisions of the Charter that had been absent from the Covenant of the League of Nations: the Secretary-General's right, under Article 99, to apprise the Security Council of "any matter which in his opinion may threaten the maintenance of international peace and security"; and his right, under Article 98, to make an annual report to the General Assembly "on the work of the Organization." Pérez de Cuéllar favored a broad interpretation of these rights (as had Dag Hammarskjöld when he gave the Cyril Foster lecture in May 1961).[5] The Secretary-General, he said, should not be self-aggrandizing or unrealistically ambitious in the performance of his political functions, but neither should he be overcautious. The Secretary-General was not just the chief administrative officer of the UN; Articles 98 and 99 attributed to him "the independent responsibilities of 'a principal organ.'" He "was thus given a reservoir of authority, a wide margin of discretion, which requires the most careful political judgement." Paralysis of the Security Council by the Cold War had led Secretaries-General to undertake peacemaking tasks, often without formal invocation of Article 99. This, said Pérez de Cuéllar, was quite proper in the circumstances, but Secretaries-General had to take care that such action did not enable member states to evade their own responsibilities under the Charter; the Secretary-General "must not become an alibi for inaction [by them]." The political functions entrusted to the Secretary-General obliged him to be the guardian of the Charter, independent of all member states and impartial in his dealings with them.

At the beginning of his mandate Boutros-Ghali would probably have agreed with Pérez de Cuéllar's lecture. He saw the Security Council summit on January 31, 1992, as the defining moment of his Secretary-

Generalship and responded enthusiastically to the Council's request for recommendations on how to strengthen the UN's capacity for preventive diplomacy, peacemaking, and peacekeeping. For the moment, expectations of a productive partnership with the Council overrode concerns that he had previously expressed about the undemocratic nature of its composition and his sympathy with the South's view that the North was giving too much attention to peace and security and not enough to economic and social development. But by the middle of 1993 strained relations with the United States over Bosnia and Somalia had undermined his optimism, and from then on, as is evident in his memoir, *Unvanquished,* he saw everything through the prism of his resentment at Washington's attitude to the United Nations.[6]

When he too delivered the Cyril Foster lecture at Oxford, also in his fifth year as Secretary-General, his perception of the Security Council was wholly different from Pérez de Cuéllar's.[7] His title for the lecture was "The Diplomatic Role of the Secretary-General," but he made only passing allusions to that role and only two references to the Council. In the field of international law, he noted its power to recommend that member states submit their disputes to the International Court of Justice; and in the field of UN reform, he said that reform of the Council's composition was at the heart of the endeavor to democratize the United Nations system. But that was all. His main themes were what he described as the "dialectics" between globalization and fragmentation and between demand and resources, plus an enumeration of the reforms of the UN that he had already achieved in New York.

Boutros-Ghali's lecture should not, however, be taken as an authoritative statement of his views on the Council. The contexts of the two lectures were very different. When Pérez de Cuéllar spoke in Oxford he had already won the confidence of the member states and knew that a second term was at his disposal if he wished it. He could afford to be analytical and reflective. He already sensed that the Cold War was thawing and that this would give the Council a new relevance. The lecture provided him with an opportunity both to reflect publicly on what the Secretary-General's relationship with the Council should be and to remind the member states that it was they, not the Secretary-General, who had the primary responsibility for the maintenance of peace and security. Boutros-Ghali's lecture, by contrast, was given after he had had a number of brushes with the Security Council and when he already feared that the United States might block his reelection. Although delivered in Oxford, his lecture was primarily addressed to the third world, restating his credentials as a critic of globalization and a champion of a more "democratic" United Nations and suggesting that his difficulties with member states had been due to their failure to respect the independence of the office of Secretary-General. The lecture was an electioneering speech, delivered in short, staccato sentences, the first shots in his campaign to win the second term that he so ardently desired.

In sum, Pérez de Cuéllar, had a clear perception of the division of responsibilities between the Council and the Secretary-General. The members had the primary responsibility for maintaining peace and security and the power of decision, but the Secretary-General also had a political role and could take initiatives of his own. Boutros-Ghali initially had some reservations about the Council's allegedly undemocratic nature but responded enthusiastically when, at the very beginning of his term, the Council invited him in effect to define the Council's agenda for the coming years, a point that he underlined by calling his report *An Agenda for Peace*.[8] However, some factors beyond his control, and some errors of his own, frustrated his hopes of a cooperative and fruitful relationship with the Council. By the end of his five years he had reverted to his misgivings about the composition of the Council and the U.S. role within it.

Harmony of Purpose Between the Council and the Secretary-General

The West's victory in the Cold War gave it an almost unchallenged dominance in the Council. Both Pérez de Cuéllar and Boutros-Ghali were, however, sons of the South, from Peru and Egypt respectively, and the South was (and still is) concerned about the direction the United Nations was taking. The developing countries argued that the maintenance of peace and security was only one of the purposes of the United Nations listed in the Charter, and they complained that the West, following the end of the Cold War, was engineering a shift of resources and political energy to peace and security at the expense of the other purposes, especially economic and social development, which in the South's view ought to have been receiving equal if not greater attention from the United Nations.

For Pérez de Cuéllar, this was a view to which lip service had to be paid. He was conscientious in carrying out the Secretary-General's duties in the economic, social, and cultural fields. But his heart was not in it; his heart was in the Security Council and the resolution of conflict, a field in which he had long been active and would soon score some important successes. His memoir of his ten years as Secretary-General, *Pilgrimage for Peace,* is entirely devoted to his endeavors in that field.[9] Only in a brief epilogue does he acknowledge the importance of economic and social issues as causes of conflict; only there does he state that development and democratization are becoming more effective instruments of peacemaking than mediation and good offices.

His relative detachment from standard third world and Latin American positions enhanced his value as a peacemaker and helped him to avoid disharmony of purpose between himself and a Council dominated by the industrialized democracies. One example, at the very beginning of his mandate, was his scrupulous impartiality after Argentina invaded the Falkland Islands. That crisis was a tough test for the organization's first Latin American Secretary-General, who had been in office for only three months when it erupted. His near success in mediating an interim agreement that, if accepted in Buenos Aires, would have averted the conflict of May–June 1982 was an impressive achievement.

Another example was his decision in April 1989 to suspend the confinement of the South African Defense Forces to their bases in Namibia after the South West African People's Organization (SWAPO), in violation of the peace settlement, had infiltrated armed fighters from Angola. Because of the permanent members' last-minute insistence on cutting the military component of the UN Transition Assistance Group (UNTAG), there were as yet no UN troops in northern Namibia to deal with this situation. The Secretary-General's special representative, Martti Ahtisaari, advised him that the peace settlement would be in peril unless the confinement of the South African troops was temporarily suspended so that they could bring the incursion under control. Almost all Pérez de Cuéllar's advisers in New York pressed him not to accept this advice. But he was persuaded by Ahtisaari's case and courageously took a decision that he knew would cause him to be vilified by the Africans and the nonaligned nations.[10]

A third example was the evolution of Pérez de Cuéllar's thinking on sovereignty. As a Latin American jurist, he came from a political culture in which sovereignty is fiercely defended. But toward the end of his Secretary-Generalship he reached the conclusion that, as he stated in a speech in Bordeaux in 1991, international law must not be allowed to stagnate; it must keep pace with changes in international life. A new balance, it seemed, was being established between the rights of states, as confirmed by the Charter, and the rights of individuals, as confirmed by the Universal Declaration of Human Rights. Did this not call into question the notion that sovereignty must in all circumstances be regarded as inviolable?

Pérez de Cuéllar had been Peru's permanent representative in New York for five years, special representative of the Secretary-General in Cyprus for three years, and Undersecretary-General in New York for another three years. He understood the New York scene well and was a skillful judge of what the Secretary-General could and could not do. It was not difficult for him to maintain a harmonious relationship with the Security Council.

Boutros-Ghali was a different story. He had had little exposure to the United Nations. During his long years as a minister in Cairo, his main responsibility had been Egypt's bilateral relations with the countries of the third world, especially those in Africa. He shared much of the third world's dissatisfaction with the existing international architecture, and as soon as he became Secretary-General he threw his energy into a series of world conferences on economic and social issues in an effort to restore balance between peace and development in the UN's work. But it would be wrong to give the impression that he uncritically accepted all nonaligned positions. Having an independent and searching mind, he was ready to stand up to pressure from the nonaligned nations if he became convinced that the greater good of the world organization would require him to sidestep their concerns.

The Security Council summit of January 31, 1992, was a case in point. It endorsed, albeit in guarded language, a number of Western ideas—preventive action, democratization, human rights, humanitarian relief, good governance—that were seen by the governments of the third world as potential threats to their sovereignty. Boutros-Ghali, however, had already espoused many of them, especially preventive action and democratization, and like Pérez de Cuéllar he did not feel wholly constrained by the need to respect sovereignty. Moreover, he knew where power lay and he knew that power could not be ignored, even if what the powerful demanded was sometimes unpleasant or unfair. The ideas that he put into his *Agenda for Peace* were thus his own ideas, not ideas foisted on him by the West. The West liked them, but they encountered some criticism in the third world, with the result that the General Assembly was never able to adopt a substantive resolution approving them.

At the beginning of Boutros-Ghali's term of office there was thus a significant but not total degree of harmony between the priorities of the Secretary-General and those of the Security Council. But it could not withstand the strains placed on his relations with Western and other powers by the Yugoslav wars, especially the one in Bosnia. As the atrocities multiplied there and in some other territories, where a UN force had been deployed, governments and public opinion increasingly placed the blame on the United Nations, in the person of the Secretary-General, rather than on the members of the Security Council who, against his advice, had given the UN Protection Force (UNPROFOR) an unimplementable mandate in Bosnia and, as is so clearly described by Mats Berdal in Chapter 30, subsequently failed to define a strategic purpose for a force that grew larger and larger.

Delivering Results

Pérez de Cuéllar's hunch was right. The Cold War did begin to thaw as he started his second term of office. As the thaw grew, the members of the Council developed new expectations of the Secretary-General. During the Cold War they had had to acknowledge that he, like them, had very few chances of success in negotiating and implementing the settlement of third world conflicts that were fueled by East-West rivalry. Where there had been some progress in peacemaking (e.g., in the case of Namibia), the lead had been taken by a group of Western countries, not by the Security Council or the Secretary-General. Now there were opportunities for Pérez de Cuéllar to start putting into practice the ideas he had aired in Oxford. Cleverly, he first tried them on a conflict that was not a proxy conflict of the Cold War and had almost no East-West content but that was damaging the interests of all the major powers.

The Iran-Iraq War had begun in 1980. The Security Council was already seized with it, so no invocation of Article 99 was required. In January 1987, Pérez de Cuéllar invited the five permanent members of the Council to meet him in private to discuss how to start a process that would lead to a negotiated settlement. Four months of secret consultations led to agreement between the permanent members on the ingredients of a draft resolution. In July 1987 the Security Council, meeting at the level of foreign ministers, adopted the resolution unanimously. It was quickly accepted by Iraq; a year later Iran accepted it and a cease-fire came into effect. Pérez de Cuéllar had succeeded in applying the principles he had outlined in Oxford; he had taken the lead, cautiously and discreetly, in getting the five permanent members to face up to their responsibilities under the Charter and define the outlines of a settlement. As he later said in his memoirs, "The adoption of this resolution marked the beginning of the disintegration of the stultifying shroud of the Cold War that had so long enveloped the Security Council."[11]

Another example of Pérez de Cuéllar's ability to take the initiative in peacemaking was in Central America. When he assumed office, three wars had been raging for some years in El Salvador, Guatemala, and Nicaragua. The Council was deeply divided; the United States supported the governments in El Salvador and Guatemala and the rebels in Nicaragua; the Soviet Union supported the government in Nicaragua and the rebels in the other two countries. In early 1983 the Council nevertheless adopted a resolution supporting a local peace initiative and asking the Secretary-General to keep it informed. This modest but useful result was achieved despite the strong opposition of the Reagan administration to any direct UN involvement in Central America and jealous protection by the Organization of American States (OAS) of its regional turf.

Within these constraints, and with rather little consultation with the Security Council, Pérez de Cuéllar quietly inserted himself into the process. By 1989, six years later, the Central American presidents, the Reagan administration, the other members of the Council, and the OAS all agreed, with varying degrees of enthusiasm, that the United Nations had a role to play in Central America, and the Council adopted a resolution that, inter alia, expressed its full support for Pérez de Cuéllar's "mission of good offices in the region." A few months later, the Council set up a UN military observer group in Central America to support the emerging peace process there. Having thus got its foot in the door, the United Nations went on to play a major role in the 1990s in helping to restore peace in all three countries. The beneficial results that Pérez de Cuéllar's initiative had in the case of El Salvador are described in detail by Blanca Antonini in Chapter 28.

This was Pérez de Cuéllar at his best. From the beginning of his term in 1982 he had had a clear vision of what he wanted to achieve. The local stirrings of peace, led by President Oscar Arias of Costa Rica, needed to be reinforced from outside the region. Reinforcement was not going to come from the superpowers; nor could the Security Council take decisive action, as long as the Cold War continued. In an initially quiet, almost clandestine way, he talked to the governments of the region about the help that the United Nations could give to their own efforts. The initial mandate that he had from the Council was not a very robust one, but he kept the more important members of the Council informed about what he was doing and weathered the storm if one of them (usually the United States) complained that he was going too far or too fast. As in some other cases, his patience, his conviction that he was doing the right thing, and his readiness to convey the same message to his interlocutors time and again built confidence in him and minimized the risk of his efforts being curtailed by the Council.

But there was one peace process in which he seemed to lose the diplomatic skills that were so evident in the Iran-Iraq and Central American cases. This was his failed effort to negotiate a settlement of the conflict in Western Sahara between Morocco and the POLISARIO Front.[12] On this matter he provided the Security Council with rather little information and withheld from it significant details, even when he was recommending that it establish an expensive peacekeeping operation to help the parties implement a negotiated peace settlement (which later turned out to be deeply flawed). He was also sparing in his provision of information to the two parties. Because Morocco was opposed to direct negotiations between them, the peace settlement was brokered through shuttle diplomacy. This is a particularly difficult technique, in which the accurate transmission of one party's position to the other is crucial to success. If the peacemaker is trying to persuade the parties to accept a compromise, it can be tempting to dilute the strength of one party's view when communicating it to the other party. But the compromise will not last long if that is the way it is brought about.

There was a second way in which the thawing of the Cold War increased the Council's expectations of the Secretary-General. When peacemaking succeeds and a peace settlement is signed, a third party is required to help the parties implement their agreement and to resolve any differing interpretations of it. By general consent, this was a role for the United Nations, and there thus evolved a new form of peacekeeping, now called "multifunctional peacekeeping." The first such operation was UNTAG in Namibia, which is described by Cedric Thornberry in Chapter 27. Its success in completing its mandate ahead of schedule and below budget, in spite of the difficult start already mentioned, enhanced the Security Council's satisfaction with the results that Pérez de Cuéllar was delivering. He could also claim credit for peacekeeping successes in monitoring the Iran-Iraq cease-fire, verifying the withdrawal of Cuban troops from Angola, and controlling the Iraq-Kuwait border after Operation Desert Storm, as well as the establishment of a UN military presence in Central America.

By the time Boutros-Ghali assumed office, there were fewer opportunities for the Secretary-General to shine in peacemaking and peacekeeping. The peacemaking stage had become crowded, and most of the peace settlements during his tenure were the work of ad hoc groups of member states, with no conspicuous successes for the United Nations other than Guatemala and, to a limited extent, Tajikistan. There were peacekeeping successes in Cambodia, Mozambique, and Eastern Slavonia, but they were overshadowed by disasters in Angola, Bosnia, Croatia, Rwanda, and Somalia and continuing stalemate in Western Sahara. As the UN's performance appeared to decline, there was a tendency to lay the blame on Boutros-Ghali, a tendency that was fueled by growing U.S. antipathy toward him. This was unfair. The paucity of peacemaking successes was mainly due to the fact that so many other peacemakers were in the field. As for peacekeeping, the disasters mostly resulted from factors outside his control—faulty mandates imposed by the Security Council, failure of the protagonists to honor agreements they had signed, reluctance of member states to provide the resources needed, overstretch in the Secretariat, and the intrinsic difficulty of the conflicts that the international community was trying to prevent, manage, or resolve.

Managing the Relationship with the Council

The two Secretaries-General differed greatly in the way they handled their relations with the Security Council. For Pérez de Cuéllar, the Council was the most important United Nations institution: All the conflicts to which he gave so much attention passed through the Council at some stage; it was the arena in which he had his successes; and he was subtle and discreet in his use of it. He almost always gave the impression of feeling comfortable in the Council, even in the hot and airless little room where sixty or more people would gather for hours of closed "informal consultations," perched on narrow seats and jostled by the endless coming and going of the

Secretary-General's staff and junior members of missions. Pérez de Cuéllar would sit there patiently, doodling, listening intently but not often speaking himself. The speaking came later in private conversations with the protagonists and their allies. He was a diplomat par excellence, always looking for a way forward, never ashamed of repeating what he had said before, always polite, almost always calm. I cannot recall a single occasion, in open session or informal consultations, when he did or said anything that offended a delegate.

Boutros-Ghali was very different. He almost always attended open meetings of the Council when he was in New York, but he soon tired of the ennui of informal consultations. Early on in his term he appointed one of his senior political advisers, Chinmaya Gharekhan, to be his special representative on the Security Council, and thereafter he attended informal consultations only when he had something important to say (which was quite often, given the expansion of peacemaking and peacekeeping during his term of office and the disasters that beset several of the UN operations). The appointment of Gharekhan made sense in terms of the management of the Secretary-General's time, and Gharekhan was liked in the Council, where he had served as India's permanent representative. But his appointment was not well received. During Pérez de Cuéllar's tenure the members had become accustomed to the presence of the Secretary-General at all their gatherings, and some felt slighted by Boutros-Ghali's frequent absences. These damaged his interests in another way; they made it more difficult for him to "get the feel" of the Council and perhaps prevented him from seeing early enough how determined the United States was to deny him a second term.

The personal styles of the two Secretaries-General also differed, and this too affected their relations with the Council. As already mentioned, Pérez de Cuéllar is invariably calm, modest, and polite. Boutros-Ghali has charm, gracious manners, and an agreeable wit, but he can become assertive in argument, speaking directly and not always resisting the temptation of the bon mot that will raise a laugh but may also cause offense. As he readily admits in his memoir, he allowed himself to make some ill-judged remarks in the Council that did not enhance his standing there. For instance, he characterized the Bosnian conflict as "the rich man's war," drawing a contrast between the West's preoccupation with the atrocities committed there and their alleged indifference to equally awful events in Somalia. And when the U.S. mission's spokesman criticized him for suggesting that the United States and the North Atlantic Treaty Organization should assume responsibility for peacekeeping in Eastern Slavonia after the signing of the Dayton Accords on Bosnia (from the negotiation of which the United Nations had been totally barred), Boutros-Ghali told the Council that he was "shocked by the vulgarity" of the spokesman's criticism. In both cases he had genuine grounds for complaint, but the infelicity of his language strengthened U.S. hostility toward him and put him on the defensive.

But these differences in personality are not sufficient to explain why Pérez de Cuéllar had an easy and confident relationship with the Security Council while Boutros-Ghali had a comparatively difficult one. A more important factor was the quantity of work that the Council was engaged in during their respective Secretary-Generalships. In the course of Pérez de Cuéllar's ten years the Council adopted an average of 22.6 resolutions per annum; in Boutros-Ghali's five years the average nearly trebled to 73.4 per annum. During Pérez de Cuéllar's first six years there were only five peacekeeping operations in the field, with a strength of barely 10,000 uniformed personnel, and of them only the UN Interim Force in Lebanon (UNIFIL) had significant difficulties. Peacekeeping began to grow from 1988 onward, and when Pérez de Cuéllar passed the baton to Boutros-Ghali in January 1992, ten operations were in the field, though their personnel still numbered only about 12,000.

Thereafter, peacekeeping expanded very rapidly. At its peak, in mid-1994, more than 75,000 uniformed personnel were deployed in seventeen operations. Four of them—in Angola, the former Yugoslavia (Bosnia and Croatia), Somalia, and Rwanda—were facing acute difficulties, and several others were unable to implement their mandates because of obstruction by one or more of the parties. These failed, or partially failed, operations undermined confidence in peacekeeping, especially in Washington, and led to a decline in peacekeeping as rapid as the post–Cold War increase. When Boutros-Ghali left at the end of 1996, eleven operations were still in the field, but all the large ones had been completed and the overall strength had fallen to less than 20,000 military and police personnel.

It was this rapid growth in field operations that gave rise to the increase in the Security Council's activity in the first half of the 1990s. But it was not matched by a commensurate increase in staff at UN Headquarters in New York, where everyone from the Secretary-General downward had a barely tolerable workload. At the same time, member states, especially the richer ones, became less and less willing to meet the costs of peacekeeping. Those costs came in two forms: the assessed contributions that member states were obliged to make to the operations' budgets; and the costs incurred by troop-contributing countries that, in the case of the developed countries, far exceeded the often delayed reimbursements they received from the United Nations. These factors added poison to the "dialectic of demand and resources" of which Boutros-Ghali had spoken at Oxford. The worst case, which haunts the United Nations to this day, was the Western powers' refusal to provide any of the 5,000 well-trained, mobile troops that the UN force commander in Rwanda sought from New York so that he could bring the 1994 genocide under control.

But the dialectic of demand and resources was not the main cause of the less than happy relationship that developed between Boutros-Ghali and the Western members of the Security Council in 1993 and 1994. The main cause was the Western powers' policy on Bosnia, which Boutros-Ghali considered, not without reason, to be a cynical attempt to transfer to him and the United Nations responsibility for atrocious events that, until 1995, the Western powers were not prepared to deal with themselves. As Pérez de Cuéllar had rightly observed in Oxford, one of the Secretary-General's duties is to remind the member states of the responsibilities that under the Charter they, not the Secretary-General, have for the maintenance of peace and security. Boutros-Ghali repeatedly conveyed this message to the Western powers on the Security Council, but they repeatedly returned the poisoned chalice to him.

His resentment at their behavior was justified. But it led him into a number of errors: complaints about double standards, demands for more peacekeeping in Africa (when, by mid-1994, seven out of seventeen peacekeeping operations were already deployed in Africa), and as already mentioned, using language about the Council and its members that some found offensive and disrespectful. These errors, combined with the personalized campaign conducted against him by Madeleine Albright, first as U.S. permanent representative to the UN and then as secretary of state, undermined the confidence that the Security Council had placed in him during his first year and added to his difficulties at a time of hectic change in the UN's role in the prevention, management, and resolution of conflict.

Conclusion

This brief and necessarily selective comparison between the two rather different Secretaries-General who led the United Nations from the certainties of the Cold War into the uncertain opportunities and perils of a conflict-ridden postwar environment suggests the following conclusions about the relationship between the Security Council and the Secretary-General:

- The organization's capacity to achieve its purposes in the field of peace and security is undermined if there is not a harmonious working relationship between these two "principal organs."
- Such a relationship will not be achieved unless each party understands the powers and prerogatives of the other. The members of the Council must understand that the Secretary-General is not just the UN's chief administrative officer and that Article 99 gives him a

political role as well. The Secretary-General must understand (as both Pérez de Cuéllar and Boutros-Ghali did) that the final power of decision lies with the Council, which must be respected.

- Both parties must do all they can to avoid public confrontations between them because such confrontations undermine the effectiveness and credibility of the Council. When powerful members of the Council decline to accept the Secretary-General's advice, as the permanent members did in 1989 over the budget for Namibia and the Western powers did in 1992 over Bosnia, the Secretary-General faces a bleak choice. He either must challenge the Council and thereby bring about a public confrontation between the two "principal organs" with responsibility for the maintenance of peace and security; or he must give in, running the risk that terrible things will happen and the UN will be blamed for them, as happened in both Namibia and Bosnia.

- The Secretary-General's ability to perform effectively in the peace and security field depends on his enjoying the confidence of the members of the Security Council. That confidence will depend to a significant extent on the personal qualities of the incumbent and the respect that he or she displays for the Council as an institution.

- To win and retain that confidence, the Secretary-General needs to be transparent in his relations with the Security Council. There have nevertheless been occasions when an initiative by a Secretary-General would not have succeeded if it had been revealed prematurely, even to the Council. That degree of secrecy was needed more often during the Cold War than it is now; the classic case was Ralph Bunche's success, during U Thant's Secretary-Generalship, in paving the way for Bahrain's independence in 1969–1970, the best example yet of preventive diplomacy.[13] Pérez de Cuéllar was right to be secretive in his delicate approach to peacemaking in the Iran-Iraq War and in Central America, but it is now clear that he was wrong to use the same tactic in Western Sahara. In the post–Cold War world, transparency should be the norm.

Notes

1. Adam Roberts and Benedict Kingsbury, *United Nations, Divided World: The UN's Roles in International Relations,* 2nd ed. (Oxford: Clarendon, 1993).

2. The Charter says "international peace and security," but the prevalence of wars within states and the Security Council's post–Cold War readiness to include them in its agenda justify the omission of "international."

3. For a definition of "proxy conflict" of the Cold War, see Marrack Goulding, *Peacemonger* (London: John Murray, 2002), p. 118.

4. Roberts and Kingsbury, *United Nations, Divided World,* pp. 125–142.

5. SG/1035, May 30, 1961. See also Brian Urquhart, *Hammarskjold* (New York: Alfred A Knopf, 1972), pp. 527–529.

6. Boutros Boutros-Ghali, *Unvanquished* (New York: I. B. Tauris, 1999).

7. The lecture has not been published.

8. Boutros Boutros-Ghali, *An Agenda for Peace* (New York: United Nations, 1995).

9. Javier Pérez de Cuéllar, *Pilgrimage for Peace* (New York: St Martin's, 1997).

10. Ibid., p. 311; Goulding, *Peacemonger,* pp. 153–154.

11. Pérez de Cuéllar, *Pilgrimage for Peace,* p. 159.

12. See Goulding, *Peacemonger,* pp. 199–214, though this is probably not yet the full story.

13. See Brian Urquhart, *Ralph Bunche: An American Life* (New York: W. W. Norton, 1993), pp. 426–429.

19

International Tribunals and Courts

Philippe Kirsch, John T. Holmes, and Mora Johnson

Of the fundamental changes to the role of the Security Council wrought by the end of the Cold War, perhaps none inspired more hope and optimism than the Council's reluctant reach into the field of international justice. Shamed into action by a world opinion shocked and outraged at the horrific crimes committed first in the former Yugoslavia and then in Rwanda, the Council, desperate to be seen to be doing something, chose to create international judicial institutions whose objectives were to punish those individually responsible for such heinous crimes. These innovative measures to combat impunity were rightly criticized at the time as being poor substitutes for bolder action that might have mitigated or even halted the carnage much sooner. Nevertheless, the creation of the two international criminal tribunals constituted an important and unprecedented step for the Security Council and gave life and hope to the fifty-year effort to create a permanent international criminal court.

The creation of the tribunals by the Security Council was of historic import. Not only had such judicial institution-building never been initiated by the Council before; in using the broad powers assigned to it under the UN Charter, the Council also made the critical link that combating impunity was a necessary measure in ending threats to international peace and security. International justice would no longer be shunted to the sidelines in the interests of realpolitik but seemingly would form a critical adjunct to ending, if not deterring, conflicts involving massive breaches of the laws of armed conflict.

A decade or so into international politics is too soon to form definitive historical conclusions. However, to the extent that emerging trends can be relied upon, the hope inspired by the Security Council's bold steps in creating the two tribunals has given way to uncertainty and even pessimism that this organ will be an engine of change in advancing the cause of international justice. Perhaps not surprisingly, courage and creativity on the

Council have given way to a return to the old habits of power politics. In this world, principles are the first casualty in the search for peace—not international peace, but peace among the membership of the Council at the time, especially the permanent five (P-5). With few exceptions, the Council, when faced with challenges where the cause of international justice could have been advanced, chose the timid course of action of doing nothing or, as in the case of Resolution 1422, taking a significant step backward.

This chapter will describe the Security Council's actions in the field of international justice starting with the establishment of the two international criminal tribunals. It will also explore the missed opportunities for action in the cases of Iraq and Cambodia and the cautious approach adopted with respect to the Sierra Leone Special Court. Finally, the chapter will explore the possibilities for the Council to use the newly established International Criminal Court (ICC) as a mechanism to deter threats to international peace and security and to punish those who choose to flaunt the international community's will to end impunity.

Prior to July 2002, the Council's inertia in following up on the promise generated through the creation of the tribunals was predominantly the result of an inability to act or to act more effectively, no doubt caused by differences of opinion among the Council's members, notably the P-5. However, the decision by the Council to adopt Resolution 1422, giving immunity to UN peacekeepers from the jurisdiction of the International Criminal Court, represents a disturbing departure in the Council's record in addressing impunity. While arguably consistent with the letter of the Rome Statute of the ICC, the resolution nonetheless represents one of the most chilling decisions by a UN organ with respect to international justice. The adoption of the resolution, coming as it did within days of the entry into force of the Rome Statute and as delegates concluded the work of the ICC Preparatory Commission, was clearly a case of realpolitik trumping the principles of justice and the fight against impunity. More disturbingly, it presages the likely failure of the Security Council, at least in the short term, to take advantage of mechanisms included in the Rome Statute to create a close relationship between the two entities.

International Criminal Tribunals

Overview
In 1992, reports of atrocities being committed against civilians in the former Yugoslavia, including "ethnic cleansing," mass rape campaigns, and the detention of civilians, deeply shocked the international community.

Sustained and widespread calls to bring perpetrators to justice, fueled by vivid media coverage of the atrocities, put pressure on the Security Council to intervene. Council resolutions around this time began to include more explicit exhortations upon parties to the conflict to adhere to international humanitarian law, as well as declarations of individual responsibility of violators under international law.[1] Resolution 771 of August 13, 1992, first hinted at genuine enforcement: the Council, invoking its powers under Chapter VII, declared that "all parties . . . shall comply with the provisions of the present resolution, failing which the Council will need to take further measures under the Charter." A few months later, the Council created a commission of experts to evaluate the information provided to the Secretary-General on breaches of humanitarian law pursuant to Resolution 771.[2] Bolstered by strong support for the creation of a tribunal by the international community, the Council adopted Resolution 808 on February 22, 1993, which created an international tribunal for the prosecution of persons responsible for serious violations of international humanitarian law committed in the territory of the former Yugoslavia since January 1, 1991. Subsequently, Resolution 827 adopted the Statute for the International Criminal Tribunal for the Former Yugoslavia (ICTY), which set out the jurisdiction of the tribunal, including crimes under its competence, as well as other issues related to the functioning of the court and its relationships with the General Assembly and member states of the UN.

Not long after the establishment of the ICTY, the Security Council was faced with another humanitarian tragedy: the Rwandan genocide. Despite growing knowledge of the scale of the atrocities being committed in Rwanda,[3] the Security Council's response was ineffective and indeed contributed to the carnage. Instead of the bolder option outlined in the Secretary-General's report and advocated by General Romeo Dallaire, Resolution 912 called on the Secretary-General to scale back the UN mission. Paralyzed by an inability to stop the carnage, the Council began to explore how to deal with the crimes being committed. At the end of April 1994, a Council presidential statement affirmed that "persons who instigate or participate in [breaches of international humanitarian law] are individually responsible."[4] It also included a thinly veiled reference to genocide as a crime punishable under international law, language repeated in Resolution 918 of May 17, although the Council avoided the use of the word "genocide" until it adopted Resolution 925.[5] On July 1 the Council requested the Secretary-General to establish a commission of experts to evaluate any evidence or information obtained regarding grave violations of humanitarian law, with a view to providing its conclusions to the Secretary-General. Despite much high-level discussion and broad public support for the creation of a tribunal, the Security Council was very slow in reaching decisions on the framework of an ad hoc tribunal for Rwanda. At least some portion of the delay can be attributed to the lack of agreement on several aspects of the proposed tribunal by the new Tutsi-led government of Rwanda, which held a seat on the Council. In the end, Rwanda voted against Resolution 955, which created the International Criminal Tribunal for Rwanda (ICTR) when adopted by the Security Council on November 8, 1994.[6]

Challenges to the Ad Hoc Tribunals

The establishment of the tribunals by the Security Council was unprecedented and at a first glance appeared bold and imaginative. Yet the reality of the Council's efforts at the time of the creation of the tribunals was less than compelling. The commission of experts established to accumulate evidence of crimes being committed in the former Yugoslavia was severely underfunded and received indifferent support from the UN Secretariat and many key UN member states. Indeed, the UN Secretariat terminated the commission itself on April 30, 1994, prior to the appointment of a prosecutor. Moreover, that appointment was delayed in part by chance (the first prosecutor decided to remain in Venezuela to join a new government) and by political machinations among the P-5, as Russia threatened to veto any candidate from a member of the North Atlantic Treaty Organization (NATO). As well, there were problems in budgeting for the tribunal. Some of these difficulties were attributed to predictable bureaucratic problems in the UN and in states, especially since the tribunals were a new phenomenon. Yet there was also little doubt that serious reservations about the tribunals existed in the Council, in the UN Secretariat, and among key states. The work of the ICTY coincided with the Dayton peace process and gave rise to fears that investigations and prosecutions of senior officials and leaders in the former Yugoslavia could hamper the peace negotiations. In the end, both processes proceeded independently of each other. The tribunals were also the subject of legal attacks by individuals and some states questioning the authority of the Security Council to establish these types of judicial institutions.

Shortly after the creation of the ICTY, the Federal Republic of Yugoslavia challenged its legality, arguing: "No independent tribunal, particularly an international tribunal can be a subsidiary organ of any body, including the Security Council."[7] Other states, notably Mexico and Cuba, also questioned the authority of the Council to establish the tribunals and subsequently refused for many years to join the consensus in the General Assembly on their financing. In addition, defendants have unsuccessfully challenged the legal bases of the tribunals, both before the tribunals themselves and before some domestic courts.[8]

The legal authority of the Security Council to create the tribunals under Chapter VII appears today to be beyond question. The ICTY decision in the Tadic case found that the broad and discretionary powers of the Security Council under Article 41 include the power to create an international criminal tribunal. The list of measures in Articles 41 and 42 is clearly not exhaustive, and others, such as peacekeeping missions, have been established under Chapter VII even though such measures are not listed in the Charter. It does seem absurd to argue that a body with the authority to legally wage war does not have the power to create a tribunal to bring justice to war criminals in the interests of restoring or maintaining international peace and security.

In conclusion, the preponderance of legal arguments supports the legality of the establishment of the ad hoc tribunals. Additionally, their legitimacy is enhanced by their reasonably effective functioning despite many challenges, their solid record of fair decisions, and the institutional oversight role of the General Assembly.

Relationship Between the Security Council and the Ad Hoc Tribunals

The statutes of the tribunals reveal considerable powers bestowed upon them by the Security Council. For example, the tribunals' primacy over domestic courts, and the obligation upon states to provide evidence or to surrender suspects, constitute significant intrusions into areas of state sovereignty. The authority of the tribunals is supported, at least in theory, by the considerable enforcement powers of the Security Council. For example, the Council could adopt a resolution under Chapter VII calling upon a particular state to comply with an order of the tribunal, on threat of sanction, if it determined that such compliance would assist its mandate of maintaining international peace and security.

In reality, the Security Council has not made extensive use of its broad powers, despite the fact that state cooperation has been uneven at best. In the early years of the ICTY, many states under the territorial jurisdiction of the tribunal did not cooperate with it until governments changed and regimes complicit in the commission of crimes were gone. At the same time, the Council was criticized for failing to move quickly to ensure the effectiveness of the tribunal. For example, the ICTY prosecutor publicly stated in 1998 that "the Security Council unanimously approved a resolution that called upon Libya to honour its pledges with respect to the transfer for trial for the two suspects in the Lockerbie bombing case. . . . This resolution stands in stark contrast with the lack of action by the Council regarding the [Vukovar] case."[9] Later, both France and Russia were accused by the prosecutor of not turning over suspects as requested by the ICTY when they had the opportunity to do so.[10] In the case of Rwanda, it is only in recent years that cooperation with the ICTR, including the surrender of accused, has improved.

More recently, the support of the international community for the tribunals has grown. The Federal Republic of Yugoslavia's handover of Slobodan Milosevic, in large part due to the diplomatic and economic pressure of the United States and the European Union, was a significant development, in that he is the first head of state tried for crimes committed while in office. However, the record remains uneven. High-profile accused remain at large. Key states still adopt ways to evade their obligations to cooperate fully with the tribunals. The Security Council, while well aware of these deficiencies and possessing the capacity to act with vigor, has been reluctant to do more than debate the issue.

The International Criminal Court

Establishment

The ad hoc approach taken by the Security Council to address global justice issues was deemed to be unsatisfactory by many states for various reasons. In addition to those few states that questioned the authority of the Council to adopt binding decisions in this field, many states believed that a more systemic, less political approach was required. The ad hoc approach addressed only specific situations that met an artificial, unwritten threshold (the "CNN factor") forcing the Council to act. Moreover, it was clearly understood that the power of the veto would preclude even a discussion of, let alone a decision to, create a tribunal with jurisdiction to review the actions of the P-5 or their close allies. In parallel to and subsequent to the creation of the tribunals, the focus on the issue of addressing impunity began to shift to the UN General Assembly.

The idea of creating a permanent international criminal court, born of the horrific events of World War II and the judicial precedents of Nuremberg and Tokyo, languished in the International Law Commission for many years due to Cold War tensions. In 1989 the concept was revived in the General Assembly by Trinidad and Tobago, although the scope of its vision was focused more on assisting small states in the fight against drug trafficking. It was only when the Security Council responded to the events in the former Yugoslavia and Rwanda through the creation of the international tribunals that work on the preparation of a draft ICC statute took on greater urgency and the emphasis shifted to war crimes, genocide, and crimes against humanity, putting drug trafficking, terrorism, and other crimes to the side. In early 1998, negotiations on a draft statute were completed (although with more than 1,500 options in the form of square brackets, alternative proposals, and so forth), and this text formed the basis for negotiations at the Rome Diplomatic Cónference on an International Criminal Court. On July 17, 1998, by a vote of 120-7 (with twenty-one abstentions), the conference adopted the Rome Statute.

Relationship Between the ICC and the Security Council

The interrelationship between the Security Council and the ICC formed a critical and controversial part of the negotiations leading up to and at the Rome Conference. Many states believed that one of the central goals of establishing an ICC was to obviate the need for the ad hoc approach taken by the Security Council. The existence of a functioning permanent court would permit the Council to refer serious situations to it for investigation and prosecution, rather than pursuing the difficult and costly process of establishing a new ad hoc tribunal. This logic held broad appeal to many delegations at Rome, but the difficulties in the negotiations came from two sources: one legal and one political. From a legal standpoint, there were justifiable concerns that an appropriate balance needed to be struck between the Council's primacy in addressing situations threatening international peace and security and the necessity of insulating the Court from overt and untoward political influence by the Council. Politically, the debate on the role of the Security Council and the ICC became enmeshed in the endless debates in New York regarding Security Council reform and expansion, particularly with respect to the use of the veto. India (and a few other states) challenged the notion that the Security Council should have any role with respect to the ICC because of the veto possessed by the P-5.

The Rome Statute envisages a close and cooperative relationship between the ICC and the Security Council, as well as significant potential for the Security Council to use its Chapter VII powers to enforce and assist the undertakings of the ICC. The nature of this relationship is defined in the Rome Statute, and additionally in the Rules of Procedure and Evidence (RPE) and the Relationship Agreement between the International Criminal Court and the United Nations, two important documents adopted by the ICC Preparatory Commission and approved by the Assembly of States Parties of the Rome Statute.[11] It is intended to be an instrument that the Council will make use of in its responsibility to maintain and restore international peace and security. It represents a carefully balanced legal and political approach to combating impunity: a treaty-based organization with its powers consented to by states, but with significant potential for Security Council involvement and enforcement. The Council could play a significant role in deterring the commission of international crimes through threats of a referral of a situation to the Court and in bringing to justice perpetrators in states not party to the statute, or through actual referrals. The

Council may also play a critical role in ensuring that states cooperate with the ICC in prosecuting cases.

Referrals by the Security Council to the ICC

Article 13(b) of the Rome Statute provides that the Security Council may refer a situation to the ICC.[12] The main purpose, of course, is to make the ICC available to the Council to investigate situations posing a threat to international peace and security. Additionally, it potentially enlarges the jurisdiction of the Court by allowing the Council to refer situations in states that are members of the UN but not parties to the Rome Statute.

Referrals are subject to certain conditions specified in the Rome Statute and the RPE. The Court may not pursue a referral relating to human rights or humanitarian law violations unless those violations relate to crimes falling within its jurisdiction. The Council cannot refer a specific case or crime to the Court: it must refer a situation. It then falls to the Court to determine if the situation should be investigated and which statute crimes are to be prosecuted. This formulation provides the option of referral by the Council yet preserves the independence of the Court. The Council can make its referral retroactive to the date of the request. However, crimes committed before the entry into force of the Rome Statute (July 1, 2002) fall outside the jurisdiction of the Court. Last, the Council must make the referral in writing, acting under Chapter VII of the UN Charter.

The Rome Statute, the RPE, and the Relationship Agreement envisage a complex, cooperative relationship between the ICC and the Security Council in how a Council referral is addressed. Provisions exist for the prosecutor and the pretrial chamber to request additional information or clarification as to the nature of the referral. There is also an obligation for the prosecutor to inform the Council of his/her intention not to proceed with an investigation, and a right of the Council to request a Court review of that decision. The relationship is founded on the independence of the Court as a judicial institution while recognizing the primary responsibility of the Security Council in maintaining international peace and security and the important role international justice can play in that regard.

The Rome Statute provides extensive safeguards, which allow states and accused the ability to challenge the jurisdiction and admissibility of any proceedings. The procedural opportunities to challenge, when the Court is dealing with a Security Council referral, are more limited but not completely absent. Some jurisdictional challenges are unavailable, such as arguing that the state in which the crimes occurred was not a party to the Rome Statute. However, a state or an accused is arguably still able to make a complementarity challenge, to the effect that a state is already investigating or prosecuting the same situation. Although the Council could, in its referral decision, seek to preclude this possibility by determining that the state in question is genuinely unwilling or unable to investigate or prosecute a case, any such determination would not be binding on the Court. If the latter is satisfied—that the state in question was genuine in its efforts to investigate and prosecute—the Court can ignore the wishes of the Council and decline to assume jurisdiction in the case or situation.

Requests by the Security Council to the ICC to Defer Action

The most contentious issue relating to the role of the Security Council in ICC undertakings is that of deferrals of investigations and prosecutions. Generally, unease about Council deferrals goes beyond concerns about political interference with the Court by the Council, or questions regarding the legal authority of the Council to seek a deferral under Chapter VII. Most objections relate to issues of inequality for P-5 countries: the fact that the P-5 possess a veto means that they could avoid Court scrutiny if a situation developed in their country or involved their nationals, a "privilege" of putting their nationals above the law that is not enjoyed by other states. At the same time, there is a recognition by most that the Council's responsibilities in the maintenance of international peace and security require that the ICC's actions not interfere with delicate proceedings in which the Council is involved.

Article 16 as agreed to at the Rome Conference strikes a delicate balance between these two concerns. It requires a resolution of the Security Council under Chapter VII to request the deferral of an investigation or prosecution, but limits the length of the deferral to twelve months, while permitting renewals. If the Court receives a valid request from the Security Council, it must comply immediately with the request.

On July 12, 2002, at the initiation of the United States, the Security Council passed Resolution 1422, which includes in its first operative paragraph that "if a case involving current or former officials or personnel from a contributing State not a Party to the Rome Statute over acts or omissions relating to a United Nations established or authorized operation, shall for a twelve-month period starting 1 July 2002 not commerce or proceed with investigation or prosecution of any such case, unless the Security Council decides otherwise."[13] The purported effect of this resolution is to prevent the Court from investigating or prosecuting any nationals of non–Rome Statute parties that participate in UN missions or regional missions that are sanctioned by the Council.[14] Under Chapter VII of the UN Charter, resolutions such as 1422 may be adopted only when the Council determines the existence of a threat to the peace. Procedurally, the Security Council did not satisfy or purport to satisfy that precondition. In addition, even if the

Council is generally granted a fair degree of latitude and deference as to its authority, there appeared to be a manifest absence of any threat to the peace in this situation.

The Council's actions were especially surprising and disturbing given the extensive safeguards contained in the Rome Statute and the RPE to prevent the kinds of politicized investigations that motivated the United States to insist on Resolution 1422 in the first place. The Court will act responsibly and should be viewed as a very valuable instrument at the disposal of the Council in its responsibilities to maintain international peace and security. It is hoped that the Council will be reflective of the costs of renewing 1422.[15] The credibility of both the Security Council and the ICC will be undermined if the responsibilities entrusted to the Council continue to be seen to be used for the questionable benefit of attempting to preemptively place some states' nationals above the rule of law.

Cooperation Between the Security Council and the ICC

The Rome Statute and the RPE provide several means through which the Council can cooperate closely with the ICC. Apart from referrals, the Council can also assist the prosecutor and the Court in investigations and prosecutions of cases not referred by the Council (e.g., provide additional information such as reports of the Secretary-General on matters already before the attention of the Council). The scope of "additional information" is broad enough to include a request to the Council to provide up-to-date information on a Council-mandated peacekeeping or enforcement mission.[16] Assuming the willingness of the Council to cooperate, it could include the Council's authorizing the commander or other members of the mission to appear before the Court to provide additional information or give testimony.[17]

Role of the Security Council in
Ensuring State Cooperation with the ICC

It is clear from the experience of ad hoc tribunals that state cooperation will be essential for the effective functioning of the ICC. The Security Council has an opportunity to play a significant role with respect to ensuring that states comply with requests from the Court—not just with respect to situations referred by the Council, but also in other instances.

Rome Statute parties will always be legally bound to respect orders and requests for assistance by the Court, but of course, some may fail to live up to their obligations. In the case of Security Council referrals, all member states of the UN, regardless of whether they are parties to the statute, will be required to cooperate with the Court. If UN member states fail to comply with requests for cooperation with the Court, regardless of whether they are parties to the statute, the Court may refer the matter to the Security Council.

The Council is clearly empowered to pass a resolution under Chapter VII requiring a particular state to comply with requests of the ICC, if it determines that such compliance will be in the interests of maintaining or restoring international peace and security once a breach of the peace has been determined to exist. This is obviously most likely to occur in the case of a Council referral of a situation to the Court. However, it is possible to envision situations in which the Council would use its powers to assist the Court even in cases that do not concern Council referrals. For example, if the ICC were to indict a notorious terrorist or war criminal based on a non-Council-referred investigation, the Council may determine that surrendering such a person to the ICC for trial would be in the interests of international peace and security, and thus order a country harboring that person to cooperate with the Court.

The Crime of Aggression

Aggression was included in the Rome Statute, but the Court will not exercise jurisdiction over the crime until "a provision is adopted in accordance with articles 121 and 123 defining the crime and setting out the conditions under which the Court shall exercise jurisdiction with respect to this crime. Such a provision shall be consistent with the relevant provisions of the Charter of the United Nations."[18] The phrase "conditions under which the Court shall exercise jurisdiction" was intended by many to refer to the role of the Security Council, as was the reference to the provision being consistent with the UN Charter.

The ongoing negotiations on aggression reveal that the above view is not shared by all. Some delegations have endeavored to develop solutions for the Court to exercise jurisdiction over the crime of aggression even absent a Security Council determination. In large part, this desire is based on the fact that the Council rarely makes determinations that an act of aggression has occurred and certainly would be unlikely to do so with respect to a member of the P-5. Although this may be true, it is unquestionable that the Court must function within the framework of the UN Charter. If the crime of aggression is to be defined and included in the statute, a role for the Council will have to be developed, consistent with its mandate under the Charter.

In conclusion, it is clear that a strong, cooperative relationship between the Security Council and the ICC is envisaged by the Rome Statute and the RPE and is critical to the success of the Court. The relationship is consistent with the respective mandates and powers of the Court and the Council.

Conclusion

If the Council, at the insistence of one of the P-5, is not prepared to use the ICC to respond to specific situations in which heinous crimes have been committed, what alternatives are available to it? The ad hoc approach of creating new tribunals remains an alternative. However, the Council has not seen fit to establish new tribunals, despite demands to do just that. The reasons for the Council's inaction have been political, as well as based on a growing concern over the costs, longevity, and perceived inefficiencies of the two international criminal tribunals. During the 1990s the U.S. delegation proposed informally to Council members that a tribunal be created to try Saddam Hussein for crimes committed during the Iran-Iraq War against his own people and for crimes committed during the Gulf War. The proposal never moved beyond informal discussions because of the lack of support among a number of Council members. The idea of creating a tribunal to prosecute the Khmer Rouge was left to the UN General Assembly to address. The closest the Council came to creating a new tribunal was with respect to Sierra Leone. The Council held extensive discussions on this issue and ultimately adopted Resolution 1315. However, the Sierra Leone Special Court is not a Chapter VII tribunal. Rather, it is a hybrid entity with voluntary funding and no specific Council enforcement mechanisms. It is often held up as the model for the future, particularly by states opposed to the ICC. It is more cost-effective than the two existing tribunals, and because it is located in Sierra Leone, it is thought to be better able to foster national reconciliation and promote the rule of law in the country. Detractors argue that the long-term success of the Sierra Leone Special Court is contingent upon the continued voluntary support of donors and the continued commitment of a fragile and poor state.

Clearly, the ICC offers many advantages over the ad hoc tribunals. It is a permanent institution with highly qualified judges and staff in place. It is conceivably ready and able to assume responsibility for a serious situation the moment the matter is referred to it by the Security Council. As the ICC was created by states through careful negotiation and direct state consent, it has a high degree of credibility and international support. Because parties to the Rome Statute directly oversee the management of the Court (e.g., in the election of judges), they have both the opportunity and a direct stake in ensuring its success. The speed of ratifications and accessions is testimony to states' willingness to support and strengthen the ICC. This active support of the international community should translate into concrete action by states, using diplomacy and other means, to pressure noncooperative states to comply with requests and orders of the Court.

Detractors of the Court, such as the United States, argue that the Rome Statute is flawed and that the Court will be subject to politically motivated manipulation. As a result, they would likely oppose close UN cooperation with the Court, including the possibility of a Security Council referral. At the same time, alternative models (ad hoc tribunals, special courts, national courts) may not prove realistic, especially in situations where a state is actively complicit in the commission of crimes. A number of states, including the Russian Federation, have publicly stated that the establishment of the ICC makes unnecessary the creation of any new ad hoc tribunals.

The apparent impasse may result in paralysis in the Security Council, at least in the short term. Over the longer term, the reluctance to embrace (or tolerate) the ICC may change. As the Court demonstrates itself to be fair, evenhanded, and effective, concerns will become less credible and diminish over time. Ratification by states of the Rome Statute is continuing at a positive pace, and it is conceivable that more than two-thirds of the UN membership will be party to the Rome Statute within a decade, thus going a long way toward making it a universal court.

The Security Council and its members cannot turn a blind eye to these developments. It will surely come to recognize that the ICC, by bringing perpetrators to justice and halting cycles of violence, also has the potential to play an invaluable role in enabling the Security Council to fulfill its responsibility of maintaining and restoring international peace and security. In so doing, the Security Council will join with the many states and representatives of civil society that have already come to this realization.

Notes

We were members of the Department of Foreign Affairs and International Trade at the time this chapter was prepared. The views contained in this chapter are personal and do not necessarily reflect the views of the government of Canada.

1. Resolution 752, May 15, 1992, and Resolution 764, July 12, 1992.
2. Resolution 780, S/RES/780 (1992). The commission concluded that war crimes, crimes against humanity, as well as crimes that could possibly constitute genocide were taking place in the former Yugoslavia, and it included a suggestion that the Security Council or another organ of the UN could establish an international criminal tribunal to try the accused. See S/25274, February 10, 1992.
3. *Special Report of the Secretary-General on the UN Assistance Mission for Rwanda,* S/1994/470, April 20, 1994.
4. S/PRST/1994/21, April 30, 1994.
5. S/RES/925, June 8, 1994.
6. S/RES/955 (1994).
7. A/48/170, May 21, 1993.
8. *Prosecutor v. Tadic* (IT-94-1-AR72), *Prosecutor v. Kanyabashi* (ICTR-96-15-T). In the case of *Re the Surrender of E. Ntakirutimana* (L-96-005, S.D. Texas), the legality of the tribunals was challenged in a U.S. domestic case.
9. ICTY press release, CC/PIU/344-E, September 9, 1998.
10. *Le Devoir,* December 16, 1997, p. A1; *National Post,* December 17, 1998, p. A14.
11. *Official Records of the First Session of the Assembly of States Parties,* September 3–10, 2002, New York, ICC-ASP/1/3.

12. Referrals may also be made by parties to the statute and the prosecutor is empowered to initiate investigations proprio motu, with the approval of the pretrial chamber of the Court.

13. S/RES/1422 (2002).

14. For example, the Council authorized the Stabilization Force for Bosnia-Herzegovina, a NATO force (see S/RES/1088 [1996]), and the International Task Force for East Timor (see S/RES/1264 [1996]).

15. Resolution 1422 was renewed by Security Council Resolution 1487 (2003).

16. That is, interim reports, or responses to specific Council requests.

17. *Rome Statute,* art. 15(2).

18. Ibid., art. 5(2).

20

Collaborating with Regional Organizations

SHEPARD FORMAN AND ANDREW GRENE

The engagement of the Security Council in post–Cold War peace and security correlates to the belief of its members that the legitimacy conveyed by the United Nations can help them achieve key objectives. Although recent debates over Iraq will likely complicate this equation in the future, the major powers have relied increasingly upon the Council as a forum to authorize military action, in order to maintain international goodwill for sensitive tasks, reduce the risk of "spoilers," and preserve international order. But their confidence has been less consistent in the ability of the United Nations to act as an "implementing agency." This is evidenced by the rapid development in the post–Cold War period of regional and multinational forces (MNFs) as alternatives to UN operations, not only for "enforcement" (a task to which they may bring important advantages) but also for peacekeeping.

This chapter focuses on a series of peacekeeping operations that were undertaken by the Security Council on the premise, drawn in part from the model of MNF partnerships, that regional organizations with a substantial military presence on the ground would play a lead political and security role. As described below, these are the operations codeployed with missions established by the Economic Community of West African States (ECOWAS) in Liberia and Sierra Leone, by the Commonwealth of Independent States (CIS) in Tajikistan and Georgia, and by the North Atlantic Treaty Organization (NATO) in the former Yugoslavia (after Dayton) and Kosovo.

In other instances,[1] regional organizations had been authorized to assist UN operations to discharge their mandates under the Secretary-General's command and control.[2] However, the operations discussed in this chapter suggest a step by the Security Council away from global responsibility for peace and security[3] and toward a regionalist approach, where, although the Council would authorize activity, it would be executed primarily by regional agencies and mechanisms.

295

This chapter reviews these experiences, which were based, in broad terms, either on a limited UN response to regional initiatives, or on the desire on the part of Security Council members to deploy a robust presence outside of a UN operational framework, and identifies certain problems that emerged in both kinds of partnership. It concludes with a review of various doctrinal and operational guidelines proposed by academics and practitioners to govern future cooperation between the UN and regional organizations in peacekeeping as a means to reduce such problems in the future.

Experimentation with Partnerships

Rise in Partnerships

"Observer" missions—UN acceptance of and support for regionally initiated actions. Despite the existence of provisions regarding regional operations in the UN Charter, it was only after the end of the Cold War, when confronted with a rush of intrastate conflicts, that the Security Council authorized operations where regional organizations took a lead role. The first such "partnership" between the Security Council and a regional organization took shape with the September 1993 authorization of a United Nations deployment in Liberia. There, Nigeria had taken the lead in deploying, through ECOWAS, a large regional force (the ECOWAS Monitoring Group [ECOMOG]) to address a chaotic civil conflict that threatened to spread beyond the country. This deployment took place in the context of a conspicuous absence of interest from external powers, including those with historical and economic ties to the West African country.

ECOMOG's efforts to impose peace quickly ran into a number of problems, attributed to causes including inexperience in such undertakings, logistical deficiencies, and wide differences of approach by key ECOWAS members, the less powerful of whom believed that their perspectives were being excluded or sidelined.[4] The force soon found itself cast in the role of combatant, rather than mediator, by the key faction leader, Charles Taylor; after an attack by Taylor's faction brought unsustainably high costs on both the rebels and on ECOMOG and its key contributors,[5] the wider international community was reluctantly drawn in through the Cotonou Agreement, which paved the way for deployment of the UN Observer Mission in Liberia (UNOMIL).

UNOMIL was presented as a symbol of international support for Liberia; it was also publicly perceived as a means to ensure that international norms were observed and to combat suggestions that ECOMOG's presence in Liberia favored regional hegemony by Nigeria. The Security

Council underlined the historic nature of its deployment, noting that this would be "the first peacekeeping mission undertaken by the United Nations in cooperation with a peacekeeping operation already set up by another organization."[6]

However, the use of the word "cooperation" implies that the two operations were comparable in role and capacity, which was far from the case. In fact, UNOMIL's tasks were essentially to "monitor" and "report," whereas ECOMOG undertook the peace enforcement tasks in question. ECOMOG and Nigeria had hoped that the deployment could be a key to obtaining desperately needed resources and logistical support. But far from being a full-scale peacekeeping operation, UNOMIL included only a handful of unarmed officers, who were dependent upon ECOMOG for their own security.

These mismatched expectations tended to create a difficult relationship between the two forces in the field. Furthermore, while ECOMOG was arguably a force for stability within an otherwise chaotic situation, it was itself accused of abuses. Yet UNOMIL's dependence upon ECOMOG limited its capacity to play an effective "monitoring" role: "although UNOMIL was expected to assume a supervisory position over ECOMOG . . . the Accord did not put in place a mechanism to make this possible."[7] Critics also argued that the UN's limited presence testified to the West's indifference to problems outside areas of its immediate strategic interests. For all of these reasons, this first "codeployment" was viewed as problematic at best (and its justification was questioned further after Taylor was elected as the country's president—the likely outcome had no regional or UN intervention taken place at all).

Even as the UN was finding its way in West Africa, the Security Council authorized two operations within the CIS that shared some key characteristics with UNOMIL. The first of these was the ongoing UN Observer Mission in Georgia (UNOMIG), which was initially authorized in August 1993 but could not be deployed until the following July. Like UNOMIL, UNOMIG is composed of unarmed observers and depends upon a much larger, armed regional force (the CIS peacekeeping force) for its ability to discharge a number of monitoring tasks—which include observing the operation of the CIS peacekeeping force. The second operation was the UN Mission of Observers in Tajikistan (UNMOT), authorized in December 1994, which was initially designed as a minimalist observer operation that could function only with close cooperation with the CIS collective peacekeeping force in Tajikistan.

As in Liberia, the impulse for action came from within the region, and was led by a key power within it, acting through a regional political/security structure. And as in the case of UNOMIL, the two CIS operations reinforced the idea that maintaining order is a regional concern that relies upon the engagement of major powers within their respective regions.

Forceful peacekeeping—the Security Council calls on NATO. The next major regional partnership, the post-Dayton engagement of NATO in Bosnia and Herzegovina, was markedly different in origin and in character. Unlike the conflicts in West Africa and the CIS, the civil war in Bosnia did not fall clearly within an acknowledged sphere of influence but rather straddled an emerging fault line of post–Cold War power relations. Therefore, in contrast to the Council's halting involvement in the former cases, where the search for a solution fell largely by default to the relevant regional power, the authorization of NATO's lead security role in Bosnia and Herzegovina was the product of intense political engagement by Council members, since it signaled significant geostrategic change.

From their inception, the UN's efforts to promote peace in the former Yugoslavia had drawn upon simultaneous work by NATO, which was initially engaged (together with the Western European Union) to undertake force-related activities that supported the peacekeeping and peacemaking role of the UN Protection Force (UNPROFOR). However, both were clearly "junior partners" to UNPROFOR, their engagement offering them—NATO in particular—a welcomed means to gain new relevance in the post–Cold War period.

NATO's role became increasingly prominent as the track of peaceful negotiations became harder to defend politically and public opinion swung behind an enforcement approach. This swing became definitive in 1995 after the massacre of civilians in Srebrenica and the shelling of a Sarajevo marketplace led to authorization of a two-week bombing campaign by NATO that, together with Croatian military success, paved the way for the Dayton Accords.

Political considerations played an important role in shaping these arrangements. Dayton came in the wake of the public debate in Washington, where the debacle in Somalia was attributed to failure by the United Nations. The strategy worked out at Dayton corresponded to the logic of Presidential Decision Directive 25, the articulation of U.S. post-Somalia peacekeeping policy, which sought to limit U.S. engagement in UN operations and urged greater consideration of regional options. It reflected U.S. political wariness of appearing to support the United Nations,[8] combined with political interest in anchoring Bosnia and Herzegovina within a Western security sphere.

While the use of NATO for *peace enforcement* activities had built upon the paradigm established with the use of MNFs in the Gulf War, Somalia, and Haiti, the Dayton Accords went further in allocating the military dimension of a *peacekeeping* operation to the Implementation Force (IFOR). This force was no longer subject to a "dual-key" formula, whereby UN consent was required for forceful action, but functioned exclusively under its own command. IFOR was given authority—although no obligation—to go beyond a military role to encompass such tasks as policing, security, and detention of war criminals.[9]

The involvement of NATO was advocated based on its military strength, and analysis by UN Secretariat officials has also noted the benefit of NATO's strong deterrent capability—but has stressed that this would have been particularly useful prior to Dayton.[10] By the time that IFOR was deployed, the overarching political agreement that had so notably been lacking during UNPROFOR's mandate had finally fallen into place; and while continued political pressure was essential, the basic prerequisite for peacekeeping was finally present. Furthermore, the overarching reality that emerges from a review of the conflict was that early external intervention, of whatever sort, was doomed because there was no agreement among the major powers, nor among regional powers, on what to do. Despite its primarily military character as a defensive alliance, NATO, like the UN, is subject to political oversight by an established body and, also like the UN, was initially paralyzed by the political reality that no consensus for action existed among major powers.

NATO's comparative influence grew still more as the UN's role was minimized even in peacebuilding—where the UN's competence had not been at issue. Responsibilities in this area were farmed out to the Organization for Security and Cooperation in Europe (OSCE), the European Union (EU), the UN high commissioner for refugees (UNHCR), and others, and a High Representative was created, which did not report to the Security Council but to an ad hoc steering committee. However, it is notable that since Dayton an extensive international presence remains in Bosnia and Herzegovina, still based on the original division of labor between NATO peacekeeping and a series of political and peacebuilding activities under the loose authority of the High Representative.

Although political problems remain outstanding in the country, the international community's pursuit of peacekeeping and peacebuilding on parallel tracks may also have contributed to delay. It has favored reduced accountability to address some of the most intractable problems, such as arrest of war criminals and law and order, which fall into an organizational and substantive gray area. It has also paved the way for relatively weak and uncoordinated support given to peacebuilding. The result has been that the international community has to some degree lacked an exit strategy by which to work itself out of a job.

Reversion to United Nations Peacekeeping
The initial impact of these experiments in codeployment and delegation was a widespread belief that regional operations, together with MNFs, were the way of the future, and that the era of expansive United Nations peacekeeping might pass as quickly as it had begun. This was reinforced when, over the next two and a half years, from December 1995 through April 1998, no new deployments were authorized, apart from a very brief operation in Guatemala. The number of United Nations peacekeepers declined steadily, from about 53,000 in November 1995, just before the Dayton Accords, to slightly more than 13,000 at the beginning of 1998; the budget for United Nations peacekeeping dropped proportionately from U.S.$3.3 billion to U.S.$907 million.[11] Peacekeeping staffing at United Nations headquarters declined by more than 20 percent, from 450 to 350.

However, even as the machinery for United Nations peacekeeping was downgraded, the need for effective peacekeeping mechanisms continued to demand attention, and a series of experiences in Europe and Africa suggested that options relying upon regional or multinational solutions could present their own problems. In Europe, efforts to rely upon either NATO or the EU to respond to the problems in Albania in 1997 proved unsuccessful when no consensus could be reached on the necessary action, forcing last-minute reliance upon an ad hoc arrangement. Meanwhile, in Zaire (now the Democratic Republic of Congo [DRC]), the Security Council authorized deployment of a multinational force to deal with the camps that came into being after the flight of the Interahamwe and Forces Armées Rwandaises from Rwanda but found that the required level of troops could not be obtained. Over the same period, countering the image of failure that had resulted from UNPROFOR, the United Nations effectively undertook an operation that required a forceful role in Eastern Slavonia.

Despite these experiences, it came as a surprise when the Security Council plunged into a new, rapid expansion of United Nations peacekeeping. Between 1998 and 2002, the Security Council authorized seven operations,[12] mostly large, reflecting a renewed recognition by the Council that deployment of a substantial United Nations operation might in the long term be crucial to ensuring success.

In Sierra Leone, in support of ECOMOG's efforts to address a civil conflict ignited by the war in Liberia, the Security Council had authorized deployment of the UN Observer Mission in Sierra Leone (UNOMSIL) in July 1998, in accordance with a peace plan organized through ECOWAS. UNOMSIL, a small observer mission that served alongside a much larger ECOMOG force, resembled UNOMIL; it included seventy unarmed observers, working under the protection of ECOMOG, who were mandated to monitor and advise efforts to disarm combatants and to document abuses. But despite high expenditure and casualties, ECOMOG proved unable to impose peace, and after a major attack on Freetown in January 1999 the Security Council abandoned the model of minimalist engagement it had used in Liberia.

In October 1999 it moved to replace UNOMSIL with the UN Mission in Sierra Leone (UNAMSIL), a major peacekeeping operation that gradually took over from the regional force. Over the following year and a half, the Security Council three times expanded the size of the operation, from 6,000 ultimately to 17,500, while giving it Chapter VII (enforcement) authority. Nigeria's key role continued to be reflected in senior military and civilian appointments and in the composition of the force. Furthermore, the operation's effectiveness was ensured by direct intervention by the United Kingdom at key moments. Nonetheless, in broad terms, UNAMSIL suggested that the United Nations might need to assume primary operational responsibility where local capacity was lacking, and that a UN peacekeeping operation could still represent a key conduit for operational engagement by major powers, in addition to conferring legitimacy and political acceptability.

This sense of "added value" on the part of the UN was further expressed with the Security Council's authorization of full-scale operations in four other countries, the Central African Republic (1998), East Timor (1999), the DRC (1999), and Ethiopia and Eritrea (2000). In the first two of these, while a high level of capacity was brought to bear for a limited period through a multinational force, its maintenance would have demanded a politically or financially unsustainable commitment by the MNF's lead country, and in the case of East Timor the need for legitimacy of action made a lead UN role desirable. In the last two, while a significant political role was played by a regional body (the Organization of African Unity), appropriate operational capacity could be brought to bear only through the United Nations.

Kosovo exemplified still another rationale for giving a major role to United Nations peacekeeping even where regional capacity existed. There, after an eleven-week bombing campaign by NATO led to the withdrawal of Serbian forces, the United Nations became at the last minute a key part of the international community's strategy for maintaining a fragile peace in the area, because of the need to ensure support by a major regional power (the Russian Federation). In contrast to the arrangements forged at Dayton, the Security Council retained an important operational role for the United Nations. While the regional dimension remained a core part of the international community's response, with NATO taking a lead role in security, and important roles in peacebuilding being played by the OSCE and the EU, no High Representative was created in Kosovo. Instead, the special representative of the Secretary-General took the lead in political activity, oversaw peacebuilding activity, and assumed responsibility for Kosovo's "transitional administration."

Finally, the decision to create a UN operation in Afghanistan in 2002 was driven, as in Kosovo, by the importance of legitimacy. Also as in Kosovo, the special representative of the Secretary-General is the clear coordinating authority for international political and peacebuilding efforts. However, its structure in several other respects represents a further experiment with delegation. Operationally, security was pursued outside the United Nations framework,[13] with peacekeeping and enforcement actions initially undertaken by separate ad hoc forces; in late 2003, NATO was once again given responsibility for peacekeeping. Individual member states have assumed the operational lead for specific peacebuilding tasks, and administrative responsibility for the country remains clearly with national authorities. As of fall 2003, it would be premature to evaluate the impact of this new arrangement, but the operation in Afghanistan will undoubtedly influence the Security Council's thinking in sculpting future operations.

Future Peace Operations

Demands

The international community is likely to face demands for peacekeeping in the future. As it has since the end of the Cold War, it will confront threats to international peace and security posed by continuing strategic shifts in power, as well as civil and interstate conflicts with the potential to destabilize broader areas. At the same time, new rationales for international action have emerged. The concept of humanitarian intervention has been developed into the ideal of a "responsibility to protect," as articulated in the report of the International Commission on Intervention and State Sovereignty.[14] This doctrine offers a new threshold for Security Council–mandated action in internal affairs even where international stability is not at stake. Moreover, the concept of international security has itself been broadened with the U.S. declaration of a global war against terrorism, which has been cited as a doctrinal basis for intervention in domestic affairs, including through force.

Many new peacekeeping operations—as well as enforcement actions— are likely to focus upon transforming the internal dynamics of their host societies through both forceful and nonforceful activities. It remains likely that the authorization for most such actions will be sought through the Security Council, which is increasingly perceived as an indispensable means to reconcile competing points of view and to create a basic level of continuity, order, and predictability as power relationships evolve. However, the agency through which Council decisions will be implemented will likely be debated at length on political and practical grounds.

As described above, the broad strength of regional organizations vis-à-vis the United Nations has generally centered on the motivation of local actors to become involved in addressing a conflict and to maintain involvement even in the face of casualties. As in the past, key Security Council members may be inclined to seek regional solutions for future operations where a conflict falls within a traditional sphere of influence, where local political support can thereby be provided, or where major powers are reluctant to deploy their own forces. This may also be driven by concerns about the perceived difficulty and cost of mustering support within the wide political arena and legislative processes of the United Nations. Reflecting these tendencies, regional peacekeeping capacity is undergoing considerable development, propelled by the interest of countries within and outside those regions.[15]

However, arguments abound on both sides regarding the degree to which regional peacekeeping—or MNFs, for that matter—represent a viable alternative to United Nations operations. For the doubters, the area with the greatest regional capacity, Europe, has comparatively low peacekeeping needs, and even here a regional response has proven problematic because of political opposition.[16] Within Africa, the Americas, and Asia, the development of peacekeeping capacity faces major political and practical obstacles, notwithstanding current initiatives; and recourse to either NATO or EU forces for out-of-area operations in these regions could meet with insurmountable political opposition both in the host region and at home.

If the Security Council were to regularly privilege regional action over UN operations, additional longer-term implications would also have to be considered. If human and financial peacekeeping resources are extensively used in regional and multinational efforts, this could complicate the deployment of UN operations. Regional deployment in Europe, particularly in combination with recourse to MNFs, could also reduce the already limited availability of well-equipped and well-trained peacekeeping troops from the North and could in turn exacerbate North-South tensions rooted in developing countries' perception that they bear an unfair portion of the UN peacekeeping burden.

Politically, reliance on regional solutions could favor the development of competing spheres of influence, thereby paradoxically increasing risks of regional conflict. Furthermore, the influence of, and the legitimacy conferred by, the Security Council can be reinforced by operational activities by the United Nations, and disparities between regional capacities can undermine the principle of a similar response to similar problems. The legitimacy of Security Council actions could be undercut by criticism that conflicts are addressed according to a de facto class system, whereby high interest by major powers translates into engagement of NATO or MNFs, moderate interest leads to the use of UN operations, and low interest leads to delegation to other regional organizations.

For those who advocate primary reliance upon UN peacekeeping, the reversion to UN peacekeeping in 1998–2002, and member states' efforts to address operational weaknesses following the blueprint of the Brahimi Report, represent positive steps toward ensuring that UN operations are a key instrument to respond to future crises. This is based on its political legitimacy (derived from the world organization's universal membership, the values anchored in the UN Charter, and the comparatively strong Secretariat); its exceptional capacity to undertake multidimensional action, based upon the breadth of its expertise and mandate; and the reduced financial and political costs implied by burden-sharing. In the future as in the past, the Security Council may be forced to assume responsibility for entire operations, or for different aspects or phases of an operation undertaken in collaboration with regional organizations, as other options become impractical, too expensive, or politically unsustainable.

Problems—and Solutions

The Security Council therefore faces not only the long-term questions explored above—the comparative advantages of a United Nations or a regional operation in response to conflict, as well as the implications of a pattern of reliance upon one or another type of solution—but also the more immediate concern of how to make partnerships between the two mechanisms as effective as possible.

In *Supplement to an Agenda for Peace* (1995), former Secretary-General Boutros Boutros-Ghali suggested that cooperation between the UN and regional organizations held great potential. But he also noted, albeit rather obliquely, the potential for problems, observing that "the political, operational and financial aspects of the arrangement give rise to questions of some delicacy." As regards the UN, two issues stand out:

- In the case of observer missions, the UN's credibility and standing can be compromised where its operations lack adequate resources to function independently alongside an operation without meaningful accountability to the Security Council.

- Where a multidimensional United Nations operation is expected to function alongside a major peacekeeping operation, there is a risk that a divorce between military and peacebuilding responsibilities can lead to funding and operational gaps, with peacebuilding being shorted and lack of an exit strategy raising overall costs. Where peacebuilding activities are delegated in such a context, the resultant lack of coordination also militates against effectiveness. In either case, the United Nations may face blame for being unable to get the job done.

While the range of capacity, philosophy, mandates, and goals of regional and subregional organizations poses an inherent difficulty for those who seek to elaborate an overarching framework for the involvement of regional organizations in Security Council–mandated peacekeeping, some broad proposals have been made to address these problems. These include the principles for consultation, UN primacy, effective division of labor, and consistency of approach as identified by Boutros-Ghali in *Supplement to an Agenda for Peace*. The Security Council has endorsed similar principles, one example being a presidential statement adopted on November 30, 1998, in the context of its review of African peacekeeping, wherein the Council calls for "a clear mandate, including a statement of objectives, rules of engagement, a well-developed plan of action, a timeframe for disengagement and arrangements for regular reporting to the Council"; recalls the United Nations "standard-setting" role; and "underlines the importance [of a] clear framework for cooperation and coordination."[17]

A variety of other possibilities could also be proposed, including:

- Standardization of the terms of authorization by the Security Council[18] and detailed clarification of required reporting and coordination arrangements.
- Explicit stipulation that peacekeepers within a Council-authorized operation be subject to international legal parameters, including international humanitarian law and, unless otherwise noted or negotiated, the jurisdiction of the International Criminal Court.
- Requirements that regional organizations maintain an ongoing relationship with the United Nations, including provision of peacekeepers to UN operations.
- Use of assessed contributions to support complementary peacebuilding activities, as has been done in East Timor. If the UN's standing is to be safeguarded, it must not combine high visibility, through presence in the field, with low capacity, authority, and resources.

• Training and resources to enhance regional and subregional capacity be channeled through the United Nations, rather than through fragmented bilateral approaches, in order to reinforce the international order envisioned in the Charter.[19]

These guidelines are based upon the premise that, despite their variety, these peacekeeping partners—the CIS, a regional organization; ECOWAS, a subregional organization; and NATO, a defensive alliance—share the attribute of a preexisting institutional framework that offers a means of some control. Unlike MNFs, all of these entities have a corporate identity and could be held accountable by the Security Council for short-term actions and, in the long-term, for formulation of a regional vision of security and participation in global efforts.

In practice, however, the Council has not generally insisted upon such principles in the case of actual regional deployments, much less for multinational forces; nor has it made its authorization of a regional action conditional upon compliance. And the membership as a whole has not shown enthusiasm for funding those elements (such as liaison officers) that would impose financial demands. Instead, it seems likely that modifications in partnership arrangements will take place on a case-by-case basis, just as the operations in Sierra Leone and Kosovo testified to the Security Council's interest in addressing the problems that occurred in Liberia and Bosnia and Herzegovina respectively.

Conclusion

As the involvement of regional organizations in peacekeeping began its rapid rise, former Secretary-General Boutros-Ghali suggested that "regional action as a matter of decentralization, delegation and cooperation with United Nations efforts could not only lighten the burden of the Council but also contribute to a deeper sense of participation, consensus and democratization in international affairs."[20] This has been characterized as a form of "subsidiarity," according to which action taken at the "lowest appropriate organizational level"[21] may favor efficiency through decentralization.

However, the case studies above suggest that reliance on regional solutions and MNFs has been spurred by political concerns as much as by a methodical assessment of the relative strengths of available instruments for intervention. In terms of burden-sharing, because many conflicts occur in developing regions, reliance on regional operations may mean that a greater burden is carried by those who are comparatively ill-equipped to do so; in other areas, such as Bosnia and Herzegovina, burden-sharing has indeed taken place but has hampered coordination and effectiveness. As for the concept of democratization, although regional action may increase the capacity of regional powers to act within their spheres of influence, there is little evidence that the regional model of peacekeeping empowers the weaker countries within that sphere.

Yet experience to date suggests that, on a case-by-case basis, regional partnerships will continue to be an attractive option for both practical and political reasons. Indeed, it is possible to imagine occasions in which the political engagement of regional organizations may be invaluable to secure the peace. However the relationship with regional organizations plays out in the future, the Security Council's approach should be informed by a full understanding of the costs and benefits of partnership arrangements as well as an awareness of the role that United Nations peacekeeping plays as an expression of, and catalyst for, international cooperation to promote peace.

Notes

The opinions expressed in this chapter are ours alone and do not necessarily reflect the official view of the United Nations. We are grateful to Feryal Cherif for her extraordinary skill in reviewing the literature and UN documents and for her general contributions to this chapter.

1. Examples are the engagement of the Organization of American States in Haiti, and the involvement of the North Atlantic Treaty Organization and the Western European Union in the former Yugoslavia before Dayton.

2. United Nations peacekeeping operations function under the operational control of the Security Council, vested in the Secretary-General. They are subject to United Nations command within the limits of a specific geographic area, to accomplish a specific mandate, and for a specified period of time. This contrasts with operations by regional organizations, which even though they may be authorized by the Security Council, do not come under the operational command of either the Council or the Secretariat.

3. This would represent a reversal from the thrust of the Charter's provisions regarding regional organizations (Chapter VIII). "Ultimately, a compromise was reached at San Francisco in which the structure adopted was fundamentally globalist, whilst making some concessions to regionalism, not least in Article 51 itself [concerning 'defensive alliances'] and in the provision of Chapter VIII of the Charter." Justin Morris and Hilaire McCoubrey, "Regional Peacekeeping in the Post–Cold War Era," *International Peacekeeping* 6, no. 2 (Summer 1999).

4. This discussion draws, inter alia, from Clement Adibe, "The Liberian Conflict and the ECOWAS-UN Partnership," in Thomas Weiss, ed., *Beyond UN Subcontracting: Task Sharing with Regional Security Arrangements and Service Providing NGOs* (London: Macmillan, 1998); and Funmi Olonisakin, "UN Co-operation with Regional Organizations in Peacekeeping," *International Peacekeeping* 3, no. 3 (Autumn 1996): 33–51.

5. The cost of involvement was particularly high for Nigeria. Clement Adibe notes that Nigerian governments spent more than U.S.$3 billion in Liberia between 1990 and 1996, and Nigerian troops constituted 70–80 percent of the total throughout. Adibe, "The Liberian Conflict."

6. S/1997/712, September 12, 1992.

7. Olonisakin, "UN Co-operation."

8. In an interesting analysis Michael MacKinnon suggests that the internal

political dynamics that drove Washington's turn away from United Nations peace-keeping distorted, rather than reflected, popular opinion in the country, and that public support for the United Nations remained potentially quite high throughout. Michael MacKinnon, *The Evolution of U.S. Peacekeeping Policy Under Clinton: A Fairweather Friend?* London/Portland: Frank Cass, 2000. See also Sarah B. Sewall, "Multilateral Peace Operations," in Stewart Patrick and Shepard Forman, eds., *Multilateralism and U.S. Foreign Policy: Ambivalent Engagement* (Boulder: Lynne Rienner, 2002).

9. This analysis draws on Ivo H. Daalder, *Getting to Dayton: The Making of America's Bosnia Policy* (Washington, D.C.: Brookings Institution, 2000).

10. This includes Boutros-Ghali's belief that NATO, because of its military capability and culture, could have been better equipped to bring peace to Bosnia in the pre-Dayton period; and within the United Nations report on the fall of Srebrenica, discussion of the problems caused by an inappropriate Secretariat philosophy of moral equivalency, in which UN neutrality had the effect of privileging one side in the conflict.

11. "Peacekeeping Expenditures: 1947–2001," table compiled by Michael Renner, senior researcher, Worldwatch Institute.

12. In Sierra Leone, the Central African Republic, Kosovo, East Timor, the DRC, Ethiopia/Eritrea, and Afghanistan.

13. The political framework for a multinational peacekeeping force was established through a Security Council resolution authorizing the International Stabilization Assistance Force.

14. International Commission on Intervention and State Sovereignty, *The Responsibility to Protect* (Ottawa: International Development Research Center, 2001). Although this text is not a United Nations document and does not represent United Nations policy, it articulates an important trend in international thinking. Already, the Security Council has "operationalized" this principle to some degree through inclusion of the protection of civilians within several recent mandates.

15. In Europe, NATO's expanding definition of its role, as well as its outreach to Russia, may make it a still more prominent peacekeeping partner in the region. The EU continues to enhance its own peacekeeping structure while the OSCE develops its peacebuilding capacity. In Africa, the Group of Eight has pledged to "provide technical and financial assistance so that, by 2010, African countries and regional and sub-regional organizations are able to engage more effectively to prevent and resolve violent conflict on the continent, as well as to undertake peace support operations in accordance with the United Nations Charter." See Jim Cason, "G-8 Leaders Promise Support, but Fail to Agree on Targets," *allafrica.com*, June 28, 2002, available at http://allafrica.com/stories/200206280176.html.

16. It is imaginable that the trend toward greater political cohesion within the European Union could ultimately undermine its acceptability as a peacekeeper. As for NATO, its future peacekeeping role may be complicated by the fact that it occupies a "gray zone" institutionally, with neither the unique legitimacy conferred by universal membership nor the flexibility of an MNF.

17. Presidential statement S/PRST/1998/35. Notably, the Council did not endorse these principles in the more binding format of a resolution.

18. To date, the Security Council's authorization of regional action has varied greatly in timing, wording, and conditions.

19. A number of these possibilities have been identified, inter alia, in Eric Berman, "The Security Council's Increasing Reliance on Burden-Sharing:

Collaboration or Abrogation?" *International Peacekeeping* 4, no. 1 (Spring 1998): 1–21.

20. Boutros Boutros-Ghali, *An Agenda for Peace* (New York: United Nations, 1995), para. 54.

21. Michele Griffin, "Retrenchment, Reform, and Regionalization: Trends in UN Peace Support Operations," *International Peacekeeping* 6, no. 1 (Spring 1999): 1–31.

21

Groups of Friends

TERESA WHITFIELD

Since the early 1990s a number of informal groups of United Nations member states have been established to support the peace-related efforts of the Secretary-General and Security Council. Such groups, most commonly known as the "Friends" of the Secretary-General, or of a particular process, vary in origin, size, and purpose, as well as in their relationships to the conflict in question. They can generally be distinguished from other international groupings of states, such as the Contact Group in the former Yugoslavia, both by their informality and by their at least implicit goal of supporting the efforts of the Secretary-General or the interests of a particular peace process being conducted under the auspices of the United Nations.[1]

In conflicts as varied as El Salvador and East Timor, Friends or analogous groups (e.g., the Core Group on East Timor) have increased the legitimacy of the peace process, enhanced the leverage of the UN Secretary-General with the parties, harnessed the competing interests of would-be rival negotiators and acted as a buffer against others, aided coordination among members of the international community both prior to and following the signing of a peace agreement, and facilitated the work of the Security Council. For the states involved they represent privileged involvement in a particular process and effective engagement within the United Nations.

But in other instances internal differences or other factors related to the groups' composition and engagement have limited their utility within a process, creating a layer of interests to be managed and negotiated in addition to those of the parties to the conflict. Groups of Friends have at times assumed an identity of their own that may be at cross-purposes to the good offices of the Secretary-General. They have led members of the Security Council to fear that their authority may be undermined by the opacity of the groups' working methods. Competing national interests have led groups' sometimes fragile unity to crack and be exploited by parties to a conflict.

Sensitivities regarding composition have in other instances led to the creation of large groups that may do no harm but are hardly well placed to do the good that is intended.

This chapter represents an attempt to review some of the key instances in which Groups of Friends have been engaged in the peace efforts of the United Nations. The subject is a complex one, for a number of reasons. The mechanism represented by these groups has evolved on an ad hoc basis, and thus no guidelines for their composition or functions exist. Diverse expectations of Groups of Friends held by members of the Secretariat, Security Council, and other member states—whether they are there to support the Secretary-General, facilitate the work of the Security Council, or effectively channel bilateral interests through the UN's machinery—lead to a confusing array of opinions as to their utility.

Although many groups are acknowledged to be helpful both by Council members and the Secretariat, others provoke comments such as "Friends—if only they were!" from exasperated officials. Individual cases offer cautionary tales underlining that a mechanism such as the Group of Friends will not be appropriate for every occasion.

Group Dynamics in a Changing Security Council

The development of the Friends mechanism can be traced to two somewhat contradictory impetuses. The first is the formation of Groups of Friends to support the peacemaking of the Secretary-General and his representatives. As will be discussed below, the mechanism was first employed in the negotiation of agreements that paved the way to the end of the civil war in El Salvador in 1992. Its utility in this instance—where the Friends were like-minded states with an interest but no overriding strategic stake in the conflict at hand—was widely recognized by the Secretariat, the member states involved, and the parties to the negotiations. Its success contributed to the creation in the early 1990s of a number of other groups—some of them specifically identified as being Friends of the Secretary-General and some not—to address conflicts in situations as diverse as Haiti and Georgia, Guatemala and Western Sahara. That these groups varied greatly not only in their origin (most were formed at the initiative of member states rather than that of the Secretary-General) but also in the rationale behind their composition can be seen as one of the factors that affected their outcome. But other factors, intrinsic to the conflict in question—including its nature and duration, the motives, coherence, and resources of the parties, the presence of spoilers, and the conflict's relationship to regional stability—also need to be considered in any comparative assessment of the role that Groups of Friends have played in the resolution of conflict.

A parallel development was the realization, through practice, that groups of key member states could work effectively to support the efforts of special representatives of the Secretary-General (SRSGs) leading complex peace operations in the field. The cases of Cambodia and Mozambique are illustrative in this regard. In both, the United Nations was charged with the implementation of far-reaching agreements. In each the relationship of the SRSG, Yasushi Akashi in the case of Cambodia, Aldo Ajello in that of Mozambique, to ambassadors of Security Council and other countries engaged in the field (the extended permanent five [P-5] in Cambodia, the Core Group on Mozambique) proved vital for the political leverage, donor support, and fluid communication with the Security Council in New York and with capitals that it brought with it. Although not specifically acknowledged as "Friends," the relationship was broadly analogous to that enjoyed by SRSGs in El Salvador and Haiti with representatives of the Groups of Friends resident in San Salvador and Port-au-Prince. This is, of course, a relationship that can and has been replicated by other SRSGs—a number of whom cultivate "friends" as important constituencies vis-à-vis both the Security Council and headquarters—meeting regularly with key ambassadors in the mission area, regardless of whether or not they are designated as a specific group.

The second impetus for the development of Friends mechanisms is less specific in origin but stems from the increased cooperation among the P-5 that derived from the end of the Cold War and the evolution of the working methods of the Council to handle the intense period of activity that followed. By the early twenty-first century most issues within the Council were staffed by identifiable groups under the coordination of a lead nation, whether or not explicitly acknowledged as such.[2] The existence of these groups represents a pragmatic response not only to the pace of work but also to the rising frustration of successive elected members of the Council, as well as a wide range of troop-contributing countries (TCCs), with the grip on the work of the Council maintained by the P-5.

P-5 control of the issues that are closest to their national interests has remained tight, whether these issues are on the agenda of the Security Council (consider the negotiations preceding Resolution 1244 on Kosovo in 1999, or the handling of Iraq in the latter part of 2002) or remain steadfastly off the agenda (Burma, Chechnya, Tibet). In areas such as these the formation of Groups of Friends would not be countenanced.[3] But on other issues a plethora of different arrangements with a wide variety of functions and incidence upon the processes with which they are engaged have evolved. While many of these groups are led by one or another of the P-3 (France, the United Kingdom, and the United States) and include others of the P-5 among their members, they provide an avenue for the "top table" engagement of elected members and interested member states from outside the Security Council. In some cases they also—like other working groups and committees of the Council—provide opportunities for elected members to demonstrate leadership on a particular issue (Norway's leadership on issues related to the Horn of Africa during 2001–2002 being an example). This can be true even after elected members leave the Council (demonstrated by Canada's role on Haiti over the years) or without states being elected to it at all (as Australia proved in the East Timor case).

At one end of the spectrum covered by these mechanisms stand the Groups of Friends operationally involved with a specific issue and meeting regularly with senior Secretariat officials to that end. Some, such as the Friends of the Secretary-General on Georgia, may work in a formal and open way, as acknowledged in the published documents of the Security Council, whereas the work of others, such as the Core Group on East Timor, has been conducted more informally and discretely. At the other end is a group such as the Friends of Guinea-Bissau, which operated as little more than a discussion group until differences between its chair, Gambia, and Guinea-Bissau overtook its utility and "group" action in support of peacebuilding in Guinea-Bissau largely passed to an ad hoc advisory group established by the Economic and Social Council (ECOSOC), working in close coordination with the newly formed Ad Hoc Working Group on Conflict Prevention and Resolution in Africa.

Between these stand groups whose primary purpose has been the preparation of resolutions, such as the Coordination and Drafting Group for the Balkans—which obviously reflects the powerful interests of the key actors in this area, France, Russia, the UK, and the United States, as well as Germany and Italy—and the Friends of Western Sahara, discussed below. Another intermediary category is represented by groups such as the Friends of the UN Mission on Ethiopia and Eritrea (UNMEE) and the Core Group on Sierra Leone, which were formed by member states (Netherlands in the case of UNMEE, the UK in that of Sierra Leone) in response to differing bilateral concerns about the respective peacekeeping operations.

A very particular case is presented by Angola, which has historically been managed within the Council by Portugal, Russia, and the United States—the Troika—which derives its status from the legal framework of the Lusaka Protocol. As the Angolan peace process reached an impasse in the late 1990s, frustration with the tight grip maintained by the Troika and the perception that it was overly beholden to the Angolan government led the Secretary-General to form a distinct group, the Friends of Angola. That group, which included the Troika, rapidly became somewhat large and unwieldy (in part as a result of difficulties that the Secretary-General will almost always encounter in assembling a Group of Friends that is neither genuinely self-selecting nor a natural grouping) and remained something of a talk-shop. However, it served to demonstrate that interest in Angola extended beyond the Troika and provided diplomatic support to missions to Angola undertaken by the Secretary-General's representative.

The Secretary-General and His Friends

The mechanism of Friends of the Secretary-General has antecedents in the use made by Secretary-General Dag Hammarskjöld of advisory committees to help guide preparations for the Atoms for Peace Conference held in Paris in August 1955 (the Advisory Committee on the Peaceful Uses of Atomic Energy), on the UN Emergency Force (UNEF) established in response to the Suez crisis of 1956 (the UNEF Advisory Committee), and on Lebanon and the Congo in 1958 and 1960 respectively.[4] Although the advisory committees had some elements in common with the Groups of Friends established in the 1990s—those related to peace operations responded to Hammarskjöld's desire to gather like-minded states around him to improve his leverage to steer complex and controversial operations through the choppy waters of the General Assembly (in the case of UNEF) and a Security Council divided by Cold War rivalries—they also differed from the concept, as pioneered in El Salvador by Javier Pérez de Cuéllar, in important regards.

In the case of UNEF and the Congo the advisory committees were formally consulted with the General Assembly and Security Council and, in the case of UNEF, mandated by a resolution (A/3302). They were made up of troop contributors to the operations (eighteen countries in the case of the Congo), and although their meetings were private, records of them were kept and circulated. Moreover, the advisory committees had as their origin the management of complex field operations rather than the support of the Secretary-General's good offices and peacemaking, for which the mechanism would be developed in the early 1990s. The difference is a fundamental one insomuch as it relates not only to the composition, functions, and utility of each particular group but also to their relationship to the Security Council, which is necessarily more nebulous when peacemaking is conducted by a Secretary-General or his representative than when an operation is established under the Council's own authority.

The Friends of the Secretary-General on El Salvador, which comprised Colombia, Mexico, Spain, and Venezuela, had a very different genesis. As the Secretary-General's personal representative for the Central American peace process, Alvaro de Soto consulted regularly with a number of countries regarding the course of the negotiations he mediated between the government of El Salvador and the guerrillas gathered in the Farabundo Martí National Liberation Front (FMLN).[5] Some of these, such as the United States and Cuba, had an obvious political stake in the outcome of the conflict, and others, such as the Nordic countries, did not. The Group of Friends, however, consisted of countries that had a demonstrated interest in the region: the three Latin American states had been involved in the earlier efforts of the Contadora Group to foster peace in Central America, and Spain, with its historic ties to the continent, was an important bridge to the European Union.

De Soto briefed ambassadors from the four countries, usually individually, in New York, El Salvador, or the country in which negotiations were taking place, on a regular basis. He used the Friends' willingness to act in support of the Secretary-General's efforts to transmit messages and exert leverage on both parties to the negotiation and—for good measure—ensured that would-be rival mediators were harnessed to the UN's effort.[6] But it was only in mid-1991, some eighteen months after initiation of the UN-led process, that the Friends first met as a group. The pressure on the parties exerted by the Friends—together with that of the United States—proved an important aspect of the fortuitous confluence of circumstances that led to the signing of agreements in the final minutes of Pérez de Cuéllar's term in office on December 31, 1991.

The group exemplified both the benefits to be accrued from the personal commitment of a representative of the Secretary-General to the cultivation of "friends," as well as the importance of personal relationships to the success of such informal mechanisms. However, it differed from many subsequent Groups of Friends in that part of its purpose was to provide a counterweight to members of the Security Council, particularly the United States, with clearly defined bilateral positions on El Salvador and, as such, to reassure the insurgents engaged in negotiations of the UN's impartiality. During implementation of the agreements, ties between the Friends and the Council were strengthened by the addition of the United States (in deference to the original Friends' preference, the United States remained a distinct member of the "four plus one"), as well as Venezuela's presence on the Council from 1992 to 1993.

From the point of view of the Secretariat, the provision of a counterweight to the United States was also a factor in the creation of the Friends of the Secretary-General on Haiti, a development encouraged by officials who had direct experience in the Salvadoran process. Like the Friends of the Secretary-General on El Salvador, and its direct descendant, the Friends on the Guatemalan Peace Process,[7] the Friends of Haiti enjoyed the benefits of emerging as a natural grouping. Canada, France, the United States, and Venezuela shared an interest in attracting increased international attention to Haiti and had identified themselves as a quadripartite group after the ousting of President Jean-Bertrand Aristide in 1991. They were approached soon afterward by the Secretary-General, who suggested they form a Group of Friends to help steer the issue of Haiti within the Security Council and General Assembly.[8]

Over the following years, as Sebastian von Einsiedel and David M. Malone describe in Chapter 31, the group was to prove a central actor—and at times the driving force—in UN involvement in Haiti. Perhaps its most salient achievement was to place and maintain Haiti on the agenda of the Security Council, a feat that required considerable diplomatic agility. However, there were always those within the Secretariat and on the Security Council who remained uneasy about the diplomatic cover provided by the Friends to the extent that the United States, galvanized by fear of uncontrolled numbers of Haitian refugees arriving on the shores of Florida, drove the issue within the United Nations. This uneasiness surfaced during the negotiation of the Governors' Island Agreement in June 1993, where the Haitian parties were strong-armed by the United States and the UN while the other Friends took a backseat. The failure to implement the agreement in the months that followed led to serious differences within the Friends during the winter and spring of 1994 as U.S. priorities rose to the fore.

The Friends and the United Nations worked well together in the mid-1990s to support peacekeeping operations whose central activity was better described as peacebuilding. But by 1997 the Haitian process had descended into a political crisis from which it has not yet recovered. Within the Security Council the Friends put up a series of staunch defenses to the efforts of Russia and especially China to downsize the UN presence in Haiti. The result was a succession of operations, the last of which was followed in March 2000 by a technical assistance mission under the authority of the General Assembly only after the Friends put intense pressure on the Secretariat to mount it.

Like Haiti, the Georgia-Abkhaz conflict generated, almost from the beginning, a Group of Friends—the Friends of Georgia—in which the regional hegemon was directly represented. Indeed, when the Friends were created, at the instigation of the French in 1993, Russia was named not only as a member of the group (the others were Germany, the UK, and the United States) but also as "facilitator" of the peace process. Over the years the role of the Friends of Georgia has shifted considerably. A self-appointed group, it resisted initial suggestions by the Secretariat to constitute itself as Friends "of the Secretary-General," although it adopted the title in 1997 both to counter well-founded Abkhaz suspicions that members of the group operated with a bias in favor of the government of Georgia and to offer support to the reinvigoration of the UN's efforts.

Successive SRSGs have drawn the Friends deeper into the substance of the negotiations, but these in turn have become bogged down as a result of actions taken by the Abkhaz (who have declared the independence of Abkhazia, ratified a constitution, and elected a president and a parliament) and the increasingly complex and sensitive dynamics of the bilateral relationship between Russia and Georgia. Consequently, some two years passed before SRSG Dieter Boden was able to achieve agreement among the Friends to a paper on basic principles for the distribution of competencies between Tbilisi and Sukhumi in December 2001, and even then it could not be presented to the parties. Attempts by the SRSG and Friends to meet with Abkhaz leaders during 2002, first in Sukhumi and then in Moscow, came to naught and threatened the confidence of the Western Friends in their Russian partner. "Sometimes Russia forgets," as one of them put it, rather dryly, that it is "a friend of the Secretary-General and not of the Abkhaz."[9]

The presence of Russia as a Friend of Georgia—which officials from the Secretariat as well as from within the Friends defend on the basis that, although Russia may be "part of the problem" presented by the Georgian-Abkhaz conflict, it is surely part of any solution and that, in any case, nothing could be done by the UN in the region without Russian consent—highlights the complications created by a Friend with an obvious political stake in the outcome of a conflict. Another kind of obstacle to a Group of Friends is presented by the case of Western Sahara. Here, seemingly irreconcilable differences between the parties—Morocco on the one hand and the POLISARIO Front on the other—are reflected within the Friends. Challenged by a report of the Secretary-General that in February 2002 requested the Security Council to make a clear choice between four policy options (S/2002/178), the group all but unraveled under the pressure of its differences.

The Friends of Western Sahara was formed in 1993 on the initiative of the United States. Like the group on Georgia, it is essentially a subgroup of the Security Council, being made up of the P-4 (the United States, France, the UK, and Russia) plus one (in Western Sahara's case, Spain). Originally perceived as being clearly pro-Morocco in their stance, the Friends began by inviting a number of elected members of the Council, representing the nonaligned movement, to join them for the duration of their stay on the Council. However, this practice ceased after several states were seen to be acting as mouthpieces for one side or the other on a deeply divisive issue.

Although the Friends were active during 1995–1996 in the resolution of problems associated with the identification process, their work has generally been conducted at the expert level, limited to the drafting of resolutions rather than direct engagement in the political process. But from 2000 on, as it became clear that the original settlement plan was no longer viable, the "proxy" relationship of some of the Friends to the parties—with France hewing most closely to Morocco's line, Russia to that of POLISARIO—

began to weigh in and complicate efforts to reach consensus. In the end, discussions on a response to the Secretary-General's February 2002 report reverted to the full fifteen members of the Security Council, who approved Resolution 429, which sent the Secretary-General and his personal envoy back to the drawing board, leaving the fate of the Friends of Western Sahara as uncertain as the process.

As Stewart Eldon demonstrates in Chapter 35, a good example of what can be derived from a group that contains neither parties nor proxies is presented by the case of the Core Group on East Timor. Composed of a mixture of P-5 (the UK and the United States) and non-Council states with a strong regional interest in the issue (Australia, Japan, and New Zealand), its members were like-minded in their concern to right the historical wrong done to East Timor, although preoccupied, if at varying levels, with the risks posed by instability in Indonesia. They counted among them Australia, a midsized country prepared to make an unprecedented diplomatic and financial commitment to the effort, and Japan, a major regional donor and member of the Association of South East Asian Nations (ASEAN) Regional Forum, pleased to be engaged in the front line of UN action. The deep pockets of the international donor community that the group collectively represented would be crucial to the UN operations deployed to East Timor from 1999 on and to the future of independent Timor Leste.

The Core Group proved an ideal buffer between the United Nations and the Security Council, particularly during the months in which the UN was effectively implementing the May 5, 1999, agreements on Indonesia's behalf, against a background of intense resistance by some Indonesian actors. While the question of East Timor was influenced within the Security Council by a number of factors—among them that it was of no strategic value to any of the powers represented on the Council and that China's traditional concerns about issues of sovereignty, particularly in Asia, were tempered by its cool relationship with Indonesia—the Secretariat would have been extremely exposed without the Core Group's ability to put its considerable weight behind the UN effort.

The View from the Council

Opinions of Groups of Friends within the Security Council are decidedly mixed. As these groups mushroomed in the late 1990s and early 2000s, so did criticism of their composition and actions. It is generally acknowledged—especially by those member states most actively represented within them—that Groups of Friends have a lot to offer the Council. Their marriage of substantive and procedural benefits through the introduction of well-grounded drafts of resolutions and other texts undoubtedly facilitates its work. But it is in the very efficiency of some of the Groups of Friends that sow the seeds of complaint among those who are not represented within them. Those who have criticized the work of the groups are generally elected members of the Council—including, in recent years, Bangladesh, Colombia, Ireland, Jamaica, New Zealand, and Singapore—concerned with issues of transparency and the usurpation of their authority as Council members by elite ownership of specific issues.[10] They object that the groups include scarce numbers of developing countries and perpetuate the sense of "us" versus "them" already present in the Council's two-tiered structure. That some Groups of Friends include nonmembers of the Council does not improve matters: it can be galling to elected members to see colleagues outside the Council have access to privileged information and influence that they do not themselves enjoy.

The extent of these rumblings in opposition to Groups of Friends varies greatly in accordance with both interest in the subject at hand and the working practices of the different groups, some of which are more sensitive to the dynamics of the Council as a whole than others. The essence of the problem is that it is difficult for the members to feel that they have much influence on the decisionmaking process if they are presented with faits accomplis by powerful and secretive Groups of Friends. "Sometimes we are not quite sure of how they arrive at the various decisions they present to us," the ambassador of Singapore complained in November 2001. "Some indication of the background that went into their thinking would be useful to us."[11] The group on Georgia is one that, in the view of several states, stepped way over the line during 2001–2002. Recalling the irritation of a meeting in which the Friends discussed a draft of the Boden paper that was not made available to other members of the Council, a representative of Colombia commented that "really there is no need to have the political discussion of Georgia on the agenda of the Security Council, because it doesn't take place in the Council."[12]

In early 1999 frustration with the control exercised over a number of the processes under the Council's authority—in particular the tight hold on Cyprus maintained by the P-5 (as one Council member recalled, "They'd come with drafts and tell the rest of us we had two hours to make up our mind"),[13] the monopolization of Georgia by its Friends, and the behavior of the Contact Group on the former Yugoslavia, which was at the time considered by many to be in the first instance an effective tool for the prevention of Security Council engagement—led to the issuance of a note by the president of the Council (Canada) on February 17, 1999. The note pointed out that "contributions by members of groups of friends and other similar arrangements" are welcome but emphasized that "the drafting of resolutions and statements by the President of the Council should be carried out in a manner that will allow adequate participation of all members of the Council" (S/1999/165).

Such criticisms reflect an uncertainty about the working methods and practice of Friends and other groups that appears to have done nothing to halt a general inclination to form more of them. This is seen most clearly in Africa, in part in reflection of the increased attention directed toward the continent by the Council since the late 1990s. In his April 1998 report on the causes of conflict in Africa, the Secretary-General offered a clear endorsement of the "group" approach to peace efforts: "The establishment of contact groups of interested countries, whether in the form of groups of 'Friends,' or a special conference as in the case of Liberia, can be effective in mobilizing international support for peace efforts" (S/1998/318). Since then the general idea that Friends and contact groups provide a positive avenue for international engagement with Africa has taken hold, despite the rather uneven performance of a number of the groups that have so far been established.

Pressure on the United Nations and the Secretary-General to maintain this direction was increased by the Africa Action Plan agreed at the Group of Eight (G8) summit in Kananaskis, Canada, during July 2002. The plan included a commitment by the G8 to "endorsing the proposals from the UN Secretary-General to set up, with the Secretary-General and other influential partners, contact groups and other influential mechanisms to work with African countries to resolve specific African conflicts."[14] Within the Security Council, this approach has found reflection in the work of the Ad Hoc Working Group on Conflict Prevention and Resolution in Africa. The working group, which was formed in February 2002 under the chairmanship of Mauritius, placed the issue of "the establishment of groups of friends for specific conflict situations" on its program of work. It has held several discussions on Groups of Friends, including within the context of an open meeting of the Council on the working group held on May 22, 2002.

Recommendations from the working group on Groups of Friends included suggestions that the groups could provide an informal framework for in-depth discussion; that they should be "relatively small (about twelve to fifteen members), but would remain open to all members"; that they have a lead nation; and that they work best if focused on implementation of agreements already agreed to by the parties to a conflict.[15] As a first attempt by the Security Council to codify the composition and practice of the mechanism, it is notable that these recommendations outline a model that would differ considerably from most of the existing groups, including the more successful among them. While the recommendations were circulated on the understanding that they had been "agreed to by members of the Security

Council," it is unlikely that they will have much bearing on the ad hoc and idiosyncratic behavior of Groups of Friends themselves, which as this chapter has demonstrated respond to a complex set of interests and circumstances that the Security Council itself is unlikely to be able to regulate.

Conclusion

The end of the Cold War saw an explosion in the formation of Friends and other groups with a wide variety of purposes and incidence upon the processes with which they have been engaged. Although Groups of Friends have on many occasions facilitated the work of the Secretary-General and Security Council, representing effective avenues for states' engagement with the United Nations, these positive outcomes are by no means guaranteed. This is not least because the groups will always be vulnerable to the potential of individual member states' interests to skew priorities away from the stipulated goals of the United Nations in a particular peace process. As such they are direct expressions of the tension between national interest and international norms that lies behind many states' engagement with the UN.

Groups of Friends formed to support the peacemaking efforts of the Secretary-General will face more stringent demands with regard to both composition and comportment than those whose primary concern is the coordination of Security Council action. Groups formed for no better reason (although it is not necessarily a bad one) than to show international support for a particular country or situation are different again. Although this diversity militates against the development of guidelines for the formation of Groups of Friends, it argues in favor of the utmost care and attention being taken at the moment of a group's inception.

As this chapter has demonstrated, the composition of a Group of Friends is all-important, determining the group's relationship to both the Security Council and the conflict in question. Most groups have involved some mixture of Security Council members (including the P-5 to ensure heavy lifting within the Council as necessary), donors, and interested regional actors. Groups intended to be operational, or to support the delicate diplomatic efforts of the Secretary-General or his representative, have been most successful when they remain small (four to six members) and represent a natural grouping of states that have at least the appearance of being self-selecting. In cases where a large number of states press for inclusion within Friends or support groups, a core group of states has been helpful. States that can be considered parties or proxies for the parties to the conflict have complicated the efforts of Groups of Friends. The inclusion of a state with an overriding strategic interest in the outcome of a particular conflict has inevitable consequences for the engagement of a Group of

Friends and its relationship to the agenda of the United Nations more generally.

Ad hoc in nature, Groups of Friends function best when acting with informality and flexibility—which also can ensure that concerns that the group might be encroaching on the prerogatives of the Council are avoided. Whether peacemaking or implementation is involved, clarity in the leadership of the effort and objectives of the process is a great asset. Friends have been most successful when like-minded enough to work together and, if working in support of the Secretary-General or his representative, willing to follow the UN lead, foregoing unilateral policy objectives or initiatives. With regard to the procedural aspects of their work in the Council, Groups of Friends have been most effective when they avoid the impression of presenting the Council with faits accomplis, ensure that Council members are adequately consulted and briefed on the issues at hand, and allow sufficient time for the decisionmaking process to run its course.

Notes

This chapter reflects work in progress for the book *Friends Indeed: The United Nations, Groups of Friends, and the Resolution of Conflict,* undertaken with the support of the Department for International Development (UK), the U.S. Institute of Peace, the Fafo Institute for Applied International Studies, Oslo, and the Ford Foundation.

1. In 1997, Marrack Goulding recommended that a clear distinction be drawn between Groups of Friends selected by the Secretary-General and self-appointed contact groups. Marrack Goulding, "Enhancing the United Nations' Effectiveness in Peace and Security," a report submitted to the Secretary-General of the United Nations, New York, June 30, 1997, mimeo, p. 74. This chapter does not address thematic Groups of Friends, such as the Friends of Rapid Reaction and the Friends of Conflict Prevention.

2. See Pascal Teixeira, *Le Conseil de Sécurité à l'aube du XXIème siècle* (Geneva: UNIDIR, 2002), pp. 12–15.

3. The Friends of Kosovo, a very large group, was formed after the passage of Resolution 1244 but is not closely engaged with the process. The Coordination and Drafting Group (CDG) coordinates Kosovo in the Council, and in the field the "Quint" of France, Germany, Italy, the UK, and the United States plays an important role. There was an attempt to form a Group of Friends of Myanmar in the early 1990s, but it did not prosper, although there is a consultative mechanism in place that meets on an irregular basis.

4. See Jochen Prantl and Jean Krasno, *Informal Ad Hoc Groupings of States and the Workings of the United Nations,* ACUNS Occasional Paper no. 3, New Haven, Conn.: Yale University, International Relations Studies and the United Nations Occasional Papers, pp. 13–28.

5. These consultations were explicitly provided for in Point 5 of the Geneva Agreement, signed by the parties in April 1990. A/45/706-S/21931, annex 1.

6. Without creating even an informal Group of Friends, de Soto, as the Secretary-General's special adviser on Cyprus, adopted a similar approach in the very different circumstances of the Cyprus conflict. In his report to the Security

Council of April 1, 2003, on his mission of good offices in Cyprus, the Secretary-General referred to several governments that "acted, in effect, as Friends of the Secretary-General, providing advice as well as diplomatic and practical support, and avoiding the temptation to duplicate or supplant my efforts—the bane of any enterprise of good offices." S/2003/398, April 1, 2003, para. 149.

7. The Guatemalan group is not addressed in this chapter, as the Guatemalan process has been conducted almost entirely under the authority of the General Assembly.

8. David M. Malone, *Decision-Making in the UN Security Council: The Case of Haiti, 1990–1997* (Oxford: Clarendon, 1998), p. 74.

9. Confidential interview, November 18, 2002.

10. See, for example, the remarks of Ireland, Jamaica, and Singapore in the wrap-up discussion on June 2001, S/PV.4343; and Singapore in the wrap-up discussion on November 2001, S/PV.4432.

11. Ambassador Kishore Mahbubani of Singapore, wrap-up discussion on the work of the Security Council in November 2001, PV.4432 p. 14.

12. Confidential interview, November 12, 2002.

13. Interview with Ambassador Andrés Franco, October 2, 2002.

14. *G-8 Africa Action Plan,* available at http://www.isa-africa.com/G8/en/planafG8.htm.

15. Letter dated August 29, 2002, from the permanent representative of Mauritius to the president of the Security Council, S/2002/979, August 30, 2002, "Recommendations of the Ad Hoc Working Group on Conflict Prevention and Resolution in Africa to the Security Council," annex.

22

Special Representatives of the Secretary-General

Connie Peck

Special representatives of the Secretary-General (SRSGs) have been a regular feature of UN practice since the early days of the organization, when it quickly became clear that the Secretary-General could not possibly carry out assignments in the field without the assistance of trusted envoys.[1] The practice continued throughout the decades but accelerated greatly with the end of the Cold War due to the increased demands for UN involvement in crises around the world. As the Security Council took on responsibility for a range of different types of peace missions, SRSGs were appointed in increasing numbers to head and implement these operations. I will argue in this chapter that SRSGs have become a major instrument for carrying out the Council's work in the area of peace and security and that a close relationship between SRSGs and the Council is required to enhance the success of peace missions.

Many of the observations in this chapter derive from the United Nations Institute for Training and Research (UNITAR) Program for Briefing and Debriefing Special and Personal Representatives and Envoys of the Secretary-General, which involves, inter alia, in-depth interviews with current and past SRSGs and the preparation of a book and set of DVDs for new SRSGs based on a distillation of the major issues raised in these interviews, as well as a regular seminar for SRSGs. The objective is to preserve and pass on the valuable lessons and experience of SRSGs and to ensure that these are used to refine and enhance UN practice.

The Relationship Between the SRSG and the Security Council

When the Security Council authorizes a new peace mission, the Secretary-General typically appoints a special representative to head the mission following consultation with the Department of Political Affairs (DPA) and the

Department of Peacekeeping Operations (DPKO), with the parties and, in some cases, with member states. SRSGs can come from inside or outside the UN system.

The nature of the relationship between SRSGs and the Council depends on the type of mission and whether it has been mandated by the Council. Peacekeeping and peacebuilding missions are usually mandated by the Security Council (although in a few cases they are mandated by the General Assembly). Most peacemaking missions, however, do *not* have Council mandates and are instead based on letters of understanding between the parties and the Secretary-General or on a framework agreement negotiated with the parties. The DPA is currently responsible for overseeing peacemaking and postconflict peacebuilding missions, and the DPKO is responsible for the oversight of all peacekeeping operations. The intensity of reporting and contact also varies depending on the degree of the crisis and the geostrategic importance of the particular situation to Council members, especially to the five permanent members.

A mission is mandated through a Security Council resolution that sets out the objectives it is to fulfill, the components of the mission, and the resources that will be sought for each component. If the mission is a new one, the mandate may be based on recommendations of an assessment/planning mission that has been sent by headquarters to the field to determine what is required. Mandates are provided for a given period specified by the Council. The Secretary-General is responsible for reporting to the Council on the progress of each peace mission and for making recommendations for action when deemed necessary. SRSGs report to the Secretary-General through the Undersecretaries-General for political affairs or peacekeeping operations, depending on which department is in the lead. Reports of the Secretary-General to the Security Council are regularly submitted to the Council and prepared by SRSGs and their staff in the field, working in close cooperation with the headquarters departments.

Following consideration of a report of the Secretary-General and discussion with the Secretary-General, the Secretariat, and/or the SRSG, the Council reconsiders the mandate for possible renewal and/or amendment. The Council can alter the mandate at any time (including modification of the objectives of the mission or its resources) in response to developments on the ground. One of the major challenges for the Security Council is therefore to provide and maintain an appropriate mandate and adequate resources for each mission. To ensure that the mandate and resources are indeed in accordance with the needs on the ground, the SRSGs (through the Secretary-General and the Secretariat) need to work closely with the Council to keep it thoroughly briefed, to offer a clear analysis of each situation, and to provide cogently argued recommendations when Council action is required.

In addition to furnishing the mandate, the Council provides overall direction with regard to the situations with which it is seized, through resolutions that instruct the Secretary-General (and, by implication, the SRSG and the mission). These also provide direction to the conflicting parties and to other member states as to how they should interact with the parties. As well, the Council may comment on the actions of regional and subregional organizations and their efforts. Thus there is an ongoing interplay between the Security Council, which provides overall direction for the mission from New York, and the SRSG, who is responsible for the day-to-day decision-making on the ground. Mediating this interaction are the Secretary-General and the Secretariat, who provide operational guidance to the SRSG and who report to the Council on the progress and problems of the mission.

The Unique Role of SRSGs in Peace Missions

Upon arrival in the mission area, an SRSG becomes the head of mission and has authority over all its components, as well as all aspects of its management and functioning. To accomplish the mission's objectives, the special representative is required to engage in constant negotiation with a wide range of actors. In conjunction with his/her senior management team, the SRSG is responsible for developing a clear analysis of the situation and further elaborating the mission's objectives and strategy. He/she also faces the challenge of harmonizing different mission cultures and components (e.g., military, police, civil affairs, electoral, human rights, administration) into a well-functioning team. The SRSG must also provide leadership and be able to communicate effectively with the diverse international and local staff, as well as the rotating national contingents of peacekeepers and police, to keep them working toward the same objectives and to maintain morale. SRSGs must also create good working relationships with staff at headquarters, who monitor and support their work in order to keep the Secretary-General, the Security Council, and the membership as a whole informed.

Crucial to their work is the development of a solid working relationship with the conflicting parties, as well as with those who surround and influence the decisionmaking process. Bringing them to a unity of purpose is not an easy task, and SRSGs must constantly engage in persuasion, problem-solving, and the skillful use of leverage to find ways around the many obstacles that constantly present themselves. Building a relationship with a broad base of civil society, especially those who support the peace process, as well as with the local population, can also help to keep the process on track and the population on one's side.

As well, SRSGs need to negotiate solid working relationships with UN specialized agencies, funds, and programs in order to overcome the inherent institutional rivalries and create an atmosphere in which the UN can truly work as a family—with coordinated objectives and approaches. Developing a close relationship with regional and subregional organizations and regional leaders is also necessary to foster a coordinated approach. Among the host of other actors that SRSGs have to work with are nongovernmental organizations, which are often pursuing their own objectives and funding but whose energy and flexibility, if harnessed appropriately, can add synergy to particular mission goals. In addition, SRSGs have to develop effective relationships with the media in order to raise international awareness and communicate with the local population about the mission's objectives and methods.

Further, SRSGs must be able to work closely with interested member states, developing the necessary relationships with ambassadors on the ground, at UN headquarters, and within relevant ministries in key capitals, to engender political support, to mobilize leverage, and to find the resources needed to sustain the mission and make a significant impact on the mission area. Finally, they must be able to develop a supportive relationship with the Security Council in order to keep the Council informed and actively engaged, as well as to ensure that the mission's mandate and resources remain appropriate to the evolving situation on the ground.

The tasks required for an SRSG managing a transitional authority in which the UN temporarily takes over the function of a government (e.g., in Cambodia, East Timor, and Kosovo) are even more challenging. SRSGs in these types of missions are given wide-ranging executive authority, which must be exercised to establish order, but which must also be carefully balanced with the need to build local capacity for governance, to create local ownership for key decisions, and to devolve institutional power to local authorities as quickly as possible.[2]

To bring such difficult missions to a successful outcome, SRSGs require excellent political, negotiation, leadership, and management skills. SRSGs also mention the need for a superabundance of optimism, persistence, and patience. The UN Panel on Peace Operations notes: "Effective, dynamic leadership can make the difference between a cohesive mission with high morale and effectiveness despite adverse circumstances and one that struggles to maintain any of those attributes. That is, the tenor of an entire mission can be heavily influenced by the character and ability of those who lead it."[3]

It should be noted, however, that not all SRSGs are appointed to head a peace mission. A few have been chosen to work on specific issues, such as the special representative for children and armed conflict or the special representative for internally displaced persons. These SRSGs are assigned to raise awareness of such major problems, to develop relevant policy, and to work with member states and the UN system to ensure that the problems receive appropriate attention and action.

Working Together to Provide
Appropriate Mandates and Adequate Resources

To carry out the objectives of peace missions in such complex situations requires a strategic approach at all levels of the UN system—in the Security Council, at UN Headquarters, and in the mission itself. Lack of a sharply defined strategic approach at any of these levels can affect the outcome of a mission. Such an approach begins with the mission mandate and the resources allocated to achieve it.

As SRSGs stressed at UNITAR's 2001 SRSG seminar, Security Council mandates should be clear with well-defined end goals, should be achievable, should fit the experience in the field, and should provide adequate human and financial resources. Agreement on mandates and resources is not, however, always easy to achieve. The fifteen governments represented on the Council each have their own individual geopolitical and domestic interests, and the compromises necessary to achieve consensus among them can sometimes result in decisions that do not match the needs on the ground. The UN reports on Srebrenica and Rwanda point to this as one of the causes of the UN's disastrous lack of action in both situations,[4] which led the UN Panel on Peace Operations to conclude: "Most [of the failures of the United Nations] occurred because the Security Council and the Member states crafted and supported ambiguous inconsistent and under-funded mandates and then stood back and watched as they failed, sometimes even adding critical public commentary as the credibility of the United Nations underwent its severest test."[5]

In the words of General Romeo Dallaire, force commander for the UN Assistance Mission in Rwanda (UNAMIR), whose forces were reduced in the face of a massive genocide in Rwanda that ultimately left 800,000 dead: "As long as these states procrastinated, bickered, and cynically pursued their own selfish foreign politics, the UN and UNAMIR could do little to stop the killing."[6] Similarly, the report on Srebrenica argues:

> In an effort to find some consensus in the Council, resolutions were adopted in which some of the more robust language favoured by non-troop contributing nations was accommodated. Chapter VII of the Charter was invoked with increasing frequency, though often without specifying what that implied in terms of UNPROFOR operations. In this way, the efforts of Member States to find compromise between divergent positions led to the UNPROFOR mandate becoming rhetorically more robust than the Force itself.[7]

Another problem worth noting is that the highly complex nature of the many situations upon which the Council must authoritatively pronounce creates a real challenge for Council members in terms of possessing sufficient familiarity with the ins and outs of each situation. It is important, therefore, that the Secretary-General, the departments, and the SRSGs view themselves not as passive recipients of mandates but rather as key actors who can, through their careful analysis and well-argued recommendations, assist the Council in the formulation or tailoring of appropriate mandates. Indeed, the Ad Hoc Working Group on Conflict Prevention and Resolution in Africa, in its recommendations on enhancing the effectiveness of SRSGs, notes: "The special representative is often the Council's primary source of information on a conflict or post-conflict situation and it is through the special representatives that many of the Council's decisions are implemented."[8]

Picking up on this issue, the UN Panel on Peace Operations recommends:

> The Secretariat must tell the Security Council what it needs to know, not what it wants to hear when recommending force and other resource levels for new missions and it must set those levels according to realistic scenarios that take into account likely challenges to implementation. Security Council mandates, in turn, should reflect the clarity that peacekeeping operations require for unity of effort when they deploy into potentially dangerous situations.[9]

The initial resources allocated to UNAMIR in Rwanda illustrate the point. Although the reconnaissance mission estimated that a force of 4,500 troops was required to fulfill the mandate, a peacekeeping force of 2,548 military personnel was recommended by the Secretariat, which feared that it would not be possible to secure Council support for the original number. The Council subsequently further limited the mandate.[10] Moreover, after the genocide began, the Council voted unanimously to cut UNAMIR to 270 personnel and to change the mandate. Although the Council reversed itself some weeks later, the reluctance of member states to contribute troops meant that, by the time they did, it was too late. A seminar organized later by the Carnegie Commission for Preventing Deadly Conflict asked a group of U.S. generals to analyze whether a relatively small force of 5,000, had it been deployed rapidly at the time of the genocide (or, implicitly, had it been in place and not removed), could have stemmed the genocide in Rwanda. The conclusion was that it indeed could have significantly altered the outcome.[11]

On a related matter, the UN Panel on Peace Operations notes: "The Secretariat must not apply best-case planning assumptions to situations where the local actors have historically exhibited worst-case behaviour."[12] In his book describing his experience as head of the UN Mission in East Timor (UNAMET), SRSG Ian Martin notes that the lack of contingency planning for the worst-case scenario became particularly critical when widespread violence broke out after the announcement of the result of the popular consultation, eventually leading to the evacuation of the mission, the local staff, and the internally displaced persons sheltering in the UN compound. He proposes that worst-case planning *must* be instituted as a matter of general practice and that the Council should take this into consideration in its own planning.[13]

There is also a strong case to be made for ensuring that mandates are changed in a timely fashion to keep pace with the changing conditions on the ground. In his book *The Shallow Graves of Rwanda,* SRSG Shaharyar Khan describes how the second UN Assistance Mission in Rwanda (UNAMIR II), which he headed, was mandated to keep the peace, but by the time it arrived, the crisis was over—the Rwandan Patriotic Army had won the war and formed a broad-based government. He argues that the failure to give UNAMIR II a new postconflict peacebuilding mandate made it much less effective than it could have been and led to its ultimate withdrawal: "UNAMIR II was the only entity with the capacity and the wherewithal to help revive the people and repair the devastated infrastructure of the country. Regrettably UNAMIR II was given neither the mandate nor the minimal finance to perform this essential post-conflict peace-building role." He suggests that a simple change in the mandate's wording, providing the following enabling clause, would have made this possible: "In addition to its peacekeeping responsibilities, UNAMIR [II] would assist, where possible, in the repair and rehabilitation of Rwanda's infrastructure."[14]

A number of relatively recent changes in practice have helped overcome some of these problems. During the tenure of Secretary-General Boutros Boutros-Ghali, reporting to the Council on missions was carried out largely by a special representative in New York who was specifically assigned to this duty. SRSGs in the field and Secretariat staff did not report directly. As one Secretariat staff member commented:

> This erected a wall between operations, program managers and the Council. Most of the time, the person reporting would have a brief prepared by the concerned department and he would read it out and then take questions. Often he wasn't familiar with the details, so he would just say, "I have taken notes; I will get back to you." Since Kofi Annan became Secretary-General, however, the direct reporting of SRSGs and those in the Secretariat who are responsible has allowed Council members to obtain a more direct account of situations on the ground. There is now a genuine dialogue which members of the Council appreciate very much.[15]

Stating its conclusions on this issue, the Independent Inquiry on Rwanda recommended: "The more direct the flow of information, the better."[16]

In interviews, SRSGs were very enthusiastic about appearing in person before the Council. They reported that the opportunity to brief the Council and answer members' questions enabled them to highlight issues of importance and to go into much more depth on key topics. SRSGs and Secretariat staff also noted that oral briefings allow discussions to be more candid and allow issues that cannot be published in a public document to be raised and discussed. Some SRSGs proposed that they should be present every time their mandates come up for renewal. It was also suggested that it can be helpful for SRSGs to call on ambassadors represented on the Security Council bilaterally before Council meetings, in order to brief them on a one-to-one basis about difficult or complex issues. Indeed, in a recent seminar organized by the permanent mission of Colombia with the support of the International Peace Academy it was suggested that the Council would like to work even more closely with SRSGs: "First and foremost, the dialogue between the special representative and the Council needs to be improved."[17]

Another factor that has improved member states' understanding of the situation on the ground is that Security Council missions have come back into vogue, following the successful Council visit to Indonesia and East Timor in 1999, which played a major part in resolving that crisis. This was the first Council mission in four years, but in the three years since there have been a number of additional such missions. These visits are used instrumentally by the Council when it feels that there is a need for stronger involvement by the international community in response to a blocked peace process. They allow Council members to see the situation firsthand and to have face-to-face meetings with key actors on the ground; they also give Council members a much clearer picture of the issues and problems, as well as the different personalities and perspectives. SRSGs report that such Council missions are highly useful in providing support to the mission and in bringing the Council's influence to bear on those who are obstructing the process.

Another way that SRSGs can affect decisionmaking on the Council is by working closely with ambassadors in the field whose countries are represented on the Security Council. Most SRSGs establish regular meetings with a core group of key ambassadors to share information, brainstorm solutions to problems, and engage in joint strategizing, so that member states feel more engaged, accept responsibility, and transmit similar recommendations back to their capitals. Even when these core groups are not formalized (see Chapter 21, on Groups of Friends, by Teresa Whitfield), SRSGs stress that a close relationship with member states gives them much greater authority and leverage in working with the parties, as well as providing useful ideas and much-needed support for their work.

Former SRSG Aldo Ajello called his group of ambassadors in Mozambique his "mini–Security Council." As he explains: "What I was doing was simple. When I briefed them each week, I was basically dictating the reports they would write to their capitals—which had two good results. First, I knew they were sending the right information. Second, I knew they were all sending the same information at the same time. So, all the capitals were reacting in the same way."[18]

Another way for SRSGs to influence policy is to visit key capitals and discuss issues directly with the policymakers there. The report of the Fafo Forum for SRSGs, titled *Command from the Saddle,* suggests that "an SRSG may find it useful to relate directly to senior officials in world capitals to reinforce a message articulated to the local diplomatic community. When backed by parallel steps at UN Headquarters, such approaches can have a useful impact on the decisions of key actors at important junctures."[19] Some SRSGs stated that they do this particularly when they believe that a member state is badly informed or has very strong vested interests that blind it to the realities of the situation. Visiting delegations from member states can be another way for SRSGs to keep key member states informed.

A further development that may also assist the strategic partnership between the SRSG/Secretariat and the Security Council is the use of a mandate implementation plan, which sets out specific goals and a time frame for achieving them (as used in the UN Mission in Bosnia and Herzegovina [UNMIBH] and the United Nations Mission of Support to East Timor [UNMISET]). It helps to ensure that the Security Council and the mission are on the same page by providing a road map that both can use to evaluate progress and to plan any changes that are needed.

Factors to Consider in Mission Mandating and Resourcing

One factor that the Council should take into account in the resourcing of missions is the difficulty of the conflict environment. Stephen Stedman, Donald Rothchild, and Elizabeth Cousens, based on their recent research on the success of implementation of peace agreements, strongly urge that if missions are to be undertaken in difficult conflict environments, they *must* be given adequate resources to succeed. The authors commissioned studies of implementation following a peace agreement in sixteen cases of civil war to determine the extent to which a number of factors affected implementation. Their findings suggest that four variables were most determinant. The three that were likely to make implementation more difficult were the presence of spoilers, the presence of disposable natural resources, and the presence of a neighboring state hostile to the peace agreement. The factor most likely to predict implementation success was the presence of major power interest.[20] Stedman and his colleagues argue that if sufficient resources cannot be provided, the UN should not become involved at all, since failed interventions can be more costly in terms of human lives than the wars themselves (e.g., Rwanda and Angola).

Another factor concerns peace agreements themselves. As one of the few SRSGs to date to have been involved in both peacemaking and implementation in the same country (Guatemala), SRSG Jean Arnault argues: "The first thing you learn by combining the two experiences is that the implementation process is as viable as the peace agreement on which it is based."[21] Several SRSGs maintain that in deciding whether or not to authorize a mission, it is incumbent on the Security Council to consider whether the agreement on which the mission will be based is appropriate and will be able to withstand the test of implementation. From my interviews with SRSGs, a number of factors emerged as essential ingredients. SRSGs proposed that the peace agreements most likely to be successfully implemented are those that contain sufficient detail and specificity, resolve all major issues, achieve agreement on how power would be shared/divided, are acceptable to a majority of constituents, meet international standards, provide clear guidelines about implementation priorities, contain realistic implementation timetables, give a lead role to the UN in implementation, and set forth an effective implementation mechanism for resolving disputes. SRSGs recommended that the Council should examine peace agreements more carefully before agreeing to implement them, especially agreements that have not been negotiated with significant UN involvement.

Working Together to Maximize Leverage

Another area where SRSGs and the Council can create synergy is in the coordinated use of leverage. Different stages of the peace process are likely to bring to the fore different kinds of leverage. Thus the main sources of leverage at the peacemaking stage are likely to be the personal suasion of the SRSG and the Secretary-General, as well as what is occurring in the negotiation process itself. Public and international opinion may also play a role. When a Group of Friends of the Secretary-General has been formed, it can provide a very useful source of influence. In some cases, other bilateral, regional, or international actors may also weigh in.

As for the peacekeeping stage, three additional factors are added to the mix. If the situation calls for it, the Council can employ a range of instruments to exert influence, including letters from the president of the Council to the parties, presidential statements, Security Council resolutions, changes in the mandate, Council visits to the mission area, and even requests for representatives of the parties to address the Council in person. These, in turn, affect the national and international image of the parties and have positive and negative consequences regarding various kinds of bilateral and multilateral assistance. As well, the Council has at its disposal a range of punitive measures that can be applied under Chapter VII.

A second factor is the presence of the peacekeeping mission itself as a source of influence—the supervision, monitoring, and reporting functions of the peacekeeping troops (whether unarmed, lightly armed, or heavily armed), military observers, civilian police, human rights monitors, civil or political affairs officers, and electoral monitors. Their actions exert a range of implicit and explicit positive and negative influences on the leaders, their constituents, and the population at large.

A third factor is the expanding involvement of the international community, where UN agencies, other multilateral and bilateral actors, as well as nongovernmental organizations become involved in humanitarian, development, or reconstruction aid. Promises of relief and reconstruction can provide a powerful set of positive incentives. It should be noted, however, that failure to deliver pledged aid can seriously undermine this useful source of leverage.

During the peacebuilding phase, the amount of potential leverage often diminishes as Council involvement lessens, the mission is downsized, and the international community's presence dwindles. The conclusion that one might draw is that the amount of leverage is greatest during the peacekeeping phase, but as Michael Doyle points out, there is a paradox in peacekeeping situations that gives the parties considerable counterleverage over the UN and the SRSG:

> The spirit of the agreement is never more exalted than at the moment of the signing of the peace treaty; the authority of the United Nations is never greater. . . . Although the United Nations has put some of its diplomatic prestige on the line, it as yet has no investment in material resources. The United Nations, in short, holds most of the cards. But as soon as the United Nations begins its investment of money, personnel and operational prestige, then the bargaining relationship alters its balance. The larger the UN investment . . . the greater the independent UN interest in success is and the greater the influence of the parties becomes. Since the parties control an essential element in the success of the mandate, their bargaining power rapidly rises.[22]

This paradox argues for SRSGs and the Security Council to consider carefully who is leveraging whom, as well as how and why.

In their interviews, SRSGs reported being keenly aware of the need to maximize the use of influence from the international community. As one SRSG stated: "It was because people were aware that I had the total support of the international community that they accepted my authority. If you think you have power because you represent the United Nations Secretariat, you'll find that this is not sufficient. People must feel that you have someone backing you. For that, the international community was my best asset."[23] Another stated: "To coordinate and spearhead international action, I had to identify countries on whose shoulders I could stand."[24] SRSGs often reminded the parties that the Security Council was following their progress and also made skillful use of ambassadors on the ground to increase their influence.

SRSGs also called for a more sophisticated use of leverage than external carrots and sticks to compel compliance. A number of SRSGs argued that the key to effective leverage is understanding parties' motivations and working from there to provide incentives that are tailored to their interests. They felt that involving the parties as partners in the mutual process of agreeing on objectives and exploring incentives was the best way to give them a greater sense of ownership and responsibility. Many SRSGs stressed that this is why inclusiveness of all the major protagonists as partners—whether at peace talks or on an implementation commission—is so important. Even where it does not seem possible for SRSGs to work with certain parties in considering how incentives can be structured (e.g., when they have excluded themselves from the process), a good understanding of their motivations is certain to assist with a more effective use of incentives. The bottom line, they argued, is that the better one understands the motivation of the parties, the more likely one is to be able to influence the process. Thus, in considering the overt use of leverage, the Council would be well advised to consult with SRSGs about what they think could be effective.

Several SRSGs argued for a greater use of positive incentives. Former special adviser Jan Egeland argued:

> When we consider using leverage, what tends to happen is that the stick becomes bigger than the carrot or the stick comes before the carrot. But we need to realize that threats backfire more often than they create progress. The most effective leverage is usually moral pressure over time or positive incentives such as recognition, invitations and assistance. This works better than negative sanctions and we need to make more use of this approach.[25]

Another suggested that "there are two main carrots, one is economic support and the other is legitimacy."[26] Research in conflict resolution also supports this conclusion. As Melanie Greenberg, John Barton, and Margaret McGuiness argue in their study of twelve conflict resolution efforts: "Positive pressure where the parties are offered a promising future seem more likely to be effective than negative pressures."[27]

Similarly, several SRSGs argued for more caution in the use of heavy-handed leverage by the Council since, as stated above, it can sometimes backfire. "Reactance" is a well-studied psychological phenomenon that typically occurs when the party trying to achieve influence does not fully take into account all the factors that affect the motivation of those they are trying to influence. In such cases, the blunt use of leverage may be seen by a party for what it is—an attempt to "manipulate" it to act in a certain manner against what it perceives to be its own interests. The party may react against the attempt to influence its behavior and refuse to comply in order to preserve its freedom of choice and control over a situation. When internal approval from followers is crucial to a leadership, not being seen by one's constituents to be caving in to external pressure may be more important to a leader than avoiding punitive sanctions—even when they are severe. In such situations, the use of sticks can backfire badly—not only failing to bring about the desired result but even causing the obstinate party to become more entrenched in its resistance to influence. SRSGs also cautioned that sticks—as well as carrots—that are not delivered as promised erode the power of both the Council and the SRSG.

Conclusion

The relationship between an SRSG and the Security Council is a bit like that between a senior staff member in a company and its board of directors. Although the board may have the power to give direction to its senior staff through its executive director, a wise board will realize that it does not usually have the detailed information to micromanage each situation and that the best way to proceed is to work closely to support those who are working on a day-to-day basis to carry out the broad objectives of the organization that have been set by the board.

By working closely with the members of the Council, the Secretary-General and his SRSGs are more likely to obtain the support they need to get the job done. This involves close collaboration with representatives of member states who are on the Council, on the ground, and in key capitals. In all cases, clear analysis and well-argued recommendations stand the best chance of being heeded. Direct reporting by the SRSG to the Council is to be encouraged, as are visits by Council members to the mission area so that they can see the situation firsthand. Since the situations into which SRSGs and missions are deployed are extraordinarily complex, a strategic partnership is crucial for meeting the many challenges that arise.

Notes

1. Representatives of the Secretary-General have various titles: special representative, personal representative, representative, envoy, special adviser, and the

like. The terms "special representative" and "SRSG" will be used in this chapter to refer to all of these.

2. For a more in-depth discussion of the many issues that this entails, see Sebastian von Einsiedel, *You the People: Transitional Administration, State-Building, and the United Nations,* report of the International Peace Academy (IPA) (New York: IPA, October 18–19, 2002).

3. *Report of the Panel on United Nations Peace Operations.* A/55/305–S/2000/809, August 21, 2000, p. 16.

4. See Ingvar Carlsson, Han Sung-Joo, and Rufus M. Kupolati. *Report of the Independent Inquiry into the Actions of the UN During the 1994 Genocide in Rwanda.* New York: United Nations, 1999; and UN General Assembly, *Report of the Secretary-General Pursuant to General Assembly Resolution 53/35: The Fall of Srebrenica,* A/54/549, November 15, 1999.

5. *Report of the Panel on United Nations Peace Operations,* pp. 44–45.

6. Romeo Dallaire, "The End of Innocence," in Jonathan Moore, ed., *Hard Choices: Moral Dilemmas in Humanitarian Intervention* (Lanham, Md.: Rowman & Littlefield, 1998), pp. 78–79.

7. UN General Assembly, *The Fall of Srebrenica,* p. 17.

8. UN Security Council, *Recommendations of the Ad Hoc Working Group on Conflict Prevention and Resolution in Africa on enhancing the effectiveness of the representatives and special representatives of the Secretary-General in Africa,* S/2002/2353, December 9, 2002, p. 3.

9. *Report of the Panel on United Nations Peace Operations,* p. x.

10. Carlsson et al., *Report of the Independent Inquiry on Rwanda,* p. 25.

11. Scott R. Feil, *How the Early Use of Force Might Have Succeeded in Rwanda,* report to the Carnegie Commission on Preventing Deadly Conflict (New York: Carnegie Corporation, 1998).

12. *Report of the Panel on United Nations Peace Operations,* A/55/305–S/2000/809, August 21, 2000, p. x.

13. Ian Martin, *Self-Determination in East Timor: The United Nations, the Ballot, and International Intervention,* International Peace Academy Occasional Paper (Boulder: Lynne Rienner, 2001), pp. 126–127.

14. Shaharyar Khan, *The Shallow Graves of Rwanda* (London: I. B. Tauris, 2000), pp. 202–203.

15. Interview with senior staff member in the Department of Peacekeeping Operations, New York, March 2002.

16. Carlsson et al., *Report of the Independent Inquiry on Rwanda,* p. 47.

17. Letter dated December 19, 2002 from the permanent representative of Colombia to the United Nations addressed to the president of the Security Council. S/2002/1388, p. 7.

18. Interview with Aldo Ajello, Brussels, November 2000.

19. Fafo Forum for SRSGs, *Command from the Saddle: Managing United Nations Peace-Building Missions,* Fafo Report no. 226 (Oslo: Fafo Institute of Applied Science, 1999), p. 39.

20. Stephen John Stedman, Donald Rothchild, and Elizabeth M. Cousens, eds., *Ending Civil Wars: The Implementation of Peace Agreements* (Boulder: Lynne Rienner, 2002).

21. Interview with Jean Arnault, Geneva, November 2001.

22. Michael W. Doyle, "War-Making and Peace-Making: The United Nations' Post–Cold War Record," in Chester A. Crocker, Fen Osler Hampson, and Pamela Aall, eds., *Turbulent Peace: The Challenges of Managing International Conflict* (Washington, D.C.: U.S. Institute of Peace, 2001), p. 542.

23. Interview with Samuel Nana-Sinkam, Geneva, January 2002.

24. Interview with Francis Okelo, Harare, March 2000.

25. Interview with Jan Egeland, Oslo, November 2000.

26. Interview with Jean Arnault, Geneva, November 2001.

27. Melanie Greenberg, John Barton, and Margaret McGuiness, *Word over War: Mediation and Arbitration to Prevent Deadly Conflict* (Lanham, Md.: Rowman & Littlefield, 2000), p. 366.

23

Pressure for
Security Council Reform

Bardo Fassbender

In a September 2002 report, UN Secretary-General Kofi Annan spoke of the "stalled process of Security Council reform." He stated that after nearly a decade of discussions in the UN, "a formula that would allow an increase in Council membership is still eluding Member States," notwithstanding the fact that "in the eyes of much of the world, the size and composition of the Security Council appear insufficiently representative."[1] Indeed, today prospects for a comprehensive reform of the Council, which would encompass both the body's composition and its decisionmaking process, are dim, and the pressure for such a reform, still strong in the early 1990s, has given way to a certain ennui or resignation of the interested governments and nongovernmental organizations. Was it an illusion to believe that the Council could be adapted, in a rational process of discussions and negotiations, to a world so different from that of 1945?

Although there is global agreement on the need for a "comprehensive reform of the Security Council in all its aspects," as the UN Millennium Declaration of September 2000 put it,[2] conflicting views of member states continue to block a solution:[3]

• All governments appear to support an enlargement of the Council in the category of nonpermanent members (which is not to say that there is a consensus on the size of such an enlarged Council, an issue that is discussed under the opposing slogans of "representativeness" and "effectiveness"). But whereas a majority of governments also wish to increase the number of permanent members, others strongly object to such a change.
• Among the supporters of more permanent seats, there is disagreement whether—in addition to the strongly underrepresented African, Latin American, and Asian countries—Germany and Japan should get such seats. The developing regions that are aspiring to permanent representation have so far been unable to decide on the states they want to nominate for perma-

nent membership. The idea of "rotating permanent members," which was advanced to overcome this difficulty, seems to be a contradictio in adjecto and is very controversial. It is not sincerely supported by the most promising possible aspirants for permanent seats among the developing countries. Allocating permanent seats not to states but to regions is also at variance with the state-centered system of the UN Charter.

   • A majority of states wants to abolish or curtail the right of veto of the permanent members, but the current permanent five (P-5) are unwilling to accept any such diminution of their status. There are also conflicting opinions about whether new permanent members should be entitled to the veto (and, if so, whether all members or only some).

   In recent months, this unfortunate situation has been exacerbated by uncertainty about the future relationship of the United States with the United Nations. Already President Bill Clinton was far from taking the lead in promoting a reform of the Security Council. Pressed by a majority in Congress openly hostile to the UN, he instead limited U.S. support for the organization to narrowly defined measures directly serving U.S. national interests. But now much more is at stake. It is unclear whether the United States, in its fully developed role as the only superpower, is at all interested in the existence of a world organization of a type represented by the existing UN. In any case it is unlikely that the current administration under George W. Bush will actively advance a major reform of the Security Council. In October 2002 one of the U.S. representatives to the United Nations, Ambassador Sichan Siv, unenthusiastically repeated that the United States supports "a reformed Council, with Japan and Germany assuming permanent seats and with an expanded number of rotating seats,"[4] but in the meantime even this minimal program has been revised in light of experiences in the current Iraq crisis.

   In this chapter, the original positions of member states regarding the composition, size, and voting procedure of the Council, as well as their modifications during the discussions that have taken place since 1992, shall be outlined. However, it is not always easy to assess the degree of these modifications and the positions taken by governments at the moment, because in general official statements of recent years have been much less detailed than those put forward between 1994 and 1997. Because of the long-lasting deadlock, in many governments questions of Security Council reform have not been thoroughly discussed at a high political level for several years.

The Course of the Debate Since 1992

Following a meeting of the Security Council at the level of heads of state and government in January 1992 and a summit meeting of the nonaligned movement in Jakarta in September 1992, almost global consent developed according to which the increase in membership of the UN, the fundamentally changed international situation after the end of the Cold War, and the new challenges faced by the organization (in areas like development, protection of the environment, and human rights, for instance) required a thorough review of the structure and working methods of the major UN organs, including the Security Council. The permanent members of the Security Council who wanted to avoid a broad review of the Council's functioning and composition were not able to contain the discussion anymore. The new current of opinion became obvious at the session of the General Assembly in November 1992.

As a result of this debate, the General Assembly adopted on December 11, 1992, Resolution 47/62, on the question of equitable representation on and increase in membership of the Security Council. In its operative part, the resolution requested the Secretary-General "to invite Member States to submit . . . written comments on a possible review of the membership of the Security Council." The Secretary-General presented the comments submitted to him in a report dated July 20, 1993, and four addenda to this report.[5] Altogether, seventy-five member states from all regions replied. The submissions can be regarded as the most comprehensive statement of the original UN member states' policies with regard to a reform of the Security Council.

On December 3, 1993, the Assembly decided "to establish an Open-Ended Working Group [OEWG] to consider all aspects of the question of an increase in the membership of the Security Council and other matters related to the Council" (Resolution 48/26).[6] In the resolution's preamble, the General Assembly recognized as the two primary reasons for the need to review the Council's membership "the substantial increase in the membership of the United Nations, especially of developing countries, as well as the changes in international relations." The mandate of the working group was extended by the General Assembly at its forty-eighth through fifty-seventh sessions. The working group adopted a program organizing the questions to be considered in two so-called clusters—first, questions of membership of the Council, including regional distribution, categories of membership, numbers, and modalities of selection; and second, "other matters related to the Council," in particular working methods and procedures. Participation in the OEWG is open to all member states.

The Open-Ended Working Group, under the chairmanship of the president of the General Assembly, began its substantive work on March 1, 1994. In the first year, the meetings were generally attended at the ambassadorial level. Since discussions of the OEWG are not open to the public and no official records are kept, the observer mainly must rely on the annual reports submitted by the group to the General Assembly, press releases of the member states' missions, and information obtained from members of delegations. Further, so-called nonpapers are presented and periodically revised by the vice chairs of the group, which try to summarize and organize the views expressed by member states, indicate major lines of thought, and identify areas of agreement. The nonpapers are not agreed upon in consultations. For this reason, it is not surprising that some member states objected to their contents and evaluations.

The special commemorative meeting of the General Assembly on the occasion of the fiftieth anniversary of the UN in October 1995 provided an opportunity for member states unanimously to reaffirm at the highest political level their agreement to expand the membership of the Security Council. At this meeting, the heads of state, government, and delegation adopted a declaration, the relevant passage of which reads as follows: "The Security Council should, *inter alia,* be expanded and its working methods continue to be reviewed in a way that will further strengthen its capacity and effectiveness, enhance its representative character and improve its working efficiency and transparency." Similarly, the UN Millennium Declaration, adopted by the heads of state and government on September 8, 2000, said that member states will intensify their efforts "to achieve a comprehensive reform of the Security Council in all its aspects."

A Summary of Current Views on
the General Structure of the Security Council

Until today, positions on concrete proposals could not be reconciled. Many states, among them the members of the African Group, seek an increase in both permanent and nonpermanent membership; they constitute a majority. Some delegations (in particular Argentina, Canada, Italy, Libya, Mexico, Pakistan, and Turkey) have supported an increase in nonpermanent membership only, and others (like South Korea and Sweden) propose a reform process in stages, the first stage being an enlargement limited to nonpermanent members. However, criteria and modalities for the election of nonpermanent members remain to be agreed upon. Proposals aiming at an introduction of new categories or types of Council membership, which had some importance in the early discussions of the Open-Ended Working Group, remain on the agenda but appear to enjoy very limited support. Views are divided on how, if there is to be an expansion in permanent membership, such members should be elected, and whether formal criteria such as those contained in Article 23, paragraph 1 of the Charter should guide such an election. In the event that there is agreement on an increase in the permanent membership, an increase only by industrialized countries is widely regarded as unacceptable.

If one takes a general look at the proposals, the question of reform of the Security Council is first of all a North-South issue. The industrialized states of the Northern Hemisphere, which make up four of the five permanent members and to which, according to the 1963 allocation, are assigned three of the ten nonpermanent seats (leaving aside the two Latin American seats), acknowledge that the increase in the general membership from fifty-one in 1945 to 113 in 1963 to 191 in 2002 suggests that the number of Council seats should again be increased. However, they want to limit an increase in the overall membership of the Council, since any such expansion necessarily amounts to a certain restraint on their influence and, according to the official reasoning, might impede the Council's ability to fulfill its mission speedily and effectively (the "efficiency and effectiveness" argument). The developing nations of the Southern Hemisphere, by contrast, tend to promote a stronger increase in the Council's membership in order to improve their representation on the body.

Of course, this contrasting of North and South holds good only in very general terms, because there are numerous differences of opinion within the two camps and overlappings of views that give developed and developing nations some common ground. There is, in particular, general agreement about the fact that the number of nonpermanent members should be increased and that the criteria contained in Article 23, paragraph 1 of the Charter should by and large remain valid. Different opinions exist as to whether additional criteria (and, if so, which) should be applied and whether the chances of smaller states being selected for nonpermanent membership by their regional groups should be enhanced. Some delegations pointed to the lack of uniformity in the way regional groups select candidates and suggested that the selection procedures could be unified to ensure equality of treatment across regions. Proposals for a new distribution of seats among regional groups, and for a new definition of these groups, usually favor the developing countries and seek to reduce the number of European and Western seats. Other proposals intend to regularize the practice of selecting certain states more often for nonpermanent membership. Views have also been expressed in support of, and against, lifting the ban on immediate reelection of nonpermanent members (Article 23, paragraph 2 of the Charter).

As regards the overall size of the Council after its reform, there was a certain convergence of positions. The figures most commonly quoted in the discussions of the Open-Ended Working Group seem to be between twenty and twenty-five, the lowest and highest figures being twenty and thirty. The African Group favors a Council of twenty-six members.

The Question of Permanent Membership
Already the George H. W. Bush administration had favored permanent membership for Japan and Germany, and President Clinton adopted this

policy. Pointing to the two states' "record of constructive global influence and their capacity to sustain heavy global responsibilities," the U.S. representative even said in 1995 that the United States "enthusiastically endorse[s] the candidacies of Japan and Germany" and that it "could not agree to a Council enlargement that did not result in their permanent membership."[7] The United States regards both countries as economically potent Western democracies that it expects substantially to share the burden the United States has to carry in the post–Cold War world. Very cautiously, the United States intimated that it could also agree to a permanent membership of other states if they were to enjoy universal support. The United States has, however, strictly opposed the idea of granting any developing country the right of veto.

For their part, Great Britain and France initially were reluctant to accept the idea of additional permanent seats. It was clear from the beginning that any such addition would give testimony to a relative loss of global power of the United Kingdom and France and might also increase Germany's regional influence in Europe, thus adding to the perceived imbalance that was brought about by Germany's reunification in 1990. However, in the 1990s both states became strong supporters of Germany's and Japan's candidacies. France later also decided to support India's aspiration to become a permanent member.

Russia's and China's statements on the subject continue to be fairly muted. Neither state appears to welcome the prospect of German and Japanese permanent membership. In a more recent Russian pronouncement, Germany and Japan were not mentioned, but India was called "a strong and worthy candidate for permanent membership."[8]

The People's Republic of China presents itself as a representative of the developing countries. Repeatedly China has declared that "at the present time, the main reform task should be the increase, as a priority, of membership of the developing countries in the Council in accordance with the principle of equitable geographical distribution."[9] It will thus not be easy to win China's support for any improvement in the position of Western capitalist states on the Council.

Since 1992, Japan and Germany increasingly stressed their "willingness" to become permanent members of the Security Council.[10] Germany also favors the inclusion of up to three developing countries (one Asian, one African, and one Latin American) in the circle of permanent members, a concept that has been described as the "two plus three" proposal and aims at creating a certain balance between developed and developing countries (or the North and the South) within the permanent membership (six developed countries compared to four developing countries). To make its candidacy even more palatable, Germany also proposed a so-called periodic review clause to be included in Article 23 of the Charter. A review, compulsorily taking place after fifteen years, was said to "guarantee that an increase in both membership categories is not irreversible."[11]

Smaller countries were generally less disturbed by possible changes within the group of leading military and economic powers, of which they clearly cannot count themselves. A number of states advocated permanent membership for Japan and Germany only if this membership would not entail the right of veto. Other states, however, opposed any new permanent seats. Pakistan, for instance, held that "centres of privileges within the UN system" are "anachronistic, anti-democratic, and contrary to the spirit of sovereign equality as enshrined in the UN Charter."[12]

At the beginning of the debate, the industrialized states in the North rather disliked the idea of creating new permanent seats for developing countries. They argued that the more players there are, the less efficient and effective the work of the Council will be. Later this position changed, particularly in view of the firm position of the African states, without which a majority necessary for Charter reform cannot be obtained. The United Kingdom declared to be in favor of "additional seats for Asia, Africa and Latin America and the Caribbean."[13] Most important, the United States announced in July 1997 that it endorsed the proposal of giving three new permanent seats to developing countries. "The regions themselves ought to decide how these seats will be filled." The Clinton administration did not take a position on the question of a veto for new permanent members, including Japan and Germany, but declared that it would oppose any solution that would infringe on the prerogatives of the current permanent members.[14]

Besides the question of the veto, it was the inability of the three regions to agree on states that would represent them as permanent members that prevented the emergence of a consensus. The candidacy of Brazil is opposed by Latin American Spanish-speaking countries, and India's claim is strongly rejected by Pakistan. In Africa, the postapartheid Republic of South Africa and Egypt emerged as strong competitors of Nigeria. Proposals favoring certain types of rotating or semipermanent seats were put forward in order to overcome these difficulties.

The views of the developing countries with regard to an increase in the number of permanent seats of the Security Council are also by no means unanimous. Common ground is still reflected by a 1995 statement of the countries of the nonaligned movement, which since then has often been repeated: "The non-aligned countries are grossly under-represented in the Council. This under-representation should, therefore, be corrected by enlargement of the Security Council. . . . The extent, nature and modalities of the expansion of the Security Council should be determined on the basis of the principles of equitable geographical distribution and sovereign equality of states."[15] However, it is still controversial exactly how these goals are to be achieved. In particular, the question of permanent membership and veto power is highly contentious. Some developing countries wish the category of permanent membership, and the veto power it entails, to be abolished altogether because of its "undemocratic character." Other countries, among them Mexico, dismiss the idea of additional permanent seats.

A larger number of developing countries, however, do not question the existence of permanent members but favor additional permanent seats for the Southern Hemisphere. In particular, the member states of the Organization of African Unity (OAU, now the African Union), though emphasizing that "ultimately . . . all members of the Security Council would be elected according to the principle of equitable geographical representation," adopted this position.[16] The key phrase referred to most often in this context stems from Article 23, paragraph 1 of the UN Charter, according to which the General Assembly, when electing the ten nonpermanent members of the Security Council, shall pay due regard "also to *equitable geographical distribution*" (emphasis added).

The developing countries in question want to extend the scope of application of the latter criterion to the selection of permanent members. In the last analysis, the criterion shall even take precedence over the others mentioned in Article 23. On September 29, 1994, the Council of Ministers of the OAU unanimously declared Africa to be entitled to two permanent seats, to be occupied on a rotating basis according to criteria to be established by the OAU.[17] The representative of Tunisia, setting forth the African proposal, expressed that Asia and Latin America should equally obtain two such seats. The demand was reiterated by the speaker of the African Group in the General Assembly in October 2002.[18]

The Western states have generally rejected the idea that the criterion of equitable geographical distribution should be decisive for the selection of permanent members and have laid more stress on the contribution of member states to the maintenance of international peace and security and the other purposes of the organization. A number of states, from the developed as well as the developing world, came forward with often lengthy catalogs of criteria that should govern the selection of permanent members or members constituting one of the differently designed groups of semipermanent members. According to most of these proposals, the criteria shall be applied only to new members. The governments of India and Nigeria have particularly stressed the importance of the population size of a given country. They hold the view that the principle of democracy entitles countries with a large population to increased rights of participation in the international sphere. The other criteria listed by India are size of economy, resilience and self-sufficiency in terms of raw-material supply and markets, troop and financial contributions to UN peacekeeping operations, and the "future potential" of a state.

However, these efforts to establish common standards for future permanent and semipermanent members of the Security Council have met with mixed response. The British ambassador called them "an academic exercise." It appears that lately only Tunisia has tried to revitalize the idea and suggested applying the following criteria for enlargement: geographical representation, economic significance and financial contributions to the UN, size of population, and identities and cultures.[19]

Proposals Regarding a Third
Category of Members of the Security Council

The idea of creating a third category of members of the Security Council—which would enjoy a "better" status than the nonpermanent members but not the privileges of the permanent members—has found substantial support during the discussions of the Open-Ended Working Group.

The respective proposals are closely linked to the problem of veto power in that one of their major concerns is to prevent further proliferation of the veto. Certain "midsized" states, realizing that their chances of becoming permanent members are minimal, see a third category as a possibility of being represented more often on the Council. Last, some governments support the idea because they fear it might not be possible at all to reach agreement on increasing permanent membership. In their opinion, the aspirations of the respective states should then, for the sake of the organization, at least be accommodated as far as possible.

According to the different motives, proposals for a third category vary. One such category would be established by adding to the current P-5 a group of permanent members without the right of veto. This concept is supported by a number of states, in particular those that regard permanent membership for Japan and Germany as a necessity but for a variety of reasons reject the right of veto. Another third category, in addition to the one just mentioned or standing by itself, would be constituted by a group of regional representatives serving a long term of office, as proposed by the Chilean government.[20]

As mentioned before, the Organization of African Unity has claimed two permanent seats for Africa. The OAU wants Asia and Latin America to be endowed equally with two seats. These seats ("permanent regional rotating seats") shall rotate among members of the respective regional group, according to criteria established by the region. Although the seats are described as a "privilege of the regions entitled to them," membership on the Council shall be governed by the rules of the Charter. What is meant by this was made clear in a statement by Tunisia on May 10, 1996: "The country which occupies that seat will have to enjoy the veto right and would not have to consult with other states of that region before exercising it." The states shall be designated by the region (for a period of approximately four to six years, with the possibility of immediate reelection) and be elected by the General Assembly. This proposal seems to be based on the idea of lifting the ban on immediate reelection of nonpermanent members (Article 23, paragraph 2 of the Charter) as advanced by Germany and other states. It goes beyond that idea in that the normal terms of two years shall be exceeded and the role of the respective regional group be strengthened. The African states see this approach as a first step toward a more far-reaching democratization of the Council: "In time, the present permanent members should also be subject to nomination by their regions and election by the General Assembly."[21]

These various proposals have, however, not passed unchallenged, again for different reasons. India and Mexico rejected the regional rotation schemes as discriminatory because only developing countries shall be submitted to this procedure. India is not inclined to share the seat to which it feels entitled with other states of the region, or to seek their support for obtaining and keeping this seat.

More widely, the idea of creating a new category of permanent members that would lack the right of veto has been criticized. According to this view, the introduction of a three-class membership system would only aggravate the current situation in which the prerogatives of the permanent members compromise the equality of states. However, a "realistic" approach led some states, among them Singapore, to the conclusion that suggestions to introduce a new class of permanent members without the veto are impractical: "No country that is capable of making a contribution as a new permanent member will accept such second class status for long."[22]

Moreover, Germany declared that if it becomes a permanent member of the Council "this has to be on an equal footing with the other permanent members, without discrimination, i.e. with the same rights and the same obligations."[23] This view is shared by the governments of other states interested in becoming permanent members.

If, therefore, the formal establishment of a third category of members of the Security Council is unlikely, a less complicated amendment to the UN Charter could lead to a similar result. Article 23, paragraph 2 of the Charter provides that a "retiring member shall not be eligible for immediate re-election." A number of states proposed to delete, or to provide for certain exceptions from, this clause. Among these states was Germany, which explained that, together with an increased number of seats on the Security Council, such a removal of the ban to reelect nonpermanent members would give Africa, Asia, and Latin America a full range of options as to which member state they want to send, and for how long, to the Security Council as their representative.[24]

The Reform of the Veto Power

The current debate among governments about the right of veto resembles very much the debate of 1945. Many governments oppose the veto for its violation of the principle of sovereign equality among states. Often the veto is also said to be inconsistent with a concept of "democracy in the United Nations," although it is doubtful whether such a concept has a firm basis in the UN Charter.[25] Radical proposals aim at a total removal of the right of veto from the Charter, whereas more cautious ones suggest certain modifications and limitations. It is interesting to note that Latin American countries figure prominently in both of these groups. A third group, partially overlapping with the first two, contests the extension of the veto power to any new permanent members of the Security Council. Among these states are Australia, Italy, Spain, Sweden, and Iceland, along with important Western European and other states.

Like countries of the nonaligned movement, the African states wish the right of veto—an "antidemocratic practice"—eventually to be eliminated. However, in case it must be maintained, Africa wants the new permanent members to enjoy the same prerogatives as the existing P-5: "No fewer than two permanent seats, with all the privileges—including the veto— attached thereto, should be allocated to Africa."[26]

In general accordance with this view, many states have come forward with specific recommendations for restrictions of the veto power or, in more general terms, with a call for a "review" of the current system of voting in the Security Council. The reasons given to support the different proposals are mainly the same as those asserted for an abolition of the veto.

The first of the specific proposals wants to limit the scope of the veto. According to a proposal of the nonaligned movement and a number of individual submissions, the right of veto should be confined to decisions made under Chapter VII of the UN Charter.[27] The second proposal aims at restricting a single permanent member's power to prevent the Council from adopting a resolution. A requirement that, for a veto to become effective, it should be exercised by at least two permanent members was suggested by the OAU and a number of other states.[28] Similar to this is a third proposal that suggests ways of overruling a veto cast by only one permanent member by a majority decision of either the Security Council or the General Assembly.

Another group of states emphasized that any new permanent members of the Security Council should not be awarded the right of veto. Such extension is regarded as furthering an inherently undemocratic privilege that should actually be restricted and eventually abolished in the post–Cold War world.

During the discussions of the Open-Ended Working Group, it was suggested that new permanent members should unilaterally declare their intention to restrict the use of the veto. In view of the position adopted by the current members of the P-5, it has been proposed that they too should be urged to limit the exercise of their veto power. Other delegations have doubts about whether such political declarations would be effective.

In comparison, the camp supporting the veto is less densely populated. However, among its residents are particularly strong states—the veto's current beneficiaries and the states aspiring to permanent membership. Only a handful of other countries have defended the veto. Australia, although believing that there are good reasons not to extend the veto to new permanent members, has acknowledged the value it has had so far as a form of "last resort" to safeguard the national interests of the strongest players in the system of collective security, "if only to ensure that they have a stronger stake in acting within the system than outside of it."[29] According to Singapore, "It is neither practical nor even desirable to do away with the veto. . . . It is a recognition of the hard reality that great powers will not consent to put their power at the disposal of a sheer majority for the implementation of decisions which they do not agree with. It is a safety valve that prevents the UN from undertaking commitments that it lacks the power to fulfil."[30]

In a statement on March 27, 1996, one of the U.S. representatives to the UN, Ambassador Karl Inderfurth, said that "the [United States] does not support any abridgement of the right of veto or its scope of application as set forth in Article 27 of the Charter."[31] The United States also discarded the idea of defining "procedural matters" as referred to in Article 27, paragraph 2 of the Charter, which some delegations saw as a way of limiting the use of the veto.

For years now, this deadlock has not been overcome, and it is unlikely that it will be overcome anytime soon. The current P-5 insist on preserving their right of veto in its given form. At the same time, the P-5, with the exception of France, do not support new permanent seats for the developing world endowed with that full-fledged right. In particular, they are not willing to accept a scheme like the African plan of "rotating permanent seats," according to which the states enjoying the right of veto would not be known in advance. For their part, the nonaligned movement and the African Union have made it clear that they expect the new African, Asian, and Latin American permanent members to enjoy the same rights as all the other permanent members and that they will not agree to any new permanent seats for industrialized states if this condition is not met. The speaker of the African Group at the fifty-seventh session of the General Assembly expressly warned that an expansion of the Council, particularly of the permanent members, would occur only if Africa were included.[32]

Conclusion

It is well known that any amendment to the UN Charter requires a vote of two-thirds of the members of the General Assembly and a ratification by two-thirds of the UN member states, including all the permanent members of the Security Council (Articles 108 and 109 of the UN Charter). After almost a decade of discussions about a reform of the Security Council, such a level of consensus does not appear to be anywhere in sight. No single state is capable of untying the Gordian knots. The only state that today could launch a reform initiative with a reasonable chance of succeeding is the United States, but there is clearly a lack of any will in this direction in Washington. Even the most modest of all Council reforms—a repeat of 1963 with a further increase in the number of nonpermanent seats from the current ten to either fifteen or seventeen, about which there was broad agreement in the Open-Ended Working Group—is unlikely to be supported by the Bush administration.

It has rightly been said that the powers of the Security Council "are a precious, but at the same time precarious trust of the international community, certainly the greatest achievement of the new world order that emerged after the catastrophe of the Second World War. . . . Each and every state should be aware of the enormity of the progress that Chapter VII of the Charter embodies compared with the earlier system of unbridled coexistence of national sovereignties."[33] And yet states are far away from uniting their strength, for the sake of their common future, in an effort to give new life and vigor to the security system of the UN Charter.

Notes

1. See *Strengthening of the United Nations: An Agenda for Further Change,* A/57/387, September 9, 2002, para. 20.
2. See Resolution 55/2 (2000), para. 30.
3. For a recent summary of the various proposals, see *Report of the Open-Ended Working Group on the Question of Equitable Representation on and Increase in the Membership of the Security Council and Other Matters Related to the Security Council,* A/56/47, 2002 annex 4.
4. Statement in the General Assembly, A/57/PV.27, October 14, 2002, p. 10.
5. UN Secretary-General, *Question of Equitable Representation on and Increase in the Membership of the Security Council,* A/48/264, July 20, 1993, and Add.1, Add.2, Add.2/Corr.1, Add.3, Add.4.
6. For an overview of the discussions of the Open-Ended Working Group, see Bardo Fassbender, *UN Security Council Reform and the Right of Veto: A Constitutional Perspective* (The Hague: Kluwer, 1998), pp. 221–275; and Ingo Winkelmann, "Bringing the Security Council into a New Era: Recent Developments in the Discussion on the Reform of the Security Council," *Max Planck Yearbook of United Nations Law* 1 (1997): 35–90.

7. Statement by Ambassador Karl Inderfurth, A/50/PV.58, November 14, 1995, p. 5.

8. Statement by Sergei Ordzhonikidze, deputy foreign minister of the Russian Federation, at the General Assembly, A/56/PV.34, October 31, 2001, p. 17.

9. Statement by Zhang Yishan at the meeting of the Open-Ended Working Group, February 2, 2003.

10. See, for example, speeches by Morihiro Hosokawa, prime minister of Japan, and Klaus Kinkel, foreign affairs minister of Germany, before the forty-eighth session of the General Assembly, September 27, 1993, and September 29, 1993, respectively.

11. See *Periodic Review Clause: Working Paper by Germany*, A/AC.247/1996/CRP.15/Rev.1, July 3, 1996, reprinted in *Report of the Open-Ended Working Group . . . Addendum*, A/50/47/Add.1, September 9, 1996, annex 14.

12. Intervention by Ambassador Ahmad Kamal before the Open-Ended Working Group, March 27, 1996, p. 2.

13. Statement by Simon Manley to the Open-Ended Working Group, March 28, 1996, UK Mission to the UN press release 023/96, March 28, 1996, p. 2.

14. See statements by a spokesman of the Department of State, July 17–18, 1997; U.S. Department of State, *Daily Press Briefing* nos. 108–109.

15. Statement of the nonaligned movement, A/AC.247/5(i), February 13, 1995, reprinted in A/49/965, September 18, 1995, p. 94.

16. See *Réformes des Nations Unies: Position africaine commune*, OAU Doc. NY/OAU/POL/84/94 Rev. 2, September 29, 1994, paras. 31, 33–34. See also *Harare Declaration of the Assembly of Heads of State and Government of the OAU on the Reform of the United Nations Security Council*, June 4, 1997; and A/AC.247/1997/CRP.11, June 27, 1997.

17. See *Réformes des Nations Unies*, para. 34.

18. See statement by Abdulmejid Hussein, representative of Ethiopia, on behalf of the African Group, A/57/PV.31, October 16, 2002, p. 19.

19. See statement by Noureddine Mejdoub, representative of Tunisia, at the General Assembly, A/57/PV.30, October 15, 2002, p. 6.

20. Statement by Chile, June 30, 1993, in UN Secretary-General, *Question of Equitable Representation*, pp. 15, 17.

21. *Réformes des Nations Unies*, para. 36; *Harare Declaration*, para. 3.

22. Speech by Wong Kan Seng, foreign affairs minister of Singapore, at the forty-eighth session of the General Assembly, October 6, 1993, p. 5.

23. Statement by Ambassador Gerhard Henze to the Open-Ended Working Group, May 17, 1994, p. 4. In essence, this position was reiterated in the statements by Ambassador Tono Eitel to the Open-Ended Working Group, March 25, 1996, p. 6, April 23, 1996, pp. 9–10.

24. Statement by Ambassador Gerhard Henze, May 17, 1994, p. 2.

25. See Fassbender, *UN Security Council Reform*, pp. 301–305.

26. Statement of the representative of Tunisia, Abdulmejid Hussein, on behalf of the African Group at the General Assembly, A/57/PV.31, October 16, 2002, p. 19.

27. See the respective statements in UN Secretary-General, *Question of Equitable Representation*, p. 25, and A/48/264 Add.3, p. 7. For a discussion of alternative proposals, see Fassbender, *UN Security Council Reform*, pp. 266–268.

28. See *Réformes des Nations Unies*, para. 33(e).

29. Statement by Australia, July 7, 1993, in UN Secretary-General, *Question of Equitable Representation*, pp. 8–9.

30. Speech by Wong Kan Seng, October 6, 1993, p. 6.
31. See U.S. Mission to the UN press release 39-(96), March 27, 1996, p. 2.
32. See statement by Abdulmejid Hussein, October 16, 2002, p. 19.
33. See Christian Tomuschat, "Using Force against Iraq," at 81.

24

The United States in the Security Council: A Faustian Bargain?

FREDERICK RAWSKI AND NATHAN MILLER

In the traditional version of the German myth, Professor Faust makes a deal with the devil for wealth and power and is thereby damned. In Goethe's Enlightenment retelling, however, Mephistopheles is recast as Faust's most valuable ally, there to guard against complacency, to prod Faust to continuous exploration and ever-greater achievement. The current relationship between the United States and the Security Council could be seen in Faustian terms, but which? On the one hand, the United States has supported innovations in Security Council practice that have expanded the responses available to the Council in a post–Cold War environment that constantly challenges traditional definitions of international peace and security. On the other hand, U.S. policy has been inconsistant at best and has often run counter to the very changes it helped foster. The Council has been forced to cater to U.S. interests, thereby undercutting its achievements and undermining its legitimacy in an effort to remain relevant.

This chapter will illustrate this contradictory dynamic through a series of brief discussions of key interactions between the Council and the United States during the 1990s. It will then turn to an argument that the apparent paradox of that dynamic rests on the mistaken—though common—conception of the United States as a unitary actor. Finally, it will examine several theories that have been proposed to explain this paradox, including the ideological pull of U.S. political history, the weight of public opinion, and the complex constitutional dynamic of U.S. domestic politics.

The Security Council During the Cold War

With the failures of the League of Nations prominent in their minds, the members of the U.S. delegation to the San Francisco Conference were enthusiastic in their support of a powerful Security Council. The initial enthusiasm abated, however, when it became apparent that the Soviet

ch had boycotted the Council during the Korean War, would
meaningful role for the Council in international affairs. For the
our decades, the Council was virtually paralyzed by the compet-
ts of the United States and the Soviet Union.

With the end of the Cold War, the Council began to reemerge as a functioning institution. Mikhail Gorbachev's 1987 announcement that the
Soviet Union was prepared to reengage with the United Nations marked the
beginning of a new era of Soviet, and then Russian, cooperation with the
United States and the Council.[1] This cooperation generated numerous successes, including unanimous resolutions establishing missions to monitor
the Iran-Iraq War and to prepare Namibia for independence. Though the
Reagan administration (1981–1989) managed to keep most U.S. military
activity out of the Council, the United States, joined by the United
Kingdom, began to exercise its veto to prevent condemnation of military
action in Grenada (1983), Libya (1986), and Panama (1989). During this
period, the United States assumed a strongly defensive posture, invoking
the veto to protect U.S. and often Israeli action from censure.

The Deal Is Struck: Progress and Innovation in the 1990s

During the 1990s the Security Council identified a number of situations as
"threats to international peace and security"—a term of art used to trigger
the exercise of the Council's enforcement power under Chapter VII of the
UN Charter—and developed novel responses, or at least novel applications
of old responses, to those threats. The leadership or strong support of the
United States led to Council innovation in several areas, including international law governing the use of force, the establishment of international
criminal tribunals, peacekeeping, and the use of economic sanctions.

Authorization for the Use of Force

Iraq—classical intervention and coalitions of the willing. The decade opened
with what would be one of its last instances of classical interstate violence,
the resolution of which marked a high point of U.S.-Council collaboration.
When Iraq invaded Kuwait in 1990, the U.S. administration under George
H. W. Bush secured Resolution 678, authorizing the use of force by a U.S.-
led coalition for the first time since the Korean War. In part to avoid a
Soviet veto, Secretary of State James Baker approached the issue of authorization incrementally, first obtaining a condemnation of the Iraqi occupation of Kuwait, followed by the imposition of sanctions and authorization
to enforce an embargo. Despite intense lobbying by the United States of
Council members during informal consultations, which contributed to a
sense that the United States was forcing its will upon the Council, the Gulf

War is widely characterized as a period of successful U.S.-Council cooperation.

The designation of Iraq's invasion and annexation of Kuwait, a paradigmatic case of interstate aggression, as a threat to international peace and security was hardly novel, but the military coalition put together by the United States under the Council's authorization for the use of force was unprecedented. Military forces from more than twenty states participated in Operation Desert Storm. The "coalition of the willing" became the template for the authorized (and unauthorized) use of force for much of the decade.

Somalia and Haiti—expanding notions of "threat to international peace and security." The United States was the driving force in the Council behind the authorization of intervention in Somalia in 1992 and Haiti in 1994, identifying humanitarian crises and disruption to democracy, respectively, as threats to international peace and security—a radical redefinition of the concept. In both cases, the Council authorized U.S.-led military forces, but not for the traditional purpose of combating international aggression. In Operation Restore Hope in Somalia, U.S. Marines were deployed to ensure the equitable distribution of humanitarian relief supplies. In Haiti, another coalition, the twenty-eight-member Multinational Force, intervened to restore ousted President Jean-Bertrand Aristide to power and halt the flow of refugees, which threatened to cause a political crisis for Bill Clinton's administration. These novel exercises of Chapter VII powers invigorated the doctrine of humanitarian intervention and bolstered arguments for an emerging right to democratic governance, themes that would return to haunt relations between the United States and the Council later in the decade.

Humanitarian Law and International Criminal Tribunals
In response to Serbian atrocities in Bosnia and Croatia, the Council in Resolution 808 designated "violations of international humanitarian law" as a separate, independent threat to international peace and security. While such a designation itself was innovative, the response the Council crafted to this new threat was even more exceptional. In May 1993 the Council passed Resolution 827, which called for the establishment of the International Criminal Tribunal for the Former Yugoslavia (ICTY). The U.S. attitude toward the ICTY was initially ambivalent, when active prosecution was seen as a potential obstacle to the negotiation of the Dayton Accords. However, in later years the United States became an ardent supporter, going so far as to threaten to withhold economic aid if the government of the former Yugoslavia failed to uphold its obligation to surrender

Slobodan Milosevic. In 1994 the United States played a key role in securing the passage of Resolution 955, establishing the International Criminal
Tribunal for Rwanda (ICTR). The rulings of the two tribunals have since
contributed to the advancement of international criminal law in a number of
areas, including command responsibility, the definition of rape as a war
crime, and the refinement of the doctrine of state responsibility.

Peacekeeping

There was a sense in the early 1990s that UN military peacekeeping had
reemerged as the tool of choice for the resolution of international conflict.
In the wake of its successful engagement with the Council during the Gulf
War, the first Bush administration committed 28,000 U.S. troops to a
Security Council–mandated operation in Somalia (the Unified Task Force
[UNITAF]) and issued a *National Security Strategy* that encouraged the
United States to take "an active role" in the "full spectrum" of UN peace-
keeping operations.[2] During his presidential campaign, then–Arkansas gov-
ernor Bill Clinton invoked Secretary-General Boutros Boutros-Ghali's call,
in *An Agenda for Peace,* for a permanent UN "rapid deployment force."
When Clinton finally took office, his first ambassador to the United
Nations, Madeleine Albright, announced a policy of "aggressive multilateralism," which included extensive U.S. engagement with the Council on the
issue of peacekeeping (partly in the hope that it would help limit U.S. military involvement overseas). The Clinton administration maintained a significant U.S. military presence in Somalia in support of the second UN operation there (UNOSOM II) and released Presidential Review Directive (PRD)
13, which among other things endorsed the hitherto inconceivable idea of
subordinating U.S. peacekeeping troops to UN operational command.

Sanctions

The end of the Cold War saw a dramatic increase in the use of sanctions by
the Security Council as an alternative or supplement to military action in
maintaining international peace and security. After imposing mandatory
sanctions only twice between 1945 and 1989, the Council did so more than
a dozen times over the course of the 1990s. The most significant of these
instances, and the one most closely bearing on the relationship of the
United States to the Council, was the imposition of severe economic sanctions against Iraq following its invasion of Kuwait in hopes of forcing its
immediate withdrawal. The sanctions, including a U.S.-led naval blockade
and an oil embargo, remained in place after the successful prosecution of
the Gulf War, with Resolution 687 setting out detailed conditions for their
removal. Despite widespread criticism of the selective enforcement and
inhumane effects of sanctions regimes in Iraq and elsewhere, frequent U.S.

engagement with the Council on the imposition of sanctions bolstered the Council's authority and gave it at least a moderately effective tool for managing international conflict.

Power at What Price?

The cooperative U.S. stance vis-à-vis the Council in the first half of the 1990s gave way to U.S. unilateral action and a progressive marginalization of the Council. U.S. aid to and support of Security Council initiatives in the 1990s never came without a price. Each of the instances of cooperation, progress, and innovation discussed in the preceding section was either immediately followed by, or set the stage for, subsequent U.S. actions that undermined the legitimacy and authority of the Council.

Authorization for the Use of Force

Iraq and implied authorization.   In the months and years after the Iraqi government agreed to the cease-fire terms laid out in Resolution 687, U.S. enforcement action became progressively more unilateral and based on increasingly tenuous legal grounds. The first Bush administration based the establishment of no-fly zones in southern and northern Iraq on the Council's finding in Resolution 688 that a "threat to international peace and security" existed in the region. Initially, both the French and British flew alongside U.S. planes patrolling the no-fly zones. The Clinton administration subsequently executed military strikes to extend the southern no-fly zone in 1996, again invoking Resolutions 678 and 688 as authority, without seeking new authorization from the Council. In light of U.S. veto power, the Council never even considered discussion of the legality of the U.S. interpretation; nor could it act after the United States, without seeking approval, fired missiles at targets in Baghdad and in southern Iraq in 1993, 1996, and 1998. The United States persisted in interpreting Iraq's "continuing breach" of Resolution 678 and the post-cease-fire resolutions as grounds for the unilateral use of force, thus weakening the authority that the Council had amassed in the aftermath of the Gulf War. Similarly, in October 2002, when the second Bush administration went to the Council seeking a new resolution authorizing the use of force against Iraq, U.S. State Department negotiators implied that a Council finding of "material breach," coupled with a threat of "serious consequences," would constitute sufficient authorization for the United States to act unilaterally if Iraq remained in violation.

Kosovo, humanitarian intervention, and no authorization.   The redefinition, in the context of Somalia and Haiti, of humanitarian crises as threats to inter-

national peace and security proved to be a compelling one. Responding to
the humanitarian crisis in Kosovo in 1997 and 1998, the international community, led by the United States, first sought a diplomatic solution. When
negotiations, set against a backdrop of near-constant threats of a military
campaign by the North Atlantic Treaty Organization (NATO), failed and
both Russia and China threatened to veto any resolution authorizing the use
of military force, NATO took action without seeking prior Council
approval. At the time, Richard Holbrooke, the U.S. special envoy, claimed
that NATO did not require authorization from the Council, though U.S.
officials would on occasion cite the Federal Republic of Yugoslavia's
breach of Resolution 1203, which invoked Chapter VII but did not explicitly authorize the use of force.

There could be no greater blow to the Council's political standing.
NATO, and the United States in particular, publicly humiliated the Council,
demonstrating that they could and would organize a "coalition of the willing" to engage in a large-scale, coordinated military action without Council
approval. To make matters worse, the rhetoric used to justify the bombing
of Kosovo was precisely the language of humanitarian intervention earlier
relied upon by Council, making it seem an institution incapable of living up
to its own standards.

The Failure of Military Peacekeeping

When eighteen U.S. soldiers were killed in Mogadishu in October 1993, the
U.S.-UN peacekeeping "partnership" unraveled almost overnight. President
Clinton ordered a full withdrawal of U.S. troops from Somalia (which at
UNITAF's peak included 37,000 U.S. soldiers) within six months. While
U.S. soldiers were still leaving the field, White House legal advisers were
hard at work drafting Presidential Decision Directive (PRD) 25, which
superseded PRD 13. PRD 25 placed strict conditions on future U.S.
involvement in UN operations, including a policy review to determine
whether U.S. participation served a legitimate foreign policy interest, a
pledge to consult Congress before voting in favor of the creation or expansion of a peacekeeping force in the Council, and a prohibition on the place-
ment of U.S. troops under UN command. Subsequent U.S. resistance to the
establishment or expansion of peacekeeping operations was largely to
blame for the Council's most shameful period of inaction. On April 21,
1994, after intense lobbying by the U.S. State Department, the Council
passed Resolution 912, recalling from Rwanda the greater part of its peacekeeping force, the UN Assistance Mission in Rwanda (UNAMIR). In the
midst of the genocide, the State Department instructed the UN ambassador
to aggressively oppose "any effort at this time to preserve a UNAMIR presence in Rwanda."[3] During the same period, the Clinton administration

refused to contribute troops to the UN Protection Force (UNPROFOR) in Bosnia-Herzegovina. After Somalia, the United States rarely endorsed military peacekeeping efforts unless they were under its control or narrowly tailored to its foreign policy, such as the post-Dayton multinational Implementation Force (IFOR) and military Kosovo Force (KFOR), both under the operational command of NATO.

Though UN peacekeeping resurfaced in the late 1990s, including the ambitious civilian "transitional administrations" such as the UN Transitional Administration in East Timor (UNTAET) and the UN Mission in Kosovo (UNMIK), there is little doubt that U.S. withdrawal of support for military peacekeeping operations in the 1990s considerably weakened the Council's ability to utilize peacekeeping as an effective tool.

Individual Criminal Accountability . . . for Some

The interplay between U.S. resistance to the establishment of the International Criminal Court (ICC) and support of the ad hoc international criminal tribunals likewise illustrates the inconsistency of the interactions between the United States and the Council. At the 1998 ICC conference in Rome, the United States argued that the Council should have an exclusive power to refer cases to the Court and maintained that, at the very least, the Court should not be able to exercise jurisdiction over nationals of states not party to the Rome Statute. When these and other demands were not met, the U.S. government began to aggressively oppose the Court's establishment.[4] This opposition culminated in the summer of 2002 when the U.S. ambassador to the UN, John Negroponte, threatened to withdraw U.S. personnel from the UN force in East Timor and vetoed the extension of the UN Mission in Bosnia and Herzegovina (UNMIBH) after the Council failed to agree upon a resolution granting immunity to U.S. peacekeepers from the ICC's jurisdiction. The Council ultimately passed Resolution 1422, prohibiting the Court from prosecuting current or former peacekeeping personnel from countries not party to the Rome Statute for a renewable twelve-month period.

At the same time, the United States has continued to support ad hoc international criminal justice efforts. The ICTY and ICTR are operating at more than capacity, and a body of ad litem judges was approved to assist them in completing their work more quickly. The United States is the principal financial backer of a Council-mandated judicial experiment in Sierra Leone and was also instrumental in the negotiations between the UN and Cambodia for a similar mechanism to try the remnants of the Khmer Rouge.

The Security Council's continued acquiescence to U.S. preferences for regional, ad hoc criminal justice risks setting up an opposition between an ad hoc, Council-controlled model and a permanent model, particularly if the ICC gets off to a rocky start. Through its attempts to keep international justice initiatives within the purview of the Council, and thus largely under the control of the United States, the United States once again succeeded in simultaneously enhancing the Council's authority and contributing to the perception that the Council can take no action at variance with U.S. interests.

The Failure of Iraqi Sanctions

There is little doubt that the continuation of the Iraqi sanctions regime throughout the 1990s has been the primary, though not the only, cause of a massive humanitarian crisis in that country. The crisis reached such proportions that the Council itself set up a "humanitarian panel" in 1999 to investigate the issue. The panel's findings described widespread problems in areas such as infant mortality, malnutrition, health care, and education and recommended loosening the sanctions in order to alleviate the crisis.[5] As the humanitarian situation worsened, the support of the international community for the sanctions regime dwindled and the United States lost key allies even within the Council. France withdrew from participation in enforcing the no-fly zones in 1998 and then–French foreign minister M. Hubert Védrine described the sanctions regime as "cruel, ineffective and dangerous."[6]

The United States remained adamant about maintaining the regime without changes, repeatedly threatening to veto any modification. As President Bill Clinton noted in 1997, "The sanctions will be there until the end of time, or as long as [Hussein] lasts."[7] This did not entirely paralyze the Council, which established the oil-for-food program, began talks on the use of more targeted "smart" sanctions, and in 2002 introduced additional reforms to the sanctions program, embodied in Resolution 1409. Nonetheless, the overall inability of the Council, in the face of U.S. intransigence, to address widely recognized problems with the sanctions regime has significantly contributed to its perception as an illegitimate tool of U.S. foreign policy.

Explaining the Paradox

Contradictory as it may seem, to describe the foregoing dynamic as a paradox is to assume incorrectly that the United States is a unitary actor of which both internal coherence and consistency over time should be expected. Quite the opposite is actually the case. U.S. foreign policy—of which its relations with the Security Council are but a part—is the product of the interplay among internal ideologies, constituencies, and political agendas that are not only often at odds with one another over the proper response to any given situation but also change configuration over time. Three such elements—a historically rooted ideology, public opinion, and congressional activism—are especially important in understanding the ambivalence of the United States toward the Council.

Ideology: The Dialectic of Exceptionalism

On his way to the American colonies, John Winthrop, the governor of Massachusetts, wrote in "A Model of Christian Charity" of his vision of Boston as a free and independent city on a hill, a beacon for all the people of the world. That conception of U.S. exceptionalism has thrived since 1630, reflected in the idea of "manifest destiny" and most recently endorsed in the second Bush administration's *National Security Strategy*, which declares that "the United States will use this moment of opportunity to extend the benefits of freedom across the globe . . . to bring the hope of democracy, development, free markets, and free trade to every corner of the world."[8] This moral imperative has often driven U.S. policy toward the establishment of institutions capable of promulgating and applying universal principles of freedom, democracy, and the rule of law. Such a motivation was apparent in President Woodrow Wilson's enthusiasm for the League of Nations and President Harry Truman's leadership in the establishment of the United Nations. The structure and authority of the Council in particular was an ideal means of propagating these universalisms, without impinging upon U.S. sovereignty.

One might expect such a drive to lead to a deep commitment to an international relations policy conducted according to democratic precepts of equality, deliberation, cooperation, and majority rule. Yet U.S. support for the international institutions it helps establish seems seldom to last past the founding. Embedded in the very notion of multilateral institutions is the ceding of some measure of sovereignty to the organization. U.S. resistance to the diminution of the brightness of the beacon on the hill leads it to pull back from multilateral commitments that threaten to interfere with its internal decisionmaking. This ideological tension was apparent in the speed with which the United States turned away from the General Assembly once its influence there waned, and in its relative preference for the Security Council—even during the Cold War—and would help explain both its long-term, albeit inconsistent, political (and financial) support of the Council as well as its fierce resistance to reform of the Council's archaic voting structure.

This dialectic between grand universalism and unilateralism fits the pattern of U.S.-Council interaction examined in this chapter.[9] It is reflected in the incongruity between the U.S. backing of ad hoc international war crimes tribunals and resistance to the ICC. It appears in the Clinton administration's willingness to invoke the high ideals of democracy and humanitarianism when seeking Council approval for U.S.-led interventions (Haiti) while resisting the use of the Council to consistently enforce those same ideals when they run counter to U.S. interests or public opinion (Rwanda). Similarly, the second Bush administration cast the imperative to attack Iraq and Afghanistan not only in security but also in humanitarian terms, emphasizing the plight of Kurds and Afghan women and even alluding to the right of the population to democratic governance. At the same time, George W. Bush tinged his rhetoric with a sly cynicism that even though Council approval of these noble aims might be politically desirable, it was by no means required.

Although neither ideology nor rhetoric themselves explain the ambivalence of U.S. relations with the Council, this dialectical and often contradictory strain of political thinking sustains a public discourse within which both domestic actors (Congress, White House, the "American people") and foreign actors (the elected ten members, the permanent five, the "international community") interact, at times promoting the Council as a vessel for the promulgation of universal values and at times deriding it as inconsequential or even a threat to U.S. sovereignty.

Public Opinion

It could be argued that public opinion in the United States moves within this dialectic as well and thereby affects relations with the Security Council insofar as it sets the boundaries within which officials must operate. It should be noted here that the U.S. public rarely takes a strong stance on particular UN activities, with striking exceptions such as the 1991 Gulf War and the failed peacekeeping operation in Somalia. At the same time, it would seem that citizens of the United States are more consistently supportive of the UN than are their leaders. Indeed, Americans polled from 1964 to 1997 generally agreed that the United States should cooperate with the UN.[10] Respondents throughout the 1990s had an overwhelmingly favorable opinion of the UN and of multilateral efforts across a broad range of subject areas including military peacekeeping, international economic regulation, and international law.[11]

One common attempt to square the poll data with the reality of U.S. engagement is to see the broad support for the UN as shallow and easily dissipated and the smaller opposition as deeply committed and immovable. Policymakers in that situation would have no incentive to cater to the interests of the fickle majority but would need to be careful of the staunch, vocal minority. This view has been challenged by some data that suggest that a portion of the majority is both strongly committed to its affirmative view and vocal.[12] One could, however, also argue that the polls reflect a multilayered attitude where considerably more Americans support the principle of the existence of the UN than support any given one of its activities.

Such an understanding would explain why attacks on the UN in general and the Security Council in particular by entrenched interests in Congress and elsewhere do not seem to generate any political accountability, because skepticism about the advisability of the United States taking international action of any kind—whether multilateral or not—in any particular situation can coexist with the desire that a multilateral mechanism be available should such action become absolutely necessary. A striking example of that coexistence came shortly after the killing of U.S. servicemen in Mogadishu: amid a massive public outcry to pull U.S. soldiers out of the peacekeeping mission, 88 percent of Americans polled agreed with the statement: "Because the world is so interconnected today, it is important for the [United States] to participate, together with other countries, in efforts to maintain peace and protect human rights."[13] Understanding the public's attitude in this way would explain why strong faith in the UN in general was accompanied in the 1990s with numbers reflecting a much lower confidence that the organization is doing a good job, and why the second Bush administration's efforts to undermine the ICC have had no domestic political consequences despite poll data indicating that the majority of Americans are in favor of it.[14]

The view sketched above would also be consistent with the dialectic of exceptionalism, where commitment to the principle of the UN corresponds to the universalist thesis, whereas ambivalence about U.S. involvement in particular operations corresponds to the inevitable unilateral antithesis. A marked exception to the ambivalence reflected in the poll data is the insistence that when international action—particularly the use of force—is necessary and/or unavoidable, the action be multilateral. For instance, in a Pew survey taken in early 2003, though 68 percent of Americans were in favor of military action in Iraq, only 26 percent supported doing so without the support of allies.[15] The second Bush administration's initial resort to the Security Council for approval for the use of force against Iraq could have been driven as much by public opinion as was President Clinton's about-face on military peacekeeping policy in the wake of Mogadishu. In a poll published on February 7, 2003, just two days after Secretary of State Colin Powell made the case for war against Iraq to the Council, only 31 percent of Americans thought the United States should proceed without UN approval and 65 percent thought that weapons inspectors should be given more time.[16] Thus one could argue that, on some issues, public opinion is an important factor driving Washington toward the Security Council. More often, it seems that public ambivalence leaves a vacuum into which other political actors may step.

Congressional Activism

The analysis of public opinion trends above, if accurate, would help to explain the dynamics of congressional support for or resistance to cooperation with the Council in the 1990s. Because in the U.S. constitutional system the power to disburse funds, including those for UN dues and foreign policy initiatives, rests with the legislative branch, Congress has had a unique power to affect U.S. foreign policy. During the 1990s, ideologues in Congress stepped in where the public stepped out. In particular, the Senate Foreign Relations Committee, under the leadership of Senator Jesse Helms, showed an increasing willingness to exert this influence to shape U.S.-UN interactions.

On the one hand, public ambivalence about U.S. engagement with the UN in a given situation gives significant leeway to entrenched interests on Capitol Hill. In that context, congressional skepticism toward international institutions dating from the Senate's refusal to ratify the Convention of the League of Nations continues to flourish today, exemplified in Helms's excoriating speech to the Council in January 2000.

Congressional initiatives in the 1990s implemented under the rubric of UN reform had a particularly negative impact on the Council's ability to deploy effective peacekeeping operations. Congressional calls for a restructuring of assessed contributions began as early as the mid-1980s and culminated with the passage of the Helms-Biden Act of 1997, which linked U.S. payment of arrears to reforms at the UN and placed a cap on contributions to peacekeeping operations. More recently, congressional opposition to both the ICC and the deployment of U.S. troops in peacekeeping operations manifested itself in the passage of the American Service Members Protection Act of 2002, which urged the president to veto any peacekeeping operation that does not exempt U.S. military personnel from the jurisdiction of the ICC. Throughout the 1990s, Congress has reinforced and sometimes gone above and beyond consecutive U.S. administrations' strong support for sanctions regimes by passing its own bills imposing sanctions against Iran, Libya, and Cuba, effectively undercutting the Council as the principal venue for the imposition and supervision of sanctions regimes.[17]

On the other hand, congressional action has at times alleviated U.S.-Council tensions by encouraging the White House to seek a more multilateral approach to conflict resolution in an attempt to soften congressional opposition to U.S. military action at home. In recent years, Congress, responding in part to public opinion, has expressed a preference for resolutions approving the use of force where a significant multilateral presence existed, such as in Operation Desert Storm and NATO action in the Balkans. After the debacle in Somalia, however, the Senate Foreign Relations Committee began to take a closer look at presidential war-making. When Bill Clinton invoked the violation of Council resolutions as authority to intervene in Haiti without going first to Congress, the Senate passed a resolution asserting that Council approval was no substitute for congressional authorization.[18] In contrast, when the second Bush administration chose to seek congressional authorization for the use of force against Iraq, Congress passed a joint resolution that invoked the Council more than twenty times and authorized the president to use military force to "enforce all relevant United Nations Security Council resolutions regarding Iraq."[19] While Congress was quick to grant Bush the right to use "all necessary force," in the subsequent months congressional reservations about the prudence of war were a major factor in the administration's decision to engage rather than ignore the Council.

Conclusion

A review of U.S.-Council relations over the course of the 1990s reveals that the United States pushes the Security Council forward at times, sponsoring genuine innovation and thereby enhancing the relevance of the Council in post–Cold War international affairs. At other times, however, and on the same or similar issues, the United States undermines the efforts of the Council and diminishes the very relevance it helped create. The paradox of that dynamic is only apparent, for it ignores the fact that U.S. interests can be fractured and the process of their determination divisive. It is a complex mixture of, among other things, public opinion, congressional activism, and executive policy, with different elements dominating depending on the time and the issue at hand. The cursory overview of some of those interests in this chapter nonetheless suggests that there may be commonalities among them that set boundaries—though perhaps broad ones—on U.S.-Council interactions.

The dynamic, then, is not a struggle for salvation or damnation between Faust and Mephistopheles but a more nuanced fluctuation between less extreme poles. If it is the case that public opinion strongly favors both multilateralism where international action is strictly necessary and the existence in principle of the UN, it is unlikely that the White House will ever take a position that definitively undermines the Council and completely extinguishes its relevance. Yet the apparent ambivalence of the public on specific issues leaves considerable latitude for other groups to push a unilateralist agenda, setting the stage for the continued undermining of the relevance and influence of the Council. The bargain is not after all Faustian.

Or at least it has not been to date. Whether this thesis holds true for the interactions of the United States and the Council in the 1990s, its continued existence is in some doubt. It remains unclear to what extent the Bush administration in its twin wars on terror and Iraq will allow itself to be constrained by any interest external to the White House, whether domestic or international. In the aftermath of September 11, 2001, the U.S. State Department, rather than seeking Chapter VII authorization, argued that U.S. military action in Afghanistan was justified as an act of self-defense under Article 51 and therefore did not require Council authorization. It appears that the Council was willing to adopt a resolution explicitly authorizing U.S. action in Afghanistan, but the United States declined to pursue this out of a desire to retain as much freedom of action in its response as possible.[20] Going even farther, the Bush administration repeated time and again its intention to go to war with Iraq with or without Council approval, in contravention not only of its obligations under the UN Charter and the wishes of its allies but also of the explicit wishes of its citizenry. In the end, the Bush administration did just that, withdrawing—in the face of the public opposition of three permanent members (France, Russia, and China)—a U.S. draft resolution and going to war in Iraq without Council approval. The determination of President George W. Bush to attack Iraq in the face of all opposition, then, seems to have been strong enough to overcome the limits described above. It may be that the Bush administration will alienate its foreign allies and domestic constituents enough that those boundaries are in the end reinforced, and that the price for violating them will prove too dear for future administrations to contemplate. Until that speculation is proven true or false, however, the consequences of the present lurch toward unilateralism for the position of the Security Council remain uncertain at best.

Notes

1. Mikhail S. Gorbachev, "Realities and Guarantees for a Secure World," *Pravda,* September 17, 1987.

2. *National Security Strategy of the United States of America,* Ref. UA U492 (Washington, D.C.: U.S. Government Printing Office, January 1993), p. 7.

3. U.S. Department of State, cable no. 099440 to U.S. Mission to the United Nations, New York, "Talking Points for UNAMIR Withdrawal," April 15, 1994.

4. Though one could argue that President Clinton's signing of the Rome Statute signaled a diminution of U.S. opposition to the Court, it could be better characterized as the symbolic act of an outgoing president, given the impossibility of Senate ratification. Even that symbolic support was quickly withdrawn by George W. Bush's administration in April 2002.

5. S/1999/356, March 30, 1999.

6. Interview with Hubert Védrine, minister of foreign affairs, in *Al Hayat,* August 1, 2000, www.info-france-usa.org/news/statmnts/2000/iraq0108.asp.

7. Barbara Crosette, "For Iraq: A Doghouse with Many Rooms," *New York Times,* November 23, 1997, quoted in David Cortright and George A. Lopez, eds., *The Sanctions Decade: Assessing UN Strategies in the 1990s* (Boulder: Lynne Rienner, 2000), p. 56.

8. Introduction to *National Security Strategy of the United States of America,* September 17, 2002, www.whitehouse.gov/nsc/nssintro.html.

9. It should be noted that "unilateralism" is meant here in the narrow sense of "acting alone" and can encompass both action and inaction. The point is that the United States either acts alone, in contravention of multilateral commitments it was often instrumental in creating, or evades them by refusing to do anything at all.

10. See Edward C. Luck, *Mixed Messages: American Politics and International Organization, 1919–1999* (Washington, D.C.: Brookings Institution, 1999), p. 262.

11. Ibid., p. 261.

12. See Steven Kull, "Public Attitudes to Multilateralism," in Stewart Patrick and Shepard Forman, eds., *Multilateralism and U.S. Foreign Policy: Ambivalent Engagement* (Boulder: Lynne Rienner, 2002), pp. 113–115.

13. Poll conducted by the Program on International Policy Attitudes, quoted in ibid., p. 101.

14. See Luck, *Mixed Messages,* p. 265; and Kull, "Public Attitudes to Multilateralism," p. 112.

15. "Public Wants Proof of Iraqi Weapons Programs," Pew Research Center for the People and the Press, January 16, 2003, http://people-press.org/reports/print.php3?pageid=664.

16. "U.S. Has Made Case Against Iraq," CBS News Poll, February 7, 2003, www.cbsnews.com/stories/2003/02/07/opinion/polls/main539763.shtml.

17. *Cuban Liberty and Democratic Solidarity Act,* Pub. L. no. 104-114, 110 Stat. 785, March 12, 1996; *Iran-Libya Sanctions Act,* Pub. L. no. 104-172, 110 Stat. 1541, August 5, 1996.

18. 140 Cong. Rec. S10397-489, daily ed., August. 3, 1994.

19. S.J. Res. 46, 107th Congress.

20. Many thanks to David Malone and Sebastian Einsiedel for pointing this out.

25

Working with Nongovernmental Organizations

JAMES A. PAUL

Beginning around 1990, nongovernmental organizations (NGOs) dramatically increased their contact with the UN Security Council. This chapter will consider why this happened, describe the new interaction, and analyze means used by NGOs to influence Council decisions. It will show that NGOs have had an impact on the Council's procedure, openness, and field of vision, as well as a few significant legal and policy issues. On many matters of great importance, however, NGOs ran into frustrating and unshakable opposition from veto-bearing permanent members, whose national interests ran counter to NGO priorities. NGOs are now more savvy about the Council and better aware of the possibilities and limitations of its realpolitik. They continue to promote a vision of legality and human security, believing that it must steadily gain ground over national interest, aggressive relations, and the headstrong use of force.

Background

At the United Nations, NGOs enjoy official status only with the Department of Public Information and with the Economic and Social Council (ECOSOC). Article 71 of the Charter speaks of NGO consultation with ECOSOC and many texts regulate these relations, but no official texts authorize or encourage NGO relations with the Security Council.[1] The organization's founders saw the need for NGO consultation on such ECOSOC issues as labor, health, and social policy. But in 1945 and for long thereafter, governments considered issues of peace and security to be their unique province. Council practice, including the formality of its deliberations and the special powers of the five permanent members (P-5), as well as outright hostility from Council members, discouraged most NGOs from working with the body for the next forty-five years. As the world changed after the Cold War, under the influence of globalization and the politics of the single superpower, NGOs began to assume a new role in the peace and security realm.

The international community of NGOs, numbering in the millions, is an extremely diverse group. Some are large international confederations, whereas others are very small local groups. Some have ample budgets, whereas others are chronically short of funds. All are private, nonprofit organizations serving public purposes, and most have specific policy mandates like disarmament or human rights. Compared to states, NGOs are very small and have no capacity to wage war, levy taxes, or enforce sovereign authority. Their strength lies in their committed members, capable staff, transnational values, and substantial moral authority.

NGOs affiliated with the UN tend to be among the largest and most important NGOs. To work effectively in the UN arena, they must demonstrate international recognition and public credibility as well as high-quality work. Secretary-General Kofi Annan has called them "the conscience of humanity." The NGOs that approached the Security Council were among the world's most respected and effective—diverse in their mandates and policy preferences but united in their interest in peace and security.

Trends Favoring NGO Involvement

Beginning in the 1990s, several trends led toward greater NGO involvement with the Security Council. First, in this period the Council assumed a much more active program of work and began to meet on an almost continuous basis. In the six years from 1988 to 1993, the Council's total number of meetings and consultations grew nearly fourfold while its total resolutions and presidential statements increased more than sixfold.[2] As the Council took unprecedented action in the area of sanctions, peacekeeping, election monitoring, policing, and postconflict peacebuilding, NGOs with international policy mandates decided that they must follow the Council's work much more closely.

Second, Council delegations (and especially those of the elected ten [E-10]) faced a large and growing policy burden as the Council took on responsibilities in dozens of active crisis areas. The smaller delegations could not keep up with this pace. They urgently sought information, expertise, and policy ideas from NGOs that could help them fulfill their responsibilities in the Council and act as a counterweight to the large mission staffs and vast intelligence capabilities of the P-5.[3] Even the larger and richer E-10 missions were grateful for assistance in policy formulation and support for their national positions with international public opinion.

Third, in this period NGOs were assuming a larger role in international affairs and a greater influence in shaping public opinion on international policy issues. Council members found it much more difficult to brush them off as insignificant or irrelevant to the Council's deliberations, since in many crisis areas NGOs remained active on the ground after the UN and government aid agencies had left the scene. Further, NGO public advocacy and media campaigns often shaped public understanding of the crises and created public pressure on governments to act. NGOs, then, increasingly appeared as actors in the policy process that could not be ignored and whose goodwill and support was useful, and at times even essential, to the success of government policies and Council initiatives.

Fourth, because the Council's work increasingly addressed civil wars, the collapse of government authority, and internal strife—not interstate wars as had been largely the case previously—its work entered an arena where the expertise and action of NGOs was especially critical. In every crisis, NGOs were present, struggling to feed the hungry, care for the sick, shelter the homeless, and protect the vulnerable. If the Council was to end such conflicts, it obviously had to seek more than formal peace agreements between belligerents. Rather, Council-built peace depended on economic and social development, respect for human rights, disarmament, and other areas of NGO expertise. Member states did not always have such benign goals in these crises, of course, but formally and publicly the Council was in the business of seeking and promoting such goals, and no state could be seen to oppose them.

And fifth, as awareness of globalization emerged, the international public began to recognize the "democratic deficit" in the global decision-making process. Such a democratic deficit was especially evident in the Security Council, with its permanent members and their veto power. Indeed, after 1990 the Council's deliberations had become more secretive and unaccountable than ever, with meetings largely held behind closed doors in private "consultations of the whole."[4] Critics of the Council, including many influential government delegations, argued that the Council's work lacked legitimacy because its practices included so little transparency or public accountability. Countries providing troops and other personnel for the Council's increasing peacekeeping missions grew irate that the Council was placing their nationals at risk with scarcely any expla-nation or accountability. The Nordic countries and Canada urged better Council consultation with troop-contributing countries while the non-aligned movement called for a full-scale reform of the membership and procedures of the Council itself. On December 3, 1993, reflecting these pressures, the General Assembly passed Resolution 48/26, setting up an Open-Ended Working Group (OEWG) on UNSC Reform.

As criticism of the Council grew, a number of delegations came to see increased Council interaction with NGOs as an essential step toward a more legitimate and effective international political and legal order. As we shall see, they felt that NGOs could join with states to produce better policy results. Some also felt that NGO partnerships could help counterbalance the power of the permanent members in the Council, especially the U.S. super-power. Powerful states, they believed, often had a nefarious self-interest in conflicts, hobbling the Council with a "foxes guarding the chicken coop" system of power. NGOs, they hoped, could expose these practices to public scrutiny and give pause to the worst abuses, yielding a more lawful, legiti-mate, and peace-promoting Council.[5]

The setting, then, proved far more advantageous than in the past for NGOs. But it still remained quite unwelcoming. Permanent members of the Council sternly resisted NGO scrutiny of their special terrain. Many elected members also had doubts, because their governments had faced negative comments from human rights organizations and other critics from the NGO community. NGOs nonetheless began to make sporadic contacts with the Council as an institution, or with individual Council members. And con-versely, Council members reached out to NGOs.

The new contacts arose mainly from urgent international crises such as the Gulf War in 1991 and the Somalia crisis in 1993. The 1994 genocide in Rwanda, during which the Council had remained shockingly inactive, alert-ed human rights and humanitarian NGOs to the need for regular communi-cation and advocacy. The Balkan wars, the conflict in Chechnya, the deep-ening Palestine crisis, and conflicts in central and western Africa had a similar effect: the post–Cold War world was obviously not going to be an era of peace, and NGOs could not count on states to solve these problems. NGOs with such concerns, however, had little or no regular representation at UN headquarters in the early 1990s. Nor were they familiar with the Council, its arcane traditions, or its secretive working methods.

Models and Beginnings

Four organizations offered models for interaction with the Council, attract-ing the interest of NGO newcomers. The Quaker United Nations Office, representing the worldwide religious organization the Society of Friends, had perhaps the longest-standing relations of any NGO with Council mem-bers. For many decades, it had organized informal gatherings of delegates and experts at nearby Quaker House to promote the peaceful settlement of disputes in a low-key atmosphere. A more recent player was the International Committee of the Red Cross (ICRC), a venerable body work-ing to protect and assist victims of armed conflicts and to defend interna-tional humanitarian law. The ICRC had set up an office in New York in the early 1980s and established regular relations with Council members. Gaining UN observer status in 1991, the ICRC strengthened its access, including regular meetings with Council presidents. Council members turned to the ICRC because of its very high reputation, its legendary neu-trality, its quiet diplomacy, and its unique sources of information on field conditions in crisis areas.[6] Though not an NGO, the ICRC was also not a state, so it bridged the two worlds and helped to erode the "states only" thinking of Council members.

The Stanley Foundation and the International Peace Academy (IPA) provided different models. Both were specialized NGOs involved in policy research and adept at organizing conferences and roundtables on key policy issues. Stanley, based in Iowa and without a direct New York presence, had nevertheless organized influential private conferences since the 1960s several times each year on peace and security issues, which Council ambassadors and high UN officials attended. The IPA, founded in 1970, had headquarters directly across the street from the UN and had built a solid reputation based upon longtime work on peacekeeping. In 1990, the IPA began a series of well-received roundtable meetings on a variety of Council issues, assembling high-ranking diplomats, executives, lawyers, academics, and others.

Such precursors had expanded Council members' comfort zones with NGOs. The newcomers of the 1990s brought a different type of NGO into the picture—large, international, membership-based NGOs like Amnesty International, Oxfam International, and Médecins sans Frontières (Doctors Without Borders). These organizations operated less discretely and often through international public campaigns, with well-orchestrated press mobilization and pressure through affiliates directly in national capitals. They were bound to encounter resistance as they approached the Council for the first time. Still, they came to the table with large information networks, field presence in conflict areas, and wide public support.

Amnesty International was one of the first NGOs of this new type to begin an active advocacy. In 1991, in the aftermath of the Gulf War, Amnesty presented a major paper to the Council advocating human rights monitors for Iraq. Amnesty's secretary-general came to New York for meetings with Council ambassadors to argue for the monitors concept. Thereafter, Amnesty sent periodic letters to the Council, and Amnesty's representative regularly attended Council meetings as an observer. The representative also met privately with Council presidents and delegations. As Amnesty's work progressed, it gained increasingly effective access to key diplomats. Behind the crisp, lawyerly positions of Amnesty lay an impressive research department and an aggressive press section in London, not to mention tens of thousands of letter-writing members ready to bombard foreign ministers and set in motion embarrassing parliamentary questions.

The NGO Working Group on the Security Council: First Steps

In May 1994, six months after the General Assembly set up the new working group on Security Council reform, a major NGO conference took place in New York on Council reform, greatly stimulating NGO thinking about the Council and building ties between NGOs and reform-minded ambassadors with Council experience. In early 1995 a group of NGOs under the leadership of Global Policy Forum founded the NGO Working Group on the Security Council to pursue reform issues.[7] After a year, as the reform process languished in the General Assembly and NGO ties to delegations grew, the group shifted its focus to "dialogue" with Council members. Skeptics thought this an unattainable goal, but success came surprisingly quickly, thanks to strong support from several E-10 members.

Ambassador Juan Somavía of Chile, a former NGO leader himself, joined the Council in January 1996 and began actively promoting Council contact with NGOs. Somavía emphasized in particular how the civil wars on the Council's agenda made action on the basis of traditional diplomacy much more difficult. "Under those conditions," he argued,

> a stronger link must evolve between the United Nations, the Security Council and organizations like Oxfam—who are on the ground, doing humanitarian work, who are touching those societies, looking into the eyes of the people in danger, learning who they are and what is going on and who the factions are and what relations people have with their leaders—much of which never gets to the table of the Security Council.[8]

In late 1996, Somavía and a number of other NGO-friendly delegates encouraged NGOs to request a monthly briefing from the Council president, as a step toward more regular interaction. As it turned out, P-5 members blocked this modest proposal when the Council took up the matter. Instead, the Council decided that members could give "national" briefings to NGOs, and Ambassador Paolo Fulci of Italy offered to oblige as soon as he stepped down from the presidency in January.

For the meeting with Fulci, the working group's leadership decided to invite a select group of respected NGO representatives, with special knowledge and program focus on the Council. Group leaders were convinced that this approach would be the most workable and most consistent with finding "legitimate" NGO voices that would command respect and access from Council members.

A Regular Meeting Process

The Fulci meeting launched a process that was soon to include virtually all Council members. Some newly elected members of 1997, notably Ambassador António Monteiro of Portugal, acted as crucial allies and sponsors in this next phase. The membership of the working group soon grew to nearly thirty, adding a number of important organizations that had set up regular representation at the UN, including Médecins sans Frontières,

Oxfam International, CARE International, and Human Rights Watch. Over the next five years, other organizations would establish a presence at the UN or strengthen their representative offices, steadily increasing the power and capacity of the NGO community.

The NGO Working Group on the Security Council eventually met each Council ambassador on a regular basis. Though the P-5 had opposed formal NGO contact, they joined this informal process with surprisingly little hesitation. Evidently, once the meetings were under way, P-5 diplomats wanted to present their own national viewpoint, and they hoped to gain NGO support for their national policies and initiatives. E-10 members were more natural partners of the NGOs, however. Most often, NGOs turned to elected members for information and joint initiatives. Elected members, lacking major power status and Council vetoes, had the most to gain by working with NGOs.

Meetings of the working group, currently held about four times per month, provide a central and ongoing point of contact between key NGOs and the Council.[9] At the same time, NGOs have developed a range of other activities and initiatives that compliment and deepen this process.

The Arria Formula

From their earliest contact with the Security Council, NGO representatives yearned to speak to the whole Council, rather than meeting with Council members individually. In the Council itself, some elected members had a similar vision. Juan Somavía was one. He believed that humanitarian NGOs would have a strong claim on the Council's attention, so he proposed that key humanitarian NGOs make presentations in an "Arria Formula" briefing, an informal process devised in 1993 to enable the Council to hear the views of outsiders.[10] The P-5 opposed this use of the Arria Formula, however, preferring that such meetings be restricted to heads of state and other top officials. Eventually, Somavía tried to modify the Arria Formula by adding non-Council delegates as well. This "Somavía Formula" briefing met on February 12, 1997, with three humanitarian NGOs—Oxfam, Médecins sans Frontières, and CARE—as well as the ICRC to discuss the crisis in the Great Lakes region of Africa. During the meeting and in a press conference afterward, the organizations were highly critical of the Council's failure to take action and to find political solutions in the region, an outcome with which P-5 delegations were not pleased.[11] The Somavía Formula never got a second chance.

Soon afterward, António Monteiro returned to the Arria Formula and argued that not only humanitarian but also human rights voices should be heard. A campaign by Portugal, with the support of Chile, Sweden, and others, culminated in the fall of 1997. After much hesitation, the Council overcame P-5 objections and agreed to hold a briefing with Pierre Sané, secretary-general of Amnesty International, on September 15, 1997. Monteiro tried hard to win further Arria-style briefings with NGOs, but the P-5 kept the matter frozen for another two and a half years. Finally, in early 2000, as delegates came to see interaction with NGOs as normal and even advantageous, the Arria possibility reappeared on the political horizon.

On April 12, 2000, Ambassador Peter van Walsum of the Netherlands convened an Arria briefing on protection of civilians in armed conflict with CARE, Oxfam, and Médecins sans Frontières, the threesome originally invited by Somavía. Canada's ambassador, Robert Fowler, president of the Council, engineered the briefing and won P-5 support. Five days later, the Council debated the issue, with the Canadian foreign minister in the presidential chair, and eventually Resolution 1296 on the same subject was adopted. NGOs were happy to debut as Canada's supporting cast. Everyone understood that the policy interests of like-minded states were crucial to NGO progress. The Arria Formula was thence open to regular NGO use.

In the next two years, the Council held five or six Arria Formula briefings annually with NGOs. No further opposition arose to NGO briefings as such, though many briefings proposed by NGOs were blocked because of political objections to the subject matter (Kashmir and Sudan being two notable cases).

As the Arria process continued, however, it lost some of its appeal. NGOs devoted much time and expense to giving the Council their very best—presenting top leaders, key policy experts, and grassroots voices from the crisis regions. But the briefings seemed to shorten, and far fewer ambassadors or other top diplomats attended. Consequently, NGOs lowered their expectations and sought briefings less eagerly than at first. Though the Arria Formula was a precedent worth gaining, it offered, on balance, only a modest payoff.

Informal Channels

In contrast to the disappointments of the Arria briefings, NGOs valued the increasing informal communication with Council delegations, especially private meetings between representatives of a single NGO and delegates from a single mission, often referred to in UN parlance as "bilateral" meetings. As we have already seen, E-10 delegations urgently needed good information as the Council expanded its scope and as the tempo of Council meetings increased. The E-10 could not get adequate information from their ministries; nor could they trust the information offered by the P-5. They found media sources often sketchy and unreliable. So they welcomed NGO information, seeing it as trustworthy, timely, and richly detailed.

In April 1994, delegations were shocked at P-5 secrecy (and Secretariat silence) as the genocide in Rwanda was unfolding. New Zealand ambassador Colin Keating, president of the Council, invited Médecins sans Frontières and the ICRC to brief him, while the Czech ambassador invited an expert from Human Rights Watch to his residence to brief all E-10 members. Rwanda firmly established NGOs as indispensable information sources.

NGOs were increasingly well equipped to provide first-rate information. As they came to know the Council and learned its program of work, they could intervene on precisely the questions delegates were grappling with. Humanitarian organizations with field operations like Médecins sans Frontières, CARE, World Vision, Save the Children, and Oxfam were especially well placed to produce strategic information. So were the big human rights organizations like Human Rights Watch and Amnesty International. By the late 1990s, NGO representatives received a steadily rising flow of daily e-mails bringing timely information from the field. About the same time, as mobile phone service grew more common and came into operation via satellite, NGO representatives could place calls to field representatives in crisis-ridden locations of Africa or Asia, garnering the latest information for a briefing with a Council ambassador.

In addition to the large, international NGOs, other influential NGO players began to take advantage of the new environment. The International Peace Academy increased the tempo of its breakfast and luncheon briefings, which offered expert analysts talking on very current topics. Ambassadors and other high-level delegates on the Council frequently attended. In 2001 the Brussels-based International Crisis Group (ICG) opened an office in New York and began to provide its own original information briefings to delegations. With a large network of researchers deployed in crisis areas, the ICG offered delegations valuable strategic information. In May 2002 an ICG representative was even invited to join the Council on its field mission to the Great Lakes region.

London-based Global Witness won standing in 1998 with a powerful report, *A Rough Trade,* that linked the diamonds sold by rebel forces of the União Nacional para a Independência Total de Angola (UNITA) in war-wracked Angola to the giant DeBeers company and other Western diamond interests. The report attracted such attention that Global Witness leaders were invited to meet with the Security Council's Angola sanctions committee less than a month after publication. Soon, under Canadian leadership, the Council toughened its sanctions enforcement, using many innovative techniques. Three years later, UNITA collapsed, unable to finance its forces, bringing an end to a terrible, decades-long civil war.

Global Witness showed how a compelling and original analysis could mobilize public support, affect government positions, and change thinking and action in the Council. In this case, the value of diamonds depended on their symbolism of purity and beauty. An international campaign associating diamonds with a corrupt, violent, and ugly civil war threatened the industry and governments that defended it. Official positions changed rapidly as the media took up the "blood diamonds" theme. This was NGO advocacy at its best and most effective.

Reports and the Internet

As NGO interest in the Council increased, and as NGO thinking about global security deepened, NGO policy papers, advocacy books, and websites had a growing sway over the shape of issues. This influence was due not to a few clever thinkers but to the unique vantage point, novel mandates, and rapid research deployment of NGOs. Ever-busier Council delegates felt compelled to read and pay attention to documents like IPA books, Médecins sans Frontières and ICG reports, and Human Rights Watch policy papers.[12]

New technologies reinforced the power of NGOs, helping them knit together and mobilize global like-minded constituencies. Computers, fax machines, and cheaper international telecommunications costs had propelled the first wave of global networking in the early 1990s. Advances in e-mail and mobile telecommunications carried the process farther still. The emerging technology of the World Wide Web gave NGOs an unparalleled new opportunity to circulate their reports directly to a global public at very low cost.

NGOs used their websites to post information and analysis on conflicts and on the work of the Security Council. These reports could reach hundreds of thousands of readers worldwide. Newspapers, television, and other media came to rely on the Internet, further magnifying the power of this new information system and the NGOs that used it to good effect. At the very end of the 1990s, Council delegations themselves started to use the Internet more commonly, for their own research on Council issues, enabling NGOs to reach them directly in this new way.

Eventually, Council delegations saw the value of establishing their own websites. By 2001, sites of larger delegations posted not only official speeches to the Council but also policy papers, news conferences, draft resolutions, and many other documents. With NGO encouragement, Slovenia (1998–1999), Canada (1999–2000), and Singapore (2001–2002) posted special web-based information during their presidencies, including extensive descriptions of the Council's work. The Council itself decided in 2001 to set up a "presidency" area on the official UN website. By early 2003 that site posted the current program of work, wrap-ups and assessments of previous months, presidential statements, resolutions, and transcripts of formal Council meetings. The site also posted streaming videos of the Council's meetings. The Council thus moved steadily away from the secrecy of the early and mid-1990s, when it did not even allow the Secretariat to tape-record press statements of the president of the Council. NGO information culture, magnified by the web, had seeped into the Council, changing its outlook and working methods.

Further Lobbying Tools

NGOs developed many more advocacy tools to sway the Council. They wrote letters to the Council, at times as individual NGOs and at times as substantial international coalitions. Well-drafted and carefully timed letters could sometimes gain the Council's attention and bring subtle influence to bear. NGOs also caught the Council's attention through conferences and meetings on Council-related policy topics. Stanley, Save the Children, the Quakers, the Mennonites, Hague Appeal for Peace, and especially the IPA organized events that attracted participation and attendance from Council delegates, nudging thinking at times in new directions.

NGOs lobbied Secretariat and other agency officials who viewed them as partners and friends and invited them to participate in task forces and special consultation meetings. NGOs especially tried to influence and improve the Council-mandated reports of the Secretary-General, typically subject to intense P-5 pressure.

To strengthen their effectiveness and coordinate their advocacy, NGOs created ad hoc like-minded policy groupings. One such cluster brought together humanitarian agencies for regular meetings. Other groups assembled organizations interested in Iraq, Israel/Palestine, women and peace and security, and children and armed conflict. International contacts and networks widened the circle of such ad hoc advocacy and magnified the influence of these groups.

Security Council field missions to crisis areas in 2000 and after attracted special NGO lobbying action. Prior to the departure of the special missions, NGOs offered delegates fresh information on the areas to be visited, and they urged that the travel programs include meetings with local NGOs. Ambassadors organizing the missions often saw NGO involvement as favorable to their national policy goals and actively sought NGO support.[13]

As NGOs gained experience in Council advocacy, many concluded that the most effective strategy combined diplomacy in New York with worldwide public advocacy campaigns. Amnesty International had discovered this formula early on. Later, similar techniques were adopted by other NGOs such as Save the Children, Oxfam, Human Rights Watch, and Global Witness. Campaigning NGOs would mobilize pressure on parliamentarians, generate press exposure, garner statements by celebrities, and sometimes stir high-profile boycotts or mass meetings. Armed with e-mail messages and the World Wide Web, NGOs could launch campaigns quickly, flexibly, and inexpensively.

Brick Walls and Paradoxes

NGOs began their work with the Security Council in the early 1990s with high hopes, idealism, and perhaps a certain amount of naïveté. Some were inclined to believe that solutions could be found to even the worst crises if only enough patience, good information, and effective analysis could be mobilized. These illusions were steadily dispelled by a close monitoring of the Council and a growing awareness of how it operated. NGOs became painfully aware how the P-5 had refused to act on the 1994 Rwanda genocide, how Council resolutions were disregarded and undermined by leading members, how powerful members sometimes issued economic threats to win important Council votes, how strategic resources like oil and diamonds could secretly drive Council deliberations, and how ambassadors could be chastised or even recalled if they angered mighty opponents.

NGOs worked steadfastly on urgent issues such as Iraq, Sudan, the Balkans, the Great Lakes, disarmament, sanctions reform, and the Israel-Palestine conflict, learning that support by a Council majority was not enough, no matter how just the cause. They faced the brick wall of P-5 vetoes, whether cast or threatened, most often by the United States. Close observation of the Council revealed an institution where, again and again, national interests prevailed over the interests of humanity and where at times power was exercised in a crude and even despotic way.

Paradoxically, though, the Council could at times overcome its worst tendencies and act wisely and well. Though all too rarely, it could rise above the squalor of state interests and bring peace to war-wracked places. So in spite of the many disillusions and setbacks, the Council offered NGOs some regular glimmers of hope.

Conclusion

In just ten years, NGOs developed a broad range of advocacy with Security Council members, from private bilateral meetings to mass-based campaigns. The influence of NGOs cannot be easily separated from the complex of pressures and influences on the Council, and NGO accomplishment always came through collaboration with Council allies and other international partners. In this light, some tentative conclusions are possible:

• *Greater Council transparency and accountability.* NGOs succeeded in learning a great deal about the Security Council and making information about its work far more available to the public. After more than a decade of

NGO action, the public knows much more about the Council than before, and citizens are in a stronger position to demand accountability for Council action.

• *Better information and analysis available to the Council.* NGOs succeeded in persuading many Council members to use and even rely on NGO information and analysis. This was especially true of the E-10, who not only welcomed such input from NGOs but actively sought it out. As a result, the P-5 intelligence monopoly was broken and the Council was much better informed, on a wider range of issues, than at the start of the 1990s and before.

• *Council procedural reforms.* NGOs successfully influenced changes in the Council's procedures, both formally and informally. Among other things, they established their own regular process of consultations with Council members, broadened the Arria Formula, gained more informative mission websites, and greatly expanded UN information on the Council and its work. They nudged the Council into new approaches to its field missions, promoted expert panels to reinforce sanctions, and joined in pressures that resulted in far more frequent open meetings.

• *Legal and political policy accomplishments.* NGOs had some limited success in influencing Security Council decisions in the legal and political domains. Such influence was clearest and strongest in "soft" policy areas like Resolution 1209 (November 19, 1998) on illicit arms flows in Africa, Resolution 1296 (April 19, 2000) on the protection of civilians in armed conflict, and Resolution 1325 (October 31, 2000) on women and peace and security. NGOs also successfully persuaded the Council to include many references to humanitarian and human rights mandates in peacekeeping and other resolutions, and they helped persuade the Council to establish three important criminal tribunals (Yugoslavia, Rwanda, and Sierra Leone). NGOs had an influence on a few hard policy areas too, such as the tightened Angola sanctions beginning in the spring of 1999, eventually ending one of Africa's most terrible civil wars, and the continuation of an arms embargo in the volatile Eritrea-Ethiopia conflict (late 2000–early 2001). In these cases, NGOs acted in coalitions with like-minded Council members, usually E-10 delegations. The P-5 permitted these decisions because they did not interpret them as a challenge to their key national interests.

• *Disappointments and blockages.* When the P-5 have strong positions, as they often do, NGOs encounter immovable opposition. On sanctions reform, Chechnya, the Middle East, Iraq, and many other important issues, even the most vigorous NGO advocacy runs into the brick wall of P-5 opposition (especially from the United States), as national interests block key NGO concerns.

• *A realist idealism.* NGOs are often dismayed and disheartened by the realpolitik that they observe and by the needless human suffering that so often results. But no one expects, after all, that the Security Council is a Boy Scout lodge or a chapter of Amnesty International. With a dose of realism, NGOs can take encouragement from the measure of their rapid, if limited, success and the breadth of their support by international public opinion. In just a decade, NGOs have established a remarkably strong standing in the Council arena. Their presence, if only on the outskirts of this states-only club, reflects tectonic shifts in the international order. Looking ahead, NGOs can hope that their work with the Security Council may eventually contribute to a stronger system of international law and a global order that will eventually ensure the values of peace, democracy, and human dignity.

Notes

1. Forty-one NGOs were first granted consultative status with ECOSOC in 1948; by 1968, 377 had that status, and by 2002 the number was over 2,000. Additionally, there were about 1,400 NGOs accredited to the Department of Public Information in 2002.

2. During this period, the number of Council meetings grew from 55 to 171 and consultations from 62 to 253. The number of resolutions grew from 20 to 93 and presidential statements from 8 to 88. Data from the UN Secretariat; see Global Policy Forum, "Table on Number of Security Council Meetings on Consultations: 1998–2002" at http://www.globalpolicy.org/security/data/secmgtab.htm and "Table on Number of Security Council Resolutions and Presidential Statements: 1998–2002" at http://www.globalpolicy.org/security/data/resolutn.htm.

3. Smaller delegations have just five or six persons on their Security Council teams. Some African members have even less. In 2002 the total UN-based diplomatic staff of states that were Council members ranged from seven (Mauritius) to 123 (United States). See Global Policy Forum "Size of Missions in the Security Council" at http://www.globalpolicy.org/security/data/tabsec.htm.

4. The Council in this period rarely met in public sessions except to pass resolutions and conduct other official business. Almost no debate took place in such sessions. These practices began to change significantly in 2000 and after.

5. Some of these perspectives are to be found in the speeches at the NGO conference on Security Council reform. See transcript in Global Policy Forum "1994 Conference on 'Reforming the Security Council'," May 23, 1994, at http://www.globalpolicy.org/security/conf94/index.htm.

6. The ICRC sends delegates to crisis areas and is also able to draw on information resources of the local Red Cross and Red Crescent societies. ICRC delegates have unique access to prisoners, prisoners of war, concentration camps, and hospitals, as well as access to high-level government officials.

7. The founding partners were Amnesty International, Earth Action, Global Policy Forum, the Lawyers Committee for Nuclear Policy, the World Council of Churches, the International Women's Tribune Center, and the World Federalist Movement.

8. Juan Somavía, "The Humanitarian Responsibilities of the United Nations Security Council: Ensuring the Security of the People," at http://www.globalpolicy.org/security/docs/somavia2.htm.

9. Typically, these meetings last an hour and a half, bringing eighteen to twenty NGO representatives in contact with an ambassador and (sometimes) other

members of the ambassador's Council team. Delegates often find these meetings a refreshing change of pace from the interminable diplomatic discourse in the Council. From just fifteen meetings in 1997, activity of the working group had grown by 2002 to forty meetings with ambassadors and five with UN Undersecretaries-General. In 2001–2002, members of the working group also met with foreign ministers of the UK and Ireland.

10. These meetings were invented by Ambassador Diego Arria of Venezuela during his term as a member of the Council. He first invited a Croat priest to talk to his colleagues over coffee in the delegates' lounge. See James A. Paul, "The Arria Formula," Global Policy Forum, February 2001, at www.globalpolicy.org/security/mtgsetc/arria.htm.

11. The United States and France both opposed action. The United States had told Council members that its intelligence satellite photos demonstrated no refugee emergency, but NGOs in the briefing testified otherwise.

12. Examples of IPA books include David Cortright and George A. Lopez, *Sanctions and the Search for Security: Challenges to UN Action* (Boulder: Lynne Rienner, 2002); and Stephen John Stedman, Donald Rothchild, and Elizabeth M. Cousens, eds., *Ending Civil Wars: The Implementation of Peace Agreements* (Boulder: Lynne Rienner, 2002).

13. UK ambassador Jeremy Greenstock invited NGOs to brief Council members at the UK mission on September 28, 2000, prior to the departure of the Council field mission to Sierra Leone. This marked the beginning of regular NGO input into field missions.

PART 4

Major UN Operations on Four Continents

26

The Middle East
Peace Process

BRUCE D. JONES

The abundant literature on the Arab-Israeli conflict contains scant reference to the role of the United Nations, but the histories of the two entities are deeply interwoven. At various points since its founding, Israel has been separated from each of its Arab neighbors by a UN peacekeeping operation; three of these operations remain in place. The Arab-Israeli theater was the site of the first UN mediator, the first UN observer mission, the first UN peacekeeping mission, and the first UN specialized agency, still its largest. Even the white and black markings that adorn UN vehicles the world over have their origins in the Middle East, where UN blue and white was avoided so as not to give rise to an appearance of bias by replicating the colors of the Israeli flag.[1]

Brian Urquhart, writing in 1995, stated that "the UN's performance in the Middle East, mixed though it has been, has not been insignificant."[2] Moreover, Urquhart suggests that the Palestinian context illustrates the real nature of the UN's capacity: to contain and limit conflict, to help its victims, and to help create conditions for settlement. However, he also notes that by the 1970s, and into the mid-1990s, the UN appeared to be peripheral.

This chapter briefly reviews the historical role of the UN Security Council and the factors that shaped and constrained its actions, from 1947 to the launch of the Madrid and Oslo processes in 1991; provides a more detailed account of the Council's role in the post–Cold War era; and identifies some of the variable and constant factors that explain the waxing and waning of the Council's role. In particular, it seeks to explain a partial resurgence in the Council's role in the period after Urquhart's comments, from the late 1990s to the time of writing (fall 2003).

Background: From Lake Success to Madrid

Mandate-Era Palestine

The Council's first actions with respect to the Middle East came neither through statement nor resolution but through the appointment (effected through the Secretary-General) on May 20, 1948, of UN mediator Count Folke Bernadotte. Bernadotte's appointment followed a turbulent period of great power debate over the best way to orchestrate British withdrawal from its mandate obligations in Palestine. Tensions between the United States, the Soviet Union, and the two European colonial powers in the Middle East, France and Britain, negated the possibility of a consensual solution within the framework of the Council. As mandatory power, Britain brought the issue to the General Assembly, which debated the Palestine issue in a special session in London and created the UN Special Commission (UNSCOM) to explore the Palestine question.[3] Its majority recommendation for an Arab state and a Jewish state was rendered void when Britain withdrew from Palestine in May 1948, sparking the Israeli declaration of independence. The Council, then housed in Lake Success, Long Island, issued a statement supporting the declaration of independence. Twenty-four hours later, five Arab states invaded Israel.

The appointment of Bernadotte as mediator in 1948 constituted the first such UN action and created a precedent that would be widely used through the next half-century. Soon thereafter, at Bernadotte's urging, the Council would take a second action that also constituted new ground for the Council, namely, the deployment of a UN observer force: the UN Truce Supervision Organization (UNTSO), headquartered in Jerusalem and deployed along truce lines along the length of Israel's borders with its Arab neighbors.

Proliferation of Peacekeepers

The UN's role in the Middle East—though not initially the Council's—expanded in 1956 following the Suez crisis, which saw France, Britain, and Israel join forces to attack Egypt following General Gamal Abdul Nasser's decision to nationalize the Suez Canal.[4] The constellation of forces arrayed against Egypt produced a temporary alignment of interest between the United States and the Soviet Union, both of which sought a solution that forestalled intervention by the other.[5] The coincidence of U.S. and Soviet interests created an environment in which the UN was seen by the United States as a useful forum in which to conduct crisis management efforts. However, the British and the French were able to forestall any Council action by vetoing two resolutions. However, the United States used a procedural motion—which cannot be vetoed—to shift the Middle East debate to the General Assembly, where the members acted under the "Uniting for

Peace" formula to pass a resolution creating the UN Emergency Force (UNEF), the UN's first peacekeeping force.[6] UNEF served as a buffer between Israeli and Egyptian forces, in what would serve as a model for so-called first-generation UN peacekeeping. Urquhart notes that the personal relationship between Secretary-General Dag Hammarskjöld and Israeli prime minister David Ben-Gurion was essential to the creation of Israeli willingness to cooperate with the UN.[7]

The Council's role expanded in 1958, when U.S. Marines landed on the beaches of Beirut in an effort to forestall what the United States believed was an incipient coup and crisis. In this context, the Council acted rapidly to authorize the UN Observer Group in Lebanon (UNOGL), which deployed only for a matter of months, providing the United States with cover under which to withdraw. It then disbanded.[8]

The outbreak of a crisis in 1967 would once again create the need for Council action. On this occasion, the UN itself became the pretext for the crisis, when Egypt demanded the withdrawal of UNEF from the Sinai, notwithstanding efforts by Secretary-General U Thant to dissuade it from this stance. The withdrawal of UNEF forces was quickly followed by Israel's strike into the Sinai and subsequently into the West Bank and the Golan Heights, all of which it captured, along with the Gaza Strip.

The crisis sparked active debate in the Council. Following a series of blocked resolutions, the Soviet Union, with support from the Arab states, introduced a text that called for Israel to fully withdraw from the territories occupied after June 4, 1967. The United States threatened to veto this formulation, seeking a less binding approach. In an effort to produce a compromise, Britain introduced a draft text whose main innovation was, famously, to remove the definitive article from the Soviet draft, while introducing the general concept of the "inadmissibility of the acquisition of territory by war." Israel was thus required by Resolution 242 to withdraw from "territories" occupied in 1967, as distinct from "the territories." The resolution passed following UK assurances to Arab states and others that the general principle allowed a comprehensive interpretation of the specific text—that is, that the resolution could be interpreted to mean that Israel should withdraw from all the territories occupied during 1967.[9] However, Britain's permanent representative, Lord Caradon, also noted that reintroducing the definite article would undermine the compromise nature of the text. Thus Resolution 242 was passed with an important degree of ambiguity regarding the status of the 1967 borders.

The passage of Resolution 242 led to a rejuvenation of international diplomatic efforts concerning the conflict, led by William Rogers, the U.S. secretary of state. Prodded by the United States, the Council once again appointed an envoy, Gunnar Jarring of Sweden. Although Rogers and Jarring both sought the launch of peace talks, neither effort bore fruit.

War in 1973—starting with a surprise attack by Egypt against Israel's forces in the Sinai, on Yom Kippur—once again brought the Middle East to the forefront of the Council's agenda. On October 25 and 27, 1973, Council resolutions authorizing UNEF II were a critical part of the disengagement package negotiated by Secretary of State Henry Kissinger.[10] This pattern continued in 1974, after a peace conference in Geneva, when the UN Disengagement Observer Force (UNDOF) was authorized to deploy as a buffer force in the Golan Heights.[11] Resolution 338 was also passed at this stage, though its only content was to restate the established principles of Resolution 242; the United States vetoed an alternate resolution introduced in August that would have stipulated that "a just solution to the problem could be achieved only on the basis of respect for the rights of all States in the area and the rights and legitimate aspirations of the Palestinians."[12]

In 1978, Israel invaded southern Lebanon, following a Palestinian attack north of Tel Aviv. As crisis unfolded in southern Lebanon, the United States sought to keep alive active negotiations on the Israeli-Egyptian front and backed efforts in the Council to restrain Israel's actions. This resulted in the creation of a new UN operation, the UN Interim Force in Lebanon (UNIFIL). Urquhart records the objections of the UN Secretariat to the creation of UNIFIL, given the absence of truce conditions under which a mission of the scale and scope of UNIFIL could play a constructive role.

The role of UN peacekeeping forces in creating buffers between Israel and its neighbors was broached again at Camp David in 1978, during negotiations convened by President Jimmy Carter. The Camp David Accords called for a UN force to be deployed between Israeli and Egyptian positions. However, Arab countries rallied against the accords (since they recognized the State of Israel) and moved to block any UN connection to the accords.[13] The result was that Israel, Egypt, and the United States ultimately agreed to the deployment of a multinational force not authorized by the Council, the Multinational Forces and Observers in Sinai (MFO Sinai). In this instance, Arab diplomacy was an obstacle to UN involvement.

In 1983 the UN ran into further obstacles that proved prescient Urquhart's concerns about UNIFIL. Following devastating attacks on U.S. forces deployed as part of a multinational force in Beirut, the United States sought to negotiate an end to Israel's siege of Beirut and to evacuate the remnants of the Palestine Liberation Organization (PLO), led by Chairman Yasser Arafat. Following a long period of stalemate in the Council, U.S. and Soviet efforts to find a solution that did not involve the other deploying ground forces ultimately led to a comprise decision to have UNIFIL increase its observer presence around Beirut. On the ground, however, UNIFIL redeployments were physically blocked by Israel.[14] A draft resolution that would have created a new UN force in Beirut was vetoed by the

Soviet Union in 1984, apparently because the text did not provide adequate guarantees of noninterference in Lebanon's internal affairs.[15]

Waning Relevance

The ability of Arab diplomacy to block the deployment of UN forces in the Sinai in 1979, following the Camp David Accords, and the fact of Israeli forces blocking the movement of UNIFIL personnel in Lebanon in 1983, ushered in a period of marginalization of the UN in the Middle East. Whereas the UN had played "an important role as a last resort and safety net when the Arab-Israeli conflict threatened to spark wider confrontations"[16] from the 1950s to the end of the 1970s, by the beginning of the 1980s the UN's role was decidedly constrained. Also constraining were two additional factors: first, the growing use of UN fora by Arab states, with support from decolonized nations, to condemn Israel actions; and second, the increasingly unequivocal backing of Israel by the United States.

The negation of the UN's active role continued into the early 1990s, notwithstanding the launch of two major peace tracks in the aftermath of the Gulf War. When in 1991 the United States convened the parties and the major international actors to the Madrid Peace Conference, the UN along with the European Union was confined to observer status. This was the result of an active decision by Israel and the United States; indeed, nonparticipation of the UN was among the conditions under which Israel agreed to attend the Madrid conference, under significant U.S. pressure.[17] This condition was laid out in a U.S. letter to the Palestinian delegation.[18] Nor was the UN involved in second-track activities, particularly the Oslo process, which culminated in October 1993 with the signing of the Declaration of Principles in Washington. Thus, both of the major breakthroughs in the peace process—Madrid and Oslo—occurred without UN involvement or support. However, both Madrid and Oslo reasserted the basic principles of peacemaking that had been outlined in Resolution 242.

Partial Reengagement After the Cold War

Although the UN had had no role in the Oslo process, the new political realities created by the agreement between Israel and the PLO created a significant new space for UN activities. With the creation of a transitional Palestinian Authority in Gaza and Hebron in 1994 came opportunities to play a role in what would later be termed "peacebuilding." Shortly after the establishment of the Palestinian National Authority (PNA) in Gaza, Secretary-General Boutros Boutros-Ghali created a new senior UN position in the Middle East, that of personal representative of the Secretary-General to the Palestine Liberation Organization and special coordinator for the Occupied Territories (UNSCO), and appointed to the post the architect of the Oslo process, Terje Roed-Larsen. Unlike Bernadotte and Jarring, Roed-Larsen was not appointed by the Council but rather by the Secretary-General.

Israel's Withdrawal from Lebanon:
Active Involvement in Peacemaking

A reengagement by the Council in the real business of peacemaking in the Middle East began after the election in 1996 of Secretary-General Kofi Annan. Early in his tenure, Annan worked to restore what by then were deeply corroded relations with Israel. Most significantly, Annan worked with member states to reach an agreement that Israel should be allowed to join the West European Group, having been effectively excluded from the Asian Group for the length of its UN membership. Moreover, Annan worked to remove the 1975 "Zionism is racism" resolution from the General Assembly's agenda. The two efforts significantly improved Israel's position at the UN and earned Annan support and trust from the Israeli leadership.

These efforts were undertaken at a time when implementation of the Oslo Accords had faltered, following the assassination of Prime Minister Yitzhak Rabin in 1995, terrorist attacks by Hamas in Israel the same year, and the election of Prime Minister Benjamin Netanyahu in 1996. Between 1996 and 1999, the process had largely stalled. However, the election in 1999 of Prime Minister Ehud Barak appeared to herald a new opportunity for peacemaking. In this context, Annan reappointed Roed-Larsen to the post of special coordinator (he had left in 1996). Once again, the appointment was made by the Secretary-General, but Annan took care to ensure that the appointment had the political support of the Council.

The combination of Annan's effort to restore relations with Israel and the reappointment of Roed-Larsen to UNSCO rapidly created new political space for the Council. In early spring 1999, Roed-Larsen was informed by Prime Minister Barak that he was contemplating a withdrawal from parts of southern Lebanon. Over a period of several weeks, in extensive discussions with Israeli officials, Roed-Larsen convinced Barak of the value of having the Council oversee and certify the withdrawal as being in compliance with Resolution 425, passed at the time of the establishment of UNIFIL. Barak ultimately acknowledged the value of working within the framework of the UN resolutions as a means of ensuring international support for the withdrawal.[19]

This created a situation that directly linked the authority and legal standing of the Council to concrete peacemaking efforts on the ground. A process was launched whereby the boundary to which Israel would withdraw was determined by a UN team of cartographers and geographers.[20] Since no formal border existed between these two parties, the UN arrived at the formula by which they would identify a line that would "correspond to the presumed international boundary" and would constitute a line beyond which the UN could certify that Israel had fully withdrawn from southern Lebanon. Because the withdrawal was seen as being in implementation of Resolution 425, the body that could certify the withdrawal was the Council itself. There followed an exhaustive process of consultations with the Council to lay the foundation for the certification, while on the ground Roed-Larsen and UNIFIL monitored the border to ensure full Israeli compliance. In May 2000 Secretary-General Annan wrote to the Council establishing the line for withdrawal, and in June 2000 he wrote to the Council noting that Israel had indeed withdrawn precisely to this line. On both occasions the Council responded with presidential statements that together constitute certification of full Israeli withdrawal from southern Lebanon.

This episode constituted a significant reentry of the Council into the process of peacemaking in the Arab-Israeli theater. Indeed, arguably not since 1948 had the Council had such a direct diplomatic role in creating the conditions for an easing of tensions between parties in the Middle East.

However, in September 2000 the outbreak of what became known as the second intifada (Al-Aqsa) presaged a return to the old role of the Council—as a forum for diplomatic maneuver between increasingly hostile Israeli and Arab representatives; as the site of repeated U.S. vetoes or threatened vetoes; and as a space within which to articulate the basic principles for future peacemaking.

Crisis in Israeli-Palestinian Relations,
Corrosion of Israeli-UN Relations

As violence flared on the ground, Middle East discussions in the Council became heated. The first major Council discussion during this period concerned a Palestinian initiative to gain Council backing for an international inquiry into Israel's actions. The United States signaled on several occasions that it would veto any such resolution. However, the United States was simultaneously attempting to resuscitate final status negotiations (which temporarily abated after intensive talks in Camp David in June 2000) and was coming under increased pressure from the Arab world to moderate its strong support for Israel.[21] Under this pressure, on October 7, 2000, the United States decided to abstain rather than veto Resolution 1322, which condemned Israel for its excessive use of force in suppressing the intifada and called for an international commission of inquiry into the violence.[22]

The subsequent months saw intensive final status negotiations between the parties, which ended without a full agreement. Such progress as did occur was then overshadowed by Barak's failure at the polls and the election of Likud leader Ariel Sharon. Though Annan and Roed-Larsen remained active at the diplomatic level, repeated Council meetings on the Middle East produced no action.

In the period after Sharon's election, a number of issues, debates, and events contributed to an erosion of relations between Israel and the Council. At the same time, however, U.S. diplomacy vis-à-vis the Arab world led to the passage of two important Council resolutions that once again played the role of establishing the basic principles for Middle East peace.

The first significant issue was that of a potential Council role in authorizing an observer or protection force for the West Bank and Gaza. This emerged as a key Palestinian goal during the first months of the intifada, and the idea had gained considerable international support. A resolution to establish an observer force was vetoed by the United States in March 2001, given strident Israeli objections to any perceived "internationalization" of the Israeli-Palestinian conflict—a position that fueled Arab anger toward the new Bush administration's Middle East policy.

Progress toward more extensive consideration of the topic was halted by a scandal that broke in October 2001 involving video evidence held by UNIFIL relating to the kidnapping by Hezbollah in October 2000 of three Israeli Defense Forces soldiers. Israel reacted furiously to the news, claiming that the incident provided clear evidence of the bias of the UN against Israel. The Secretary-General launched an investigation and determined that indeed "serious mistakes were made" by UNIFIL. The report, however, did not forestall a widespread perception within Israel that the Council could not be considered a reliable forum for managing the conflict with the Palestinians.[23]

The tenor of debate within the Council was temporarily transformed by the September 11, 2001, terrorist attacks on the United States. These attacks ultimately created new tensions between the United States and the Arab world but initially also created new support for the United States in moderate Arab capitals. This support, or sympathy, helped facilitate the rapid Council response to the attacks in the form of Resolution 1373, which created a new international framework for states' efforts to combat terrorism. Although addressing a global issue, Council action related to terrorism had particular salience in the Middle East and became part of the context of the overall balance of relations between the United States and Middle Eastern states, especially the moderate Arab states—from whom the United States, with the support of the Council, now expected a range of actions against domestic Islamist groups.

This pressure on the Arab world created its own pressure on the United States. As the United States began to prepare for its military campaign against Afghanistan, its Arab allies sought to avoid the perception, which was growing among Arab populations, that the Council was simply an instrument of U.S. power that was willing to act forcefully when a Muslim state had committed atrocities but was unwilling to rein in Israeli actions seen in the Arab world and in other countries as similarly atrocious. Through the nonaligned movement, the Palestinian representatives at the UN repeatedly sought to take advantage of this pressure, drafting several resolutions and introducing some of them to informal Council discussions. However, the Palestinians encountered significant resistance in the post–September 11 environment. Most members of the Council now attached greater importance to maintaining "Council unity"—that is, not generating a situation in which the United States was forced to veto a resolution.

Rather, the United States sought to balance its position vis-à-vis the Arab world with declarative support for elements of the Palestinian position. Most important, President Bush spoke to the UN General Assembly in November 2001 and affirmed his support for the creation of a "state of Palestine" as the necessary endpoint of final status negotiations between Israel and the Palestinians.

However, declarative balance was not matched by a U.S. willingness to pressure Israel to alter its actions in the West Bank and Gaza. Even as the U.S. war in Afghanistan was under way, with support from moderate Arab states, the United States vetoed a resolution that called on Israel to withdraw its forces from Palestinian-controlled areas. Palestinian and Arab anger grew, and Arab pressure on the United States continued to mount. Ultimately, faced with both intense Arab pressure and growing European discontent about its policies, the United States felt compelled to act. In March 2002 U.S. permanent representative John Negroponte introduced and secured passage of Resolution 1397, which formalized President Bush's earlier statements and affirmed "a vision of a region where two states, Israel and Palestine, live side by side within recognized and secure borders." As soon as it was passed, Resolution 1397 became the new benchmark for peacemaking in the Middle East, with the principle of Palestinian statehood established alongside land for peace (in Resolution 242) as the presumptive endpoint of the Middle East conflict.

None of these developments served to improve Israel's perception of the Council; rather, they reinforced the Israeli perception of the UN as an Arab-dominated body. This was further reinforced in January 2002 by the accession of Syria to a nonpermanent seat on the Council.

Given Israel's negative perception of the Council, and U.S. willingness to use its veto to block measures such as the deployment of peacekeeping forces, the Council's role became once again fairly marginal. In a series of statements in 2002, as well as in Resolution 1402, the Council confined itself to chiding Israel and the Palestinian Authority for their continued use of violence and terrorism, and to lending declarative support for "the Quartet"—a new mediating body, comprising the United States, Russia, the European Union, and the UN, that had been established at the initiative of Roed-Larsen and Secretary-General Annan.[24]

However, for many governments in the Council, this was far from a comfortable position, and an effort was often made to redress Israeli concerns and perceptions by issuing strong presidential statements or press releases condemning terrorist actions against Israeli citizens, usually balanced by some statement critical of Israel's use of force in populated Palestinian areas. These statements were noted by Israel but not seen as carrying the full weight of the Council. As this chapter was being written, the Council took further action in this vein, passing Resolution 1450, which condemned attacks of terrorism specifically against Israeli (and Kenyan) citizens, following twin terrorist attacks (claimed by Al-Qaida) against an Israeli airliner and hotel in Mombasa. In official statements, Israeli diplomatic officials called this resolution "a psychological turning point" in Israel's perception of the UN. Of course, whether this proves to be such a turning point remains to be seen. The fact that shortly thereafter the United States vetoed a draft resolution condemning Israel gives room for doubt.

Explaining the Variation in Security Council Action

No issue has been on the agenda of the Council as long as that of the Middle East; nor has any issue generated as many resolutions (244) or as many vetoes (forty-five). Putting aside routine resolutions pertaining to the renewal of UNTSO, UNEF, UNIFIL, and UNDOF (themselves an indicator of sustained Council involvement in the Middle East), there have been a total of 128 substantive resolutions on various aspects of the Arab-Israeli conflict. An analysis of the evolution of patterns in voting, censure, and vetoes is instructive.

Votes and Vetoes

In the 1940s and 1950s, a total of thirty-seven substantive resolutions on the Middle East were passed (see Table 26.1). Of these, the majority were what might be termed "general peacemaking" resolutions—that is, resolutions that expressed concern and laid out a series of proposed steps for each party to take. In addition, three resolutions in the 1950s censured Israel for its actions.[25] One resolution implicitly censured Egypt for interfering with the passage through the Suez Canal of goods destined for Israel;[26] in this

Table 26.1 Substantive UNSC Resolutions and Vetoes on the Middle East[a]

	Total Resolutions on the Arab-Israeli Conflict	Resolutions Critical of Israel[b]	Resolutions Critical of Arabs[c]	Vetoes by the United States	Vetoes by the Soviet Union	Total Vetoes on all Resolutions
1940–1949	19	0	0	0	2	44
1950–1959	18	3	1	0	6	45
1960–1969	22	10	0	0	3	19
1970–1979	21	12	0	6	0	34
1980–1989	29	19	0	21	1	49
1990–1999	9	7	0	5	0	9
2000–2002	6	1	0	3	0	4

Notes: a. Does not include periodic resolutions for the renewal of UNTSO, UNEF, UNIFIL, and UNDOF mandates.

b. Refers to resolutions that condemn/deplore Israeli actions, without a balancing reference to actions by Arab states.

c. Refers to resolutions that condemn/deplore Arab actions without a balancing reference to actions by Israel.

resolution, however, the words "condemn" or "censure" were not used for fear of a Soviet veto. The Soviet Union vetoed two resolutions in the 1940s and a further six resolutions in the 1950s, the majority of which either contained draft language criticizing or condemning Egypt, or called for an expansion of Council peacemaking activities (observers, etc.). The Soviet Union also used its veto power repeatedly to block Jordanian membership in the UN. France also used its veto twice during the 1950s to block complaints by Egypt against British and French actions in the Suez.

The 1960s showed a sharp increase in the number of resolutions that critiqued, condemned, or censured Israel for its various actions—fully ten out of twenty-two substantive resolutions. Several of these pertained to Israeli actions in Jerusalem that were seen as threatening to the maintenance of the status quo in that divided city. Three resolutions critical of Arab states were vetoed by the Soviet Union.

Interestingly, given the later history, the United States vetoed none of the 1960s resolutions critical of Israel. However, there was a sharp change in this pattern of behavior in the 1970s, when, of a total of twenty-one substantive resolutions on the Middle East, twelve censured Israeli actions, and none censured Arab actions. However, the 1970s also saw the United States use its veto six times, in each case to block resolutions that condemned Israel but not the Arab states. Both aspects of this pattern accelerated in the 1980s. Of twenty-nine substantive resolutions passed on the Middle East, nineteen censured Israeli actions, and none censured Arab actions.

However, the United States vetoed a further twenty resolutions that were critical of Israel and one additional Middle East resolution.

Factors Explaining the Variation

Historically, three factors appear to explain the variation in the Council's role (and in its voting patterns). First, in the 1940s, the 1950s, and to a lesser extent the 1960s, U.S.-Soviet relations were the driving factor in determining when and where the Council could play an active role. This more than any other factor determined the course of UN involvement, generating UN action when the interests of the two superpowers were aligned or when each feared the other's engagement more than collective action.

Second, U.S. relations with Israel clearly influenced Council actions through the 1970s and 1980s. During this period, U.S. attitudes in the Council reflected not only U.S.-Soviet concerns but also the consolidation of the U.S.-Israeli alliance, as well as an increasing concern by U.S. administrations to protect Israel from Arab/Soviet criticism. U.S. foreign policy to Israel and the Middle East in turn reflects in part domestic politics, including the influence of the Israeli lobby in Washington.

Third, U.S. relations with the Arab world also shaped Council action. During the 1970s and 1980s in particular, for every resolution critical of Israel vetoed by the United States, another resolution was allowed to pass, often with a U.S. abstention (and often after negotiations that watered down the text from outright censure to a softer form of critique). As was the case in the more recent period, repeated U.S. vetoes of resolutions criticizing Israel created unease in the Arab world. The United States faced pressure in the Council to balance its Middle East diplomacy, which was often seen as biased toward Israel. During the 1980s the United States abstained from six resolutions that criticized Israel for its actions.

Thus, shifting U.S.-Soviet relations, an evolving U.S.-Israeli alliance, and a corresponding need for balancing measures in the U.S.-Arab relationship—in short, U.S. foreign policy—largely explains the variation in voting and vetoing patterns in the Council. However, this is not the same as explaining the effectiveness (or not) of Council action.

Factors Relating to Effectiveness

The effectiveness of the Council—roughly defined as having a discernible impact on the political or military postures of the parties to the Arab-Israeli conflict—appears to have varied in an almost precisely inverse relationship to the degree of polarization in the Council. Thus, during the 1950s and 1960s, as described earlier in this chapter, the Council played a substantive role in helping the parties to escape from crises, usually by endorsing agreements negotiated on the ground, and by deploying UN observers or peacekeepers to help maintain truce conditions. The last period in which this factor characterized Council actions was 1973–1974. By the late 1970s, as the number of censuring resolutions began to rise, and vetoes also began to rise, the number of concrete actions by the Council began to diminish, with the exception of the creation of UNIFIL. By the 1980s, as debate within the Council became highly polarized, the Council's role on the ground was virtually nonexistent. Thus—unsurprisingly—Council effectiveness is in part a function of unity.

The marginalization of the Council continued into the mid-1990s, when three factors came into play: a tempering of U.S.-Russian tensions after the end of the Cold War; positive relations between the Israeli political leadership and the UN Secretary-General; and the existence of a direct relationship between Council actions and actions by UN political actors on the ground. An end to Cold War rivalries created space. Annan's relations with the Israeli leadership created opportunity. And Roed-Larsen's presence and access on the ground created capacity. The effectiveness of Council actions in 1999–2000 is a function of the direct connection between these elements.

Finally, the effectiveness of the Council is clearly enhanced when it is *led* by the United States, as opposed to simply not being blocked by the United States. This is seen in the immediate importance attached to Resolution 1397, introduced by the United States in 2002. This resolution, outlining a vision of two states, instantly changed the baseline for future peacemaking efforts, becoming the standard reference for almost all U.S., Western, and Arab statements of goals or intent.

Conclusion

In referring to the effectiveness of the Council, a degree of skepticism is called for. Important as Resolution 1397 is in establishing parameters for peacemaking, it could well remain unimplemented, alongside Resolutions 242 and 338. The main factors determining whether the Council will play a role in its possible implementation will be the evolving U.S. alliance with Israel, as well as the U.S. need to balance that alliance with some gestures to the Arab world. In this, rhetorical and declarative gestures, such as Resolution 1397, have limited the fallout between the United States and moderate Arab regimes. However, in a context of the vexed U.S. relationship with Iraq, mere declarative progress may be inadequate to contain Arab popular anger about U.S. policy in the Middle East. Additional factors that may contribute to the Council playing a constructive role include the nature of relations between the Israelis and the UN Secretary-General and his representatives; a direct relationship between Council statements and real peacemaking initiatives on the ground; and avoiding the polarization that characterized Middle East debates in the Council in the 1970s and 1980s.

Notes

This chapter benefited from research assistance from Feryal Cherif, of the Center on International Cooperation, and Candace Karp, of the Office of the United Nations Special Coordinator in the Occupied Territories (UNSCO), whose own writings on U.S. policy in the Middle East influenced the background section. The views expressed in this chapter are mine alone and do not necessarily reflect the views or policies of the United Nations.

1. Kati Marton, *A Death in Jerusalem: The Assassination by Extremists of the First Middle East Peacemaker* (New York: Pantheon, 1994), chap. 1.

2. Brian Urquhart, "The United Nations in the Middle East: A Fifty-Year Retrospective," *Middle East Journal* 49, no. 4 (Autumn 1995): 579.

3. Marton, *Death in Jerusalem,* chaps. 1–2.

4. Charles D. Smith, *Palestine and the Arab-Israeli Conflict,* 4th ed. (Boston: Bedford/St. Martin's, 2001), p. 183.

5. This section draws in substantial part on William Quandt's authoritative study, *Peace Process: American Diplomacy and the Arab-Israeli Conflict Since 1967,* rev. ed. (Washington, D.C.: Brookings Institution, 2001).

6. Derek Boothby, *The United Nations and Disarmament,* International Relations Studies and the United Nations, Occasional Paper no. 1 (New Haven, Conn.: Academic Council of the United Nations, 2002).

7. Urquhart, "The United Nations in the Middle East," p. 574.

8. Resolution 128, June 11, 1958.

9. Candace Karp, *US Policy Towards Jerusalem and the Occupied Arab Territories 1948 and 1967* (Jerusalem: Passia, December 2001).

10. Resolution 340, October 25, 1973; and Resolution 341, October 27, 1973.

11. Resolution 250, May 31, 1974.

12. Resolution 338, October 22, 1973; and Global Issues Research Group, Foreign and Commonwealth Office, *Research Analysts Memorandum: Table of Vetoed Draft Resolutions in the United Nations Security Council, 1946–1998* (London: Global Issues Research Group, September 1999), p. 28.

13. Richard W. Nelson, "Multinational Peacekeeping in the Middle East and the United Nations Model," *International Affairs* 6, no. 1 (Winter 1984–1985): 68.

14. Ibid., p. 79.

15. Ibid., p. 72.

16. Urquhart, "The United Nations in the Middle East," p. 579.

17. Stephen Zunes, "The U.S. and the Breakdown of the Israel-Palestinian Peace Process," *Middle East Policy* 8, no. 4 (December 2001): 76; "Points Agreed Upon by Israel and the United States on the Question of the Proposed Conference," *Middle East Bulletin* 5, August 4, 1991; and John Quigley, "The United Nations Security Council: Promethean Protector or Helpless Hostage?" *Texas International Law Journal* 35 (Spring 2000): 161–162.

18. "U.S.-Soviet Letter of Invitation to the Peace Talks in Madrid," October 30, 1991, www.palestine-un.org/peace/m_a.html.

19. Author's field notes.

20. Frederic Hof, "A Practical Line: The Line of Withdrawal from Lebanon and Its Potential Applicability to the Golan Heights," *Middle East Journal* 55, no. 1 (Winter 2001): 35–42.

21. William Quandt, "Clinton and the Arab-Israeli Conflict: The Limits of Incrementalism," *Journal of Palestine Studies* 30, no. 2 (Winter 2001): 26–40; and author's field notes.

22. Kirsten Schulze, "Camp David and the Al-Aqsa Intifada: An Assessment of the States of the Israeli-Palestinian Peace Process, July–December 2000," *Studies in Conflict and Terrorism* 24, no. 3 (May–June 2001): 222.

23. Author's field notes.

24. Ibid.

25. Resolution 101, November 24, 1953, condemned Israel's actions in Qibya; Resolution 106, March 29, 1955, condemned the Israeli attack on the Gaza Strip; and Resolution 111, January 19, 1956, condemned the Israeli attack on Syria.

26. Resolution 95, September 1, 1951.

27

Namibia

Cedric Thornberry

One may safely suppose that there have not been many UN Security Council resolutions whose designation came to be widely worn on T-shirts throughout the length and breadth of a whole country. One such was Resolution 435 of 1978, which definitively set out the detail of an internationally approved plan for Namibia's independence from South Africa. As the years after the resolution's adoption drifted by, the legend on the T-shirts grew more insistent: "435" became "Implement 435," then "Implement 435 now!"

With the possible exception of the Palestinian issue, the Namibia question was the most enduring of disputes involving the organized international community—initially the League of Nations, then the UN. It first surfaced in 1920 and was laid to rest only in 1989–1990 as the Berlin Wall tumbled, a new international community was born, and South Africa took its first step toward a new political beginning.

Of the UN's principal organs, only the Economic and Social Council did not at one time or another assume the lead role on behalf of the membership. The Trusteeship Council, General Assembly, International Court of Justice (ICJ), and Secretariat built up a compendious repertoire of practice aimed at divesting South Africa of its vast, dusty, remote, unwilling dependency. In this evolution, the Security Council came rather late onto the scene.

A prisoner, perhaps, of its own rhetoric (and that of the Assembly), during too long a gestation, the Council had great difficulty in overcoming the mistrust of many members over Namibia. It was thus hampered in providing the necessary help for the UN Transition Assistance Group (UNTAG) to fulfill its mission. Instead this had to come from ad hoc groups whose interests—and those of the Council at the time—converged.

Equivocation and a Turning Point

Namibia, then known as South West Africa, had been a German colony until its conquest by South Africa in 1915. The League of Nations placed it under the new mandate system, as a "class C" territory—one that could be administered under the laws of the mandatory as an integral portion of itself. The mandate was conferred on the United Kingdom on behalf of South Africa. Problems arose early in the mandate's history, with South Africa requesting but being refused permission to effect formal annexation and incurring criticism in the Mandates Commission for its practices in South West Africa.[1]

On the UN's establishment, South Africa refused to place the territory under the new trusteeship system. The ICJ, though agreeing that South Africa was under no obligation to do so, also denied its right to change its constitutional status and held that the mandate was still in force. Three equivocal advisory opinions were given by the ICJ on the legal status of South West Africa in 1950, 1955, and 1956, each at the behest of the General Assembly.[2] The 1960s saw further inconclusive litigation when Ethiopia and Liberia, former members of the League, invited the ICJ to find that South Africa was in breach of its obligations as mandatory. Surprisingly, the ICJ, having heard arguments for four years, and having earlier declared the case admissible, in effect reversed itself, deciding (by the president's casting vote) that Ethiopia and Liberia had no legal right or interest in the issues they had brought before it.[3]

Its decision brought about general rejoicing in white South West Africa and in South Africa, which because of apartheid had been for many the real target of pressure via its international territory. The name "South West Africa" was soon officially changed by a furious General Assembly to "Namibia." It also marked a turning point, as one can now see. In light of the new international climate in which the international protection of human rights began to be seen as more than a mere slogan, pressures began to build.

The Council's Delayed Entry

The South West Africa People's Organization (SWAPO) decided at this stage that it would if necessary employ all possible means to achieve national liberation—including armed struggle. Later that year the Assembly revoked the mandate and determined that Namibia was thenceforth the direct responsibility of the UN.[4] It created the UN Council for Namibia to administer the country until independence. In Resolutions 264 and 269 of 1969 the Security Council endorsed the Assembly's actions. Would such resolutions have more than a purely academic significance? There had been so much rhetoric over the years, without effective action.

For a while, the pace quickened. In Resolution 276 of 1970 the Council endorsed the Assembly's decision that South Africa's presence in Namibia was illegal. Shortly after, it decided to request, itself, an advisory opinion of the Court as to the legal consequences for states of South Africa's continued presence in Namibia, despite Resolution 276. Not everyone saw this as a new delaying tactic.

On June 29, 1971, the ICJ confirmed the Assembly's revocation of the mandate, stating that South Africa must withdraw its administration and end its occupation, and that member states must refrain from providing any support to South Africa in Namibia.[5] The resolution and advisory opinion were seen within Namibia as being of considerable importance, because they set out definitively the duties of South Africa and of other governments and interests in regard to the territory's unique position—and, of course, its mineral wealth.

For a while, the Council, Assembly, and ICJ rested upon their laurels while the new UN Council for Namibia (whose members were elected by the General Assembly) and commissioner for Namibia, Sean MacBride of Ireland, became active in mobilizing international opinion, publicizing the Namibian situation, and providing education and training for the long-neglected inhabitants. South Africa did not recognize either Council or commissioner. Instead, it pressed ahead with preparations for its own, strictly controlled plan for devolution of "government"—on an ethnic basis—for Namibia. The Council's passivity encouraged further cynicism among, in particular, the nonaligned movement as to the motivation of its Western permanent members.

At this time, SWAPO and other black nationalists within Namibia were especially harassed and imprisoned but were themselves taking the initiative, in and out of court, to lecture judges, international observers, and the press as to why it was the local authorities, including the judiciary, and not they themselves, who were now illegal. South Africa was also coming under increasing internal pressure from Namibia's powerful churches and a nascent trade union movement.[6]

Another thunderbolt fell: the Portuguese dictatorship crashed, and Angola became independent in 1974. South Africa expedited its plans toward an "internal settlement," though perhaps realizing that this would not long hold international pressures at bay. SWAPO fighters moved into southern Angola and began to cross into Namibia. When South Africa entered the postindependence civil war that plagued Angola for so many years and advanced almost to Luanda, Cuban regular troops arrived and, on South Africa's withdrawal, were deployed not far from the Namibian border. It seemed, once more, that the net was closing.

It was in this environment that, on January 30, 1976, the Council negotiated and unanimously adopted Resolution 385, which condemned South

African policy toward Namibia for a wide range of reasons: its discriminatory laws, repressively applied; its continued illegal occupation; its military buildup in the territory; its "bantustan" policy in Namibia; and its evasion of the UN's demand for free elections under UN supervision and control. The Council required South Africa to make "a solemn declaration" accepting the various provisions of the resolution and also endorsing the territorial integrity and unity of Namibia as a nation. It required South Africa to withdraw its illegal administration from Namibia and to transfer power to the Namibian people, with UN help. It demanded the possibility of return for all Namibian exiles and the release of all political prisoners. Significantly, the resolution, in its final paragraph, stated that the Council would remain seized of the matter and that it would meet again on or before August 31, 1976, to determine South Africa's compliance and, failing compliance, to consider taking appropriate measures under the UN Charter. As to this, Resolution 385 made no reference, however passing, to Chapter VII of the Charter.

Three Triple Vetoes and a Proposal for Settlement

Later in 1976, UN members heard that South Africa had failed to comply with Resolution 385. Three draft resolutions were brought forward by members of the nonaligned movement that would have imposed mandatory sanctions for such failure. In October, Britain, France, and the United States cast a triple veto against each resolution. Lord (Ivor) Richard, then British ambassador to the UN, later told me that he had subsequently advised the British foreign secretary that the vetoes could not be justified and had also been contrary to British national interest. Britain, he believed, should join with its Western colleagues in finding a means to bring Namibia to genuine independence in accordance with Resolution 385. The three Western permanent members consulted among themselves. They agreed that action must quickly be taken to remove this area of friction that was undermining the West's position on a range of unrelated but important matters. But essentially, most wanted the Namibia question to just go away.

Realizing, however, that a "UN settlement" was unavoidable, given Namibia's international status, they did not want to legitimize any further Soviet or Chinese involvement in the affairs of southern Africa. Both governments were becoming more active in the economic, infrastructural, and strategic affairs of the region.

Meanwhile, South Africa was being unhelpful by delaying its acceptance of Resolution 385. The need to veto the nonaligned resolutions made the Western permanent members' dilemma all the more poignant. This pain was not universally shared. By 1977 Canada and Germany had joined the three Western permanent members in the Council. The search began among those five Western nations for an independence—and a process—that would satisfy the Council, the Frontline States (Angola, Mozambique, Tanzania, Zambia, Zimbabwe, and sometimes Nigeria), South Africa, and SWAPO. The search was conducted in a semiclandestine way, alongside the Council rather than within it, because of the Western Contact Group's concern that the Soviet Union or China might wreck the negotiating process.[7]

Intensive discussions took place over the next year to try to find an acceptable program. They occurred under the sudden shadow of major change in Moscow. Though there were gaps in the agreement that was eventually achieved, some of which almost derailed the settlement proposal in the earliest stages of its implementation, a remarkable level of consensus was reached by the Contact Group with the parties and with the Frontline States. On April 10, 1978, an agreement was presented to the Security Council, together with a detailed timetable for the settlement proposal (S/12636). Commissioner for Namibia Martti Ahtisaari, a diplomat and later president of Finland, had been kept in the picture throughout by the negotiators.

The settlement proposal stated that it addressed itself to all the elements of Resolution 385 (1976) but that the central feature of that resolution, and of the proposal, was the holding of free and fair elections for Namibia as a single entity under the supervision and control of the United Nations. Among the nonaligned movement, reaction to the document was guarded. Especially difficult for many to accept was the idea of joint responsibility on the part of the UN and South Africa, which was to keep its administration in place until independence. Indeed, the principal executive was to be a South African–appointed Administrator-General. A number of the provisions of earlier resolutions and judgments were not strictly complied with in the document, and the proposal itself emphasized that it was just a "working arrangement" and was not to "constitute recognition of the South African presence in and administration of Namibia."

Nevertheless, many countries felt that the Western permanent members had for years been obstructing essential democratic change in southern Africa for reasons that had nothing to do with either human rights or democracy. Many thus remained suspicious and wondered, for instance, what would happen if the process broke down (as many expected). A great deal, it was emphasized at the time, would depend on the special representative of the Secretary-General (SRSG) and how he would stand up to continuous South African pressure. It was also felt that, however closely South Africa was supervised and controlled in the holding of elections, it would certainly cheat and the self-determination process would not be "free and fair." However, all decisions of any significance on the part of the Administrator-General (Louis Pienaar, a former South African ambassador and subsequent government minister) would require Ahtisaari's agreement.

Resolution 431 of 1978 took note of the settlement proposal and of the Secretary-General's appointment of Ahtisaari and called for a report as to how the proposal would be carried out. After a major survey mission led by the new SRSG, a report was prepared for the Council showing how the proposal would be implemented and pointing out a number of gaps or other defects—for instance, the proposal did not include, specifically, any UN police to watch over the activities of their opposites among the South West African Police (SWAPOL), and the Secretary-General had had to invent them (S/12827).

The Secretary-General's report was approved by the Security Council in Resolution 435 of September 29, 1978. The resolution also approved the establishment of UNTAG, which then remained in being, in nuclear form only, until implementation began eleven years later. A few senior Secretariat members continued to support the SRSG until independence. This "leadership group" was convened occasionally from other duties to update and coordinate the UN's operational planning and help to conduct further negotiations.

There was no substantive opposition to the resolution or its related report. Instead, there was some preliminary skirmishing, with markers being laid down for another day, around the question of sufficiency of the military component and, by implication, the adequacy of the financial arrangements. Moreover, though no budget was established at this time, UN Secretary-General Kurt Waldheim emphasized that it would be a costly operation and that the resources required would stretch the capacity of the Security Council and its members to the utmost.

Ten More Years

Though on that misty September afternoon in New York few expected that South Africa would leap to implement Resolution 435, even fewer could have imagined a delay of more than ten years before the independence process began. At times there may have been doubts that it would ever be implemented, but as the years passed and the new U.S. government trimmed its ideology and pragmatically inspected its options, it emerged that Resolution 435 had become a sacred icon and that no settlement in southern Africa would have legitimacy or durability unless conducted by the UN in accordance with its terms. However, South Africa used a variety of pretexts to delay its implementation in the hope that, meanwhile, something might turn up.

The immediate cause for delay was the election as U.S. president of Ronald Reagan, who during his campaign had introduced new tones in speaking of South Africa. He called for a full review of U.S. policy on Africa, and this took place under a new assistant secretary of state for Africa, Chester Crocker. The new U.S. policy was less confrontational than that of former president Jimmy Carter. Crocker called his philosophy toward South Africa one of "constructive engagement." It had initially seemed possible, under "neoconservative" pressures in the new U.S. administration, that negotiations with South Africa might have to start again from the beginning.

Discussions under the aegis of a new UN Secretary-General, Javier Pérez de Cuéllar, recommenced in late 1981, and the Western Contact Group began to meet again. In 1982 it sent to the Secretary-General the text of a document on principles concerning the Constituent Assembly and the constitution for an independent Namibia. This was published as a document of the Security Council (S/15287) and was followed in 1983 by a report to the Council on the overall situation regarding Namibia by the Secretary-General on May 19, 1983 (S/15776). The report stated that the delay in implementing Resolution 435 was having widespread destructive consequences in the region. "Factors which lie outside the scope of Resolution 435" were being advanced to delay its implementation.

The reference was to what became known as "linkage"—the proposition that there could be no implementation of Resolution 435 without parallel progress on the withdrawal of Cuban troops from Angola. For at least a decade the leaders of the South African National Party had been warning their electorate of the growing "encirclement" of southern Africa by "international communism." A major task for negotiators in 1988–1989, nearing the end of the process, was to convince South Africa that Moscow was really disengaging from southern Africa, and that it was not merely regrouping its forces. In 1988, during discussions led by the United States and directly involving Angola, Cuba, and South Africa, as well as the Soviet Union, Cuba began to show genuine interest in arranging an honorable departure from Angola.[8] The parties established agreed principles for a peaceful settlement in South West Africa and a series of steps necessary to prepare the way for the independence of Namibia in accordance with Resolution 435 as well as for the withdrawal of Cuban troops from Angola.

The UN was not officially present at these talks, which took place in London, Cairo, New York, Geneva, and Brazzaville. However, SRSG Ahtisaari was available for consultation. Those concerned agreed that implementation of the Namibian settlement should begin on April 1, 1989, and that they would establish a tripartite joint commission, which the United States and Soviet Union would also attend as "observers."

The parties met in the Trusteeship Council Chamber at UN headquarters on December 22, 1988. Tripartite and bilateral agreements were publicly signed. Two days before, the Security Council in Resolution 626 had

created the UN Angola Verification Mission (UNAVEM) to verify implementation of the Angolan-Cuban Accords, by which the Cuban military
presence would be steadily phased out over a period of thirty-one months
(South African troops were to leave Namibia, as set out in Resolution 435,
by one week after the Constituent Assembly elections—that is, about seven
months from the date of implementation).

Brave New World Order?

The Secretary-General appeared to have three clear months in which to create and transport to Namibia a huge international operation that would be
called the UN Transition Assistance Group. Planning the UNTAG operation
had been an intermittent though steady process since 1978. As regards
logistics, most items would have to be imported, as Namibia's resources
did not come close to supporting such a mission. Pérez de Cuéllar hoped
that budgetary and enabling resolutions would be quickly drafted and
adopted. But first the Security Council and then the General Assembly
stalled.

The permanent five (P-5) and other major contributors asserted that
UNTAG's estimated cost, about U.S.$700 million, was excessive. The
Secretary-General responded that unless its tasks were reduced, it would
not be possible to make appreciable savings. The nonaligned movement,
spearheaded by the Frontline States, objected to any reduction in the size or
competence of the mission. In particular, the nonaligned movement objected to reducing the size of the military component. It emerged that the military component of UNTAG would account for approximately 75 percent of
the cost of the mission.

Responding to the Council's intensely lobbied and heavily debated
Resolution 629 of January 16, 1989, the Secretary-General produced a
report that gave an update of his preparations for the implementation of
Resolution 435. In response to the Council's plea that he should bring forward whatever cost-saving measures possible that would not prejudice the
operation's effectiveness, he was able to make some savings by juggling
the structure and deployment of the battalions.

This confrontation between the P-5 and nonaligned movement gathered momentum, generating much heat and a great deal of mistrust. Each
side of the controversy was working toward scarcely hidden longer-term
agendas. The P-5 believed that UNTAG would largely be a political and
police operation, with UNTAG's military underemployed once South
African troops had mostly been repatriated after the mission's first two
months. Indeed, they would be considerably reduced and confined to two
bases from the date of implementation. They also thought that this would
be just the first of a number of large, complex, costly peace support mis-

sions that the UN would have to deploy in the coming years, and that a number of political or political/financial battles might as well be fought over Namibia rather than over some other conflict in the future.

The nonaligned movement had long been suspicious of the West's attitudes on apartheid and Namibian freedom, some believing that the West would be content to see Namibia emerge as the puppet state of a racist South Africa. For quite a time into the life of the mission they tended to associate the number of UN troops with UNTAG's potency. At UNTAG headquarters, where I served at the time as the assistant to the SRSG, we did not agree, believing that, while a military role would be necessary for UNTAG, it would be a highly political affair whose success or failure would depend largely on our ability to seize the initiative throughout the country.

In his report of January 23, 1989 (S/20412), the Secretary-General attempted the nearly impossible task of placating each side of the argument. It raged for a further three weeks in the Council until Resolution 632 was adopted on February 16, 1989. The resolution essentially approved what the Secretary-General had presented and what he felt was essential. On that day, Pérez de Cuéllar sent his proposed budget to the General Assembly. Instead of the widely believed cost of approximately U.S.$700 million, the overall figure was estimated at U.S.$416 million. It had been anticipated that the budget would now sail through the Assembly and its committees. Though the Assembly was supposed to have exclusive authority over financial matters, there had been nearly two months' discussion in the Council on the whole range of issues, real and imaginary, connected to putting a mission in the field. It came as an unpleasant surprise to many Security Council members—and to the Secretariat—that some countries now wanted to discuss these matters further in the framework of the General Assembly, although its Advisory Committee on Administrative and Budgetary Questions (ACABQ) had been very supportive, uncharacteristically wondering aloud if UNTAG's budget was not somewhat meager for the tasks ahead of it. And at times vehemently angry debate broke out again in the Assembly's Fifth Committee when it received the ACABQ's report. After prolonged late-night discussions, the Assembly on March 1 adopted the budget, thus finally permitting the Secretary-General to implement the array of necessary preparations. Most were set in motion by close of business that same day. But he had informed the membership that, because of the delays in Council and Assembly, he would no longer be able to achieve full operational capability on April 1, the predetermined date for the commencement of implementation.

On that date, when a cease-fire in the conflict between South Africa and SWAPO's People's Liberation Army of Namibia (PLAN) had been signed in detail, PLAN fighters instead moved across the border. Some members of the nonaligned movement had indeed previously informed the Secretary-General that, for some reason, SWAPO was looking for more time to prepare itself and that other nonaligned members were filibustering. But no convincing evidence has to date emerged, nor any confirmation on the part of any who were directly involved during what turned out to be a tragic and controversial period in Namibian history—and a significant one in the context of the Security Council.

The Joint Commission and the Tragic Events of April 1, 1989

On the night of April 1, 1989, Ahtisaari had to deal with a situation in which the South Africans demanded the right to release some of their troops, confined to base since that morning in accordance with Resolution 435 in order to deal with what they regarded as a mass invasion by PLAN. The troops that were requested, South Africa said, were to support its police, who had been confronted during the previous twenty-four hours by an influx of heavily armed SWAPO personnel with whom battle had been joined across a front of several hundred kilometers. Ahtisaari had arrived in Windhoek on March 31, 1989, the beginning of implementation having been set for the next day, on which a comprehensive cease-fire was also to come into effect. UNTAG, however, had only the most skeletal presence in the territory, as the Secretary-General had warned that it would during the previous three months' wrangling in New York.

It quickly emerged, when UNTAG insisted on questioning the few prisoners taken by South Africa that day, that SWAPO's troops had been ordered across the Angolan-Namibian border by their commanders in pursuit of the political objective of claiming and establishing military bases in northern Namibia—a claim that had been refuted many times in the previous decade but about which the SWAPO leadership felt strongly. During the next few weeks more than 300 young men on both sides of the conflict were killed—a higher casualty rate than during any previous period of the more than twenty years of armed conflict on the Namibian border; it was a futile and tragic sacrifice.

Early on April 2, Ahtisaari had received the report of his own senior personnel, civilian and military, whom he had sent to the border to investigate. They had been keeping him and the office of the Secretary-General updated. He now sent, at that office's request, a draft report for the Secretary-General to the Security Council. Ahtisaari was sure that only immediate and unequivocal decisions by the Council, together with a frank and open sharing of information with the media, could stop the carnage. Maximum diplomatic pressure, he also believed, had to be exerted on both sides to achieve this and to drag them away from one another's throats. In the next weeks, and as a part of this strategy, UNTAG took and maintained the initiative as regards public information.

The acute political problem that the Secretary-General faced in New York was that South Africa was, in international politics, virtually an outcast, whereas SWAPO had for years been anointed with most moral and political virtues by much of the UN membership. For the Secretary-General to state baldly, in a report to the Council in the first twenty-four hours of the independence process, that SWAPO had breached all its cease-fire undertakings (in a disingenuous atmosphere), and that he, acting on the advice of his special representative, had turned elements of the South African Defense Forces loose on the "freedom fighters," would confirm the worst fears of many members, of whom perhaps a majority already suspected that a duplicitous sellout was under way. Throughout the first months of the UNTAG mission, there was a tendency in some quarters to swallow, undiluted, much liberation rhetoric (though this had in many ways previously played a useful function in keeping the Namibian issue before the public).

Ahtisaari's draft report, deliberately unequivocal, was rejected by the Secretary-General's office, which instead desired something "more balanced," meaning a report that did not so categorically state that SWAPO was responsible for the cease-fire breach. During the week after the incursion major efforts continued on the part of the Secretary-General to bring about a cease-fire. Several meetings of the Council took place. Some members expressed unease about what was being reported to them in New York, suggesting that they were being given heavily edited actuality. Meanwhile, in Namibia, UNTAG was briefing the world's press each day on what was actually happening on the operational side, and this disparity was also confusing some members.

This tragic situation came to an end quite suddenly. The Frontline presidents met in camera in a stormy session, and high officials of Angola and Cuba called on SWAPO's president during the night of April 7–8. They invited him to implement a cease-fire at once and to withdraw his fighters to their previously agreed cease-fire lines. On April 8–9, the Joint Commission, consisting of Angola, Cuba, and South Africa, together with the United States and Soviet Union and, on this occasion and subsequently, the South African Administrator-General, representing the Namibian political parties, and UNTAG, met in plenary session at ministerial level at Mount Etjo in Namibia to decide what was to be done to restore the implementation of Resolution 435.

With the Administrator-General and myself conscripted to act as legal advisers and draftsmen, the parties drew up a program intended to establish a cease-fire, a safe withdrawal of fighters, a return to base as soon as possible of South African troops, and a declaration, aimed at the SWAPO per-

sonnel in the bush, to be read on all Namibian radio stations on the night of
April 9 by the SRSG and the Administrator-General.

The Joint Commission met frequently over the next weeks to oversee
the implementation of the Mount Etjo Agreement, and the Secretary-
General, in a report to the Council, approved of it. But five weeks elapsed
before confinement to base was again achieved. Thus UNTAG in mid-May
1989 found that its operational deadlines had been truncated. During the
next months it moved at speed and overtook the timetable that had been
incorporated into Resolution 435.

It established duty stations at about 200 places throughout the territory
and, first and foremost, tried to ensure that the Namibian people were fully
informed about the self-determination process, mainly through its forty-two
political and information offices. It broadcast more than 200 radio programs, all in multiple languages, and forty peak-hour television broadcasts.
It moved quickly to repeal a web of repressive and discriminatory laws and
to release political prisoners and detainees. Within its timetable it arranged,
with the UN High Commissioner for Refugees, to bring back and resettle in
Namibia many thousands of the Namibian diaspora who had been scattered
throughout forty-six countries. Before they could return, a comprehensive
amnesty was negotiated.

Although the Administrator-General did not oppose any of these measures as such, his style frequently was to argue against one or more aspects
of UNTAG's approach to the matters in question, and the negotiating
process was almost always arduous. Establishing a law for the registration
of voters, and an electoral law itself, proved especially difficult, and the
negotiations almost faltered. At a critical moment, when South African
murder squads began to operate in the country, UNTAG advanced one of its
basic objectives—to initiate reconciliation and mutual tolerance among the
various political parties and interest groups—by negotiating with them a
code of conduct for the elections, together with a simple procedure for its
implementation. This helped in calming and unifying the negotiation
process.

Perhaps the most difficult of UNTAG's tasks in restoring order and
building a sense of security in the country related to SWAPOL. There were
two problems—the colonialist and often racist mentality of the "regular"
police, and their often inadequate response in confronting matters of ordinary crime and law and order; and the continued existence of *koevoet*
("crowbar") battalions, counterinsurgency forces officially described as
"police."

The *koevoet* problem was especially intransigent. They terrorized large
swathes of northern Namibia, their activities being largely aimed at
SWAPO supporters. Indeed, during the 1980s South Africa had relied heavily on its *koevoet* battalions—some being PLAN personnel who had been

captured and "turned"—to defend northern Namibia against their former comrades. *Koevoet* platoons, armed to the teeth, often rode through the countryside in their high, heavy, mine-resistant trucks, casually destroying villages and crops and dealing out murder and violence to the population. Ahtisaari had first demanded their removal in June 1989 when it became evident that they were unwilling to be effectively monitored and that South Africa was not agreeable to removing their command structures—which were usually white and South African.

Though it did not specifically deal with the issue of bias in broadcasting, one of the few other unresolved issues between the Administrator-General and UNTAG, the Council was willing to act on the police question; on August 29, 1989, it demanded the disbandment of *koevoet* battalions and the dismantling of their command structures. The vast majority were not disbanded, however, until just before the November elections.

The Administrator-General repeatedly contended that he needed *koevoet* forces to defend Namibia against another attack by SWAPO fighters who were, he said, still present north of the Namibian border. He cited "reliable intelligence sources." The Joint Commission became actively seized of this matter and conducted various sweeps with the Angolan authorities. Though it was especially hard to prove a negative in the kind of territory that characterizes southern Angola, the commission set up its own search machinery. Both UNTAG and the Administer-General's representative were invited to sit on its joint intelligence committee and make use of it as appropriate. The commission could investigate at a few hours' notice. The chairmanship of the mechanism rotated among its members, with UNTAG fulfilling the role in due course.

Namibia's manifestly free and fair elections took place, with a more than 97 percent turnout of the registered electorate, during the same week of November 1989 in which the people of Berlin stormed their wall. The results were important not only—and primarily—for the people of Namibia. A wide range of innovation is associated with the UN's Namibia operation, but perhaps the most important was that the UN had shown that it had sufficient flexibility to be able effectively to adapt its evolutionary mechanism of international peacekeeping to a variety of international crisis situations—if the mission in question had sufficient resources and continuing full support from the Security Council. However, during the following decade it was pressed into service in numerous situations without, in many cases, adequate compliance with the quite basic and down-to-earth criteria on which previous experience should have insisted.

The impact of UNTAG's success, and especially its manner, also significantly affected the process that was about to unveil in South Africa. According to former South African foreign minister Pik Botha, the Namibian operation was "probably the most important event in southern

Africa in the previous forty years," clearing the way for the release of Nelson Mandela and for the momentous happenings that followed.[9]

But why, after so many years of noncooperation over Namibia, did South Africa so suddenly turn 180 degrees? First, the government was a coalition of interests and preferences, some being quite contradictory. In 1988–1989 senior members were already deep into secret talks with Nelson Mandela and the African National Congress. Apartheid was entering its terminal crisis through overextension and because of military and economic sanctions. South Africa also faced growing pressures from Western leaders, the continuing cost of wars on diverse fronts, and the need, argued strongly by some ministers, to negotiate with the outside world while it still could, that is, before time and resources ran out. Key Afrikaner members had a realistic understanding of their country's plight. Daily, the Angolans and Cubans grew stronger, and Pretoria had lost aerial supremacy. It had no attack helicopters, and no prospect of acquiring any, and was losing its few remaining fixed-wing aircraft. The war was increasingly unpopular, and its human and material costs were biting ever more deeply. Some saw events in Moscow—if they were what they seemed—to provide the making of a providential solution. Their impact, through Soviet disengagement in Africa, could perhaps help bring about a solution short of surrender. And, after all, they hoped the Namibian election process could be "helped" so as to bring about a "satisfactory" result.[10] Above all, what had to be avoided in Namibia was some great political disaster along the way.

The Role of the Security Council in Securing Namibia's Independence

The question of Namibia came late to the Council. One reason for this was that some of the most influential members preferred to keep it in the Assembly and ICJ. They did not care to have it become an international peace and security question directly involving all members of the Council, especially the Soviet Union and China. They wished it to be a matter for negotiation rather than confrontation. When the end came, after the possibility for confrontation had been suppressed in October 1976 (at least for the time being), it did indeed come via negotiation, though the possibility of further sanctions was clearly never far from South African ministerial minds during rough patches of the implementation.

The route of peaceful negotiation was taken outside the Council by the Western permanent three's Contact Group (soon joined by Canada and Germany). When President Reagan assumed the U.S. presidency, it was initially the United States that, by way of Chester Crocker's lonely quest, reinstated the negotiating process and finally corralled Angola, Cuba, and South Africa and pushed them into a sometimes reluctant embrace. And when the events of April 1, 1989, threatened to destroy the "linkage" consensus, it was the Joint Commission that took hold of the situation and dragged Resolution 435 back on track. When South African military intelligence (mainly) tried once again to derail Resolution 435 in the weeks before the election, the Joint Commission again rode to the rescue, creating an operational intelligence body that carried out short-notice inspections on both sides of the Angolan-Namibian border and hilariously deflated a last-ditch attempt by those units to destroy the peaceful process.

On major issues during the twelve months of UNTAG's mandate, such as the continuance of *koevoet* forces despite South African promises, pressures may also have been exerted by the Security Council. But the Council was somewhat remote from events on the ground, and primary support to the mission—so essential to its success—was habitually provided by one or more members of the Western Contact Group, or of the Frontline States, or above all, by the Joint Commission, collectively. In Windhoek itself, where there were nearly two dozen "observer missions" during implementation, the diplomatic community was very supportive of UNTAG as the mission progressed.

For many years, there had been not only a dispute but also brooding ill will over Namibia, the vulnerable international heel of South Africa, and its hated apartheid system. Some Western countries had come to be seen by the nonaligned movement as South Africa's ultimate defenders in international bodies. This had led to a poisonous buildup of suspicion. The vividness of Council and Assembly debates during January–February 1989, as the Secretariat tried to prepare for its demanding role, was traumatic, their fervor jeopardizing even the start date and practicality of independence for Namibia under Resolution 435.

And although UNTAG was the first UN peacekeeping mission to be truly universal in terms of its members' and contingent contributors' nationalities (as well as the first to be gender-blind in recruiting and then assigning staff throughout the country), the preimplementation atmosphere in some matters stretched supranational loyalty among its staff to an extreme.

Also, while the Joint Commission's assistance to UNTAG was probably essential to its success at various critical points, it sometimes forgot that the UN operation came under not its, but the Security Council's, authority, and the Secretary-General and Ahtisaari had to remind the commission. But the composition of the commission helped to prevent more negative reactions in New York and nonaligned capitals to its activities.

It was not possible to insulate either the Council or UNTAG against all of the mischief wrought by the fallout from the appalling system of apartheid. This was principally seen in the divisions that afflicted the Council in the months before implementation began, which peaked around the events of April 1, 1989. It had pervaded the extreme rhetoric that sometimes seemed to destroy any hope of a rational political process. Overall, the Council's tasks would have been easier had its political masters been more timely, as, without a shadow of doubt, history will insist they should have been.

Notes

1. Sara Pienaar, *South Africa and International Relations Between the Two World Wars* (Johannesburg, Witwatersrand University Press, 1987).

2. *International Status of South West Africa Case,* ICJ Reports (1950); *South West Africa (Voting Procedure) Case,* ICJ Reports (1955); *South West Africa (Petitioners) Case,* ICJ Reports (1956).

3. *South West Africa Case (Second Phase),* ICJ Reports (1966).

4. By Resolution 2145, para. 21.

5. ICJ Reports (1971).

6. See especially Peter Katjavivi, *A History of Resistance in Namibia* (London: Currey, 1988); and David Soggot, *Namibia: The Violent Heritage* (London: Collins, 1986).

7. Heribert Weiland and Matthew Braham, eds., *The Namibian Peace Process: Implications and Lessons for the Future* (Freiburg: Arnold Bergstraesser Institut/International Peace Academy, 1994).

8. Chester Crocker, *High Noon in South Africa: Making Peace in a Rough Neighborhood* (New York: W. W. Norton, 1992).

9. Interview with Pik Botha, 1998.

10. See Cedric Thornberry, *The People Must First Lose Their Fear* (forthcoming from Gamsberg-Macmillan), for an account of various attempts to rig Namibia's Constituent Assembly election of 1989.

28

El Salvador

Blanca Antonini

The UN Security Council played a key role in the peace process that brought to an end war in El Salvador. The conflict had cost 75,000 deaths and wreaked enormous suffering on the Salvadorian people. The Council gave international endorsement to the UN-brokered negotiations between the government of El Salvador and an insurgent movement, the Farabundo Martí National Liberation Front (FMLN). During the phase of implementation of the agreements, the Council was a driving force that encouraged the parties into compliance.

A specific set of factors, circumstances, and strategic decisions led to meaningful and opportune Council intervention. During the two-year negotiation process, action by the Council was decisive, though limited: it relied heavily on another key player, the Secretary-General of the United Nations, and tailored its intervention to the needs and pace of the negotiations conducted by Alvaro de Soto, the personal representative of Secretary-General Javier Pérez de Cuéllar. Strategic and synchronized intervention by the Friends of the Secretary-General (Colombia, Mexico, Spain, and Venezuela) was a valuable element in prodding the process along, as was the role of the United States when it decided to put its weight behind the UN-led process by leveraging incentives and conditionalities.

The Regional Context
Tension and armed conflict spread throughout most of the Central American region during the 1980s. In El Salvador, social upheaval resulted from several factors. Political and economic exclusion, recourse to the armed forces as the guarantor of the established order, massive human rights abuses, militant opposition to authoritarian governments, and the confluence of resistance groups into a single guerrilla front, the FMLN, had led to the outbreak of all-out war. The two strong contenders, their military

423

power bolstered by aid supplied by the United States or their Soviet Union–backed hemispheric allies, respectively, were confronted in a war where the principal victims were civilians. Armed conflict also raged in Nicaragua and Guatemala.

The reality of the Cold War and the preeminence of the doctrine of spheres of influence had largely excluded the Western Hemisphere from the collective remedies envisaged by the UN Charter to resolve conflict. The initiative in dealing with the Central American crisis had been assumed in 1983 by the so-called Contadora Group—Colombia, Mexico, Panama, and Venezuela—eventually joined by the Support Group—Argentina, Brazil, Peru, and Uruguay. Although the United Nations had first been seized of the situation in El Salvador through the human rights window in 1981, when it came to peacemaking it had taken a backseat, limiting its involvement to expressions of support for the regional initiatives. Hopes to see the conflicts in the region resolved through this channel were soon to be dashed, however, as the proposed solutions failed to address the conflicting interests stemming from superpower rivalry. By 1987 it had become clear that the process was in need of redirection. The drive for change would come from the Central American region. In August, at the initiative of President Oscar Arias of Costa Rica, the five Central American presidents signed the "Procedure for the Establishment of a Firm and Lasting Peace in Central America," otherwise called the Esquipulas II Agreement, a major breakthrough in addressing the crisis. Esquipulas and subsequent agreements by the Central American presidents would obtain the "firm support" of the Security Council in July 1989.

The agreement placed considerable emphasis on actions by Central American governments to promote dialogue and reconciliation. It also stipulated security commitments that would eventually be verified by the UN Observer Group in Central America (ONUCA), an operation authorized by the Council in 1989 and the first of its kind to be deployed on the American continent. The Council also endorsed a direct involvement of the Secretary-General through his good offices.

The UN as Impartial Broker

By requesting the Secretary-General to exercise his good offices, the Council had laid a thin, though definite, basis to justify the key diplomatic role that Alvaro de Soto, his personal representative, would play in the negotiations. At the UN and among interested observers, it had become clear that the Salvadoran conflict could not be dismissed merely as a byproduct of the Cold War era. Reflecting deep cleavages in society, the conflict found its sustenance in the grievances and disenfranchisement of vast sectors. Finding a durable solution would require profound institutional and political reforms, which could not be achieved without considerable outside pressure.

The Esquipulas initiative gave the quest for peace political momentum. But having been conceived by governments, its main purpose was to strengthen the institutional system without opening it to negotiations, and its starting point was to ensure the disbandment of insurgent forces. Rebel movements therefore dismissed the proposed national dialogue as a means to legitimize and perpetuate the established order.

Several factors placed the UN representative in the best position to turn the opportunities provided by a rare confluence of external and domestic circumstances into a successful bid for negotiations, fleshing out the specifics for El Salvador of the provisions contained in Esquipulas II. The UN representative had a specific advantage—he was not acting on behalf of a vested national interest and could therefore evoke the minimum trust that is the prerequisite of a serious negotiation. As the representative of a universally recognized authority, he was in a privileged position to engage a legal government and an illegal insurgency as equal parties at the negotiating table.[1]

In September 1989 the government of President Alfredo Cristiani of El Salvador and the insurgents engaged in talks to which a representative of the Secretary-General had been invited as a witness. The talks failed to produce results, and a new wave of violence ensued. The FMLN launched its broadest offensive ever, including in neighborhoods of San Salvador thus far spared from the war. For several days, El Salvador made headlines in the major international media. On November 14, in the dead of night, six respected Jesuit priests, their housekeeper, and her daughter were snatched from their bedrooms and summarily killed in the premises of the José Simeón Cañas University of Central America in San Salvador. The culprits were armed elements who were generally believed, as would later be proven, to be soldiers under military command.

These events had an enormous impact on the process. Although the FMLN had demonstrated military strength, the offensive had not resulted in the popular uprising that some of its commanders had expected. On the government side, it became clear that military victory was unviable or too costly. The pain caused by the renewed fighting, with its hundreds of deaths and thousands of casualties, and the domestic and international uproar caused by the ruthless killings on the university campus would put additional pressure on both sides to seek a political negotiation.[2]

Meanwhile, the summit of the superpowers held in Malta on December 2, 1989, confirmed their newfound willingness to seek common ground to defuse the crisis in the region. Reflecting this mood, the president of the Security Council issued a statement on December 8 expressing members' grave concern over the situation in the region and appealed to all states, "in particular those which [had] links in the region and interests in it," to immediately halt the open or covert supply of aid to irregular forces or insurrectional movements. Four days later, the Central American presidents, gathering in San Francisco de Coronado, Costa Rica, demanded that the FMLN cease hostilities and asked the Secretary-General to do everything within his power "to ensure the resumption of the dialogue." The FMLN and soon thereafter President Cristiani would request the Secretary-General's assistance to engage in an uninterrupted negotiation to settle the conflict.

During the following nine weeks, the personal representative had intensive consultations with both parties to define the way forward. In order to avoid the pitfalls of earlier attempts, it was necessary to secure the commitment of both sides to a set of ground rules with sound procedural bases and a clear and acceptable role for the United Nations. Consultations culminated at the Palais des Nations in Geneva on April 4, 1990, as representatives of the Salvadoran government and the FMLN, in the presence of the Secretary-General, signed the Geneva Agreement, which laid down the principles that would guide the two-year-long negotiations. Direct negotiations would be conducted with the active participation of the Secretary-General or his representative, who would also play an intermediary role. The Secretary-General, at his discretion, would maintain confidential contacts with governments able to contribute to the process through their advice and support. Rather than a continuation of earlier dialogues, these understandings marked the beginning of a new process.

The Dynamic of Negotiations

The following round of talks would take place in Caracas, Venezuela, and result in an agreed agenda and a timetable. The parties committed themselves to a two-phase negotiation. A cease-fire would not be a prerequisite to initiate substantive negotiations on all subjects. Outstanding commitments would be negotiated in the second phase, after the cease-fire and an end of the confrontation. Guarantees and conditions would have to be reached before proceeding to the reintegration of members of the FMLN into the institutional life of the country.

The first substantive agreement, signed in San José, Costa Rica, in July 1990, dealt with human rights and humanitarian standards. The significance of the San José Agreement—as it came to be known—stemmed not only from the array of obligations accepted by both sides but also from the strong verification powers assigned to the UN through the establishment of a ground presence. The San José Agreement was a fundamental building block in the process and fostered confidence among the war-weary population. A further boost to the talks resulted from both sides' request that, even in the absence of a cease-fire, the UN should make preparations for a verification mission. The Council agreed to the establishment of a small preparatory office in El Salvador one month after San José.

In El Salvador, the human rights agreement would not pass without resistance. The stern obligations it entailed and the provisions for strict international oversight caused jitters on both sides. Within the FMLN rank and file it was feared that the accord would give the government an unwarranted edge when it had in fact shown no willingness to make substantive concessions on its armed forces. It was feared that the accord would tie the rebels' hands without exacting a commensurate price from the army. The international verification provisions also provoked grumblings among the right, loath to the idea of negotiations. Bringing the constituencies of both sides fully onboard would require more time.

The tension between the government's interest in achieving an early cease-fire and the insurgency's reluctance to yield on its trump card would be felt throughout the process. Pressures increased as the negotiations approached September 15, 1990, the target date to achieve the initial objective. The text of a possible Security Council resolution urging a cease-fire, drafted by the United States in consultation with the Salvadorian government, made its way to the offices of several Council members in early September but never reached the status of a formal proposal: in discussions with the Secretary-General and his representative, interested diplomats came to realize that the initiative was premature, and the idea was set aside. It became clear that obtaining the main concession that the FMLN could give—a verifiable and irreversible cease-fire—would require an agreement on the armed forces, the touchiest and most difficult item on the agenda.

This issue would resurface three months after San José, as the parties, realizing that a more active UN role would be necessary to jump-start the process, asked de Soto to submit a nonpaper on the armed forces. The UN text was a carefully crafted document that articulated in a single body the various elements raised in frequent and often lengthy exchanges between the two sides. The text would be the basis for the final agreement, a blueprint for the transformation of the armed forces into an instrument of a democratic state subject to its laws and controls and fully accountable for its actions. From then on, the only written proposals at the negotiating table would be those of the Secretary-General's representative. This would change de Soto's intermediary role to that of a de facto, if not de jure, mediator.

Further internal and external pressures were again exerted to achieve a peace agreement by the end of 1990 to ensure the FMLN's participation in the March 1991 elections. The Secretary-General informed the Council that problems encountered in seeking agreement on the armed forces had impeded progress on other matters on the agenda. With guarded optimism, he expressed his belief that, with the necessary political will and the support of outside powers, the goal of peace in El Salvador would be achieved in the not too distant future. But the Secretary-General declined to recommend that the UN observe the March elections as requested by the government—it was not yet the practice of the UN to observe elections in an independent country, although this had been done in exceptional cases such as Nicaragua and Haiti. Most important, the Secretary-General noted that the electoral system was one of the items on the Caracas Agenda that the parties had to broach (S/22031, December 21, 1990).

The parties of the moderate left close to the FMLN, grouped in Convergencia Democrática, eventually took part in the elections for the first time since the war. In a sign of changing times, also for the first time the FMLN refrained from disrupting the polls.

If artificial deadlines had proven insufficient to move the process forward, deadlines instrumental to the substance of the negotiations would be decisive to reach agreements. Constitutional reforms required approval by the existing Legislative Assembly before its term of office expired on April 30, 1991.[3] According to the constitution, reforms had to be passed by two successive assemblies. Failing approval by the legislature in place, ratification would be deferred until 1994. This would entail a dangerous loss of momentum.

In April, the parties met in Mexico City to discuss constitutional reforms. Negotiations were lengthy and often tense, as both sides reacted to a barrage of sometimes inflammatory statements from military officers and extreme right-wing sectors in El Salvador who balked at any constitutional change. After twenty-three days of virtual retreat, agreement was reached on a broad set of reforms, including an overhaul of the armed forces, the assignment of law and order responsibilities to a new civil police, provisions to ensure the independence of the judiciary, and the creation of the Counsel for the Defense of Human Rights and of the Supreme Electoral Tribunal. These wide-ranging reforms were soon approved by the outgoing assembly. The parties also agreed to the establishment of a truth commission that would investigate abuses committed during the war. While no agreement was reached on a cease-fire, it seemed clear that the process had become irreversible.

The Fundamental Quid Pro Quo

The moment to grapple with the fundamental quid pro quo of the process was fast approaching. As the negotiators were soon to realize, the scheme conceived in Caracas, with its two-phased approach, had become an obstacle to progress: the FMLN would not lay down its weapons before bringing to closure the outstanding political commitments. In September 1991, by agreement between the parties and at the Secretary-General's initiative, the negotiations were compressed into a single phase with the blessing of the Security Council.

This would not come without difficulties. Several rounds of talks held after the Mexico City meeting had failed to make progress, and international pressure on the UN intensified. On August 17, 1991, the U.S. secretary of state, James Baker, and the Soviet minister of foreign affairs, Aleksandr Bessmertnykh, in a joint letter to the Secretary-General, stated they were "deeply concerned" and called on him to "take personal leadership of the negotiating process." They were ready to extend their full cooperation, "in the context of the Security Council and bilaterally" and to join with the Friends. The Secretary-General replied by confirming his continuous engagement through his personal representative or directly, when the level of representation of the parties so justified.[4]

Later that month, the Secretary-General invited President Cristiani for consultations; the FMLN general command was also invited. On September 25, 1991, after a week of intensive negotiations, the parties agreed to a "compressed agenda" covering all outstanding matters. A separate, confidential understanding established that members of the FMLN and the existing National Police would be able to join a new National Civil Police, and the FMLN accepted to waive its demand that the armed forces be disbanded. Agreement was also reached on the establishment of a national mechanism to monitor compliance with the accords. The Friends, the United States, and the Soviet Union were actively involved in the consultations leading to the accords.

Patience and consistency had been rewarded—the tide turned again in favor of the UN-led process. On September 30 the Security Council welcomed the agreement, congratulating the Secretary-General and his personal representative "for their skillful and tireless efforts" and urged both parties to reach a peaceful settlement at the earliest possible date.

As the talks continued, another deadline was looming: at the end of the year, Secretary-General Pérez de Cuéllar would leave office. In December, once again, he invited the highest-ranking representatives of both parties to New York. Simultaneous negotiations were initiated under the general direction of the principal mediator to deal with the gamut of pending agenda items. On the freezing morning of Christmas 1991, the FMLN, sitting at a table with Undersecretary-General Marrack Goulding, agreed to the basic elements of his proposal: the cease-fire would be of predetermined duration, verifiable, and lead to the disbandment of the FMLN's military structure. Only after this major breakthrough would President Cristiani join his team in New York. At midnight on December 31, agreement had been achieved on all substantive issues. The implementation timetable and the procedures for the FMLN's reintegration into civilian life would be finalized in the first half of January, after nine days of frenzied talks and a mere three days ahead of the solemn signature of the peace accord at Chapultepec, Mexico, on January 16, 1992.[5]

ONUSAL

After the signature of the peace accord, Security Council involvement in El Salvador evolved, in parallel to the establishment of the UN Observer Mission in El Salvador (ONUSAL), to become the key international authority pressing for compliance with the wide array of undertakings set out in the agreements. On the basis of reports from the mission, the Council would be seized of the issue of El Salvador from the initiation of a cease-fire in 1992 through the phasing out of the mission in 1995. Reports were submitted at regular six-month intervals coinciding with the extension of ONUSAL's mandate or when the situation so warranted. In addition to its official reports, the UN kept the Council informed through frequent informal briefings.

The Council's almost daily informal nonpublic meetings—a working modality introduced at that time—greatly facilitated the flow of information. Another significant factor that enhanced the Council's monitoring role was the presence in that organ of two members of the original group of Friends—Venezuela in 1992–1993 and Spain in 1993–1994—as well as the close involvement of the United States with El Salvador. As implementation began, the four Friends, soon to be joined by the United States in a group informally called the "four plus one," had recast themselves as the Friends of the Salvadoran Peace Process and played an active role in providing assistance and support to the implementation process, monitoring compliance, and drawing attention to delays, distortions, or outright violations of the accords. By making the release of funds dependent on the Security Council's assessment of implementation, the United States was a particularly effective engine behind implementation.

In 1990 the Security Council had approved the establishment of a single integrated mission that would verify all the agreements. An argument in favor of having an operation separate from ONUCA was to ensure proper coordination of operations on the ground and a rational use of resources. Furthermore, only an operation whose mandate was tailored to the accords would have the confidence of the FMLN, which was reluctant to recognize the authority of ONUCA, set up to verify the Esquipulas security commitments and therefore considered inimical to its interests.

As previously noted, ONUSAL established its first component, its human rights division, before a cease-fire was in place. Its presence on the ground served to alleviate the effects of the war on the civilian population, constituted a significant confidence-building measure, and signaled the parties' commitment to the peace process. It was the first time that a UN human rights operation was deployed throughout the territory of a country for a lengthy period and had such intrusive powers.

On January 14, 1992, the Council decided to expand the mandate and increase the strength of ONUSAL to include 380 military observers and 631 police monitors. After that, the composition and strength of the mission would vary as agreements were implemented, depending on evolving verification needs. In addition to its human rights division, the structure of ONUSAL would eventually incorporate a military, a police, and, following a specific request from the government in January 1993, an electoral division. They were placed under the authority of a civilian head of mission, who was also the special representative of the Secretary-General (SRSG) for El Salvador, a position initially encumbered by Iqbal Riza. Although this was also true for the human rights division, provisions had been made to give the latter a high level of autonomy, as borne out by the fact that it had its own direct reporting channel to the General Assembly and the Security Council. The role of the SRSG would prove to be particularly important: in addition to ensuring the internal cohesiveness of the mission, he was increasingly called upon to bring the parties together on the way forward. Despite the deep-rooted mistrust of hard-liners, he gradually gained the confidence of all sectors of Salvadoran society. Both the government and the former guerrilla commanders would come to rely on him in searching for solutions to many of the problems that arose in the immediate aftermath of the war.

The end of armed confrontation and the return of former FMLN commanders to El Salvador soon after Chapultepec were clear signs of the parties' commitment and willingness to embark on the road to peace. But the Security Council's close supervision of implementation through ONUSAL's verification proved to be crucial in keeping the process on track and driving the parties to compliance, particularly at critical junctures.

The implementation schedule was a carefully woven plan that sought the staggered demobilization of FMLN contingents in five phases, timed to coincide with a number of state actions designed to facilitate the former combatants' effective and safe reintegration. Although it had been determined that one breach of the agreement could not be used to justify another, the balanced synchronization of actions was key to secure the continued commitment of the parties to the process.

In keeping with this logic, the definitive end of the armed conflict was to be achieved on October 31, 1992, nine months after the formal establishment of a cease-fire. As the deadline approached, it became clear that it would not be met—the FMLN refused to budge given failure to make progress in key political accords, especially regarding political participation, recruitment into the National Civil Police, and land distribution.[6]

The head of mission, with decisive help provided by Goulding and de Soto during visits from New York, took on an active mediator's role. Substantive proposals on the key issues included a plan for the purchase of land plots at favorable conditions. The Council was kept constantly informed of developments through briefings and formal communications and gave its blessing to these undertakings. The process thus reenergized, on December 15, 1992, six weeks after originally planned, the Secretary-General declared that the armed conflict in El Salvador had "come to an end" and the first goal of the agreements had been achieved. The Russian Federation's Ministry of Foreign Affairs and the U.S. State Department hailed the breakthrough and reiterated their readiness to continue to contribute to the peace process.

But important substantive commitments remained outstanding, and delays in compliance persisted. The dismissal of military officers on grounds of bad behavior, recommended by an ad hoc commission, was completed months later than originally scheduled and not before several reminders from the UN, of which the Council was kept informed. In May 1993 the Secretary-General alluded to difficulties on the path to national reconciliation due to such factors as persistent polarization and distrust, conflicting interpretation of the agreements, and the inability by the administrative and organizational structures on both sides to manage the implementation of such a complex set of agreements. The good-offices role of the head of mission acquired ever more significance in eliciting the support of the parties for proposals to reschedule implementation. Similarly important was the regular flow of information to keep the Council onboard and to ensure its continuous engagement.

A critical juncture of the process came in March 1993, as the Truth Commission issued its report. Based on investigations conducted by the commission and numerous testimonies taken from witnesses, the report described some of the worst human rights violations committed during the civil war and indicated individual responsibilities. It made recommendations that the parties had undertaken to comply, including the dismissal from police or military duty of responsible individuals, their exclusion from public office for a decade, and deep structural and institutional reforms designed to prevent a repetition of the violations that characterized the war years. In welcoming the Truth Commission report, the president of the Security Council underlined the need for the parties to comply with its recommendations.

Notwithstanding the Council's admonitions, publication of the report heightened tensions to a level that had not been experienced since Chapultepec. The high command of the armed forces, the president of the Supreme Court, and other high state representatives publicly rejected the report. The specter of a military takeover appeared possible. The Legislative Assembly convened in an emergency session to approve by simple majority a blanket amnesty for all crimes committed during the civil war. Compliance with the Truth Commission's recommendations would prove slower and more difficult than other undertakings, and although the Secretary-General subsequently reported regularly on progress in implementation, some of the recommendations were never carried through.

A serious jolt to the process came in May 1993, as an accidental explosion in Managua, Nicaragua, revealed the existence of large caches of weapons, including surface-to-air missiles, owned by structures under the FMLN command. The UN was quick to react. The FMLN leadership was warned that the incident raised serious questions of confidence and trust and could put in jeopardy the process itself. The Council, which was continuously kept abreast of developments, on June 11 called the maintenance of clandestine arms deposits "the most serious violation to date" of the commitments undertaken in the peace accord.

The FMLN reacted positively to this stern remonstration. Its specialized personnel were placed at the disposal of ONUSAL to cooperate in the identification of all remaining clandestine deposits. ONUSAL's specialized observers were deployed to areas identified by the FMLN, both in El Salvador and in neighboring countries whose support was necessary, and proceeded to destroy the illegally kept weapons. Later in June 1993, the Secretary-General was in a position to state that it was an indication of the strength and irreversibility of the process that such a serious incident had not derailed implementation of the accord.

In March 1994, El Salvador was to hold its first postconflict elections for the presidency, the vice presidency, all members of the Legislative Assembly, municipal authorities, and representatives to the Central American parliament. For the first time, the FMLN would participate as a legitimate political party. The electoral division of ONUSAL would verify the electoral campaign, observe the elections, and support the Supreme Electoral Tribunal in the registration and the delivery of voter cards.

As the opening of the electoral campaign approached, a deterioration of the human rights situation became evident. Violent incidents, including arbitrary executions, were again on the rise. Two FMLN leaders and several lesser-known politicians were killed, raising serious fears that death squads continued to operate. Recalling that a thorough investigation of illegal armed groups and their full eradication had been recommended by the Truth Commission, the Secretary-General instructed the human rights division of ONUSAL to work with the Salvadoran government on this issue. In a presidential statement, the Security Council expressed "shock and concern" at the killings and approved the Secretary-General's decision. In

December, the government agreed to the establishment of a joint group for the investigation of politically motivated illegal armed groups; it was endorsed by the Security Council, and its findings would be brought before the Council in July 1994.

As President Cristiani's term of office came to an end, securing a commitment from the incoming administration of President Calderon Sol became essential to comply with outstanding obligations. This required active mission involvement and Council monitoring. In September, a joint declaration by the government and the FMLN announced their intention to cooperate closely and to establish a joint mechanism, with the participation of ONUSAL, to determine the measures necessary to comply with the agreements.

By the time of ONUSAL's complete withdrawal in April 1995, and as several important agreements remained to be fulfilled, the Security Council agreed to a post-ONUSAL arrangement to ensure appropriate UN verification of outstanding commitments while lending continued UN good offices to support implementation. These tasks would be carried out by a small team from the mission, which initially took the name Mission of the United Nations in El Salvador (MINUSAL). The Council would no longer be seized of the matter—reports on the process would be addressed to the General Assembly.[7]

Conclusion

The end of the Cold War opened the way to a new era in hemispheric relations that, along with the willingness of both parties to pursue a political solution, enabled the Council to move close to fulfilling its stated goal of maintaining international peace and security. During the negotiations, this purpose was achieved through measured intervention, tailored to the needs of the talks, rather than through activism. The personality of the main UN negotiator was a significant factor. Patience, consistency, a rare capacity to understand the motives behind both sides' positions, a combination of restraint with decisive and timely action, and the ability to weave into the process the major international actors became essential ingredients in bringing the parties together.

During implementation, periodic reports from ONUSAL enabled the Council to monitor compliance continuously and, to a large extent, effectively. The specific interest of the United States, Spain, and Venezuela—the latter two as elected members to the Council—turned El Salvador into an important item on the Council's agenda.

With its various components and a mandate designed to verify a complex gamut of agreements ranging from cease-fire and demobilization to human rights practices, numerous structural, institutional, and legal reforms as well as measures to ensure the political, social, and economic reintegration of former combatants, ONUSAL set precedents in many respects and has often been hailed as the first example of a second-generation peacekeeping operation. The Secretary-General called the UN intervention in El Salvador "a pioneering experience."

ONUSAL became a model for later peacekeeping operations that sought durable solutions to internal conflicts through institution-building. In this context, it would become clear after the mission was established that the typical verification functions had to be combined with a capacity to provide technical assistance. During its initial stages, ONUSAL placed emphasis on monitoring cases of abuse. As the methodology for investigating cases evolved, the formulation of recommendations to avoid recurrence of violations and on ways to follow up on their implementation acquired preeminence. The recommendations enabled the mission to identify flaws in the legal system and in the institutions on which the enjoyment of human rights largely depends, namely, the judiciary, the police, and the figure of the ombudsman.

In retrospect, it can be said that ONUSAL would have benefited from a clear and well-defined strategy to ensure the link between peacekeeping and institution-building functions since its inception. Such a strategy requires a cohesive response from the UN system and all relevant cooperation agencies, as well as the continued and consistent commitment of donors to the long-term objectives of democratization.

Advances were noticeable in areas that had enjoyed broad support among most sectors, domestically and internationally, and for which provisions had been negotiated directly by the parties. They included the end of hostilities, reform of the armed forces, establishment of a civil police, and political participation. Success was mixed in the case of accords that had not been negotiated directly by the parties, though they had been accepted in advance through the establishment of agreed-upon mechanisms, such as the Truth Commission. Economic and social policies were left to a national forum, a mechanism that proved to be largely ineffective in reaching meaningful understandings. Economic reintegration programs, including the land program, provided valuable outlets for former combatants, though its implementation was far too complex and slow.

Active Council involvement was an essential driving force behind the peace process. But neither the Council nor the UN arrangements that succeeded ONUSAL could substitute for domestic institutions and political forces. In announcing the end of UN verification functions in El Salvador in December 2002, the Secretary-General noted that work toward full democratization, effective rule of law, and the consolidation of peace were far from over and would require renewed national commitment.[8]

Notes

1. Michael Doyle, Ian Johnstone, and Robert Orr, eds., *Multidimensional Peacekeeping: Lessons from Cambodia and El Salvador* (New York: International Peace Academy, 1995).

2. Martha Doggett. *Death Foretold: The Jesuit Murders in El Salvador* (Washington, D.C.: Georgetown University Press, 1993).

3. Joseph Sullivan, "How Peace Came to El Salvador," *Orbis Magazine,* Winter 1994, pp. 83–93.

4. Alvaro de Soto, "Ending Violent Conflict in El Salvador," in Chester Crocker, Fen Osler Hampson, and Pamela Aall, eds., *Herding Cats: Multiparty Mediation in a Complex World* (Washington, D.C.: U.S. Institute of Peace, 1999), pp. 345–386

5. Marrack Goulding, *Peacemonger* (London: John Murray, 2002), pp. 235–236.

6. Alvaro de Soto and Graciana del Castillo, "Implementation of Comprehensive Peace Agreements: Staying the Course in El Salvador," *Global Governance* 1, no. 2 (May–August 1995): 189–203.

7. Teresa Whitfield, *Staying the Course in El Salvador: Honoring Human Rights—From Peace to Justice* (Washington, D.C.: Aspen Institute, 1998), pp. 163–187.

8. A/57/384/Add.1, December 17, 2002.

29

Mozambique

ALDO AJELLO AND PATRICK WITTMANN

In typical reviews of an unprecedented period in the number and nature of UN peacekeeping operations, the successes tend to be underreported. Failed operations launch deep introspection exercises among international organizations and national governments, all eager not to repeat the mistakes of the past. But a case can be made for taking more time to study the successes. They, too, offer lessons about how to do things right in the future.

This chapter seeks to shed light on how the Security Council and the UN operation it mandated succeeded in Mozambique, with a focus on the following elements: direct involvement, cooperation, and material support of Council members and other countries; the quality and nature of Council engagement and decisionmaking; the role of coordination between the special representative of the Secretary-General (SRSG) and the local diplomatic community in "engineering" Security Council engagement; preconditions such as a sound peace agreement and clarity about the UN's role in implementing it; flexibility in the interpretation of mandates, timetables, and procedures; and approaches to avoiding past mistakes, in this instance those affecting the UN's role in Angola.[1]

The UN Operation in Mozambique (ONUMOZ), launched by the Security Council through Resolution 797 of December 16, 1992, was one of the most ambitious, multifaceted missions undertaken by the UN up to that time. Its mandate encompassed political, military, humanitarian, and electoral responsibilities not only for the pacification of a war-torn country but also for its transformation from a single-party state to a multiparty democracy. As such, ONUMOZ was an important UN foray into nation-building, one of its more successful efforts judging from Mozambique's track record to date.

When Secretary-General Boutros Boutros-Ghali formally sought the Security Council's approval of the ONUMOZ mandate in late 1992, he warned of the risks inherent in such an ambitious undertaking.[2] The

437

Council's willingness to authorize an operation of such significant scope and cost was an example of the continuing "euphoria" and cooperation among the permanent five (P-5) that marked Council dynamics in the early post–Cold War years. The acceptance of this risk was also informed by the relatively auspicious conditions that prevailed on the ground in Mozambique and the wider region, as well as the quality of the negotiations that preceded the UN's involvement. Perhaps more remarkable was the Council's resolve in sustaining the Mozambique operation (including extending it for another year) through a turbulent period in which other UN operations—in Angola, Rwanda, and Somalia—had failed or were unraveling. This can be attributed to a number of factors, not least the need, against this dire backdrop, to deliver a UN success in Africa.[3] The prior involvement of permanent Council members Britain, France, and the United States as observers of the Rome peace process, and their subsequent accompaniment of the UN mission through the implementation phase, were critical to the Council's approval of a sweeping mandate for ONUMOZ in Resolution 797, the dedication of adequate resources to realize it, and the continued, helpful engagement of the Council through the end of the mission's mandate in December 1994. The clear stake in the success or failure of ONUMOZ of three permanent members proved determinant and was leveraged to maximum effect by the SRSG, Aldo Ajello, in the achievement of results.

The 1992 General Peace Agreement and Its Timetable
An important early ingredient of success was the general peace agreement of October 1992, the product of two years of intense negotiations in Rome between the formerly Soviet-backed Mozambican government and the Mozambique National Resistance (Renamo), a South African–supported right-wing rebel force. The Italian government together with the Saint Egidio community, an order of Catholic lay brothers, mediated. Four countries, France, Portugal (Mozambique's former colonial master), Britain, and the United States, acted as observers.

The general peace agreement was a thoroughly negotiated, comprehensive text. It included prior agreement between the parties on most of the tough issues and took precedence over all other national legislation in Mozambique, including the constitution.[4] The status and soundness of the agreement, the equality it accorded to the parties, and the habit of cooperation it engendered between them proved to be crucial in building confidence between the parties throughout the peace process. In particular, it contributed to the relatively permissive environment during the seven-month interregnum between the signing of the accord and the deployment to full strength of the UN mission, a time that could otherwise have witnessed mischief or backsliding by the parties.

Although the UN did not play a central role in negotiating the general peace agreement, it became involved when its technical expertise and political legitimacy were needed to move the Rome process forward.[5] Eventually, the two sides agreed on the need for the UN to lead the implementation of the agreement. Once this request was made to the UN, efforts were made to ensure that the UN was clearly put in the driver's seat of peace implementation. This key factor in the future effectiveness of the UN was a lesson learned from Angola, where the UN had been relegated to the role of observer with limited power to influence the course of events, a status that made it the perfect scapegoat for all that went wrong there. UN officials, including the Secretary-General, pointing to the UN's miscarried mission in Angola, lobbied for UN leadership of international efforts in Mozambique. The Security Council, having also internalized the lessons of Angola, concurred in approving the ONUMOZ mandate. Sadly, similar vigilance has not always been in evidence with respect to subsequent peace agreements that the UN has been asked to implement—for example, the 1999 Lomé Accord on Sierra Leone—with predictable consequences.

In Mozambique, the UN was the locomotive moving the entire process forward. It presided over the strong political structure established by the general peace agreement, which included various commissions with genuine decisionmaking power. The main body was the Supervision and Monitoring Commission, chaired by the SRSG. It was composed of the two parties and an international membership that was expanded from the peace agreement, namely, France, Germany, Italy, Portugal, Britain, the United States, and the Organization of African Unity (OAU). The commission was empowered to act on all matters related to the implementation of the peace agreement.

The SRSG made full use of all the powers accorded to him by the peace agreement and the UN's lead role. Occasionally he was accused of exceeding his remit, but he interpreted his mandate broadly to ensure that ONUMOZ took the initiative early on and kept it firmly until the end of the mission. The UN had to drive events, not be driven by them. This proactive posture kept the process on track, reducing the capacity of the parties to induce delay and attribute the responsibility to others.

Although on most counts a model arrangement, the general peace agreement was plagued by an unrealistic timetable. According to the original plan, deployment of UN forces was to take place within a few weeks, demobilization within a few months, and elections in one year. In reality, it took seven months to deploy the UN military contingent. Protracted and difficult negotiations were necessary for the full demobilization of government and Renamo troops and for the formation of the new, unified army. Two years rather than one were required before elections could be held.

There was some criticism in the media and elsewhere of these delays, in particular the lag between the approval of the ONUMOZ mandate in December 1992 and its deployment to full strength in May 1993. But the initial delays provided needed breathing space for resolving difficulties faced by the parties—for example, Renamo's lack of qualified officials to participate in the peace commissions and the government's misgivings about ceding some of its sovereignty to the peace operation. During this period, ONUMOZ was able to lay the groundwork for smooth implementation of the peace agreement when the time was ripe. Every peace process has its own dynamic, and the role of the facilitator is to move forward in sync with it while discouraging frivolous delay. It is not to impose often experimental but arbitrary formulas developed thousands of kilometers away.

Fortunately, the Security Council proved to be flexible and pragmatic regarding the timetable. Excellent communication, coordination, and feedback between the SRSG and local ambassadors of Council members in the field helped. So did the positive disposition and confidence in local UN actors of the Council in New York. There is often a tension between allowing substantive criteria to dictate timetables and the need for the pressure of timetables to encourage the parties to fulfill their obligations. In the case of Mozambique, this tension was managed effectively and in general encouraged a climate of compliance by the parties. With the connivance of the Security Council, the SRSG was able to induce greater cooperation by using the threat of deadlines and the prospect of withdrawal of the UN operation. This leverage was enhanced by the confidence he had that the Council, within reason, would agree to extend deadlines to accommodate legitimate difficulties and concerns of the parties in meeting their obligations. The challenge was to extract maximum cooperation from the parties before agreeing to allow for more time. On Mozambique, despite the knowledge that the timetable agreed to in Rome was unworkable in practice, the Council did not formally agree to a substantial extension of the ONUMOZ mandate until halfway through the peace process, in November 1993, when it passed Resolution 882. And it only did so after major logjams were broken on demobilization and the electoral process.[6]

Local Coordination of Strategy and the Engineering of Security Council Engagement

Early on, the SRSG initiated coordination of strategy and policy with the Maputo-based diplomatic community, particularly ambassadors of Security Council countries. This approach geared toward presenting a united front not only to the parties but also to the Council in New York. In particular, it served to "engineer" the engagement of the Council at key junctures in the process and to elicit decisions from it that supported the SRSG's strategy. During the life of ONUMOZ, the Council adopted nine resolutions and issued four presidential statements, as well as frequent presidential press statements, all of which served a variety of purposes. These included extensions or modifications to the ONUMOZ mandate and expressions of concern over cease-fire violations, delays in assembly and demobilization of troops, and the formation of the new armed forces. These Council pronouncements ranged from generalized calls for more cooperative behavior by the parties to highly focused entreaties to resolve specific issues. Other Council activities, such as the holding of informal consultations to discuss problems in the peace process, were also important in influencing the attitude of the parties. These actions were designed to be supportive of the SRSG's decisions and the positions he took toward the parties. The impetus for them came largely from the SRSG with the support of the local ambassadors. His systematic cultivation of relations with the Council contributed to making it responsive to his initiatives.

This approach proved helpful in confronting one of the early challenges he faced, namely, establishing the political structure foreseen in the general peace agreement. Renamo was ill-prepared to participate as a full partner in this process. Its office in Maputo was little more than a mailbox and had no decisionmaking power. In order to communicate with Renamo, the SRSG had to travel to the bush. Two days after arriving in Maputo on October 15, 1992, he called on Renamo leader Afonso Dhlakama at his headquarters in Maringue in central Mozambique. Dhlakama's distrust of the government was palpable. He was not prepared to make any move until a significant number of UN troops were deployed to Mozambique. He had no intention of going to Maputo or sending a delegation there until the government had provided "suitable accommodations" for him and his team.

Shortly after this encounter, Renamo launched an attack, capturing four towns. This serious incident occurred with only twenty-five UN military observers on the ground and no crisis management mechanism in place. The SRSG called a meeting with the ambassadors of France, Portugal, Italy, Britain, and the United States, which resulted in a strong statement by the Security Council expressing concern with the cease-fire violations and calling on the parties to cooperate with the SRSG.[7] With this solid international backing, the latter was able to convene a meeting of the two parties and publicly urge Dhlakama to comply despite the absence of the "suitable accommodations" he demanded as a precondition.

Dhlakama, interested in obtaining international recognition, responded by sending a high-level delegation led by his de facto second in command. Within a few days, full agreement was reached on the political structure that would guide the peace process. The Supervision and Monitoring Commission was to begin functioning immediately, and instruments were provided for the management of the crisis. Soon afterward the SRSG returned to Maringue to consolidate this psychological advantage. He stressed to Dhlakama that there was little further benefit to be derived from displaying "muscle." The latter undertook to avoid further military attacks. Surprisingly to many observers, he kept his word throughout the peace process.

Two conclusions were drawn from this crisis. The first related to the importance that Dhlakama attached to recognition by the international community. Used properly, this could provide powerful leverage. The second was the value of the support of the wider diplomatic community for the SRSG and his mission, particularly when it spoke with a single voice. This unity of purpose produced two important results. First, there was no scope for either the government or Renamo to play one country against another, or against the SRSG. Second, the parties' perception of the SRSG's role changed dramatically. They subsequently viewed him not as the delegate of a remote bureaucracy in New York but as the representative of the international community. Each time the SRSG had to take a tough position against either party in order to keep the peace process on track, it was clear that he spoke on its behalf, a fact that was reinforced by strategically timed messages from the Security Council itself. And the international community, particularly the Council, did not remain an abstract entity. It was represented in person by local ambassadors who were active players in the peace process and who backed the SRSG in every important forum, whether vis-à-vis the media, in the peace commissions, or in confidential settings with the parties.

The unity of purpose of the international community and its capacity to speak with one voice in support of the SRSG resulted from hard work. He held regular briefings and consultations with the local diplomatic community, paying special attention to the international members of the Supervision and Monitoring Commission and the three permanent Council members who were part of it. They were fully involved in the decisionmaking process. No important initiative was taken by ONUMOZ without their prior agreement. Consequently, a common political analysis of the situation on the ground was reported back to capitals and to UN delegations in New York. This intensive coordination, while time-consuming, paid solid dividends of international support and translated into supportive decisions taken by the Council in New York.

A good example of this interaction was the process of regular reporting by the Secretary-General to the Security Council. According to established UN procedure, the first version of a Secretary-General's report to the Security Council on a UN peacekeeping operation is drafted by the mission in the field. In the case of ONUMOZ, the SRSG took the initiative of consulting on the early drafts among the members of the Supervision and Monitoring Commission and ensuring their prior agreement on the content. Representatives of the other Council members based in Maputo were also consulted. Particular attention was paid to the recommendations for action to be approved by the Council. These "observations" often constitute the basis for Council resolutions (or other outputs). By the time the draft reports reached New York, Council delegations had already received perspectives and instructions from their capitals, which had been briefed beforehand by their posts in Maputo. Described later by one observer as the "shadow" Security Council, the involvement of local Council ambassadors in Maputo proved unorthodox but extremely effective. With hard work and help from the UN Secretariat in New York, the final text of the Secretary-General's report generally remained unchanged from the SRSG's draft and was always consistent with needs in the field. For the subsequent Council decisions, it helped greatly that the UN Secretariat usually wrote prepared early drafts, drawing on the language of the Secretary-General's reports.

Another result of this "shadow" Security Council was the process that led to the August 1994 mission to Mozambique of Security Council members. The SRSG suggested the mission at a crucial time, when tensions between the government and ONUMOZ had been escalating dangerously. ONUMOZ had been pressuring the government to complete the demobilization of its troops in time for the elections in October 1994. Beginning around April 1994, the government started exhibiting the same reluctance to demobilize that Renamo had exhibited earlier in the peace process, albeit for different reasons. The source of the problem was the government's military leadership, which since Mozambique's independence had tended to operate beyond political control. President Joaquim Chissano was not in a position to give orders to his generals. He was, however, an extraordinarily effective mediator. Rather than ordering his generals to demobilize, he had to persuade them by mediating between the supporters of immediate demobilization and their opponents.

Unfortunately, the constituency in favor of immediate demobilization was almost nonexistent within the ruling party, the Front for the Liberation of Mozambique (Frelimo). It therefore had to be created outside of Frelimo by the international community. ONUMOZ and the international members of the Supervision and Monitoring Commission launched a campaign to denounce obstructionism by the army and put constant pressure on President Chissano and the government for immediate demobilization. This local pressure was reinforced by the Security Council, which had been kept abreast of the problem by the international actors in Maputo. Council members discussed sending a mission. When the government became aware of these deliberations, it realized that the Council was taking its obstructionism seriously. The result was a tense, confrontational atmosphere—but also a clear message that was received by the hard-liners in the army and the government. In the end, it gave Chissano the space he needed to conduct his mediation and convince the army to demobilize. The mission of Council members reinforced the united front of the international community and put the demobilization process back on track.[8] It was an early example of a technique that has since been used to good effect by the Council to influence the behavior of parties to a conflict—for example, when it dispatched a mission to Indonesia in 1999 to obtain Jakarta's consent to deployment of the International Force for East Timor (INTERFET).

Flexible Interpretation of Mandates: Demobilization and Reintegration of Soldiers

Security Council mandates tend to be drafted conservatively, at times even bureaucratically. This can pose problems for an SRSG. He or she faces the choice of either violating the mandate or overstepping it in an arbitrary way. This can create conflicts with the (military) UN force commander. Even worse, if the mandate is slavishly respected, by denying the SRSG the tools needed to fulfill the mission, failure can ensue. ONUMOZ suffered from this to a certain extent, but at the end of the day, through creativity, local innovation, cooperation from key countries including Security Council members, and the mobilization of extra resources for strategic priorities, the SRSG was able to apply an expansive interpretation to the ONUMOZ mandate to make it serve the actual needs of peacekeeping in Mozambique.

A number of innovations were tailor-made by the SRSG with the support of the local diplomatic community. An important example was the reintegration support scheme for demobilized soldiers. Under the general peace agreement, the government was to provide each demobilized soldier with six months' salary. This was obviously insufficient to cover the time necessary for their reintegration into civil society. A large number of demobilized soldiers without money or work and with easy access to weapons would have created a real risk of violence, banditry, and major disruption during the election campaign to come. To preclude such disaster, a decision was taken by the SRSG and ambassadors of donor countries to create the reintegration scheme, a trust fund combining monies from the government and the international community. The scheme provided a further eighteen months' wages to each demobilized soldier.

The reintegration support scheme was driven by the experience of Angola, where both parties had kept soldiers in reserve as a kind of insurance policy pending the outcome of elections. In Mozambique, the prospect of an additional eighteen months' salary for any demobilized soldier created a strong incentive to disarm. Fearing the loss of this benefit, the first to show up for demobilization were the very soldiers who had been held in reserve. One battalion of government soldiers nearly mutinied, demanding demobilization on the spot within twenty-four hours. The reintegration scheme played a fundamental role in preventing a return to violence and banditry, helping to create a peaceful environment throughout the electoral process. The demobilization and reintegration of more than 80,000 combatants was probably the most spectacular achievement of ONUMOZ.

Transforming Renamo into a Political Force

At the beginning of the peace process it was clear that Dhlakama wanted to keep his troops in the bush as long as possible in order to preserve his bargaining power at the negotiating table. Dhlakama's reluctance to give up his principal bargaining chip was understandable, given that the government enjoyed the many (nonmilitary) advantages of incumbency. In exchange for demobilization, Dhlakama insisted on acquiring the financial resources necessary to compete in the elections and give him some status as a political leader.

Following consultations between the SRSG, members of the Supervision and Monitoring Commission, and the major donors, it was agreed that a UN trust fund should be created to provide Renamo with the resources needed to transform itself into a political party. This initiative was highly unconventional—and even considered politically incorrect in some circles. Notwithstanding, U.S.$17.5 million was raised. Italy was the largest single donor, with important contributions from the United States, Britain, Portugal, South Africa, and the Nordic countries. Once the trust fund was established and shown to be effective, Dhlakama was ready to start demobilization. An added impetus was given by the UN Secretary-General's visit in October 1993, when Dhlakama formally agreed.

Instruments such as the reintegration support scheme and the trust fund for Renamo were essential lubricants of the peace process. They provided much-needed support for the parties to fulfill their commitments and in turn helped ONUMOZ realize its mandate.

Sticks as Well as Carrots

To bring about Renamo's demobilization, the carrot of the trust fund had to be reinforced by a stick. For Dhlakama, the UN troops in Mozambique were a safety net, a kind of alternative life insurance for him in his new role as a political rather than military leader. He also likely believed that by delaying demobilization he could push back the date for elections, thereby giving Renamo more time to increase its electoral advantage.[9] The SRSG gave the Renamo leader the choice of delaying demobilization but having elections without the guarantee of UN troops, because the international community would not bear the high cost of them indefinitely (the military component was the single most costly element of ONUMOZ). If demobilization did not start in early 1994, the SRSG threatened to advise the Security Council to begin withdrawing UN troops. He ensured that this threat was substantiated by the Security Council, which began to press for a reduction in the number of UN troops in Mozambique. This pressure mounted with the Council's agreement to increase the civilian police component of ONUMOZ by 1,000, the cost of which would have to be offset by troop reductions. On February 23, 1994, the Security Council passed Resolution 898, authorizing the enhanced civilian police deployment. The Council also called on the Secretary-General to prepare a proposal for the gradual drawdown of ONUMOZ military personnel and for the full withdrawal of UN troops after the elections. The resolution also insisted that the elections be held no later than October 1994.

Material Support of Third Countries: Training the New Armed Forces

In addition to the trust funds, another area where direct involvement and material support by third countries proved vital was in the formation of the new, unified armed forces of Mozambique. During the peace negotiations, observer countries France, Portugal, and Britain had agreed to assist in the formation and training of the new army and duly provided military trainers and equipment.

Creating a new army composed of former warring factions was a fundamental element of the peace agreement and a necessary confidence-building measure. It had to remain viable throughout the peace process, particularly as a way of managing what was initially expected to be a significant number of combatants who would not opt for demobilization. The promise of the new army was also a key condition, particularly for the government, for allowing troops to be demobilized. For the better part of the peace process, the government continued to insist on a 30,000-strong army, despite the challenges encountered in establishing the necessary facilities. Without the support of outsiders, the new army would not have been an option given the Mozambican government's incapacity to pay for it. (As it turned out, it proved to be impossible to find enough volunteers to reach the proposed strength because of the overwhelming desire of war-weary combatants to return to civilian life.)

Elections

Coordination between the SRSG and the international community remained crucial right until the last major crisis, when on the eve of the elections

Dhlakama made the dramatic announcement that Renamo would not participate. He had become convinced that the government was planning massive
electoral fraud. His suspicion of a wider conspiracy peaked during the summit of the Frontline States in Harare on October 25, 1994. Dhlakama had
been invited by President Robert Mugabe of Zimbabwe to address the summit, but Chissano blocked his participation. The summit communiqué was
clear and tough. It called on Renamo to accept the results of the elections or
face "appropriate measures," including military intervention if necessary.
No mention was made of elections being free and fair.

Dhlakama now believed that neighboring countries and the wider international community were ready to sanction electoral fraud to ensure the
stability of the region and preserve their investment in the peace process.
Just after Renamo's withdrawal from the elections was announced, the
SRSG reached Dhlakama by phone in a bid to change his mind. Sounding
firm in his resolve, Dhlakama expressed confidence that the international
community would "understand" his decision.

Once again, Dhlakama's desire for international recognition provided
the key to resolving the crisis. During several crucial hours, the diplomatic
corps in Maputo worked with the SRSG to mobilize as many leaders as
possible to send an unequivocal message to Dhlakama that the international
community did *not* understand his decision and that he was losing all the
credit he had built up over the past two years. Messages were obtained
from the Secretary-General and the Security Council urging Dhlakama to
reconsider his decision to withdraw.[10] That night at 2:00 A.M., Dhlakama
said he was ready to participate in the elections on the condition that every
complaint presented by Renamo would be fully investigated and the elections nullified if any significant fraud was uncovered. A declaration to that
effect was drafted during the night and signed the morning after. The crisis
was resolved. The elections took place in an exemplary way. The result was
accepted by all, and a few weeks later Chissano was inaugurated as the first
democratically elected president of Mozambique. The mandate of ONU-
MOZ was over, and the mission was successfully accomplished.

Conclusion

The decisive factor in the success of ONUMOZ was the strong desire for
peace of both parties. Without it, efforts by outsiders could only go so far.
Even more robust operations have their limits, if the parties are willing or
able to pursue military options. This was not the case in Mozambique,
where both the government and Renamo were spent forces. Unlike in
Angola, they lacked independent sources of revenue for waging war.

Nevertheless, peacekeeping in a relatively permissive environment
such as Mozambique still requires the dedication of the necessary

resources. In the case of ONUMOZ, those resources were provided. ONU-MOZ benefited from the failure in Angola and other operations in Africa where fewer resources had been applied to tougher situations. The peace operation was of a sufficient size (just more than 7,000 troops at its peak) and quality to build confidence and serve as a deterrent. There was also the political will to provide supplementary resources for expedients such as the trust funds. The other key lesson from Angola that was rigorously applied in Mozambique by the Council was the absolute imperative of demilitarization before elections, even if it entailed significant delays in the implementation timetable (and increased costs for the international community).

The strong UN-led political structure established to manage and drive the peace process was also critical. It gave the parties an equal role in the decisionmaking process, thereby reducing the advantage of the ruling party. It provided an added confidence-building measure.

The active engagement and coordination of the international community both locally and at the level of the Security Council are vital. The SRSG should view such coordination as an essential part of his or her mandate. In Mozambique, the SRSG worked to make the Council responsive to his needs and priorities, calling on it a number of times for reinforcement, and knew that it was available in reserve if he needed to invoke its added weight. The Council's responsiveness gave him the authority he needed to succeed. The situation in Mozambique proved fertile for such direct engagement by the Security Council and the wider international community. This was due in the case of the government to its near total dependence on foreign aid. For Renamo, the desire for recognition by the international community as it sought to assert itself as a serious political player in Mozambique's future was the key factor. Such dynamics should be exploited more fully by the Security Council in other contexts.

ONUMOZ succeeded despite no major power, whether from the region, the permanent five, or another important country, taking a leadership role in the operation either as a troop contributor or as a political patron. Subsequent operations, such as the UN Mission in Sierra Leone (UNAMSIL) or the UN Transitional Administration in East Timor (UNTAET), depended on the vital contributions of single nations, respectively Britain and Australia. In the case of Mozambique, a different constellation emerged. Although no single country drove the process, it was closely accompanied by a concert of sympathetic powers, including Italy (from the outset, as one of the mediators together with the Saint Egidio community), France, Portugal, Britain, and the United States (first as observers of the Rome negotiations and later as members of the Supervision and Monitoring Commission). Germany joined the Supervision and Monitoring Commission later. This idiosyncratic formula was in part the result of the unconventional means by which the Mozambique peace effort started, namely, joint mediation by Saint Egidio and the Italian government.[11] Each participating country placed its political and diplomatic assets at the disposal initially of the mediation effort and later of the UN operation. A number of them made substantial material and financial contributions, particularly Italy, which provided the first infantry battalion to ONUMOZ and the major contribution to the Renamo trust fund (in addition to its vital role during the prior peace negotiations). In-kind assistance from Portugal, France, and Britain was critical to the formation of the new armed forces. ONUMOZ benefited from a high level of cooperation from and between these countries.[12] Of vital importance was the favorable disposition and unity of purpose of Security Council permanent members France, Britain, and the United States. Their investment and stake in the Mozambique peace process were key to securing meaningful Council engagement in support of ONUMOZ.

The absence of direct national interest and influence of a single power may have contributed to ONUMOZ's success. This situation created the space the SRSG needed to play the central peacekeeping and peacebuilding role. He was able to conduct the peace operation with the cooperation and active support of several influential countries. Equally, however, he was able to do so without undue influence of any political, economic, or other agendas on their part.

After Mozambique, the experience of UN peacekeeping in Africa suggests that a similarly favorable convergence of circumstances may not soon materialize. The Council's acceptance of risk in Mozambique has been replaced by deep risk aversion born of UN failures in Africa and Europe and other factors documented elsewhere in this volume, although the UN Organization Mission in the Democratic Republic of Congo (MONUC) is a brave undertaking. Today, other security challenges dominate the international agenda and divert attention from African conflicts, with the risk that Africa could become what one African observer has called the world's "strategic ghetto."

Nevertheless, many of the innovations tried with success by ONUMOZ can and should be used in other peacekeeping contexts. The decisions taken by the Security Council about which peacekeeping challenges to take on and which to avoid need to be informed by the accumulated experience. Once the decision to become engaged has been taken, the lessons of both the successes and the failures need to be applied.

Notes

1. For two books on the UN Peacekeeping Mission in Mozambique, see Richard Synge, *Mozambique: UN Peacekeeping in Action, 1992–1994* (Washington, D.C.: USIP, 1997); and Dennis C. Jett, *Why Peacekeeping Fails* (Houndmills, UK: Palgrave, 2000).

2. Ibid., p. 26.

3. The need for a UN success in Africa was expressed to the Mozambican parties emphatically by Secretary-General Boutros-Ghali during his visit to Mozambique in October 1993. He raised the specter of Angola and appealed to the parties to avoid that tragic scenario.

4. For an authoritative study of the Rome negotiations, see Cameron Hume, *Ending Mozambique's War* (Washington, D.C.: U.S. Institute of Peace, 1994).

5. Ibid., p. 94.

6. The agreements between the parties on electoral and demobilization issues had been the subject of protracted negotiations that necessitated a visit by the Secretary-General on October 17–20, 1993. Renamo's cooperation required guarantees from the SRSG that the trust fund to transform the rebel movement into political party would become operational promptly.

7. Statement by the president of the Security Council, S/24719, October 27, 1992.

8. For a report of the results of the Security Council mission, see *United Nations: The United Nations in Mozambique*, United Nations Blue Book Series (New York: United Nations, 1995), pp. 258–267.

9. See Alex Vines, *Renamo: From Terrorism to Democracy in Mozambique?* (London: James Currey, 1996), p. 148.

10. United Nations, *The United Nations and Mozambique*, p. 285.

11. See Hume, *Ending Mozambique's War.*

12. For an excellent discussion of peacekeeping cooperation between France, Britain, and the United States, see Mats Berdal, "American, French, and British Peacekeeping in Africa after the Cold War," in Oliver Furley and Roy May, eds., *Peacekeeping in Africa* (London: Ashgate, 1998), pp. 49–71.

30

Bosnia

Mats Berdal

The Security Council's handling of the war in Bosnia between 1992 and 1995 remains one of the most controversial of all its efforts to deal with violent conflict in the international system after the Cold War. In spite of numerous resolutions and the presence of a large-scale peacekeeping force on the ground, a savage and merciless war persisted, albeit at varying levels of intensity, for more than three years. When the war finally did come to an end, it was only after a bloody denouement that included the fall, at a terrible cost in human lives, of what the Council had earlier designated the "safe area" of Srebrenica.

This chapter examines the Security Council's approach to the war, the positions taken by key member states, and the consequences that flowed from actions taken, as well as some of those not taken, by the Council as a whole. To this end, the chapter is framed around two central questions: What were the driving factors behind Council decisionmaking and how did the cumulative impact of its decisions influence the nature of the UN's activities on the ground? Why did the central issue of the use of military force prove so divisive within the Council?

May 1995: A Vignette and Argument in Brief

In May 1995, as Bosnia and Herzegovina (hereafter Bosnia) was rapidly returning to a state of full-scale war, the commander of UN forces for the whole of the former Yugoslavia, General Bernard Janvier, was preparing to leave his headquarters in Zagreb for New York. The Council was awaiting a report from the Secretary-General, Boutros Boutros-Ghali, on the state of the UN's mission, and Janvier was scheduled to brief its members.[1] On the eve of his trip he received an assessment from his commander in Sarajevo, General Rupert Smith, on the immediate challenges facing UN forces in Bosnia. Noting how matters had deteriorated since the collapse of the fragile cease-fire negotiated by former president Jimmy Carter in late 1994, and convinced that "both sides intend to fight to a solution," Smith carefully spelled out three possible options for the UN force: muddle on, a "stronger military response," or withdrawal. The first and last of these were not, he assumed, realistic options. As for the second, he candidly identified, as he had on previous occasions, the implications it carried for the Security Council. He wrote that it would have to answer "the fundamental question of whether the UN should enforce and escalate for aims other than self-defence." It would take two more months and many more deaths before key Council members, as well as many of the countries providing troops to UN in Bosnia, were prepared seriously to confront Smith's question. And even then, it was only because events meant doing so could no longer be post-poned.

Smith's letter to Janvier in May 1995 points to a basic political reality of the period between 1992 and the summer of 1995 that does much to explain why the Bosnian war came to represent such a sorry chapter in the Council's history: throughout this period key Council members proved unable to forge a common *strategic* purpose that went beyond a limited set of objectives on which they could all agree. The tireless pursuit of more easily agreed-upon goals—including the provision of humanitarian relief and other efforts to mitigate and contain the conflict—should not be dismissed as insignificant or entirely wasted. They did not, however, provide strategic direction for a large-scale military force that was plainly configured for peacekeeping of a traditional kind but that was operating in an environment where, for much of the time, there was no peace to keep. Operationally, the absence of such direction and the reactive nature of Council decisionmaking had the effect of generating ever more conflicting demands on UN forces in the field, to the point, when Janvier set off to brief the Council in May 1995, of near paralysis.

The political compromises and divisions among permanent and non-permanent members of the Council that gave rise to this state of affairs were a source of deep and growing frustration among UN officials, both in New York and at the subordinate headquarters in the field. This was particularly true with respect to Bosnia, the focus of this chapter. The failure to halt the war and, with it, mounting evidence of cruelty and barbarism produced an increasing number of resolutions—a majority of them adopted under Chapter VII of the UN Charter—aimed at demonstrating resolve rather than confronting the substantive but deeply divisive issues at the heart of the conflict. Starting with Resolution 713 in September 1991, which placed an arms embargo on the whole of the former Yugoslavia, and ending with Resolution 1021, welcoming the signing of the Dayton Accords, the Security Council passed eighty-three resolutions relating to the former Yugoslavia. This impressive number did not, however, reflect any agreement on the causes of the conflict, the wider issues at stake, and how best to address them. Until the summer of 1995, member states proved fundamentally unwilling to reconfigure the mission and provide the resources necessary for operations other than peacekeeping.

The Limits of Involvement:
The Security Council and Bosnia, March 1992–July 1995

The war in Bosnia began in late March 1992, when fighting broke out between Croat forces, supported by recently formed Muslim militias, and Serb paramilitaries near the strategically important Posavina corridor, which linked Serb-inhabited strongholds in northern Bosnia with Serbia proper. Bosnian Serbs, unwilling to accept the prospect of minority status within an independent Bosnia, had boycotted a referendum on independence held in late February. (Croatia and Slovenia had been recognized by the European Community [EC] on January 15, 1992.) The war intensified dramatically after the formal recognition of Bosnia by the EC on April 6, 1992. Over the course of the next three months, a murderous onslaught by Serb paramilitary forces, aided by the Yugoslav army, resulted in Bosnian Serb forces securing control of more than 60 percent of the territory of the newly recognized republic. That figure remained fairly constant until the military campaigns in the summer of 1995.

At the recommendation of the UN Secretariat and following a fact-finding mission to the region by Marrack Goulding, Undersecretary-General in charge of UN peacekeeping, the Security Council initially decided against the deployment of a peacekeeping force to the country, accepting the argument that "in its present phase" the conflict was not "susceptible to the UN peacekeeping treatment."[2] Moreover, by this time, in mid-May 1992, UN peacekeepers were already deployed, and running into difficulties and criticism, in neighboring Croatia.[3]

As the full extent of the conflict in Bosnia and its humanitarian consequences became ever more apparent in the summer of 1992, pressures on the Council to act and for the UN to become more directly involved intensified. Thus, on September 14, 1992, the Council, adopting Resolution 776, formally authorized the enlargement of the UN Protection Force (UNPROFOR, the acronym initially given to the UN force in Croatia) to support the efforts of the UN high commissioner for refugees (UNHCR) to deliver humanitarian relief throughout Bosnia on the basis of "normal" peacekeeping principles. By late autumn 1992 the overall objectives for the former Yugoslavia on which Council members were able to agree, and which would continue to define the common ground for Council action until summer 1995, had crystallized. These were threefold: first, relieving as far as possible the human suffering caused by the wars, initially by operating the

Sarajevo airport and by protecting UNHCR convoys; second, containing the conflict to the territories of the former Yugoslavia; and third, facilitating the efforts of the warring parties themselves to reach a political settlement. In the course of the mission, the mandate evolved and new tasks were added onto existing ones, yet the deployment of UN troops remained geared toward the achievement of these three basic purposes.

The limited and reactive nature of these goals reflected disagreements among member states about the origins and the nature of the conflict, disagreements that had been evident during the war in Croatia the previous year and that became more acute as the conflict wore on. Yet as David Hannay was later to write, initially at least, one point united them all: a "determination not to be drawn into the fighting themselves."[4]

In the case of the UK, which came to provide the largest number of peacekeepers on the ground in Bosnia, the initial decision to send troops was pushed through a deeply reluctant cabinet by Prime Minister John Major and his foreign secretary, Douglas Hurd. The "determination not to be drawn into the fighting" was, if anything, more pronounced in the United States and became even more so after the debacle in Somalia in the autumn of 1993.

As the war in Bosnia continued, an increasing number of member states, notably the United States, Germany, and several prominent members of the nonaligned caucus, questioned the wisdom and the viability of the initial assumptions on which UN involvement had been based. Yet the Council and other troop-contributing countries displayed little or no willingness to move toward taking enforcement action. Nor did the United States or Germany suggest they might provide troops for such action themselves. In short, UNPROFOR remained a "peacekeeping" mission—lightly equipped, widely dispersed, and vulnerable—in the midst of an ongoing war. The result was an ever-widening list of Council resolutions and presidential statements aimed at addressing specific contingencies arising in the field and adopted under Chapter VII of the Charter, with a view not to enforcing or imposing a solution but to demonstrating resolve. As the war dragged on, conflicting pressures on UNPROFOR—urged to take more forceful action, though without changing the peacekeeping basis of its mandate—only intensified.

Consequences of Council Action: U.S.-European Tensions and the "Safe Areas" Regime

The establishment of the "safe areas" regime in Bosnia in May and June 1993 provides the clearest example of how tensions within the Council and among member states ushered in decisions that were ultimately to have catastrophic consequences on the ground. In the spring and summer of 1993, against the backdrop of a major Bosnian Serb offensive in eastern Bosnia, the Council passed a series of resolutions conferring safe-area status on the towns of Sarajevo, Tuzla, Zepa, Gorazde, Bihac, and Srebrenica.[5] The critical resolution—836, passed on June 4, 1993, under Chapter VII of the Charter—extended the mandate of UNPROFOR to enable it "to deter attacks against the safe areas" and decided that member states, "acting nationally or through regional organisations or arrangements, may take, under the authority of the Security Council . . . all necessary measures, through the use of air power, in and around the safe areas in the Republic of Bosnia and Herzegovina, to support UNPROFOR in the performance of its mandate."[6] The tough wording notwithstanding, to the sponsors of the resolution, France and Britain, 836 did not signify any commitment actually to "protect" or "defend" the designated areas.[7] Although their establishment was intended to address an increasingly desperate situation on the ground, London and Paris were also responding to other pressures. In particular, the creation of safe areas served to forestall growing pressure from the new U.S. administration for the adoption of a "lift and strike" policy—that is, for a partial lifting of the arms embargo as it applied to the Bosnian government combined with air strikes against Bosnian Serb targets throughout Bosnia. Pressures for more forceful action against the Bosnian Serbs did not, however, come only from the United States. The nonaligned caucus, represented by Venezuela and Pakistan, which were then on the Council, also played a key role in the actions and decisions that led to the creation of the safe-area regime (in the end, though, both countries chose to abstain on Resolution 836).

The implementation of the safe-area concept soon ran into major difficulties as, initially, few countries offered to make *additional* troops available to meet even the "light minimum option" of 7,600 troops that had been agreed by the Council.[8] In late October 1993—more than four months after the adoption of Resolution 836—General Jean Cot, the UN force commander at the time, informed New York that "until arrival of Dutchbat [the promised Dutch battalion] in January 1994, I have no force to put into the three eastern enclaves," and that in the meantime Gorazde was only monitored by one team of UN military observers.[9]

But just as serious in the long run were the continuing tensions among key Council members about the appropriate policy toward Bosnia and, resulting from these tensions, the failure to align activities on the ground with diplomatic efforts, such as they were, aimed at reaching an overall political settlement. At the time of its adoption, Resolution 836 was justified in the only way that it could be justified: a short-term initiative to stabilize a precarious humanitarian situation and to buy time for diplomatic efforts to bear fruit. The sponsors of the resolution were not blind to what Boutros Boutros-Ghali would later refer to as the "inherent deficiencies of the safe-area regime"; yet they still hoped in May and June 1993 that a political breakthrough toward a settlement would prevent these deficiencies from becoming too acute. Madeleine Albright, U.S. permanent representative, declared that the resolution was "an intermediate step—no more, no less."[10] Ambassador Jean-Bernard Merimée, explaining France's sponsorship of the resolution, made it clear that "the designation and protection of the safe areas [was] not an end in itself, but only a temporary measure: a step towards a just and lasting political solution."[11] Yet this is precisely where progress continued to prove most elusive.

Given that UNPROFOR was already overstretched and unable to meet the expectations of the Sarajevo government, the continuation of the war meant that the disjunction between Security Council decisions and UNPROFOR activities on the ground only widened further. After the collapse of the European Union Action Plan in late 1993, the third peace plan to be presented to the parties, more than sixteen months were to pass before all three parties to the Bosnian conflict would again be present at negotiations. In the intervening period, the number of agreements, partial cease-fires, military exclusion zones, and ultimatums that UNPROFOR was given the task of supervising and monitoring—issued not just by the Security Council but now also by the North Atlantic Treaty Organization (NATO)—continued to grow. By early 1995 the remarkable list of agreements whose implementation the UN was committed to support included the Sarajevo Airport Agreement of June 1992, the Srebrenica Agreement of April 1993, the Srebrenica and Zepa Agreements of May 1993, the Mount Igman Demilitarized Zone Agreement of August 1993, the Sarajevo Airport Agreement of February 1994, the agreement on the use of civilian traffic across the Sarajevo airport of March 1994, the Gorazde Agreement of April 1994, and the Anti-Sniping Agreement of August 1994.[12] In addition to this came the commitments arising out of the cease-fire in 1994 between the Bosnian Croat and government forces in central Bosnia. And all the while, as Nicholas Morris has since perceptively observed, the humanitarian operation itself "increasingly became a factor in the political considerations of the parties to the conflict and of the international community."[13]

The deepening of tensions between the Americans, on the one hand, and European troop contributors, above all France and Britain, on the other, provides the key to understanding dynamics of Council decisionmaking following the creation of the safe-area regime. Whereas Bill Clinton as presidential candidate had promised tough military action against Bosnian Serbs and initially encouraged the view that he would deliver on his promise, the failure to make progress in the wake of Resolution 836, followed soon afterward by humiliating setbacks in Somalia and Haiti, contributed to what Ambassador Albright pointedly told a congressional committee was "a period of recalibrating our expectations."[14] The result of this process did not, however, have the effect of dampening tensions with the Europeans over Bosnia policy. Indeed, in many ways it had the very opposite effect. On the one hand, foreign policy setbacks made the Clinton administration far more sensitive to domestic and specifically congressional criticism of its Bosnia policy and thus more susceptible to domestic political pressure for "action" to be taken. On the other hand, events in Somalia in particular only reinforced a determination *not* to become involved militarily. The result was a pattern of being "in" politically and "out" militarily, which the Europeans, above all Britain, France, and to a lesser degree Russia, resented. In their view, the U.S. attitude acted as an obstacle to end the war because it provided a powerful disincentive for the parties to stop fighting. As long as none of the external powers were prepared to impose a solution by force of arms, while at the same time continuing to differ profoundly on the way forward, the warring parties would persist in seeking to obtain a decisive political or military advantage. In the second half of 1994, mounting evidence of covert U.S. support for the Bosnian-Croat federation in violation of the arms embargo only added further to the transatlantic tensions.[15] The effect of these tensions, not just on Council decisionmaking but on other efforts to bring the war to an end—notably those of the International Conference on the Former Yugoslavia (ICFY) and from April 1994 onward the Contact Group for Bosnia—were profound. As David Hannay acknowledged not long after leaving New York, the fact that a "more robust and less vulnerable policy" was not adopted in Bosnia before the summer of 1995 "was more due to the tensions between those member states with troops on the ground and those like the US without, than it was to any disembodied entity thought of as 'the UN' pursuing a policy of excessive caution."[16]

Russian and Chinese Security Council Priorities

From early 1993 onward, then, policy differences and simmering tensions between the United States on the one hand and Britain and France on the other provided the most significant fault line within the Council. This is not, of course, to suggest that London and Paris always saw eye to eye on the conflict and its management through the UN. Nor does it mean that Russia and China, the other two permanent members of the Council, had no views or interests of their own that they sought to advance within the Council chamber. It is a striking feature of both Russian and Chinese policy toward Bosnia, however, that it was driven *primarily* by considerations extraneous to the conflict itself. Put more bluntly, Russian diplomatic actions and Chinese voting behavior reflected concerns *other* than the effect that their policies might have had on the course of the conflict and the UN's involvement in it.

In the case of Russia, the critical backdrop to an understanding of its policies was the recent dissolution of the Soviet Union and Moscow's associated loss of empire. Although the dissolution itself was blissfully peaceful, the loss of superpower status was traumatic and induced within the Russian foreign policy elite an acute concern about its status as a great power alongside other Council members. Although many—including the Bosnian government in Sarajevo and influential members of the U.S. Congress—saw in Moscow's Balkan policies the influence of supposedly deeply felt and long-standing pan-Slav sentiments, there is very little evidence indicating that such sentiments shaped policy in any decisive fashion. The communist-nationalist opposition and its media outlets were often vocal in expressing support for their "Serbian brothers," but President Boris Yeltsin and Foreign Minister Andrey Kozyrev's chief priority remained focused on the perceived need to assert Russia's credentials as major power and constructive partner of the West on the international stage.[17] To this end, diplomatic initiatives (such as the effort in the spring of 1993 to save the faltering Vance-Owen plan and Vitaly Churkin's intensive shuttle diplomacy in 1994) were geared, above all, toward strengthening Russia's international standing and avoiding diplomatic marginalization. If meeting those key objectives required that relations with Russia's "Bosnian Serb brothers" be severed, then Moscow had few qualms about doing so as, indeed, events in 1994 and 1995 were to show. Insofar as Russia developed distinctive views on the *substantive* issues raised by UNPROFOR's mission in Bosnia, they tended to echo the positions of Britain and France. Still, Moscow was not deeply wedded to any particular policy or initiative and remained principally concerned about proving that it was "the diplomatic successor to the USSR not just in name but also in might and importance."[18]

Unlike Russia, China did not launch any diplomatic initiatives of its own in relation to the Bosnian conflict. Indeed, its voting behavior in the Security Council was primarily designed, through abstentions rather than vetoes, to register Chinese disquiet with the UN's growing involvement in the internal affairs of member states and, in particular, with what appeared to be an increased readiness to invoke Chapter VII with respect to humanitarian emergencies. China's anxieties about this trend led it to abstain on a large number of Chapter VII resolutions relating to Bosnia.[19] These included, inter alia, resolutions authorizing the delivery of humanitarian assistance to parts of the country and the further expansion of UNPROFOR's mandate; the decision to impose a ban on military flights over Bosnia; and the Council's demand in May 1995 for the release of UN personnel held hostage by the Bosnian Serb army. In all these cases, Chinese policy conformed to a "pattern of cautious, coherent dissent on particular issues, such as use of force, humanitarian intervention and the setting up of tribunals."[20]

China's chief priority, then, was not by its actions to influence the course of the conflict or the UN's handling of it. It was instead to express its disapproval of what it saw as the erosion, encouraged and supported by Western countries, of key Charter principles—above all, that of nonintervention in the internal affairs of member states. In doing so, China claimed to be defending the views and interests of developing countries and the nonaligned movement, though as we have seen above, what many of these countries wanted was *more* and not less intervention in Bosnia.

The Resort to Chapter VII and the Question of Use of Force

At the heart of the disagreements over the Council's handling of the war in Bosnia was the question of the use of force. Since the end of UNPROFOR's mission in 1995, several public inquiries—including one by the UN Secretariat itself as well as others ordered by national governments—into the circumstances surrounding the fall of the Srebrenica enclave in July 1995 have kept the debate on the use of force alive.[21] In essence it is a debate that has centered around one key question: Should UNPROFOR have taken *enforcement* action much earlier on in the conflict in order to impose a settlement on recalcitrant parties?

The view that UNPROFOR "failed" to take such action when in fact there was nothing to prevent it from doing so is based on a combination of two arguments: first, that UNPROFOR did not act on Chapter VII resolutions that explicitly allowed for "all necessary measures" to be used; and second, that the manner in which the parties were finally brought to the negotiating table (emphasizing, in particular, the role played by NATO's extensive use of airpower in August and September 1995) shows that a more forceful approach had always been an option. Though flawed in important respects, both arguments merit closer attention, as they highlight key aspects of the Security Council's approach to the war in Bosnia.

The Use of Chapter VII and the Bosnian Conflict

Throughout the Cold War, determining "the existence of any threat to the peace, breach of the peace or act of aggression" (Article 39 of the Charter) was not something on which the Security Council, for obvious reasons, could easily agree. For the first forty-four years of its existence, the Council adopted only twenty-two resolutions that "cited Chapter VII, or used its wording."[22] By contrast, between 1990 and 1999 the Council passed 174 Chapter VII resolutions.[23] A disproportionate number of these were adopted in relation to the conflict in the former Yugoslavia and, in particular, in relation to the war in Bosnia. As indicated elsewhere in this book, the increased resort to Chapter VII in the 1990s is suggestive of a greater willingness on the part of the "international community" to treat intrastate or internal conflict as matters of legitimate international concern and, in extreme cases, to take enforcement action in response to massive violations of human rights. Even though the Security Council has been highly selective in its commitment to address such violations, there are still good grounds for seeing the post–Cold War period as marking a normative shift in attitudes and practices toward internal conflict.

The use of Chapter VII during the war in Bosnia, however, also points to another, more instrumental reason for its frequent application, one that had little to do with any emerging consensus among member states around a broader and more permissive interpretation of threats to international peace and security. The fact is that by invoking Chapter VII the Council was often just as concerned with conveying the impression of resolve as it was with taking meaningful action on the ground. As the story of Resolution 836 illustrates only too clearly, using Chapter VII language did not mean that the Council was prepared to abandon UNPROFOR's core objectives. The circumstances surrounding the adoption of other hard-hitting resolutions, including those designed to meet concerns about security of UNPROFOR personnel and the restrictions placed on their freedom of movement by the warring parties, tell the same story.[24] The Council simply had no intention of abandoning "peacekeeping" principles in favor of enforcement.

It might still be argued, as indeed it was by critics of the UN operation at the time, that resolutions allowing for "all necessary measures" did nonetheless provide UN forces with the appropriate mandate for taking coercive action and that, ipso facto, there was nothing preventing them from doing so. The difficulty with this argument is that although it is true that the Council passed new and "tougher" resolutions authorizing the use of force, it expressly did not annul its earlier resolutions. As a result, UNPROFOR was left with the "challenge of reconciling its authority to use force with its obligation to perform all the other tasks mandated by the Security Council—tasks which required the co-operation of, and deployment amongst, all parties to conflict."[25]

The Use of Force in 1995:
Abandoning Peacekeeping in Favor of Enforcement

The NATO-led military campaign against Bosnian Serb forces, involving the extensive use of airpower and artillery over a two-week period in late August and early September 1995, played an important role in bringing about the conditions that allowed for the establishment of a permanent cease-fire and for an overall settlement to the conflict in Bosnia. The campaign and the events surrounding it, however, have given rise to many myths, encouraged in part by the self-serving and less-than-accurate accounts provided by some of the actors involved at the time.[26] Perhaps the most persistent myth has been that it was coercive airpower *alone* that forced the Bosnian Serbs to the negotiating table and that the failure to use airpower in this fashion earlier in the conflict had needlessly prolonged the war. The belief of Western leaders in March 1999 that the "short, sharp shock" of an air campaign would rapidly lead Slobodan Milosevic to cave in and abandon his repressive policies in Kosovo reflected this particular reading of the way in which the war in Bosnia had been brought to an end. Reality, as is so often the case, was more complex. The significance of Operation Deliberate Force—the name given to the military operation against the Bosnian Serb army in 1995—can be assessed only in conjunction with several other developments that, in the summer and early autumn of 1995, *combined* to create conditions that until then had not existed for the effective application of military force.

The first of these was the weakening of the military position of the Bosnian Serbs and the loss of their ability to hold vulnerable UN forces ransom. Reaching this stage, however, involved a process that began well before the NATO-led air campaign in late August and early September. Specifically, the spectacular success of Croat military offensives, first in Sector West (one of the UN's "protected areas" in Croatia) in May 1995, and later in the Krajina region in August, had dramatically altered the strategic predicament of the Bosnian Serbs. The Croat offensives, supported and strongly encouraged by the United States and resulting in a massive displacement of Croatian Serbs, were one of the preconditions for the effective use of force by NATO and the UN in September. So was the withdrawal of UNPROFOR troops from exposed and indefensible positions in Bosnian Serb–controlled territory, a process that started in June with the removal of UN peacekeepers from the weapon collection points around Sarajevo and Gorazde and completed with the stealthy withdrawal of British troops from Gorazde on the eve of Operation Deliberate Force in late August. In the meantime, the other two eastern enclaves of Srebrenica and Zepa had, at a terrible cost in human lives, fallen to Bosnian Serbian forces. The removal of troops from vulnerable and isolated locations, a policy actively pursued by General Rupert Smith after the "hostage crisis" in late May 1995, significantly reduced the scope for politically paralyzing action on the part of the Bosnian Serb leadership in the event of renewed crisis. In yet another development, British and French forces deployed a rapid reaction force to Bosnia in June and July, providing for the very first time mortar and artillery support on Mount Igman near Sarajevo. This gave UN forces a capability that had hitherto been lacking. A final, though crucial factor preparing the ground for a more forceful military action was the agreement, reached only after the disaster of Srebrenica in July 1995, to simplify command and control arrangements for the use of NATO airpower in support of UN forces. Significantly, the agreement, enshrined in a memorandum of understanding between the Commander in Chief, Allied Forces Southern Europe (CINCSOUTH), and the UN force commander held that the conditions triggering "graduated air operations" would now be "determined by the common judgement of NATO and UN military commanders."[27]

Taken together, the combined effect of these developments was to prepare the ground for the second option outlined by General Smith in his letter to Janvier in May: a deliberate transition from peacekeeping to *enforcement* action or, more precisely, war-fighting. Thus the necessary steps, which until then had been consistently rejected by the Security Council and troop-contributing countries, were finally taken. It signaled a definite break with the efforts of UN forces over the previous three years to maintain neutrality and impartiality in relation to the parties.

It is important to stress that this move to enforcement and the enabling steps that made it possible did not come about as a result of any carefully considered and deliberate strategy agreed by Council members. At the time, it was not at all clear, for example, whether the rapid reaction force was designed to cover the withdrawal of UN troops from Bosnia or whether it was intended to give UN forces a war-fighting capability. Certainly, the British government was anxious not to raise expectations about the effect of their reinforcements and continued to stress the need for "local consent" and adherence to "peacekeeping principles." When European Union (EU) and NATO ministers and their chiefs of staff met in Paris on June 3, 1995, during the hostage crisis, they also reaffirmed that UNPROFOR's "mission was not to enforce a solution by military force, but to operate in support of the peace process, to ensure essential humanitarian aid to the civilian population and to monitor cease-fire concluded between belligerents."[28] The problem was that, by this time, these objectives had simply ceased to have much meaning on the ground. The stark reality of the situation was more honestly spelled out by Rupert Smith in a note, prepared a few days after the meeting of EU and NATO ministers, for Yasushi Akashi, special representative of the Secretary-General, and other senior UNPROFOR officials. Reviewing various reinforcement plans for UNPROFOR then being discussed, he concluded: "we face a simple but difficult choice between being prepared to fight and escalate or not. Attempts at finding a middle ground are doomed to disappointment and possibly disaster when standing in middle of someone else's war."[29] In an effort to break the stalemate and avert possible "disaster," General Smith and his staff in Sarajevo had, in the late winter and early spring of 1995, worked on and developed a detailed plan for the forceful replenishment by air of the besieged enclaves in eastern

Bosnia. Anticipating, soon after his arrival in the country, that the situation in the eastern enclaves—especially in Srebrenica and Zepa—was likely to deteriorate in the coming months, General Smith authorized planning to proceed for a helicopter resupply operation. The purpose of the plan, finalized in late April and greeted with skepticism by UN officials in Zagreb and New York, was expressly "to seek to face down General Mladic, by carrying out a notified helicopter resupply with armed escorts and NATO air support with the clear intention of reacting violently to any interference."[30] In other words, the plan was designed to confront the Bosnian Serb army and, as such, could be undertaken, as Smith fully recognized and told his superiors, only if troop-contributing countries were prepared not only to risk the loss of aircraft but also to escalate for aims other than self-defense. Enthusiasm for the concept in the capitals and among the major troop-contributing countries, when they were first sounded out in April, was decidedly mixed. Crucially, key Security Council members, notably the UK, were unsupportive. In the end, the plan was overtaken by events on the ground, and in the aftermath of the hostage crisis it was effectively shelved. "Muddling on" remained, for a few more fateful weeks, the preferred option.

Conclusion

The divided, hesitant, and largely reactive nature of the response by the "international community" to the disintegration of Yugoslavia provides the essential backdrop against which the history of UN operations in the Balkans must be viewed. The divisions were mirrored in the decisions and actions of the Security Council. There was a certain paradox in this: as the gradual but inexorable collapse of Yugoslavia gathered pace in the late 1980s and early 1990s, optimism about the UN's post–Cold war role in the field of peace and security reached its peak. As Boutros-Ghali put it in *An Agenda for Peace*—a report commissioned by the Council a few months before the explosion of violence in Bosnia—the "organisation must never again be crippled as it was in the era that has now passed."[31] That kind of optimism rested crucially on the belief that the Security Council, no longer at the mercy of East-West rivalry, would "finally" be able to assume the role originally envisaged for it. It was a belief that was reinforced by the Council's response to Iraq's invasion of Kuwait in August 1990. That case, however, was unique: one state had invaded and annexed another; it could hardly be more clear-cut. Bosnia—and on this the Council did agree—was very different.

More than any other conflict in the 1990s, the war in Bosnia and the UN's handling of it helped shatter the optimism that characterized early debates about the likely impact of the end of the Cold War for the UN's peace and security role. In particular, it brought home that civil wars—or, more precisely in the case of the former Yugoslavia, conflicts that could not easily be categorized as either internal or international in nature—posed unique challenges for the Council. However, such conflicts, by their very nature, often raise issues on which consensus for action will always be difficult to obtain. How, for example, when multiethnic entities look set to collapse does one reconcile the principle of self-determination with the principle that borders should not be changed by use of force? Yet the attitudes of individual states toward conflicts of this kind—and this was certainly the case for key European countries in relation to Bosnia—are bound to be colored by historical memories, fears, and considerations of national interest. At the same time, a large number of other states, whose views China has often claimed to represent on the Council, have continued to express grave misgivings about intervening *at all* in internal conflicts. In a broader sense, therefore, the war in Bosnia undermined the belief, surprisingly widespread in the early 1990s, that the end of the Cold War also signaled the end of conflicts of interest and value among member states of the UN. If this was indeed one casualty of the UN's involvement, it is perhaps not one to be mourned. The belief was always misplaced, as the history of the Council since has regularly demonstrated.

This is not to suggest that the Council cannot or should not continue to be regarded as a preeminent forum for the discussion, management, and, when circumstances permit, orchestration of collective responses to problems of international security. To do that effectively, another important lesson will need to be drawn from the Council's Bosnia experience, namely, that there are real dangers of allowing disunity and tensions among member states to fester over an extended period, especially if the organization is, at the same time, being asked to take on peacekeeping or, more ambitiously but much less likely after Bosnia, enforcement tasks. Whether that lesson has been fully absorbed is still far from clear.

Notes

This chapter draws in part from Mats Berdal, "The United Nations in Bosnia, 1992-95: Faithful Scapegoat to the World?" in J. Krasno, B. Hayes, and D. Daniel, eds., *Leveraging for Success in UN Peace Operations* (Westport, CT: Praeger, 2003).
    1. For the purpose of this chapter, "UNPROFOR" refers only to the UN operation in Bosnia and Herzegovina, even though, technically speaking, it was only in March 1995 that the name came to be associated exclusively with the UN presence in that country. At the same time, the UN mission in Croatia was renamed UNCRO (UN Confidence Restoration Operation in Croatia), and the UN force in Macedonia was given the name of UNPREDEP (UN Preventive Deployment Force). For details, see Resolutions 981, 982, and 983.
    2. *Report of the Secretary-General,* S/23900, May 12, 1992; and Resolution

752, May 15, 1992. For a personal account of the trip and the events surrounding it, see Marrack Goulding, *Peacemonger* (London: John Murray, 2002), pp. 311–315.

3. Under Resolution 743, adopted February 21, 1992, a UN force was mandated to create three UN "protected areas" in Croatia.

4. David Hannay, "The UN's Role in Bosnia Assessed," *Oxford International Review* 7, no. 2 (Spring 1996): 5. Hannay served as UK permanent representative in New York throughout the conflict.

5. See Resolutions 819, 824, and 836 of May and June 1993.

6. Resolution 836, June 4, 1993, paras. 5, 9.

7. "Subject: Implementation of Security Council SCR 836 (1993)—"Safe Areas" in Bosnia and Herzegovina, To: Stoltenberg, Zagreb for Wahlgren, From: K. Annan," UN Headquarters, June 7, 1993.

8. Iran offered 10,000 troops or "a complete mechanised division," an offer that was politely turned down!

9. From Force Commander Jean Cot to Secretary-General Kofi Annan, October 24, 1993. Annan, in his reply, informed Cot that by the time the Dutch battalion deploys "you will have 5,010 troops of the authorised strength of 7,600 all ranks."

10. *Debate*, S/PV3228, June 4, 1993, in D. Bethlehem and Marc Weller, eds., *The "Yugoslav" Crisis in International Law: General Issues*, pt. 1 (Cambridge: Cambridge University Press, 1996), p. 295.

11. Ibid., p. 287.

12. *Cessation of Hostilities Agreement*, December 31, 1994, para. 6.

13. Nicholas Morris, "Humanitarian Action in the Balkans," draft chapter to appear in Jennifer M. Welsh, ed., *Humanitarian Intervention and International Relations* (Oxford: Oxford University Press, 2004). Morris was special envoy of the UNHCR for the former Yugoslavia in 1993–1994.

14. *Statement of Ambassador M. Albright*, Hearing Before the Subcommittee on International Security, International Organizations, and Human Rights of the Committee on Foreign Affairs, House of Representatives, 103rd Congress, May 17, 1994, p. 8.

15. Resolution 713, September 25, 1991. For details on the violations of the arms embargo, see Brendan O'Shea, *Crisis at Bihac: Bosnia's Bloody Battlefield* (Gloucestershire: Sutton Publishing, 1998).

16. Hannay, "The UN's Role in Bosnia Assessed," p. 9.

17. Christina von Siemens, "Russia's Policy Towards the War in Bosnia-Herzegovina (1992–1995)," M.Phil. diss., University of Oxford, April 2001, p. 54.

18. Ibid., p. 33.

19. Sally Morphet, "China as a Permanent Member of the Security Council: October 1971–December 1999," *Security Dialogue* 31, no.2 (June 2000): 154.

20. Ibid., p. 161.

21. For the report by the UN Secretariat, see *Report of the Secretary-General Pursuant to General Assembly Resolution 53/35: The Fall of Srebrenica*, A/54/549, November 15, 1999.

22. Sydney D. Bailey and Sam Daws, *The Procedure of the UN Security Council*, 3rd ed. (Oxford: Clarendon, 1998), p. 273.

23. Morphet, "China as a Permanent Member," p. 154.

24. See Resolutions 807 and 847.

25. Shashi Tharoor, "Should UN Peacekeeping Go 'Back to Basics'?" *Survival* 37, no. 4 (Winter 1995–1996): 59.

26. See, for example, Richard Holbrooke, *To End a War* (New York: Random House, 1998).

27. *Force Commander's End of Mission Report,* Headquarters UN Peace Forces, Zagreb, January 31, 1996.

28. Ibid.

29. UNPROFOR Reinforcements (internal UN document), BHC, June 6, 1995.

30. *BHC Situation Report,* April 5, 1995, and interviews with former UNPRO-FOR staff, 1997 and 1998. The objective of "facing down" the Bosnian Serb army led staff involved in the details of preparing the plan to refer to it jokingly as the "plan for World War III." In message sent to Kofi Annan, head of the Department of Peacekeeping Operations (DPKO) in New York, on April 18, General Janvier noted that the proposed helicopter resupply operation of the enclaves "may need to be conducted anytime from 1 May onwards if the current situation does not improve." Janvier also emphasized General Smith's commitment to the option, which if endorsed by the Secretariat and supported by member states was clearly intended to do more than just address the immediate problem of resupply: "Commander BCH sees it as vital to pursue this policy. . . . The present situation cannot be viewed as a simple resupply problem." "Subject: Air Supply of Eastern Enclaves," General Javier to K. Annan, DPKO, April 18, 1995.

31. UN Secretary-General, *An Agenda for Peace: Preventive Diplomacy, Peacemaking, and Peacekeeping (Report of the Secretary-General Pursuant to the Statement Adopted by the Summit Meeting of the Security Council on 31 January 1992),* A/47/277-S/24111, June 17, 1992.

31

Haiti

SEBASTIAN VON EINSIEDEL AND DAVID M. MALONE

Between 1990 and 2000, the UN Security Council was involved in a broad range of activities in support of democracy in Haiti. The case offers the first, and to date the only, instance of the Council authorizing the use of force to effect the restoration of democracy within a member state. The case sheds light on how leadership is exercised, coalitions are built, and burden-sharing is negotiated within the Council. It also highlights how the UN can work in partnership with a regional organization. It shows the Council improvising in response to immediate stimuli. Most important, the case of Haiti presents an instance in which UN operations were broadly successful—yet the patient failed to recover. It provides sobering lessons on the Council's readiness for overseeing long-term peacebuilding.

Haiti in Context: Crisis of Democracy

Haiti shares the Caribbean Island of Hispaniola with the Dominican Republic and has a population of approximately 8 million inhabitants.[1] The colonial conquest, which began in 1492, led to the eradication of the original inhabitants.[2] They were soon replaced with slaves from Africa. In the eighteenth century Haiti (then known as Saint Domingue) generated more wealth for France than all the Spanish colonies in the Americas combined. Following a thirteen-year independence movement, the Republic of Haiti was proclaimed on January 1, 1804. Failing to solve the inherited predicaments of colonialism and to address effectively other challenges that emerged from the diplomatic and economic isolation of this first independent black republic, Haiti has had twenty-one constitutions and forty-two heads of state (nine of whom declared themselves heads of state for life and twenty-nine of whom were assassinated or overthrown).

Guided by their fear of foreign attacks and their haste to consolidate Haiti's sovereignty through international recognition of its independence, early leaders adopted national and foreign policies that suffocated democracy and economic development while maintaining a large army, the needs of which prevailed over those of the population.

The tradition of "one-man rule" flourished through a system of institutional corruption. When seven presidents (four of whom were assassinated) failed in succession to consolidate their grip on power from 1911 to 1915, U.S. Marines landed in Haiti to safeguard U.S. interests at a time of increased international tensions accompanying World War I. The U.S. occupation, which lasted until 1934, failed to produce a more responsive governing system. The notoriously brutal president François (Papa Doc) Duvalier rose to power in 1957, never effectively challenged by the international community. The economic and political modernization strategies perpetrated by his feckless son, Jean-Claude (Baby Doc), who succeeded him in 1971, could not contain growing popular discontent, leading to his removal in 1986.

Early Security Council Involvement

When Haiti in February 1990 sought assistance from the Organization of American States (OAS) and the United Nations for elections, the challenges to genuine democracy in Haiti were immense.[3] The UN response itself nearly fell victim to a struggle for primary responsibility over UN involvement in elections between the Security Council and the General Assembly, pitting several of the permanent five (P-5), eager to expand the Council's turf, against Cuba, Colombia, and other nonaligned members of the Council that did not wish to see the Assembly's field of competence eroded.[4] The Council eventually stood down, leaving the Assembly in the lead.[5]

The elections in December 1990, monitored by several hundred UN observers as well as an OAS observer mission, unfolded well, bringing to power a young Roman Catholic priest and partisan of liberation theology, Jean-Bertrand Aristide.[6] Aristide's government, using the limited resources at its disposal, made serious efforts to address the country's formidable challenges, with uneven skill and results. However, faced with numerous obstacles, Aristide's exercise of power became increasingly personalized and authoritarian. On September 29, 1991, Raoul Cédras, the commander of Haiti's armed forces, overthrew his government.

Aftermath of the Coup

Under strong pressure from France and the United States, the putschists allowed Aristide to leave the country. Venezuelan president Carlos Andres Pérez convinced him to mobilize the international community, notably through the OAS and the UN.[7] The OAS Council reacted decisively. The day after the coup, it convened an urgent meeting to address the crisis, based on the provisions of the new Santiago Declaration, approved three months earlier to foster democracy, development, and the renewal of the inter-American system.[8] The OAS rejected the coup, calling for the "diplomatic isolation" of the military regime.

The UN Secretary-General issued a statement expressing his concern over events in Haiti and "the grave threats to democracy . . . established with the assistance of the United Nations."[9] Agreement by the Council to receive Aristide in a formal session on October 3 was a clear indication of Council support for his restoration. Aristide sought a clear stand in favor of democracy in Haiti. The president of the Security Council condemned "the violent usurpation of legitimate democratic authority and power" in Haiti and called for "the immediate reversal of the situation."[10]

The Council took no action at this stage. The OAS on October 8 adopted a resolution urging member states to impose a trade embargo on Haiti.[11] The UN General Assembly on October 11 demanded "the immediate restoration of the legitimate government."[12] The resolution's key provision appealed to UN member states "to take measures in support of the resolutions of the Organization of American States," thus inviting them to apply voluntarily the sanctions against Haiti agreed within the OAS. The OAS embargo began to produce some effects by the end of October 1991, but "exemptions" covering supplies for U.S.-owned local industries severely undermined the effectiveness of the sanctions. Meanwhile, large numbers of Haitians took to the seas, threatening to engulf Florida with boat-going refugees.

In order to sustain momentum at the UN, a grouping of Canada, France, the United States, and Venezuela was constituted in mid-1992 as the Quadripartite Group and, late that same year, as the Group of Friends of the Secretary-General on Haiti. In its efforts to overcome resistance to greater Security Council involvement on Haiti, it argued that the crisis risked undermining other fragile democracies in Latin American and the Caribbean, and that large outflows of refugees were likely to have destabilizing regional effects.

On November 24, 1992, the General Assembly condemned a rising tide of human rights violations in Haiti and requested the UN Secretary-General to assist, in cooperation with the OAS, in the solution of the Haitian crisis.[13] UN Secretary-General Boutros Boutros-Ghali now adopted a proactive approach. On December 11 he appointed Dante Caputo, a former president of the UN General Assembly and former foreign minister of Argentina, as his special envoy for Haiti.[14]

Caputo, with strong support from the Friends, laid the groundwork for a joint deployment of UN and OAS staff, known as the International

Civilian Mission in Haiti (MICIVIH), to monitor human rights in Haiti. The UN and OAS announced on February 9, 1993, that agreement had been reached with all parties on the modalities of deployment.[15] MICIVIH was to prove perhaps the most successful multilateral effort in Haiti of the 1990s.

Security Council Involvement

Caputo believed that the hoped-for improvement in human rights could lead to a degree of political dialogue. He mooted a 500-strong international police presence to forestall violence. Less publicized than the inflexibility of the military were reservations by Aristide over the proposed international "presence," given Haiti's constitutional provisions against foreign military intervention.

By May 1993, consensus emerged among the Friends that UN mandatory sanctions were required to nudge Cédras. On June 7, Aristide requested that the Council make "universal and mandatory" the OAS sanctions of 1991.[16] Anticipating objections on humanitarian and legal grounds, the Friends did not seek to universalize the broad OAS sanctions but focused on weapons and oil, the latter seen as the de facto regime's Achilles' heel. Countries that in other circumstances would have opposed the imposition of sanctions in support of democracy, such as China, acquiesced due to strong lobbying from Latin American and Caribbean countries. On June 16, 1993, the Security Council unanimously adopted Resolution 841, instituting mandatory sanctions on weapons, oil, and petroleum products against Haiti.[17]

The Governors' Island Agreement

Cédras now agreed to negotiate.[18] Caputo convened a meeting involving both Aristide and Cédras on June 27, 1993, at Governors' Island. Cédras insisted on a lifting of the embargo and a resumption of international assistance in exchange for the return of Aristide only six to eight months later. Caputo held firm on an early, set date for Aristide's return. However, Aristide signed reluctantly an agreement he believed provided insufficient guarantees for his return to Haiti. The agreement foresaw successively a new civilian government, the suspension of sanctions, the deployment of UN peacekeepers, an amnesty, retirement of Cédras, and the return of Aristide. Aristide derided it "because it imposed obligations equally on felons and on the legitimate authorities of Haiti."[19] Nongovernmental organizations took issue with its failure to mention human rights. In fact, its most serious flaw lay in a critical path for implementation that was too long and a deployment of the UN peacekeeping operation (PKO) too late in the process.

Its application proved uneven, but plans proceeded for the peacekeeping force, the UN Mission in Haiti (UNMIH), with 100 Canadian and 100 French police at its core. Washington agreed to provide troops for a small peacekeeping force also including Canadians and some others. With the ratification of a new prime minister selected by Aristide, the Council in Resolution 861 of August 27 suspended the sanctions against Haiti. However, the human rights situation in Haiti deteriorated sharply. Upon the arrival of the USS *Harlan County* in Port-au-Prince harbor on October 11, carrying the bulk of the U.S. and Canadian UN peacekeepers, thugs in the pay of the de facto regime prevented the landing of the troops, screaming, "We are going to turn this into another Somalia!"[20]

This incident challenged U.S. resolve, at a time when Washington was in shock over eighteen U.S. Army Rangers killed eight days earlier in Mogadishu. On October 12, without U.S. consultation of the UN, the *Harlan County* received orders to depart Haitian waters. From this astonishing failure of U.S. nerve, at least one lesson was learned: when the UN in 1994 prepared for UNMIH redeployment, roughly ten times more military personnel were planned than in 1993.

The Council reimposed sanctions on October 13 in Resolution 873. The Clinton administration needed more to cover its embarrassment. On October 16, the Council adopted Resolution 875, imposing a naval blockade on Haiti. China's reservations were allayed by the resolution's assertion that "unique and exceptional circumstances" required the measures.[21] The blockade was enforced by U.S., Canadian, Argentine, French, Dutch, and UK ships.

On October 25 the Council warned of additional sanctions, but among the Friends there were doubts.[22] The humanitarian toll of existing sanctions was heavy, with the poor hardest-hit. The naval blockade, on its surface a very strong measure, in fact signaled desperation following the collapse of the Governors' Island Agreement. The blockade could not be effective, due to Haiti's extensive land border with the Dominican Republic (which did not enforce the sanctions). However, the humanitarian and economic costs of the embargo were to prove lastingly crippling for Haiti.

A Showdown in Washington

The United States, powerless now to influence the military regime, turned its diplomatic guns on Aristide, warning him of the need to compromise.[23] Aristide, hitherto publicly opposed to military intervention to restore him to power, in early January 1994 signaled support for a surgical intervention to overthrow the de facto regime. The United States was not yet willing to adopt this course and exerted pressure on Aristide to yield more to his opponents, creating splits among the Friends. Aristide began to play the "immigration card," implicitly threatening further floods of boat-going Haitian refugees, in an effort to create pressure on the United States.[24]

Aristide's backers included Democratic members of Congress, Hollywood royalty, and much of the quality media in the United States. The Congressional Black Caucus, under its chairman, Kwesi Mfume, began agitating energetically for a more sympathetic U.S. policy.[25] Six congressmen who chained themselves to the White House fence were arrested amid a blaze of publicity. Randall Robinson, chairman of TransAfrica, an organization addressing foreign policy issues of interest to U.S. blacks, launched a hunger strike on April 12, 1994, calling the administration's policy of forced repatriation of Haitian refugees "cruel and . . . profoundly racist."[26] On April 21, Aristide, at Robinson's side, denounced the policy: "It's a cynical joke, it's a racist policy."[27]

The Clinton administration buckled. On April 21 it affirmed its support for Aristide, expressing commitment to secure the Dominican Republic–Haiti border against sanctions violations. On May 8, after the White House announced that the United States would no longer automatically send boat-going Haitian refugees back to Haiti, Robinson ended his hunger strike. In his showdown with the administration, Aristide had won.

Endgame at the United Nations: The Adoption of Resolution 940

A new, stronger sanctions regime came into effect on May 21, 1994. The Dominican Republic was pressured to accept a multination embargo monitoring mission.[28] The United States imposed additional financial sanctions against Haiti,[29] prohibited scheduled passenger services,[30] and blocked all U.S. assets of Haitian citizens resident in Haiti.[31] The endgame was nigh.

The Friends agreed that UNMIH's mandate could not, as in 1993, simply consist of training and engineering projects but had to envisage self-defense and security for senior Haitian officials and key installations. When this was first discussed in the Council, the Russian Federation threatened a veto, due to U.S. lack of support for a Commonwealth of Independent States (CIS) peacekeeping mission in Georgia.[32] Moscow complained that the case for a large UN force in Haiti had not been made, griped about double standards, and hinted that it did not wish to foot a large bill for a reconfigured UNMIH.[33] The Russians were also upset that France was not more helpful on Georgia, given the support Moscow had provided to Paris when it was desperately seeking Council votes for Operation Turquoise in Rwanda. Accommodations were soon reached among the United States, the

Russian Federation, and France on their respective issues of concern, triggering some criticism over P-5 backroom deals.

Although the United States had wanted a UN force, if only because the UN flag would be useful in attracting participation by a number of countries, Boutros-Ghali, believing that the UN had neither the resources nor the capacity to enforce Aristide's return, preferred a U.S.-led multinational force (MNF). The UN's involvement in Rwanda, where its small force was overwhelmed by local violence only a month earlier, and its recent setbacks in Somalia, contributed to his caution.[34] In the end, the Friends agreed on a non-UN MNF under Chapter VII, followed, once a "secure and stable environment" had been established, by a Chapter VI UN PKO.

Following receipt of a letter of support from Aristide, the Council adopted Resolution 940 on July 31, 1994, by twelve votes in favor and two abstentions (Brazil and China), authorizing the MNF.[35] In the debate marking the resolution's adoption, Mexico, Cuba, Nicaragua, and Uruguay criticized the decision, rejecting resort to Chapter VII provisions in the Western Hemisphere.[36] Venezuela also telegraphed its discomfort. Brazil, in explaining its abstention, noted that action to restore Aristide could be seen as strengthening democracy throughout the hemisphere but stated that Brazil's constitution and political traditions precluded support for military intervention. China harped on its attachment to the peaceful settlement of disputes and to the principle of nonintervention but did state that, once adopted, Council resolutions had to be respected.

The adoption of Resolution 940 was groundbreaking in several respects. It marked the first time the United States had sought UN authority for the use of force within its own hemisphere. (The contrast with its unilateral action against General Manuel Noriega's government in Panama in 1989 is stark.)[37] The resolution was also unprecedented in authorizing force to remove one regime and install another within a member state.

Aristide's Return

By September 15, 1994, the Pentagon had recruited nineteen countries with a total of 2,000 troops to join U.S. forces within the MNF, including Argentina, Australia, Belgium, Bolivia, Israel, Jordan, the Netherlands, many Caribbean and Central American countries, and the UK. However, Canada, Venezuela, and France did not join in.[38]

On September 16 in a political coup de théatre, former president Jimmy Carter led a U.S. mission to Haiti in a final attempt to secure the departure of the Haitian military leadership. When word arrived on September 18 that military aircraft were preparing to take off from Fort Bragg, North Carolina, for Haiti, Cédras agreed to leave.[39] The MNF thereupon deployed smoothly, accompanied by the small UN team charged with monitoring it.[40] On October 16 the Council lifted sanctions and the blockade, the day after Aristide's return to Haiti.[41]

Peacekeeping

The UN's most pressing priority now was that of institution-building, to achieve a sustainable democracy, including support for credible elections to a bewildering range of national offices. Fears of violence in Haiti immediately following Aristide's return initially proved unfounded. He worked to promote calm, consulting members of the economic elite who might have preferred a return to the old order but could no longer count on the armed forces to secure this end.

In January 1995 the U.S. MNF commander certified a "secure and stable environment,"[42] and the handover from the MNF to UNMIH, comprising 6,000 troops and almost 800 civilian police officers, took place in March.[43] UNMIH's mission was to provide security, stabilize the country, create a new police force, and professionalize the Haitian armed forces (which Aristide eliminated altogether in stages through early 1995).

In February 1996 Aristide was succeeded by the more pragmatic and business-oriented René Préval. An early challenge arose in connection with the renewal of UNMIH's mandate. Aristide had received U.S.$20 million from Taiwan at the time of a breakdown in cooperation with the International Monetary Fund (IMF) and the International Bank for Reconstruction and Development (IBRD) over his resistance to privatization of several loss-making national enterprises. Taiwan's vice president was also the most senior guest at Préval's inauguration. This enraged the Chinese government, already irritated with Aristide for promoting Taiwan membership in the UN in 1993. China now hinted that it was inclined to oppose an extension of even a smaller UNMIH. This was countered by Latin American and Caribbean countries and by the nonaligned movement, with which the Chinese had traditionally asserted solidarity. China ultimately consented only to 1,200 military and 300 police. Canada, which had agreed to take over military command of the mission, refused to contemplate this without the personnel it believed necessary. At the last moment, it offered to dispatch 700 soldiers on its own account, to work alongside those the Council could mandate. Russia, meanwhile, sought to exchange its support for UNMIH extension for authorization of a UN PKO in Tajikistan.

Peacebuilding

The peaceful transfer of power in early 1996 through generally free and fair elections seemed to constitute a significant step toward democracy in Haiti.

The UNMIH operation itself, which ended in June 1996, was also seen as a success, attributed to a clear mandate and good planning for a smooth transition between the MNF and the follow-on UN force.[44] Although UNMIH was a success on its own terms, the Council's broader peacebuilding efforts failed. Establishing a new police force respecting human rights and immune to politicization proved a difficult, slow process. Disaffection among former army personnel and the continued existence of paramilitary networks kept the security situation fragile. Poor economic prospects were aggravated by a political impasse resulting from the legislative elections of April 1997.

The mandate of UNMIH's three follow-up missions (the UN Support Mission in Haiti [UNSMIH] from June 1996 to July 1997, the UN Transition Mission in Haiti [UNTMIH] from July 1997 to November 1997, and the UN Civilian Police Mission in Haiti [MIPONUH] from November 1997 to March 2000) became increasingly narrow. The central task (staffed by 300 international civilian police) remained assistance in establishing and training an effective national police force. The UN missions were also encouraged to coordinate activities of the UN system in Haiti aimed at institution-building, national reconciliation, and economic rehabilitation.[45] The military dimension of these missions progressively faded until the last UN military personnel were withdrawn in November 1997.

The Group of Friends continued to be deeply involved, locally meeting with the special representative of the Secretary-General on a weekly basis to provide him with support.[46] However, a succession of constitutional crises, initiated with the resignation of Prime Minister Rosny Smarth in June 1997, was to undermine international objectives. Aristide and his supporters were now pitted against former allies in an increasingly bitter feud.[47] Préval's government was largely paralyzed, and Aristide's return to power in 2000 did nothing to improve the situation. International efforts to promote political dialogue among Haitians came to nothing.[48] The Security Council focused on process (free and fair elections) and, like the Friends, refused to take sides in the bitter political polemics.

The political crisis dealt a further blow to the country's already dismal economy.[49] In 1995, Haitian per capita gross domestic product (GDP), at U.S.$242.1, was by far the lowest in the Western Hemisphere.[50] Haiti ranked only 148 out of 174 in the 1992 UN Development Programme's global Human Development Index.[51] The World Bank and others estimated that the sanctions regime might have cost the country up to 30 percent of its GDP.[52] Investment failed to materialize given the uncertain political and security situations. What modest signs of life the economy showed in 1995 and 1996 were due entirely to massive infusions of foreign assistance, but donors rapidly grew disenchanted with Aristide's political and economic management priorities.[53] Between 1995 and 1998, foreign aid payments dropped by about 35 percent, ostensibly due to limited absorptive capacity and nonapproval of available loans by the Haitian parliament, but donor irritation played a significant role.[54] By mid-1998, at least U.S.$340 million in aid was held up by foreign exasperation at the lack of a trustworthy government.[55] A 1998 World Bank report pointed to "political instability, woefully poor governance, and corruption"—in spite of the considerable international efforts.[56]

The security situation also deteriorated, with a rising number of murders and assaults against human rights activists and high-profile political figures in 1999. The police initially performed reasonably well, with a 1998 United States Information Service poll showing that 70 percent of Haitians had confidence in them.[57] In the Haitian context, the police's political neutrality was remarkable.[58] However, it came under attack for its violent performance in confronting antigovernment demonstrations in Port-au-Prince in May 1999.[59] By November 1999, of the original 5,300-strong force, about 1,000 had to be dismissed for corruption, drug offenses, and human rights abuses.[60] And during the general elections in early 2000 the police were passive in the face of violent demonstrations by Aristide's supporters.[61]

The mushrooming drug trade, which according to one estimate increased fourfold in 1997–1998,[62] offered a potent incentive for corrupt behavior. Deportations of approximately 300 Haitian criminals annually from the United States did not help.[63] The MNF had decided against disarming the country in 1994, and small arms remained rife. Finally, the lamentable local judicial system impeded police efforts to combat crime.[64]

An Exit Strategy?

Throughout 1999, nervousness increased in Haiti over the scheduled end of the UN's peacekeeping presence.[65] However, China had not overcome its reservations toward the mission.[66] Russia was also lukewarm at best.[67] Had the United States thrown its weight behind an extension of MIPONUH, this might have been agreed.[68] But Washington was increasingly frustrated with "Mr. Préval's passivity and Mr. Aristide's duplicity."[69] In mid-1999 the Pentagon decided to pull out its remaining 500 soldiers, who were performing nation-building tasks outside the UN mission.[70] Republicans in Congress seized every opportunity to undermine the Clinton administration's efforts to support Haiti, for instance sitting on funding for MICIVIH, which was slated to start its phaseout.[71] Moreover, Haitians themselves were unhappy with any continued foreign military presence on their soil, which reinforced the view of those Council members who began to see the situation in Haiti as more a matter of development than a question of international peace and security.[72]

In the face of these difficulties, the Group of Friends tried to move the issue to the General Assembly in an attempt to secure a continued UN presence in Haiti. On December 17, 1999, the General Assembly mandated a drastically reduced follow-up mission, the International Support Mission in Haiti (MICAH), of civilian support in Haiti.[73] With the withdrawal of MIPONUH in March 2000, a decade of Security Council involvement in Haiti came to an end. The Friends, with strong support from the Italian president of the UN Economic and Social Council (ECOSOC), sought to place this UN organ in charge of overseeing the UN's continued peacebuilding efforts in Haiti, but the results were disappointing. Meeting only once a year and not being imbued with the power of mandating and ending a mission, ECOSOC was even less well positioned than the Council to manage a complex peacebuilding mission.[74]

In May 2000, general elections finally took place but resulted in further dissension. Just as Aristide was elected as president for a second time, Kofi Annan recommended the termination of MICAH in February 2001. He contended that the climate of instability made it inadvisable to extend the mission, but funding constraints weighed heavily.[75] The pullout came at a time when the "human rights situation in Haiti was more serious than at any time since the 1994 return to democracy."[76]

Conclusion

The Council's involvement in Haiti resulted from UN-monitored elections there a year earlier. It was driven strongly by the domestic interest of the United States to contain refugee flows to Florida. U.S. dominance of the issue at the UN was moderated within the Group of Friends and, occasionally, by interested Latin American countries such as Brazil. But once Washington lost interest and became increasingly hostile to Aristide, there was little these other countries could do to sustain peacekeeping or credible peacebuilding in Haiti. The willingness of China in 1996 to disrupt its normally close relations with the nonaligned movement, and to inconvenience the Council, over Haitian ties to Taiwan also demonstrate the importance of national interests as the prime motivator for Council members.

The UN exited Haiti without a strategy for the future, leaving the OAS once again in the lead, promoting political compromise and sensible economic policies through the good offices of the energetic and much admired OAS assistant secretary-general, Luigi Einaudi.[77] As of mid-2003, Haiti remains in perpetual political upheaval and economic despondency.[78]

The new engagement of the OAS in the promotion of democracy, further to the Santiago Declaration, was severely tested by Haiti, and the OAS, though shrinking from association with the use of force, performed well. Its joint sponsorship with the UN of MICIVIH played a valuable role at the worst point of the crisis and beyond in defense of human rights.

The Council's growing ambivalence toward mandatory economic sanctions was reinforced by the Haiti experience. The Haiti sanctions policy exacted a significant humanitarian toll and produced lasting economic costs that UN and other multilateral actors were later unable to counteract. Adding insult to injury, the sanctions significantly enriched the de facto regime. Unfortunately, such is the aversion to use of force that the Council is more inclined toward imposition of sanctions, even draconian ones, than toward credible threats of military force. Yet against a relatively weak adversary, the threat of force would have stood a much better chance of bringing the de facto regime to heel after the coup.

The Haiti case provides evidence of the tradeoffs routinely engineered by and among the P-5. Such mutual accommodations today seem more routine, notably those involving the former colonial powers in Africa (on such issues as Sierra Leone, the Central African Republic, Côte d'Ivoire, and the Democratic Republic of Congo).

The tendency of the Council in addressing conflict to aim for a ceasefire followed by neutral mediation of differences may not be the appropriate course in every instance. Both Aristide and Cédras undermined the Governors' Island Agreement, which they signed under great international pressure. Had the agreement been fully implemented, a showdown between the military and Aristide, with unpredictable results, would probably only have been postponed.

The UN's financial constraints in Haiti eventually became crippling. MICIVIH's modest funding requirements became problematic as early as 1996 and the mission terminated for lack of funding in 2000. UNMIH's follow-on missions were not supported by reliable funding arrangements and were saddled with impractically short mandates. "The fact that these had to be renegotiated every few months . . . hampered UNMIH's ability to gain the initiative or to maintain momentum" vis-à-vis the Haitian parties.[79] The Secretariat commented on "leaving the peacekeeping operation as an insufficient single prong in what was intended to be a multipronged strategy," seriously short-changing peacebuilding objectives.[80] The Haiti case suggests that the UN remains woefully unprepared, through its intergovernmental decisionmaking and funding approaches, as well as in its institutional culture, to lead effectively on medium-term peacebuilding efforts. A more sweeping criticism of the UN's peacebuilding activities is that it failed to address the lack of consensus between the country's different sectors on fundamental social and economic goals and on the means for achieving them.[81]

It is tempting to blame the international actors for the sorry outcome. But the Haiti case demonstrates that local actors matter critically in the success of UN mediation and peacebuilding activities. The international community supported to the hilt Jean-Bertrand Aristide's restoration to power in circumstances still unique to international relations. It was poorly repaid. Adhering to established patterns of Haitian political life, Aristide and his opponents have reverted to "winner-take-all" strategies precluding compromise or any serious commitment to national interests. In these circumstances, the conditionalities donor governments and institutions attempted to use as leverage for better policies failed miserably. International interveners have not developed alternative strategies. The Haitian political community has squandered not only considerable international goodwill but also the huge resources poured into its stabilization in the years 1994–1997. Myopic, self-serving Haitian leadership has plunged the country back into a crisis both familiar and desperately sad.

Notes

1. This section draws heavily upon Marlye Gélin-Adams and David M. Malone, "Haiti: A Case of Endemic Weakness," in Robert Rotberg, ed., *State Failure and State Weakness in a Time of Terror* (Washington, D.C.: Brookings Institution, 2003).

2. Many distinguished Haitian scholars, including Patrick Bellegard-Smith and Michel-Rolph Trouillot, have surveyed Haiti's history in a number of riveting books. For a comprehensive overview, see the magisterial study by Robert Debs Heinl Jr., Nancy Gordon Heinl, and Michael Heinl, *Written in Blood* (Boston: University Press of America, 1996).

3. Much of the chronology provided here is drawn from David M. Malone, *Decision-Making in the UN Security Council: The Case of Haiti, 1990–1997* (Oxford: Clarendon, 1998).

4. For more details, see United Nations, *Les Nations Unies et Haiti 1990–96* (New York: United Nations, 1996), pp. 10–15.

5. S/21847, October 5, 1990.

6. A/45/870/Add.1, February 22, 1991.

7. Aristide's version of these events appears in Pierre Mouterde and Christophe Wargny, *Apre Bal, Tambou Lou* (Paris: Austral, 1996), pp. 85–97.

8. See also OAS–AG/RES 1080 (XXI-0/91), June 5, 1991, the declaration's enabling resolution.

9. SG/SM4627 HI/4, October 1, 1990.

10. Ibid.

11. OAS–MRE/RES doc.3/91OAS and OAS–MRE/RES 2/91.

12. Resolution 46/7, October 11, 1991.

13. A separate, very strong resolution on human rights in Haiti was also adopted by the General Assembly on December 2, 1992 (A/C.3/47/L.73).

14. On January 13, 1993, Caputo was named special envoy for Haiti of the OAS as well as of the UN, an innovation in cooperation between the UN and regional organizations.

15. UN Press Release SG/1982-HI/10, February 9, 1993.

16. S/25985, June 7, 1993.

17. In an OAS Council meeting on June 22, Baena Soares suggested that the

UN resolution created a "serious mutation" in the international treatment of the Haiti crisis, but even those OAS members opposed to the UN measures were not prepared to fight a rear-guard action.

18. Document 68 in: United Nations, *Les Nations Unis et Haiti, 1990–96,* p. 308.

19. Interview with Jean-Bertrand Aristide, Port-au-Prince, May 21, 1996.

20. Howard French, *New York Times,* October 12, 1993.

21. S/PV.3293, October 16, 1993.

22. S/26633, October 25, 1993.

23. A/48/766 and S/26881, December 15, 1993.

24. Donald E. Schulz and Marcella Gabriel, *Reconciling the Irreconcilable: The Troubled Outlook for U.S. Policy Toward Haiti* (Washington, D.C.: U.S. Army War College, Strategic Studies Institute, 1994), pp. 46–48.

25. See Kwesi Mfume, *No Free Ride: From the Mean Streets to the Mainstream* (New York: One World–Balantine Books, 1996), pp. 338–345.

26. Reuters dispatch by Alan Elsner from Washington, D.C., April 12, 1994.

27. Ibid., April 21, 1994.

28. The United States pulled together the Multinational Observer Group of eighty-eight members, the bulk of them U.S. entities, with fifteen Canadian and a contingent of Argentinean entities joining them. The group operated only from August 30 until the lifting of sanctions on October 16, 1994.

29. Executive Order 12920, June 10, 1994.

30. Department of Transportation Order 94-6-28, June 17, 1994.

31. Executive Order 12922, June 22, 1994.

32. Resolution 929, June 22, 1994.

33. S/PV.3397, June 30, 1994.

34. See *Yearbook of the United Nations, 1994,* vol. 48 (The Hague: Martinus Nijhoff, 1995), pp. 281–317.

35. S/1994/910, July 30, 1994.

36. S/PV.3413, July 31, 1994.

37. On Panama, the United States, joined by the UK and France, had to veto a Council resolution strongly deploring its intervention (S/21048, vetoed on December 23, 1989).

38. Paris argued that France was already overextended in the former Yugoslavia, in a UN operation under political fire in Washington. France did offer UNMIH 100 police and several military observers. Canada had long sought to stave off the use of force in Haiti, preferring "total" sanctions. Canada participated in the UNMIH advance team and offered UNMIH 100 police, the police commander, 600 troops, and the military chief of staff. Venezuela participated neither in the MNF nor in UNMIH.

39. Colin Powell, *My American Journey* (New York: Random House, 1995), p. 600; and Robert A. Pastor, "The Clinton Administration and the Americas: The Postwar Rhythm and Blues," *Journal of Inter-American Studies and World Affairs* 38, no. 4 (Winter 1996): 106.

40. S/1994/1143, September 28, 1994.

41. Resolution 944 and S/PV.3430, September 29, 1994.

42. Resolution 975 (1995).

43. Annex II of S/1995/55, January 19, 1995; S/1995/46, January 17, 1995; S/1995/305, April 13, 1995.

44. U.S. Army Peacekeeping Institute, *Success in Peacekeeping: United Nations Mission in Haiti—The Military Perspective* (Carlisle Barracks, Penn.: U.S. Army Peacekeeping Institute, 1996), p. 19.

45. This task was only spelled out once, in Resolution 1063 (1996), which declared the Council would support the role of the special representative of the Secretary-General in this coordination effort.

46. Interview with Julian Harston, former representative of the Secretary-General in Haiti, New York, February 5, 2003.

47. S/1998/144, February 20, 1998.

48. S/1998/796, August 24, 1998.

49. World Bank Group, *Haiti: The Challenges of Poverty Reduction* (Washington, D.C.: World Bank Group, August 1998).

50. IBRD Haiti Assistance Strategy Document 15945-HA, August 13, 1996.

51. Ibid.

52. Richard Garfield, *The Impact of Economic Sanctions on Health and Well-Being,* Relief and Rehabilitation Network Paper no. 31 (London: Overseas Development Institute, November 1999).

53. S/1995/149, February 21, 1995.

54. *Report of the Ad Hoc Advisory Group on Haiti,* ECOSOC doc. E/1999/103, July 2, 1999. See also "Help Wanted: One Government," *The Economist,* July 25, 1998.

55. "Help Wanted," *The Economist.*

56. World Bank Group, *Haiti.*

57. S/1998/1064, November 11, 1998.

58. S/1999/181, February 19, 1999.

59. S/1999/908, August 24, 1999.

60. David Gonzalez, "Civilian Police Force Brings New Problems to Haiti," *New York Times,* November 26, 1999.

61. *Report of the Secretary-General to the General Assembly on the International Civilian Support Mission in Haiti,* A/55/154, July 17, 2000.

62. "Help Wanted," *The Economist.* See also S/1999/908, August 24, 1999; and Serge Kovalski, "Haitian Police Tinged by Thin Blue Line," *Washington Post,* October 23, 1999.

63. Serge Kovalski, "Haiti's Police Accused of Lawlessness," *Washington Post,* September 28, 1999.

64. S/1998/796, August 24, 1998.

65. S/1999/579, May 18, 1999.

66. Barbara Crossette, "UN Diplomats Search for Ways to Avoid Violence in Haiti," *New York Times,* August 27, 1999.

67. *United Nations Daily Highlights,* 98-11-25, www.hri.org/news/world/undh/1998/98-11-25.undh.html.

68. Confidential interviews, February 13, 2003.

69. Larry Rohter, "Political Feuds Rack Haiti: So Much for Its High Hopes," *New York Times,* October 18, 1998.

70. David Gonzalez, "Haiti's Paralysis Spreads as U.S. Troops Pack Up," *New York Times,* November 10, 1999.

71. Jennifer Bauduy, "U.S. Forces UN to Reduce Haiti Human Rights Mission," Reuters, June 16, 1999.

72. Mission of Netherlands to the United Nations, "No Exit Without Strategy," background paper for an open debate in the Security Council, New York, October 2000; interview with Michel Duval, former Deputy Permanent Representative of Canada to the United Nations, New York, March 10, 2003.

73. Resolution A/54/193.

74. Interview with Michel Duval, March 10, 2003.

75. A/55/154, July 17, 2000; and "Haiti," *Amnesty International Annual Report, 2001.*

76. Ibid.

77. Lotta Hagman, "Lessons Learned: Peacebuilding in Haiti," International Peace Academy conference report, January 23–24, 2002.

78. See Peter Dailey, "Haiti: The Fall of the House of Aristide," *New York Review of Books,* March 13, 2003. See also Peter Daily, "Haiti's Betrayal," *New York Review of Books,* March 27, 2003.

79. Mission of Netherlands to the United Nations, "No Exit Without Strategy."

80. S/2001/394, April 20, 2001.

81. Chetan Kumar, "Sustainable Peace as Sustainable Democracy: The Experience of Haiti," Politik und Gesellschaft Online, April 1999, www.fes.de/ipg/ipg4_99/artkumar.htm.

32

Rwanda

HOWARD ADELMAN AND ASTRI SUHRKE

On April 6, 1994, the plane of President Juvenal Habyarimana of Rwanda was shot down and the president killed. An extremist coup effectively ended the attempts to implement the Arusha Accords to end the four-year civil war. Once again, war resumed between the Forces Armées Rwandaises (FAR) and the Rwandan Patriotic Front (RPF). At the same time, a second full-scale war of the government against the Tutsi and moderate Hutu civilian population of Rwanda began. By July 1994, up to 800,000 civilians had been intentionally slaughtered in a horrendous genocide at a time when United Nations peacekeepers were in the country—albeit in reduced numbers—and when those same peacekeepers controlled the airport in Kigali. Both the civil war and the genocide ended when the extremist government and its army fled into exile in Zaire in July 1994. These events have been widely condemned and negatively evaluated by the international commission established by the UN to examine its performance in relation to the genocide.[1]

An extensive scholarship and an overwhelming consensus now exist on most of the facts, a majority of the interpretations, and even on the evaluation of what happened (e.g., see Chapter 32.1 by Colin Keating for a firsthand, insightful account). There is comparatively less analysis of the role of the UN Security Council and the reasons for its actions. For example, Michael Barnett's general analysis of the role of the UN stresses the pattern of self-protection that led to a culture of indifference and emphasizes the role of the Secretariat.[2] Other authors have stressed resource restraints,[3] the importance of U.S. positions,[4] or personality factors.[5] Building on this analysis, this chapter will focus on the Security Council and add an original dimension by analyzing in detail the early role of the Council, which has been sketchily covered by others.

Much attention has been spent on the failure to prevent or mitigate the genocide in Rwanda. As horrific as that failure was, we argue in this chapter that the failure was much broader and entailed undermining the 1951 Genocide Convention as well as the legitimacy of the Security Council by revealing the structural weakness of the Council manifested in the lack of accountability, the nonaffirmation of prevailing legal principles, and the nonrepresentative nature of the Council's composition. Rwanda became the benchmark of how the Council should *not* behave in many areas, whether from the perspective of state interests and power, regime-building, or the above norms.

The Rwanda case also illustrates the dynamic of how the Council deals with a "low-priority" matter. The collective passivity amounted in this case to a monumental failure of omission, although failure may also, of course, result from acts of commission (as in the recent controversy over the Council's role in authorizing war against Iraq).

The Framework of Analysis

At the core of the Security Council's mandate to promote international peace and security is the need to make decisions about the use of military force—whether or not force should be deployed, where, how, and how much. Rwanda in 1994 is an illustration of precisely this point, though the use of constructive diplomacy and the use of coercive diplomacy (the conjunction of the threat of force with diplomacy) were also available as tools. As we shall see, the Council did not employ either diplomacy or force constructively.

Within the overarching theme that links alternative strategies with the objective of enhancing peace and security, one set of considerations is realpolitik as conventionally defined. In a Security Council setting, three distinct sets of interests can here be identified: the interests and power of the most powerful members; the interests of the smaller states; and the collective interests of the members as a whole operating under a collective mandate to enhance the conditions for peace and security even in arenas where the major powers are not directly affected but where the Council has the role of a safety net to catch security issues that are not dealt with elsewhere. Promoting these interests in the Security Council involves issues such as agenda-setting, the engagement (or restrictions) of the great powers—above all the United States—and the mobilization of military and financial resources for action.

A second set of issues concerns regime-building in the tradition of liberal internationalism, which envisions the construction of international institutions and mechanisms to enable individual state interests to be fulfilled in a positive-sum way through, and under, a collective set of rules and within a common institutional framework. The strength of such a regime depends not only on the "enlightened self-interests" of states but also on organizational functions such as the relationship of the UN to regional organizations, the interaction between headquarters and the field, the relations between the diplomats and the mandarins, and more generally, the role of the Secretariat as the "sixth permanent member" of the Security Council. The Secretary-General and his staff played a particularly important role in the Rwanda case in initiating policy and defining the situation and associated policy options for the Council. The various dimensions of this web of connections involve issues of information capacity, institutional memory, the formal and informal rules of decisionmaking, and finally the role of the Council as an agent of legitimation and delegitimation.

On the prescriptive as opposed to the descriptive level of interests and regime rules and institutions are to be found a third set of issues that include the role of the Security Council in interpreting, consolidating, and expanding international law as well as upholding (or undercutting) procedural norms such as transparency and accountability. We will examine the role of the Security Council in the Rwandan genocide on all three levels.

Bystander to Civil War

When the RPF invaded Rwanda from Uganda in October 1990, the presidents of both Rwanda and Uganda were at UN Headquarters, staying in the same hotel. Yoweri Museveni of Uganda, then also holding the chair of the Organization of African Unity (OAU), woke up Juvenal Habyarimana, president of Rwanda, and informed him that, to his claimed surprise, the Rwandan Tutsi in the Ugandan army had deserted and invaded Rwanda. Habyarimana, for his part, insisted that this was a foreign invasion, sponsored and supported by Uganda, rather than a rebellion, but neither he nor anyone else called on the Security Council to take action. Instead, Habyarimana flew home, stopping en route to obtain help from his longstanding ally, France, and Rwanda's previous colonial ruler, Belgium, to repel the invaders. This was in sharp contrast to events only two months earlier, when the Council quickly became engaged to consider the implications for "international peace and security" when Kuwait was invaded by Iraq. While often overlooked, this fact is noteworthy given that protection of the sanctity of states from foreign invasions is central to the Security Council's responsibility under the UN Charter.

The early indifference of the Council is symptomatic of a pattern that prevailed for almost three years while the belligerents fought their way toward a standstill and a peace agreement. The Security Council did not place the conflict on its agenda until March 1993. When the Council did become involved, it was a conditional rather than proactive form of diplomacy; the Council in effect made its involvement conditional upon prior commitment from the local parties to maintain the peace. This diplomatic pattern solidified as the crisis unfolded.

The UN Secretariat at first merely sent observers to the peace negotiations. Outside the Council, however, a number of states in the region (especially neighboring Zaire, Tanzania, and Uganda) and in Europe (Belgium and France) became involved in varying capacities, alternatively to promote peace talks or to support one of the belligerents. France and Uganda at times did both. France, Belgium, and the OAU helped initiate peace negotiations, and the OAU in mid-1992 sent a small military observer group to monitor a recently concluded cease-fire. At various times, other actors appeared on the stage as well, including Egypt (as a conduit for arms), the United States, Canada, the European Union, the Holy See, and Switzerland (to support mediation).

Given this considerable activity to promote a peace settlement, it could be argued that the Security Council could justifiably stand on the sidelines if it defined itself as a safety net and diplomatic arena of last resort. Rwanda, as noted, though claiming to have been invaded, never formally appealed to the Security Council for support. This was evidently a joint decision by Habyarimana and his close allies in the French government, who initially preferred to keep the matter outside the Security Council. Instead, France sent a small military force (Force Noroît) as well as increased military assistance to help Habyarimana repel the RPF. However, the unfolding civil war had all the hallmarks of external involvement on both sides. Uganda's indirect support was widely suspected at the time and has been documented in retrospect.[6]

Over the Threshold of Attention

By early 1993 the situation in Rwanda had clearly worsened. Information about systematic killings of civilians began to be publicized. At this time, the Security Council for the first time formally engaged itself in Rwanda. In response to allegations that Uganda was behind the new RPF renewal of hostilities and the denial by the UN permanent representative of Uganda on February 22, 1993,[7] the Ugandan government asked the UN to send an observer mission to verify that Uganda was not involved. The permanent representative of Rwanda, on February 28, formally requested that the Security Council take up the matter and provide an observer/monitoring force on the Uganda-Rwanda border in the face of the rapid and devastating advance by the RPF in February 1993.[8] When the RPF responded on March 4 by calling for an expanded OAU force to monitor the newly concluded cease-fire (OAU observers had been deployed the previous year), and to authorize "an international force to maintain the cease-fire" between the belligerent forces of the RPF and the Rwandan government as well as monitor the border area, the Rwandan and French governments also requested an urgent meeting of the Security Council to discuss the issue. Invoking the criteria for Council attention, the Rwandan government claimed that "deterioration of conditions in [Rwanda] is a threat to peace and security in the region."[9]

In contrast to the RPF request, France and Rwanda wanted the UN to freeze the military situation before the RPF advanced farther, and to preempt a larger OAU role. The OAU was widely considered partial to the RPF. This predisposition, plus evident weaknesses in the early deployment, suggested to France and Rwanda that the OAU would not effectively monitor the cease-fire and the buffer zone established between the two Rwandan parties. Another concern was the likelihood that French forces would have to be withdrawn as part of the cease-fire agreement, certainly as part of the final peace agreement currently under discussion. The RPF's demand to this effect was foreshadowed in the earlier cease-fire agreement of July 1992 and explicitly stated at the summit meeting between the two Rwandan parties in Dar-es-Salaam in March of that year. To the French and Rwandese governments, a UN force was more likely to safeguard their joint interests than a probably weak and pro-RPF force led by the OAU. If the UN organized the interpositional force, France's role on the Security Council provided some assurance that French-Rwandan concerns would be taken into account in the formation and deployment of the force.

OAU Secretary-General Salim A. Salim had traveled to the Dar-es-Salaam summit to promote the role of OAU in the peace process. The OAU already had a small contingent of military observers in Rwanda and was actively involved in the Arusha talks as well. The summit meeting agreed to expand the existing OAU monitoring force and to give the Neutral Military Observer Group (NMOG) alone the task of monitoring the cease-fire. In Salim's thinking, monitoring was essential to confidence-building and hence the peace process. In a broader peacekeeping role, the OAU clearly needed the support from the UN. The joint communiqué from the Dar-es-Salaam summit requested UN support for the recently concluded cease-fire and called for the establishment of "a neutral international force which shall be organized under the aegis of the Organization of African Unity (OAU) and the United Nations."[10] Three days later, the separate requests of France and Rwanda made it possible for the UN to play an active role in shaping that force.

The French-Rwandan initiative was essential to get the Rwanda conflict over the Security Council's threshold of significance and onto the agenda. The threshold was mainly determined by the marginal importance of Rwanda to all of the permanent five except France, and the preoccupation of the Council with other conflicts that on a grim scale of comparison seemed more violent (notably war and ethnic cleansing in Bosnia, and civil war and famine in Somalia). Moreover, in a low-priority case like Rwanda, the Council was evidently reluctant to engage itself until there were clear signs that the parties themselves were willing to settle, though since mid-1992 France had futilely attempted to table the Rwanda conflict before the Security Council. Now, with yet another cease-fire and dramatic changes on the ground that were likely to accelerate the peace talks, the Council accepted the case.

The timing suggests a limited vision of the Council's role in support of international peace and security in cases that at the outset had a low-priority imprint. The Council seemed to be prepared to engage only when the conflict had virtually ended—that is, when a cease-fire had been concluded and a peace agreement was on the near horizon—rather than undertake preventive and mediation measures under Chapter VI. It was an essentially reactive and contingent mode of engagement that was dependent upon prior progress on the ground.

An Ambiguous Resolution

Once placed on the Council's table, issues relating to capacity, financing, and the role of the United States began to play a role in how the agenda item was handled. Throughout, the continued marginality of the Rwanda issue to both U.S. foreign and domestic policy played a major role. Initially, however, regime issues took center stage, particularly the UN's relationship with the OAU.

The differing perspectives between the two Rwandan parties on the role of the OAU versus the UN in monitoring the peace, noted above, were reproduced in the Security Council and expressed in the ambiguities of Resolution 812 of March 12, 1993, which formalized the UN's entry into the conflict. The Dar-es-Salaam communiqué bore the imprint of the RPF and OAU and had called for a neutral international force to be established "under the aegis of" both organizations; the French responded by initiating a resolution in the Security Council that subtly but clearly shifted the balance in favor of the UN. The French draft called for a UN force in Rwanda that would operate "in conjunction with" the OAU.[11] The draft resolution was subsequently watered down by nonaligned members of the Council and some European representatives who cautioned that the text might be viewed as an attempt by Paris to salvage its influence in Rwanda and warned against sidelining the OAU.[12] The language in the final resolution was softened but at the same time made more ambiguous. The resolution provided for three apparently simultaneous measures: (1) deployment of UN observers on the Rwanda-Uganda border (Article 3); (2) possible UN support to the OAU force "for the monitoring of the cease-fire" (Article 2);

and (3) "possible establishment, under the aegis of the Organization of African Unity and the United Nations, of an international force entrusted, *inter alia,* with humanitarian assistance and the protection of the civilian population" (Article 2). The critical points regarding areas of operation, as well as the relationship between the OAU and the UN, which were at the heart of disagreement between the Rwandan parties and their supporters, were not specified but explicitly left for the Secretary-General to work out in consultation with his OAU counterpart.

The ambiguity provided an entry point for UN Secretary-General Boutros Boutros-Ghali to effectively undermine the OAU in the monitoring process and firmly place the UN in the lead. Boutros-Ghali did not favor a UN Protection Force model for Rwanda, nor UN support for the OAU's observer force. Rather, his strategy followed a conventional and contingent peacekeeping model of inserting a UN force only when the parties already had made peace. Moreover, the external responsibility for supporting the peace process was moved from an admittedly weak OAU to the UN, which possessed a potentially formidable collective capacity but, as it turned out, one that it was unwilling to exercise.

The strategy of Boutros-Ghali was simple but effective. He refused to intercede for Salim in the Security Council to ask support for NMOG, arguing that the Council would be unlikely to assist an operation that was outside UN control.[13] As a result, the best option was for the UN and the OAU to cooperate "with the United Nations exercising command and control."[14] At the same time, he let Salim know that he himself preferred to wait for the outcome of the Arusha peace talks before deciding on the details of the envisaged force.[15] Given the OAU's admitted weakness, Salim took note of "institutional difficulties" and, lacking any allies among the permanent five, bowed out of any further discussion on how the two organizations could collaborate on a future force to promote or keep the peace. The international force envisaged "under the aegis" of both the UN and the OAU never materialized, and the UN Assistance Mission in Rwanda (UNAMIR), which appeared instead, was not mandated to protect civilians and was conceived as a classic peacekeeping operation that required prior peace on the ground.

Boutros-Ghali's policy made him a de facto ally of the strategy that France and the government of Rwanda pursued in the Security Council. The position reflected in part his reliance on France to compensate for general lack of U.S. support for his role as Secretary-General. Organizational interests and distrust of the OAU's effectiveness might have been important as well, as might more partisan concerns. Some observers recalled that Boutros-Ghali, as Egypt's minister of state for foreign affairs, had been instrumental in facilitating arms transfers to Rwanda after the RPF's invasion, thereby reversing Egypt's policy of not supplying arms to Rwanda.[16]

Establishing UNAMIR

Military failure compounded the diplomatic failure. Issues of military capacity and financing as well as regime issues, such as information and analysis, became more predominant in the next phase of the Security Council's involvement in three critical sets of events: (1) preparations for and authorization of UNAMIR; (2) delays in implementation of the peace agreement; and (3) cumulative evidence that a genocide was being planned. All events have been critically examined by scholars, journalists, and two commissions of inquiry.[17]

As for the first set of events, there is general agreement that UNAMIR's design was heavily influenced by the negative experiences of the UN-U.S. operations in the Somalia operation, a short-term institutional memory that would later reinforce and distort a pattern that had already been set. Resource constraints reflected the explosion of UN peacekeeping activities in the immediate post–Cold War world as well as the newly pronounced U.S. doctrine (Presidential Decision Directive 25) to limit its support for such operations.[18] Under the formula for assessed contributions, the United States was required to pay more than one-fourth of the costs of UN peacekeeping operations. The Clinton administration was particularly sensitive to congressional criticism of the cost of the U.S. share of UN peacekeeping, which had increased a stunning 370 percent from 1992 to 1993.[19]

These factors were played out against the background of the relative indifference to Rwanda that had characterized the Council's initial position. France's lone crusade to involve the Council was a two-edged sword, because its motives were suspect and because, being an ally of the government, it could not contribute a UN force that was supposed to be neutral.[20] That left the proposed UNAMIR with no powerful "patron" on the Council. The Secretariat, which in March–April 1993 had championed a UN role over the OAU, had by the fall firmly settled on a low-cost, low-risk operation. The UN leadership wanted command and control, but not sufficient control to assume a major responsibility for implementing the agreement.

The decisionmaking role of the Secretariat in relation to the Security Council becomes more important in this period because of its statutory role in the planning of the UN operation and because several Council members had little independent information from the field. The Secretariat, particularly the Department of Peacekeeping Operations (DPKO), which undertook the planning with guidance from the office of the Secretary-General, must therefore take considerable responsibility for the process that gave UNAMIR its final shape. Two aspects are critical in this regard.

First, the Secretariat recommended a much narrower mandate for UNAMIR than that called for in the Arusha Accords and what the parties to the agreement considered necessary to sustain the peace. This applies to three important points: geographic area to be secured, protection of civilians, and confiscation of illegal arms. The provisions in Arusha were watered down somewhat by the UN Reconnaissance Mission to Rwanda in late August, headed by the subsequent force commander, General Romeo Dallaire, but even more decisively reduced to a minimalist mandate in the proposals forwarded by the Secretariat to the Security Council and as finally approved.[21]

Unlike the Arusha Accords, the mandate proposed by the Secretariat and approved by the Council had no provisions for protecting civilians, collecting illegal arms, or taking action against armed gangs.[22] Securing "the country" was now limited to securing the capital city, Kigali. The principal function of the force had been narrowed primarily to monitoring the compliance of the two parties with regard to the military aspects of the agreement (demobilization, demining, and integration of their armed forces) and supporting the formation of a transitional government by securing a weapons-free zone in the capital. A small civilian police force (of sixty) was to verify maintenance of law and order.

Second, and as a result of the narrowed mandate, the size of the force was reduced correspondingly, ending up with slightly more than 2,500 peacekeepers. By contrast, General Dallaire had originally envisaged 8,000 peacekeepers, hoped for 5,000, but finally agreed to request only 2,500 as a feasible number that might be approved.[23]

From a decisionmaking perspective, the significant aspect of this process is that the Secretariat did not formally forward to the Security Council the contradictory information in the larger picture and the different policy options this might entail, as Keating emphasizes in this volume (Chapter 32.1). The omissions are striking in the two main reports in this earlier period, the Secretary-General's August 24, 1993, report on the Arusha Accords,[24] and his September 24 report recommending the establishment of UNAMIR, which lacked a broader political analysis.[25] The Secretariat did not mention that the proposed UN mission differed from that envisaged in the Arusha Accords on several critical points. Human rights concerns were not integrated with an analysis of deployment; there was no reference to the report of the UN special rapporteur, completed in August 1993, which concluded that the civilian Tutsi population was subject to genocidal violence;[26] nor was there reference to a similar report publicized earlier in the year by a panel of international human rights groups.[27] The Secretariat recommended deployment without reiterating concerns expressed in Kigali, inter alia to the Secretary-General's reconnaissance mission, that interethnic tension and opposition to the agreement by a militant third party posed serious obstacles to implementation. As subsequent scholarship has established, these concerns were widespread at the time.[28] Indeed, they were reflected in the clauses of the Arusha Accords that called for an international peacekeeping force with a comprehensive mandate, above all to collect illegal arms, neutralize armed gangs, and protect civilians.

The impression conveyed by the September 24 report was that implementation merely depended on two conditions: that the two sides complied with their commitments, and that UN members provided the human and financial resources specified, the latter an enormous problem in itself, as Marrack Goulding makes clear in this volume (see Chapter 18). If a third party were out to spoil the agreement, UNAMIR's role as a mere facilitator would be insufficient. This possibility and related consequences were not spelled out for the Security Council. Of course, Council members could make their own assessment based on an analysis of the Arusha Accords, but this was legitimately the function of the Secretariat and was crucial to the role of the elected ten, who were learning on the job and generally lacked an independent source of information.

The failure of the Secretariat to provide strategic options in a meaningful sense of the word can be readily explained with reference to the dynamic of "anticipatory veto." Given close and informal relations between the Secretariat and the Security Council, an unspoken rule in the Secretariat was to discern what the Council was likely to accept, then to prepare policy options within this range. It was a potentially dysfunctional decisionmaking process that in the Rwanda case contributed to disaster.

The Secretariat's reporting on the mission to the Security Council had a similar dysfunctional characteristic. The reports were generally of poor quality, offered little analysis of the implications of core issues and events, and were overly eager to present good news. Thus, at the end of 1993 the Secretariat reported that the installation of the transitional government was likely "by the end of the month,"[29] although in fact it was "nowhere in sight."[30] The massacres and massive displacement of Hutu in neighboring Burundi were characterized as a "potentially destabilizing situation,"[31] although it was evident to even casual observers in Kigali that the destabilization was actual and instant.[32] This report of December 30 noted the intention of a "well-armed and reportedly ruthless group to disrupt and even derail the peace process"[33] but did not discuss the implications with respect to UNAMIR's mandate and force. The deteriorating situation on the ground in Rwanda was not contrasted with the slow and inadequate deployment of the mission.

During the next three months—in what turned out to be the countdown to the start of the genocide and the resumption of civil war—there was a striking contrast between the internal and external communications in the United Nations. The details have since been presented in the scholarly literature and can be summarized here.[34] The reporting from the Secretariat to the Council that was in the public domain (external) differed sharply from the information that passed from the field to the headquarters (internal). In particular, the increasingly desperate calls from the force commander to exercise his mandate to the limit (and possibly beyond) in order to recover illegal arms, and for rapid transfer of equipment promised for his bare-bones force, were not shared with the Security Council through formal reporting channels. Nor was evidence that surfaced in early 1994 regarding a planned genocide, notably the famous cable from Dallaire to the DPKO on January 11.[35] On the whole, the external reporting had a reasonably optimistic tone with respect to what the UN mission was doing, with the concern focused on the failure of the Rwandan parties to keep to the implementation schedule.

Security Council members nevertheless had access to a vast network of informal information in the UN system. Some naturally had more access than others; most famously, Kofi Annan, then head of the DPKO, shared the January 11 cable with only some members of the Security Council and outside the Council chamber. "Bad news" information also originated from outside the UN system. The Belgian foreign minister on February 11 asked the Security Council to authorize "a firmer stance on the part of UNAMIR with respect to security" in view of increasing violence on the ground and the failure the Rwandan parties to form a transitional government.[36] In addition, the major Western powers all had embassies in Kigali; so did the principal African country on the Council, Nigeria. All the African countries could draw on OAU channels as well. As Keating describes in Chapter 32.1, members of the Council had to go outside the confines of the information flow in the UN to become better informed of what was happening in Rwanda, and some did.

The Council clearly was capable of making demands on the Secretariat for better options (as it did in mid-April 1994, after the crisis had erupted) and for criticizing its judgment (as it did when the Secretary-General in mid-April blamed Belgium for jeopardizing UNAMIR).[37] However, prior to mid-April 1996, the continued low priority assigned to the Rwanda conflict was reflected in the Council's generally passive role. The Council did not request further information regarding the possibility that the militant third party might "spoil" the Arusha Accords, nor did it ask for options to strengthen UNAMIR's stance in response to the Belgian request.

Consistent with its lack of demand for critical information and options, the Council continued to operate in a mode where UNAMIR's presence was made contingent upon local progress rather than being actively used to strengthen the peace process. When the implementation of the Arusha Accords stalled and the fragile peace was punctuated by increasing violence, the Council did *not* respond by engaging the UN with greater determination (e.g., by strengthening the modest UN force in place). Rather, the Council threatened to withdraw UNAMIR unless the Rwandan parties stuck to their agreement.[38] This happened in both January and on April 5, 1994—the day before the genocide started. Because the UN force presence had initially been made contingent upon progress toward peace on the ground, the logical conclusion was to withdraw when the peace process finally collapsed and the genocide erupted, which the Security Council promptly did.

Crisis

As evidence of large-scale violence mounted during the first week of crisis (April 6–13, 1994), the Council responded to the tone set by the United States and the United Kingdom and opted for de facto withdrawal (see Keating, Chapter 32.1). Other members on the Council, led by Nigeria, argued for strengthening UNAMIR and on April 13 circulated a draft proposal on behalf of the nonaligned members that proposed increasing the strength of UNAMIR and enlarging its mandate to "enable it to contribute to the restoration of law and order."[39] By that time, however, only a rapid offer of new troops could have made the resolution meaningful. Belgium, which had provided one of the two well-functioning contingents of UNAMIR, had announced the previous day that it would withdraw its troops in view of the murder of ten of its peacekeepers. The governments of other troop-contributing countries threatened the same, indifferent to the willingness of the military forces in the field to continue to play a part. Italy, Belgium, and France sent expeditionary forces, but only in order to evacuate their nationals; none of the latter offered troops to stabilize the situation or deter further violence. The United States, supported by the United Kingdom and urged on by Belgium, strongly argued against further commitment. As a result, and given that the large-scale slaughters already under way had not yet been labeled "genocide" but were readily accepted as "normal" for the region, the nonaligned draft resolution did not even come to a vote and died quietly.

It may be correct that the Council at that time was not aware that the genocide was being planned.[40] During the first week the fog of renewed civil war clouded the genocide under way. Yet lack of awareness on this point certainly does not explain why the Council's first response after April 6 was to disengage, and the only real debate was whether to disengage fully or to leave a remnant in place in order to be in a better position to restart the operation (see Chapter 32.1). On the contrary, the more evidence of an unfolding genocide accumulated, the more anxious two of the main players—the United States and the United Kingdom—became to deny that the violence indeed constituted a genocide and thus a ground for intervention.[41] Denying that the slaughters constituted a genocide, and hence a compelling reason for intervention, might also have suited other members of the Council, notably China.

Conclusion

The Rwanda case invites further reflection on the material, institutional, and normative boundaries that support, but also limit, the operations of the Council in this type of situation. Whether or not one agrees with Thomas Weiss's argument in this volume on the emergence of a "humanitarian impulse" with respect to victims of war (see Chapter 3), this chapter deals with the failure to prevent such victimization in the first place, partially because of what Weiss himself describes as the UN's demonstrated inability to conduct enforcement operations and the unwillingness by major powers to spend money, matched by an unwillingness to run risks. Others in this volume (e.g., Steven Ratner, Chapter 37) have noted if not celebrated the role of the Security Council in creating new rules in international law, as in establishing war crimes tribunals in civil wars, in interpreting the UN Charter in a robust way (the Kurds in Iraq, Haiti, etc.), and most significant, as being a catalyst for others to assume responsibility for international law in areas of security. Yet if the Security Council can serve in raising the international moral and legal standards higher, it can serve to lower them as well. The Rwanda case highlights the role of the Council in undermining international law by narrowing the interpretation of the Genocide Convention. Furthermore, by not asserting its role in the area of preventive diplomacy (Chapter VI), and by adopting a passive and contingent role in relation to security (Chapter VII), the Council failed in its promotional role in relation to the UN Charter as a whole. Only after the genocide was incontestably a fact did the Security Council try to reverse itself. Although authorizing reengagement and a new force in May 1994 (the so-called UNAMIR II), the Council had missed a critical opportunity to clarify the legal and moral responsibilities of states in relation to genocide.

The lack of transparency in the decisionmaking process at the time is noteworthy and continued to some extent afterward despite the appointment of a UN-initiated commission of inquiry. The selective version of the history of the mission presented in the official UN "blue book" functions effectively as a cover-up rather than a full disclosure of relevant documentation.[42] And despite the apologies and inquiries and efforts to describe, explain, recommend, and allocate blame, no one was in the end held accountable for possibly the greatest failure of the UN in its history. Heads did not roll among the diplomats or in the Secretariat. Kofi Annan, who was head of the DPKO at the time, went on to become Secretary-General, taking with him his closest staff, who had been central in the decisionmaking process on Rwanda. Overall, the weak accountability mechanisms in relation to disasters like Rwanda constitute a fundamental structural weakness of the UN system.

Which model best explains what happened? One model would envisage the Security Council as the pinnacle representation of a club of sovereign states somewhat frozen in time but ultimately representing the interests and powers of states in managing violent conflict around the globe. This model provides coherence to the narrative as told in this chapter: the major powers played the prime role in setting the agenda and in determining the parameters within which the Council operated. It suggests the need for a great power patron if the Council is to engage in a conflict. France was the patron of the regime, but France was compromised and the Tutsi lacked a patron. Hence we see the passive and contingent engagement. If this model—and only this model—is also held up as the normative framework for judging the actions of the Council, it seems that the Council behaved "correctly" by not engaging the organization in a conflict that was of limited interest to the state system as a whole.

However, if the normative model is a Council that is representative not only of the "international system" as the aggregate interests of state but also of an "international society," which as Hedley Bull forcefully argued is more than the sum of its composite state parts by forming a community bound by certain norms,[43] then the Council clearly failed. It did not represent a fundamental and positively codified norm against genocide and, by extension, did not represent the interests of millions of people who continue to be victimized by their own states.

In a related normative model the Security Council is seen as a moral authority with responsibility to articulate and affirm norms and to identify those who violate norms. By this criterion, the Security Council proved most deficient. The deficiency has been widely recognized: just as "Munich" became subsequently an icon of appeasement, "Rwanda" has become an icon of moral indifference and the failure of responsibility among bystanders.

However, the Rwanda case also suggests that the Council could function in a manner that is normatively acceptable yet that takes the reality of the club of sovereign states as its point of departure. Even in its lowest hour, the proceedings in the Council opened some room for maneuver for states that considered alternative action. If they had been able to back up their concerns with diplomatic, military, and financial resources, their brief but significant efforts in the Council to consider preventive actions and alternatives to withdrawal might have had an effect. None of these were major powers on a global scale but included representatives of smaller European states (Czechoslovakia and New Zealand) and a regional middle power (Nigeria). With proper support, such states may provide a safety-net function on the Council by drawing attention to conflicts that have low priority for the major powers but that are important to regional states and, above all, to the peoples most directly affected.

If the Council is to function in this manner, it requires either a different kind of support function from the Secretariat than that provided in the Rwanda case, or alternative sources of information and strategic planning. The Rwanda case illustrates how, when a generally low-priority conflict eventually gets the attention of the Security Council, the Secretariat assumes a particularly important decisionmaking role by virtue of its provision of information and strategic planning. The Secretariat evidently saw itself as primarily accountable to the permanent five, and it reacted within the perceived guidelines of the Council for a low-priority conflict—to define the problem as manageable and the proposed option as low-cost and low-risk. However, if the elected ten develop independent sources of information, and can pool these and other resources necessary for action, then a shift can take place. The closed loop that became the modus operandi in the decisive phases of the UN reaction to the Rwanda crisis—and when a UN presence was seen as contingent upon prior local progress toward peace, rather than a force to bring this about—can be opened up.

Notes

1. Ingvar Carlsson, Han Sung-Joo, and Rufus M. Kupolati, *Report of the Independent Inquiry into the Actions of the UN During the 1994 Genocide in Rwanda* (New York: United Nations, 1999).
2. Michael Barnett, *Eyewitness to a Genocide: The United Nations and Rwanda* (Ithaca: Cornell University Press, 2002).
3. United Nations, Department of Peacekeeping Operations, *Comprehensive Report on Lessons Learned from United Nations Assistance Mission for Rwanda (UNAMIR)* (New York: United Nations, 1996).
4. Samantha Power, *"A Problem from Hell": America and the Age of Genocide* (New York: Basic Books, 2002).
5. Linda R. Melvern, *A People Betrayed: The Role of the West in Rwanda's Genocide* (London: Zed Books, 2000).
6. Bruce Jones, *Peacemaking in Rwanda: The Dynamics of Failure* (Boulder: Lynne Rienner, 2001), p. 69; Ogenga Otunnu, "Rwandese Refugees and Immigrants in Rwanda" in Howard Adelman and Astri Suhrke, eds., *The Path of a Genocide: The Rwanda Crisis from Uganda to Zaire* (Rutgers, N.J.: Transaction Books, 1999), pp. 3–29.
7. United Nations, Department of Public Information (DPI), S/25356, 1996, p. 151.
8. Ibid., S/25355, 1996, p. 152.
9. Ibid., S/25363, 1996, p. 153.
10. Ibid., S/25385, 1996, p. 155.
11. Ibid., S/25400, 1996.
12. Howard Adelman, Astri Suhrke, and Bruce Jones, *Early Warning and Conflict Management in Rwanda: Study II of the Joint Evaluation of Emergency Assistance in Rwanda* (Copenhagen: DANIDA, 1996), p. 27.
13. United Nations, DPI, Doc. 11, 1996, p. 159.

14. Ibid.

15. United Nations, DPI, Doc. 9, 1996, p. 158.

16. Melvern, *A People Betrayed*, pp. 31–29.

17. Carlsson, Sung-Joo, and Kupolati, *Report of the Independent Inquiry;* Organization of African Unity, International Panel of Eminent Personalities to Investigate the 1994 Genocide in Rwanda and the Surrounding Events, *Rwanda: The Preventable Failure* (Addis Ababa, Ethiopia: Organization of African Unity, 2000).

18. Barnett, *Eyewitness to a Genocide*, p. 66; Power, *"A Problem from Hell,"* pp. 340–341; Alison L. des Forges, *"Leave None to Tell the Story": Genocide in Rwanda* (New York: Human Rights Watch, 1999), p. 199; Jones, *Peacemaking in Rwanda*, p. 106; Nicholas J. Wheeler, *Saving Strangers: Humanitarian Intervention in International Society* (Oxford: Oxford University Press, 2000), p. 241.

19. Adelman, Suhrke, and Jones, *Early Warning and Conflict Management in Rwanda*, p. 36.

20. Agnes Callamard, "French Policy and Practice in Rwanda," in Adelman, Suhrke, and Jones, *Early Warning and Conflict Management in Rwanda*.

21. Adelman, Suhrke, and Jones, *Early Warning and Conflict Management in Rwanda*, p. 89.

22. Resolution 872, October 5, 1993.

23. Jones, *Peacemaking in Rwanda*, p. 105; Barnett, *Eyewitness to a Genocide*, p. 66; Power, *"A Problem from Hell,"* 340–341.

24. S/26350, August 24, 1993.

25. *Report of the Secretary-General on Rwanda*, S/26488, September 24, 1993.

26. E/CN.4/1994/Add.1.

27. Fédération Internationale des Ligues des Droits de l'Homme, Report of the International Commission of Investigation of Human Rights Violations in Rwanda Since October 1, 1990. Paris/Washington, March 1993.

28. Des Forges, *"Leave None to Tell the Story,"* pp. 125–126; Mahmood Mamdani, *When Victims Become Killers: Colonialism, Nativism, and the Genocide in Rwanda* (Princeton: Princeton University Press, 2001), pp. 189–191; Melvern, *A People Betrayed*, pp. 62–65.

29. *Report of the Secretary-General on the United Nations Assistance Mission to Rwanda*, S/26927, December 30, 1993, para 12.

30. Barnett, *Eyewitness to a Genocide*, p. 75.

31. *Report of the Secretary-General on the United Nations Assistance Mission to Rwanda*, para 16.

32. Adelman, Suhrke, and Jones, *Early Warning and Conflict Management in Rwanda*.

33. *Report of the Secretary-General on the United Nations Assistance Mission to Rwanda*, para. 18.

34. Barnett, *Eyewitness to a Genocide;* des Forges, *"Leave None to Tell the Story";* Carlsson, Sung-Joo, and Kupolati, *Report of the Independent Inquiry*.

35. Reproduced in Adelman and Suhrke, *The Path of a Genocide*.

36. United Nations, Doc. 34, 1996, p. 244.

37. Adelman, Suhrke, and Jones, *Early Warning and Conflict Management in Rwanda*, pp. 43–44.

38. UN, DPI 1996, p. 242; Barnett, *Eyewitness to a Genocide*, 76.

39. Typescript document, April 13, 1994, para 5.

40. Jones, *Peacemaking in Rwanda*, p. 115.

41. Holly J. Burkhalter, "The Question of Genocide: The Clinton Administration and Rwanda," *World Policy Journal* 11, no. 4 (1994–1995): 44–54; Power, *"A Problem from Hell"*; Peter Ronayne and Joel H. Rosenthal, *Never Again? The United States and the Prevention and Punishment of Genocide Since the Holocaust* (Lanham, Md.: Rowman & Littlefield, 2001); Astri Suhrke and Bruce D. Jones, "Preventive Diplomacy in Rwanda: Failure to Act, or Failure of Actions Taken?" in Bruce W. Jentleson, ed., *Opportunities Missed and Opportunities Seized: Preventive Diplomacy in the Post-Cold War World* (Lanham, Md.: Rowman & Littlefield, 2000).

42. United Nations, Department of Public Information, S/25356, 1996.

43. Hedley Bull, *The Anarchical Society* (London: Macmillan, 1977).

An Insider's Account

COLIN KEATING

The tragedy of the genocide in Rwanda has haunted the international community since April–May 1994. I served as New Zealand's ambassador to the Security Council in 1993–1994. This chapter records my personal recollections and my thoughts about the lessons that should be drawn from the Council's handling of the Rwanda tragedy—lessons about process, preparedness, and most important, political will.

In February 1993 the question of Rwanda came to the Security Council as more or less a conventional civil war. After considerable reluctance, due to the pressure on the UN's peacekeeping resources in other parts of the world, the Council was persuaded that UN observers could assist in containing the cross-border elements of the conflict. Accordingly in June 1993, the UN Mission for Uganda-Rwanda (UNOMUR) was created to monitor the situation on the border between Uganda and Rwanda.[1]

UNOMUR achieved very little. Its mandate and resources were too modest to affect the situation. But this phase of the UN involvement in Rwanda influenced the way in which events were to unfold in 1994. First, it involved the UN in the peace-negotiating process between the factions involved in the Rwanda civil war that led to the Arusha Accords of August 1993, which established a cease-fire and contained a power-sharing agreement. Second, it led to the members of the Security Council seeing Rwanda as a small civil war rather than the smoldering volcano that it really was.

In mid-1993 the Council was preoccupied with desperate situations in Bosnia and Somalia. The list of crises extended from Iraq to North Korea to Haiti. These issues demanded so much time and political energy that Rwanda unfortunately did not receive quality attention.

I believe that the Rwanda experience proves that the United Nations must drastically improve the quality of the background information received by members of the Security Council about situations that come before them. It is clear with hindsight that, even in 1993, the situation in

Rwanda was much more complex and dangerous than was ever indicated to the members of the Council. It is true that the Secretariat followed existing conventions in reporting to the Council and that its sources of information were very limited. But there were a very large number of people in academia, in nongovernmental organizations (NGOs), in private life, and in the UN agencies who knew much more about Rwanda. Had the Council been exposed to a slice of this wisdom, it might have proceeded quite differently at a later time when confronted with a crisis.

The solution is not to ask the Secretariat to write even longer formal reports. It seems to me essential that, when a new situation comes before the Council, opportunities should be taken to present background briefings systematically and informally to Council members, using independent facilitation.

Another failure by the Security Council, which had its roots in the events of 1993, was the collective misunderstanding of the Arusha peace-negotiation process. Despite its request to the Secretary-General in Resolution 812 of March 12, the Council was not engaged in the Arusha process. As a result, when the Arusha talks concluded in August 1993 with a recommendation for a UN peacekeeping operation, there was anxiety in some parts of the Council that the peace process had effectively "boxed in" the United Nations and predetermined a key issue, which was not the prerogative of the negotiators. The parties had drafted provisions in the peace agreement with implications for UN action. These were predicated on the Council saying yes to the adoption of a resolution for a peacekeeping operation. This situation caused a sense of irritation with Rwanda on the part of some Council members, which may well have played a part in conditioning subsequent responses in 1994.

My conclusion is that, if it becomes clear that a Security Council–mandated operation might become an essential component of the willingness of the parties to commit to peace, then it is critical that the Council should be involved in the peacebuilding phase well before implicit commitments are entered into. Neither the Secretariat nor the facilitators of a peacemaking process have exclusive responsibility for preventive diplomacy. The parties to a conflict cannot bind the Security Council. The Council should therefore be much more actively involved in peace processes prior to their conclusion. And this suggests a more systematic process including the use of more visiting missions.

Although not an excuse for what happened later, it certainly helps in understanding subsequent events to appreciate that the Council members were generally beguiled by the outcome of the Arusha process. In their ignorance about the real situation, Council members were completely won over by the joint Rwandan government–Rwandan Patriotic Front (RPF) delegation that came to New York to trumpet the success of the peace negotiations. Given the "bad news" stories emerging on all other fronts on the Council's agenda at that time, it is easy to understand that members had little incentive to look into the problem more deeply. They were only too eager to see the positive—the end of the civil war. And so, in October 1993 a new peacekeeping operation, the UN Assistance Mission in Rwanda (UNAMIR), was created.[2] On the face of it, it seemed like a success story—one small positive ray of light in an otherwise incredibly gloomy year.

This general sense of enthusiasm about the Arusha peace process led not only to false political assumptions but also, as subsequent events showed, to unsound military decisions. UNAMIR was given a more robust mandate than was normal—to "contribute to the security of the city of Kigali inter alia within a weapons-secure area."[3] But the force structure given to the UNAMIR Force Commander—in particular the equipment and readiness levels of the force—bore no relationship to what was really needed.

Preparedness is perhaps the most difficult ongoing issue for the United Nations and will remain so in the future. But the UN has had to painfully relearn this lesson too often—go in too light and in the end, instead of keeping the peace, the blue helmets become a vulnerable target, or as in both Rwanda and Srebrenica,[4] the United Nations is simply unable to deliver on the humanitarian expectations of the international community.

We now know that the signs were there, very soon after Arusha, that all was not well. There was information available to the UN Secretariat, at least as early as January 11, 1994, when the force commander, General Romeo Dallaire, sent his famous cable to New York indicating that genocide was a serious possibility. UNAMIR was not in the benign environment that the Council assumed.

But the Secretary-General's report of December 30, 1993, had only the most oblique references to "violent incidents" and a "ruthless group." More important, the conclusions in that report seemed to Council members to be generally positive. As a result, the Council's response in Resolution 893 of January 6, 1994, passed over the security situation with only a preambular paragraph. Also—and this is reflected in the operative paragraphs—Resolution 893 demonstrated a growing concern about the cost of UNAMIR.

Clearly the Secretariat chose in December and January to proceed very discreetly with the information that it had. Perhaps it felt it was too risky to be frank with the Council, because the government of Rwanda had just been elected to the Council as a nonpermanent member.

This seems to me to demonstrate an important lesson for the international community. In my view, the General Assembly should be much more careful in the future about electing as a member of the Council a state that is the subject of an item on the Council's agenda. Articles 31 and 32 of the UN Charter already make formal provision for an appropriate role by member states with particular interests on issues before the Security Council. They envisage participation without the right to vote. But because Rwanda was elected to the Council with a right to vote, and in particular the right to participate in procedural decisions, it had a very significant capacity to block the required consensus at certain critical points. Rwanda was able to present significant obstacles to Council action during the time of crisis. This problem should not be repeated.

But the fact that Rwanda had a seat on the Council, whether or not this is the reason that the January 11, 1994, report from Kigali to New York was not revealed to the Council, should have stimulated the Secretariat to be much more innovative in ensuring that all other Council members were effectively briefed. In this case, it was particularly essential because General Dallaire's report revealed so transparently that the optimistic assumptions on which the Council had operated were false.

To understand the background to this apparent failure of communication, it must be remembered that in 1993–1994 there was constant tension between the Security Council and Secretary-General Boutros Boutros-Ghali about the appropriate level of Security Council involvement in decisionmaking. The Secretary-General detested what he called "micromanagement" by the member states in the Security Council. He even went so far as to issue an edict that the Undersecretary-General responsible for peacekeeping was not to appear in the Council. Secretariat advice was to be filtered through Boutros-Ghali's personal representative.

Throughout 1993–1994, I and some others on the Council had been in a sustained dispute with the Secretary-General about his policy of seeking to manage operations without any transparency or accountability to the Council and his personal inclination to selectively deal in only a few permanent members for discussion of difficult issues. The legitimizing role of the Security Council was being undermined, in particular with respect to the major political and military issues on its agenda. To me these are precisely the areas where political accountability should rest with national governments exercising their voice through their representatives on the Security Council. My position was that the Council not only had a right to know the details about its peacekeeping but also had a right and duty to decide the issues when human life was at stake. It was a difficult and sensitive period for Secretariat officials. I believe that the caution on the part of the Secretariat in early 1994 may have been largely influenced by the Secretary-General's personal contest with the member states on this issue.

The net result was that political representatives in New York only dimly perceived the steady deterioration in the Rwandan security situation. According to the Secretariat's reporting to the Security Council, the situation was an extension of the problem of the civil war. The deeper and more dangerous problem of a monumental threat to human life was ignored.

A strange dynamic came about in the Security Council in February and March 1994 because of this perception. The problems being encountered by UN peacekeeping operations elsewhere, as well as the spiraling costs of peacekeeping operations,[5] caused political pressure, particularly from the United States, for the United Nations to be able to demonstrate that it could "shut down" a peacekeeping operation. It almost did not matter which operation; the momentum was for a symbolic closure. UNAMIR quickly became the target. Other members of the Council such as New Zealand resisted this, making the point that if cuts were to be made, they should not be made to one of the African peacekeeping operations.

UNAMIR's initial mandate was due to expire on April 5, and the Secretary-General's report on the extension of the mandate created a focus for this particular debate to be played out.[6] For the first time, in the report of March 30, Council members saw a brief reference to "ethnic crimes," although the report attributed most incidences to "banditry," and again the conclusions were optimistic in tone.

Several of the larger financial contributors, with the notable exception of France, seemed determined to shut down UNAMIR unless the peace process was put back on track quickly. The majority of the Council members were very unhappy about this. But February–March 1994 was a very bad time for the Council. There was renewed chaos in Bosnia. Mortar shells hit the Sarajevo market.[7] In Somalia, U.S. forces were departing.[8] Crisis loomed in Asia over the North Korean nuclear issue. Rwanda still seemed much quieter than other trouble spots.

Resolution 909, adopted on April 5, 1994, must be seen in this context. The only basis on which certain veto-holders in the Security Council would agree to an extension of the mandate was by giving UNAMIR a short lease on life. Rwanda was effectively told that UNAMIR had only six weeks of life if the situation continued to be stalemated.

Throughout these months, the Rwandan government, as a Council member, was privy to all these discussions. How was the debate being read back in Kigali—especially by hard-line Hutu who wished Arusha to fail? Clearly those nations threatening to terminate UNAMIR thought they were applying leverage, which would positively reinforce the Arusha process. They seemed to be proceeding on the assumption that the parties really wanted peace and that they valued the UN presence. Now, with the benefit of hindsight, we know that the opposite was the case. The hard-line Hutu did not want peace. And they had access to a privileged insider's view of the discussions in the Council. Perhaps they read the mood of the major contributors very accurately and concluded that the interests of the Hutu extremists and the big powers actually coincided. Perhaps this led them in the direction of a dramatic act to end the Arusha process in the confident belief that this would precipitate a decision by the Security Council to pull out the UN forces—a decision that reports from their delegation in New York must surely have suggested was the inevitable consequence.

The essential lesson emerging here is that the Security Council must never again use the practice of imposing artificial reductions in mandate terms as supposed levers to secure negotiating outcomes in peace processes. There is no evidence that this tactic has worked in the past. To the contrary, in almost every situation there will be protagonists whose interests will be enhanced by the UN withdrawal. If the Council uses such tactics, it risks playing into the hands of one of the parties and destabilizing the situation.

I shall now turn to the events of April 1994. I assumed the presidency of the Security Council on April 1. It was Good Friday—a holiday—and the UN was closed. Early in the morning on Saturday, April 2, the chargé at the permanent mission of Bosnia and Herzegovina phoned me at home to advise that the Serbs had begun a massive attack on the UN-protected area of Gorazde. This crisis occupied almost all of the Easter weekend. But I did find a short time to dip into some historical papers about Rwanda.

I was surprised to learn that the previous instability in that country had involved mass murders of Tutsi civilians that seemed to verge on genocide. Moreover, it was clear that the ethnic complexity of the situation had been significantly underestimated in the reporting to the Council. It seemed beyond doubt that Tutsi had been ethnically cleansed in recent years. But large numbers of Tutsi still lived in communes with Hutu majorities. Bearing in mind the elements of the crisis that the Council was dealing with in Bosnia, the situation in Rwanda seemed to have all too many parallels. Civil war did not seem the appropriate description. The more I read, the more I understood the significance of the events in Burundi, where a few months earlier, in October, there had been massive loss of civilian life involving the same ethnic groups.[9] The whole region was a powder keg, and the match was about to be lit.

When the news came in to the Council on April 6 that the presidents of both Rwanda and Burundi had been killed in a suspicious plane crash, I sensed that an awful tragedy was at hand. The initial reaction by many Council members was influenced by the repeated advice from the Secretary-General's representative that the situation was being driven by the civil war and that the real need was to focus on how to produce a cease-fire. Not surprisingly, those Council members who a few weeks earlier had been advocating a tough line on compliance with the Arusha Accords and the need to "close down" UNAMIR if there was further backsliding, now spoke very bluntly about the need for the Council to have the courage to carry out the threat that was implicit in Resolution 909. They began to suggest withdrawing the force. This trend was acutely reinforced after the murder of ten Belgian peacekeepers by Hutu militias when the Belgian government initiated a major diplomatic campaign to persuade the United Nations to leave.

In the midst of this the Council was briefed by France and the United States about the operation being mounted to extract foreign nationals from Rwanda. It was clear that many in the Council were uncomfortable that while this robust military intervention was under way, reports of mass murder were beginning to filter in.

In the absence of good information from the Secretariat, I began having personal meetings—sometimes two or three times a day—with the New York representatives of the International Committee of the Red Cross (ICRC) and Médécins sans Frontières (MSF). I was then able to orally brief the Council on what I was being told. This also provided a factual framework against which I, as president of the Council, could speak more authoritatively to the media about the situation.

The representative of the Secretary-General continued to report that the special representative of the Secretary-General (SRSG) in Kigali considered the key issue to be the fighting between the RPF and the remnants of the Hutu government. These oral reports significantly muddied the waters. The media, the NGOs, and the force commander had a much clearer view of the situation.

The Council was now in a major difficulty. Not only were some of its most powerful members insisting on the termination of the mandate, consistent with the threat they had written into Resolution 909, but in its midst the Council had the representative of the Hutu regime, who naturally sought to focus the discussion on the RPF actions and ignore what was happening in territory held by the Rwandan government. Furthermore, given the principle of consensus, he was able to effectively block for several weeks a concerted position in the nonaligned caucus in the Council. On occasions, he was able to filibuster discussion on Council positions in informal consultations.

As the days passed, the advocates of closing down UNAMIR pressed their case with increasing vigor. And a new feature emerged. Increasingly I was under pressure, as was the Department of Peacekeeping Operations (DPKO) in the Secretariat, from troop-contributing countries (TCCs) that were extremely anxious about the safety and security of their soldiers deployed with UNAMIR. Many believed that their soldiers were exposed to unreasonable risks. Like the Council, they had been led into believing that UNAMIR was essentially in a benign environment. Their governments and their public opinion had seen what had happened to the Belgian contingent.

I was given clear and compelling evidence from the Secretariat, reinforced by my daily meetings with ambassadors from TCCs, that not only was there a problem with the TCCs at a governmental level, but there was also a serious problem with many of the contingents in the field. The United Nations was reaping what the Council had sown by deploying a force with inadequate equipment, training, and firepower. The force was really only suitable for a benign environment. Without the Belgians, they were in deep trouble. Desertion was beginning to occur and, in the Secretariat's judgment, and from the advice that I was receiving from the ambassadors of TCCs, it was only a matter of days before the troop-contributing governments unilaterally withdrew their troops from the force. At that point UNAMIR would have collapsed, which would have been an ignominious failure for the United Nations. At the same time, I was hearing from the ICRC and MSF that Rwanda faced an emerging crisis involving civilian casualties of massive proportions.

The real challenge was not to save face for the United Nations but to try to maneuver the Council into a position that would allow UNAMIR to remain with at least some capacity to protect civilians until a substantial intervention force could be marshaled. The problem was how to achieve this strategy. I knew I could really rely on only four colleagues in the Council, the ambassadors of the Czech Republic, Spain, Nigeria, and Djibouti. They indicated that they would support a strategy to preserve the UN presence in Rwanda to provide protection for civilians.

The second requirement was a nucleus of committed soldiers in the field. An important factor at this time was the reference in Resolution 872 to "contributing to a weapons-free zone in Kigali." This provided a basis for the force commander to interpret his rules of engagement so as to allow whatever robust action was possible in order to protect civilians. The heroism of General Dallaire and his troops, who provided protection for groups of civilians, must be acknowledged.

The third requirement was the cooperation of the Secretariat. I began to deal directly with the DPKO, which was happy to have political leadership in this direction. It confirmed that General Dallaire, the force commander, was willing and able to take protective action with whatever troops he could muster from UNAMIR. We established that both the Canadian and Ghanaian contingents would stand firm. Dallaire advised that his objective was to save lives in the immediate vicinity of Kigali and build a bridgehead for a rapid reinforcement of the UN presence as soon as that would be politically and militarily possible. But he and the DPKO needed time to develop a plan, and they needed New York to deal with the problem of the contingents who were either about to desert or whose governments were about to unilaterally recall them.

Within the Council, support for an immediate termination of the mission had now swelled to a clear majority. Given these circumstances, it would have been fatal to have tabled any proposal for decision that would be vetoed or might not secure a majority.

It became clear that a possible way forward to secure Council agreement on keeping UNAMIR in place, and to respond to the concerns of TCCs that were on the point of leaving, was a compromise proposal that the Council would downsize the UNAMIR force but, in return, extend the mandate. The downsizing meant little more than the Council acquiescing in what would happen anyway. Had we retained the status quo, most of the blue helmets would have voted with their feet and departed, and in a chaotic manner that would have increased the risk to all, humiliated the United Nations, and done nothing to save any Rwandan civilians. But in return for the downsizing we achieved agreement on an extended mandate—some breathing space in which the plans could be developed to reinforce the operation and begin a serious effort to protect civilians.

It was inevitable that Resolution 912 of April 21, 1994, which decided to downsize the UNAMIR force, would be misunderstood and criticized. But even with the benefit of hindsight, I still consider it the only viable option at that time with any possibility of a good outcome.

The small group of countries seeking to preserve the mandate, to keep the force in place, and to reinforce it as soon as possible were only too conscious that if the majority in the Council had prevailed at that time and the United Nations had left Kigali in such circumstances, there would have been no possibility of return.

The second feature of the strategy that this group of countries was pursuing was driven progressively by what the NGO community was telling us from about April 14–15 that genocide was most definitely taking place in Rwanda. An important goal for this group at Council meetings each day was therefore to try to get the Council to focus not on the fighting between the Rwandan government and the RPF, but rather on what was happening in the towns and villages throughout Rwanda. Most important, we tried to persuade the Council to name what was happening as "genocide." The objective was to build international support for reinforcement of UNAMIR. But this strategy ran into some very heavy roadblocks. No one was surprised about initial U.S. opposition. The United States had stood outside the Genocide Convention for many years.[10] China's opposition, although muted in public, was very vigorous in private conversation. It had a rooted opposition to the introduction of any human rights language in the Security Council and saw the Genocide Convention in that capacity. The United Kingdom's position was more pragmatic, but its interventions were clearly in a negative direction. Disappointingly, although Nigeria and Djibouti tried to assist as best they could, the nonaligned caucus was impotent on the issue. This was not only because of the Rwandan delegation, but also because of a more general reluctance to name and shame.

At the end of April the Council finally agreed to a presidential statement addressing the true situation.[11] It used words drawn specifically from the Genocide Convention. Sadly, it was still not possible to reach agreement on the use of the word "genocide." Indeed, even this outcome was possible only because of a draft resolution tabled by New Zealand, from the chair, threatening to force a vote that would have publicly exposed those countries that were resisting.[12]

At this point there was a sense that the Council was about to turn the corner and that the first few weeks of May would bring decisive action to reinforce UNAMIR with a force capable of doing what General Dallaire had been urging. He had been given time to develop a plan. A military operational strategy was now available. The Secretariat had resolved its internal position and was now strongly in favor of forceful action by the Council to reinforce UNAMIR.

On May 6, exactly one month after the Rwandan president's plane went down in Kigali, resolutions were presented to the Council by the New Zealand delegation and by the nonaligned movement. Secretariat recommendations were presented to the Council on May 13.[13] General Dallaire's plan had resolved most of the technical problems. In my view, at that point there were thirteen or perhaps fourteen votes in favor of a draft resolution. The resolution was "put in blue," meaning that it could be adopted within twenty-four hours. Four days later there was still no agreement. The momentum slipped away because the United States, a vetoholder, had indicated that it had fundamental problems with deploying a reinforced UNAMIR. As a result, Resolution 918, adopted on May 17, was no more than a faint step forward. The deployment and reinforcement was delayed because of disagreement over whether the force commander's plan for an "inside-out" operation was militarily the most feasible, or whether, as the United States believed, an "outside-in" strategy should be pursued instead.

It was an almost surreal issue. While thousands of human beings were being slaughtered every day, ambassadors argued fitfully in New York for weeks about military tactics. This situation cried out for professional military and technical advisers to sit together with the Secretariat's chief military adviser and quickly work through the military issues. It was particularly frustrating for New Zealand—which only a few weeks earlier had proposed in the Council's Working Group on the "Agenda for Peace" the idea of constituting a standing technical working group of the Council precisely to deal quickly and professionally with military issues at the working level.

The Military Staff Committee is almost certainly not capable of resurrection, and given its constitutional composition the United Nations as a whole would rightly oppose its reactivation.[14] But if modernizing the

Security Council is to be a serious consideration, then the mechanism by which it consults on technical military issues must be updated.

Finally, it is important to address squarely the question of political will. The argument is often made that no one was willing to contribute troops for a reinforced UNAMIR. This is not true. Troops were on offer, but equipment and transportation were required. Matching them up was never going to be easy, but it was never seriously tried. It must be remembered that aircraft, logistics, and money were conjured up in April 1994 for the evacuation of a small number of foreign nationals.[15] Again for Operation Turquoise, the aircraft, logistics, and money could be found.[16] And yet again aircraft, logistics, and money could be found a few weeks later for an intervention to feed millions of Hutu refugees in Goma.[17] Resources could have been made available for an operation reinforcing UNAMIR in May 1994, but resources were not the problem. The problem was a lack of political will to take another risk in Africa, following the U.S. experiences in Somalia.

One of the key reasons why the troops and resources never came together and the military plan was never finalized was because the Security Council was unable to show the leadership expected of it. Normally the Security Council is the focus of collective leadership. It decides to act. That decision constitutes a call to the member states to exercise collective security responsibilities. In May and June 1994, because of the threatened U.S. veto, the Council was not able to agree to deploy. That signal and lack of leadership were anything but a call to act, and as a result member states also held back.

If the international community is ever to be able to act effectively for human protection purposes, then it must pay attention to the recommendation of the Commission on Intervention and State Sovereignty.[18] The commission urged that permanent members of the Security Council should agree not to apply their veto power in matters where their vital state interests are not involved, and certainly not to obstruct the passage of resolutions authorizing intervention for human protection purposes for which there is otherwise majority support. If this recommendation is applied in the future, and if the Council shows the necessary leadership, troop-contributing countries will have clear and credible signals upon which to base their decisions to commit contingents to such an operation.

Conclusion

Much has been done to improve process in the Security Council since the early 1990s. But much more remains to be done. Change has barely kept up with the rising expectations of the wider membership. And there remains the question of political will. In the early 1990s, at the end of the Cold War, the positions of many governments reflected a desire among their populations for a peace dividend, for a withdrawal from situations that involved risk or the possibility of casualties. Perhaps now there is a wider recognition that no part of the world is so far away that massive violations of human rights, orchestrated attacks on civilians, or the perpetration of terror can be ignored. But as new lessons are being learned, we must ensure that the lessons from Rwanda will not be forgotten.

Notes

1. Resolution 846, June 22, 1993.
2. Resolution 872, October 5, 1993.
3. Ibid., para. 3.
4. *Report of the Secretary-General Pursuant to General Assembly Resolution 53/35: The Fall of Srebrenica,* A/54/549, November 15, 1999.
5. In 1990 peacekeeping expenditures totaled U.S.$464 million. In 1994 they had risen to U.S.$3,342 million. See Michael Renner, "Peacekeeping Expenditures 1947–2001," Global Policy Forum, www.globalpolicy.org/finance/tables/pko$$.htm.
6. S/1994/360, March 30, 1994.
7. Tony Smith, "Shelling of Sarajevo Market Kills Sixty-six, Wounds Hundreds," *Washington Post,* February 6, 1994.
8. Keith B. Richburg, "GIs Quitting Somalia Leave by Back Door; Troubles Endure as Operation Winds Down," *Washington Post,* March 7, 1994.
9. Mark Huband, "Burundi Bloodbath Runs Its Course as the West Looks On," *The Guardian,* October 31, 1993.
10. Even though the United States was one of the first signatories of the 1948 Convention on the Prevention and Punishment of the Crime of Genocide in 1948, it did not ratify it until 1988, and then only with reservations.
11. S/PRST/1994/21, April 30, 1994.
12. Linda R. Melvern, *A People Betrayed: The Role of the West in Rwanda's Genocide* (London: Zed Books, 2000).
13. S/1994/565, May 13, 1994.
14. The provision for a military staff committee was laid down in Article 47 of the *Charter of the United Nations.*
15. Tyler Marshall, "Belgians Fleeing Rwanda as Ethnic Killings Mount in Central Africa: Many Foreigners Still Await Rescue in Beleaguered Capital, Cease-Fire Accord Fails to Take Hold," *Los Angeles Times,* April 12, 1994.
16. Richard Dowden, "French 'Invasion' of Rwanda Underway," *The Independent,* June 22, 1994.
17. Tom Rhodes, "West Steps Up Aid Airlift for Rwanda," *The Times of London,* July 23, 1994.
18. International Commission on Intervention and State Sovereignty, *The Responsibility to Protect* (Ottawa: International Development Research Center, 2001).

An African Perspective

Ibrahim A. Gambari

Nigeria served a two-year term (1994–1995) as one of three African non-permanent members of the Security Council—a period that coincided with momentous changes in the international political environment. A few years earlier, the Cold War had come to an end. The euphoria that followed the downing of the Berlin Wall and the defeat of Iraq in the Gulf War by a U.S.-led international coalition of forces authorized by the Security Council may have encouraged the grandiose declaration about the arrival of a "new world order." In this atmosphere, a famous scholar, Francis Fukuyama, claimed that we have come to the "end of history," precipitated by the apparent victory of the free market and liberal democracy over command economies and totalitarian political systems.

However, the crises in the Balkans, Burundi, and Rwanda, for which the UN appeared to be ill-prepared, soon led to the sober realization that the world remained a dangerous place. Indeed, the root causes of conflicts and instability, especially those with economic origins, or with deep historical and ethnic antagonisms, did not disappear with the end of the Cold War. Rather, the case of Rwanda became emblematic of post–Cold War intrastate conflict and exemplified the debility of the Security Council in addressing them.

Of course, when member states of the United Nations collectively make disastrous decisions such as in Somalia, Bosnia, and Rwanda, there is a tendency to place the blame on the world body, especially its Secretary-General. Yet the late Lord Caradon's remark, made decades ago, that there is nothing wrong with the United Nations that is not attributable to its members, remains very relevant. The United Nations is nothing more than an aggregation and tool of its members that can only be as effective and responsive to world crises as member states, especially the most powerful ones, want it to be. And it is from this perspective, as an African member of the Security Council, that I make my contribution to this book.

The end of the Cold War presented Africa and the international community with the opportunity to resolve some of the long-standing and internecine conflicts on the continent (Namibia, South Africa, Angola, and Mozambique). On the flip side, however, the disappearance of the ideological rivalry, and its induced competition for friends and influence within Africa by the erstwhile superpower adversaries, unleashed some of the negative forces of subnationalism and ethnic rivalry. Local leaders, with the help of powerful external patrons, had previously suppressed many of these. Consequently, some of the client states that were artificially held together came unhinged, resulting in a new wave of conflicts in Africa from Liberia to Somalia to Rwanda and Burundi, among others. The post–Cold War era, therefore, presented the continent with positive opportunities hitherto unavailable while also presenting an array of new pitfalls. The combination of old and new types of conflict in Africa invariably meant that the majority of issues that were before the UN Security Council were African ones.

In this regard, and in the effort to promote the cause of peace in Africa, the Nigerian delegation made it a cardinal and guiding principle in all its activities while on the Council to work as hard as it could, in cooperation and collaboration with other Council members, to try to decongest the Council's agenda of African issues. This approach was informed by the feeling that the multiplicity of crises raging on the African continent have sapped the continent's meager and much needed resources and have made it unsuitable for longer-term investment. The approach adopted by the Nigerian delegation was cooperative and began with consulting the other African members of the Council, before moving to encompass all non-aligned members of the Council and subsequently all other interested Council members.

As chief delegate of Nigeria during the events leading up to the Rwandan crisis of 1994 and the genocide that followed, I was an observer-participant in the decisionmaking process in the Security Council and therefore in a privileged position to explain things the way I saw them at close range. Without a doubt, it was the Security Council, especially its most powerful members, as well as the international community as a whole, that failed the people of Rwanda in their gravest hour of need.

The Genocide in Rwanda
and the Security Council Response

The controversy over the culpability of the international community for its failure to prevent the genocide in Rwanda is one that will not go away. In February 1998, in his testimony at the International Criminal Tribunal for Rwanda (Arusha, Tanzania), General Romeo Dallaire, the former force

commander of the UN Assistance Mission in Rwanda (UNAMIR), confessed that "with a well-armed group of 5,000 men [and a proper mandate]
the United Nations could have stopped the slaughter of hundreds of thousands of Rwandans."[1] It must remain the eternal anguish for General
Dallaire that, despite his attempts to warn his superiors in New York as
early as January 1994, and his belief that the Security Council had the
means and power to stop the massacres, the tragedy in Rwanda, which
began on April 6, 1994, ended with the death of more than 800,000 people,
mostly Tutsi and some "moderate" Hutu.

General Dallaire did offer some excuses for the UN's reluctance to act
to prevent or stem the genocide by pointing out that "this was April, 1994:
the Americans had lost 18 soldiers in Mogadishu [Somalia], the Pakistanis
had also lost several in Somalia while the UN [forces] were spread out in
16 or 17 different Missions around the world."[2] The fact, nonetheless, was
that following the deaths in a suspicious aircraft crash on April 6, 1994, of
Rwandan president Juvenal Habyarimana, a Hutu, and the president of
Burundi, who was accompanying him, Hutu extremists began the massacres. This triggered the resumption of fighting by the Tutsi-dominated
Rwandan Patriotic Front (RPF) until the RPF troops put a stop to the
killings and took over the capital of Kigali in July 1994.[3]

At this critical stage, rather than act to prevent or halt the massacre, the
UN peacekeepers unfortunately became part of the problem. Indeed, "right
from the beginning of the Mission, UNAMIR was beset with logistic problems . . . almost all the contingents came from developing countries with
weak logistics bases at home. UNAMIR was also operating on a 'shoe-
string' budget before the Civil War broke out on April 6, 1994."[4] There
were also serious complaints about dogmatic interpretation of UN regulations by UNAMIR's administration,[5] which was generally regarded as
incompetent, and the disconnect between Security Council mandates and
the resources provided (or not provided) to implement them. Although it
came too late for the people of Rwanda, these and other related structural
issues were to be addressed later in the famous Brahimi Report on future
UN missions.

When ten Belgian soldiers serving in UNAMIR were killed on April 7,
1994, Brussels withdrew its battalion from the mission. As a consequence,
Bangladesh decided to withdraw its own contingent, and by April 19, 1994,
the first batch of UNAMIR soldiers were evacuated to Nairobi, Kenya. In a
real sense, therefore, the Belgians triggered the collapse of UNAMIR. In
hindsight, one of the most serious flaws in the Security Council–mandated
mission in Rwanda was that Belgium, a former colonial power in that
region, was allowed to participate in the mission. As such, it was not perceived as an impartial actor in the history and politics of Rwanda.

In any case, the reality at UN Headquarters was that many member states, especially those that were troop-contributing countries to UNAMIR, seemed mainly concerned about their troops and the potential political repercussions in their respective capitals of dead peacekeepers returning home in body bags. Justifiable and legitimate as these concerns were, it is my view that those countries, in large part, ignored the moral and overriding duty to help save hapless and defenseless civilians, including innocent women and children, who were being massacred. The Ghanaian battalion of less than 500, which stayed back, demonstrated clearly how much difference a well-equipped UN force with a robust mandate could have been able to accomplish in terms of saving human lives in the situation. Ghanaian brigadier-general Henry Kwami Anyidoho, deputy force commander of UNAMIR, was determined, and the Ghanaian government agreed with him, that UNAMIR should not shut down and that the Ghanaian battalion should stay and become by default the backbone of a residual UN force. The Ghanaians and the Tunisians of the residual force earned well-deserved praise for their courageous dedication and success in saving thousands of Rwandans who otherwise would have been victims of genocide.

Nonetheless, given the critical situation that prevailed at that time, with no realistic prospect of the two opposing forces agreeing on an effective cease-fire in the immediate future, and the need for the UN to maintain its efforts to help stop the genocide, the Secretary-General sent a report to the Security Council on April 20, 1994.[6] In it, he presented the Council with three alternatives to the status quo for its consideration, before the decision to reduce UNAMIR force level was taken.

The first alternative was the deployment of immediate and massive reinforcement of UNAMIR and a change in its mandate so that it would be equipped and authorized to coerce the opposing forces into a cease-fire, and to attempt to restore law and order and put an end to the killings. This alternative had the added advantage of "preventing the repercussions of the violence" from spreading to neighboring countries and leading to regional instability. It would have required the Council to deploy several thousand additional troops and UNAMIR to be given enforcement powers under Chapter VII of the UN Charter. Considering the fiasco in Somalia, this was not considered a politically feasible option by some members of the Security Council.

The second alternative was essentially a reduction in the deployment to a small group, to be headed by the force commander and to remain in Kigali to act as intermediary between the two parties in an attempt to bring them to an agreement on a cease-fire, in addition to assisting in the resumption of humanitarian relief operations. For this reduced mandate, the Secretary-General estimated a force strength of about 270 observers.

The third alternative, which the Secretary-General had stated clearly that he did not favor, was a complete withdrawal of UNAMIR. This he feared would amount to a complete abandonment of the people of Rwanda and a total betrayal of all the ideals of the United Nations and hopes of collective security.

The bombshell came on April 21, 1994, when, by its now infamous Resolution 912, the Security Council called for a reduction of UNAMIR forces from 2,558 to 270—all ranks. I believe this represented a collective failure of all members of the international community and in particular members of the Security Council. One could argue with much justification that the Secretary-General should have identified the first option as his preferred alternative and pushed for its acceptance by the Council. Assuming such a clear position may not have altered the course of events, especially in the face of strong opposition from key Council members, but this strategy was not even attempted. It is the duty of the Secretary-General to persuade the Council to do the right thing under these circumstances.

Several troubling questions were asked that must have captured the frustrations and anguish of UNAMIR's force commanders at the time: What could they do on the ground with a force of 270 in the face of all the hostilities? What made the Security Council take such a decision? Was the world to abandon Rwanda? Was it because the operation was in a developing country or more pointedly on the "dark continent"?[7] In a statement explaining Nigeria's vote in favor of Resolution 912, the delegation warned that the issue of the unfolding tragedy in Rwanda transcended politics; rather it was a moral question and went to the heart of the credibility of the United Nations, with implications that would echo well beyond Rwanda.[8]

Nigeria like many other Council members was slow in grasping the implications of what was happening in Rwanda, especially at the commencement of what became full-scale genocide. Without a resident diplomatic mission in Kigali, the delegation in New York relied almost entirely on UN sources for information about the developments in Rwanda. In spite of the limited information, however, the Nigerian delegation's Afrocentric instinct dictated its repeated calls for more UN forces to be deployed through UNAMIR, as was eventually approved by the Council through Resolution 912. The record of the Council's open meetings on the subject does not fully reflect the Nigerian delegation's efforts in this regard. For example, its stubborn insistence, even when it was completely isolated, as well as the understanding of New Zealand's ambassador Colin Keating, president of the Council in April 1994, that ensured that Resolution 912, which was adopted late in the evening of April 21, was not simply an intermission in the lengthy debate on Bosnia that had been taking place throughout that day.

Contrary to the attempts by some Council members to quietly and quickly adopt Resolution 912 without any statements, the Nigerian delegation insisted on the right of all delegations who wanted to explain their votes to do so. And the delegation took advantage of the opportunity to make the Nigerian position clear: Nigeria was not entirely happy with the Council's decision. Although we expressed serious reservations in our support for that resolution, in retrospect the Nigerian delegation should probably have abstained on the voting as we later did on Resolution 929 (1994), authorizing France's Operation Turquoise. Why did Nigeria and the other African members of the Security Council fail to persuade the Council to act differently? A number of reasons may be given.

First, there was only one African country contributing troops to UNAMIR (Ghana), and it was neither the most influential on the ground in Kigali nor a member of the Council. Hence Nigeria and other African members of the Council had little or no leverage over the position of the other troop-contributing countries, which were pushing for and indeed commencing the pullout of their troops from UNAMIR. Second, the members of the nonaligned movement were never given the opportunity to initiate and present draft resolutions concerning conflicts in which they had direct interest or affinity. Third, the Belgians were not content with withdrawing their own troops from UNAMIR; they also decided to use their considerable diplomatic leverage to lobby vigorously with North Atlantic Treaty Organization (NATO) allies on the Council to put an end to the entire peacekeeping operation. Fourth, the United States was initially in support of total withdrawal of UNAMIR and had to be persuaded to accept a drastic drawdown of the military personnel as a compromise solution. Fifth, events were moving so rapidly on the ground in Rwanda that the leadership of the Organization of African Unity did not have the opportunity to organize diplomatic lobbying efforts in the key Western capitals to strengthen the hands of the African members of the Security Council. Finally, in the post–Cold War environment there was considerable pressure on all members to have Security Council resolutions adopted by consensus, and in almost all the cases in 1994–1995 this was indeed the case.

In my view the Council had the option and the responsibility to garner the necessary political will on the part of its members, particularly the permanent members, in order to authorize the deployment of additional troops. The situation desperately warranted such an action in order to put an end to the violence. Some delegations, like Nigeria's, argued hopelessly against cutting and running from Rwanda. They were of course overwhelmed and presented with a fait accompli in the form of deserting peacekeepers and went along with Resolution 912.

To underscore the point about lack of political will, one only needs to consider how long it took to get the force strength of UNAMIR II up to the authorized level of 5,500 following Resolution 918 of May 17, 1994, which was adopted during Nigeria's presidency of the Council. It took more than three months to deploy the first batch of troops. In this situation, the anger of the existing government of Rwanda at the abandonment of its people by the UN is understandable and justified.

Furthermore, logistical problems were also responsible for the delay between the authorization of the expanded UNAMIR, the contribution of sufficient numbers of troops, and their actual deployment in Rwanda. The principal lesson here is that even when African states were persuaded to contribute troops to an international peacekeeping force (some countries outside the continent were reluctant to do so for conflicts in Africa), the constraints posed by logistics problems such as equipment for the troops, airlifting, and communication facilities are enormous. For example, as Deputy Force Commander Anyidoho pointed out, the Zambian troops for the expanded UNAMIR took a "ridiculously" long time in arriving in Kigali. The contingent elements of the Zambian troops, trained on Dutch equipment, arrived on August 26, 1994; however, their colleagues who formed part of the advanced party of the same battalion did not arrive until October 30, 1994.

The tragedy in Rwanda also illustrates an enormous contrast between the will of the international community as a whole to act promptly and massively to prevent or halt genocide, on the one hand, and the boldness of the French to launch Operation Turquoise as a humanitarian initiative, on the other. As the civil war in Rwanda escalated, hundreds of thousands of Rwandans perished from the massacres, diseases, and hunger, and noncombatants fled to neighboring countries in enormous proportions. While the entire world watched the ongoing tragedy unfold without any extraordinary action to avoid or mitigate the human sufferings, the French government decided to launch a humanitarian action in Rwanda to protect the Tutsi minority and moderate Hutu who were the main targets of the so-called presidential guards and the militias.

The Rwandan government forces welcomed the French initiative; however, UNAMIR initially had mixed reactions to the deployment. On June 22, 1994, the Security Council, in Resolution 929, authorized the government of France to carry out humanitarian operations in Rwanda under Chapter VII of the UN Charter. This was in contrast to the mandate of UNAMIR, which was based on Chapter VI of the Charter—that is, peaceful settlement of disputes in light of the challenges facing it before and during the civil war in Rwanda. In the informal discussions in the Security Council that followed the adoption of Resolution 929, several members, especially those from the developing countries, were uneasy about the French initiative in view of the latter's history of interventions in African conflicts. In spite of the Nigerian delegation's characterization of Resolution 929 as a "reluctant decision of a divided Security Council,"[9] the authorization was given to France to go ahead with its unilateral operation. UNAMIR was asked by the Council to work in cooperation with the French initiative, although it was to maintain a distinct identity. Consequently, the French established a "humanitarian protection zone" in the southwestern sector of Rwanda. The whole idea was opposed by the RPF on the grounds that it was an act designed to protect the Hutu and government "killers"; this point of view was also shared by some Western observers. Nonetheless, UNAMIR cooperated fully and successfully with Operation Turquoise and eventually took over the initiative.

Conclusion

In my experience on the Security Council and since then, I think that it would be misleading to regard the Council as an organic body that always acts to uphold the aims and objectives of the UN Charter. In reality, the Council is first and foremost a political institution that functions in concentric circles of interests and influence. The outer ring of that circle consists of the nonpermanent members that do not belong to the nonaligned movement unless they have other connections with NATO members. The next inward circle comprises the nonaligned movement, whose members meet fairly regularly and try, with sporadic success, to harmonize their positions on issues before the Council. Then there are the five permanent members (the P-5, the P-4 plus China, the circle of the P-3 [France, Britain, and the United States]), and finally the most powerful inner circle, the P-1, which is, of course, the United States. However, as the head of the Nigerian delegation, I felt that the exercise of preponderant power required the assumption of commensurate responsibility especially in protecting the weak and powerless.

Hence it is a matter of great regret that at the time when neighboring and other African countries as well as some other members of the international community were struggling to cope with the genocide in Rwanda and its immediate aftermath, U.S. officials would not allow the word "genocide" be used in public comments and in particular during the deliberations of the Security Council. This was apparently because of the fear in Washington that to do so could have increased domestic and international as well as legal pressure (under the Genocide Convention) for intervention to stop the carnage.

However, there was an apparent reversal of U.S. policy on this issue by President Bill Clinton in his decision to make a stopover in Kigali on March 25, 1998, during his visit to the African continent. He seized the opportunity in a public event to "address and acknowledge the genocide and the humanitarian crisis that ensued." This gesture is, of course, of little comfort to the victims of the genocide, but it is better late than never for the only superpower left in the post–Cold War era to openly address and acknowledge the horrendous crime against humanity in Rwanda. This apology, however belated, was made to coincide with the fiftieth anniversary of the International Convention Against Genocide and the International Convention on Human Rights. It is a grim reminder that so much time has elapsed and, in many ways, so little has been accomplished by the international community in preventing the recurrence of genocide and other crimes against humanity.

The 1994 genocide in Rwanda will remain a terrible stain on the credibility of the Security Council that neither the Carlsson Report (commissioned in good faith by the current Secretary-General, Kofi Annan) nor that by the Panel of Eminent Persons (commissioned by the Organization of African Unity) can erase. Perhaps the tragedy of Rwanda and the clear failure of the most powerful members of the Security Council to take meaningful action to prevent the genocide would provide further justification, if any were needed, for the much delayed reform of the Security Council.

Notes

1. *Christian Science Monitor,* February 27, 1998, p. 7.
2. Ibid.
3. An inside story of the massacres and the events that immediately preceded the civil war of April–July 1994, the war itself, and its immediate aftermath is very well told in the "personal account" provided by General Henry Kwami Anyidoho, who was deputy to General Dallaire in UNAMIR, in his book *Guns over Kigali: The Rwandese Civil War, 1994* (Accra: Woeli, 1997).
4. Ibid.
5. Ibid.
6. S/1994/470, April 20, 1994.
7. Ibid.
8. See William Shawcross, *Deliver Us from Evil: Peacekeepers, Warlords, and a World of Endless Conflict* (New York: Simon & Schuster, 2000), p. 138.
9. Anyidoho, *Guns over Kigali.*

33

Sierra Leone

John Hirsch

Against the backdrop of the collapse of United Nations operations in Somalia and Rwanda in the mid-1990s, the Security Council's recent role in Sierra Leone reflects a new resolve to persevere and sustain a complex United Nations peace operation in Africa. The transformation of the UN Mission in Sierra Leone (UNAMSIL) from the vulnerable peacekeeping force of May 2000, when 500 peacekeepers were taken hostage by the Revolutionary United Front (RUF), to the robust operation that subsequently conducted disarmament and demobilization and facilitated the May 2002 elections, constitutes one of the more remarkable stories of the Security Council in the post–Cold War era. It is all the more so given the reality that Sierra Leone is of neither strategic nor economic significance on the global stage. With the leading role of the United Kingdom in the Security Council and the presence at the time of the UN's largest active peacekeeping force to provide security until a new army can be trained, Sierra Leone has a new albeit precarious opportunity to become a relatively stable democratic state in West Africa.

The struggle between the RUF and three successive governments raged throughout the 1990s against the backdrop of three decades of state disintegration. In the early 1990s the rebels made common cause with disaffected elements of the ill-equipped and poorly paid Sierra Leonean army to plunder the country's resources and inflict terrible atrocities on a defenseless population. Supported by Libya's Muammar Qaddafi and abetted by arms from Charles Taylor's rebel movement in Liberia, the RUF captured the country's key economic assets, rutile and aluminum mines, and took control of the easternmost diamond areas. The rebel advance on the capital was halted in April 1995 only by the arrival of Executive Outcomes (EO), a South African mercenary organization. The first peace agreement between the government of Ahmed Tejan Kabbah and the RUF in Abidjan in November 1996 provided for the withdrawal of foreign forces as part of a broad disarmament process. President Kabbah's precipitate decision in January 1997 to have EO leave the country, however, proved a fatal mistake. Disgruntled junior army officers seized power four months later, sending Kabbah into exile and inviting the RUF to join them in Freetown. After two years of valiant efforts by peacekeepers of the Economic Community of West African States Monitoring Group (ECOMOG), a further peace agreement was signed in Lomé, Togo, in July 1999, opening the way for the deployment of a United Nations peacekeeping force later that year.

The Security Council's role on the Sierra Leone crisis can be broadly divided into two phases: (1) from the dispatch of a special envoy in early 1995 to the conclusion of the Lomé Peace Agreement of July 8, 1999; and (2) from the establishment of UNAMSIL in October 1999 to the present. The Council's role over these phases shifted dramatically: In the first phase it was limited and reactive, leaving the initiative for whatever action was taken to end the war largely in the hands of the regional leadership of the Economic Community of West African States (ECOWAS); in the second phase the Council under UK leadership became proactive, approving an assertive mandate, expanding UNAMSIL's troop strength to 17,500, adopting a two-track strategy of military pressure and negotiations with the RUF, authorizing establishment of the Sierra Leone Special Court, and applying sanctions against Liberia. These developments were not without difficulty, as the departure of India and Jordan underscored tensions between the Council, the Secretariat, and major troop-contributing countries. The council's relations with ECOWAS also were strained, as some regional leaders sought to delay international sanctions against the Taylor regime in Monrovia.

The regional priorities and interests of the United States and the United Kingdom largely determined the timing and nature of the Security Council's role in Sierra Leone. The disinclination of the United States to engage on Liberia confined the Council's engagement with West Africa for most of the 1990s, while the UK's historic relationship with Sierra Leone ultimately led to its far more energetic involvement by the end of the decade. This chapter will examine the major turning points in the Security Council's approach toward the crisis in Sierra Leone, highlighting the complex relationships among the major international, regional, and local actors. In conclusion I will seek to draw some lessons relevant to future United Nations peacekeeping and peacebuilding operations in Africa.

The International and Regional Context

For years the Sierra Leone crisis, which erupted in cross-border warfare in March 1991, was largely ignored by the international community, including the Security Council. The international climate for United Nations peace operations in Africa had deteriorated sharply throughout the decade. The disastrous failures in Somalia, Bosnia, and Rwanda sapped the Council's willingness, especially that of the United States, to authorize and engage in further United Nations peacekeeping operations in Africa. Presidential Decision Directive 25 set the bar for U.S. support for peacekeeping so high as to make further operations in high-risk environments such as Sierra Leone highly problematic.[1]

In West Africa, Security Council attention (though not action) in the early 1990s was focused on the war in Liberia. Due to reluctance to engage on the part of the United States and opposition to discuss the issue in the Security Council on the part of its African members, primary responsibility for seeking to restore peace devolved to ECOWAS and its military arm, ECOMOG. Nigeria dominated ECOWAS's political and military decisions, at times to the dismay of its smaller partner states. The Council stepped back, unwilling either to play a significant role itself or to give tangible support to ECOMOG given strong opposition in the West to General Sani Abacha's brutal dictatorship. The United States and some of its European Union (EU) allies subsequently organized logistical support for ECOMOG without Council action.[2]

On the diplomatic front, Secretary-General Boutros Boutros-Ghali authorized the UN to sponsor peace negotiations together with ECOWAS. The Cotonou Agreement of July 1993 was the first of fourteen agreements leading to the elections of August 1997, which finally brought Charles Taylor to power. Security Council action was limited operationally to the establishment of the small UN Observer Mission in Liberia (UNOMIL) in July 1993 to monitor the cease-fire, and unofficially to keep an eye on ECOMOG forces, which were accused of looting and human rights violations.

Against this backdrop the ongoing war in Sierra Leone received only minor attention in New York. There was little apparent focus on the regional context, in which Taylor and RUF leader Foday Sankoh under Libyan tutelage engaged in arms-for-diamonds transactions; nor was their focus on the emerging *sobel* phenomenon—soldiers by day, rebels by night. Burkina Faso's role as a conduit for arms supplies from the Ukraine and other Eastern European sources became an issue of concern only later. The disinclination to grasp the interaction between developments in Liberia and Sierra Leone, and the broader regional setting, reflected the proclivity of the United Nations and the three key members of the Security Council—the United States, the UK, and France—to take a severely compartmentalized approach to the subregion. In effect, the United States confined its interest to Liberia, hoping to reduce its involvement through the holding of elections; the UK encouraged and supported the 1996 elections in its historic colony Sierra Leone but had no diplomatic representation in either Liberia or Guinea; and France maintained its support for Lansana Conté in Guinea and focused on its broader francophone interests. Regional states also played only a limited role in containing the war. Nigerian and Guinean units, through separate bilateral agreements with the National Provisional Ruling Council (which had seized power in April 1992), maintained a security cordon in and around Freetown but (except for a few encounters upcountry) generally avoided direct engagement with the RUF. Some Ghanaian forces also were present in a passive role. As the rebel forces drew near to the capital in March 1995, the National Provisional Ruling Council brought in the South African mercenary organization Executive Outcomes to push the RUF back and recapture the aluminum and rutile mines in the southeast.

Phase One: Limited Engagement—From Abidjan to Lomé

The Secretary-General's appointment of Berhanu Dinka in March 1995 as his special envoy marked the beginning of direct United Nations involvement in the conflict. Dinka was a principal mediator in the nine months of negotiations between the newly elected Kabbah government and the RUF. The United Nations was one of the four moral guarantors of the Abidjan Agreement of November 1996 (together with the Organization of African Unity [OAU], the Commonwealth, and Côte d'Ivoire), which gave the RUF a blanket amnesty, the same proviso that proved so controversial in the Lomé Agreement less than three years later. The peace agreement also provided for a neutral monitoring group to track breaches of the cease-fire. This provision was seen at UN headquarters as the opening for a possible UN peacekeeping force. A UN planning team led by Indian general Yogesh Saksena visited the region at the beginning of 1997. Sankoh rebuffed the team's proposal for a 750-strong peacekeeping force, declaring the UN as not being impartial while concealing his intention to renew the war. International efforts to establish a peacekeeping operation simply stopped. The Council was never called upon to act, saving the permanent members, especially the United States, from having to vote. In retrospect this can be seen as one of the missed opportunities to stabilize the situation before it deteriorated so severely.

The inability to implement the Abidjan Agreement became quickly evident as communication between Kabbah and Sankoh collapsed in rancorous counteraccusations of bad faith while Sankoh stalled on appointments to the Disarmament and Demobilization Committee. The moral guarantors failed to react. The precipitate departure of Executive Outcomes, Sankoh's arrest in Nigeria in early March, and the resumption of RUF military operations distracted regional and international attention from the junior soldiers who plotted and carried out a coup on May 25, 1997, that led to the establishment of the Armed Forces Revolutionary Council (AFRC)/RUF junta. The junta's massive violence against the civilian population in Freetown during its eight-month control of the capital precipitated the next turning point in Security Council engagement.[3]

ECOWAS and the Security Council Adopt Sanctions

Secretary-General Kofi Annan's speech at the OAU Harare summit on June 2, 1997, condemning the AFRC/RUF coup won strong support from African leaders (even though many of them had come to power themselves through coups). Significantly the OAU devolved responsibility for seeking to restore President Kabbah on ECOWAS rather than on the Security Council, reflecting the hope that the regional organization could dislodge the junta either by quick military action (the Nigerian preference) or by dialogue and negotiation (the Ghanaian and Ivorian preferences). ECOWAS adopted regional sanctions at the Abuja summit in August 1997, imposing an embargo on arms imports, petroleum products, and international travel by the junta leaders, while gearing up for military action if the junta remained obdurate. After these and following events failed to coerce the junta to relinquish power, the stage was set for the military showdown that forced the junta out of the capital in February 1998.[4] Colonel Maxwell Khobe, the ECOMOG force commander on the ground, ramped up preparations for military action.

Over the preceding summer the Security Council was called upon by ECOWAS to buttress its regional sanctions with broader international action. The Council was motivated in part by the desire, expressed particularly by Sweden and Cape Verde, to prevent massive civilian casualties and to avoid military action in Freetown. The Council, consistent with its recent adoption of targeted sanctions on Libya, Sudan, and others, adopted Resolution 1132 on October 7, 1997, imposing mandatory sanctions on the AFRC/RUF junta. In particular the Council, acting under Chapters VII and VIII of the UN Charter, prohibited all arms and other military equipment as well as petroleum and petroleum products from entering Sierra Leone.[5]

The United Kingdom took the lead in drafting this resolution and pressing for its adoption in the Council. This was to prove a source of considerable embarrassment for the British government when several months later the so-called Sandline controversy exploded in the British press. At issue was the action of Sandline, a private British security company, in seeking to arrange the transfer of weapons to ECOMOG and the Civil Defense Forces in apparent contravention of the resolution and with alleged concurrence of British officials. The subsequent parliamentary inquiry, which garnered media headlines for weeks, revealed confusion among foreign office officials as to whether the embargo applied only to the military junta or to all arms and weapons transfers, but it did not find anyone in violation of British law.[6]

After the ouster of the junta by ECOMOG forces under Nigerian command in February 1998 and Kabbah's return to Freetown the next month, the Council lifted the arms embargo on the Sierra Leone government but retained the embargo and the travel ban on "nongovernmental forces"— that is, the RUF. In July 2000 the Security Council adopted sanctions on illegal diamond exports, seeking to block their transit through Liberia and Côte d'Ivoire to the diamond bourses of Europe.[7] These moves reflected the Council's growing awareness, largely under pressure from nongovernmental organizations, that the illicit diamond trade was among the major factors in protracting the war.

From the Lomé Agreement to the May 2000 Hostage Crisis

It is important to place the controversial Lomé Agreement of July 7, 1999, within the context of the evolving political and military situation on the ground. After being driven out of Freetown in February 1998, the RUF had regrouped in eastern Sierra Leone, continuing to inflict casualties on ECOMOG soldiers. With the advent of a democratic government in Nigeria, pressure for a drawdown of Nigerian forces mounted. With no alternative military option at hand, regional and international pressure for a negotiated solution mounted. Sankoh was allowed to leave his prison cell in Freetown (he had been condemned to death for earlier crimes) and lead the RUF delegation in Lomé. The RUF demanded a power-sharing position in the government and continued access to the country's key economic resources, the diamond fields of the east, in return for their agreement to disarm and end the conflict. While his advisers felt it was a bad deal, Kabbah ceded to international pressures, buttressed perhaps by his own optimistic view that Sankoh finally was ready for peace. It was to prove a singularly unfortunate combination of external and internal factors, precipitating the further crisis of UN peacekeepers as hostages less than a year later.

The UN's participation in the negotiations was left to the Secretary-General and his special envoy at the time, Francis Okelo. Togolese foreign minister Joseph Koffigoh represented ECOWAS in the six weeks of negotiations. A major player although not present at the talks was the U.S. special envoy, Jesse Jackson, who in May pressed Kabbah to go without his advisers to Lomé to agree to a cease-fire with the RUF. Many in Sierra Leone argued that Jackson's pressure forced Kabbah to enter negotiations from a weak position and that allowing several more weeks for ECOMOG forces to continue fighting would have changed the diplomatic equation significantly. Jackson earned the opprobrium of many Sierra Leoneans once the terms of the agreement became public.[8] His relationship with Charles

Taylor led to speculation as to whether he, knowingly or otherwise, helped to benefit the RUF.

While the Security Council did not play an active role in the negotiation of the Lomé Agreement, it was to become deeply involved in its implementation. As one Security Council ambassador has expressed it, the Lomé Agreement was "a deal with the Devil." The agreement provided a blanket amnesty for the war crimes of the RUF, although UN special envoy Okelo at the last moment appended a handwritten note that the amnesty did not cover crimes against humanity, acts of genocide, or other violations of international humanitarian law, setting the stage for the establishment of the Sierra Leone Special Court three years later. The Lomé Agreement also gave Foday Sankoh the chairmanship of the Commission for the Management of Strategic Resources (i.e., diamonds), described by one observer as putting the fox in charge of the chicken coop.

From the Council's perspective, however, the agreement provided the essential framework for the establishment of a new peacekeeping force, UNAMSIL, and thus the agreement, however flawed, must be regarded as essential. Indeed, even though a number of the agreement's provisions are simply no longer applicable (e.g., the above-noted commission), it remains the legal instrument upon which the peace process and UNAMSIL's role are based.[9]

The Security Council established UNAMSIL on October 22, 1999, three months after the Lomé Agreement was signed, initially working in coordination with the remaining ECOMOG forces. In its initial phase, the Council remained largely reactive. The Secretariat, working on the assumption that the force was operating in a noncoercive setting, and perhaps adapting to what it thought the traffic from the permanent five (P-5) would bear, had proposed a 6,000-strong force from seven developing countries to carry out the complex task of disarming and demobilizing an estimated 45,000 combatants and supporting preparations for national elections (then expected in 2001). This number was also predicated on the assumption that ECOMOG would remain in Sierra Leone. However, as pressures for further drawdown of Nigerian soldiers continued, ECOMOG abruptly withdrew, with little coordination with UNAMSIL, leaving the UN force to cover the country with inadequate troops. In the first three months of 2000, the situation quickly deteriorated. Initial deployments of Indian, Kenyan, and Zambian forces to replace outgoing Nigerian units created a sense of vulnerability that was exploited by the RUF in a series of encounters in which isolated pockets of UNAMSIL troops were forced to surrender their arms and equipment. In May 2000 the RUF seized 500 Kenyan and Zambian peacekeepers as hostages—precisely at the moment of final handover from ECOMOG when UN forces were at their weakest. For Sankoh and the RUF it would be their last pyrrhic victory.

Phase Two:
From the Hostage Crisis to the May 2002 Elections

The hostage crisis clearly constituted the major turning point for the Security Council, the UN Secretariat, and UNAMSIL headquarters in Freetown, galvanizing the key political and operational players to revise their assumptions and strategy. While the crisis caught everyone off-guard, the subsequent Security Council response showed both determination to persevere at the political level (in contrast to Somalia and Rwanda) as well as the capacity of UNAMSIL, under the leadership of the special representative of the Secretary-General (SRSG), Oluyemi Adeniji, to devise a new, more proactive approach. The Department of Peacekeeping Operations (DPKO) dispatched a mission led by Lieutenant General Manfred Eisele, which developed a number of key recommendations. These were subsequently accepted by the Security Council, in particular the adoption of a more robust mandate and support for a number of operational steps to enable the mission to recover and consolidate. The revitalization of a two-track strategy based on enhanced enforcement and continuing dialogue with the RUF was based on a growing realization that the more effective UNAMSIL became, the more the RUF's military option receded. The mission needed to be in a position to create the space for a negotiated political solution, linking the RUF's participation in the disarmament, demobilization, and reintegration process with the opportunity to take part in the upcoming elections.

The new direction of the UN strategy entailed significant political as well as operational costs. UNAMSIL force commander General Vijay Jetley was caught in the eye of the storm. As noted above, his decision before the hostage crisis to proceed with deployments throughout the country with insufficient troops had rendered Zambian and Kenyan troops vulnerable. A confidential memo critical of the performance of Nigerian troops was leaked to the press, evoking an angry Nigerian response. As the pressure mounted, Jetley resigned, precipitating a strong reaction in the Indian parliament and the withdrawal of the Indian contingent. At the same time, Jordan withdrew its battalion out of frustration that the Council was demanding its acceptance of the more robust mandate, while the UK, itself responsible for establishing the new requirements, was unwilling to place its own troops under UN command. Jordan, however, left a medical unit, which at the time of this writing still operated the UNAMSIL hospital in Freetown.

Major changes of the UNAMSIL command structure were made that enabled UNAMSIL, inter alia, to focus both on its ongoing operational requirements as well as on longer-term planning for the reintegration of former combatants and reconstruction of the country's depleted human capital and managerial capacity. Despite some criticism that UNAMSIL should move more quickly to take control in the north and east, UNAMSIL and the

DPKO insisted that the force needed to be fully consolidated and balanced before deployment beyond Freetown and the Lungi Peninsula. The arrival of the Bangladeshi and later the Pakistani contingents made that possible.

From Abuja I to Abuja II

UNAMSIL's dual-track strategy of renewed negotiations with the RUF while strengthening the force's posture and mandate produced results. The government and the RUF entered into a new cease-fire agreement (Abuja I) on November 10, 2000, under the aegis of SRSG Adeniji and Nigerian president Olusegun Obasanjo. The RUF promised to cooperate with the disarmament and demobilization program, to return weapons seized from UNAMSIL, to facilitate the opening of roads, and to allow humanitarian assistance to reach the beleaguered civilian population in Kailahun in the eastern reaches of the country. The deployment of Bangladeshi and Pakistani troops in the first quarter of 2001 and the air bombardments from Guinean airplanes finally broke the remaining RUF resistance. At a follow-up meeting in Abuja on May 2, 2001 (Abuja II), the government and the RUF undertook to remove remaining roadblocks and to proceed with simultaneous disarmament of RUF and the Civil Defense Forces, and the RUF again promised to return captured UNAMSIL weapons.[10] Behind the scenes, SRSG Adeniji's patient diplomacy persuaded the residual RUF forces in the north to withdraw from the area in exchange for an end to Guinean bombing. On the ground, Brigadier-General Ahmed Shaja Pasha, who commanded the 4,200-strong Pakistani contingent, persuaded the RUF to let his troops advance into Kailahun without ever firing a shot—a combination of skillful persuasion with the backup of a robust force.[11]

The British Role

The United Kingdom played an important multifaceted role both in the immediate days of the hostage crisis and thereafter. Prime Minister Tony Blair took the political decision to immediately deploy 600 British forces and a Royal Navy task force to Freetown. While the deployment was presented initially as limited to the evacuation of British nationals, it quickly expanded into the defense of Freetown and the western region, including the international airport. Foreign Secretary Robin Cook lobbied for EU support, and Development Minister Claire Short committed funding for longer-term reconstruction. The British troop presence in Freetown and at the Lungi airport was widely regarded as providing a major measure of psychological reassurance. The UK also took the lead in the Security Council, drafting the mandate for a strengthened UNAMSIL and the progressive enlargement of the force initially to 11,000 and thereafter to 17,500 troops.

On the ground, British forces confronted and disarmed the so-called West Side Boys, who were wreaking havoc in the western province (adjacent to the capital). All this, however, also had a cost. The British refusal to place their forces under UNAMSIL command fueled some resentment at UNAMSIL headquarters and in the DPKO and was directly responsible, as noted above, for Jordan's decision to withdraw its forces. The British contended that their responsibilities in Bosnia and Kosovo under the North Atlantic Treaty Organization (NATO) precluded committing their forces to a UN peacekeeping mission of uncertain duration, but they also had reservations about placing British forces under any non-NATO command (this was similar to the U.S. position toward the second UN operation in Somalia). A compromise was reached with the UK contribution of eight staff officers to enhance UNAMSIL headquarters capability. Ironically, the British decision to train a new Sierra Leonean army will entail an even longer-term undertaking.

The U.S. Role

The United States also played a major part in strengthening the Security Council's commitment to a more forceful and effective UN role. Ambassador Richard Holbrooke visited the region in November 1999, two months after his appointment as U.S. permanent representative, and returned with a series of recommendations for stronger U.S. engagement with peacekeeping in Africa. He dedicated the U.S. presidency of the Council in January 2000 entirely to African security issues. In the immediate aftermath of the hostage crisis, and with clear memories of Somalia and Rwanda, Holbrooke pressed Washington to "push back hard" against the RUF. Holbrooke also played a leading role in the Council's establishment of the Sierra Leone Special Court (see below) to try Foday Sankoh and others primarily responsible for the atrocities committed by the RUF.[12] On the operational level, in close consultation with London the United States established Operation Focus Relief, whereby U.S. special forces provided training for six battalions from Nigeria and Ghana who subsequently became members of UNAMSIL.

Sanctions on Liberia

The Security Council mission to Sierra Leone and Liberia in October 2000, led by Ambassador Jeremy Greenstock, constituted a further important turning point in the evolution of the UN's approach to the crisis in Sierra Leone. The Council obtained firsthand information about the regional context and a vivid personal sense of the issues at stake. The increased use of such missions has become an important policy instrument. In this case, the Council heard from many quarters that Charles Taylor was continuing covert military support to the RUF, including providing haven for Sam Bockarie (Sankoh's second in command) after Sankoh's arrest, and facilitating the illegal transit of Sierra Leonean diamonds through Liberia. The Council members were unpersuaded by Taylor's denials and in March 2001 adopted tough travel sanctions and an arms embargo. Timber exports were exempted from the trade sanctions, apparently at France's insistence. Actual implementation was deferred for two months at the behest of ECOWAS, which at Taylor's urging tried unsuccessfully to dissuade the Council from taking action. ECOWAS leaders apparently had contradictory motives, including continued reluctance to punish an African leader and Obasanjo's hope that Taylor could still be turned into a responsible leader through diplomatic means.[13] It was an important illustration of the need for the UN and ECOWAS to work in tandem if Liberia's support for the RUF was to be effectively blocked. Despite repeated appeals from Liberia, the sanctions were renewed annually since.[14]

The Special Court

At the request of the Security Council, the Secretary-General and the Sierra Leonean government entered into a formal agreement in October 2000 to establish the Sierra Leone Special Court, an independent body. Although the Security Council has no formal control over the court, it will have to deal with the political consequences of the court's decisions as they impact on the longer-term prospects for durable peace. The court is authorized "to prosecute persons who bear the greatest responsibility for the commission of crimes against humanity, war crimes and other serious violations of international humanitarian law."[15] As noted earlier, in July 1999 UN special envoy Francis Okelo appended a disclaimer to his signature on the Lomé Agreement that the amnesty provision granted to the RUF in the view of the United Nations did not apply to these categories of crimes. The UN and the Sierra Leonean government agreed that the beginning date of its temporal jurisdiction would be November 30, 1996, marking the conclusion of the Abidjan Agreement. The Secretary-General suggested that those "most responsible" should include the political or military leadership who ordered these crimes to be committed but could also apply to others farther down the chain of command depending on the gravity, seriousness, or massive scale of their crimes. The prosecutor, David Crane, indicated that he would not be bound by political considerations in deciding who to prosecute.[16]

On March 10, 2003, after six months of investigations, the prosecutor handed down initial indictments against seven Sierra Leoneans, including Foday Sankoh, three of his senior RUF associates, and Sam Hinga Norman (at the time minister of the interior), who were immediately taken into custody and imprisoned pending their trials. Former AFRC junta head Johnny

Paul Koroma, who had fled the city in apparent anticipation of the court's action, and the notorious RUF deputy commander, Sam Bockarie, were indicted in absentia. Subsequently Bockarie was killed under controversial circumstances in Liberia on May 6, 2003. The Liberian government vigorously denied that Charles Taylor ordered his assassination to avoid potentially incriminating testimony were he to stand trial. Koroma is also believed to have been killed around the same time, although there is no conclusive evidence of his death. A sealed indictment against Charles Taylor was presented on June 7, 2003, during his attendance at a special ECOWAS summit in Accra, Ghana, seeking to resolve the Liberian civil war. Taylor, under intense international pressure to step down, went into exile in Nigeria on August 11, 2003. Two weeks earlier, Foday Sankoh died in a Freetown hospital. As of this writing nine Sierra Leoneans from all major factions are in the custody of the Special Court; their trials will begin in early 2004. The indictment against Taylor remains in force, and the Nigerian leadership faces demands from governments and human rights groups to hand over Taylor to the Special Court.

The arrest of Chief Norman has inevitably stirred controversy. Prosecutor David Crane has asserted that no one is above the law and that it is important to demonstrate to the Sierra Leonean public that its actions are balanced, not aimed only against the rebels. In contrast, others have contended that such equivalence is inappropriate as Norman, serving as Kabbah's deputy defense minister at the time of the May 1997 coup, acted courageously to defend democracy against the rebels, mobilizing the Civil Defense Forces to fight alongside ECOWAS forces in ejecting the junta from control of the capital.

As in other countries emerging from protracted conflict, Sierra Leoneans will have to deal with the competing claims of peace and justice. In this regard the role of the Truth and Reconciliation Commission (TRC) remains as important as the work of the Special Court in clarifying the historical record of accountability for the profound suffering inflicted on an innocent population. Despite severe funding constraints, controversial staff appointments, and limited time under its existing mandate, the TRC conducted hearings throughout the country. In 2003, depositions were taken from almost 9,000 citizens in an effort to "get at the truth in order to avoid a repetition" of the war and its concomitant atrocities. Testimony has pointed to atrocities committed by both the RUF and the CDF. President Kabbah's testimony and imposed limitations on questioning him have raised concerns about the potential politicization of the proceedings.[17] Nonetheless, publication of the TRC's report, expected in early 2004, has the potential to be an important event for the country provided that it is properly disseminated, through radio and other means, and not allowed to languish as a formal document of the United Nations.

Lessons Learned

Several broad lessons relevant to future United Nations peace operations in Africa and elsewhere can be derived from the Sierra Leone experience. Foremost, the Security Council must develop a closer and more effective engagement with other regional and bilateral actors at all phases of planning and implementation of a peacekeeping mission. ECOWAS and its military arm, ECOMOG, played a major role in restoring President Kabbah to office and in seeking to compel the RUF to end the war, yet planning for the handover from ECOMOG to UNAMSIL proved particularly complicated. At various times the UN and ECOWAS appeared to be working at cross-purposes—for example, in the decision to impose sanctions on Liberia.

Strong leadership by a P-5 state, in this case the United Kingdom, was essential to ensure sustained Council engagement. This was particularly important in the immediate aftermath of the May 2000 hostage crisis, as well as in maintaining the focus on the requirements for long-term peacebuilding.

The Security Council and the Secretariat need to establish better lines of communication with troop-contributing countries both in the formulation of the mandate of a peacekeeping force and in its implementation. As the Council's relationship with India and Jordan demonstrated, this has become more important than it was a decade ago. Virtually all troop contributors come from the developing world, and fewer countries overall are prepared to take part in Chapter VII enforcement operations.

The Council needs to recognize the regional political and economic dimensions of intrastate conflicts and incorporate them into shaping its mandates and guidance to the Secretary-General. The establishment of a UN regional office in Dakar at the level of an SRSG provides a unique opportunity for the United Nations to forge a closer and more effective relationship with the ECOWAS Secretariat, although it would be better to have the two offices located together in Abuja.

Resources, material and human, remain fundamental, as does strong leadership, both in the field and at UN Headquarters, capable of inspiring work with others both inside and outside the UN system. The integration of military and civilian cultures operating under stress requires the highest caliber of professionalism and ability.

Conclusion

Sierra Leone represents a major test case for the Security Council's approach to complex peace operations. The recovery and refocus of the UNAMSIL mission demonstrates the ability of the United Nations system to learn from past mistakes. The flexibility at all levels to adapt positively in a difficult situation is highly commendable. The government and people of Sierra Leone stood steadfast through some of the most brutal experiences in recent warfare, and the conduct of the May 2002 elections was satisfactory overall, albeit with some regrettable electoral fraud.

That said, major challenges lie ahead both for the country and the United Nations. The transition phase is posited on a drawdown of UNAMSIL forces in conjunction with certain key benchmarks, particularly the development and training of a new Sierra Leonean army and a revitalized police force.[18] The Security Council has revised its drawdown plan several times and as of this writing envisages full withdrawal by December 2004 (in August 2003 troop strength was 12,311),[19] with periodic review of the capacity of the army and police to carry out their security responsibilities. These are major challenges whose objective measurement will be problematic. At the same time, the security situation will inevitably remain connected to broader regional developments in the Mano River region. The deployment of West African peacekeepers (ECOMIL), Charles Taylor's exile, and the establishment of UNMIL, a 15,000-strong UN peacekeeping force, provide a new opportunity to restore peace not only to Liberia but also to the subregion.[20] The UN and ECOWAS need to develop an agreed sustainable strategy to prevent renewed fighting among the Liberian factions as well as to prevent the spillover of such fighting into Sierra Leone.

On the development side, the mobilization of resources for national reconstruction will remain difficult, exacerbated by the UN's pattern of making multiple requests for voluntary contributions to other operations (e.g., Afghanistan, Bosnia, Kosovo, East Timor). Making development an integral part of a peacekeeping operation from the outset, both in planning and in implementation, is also essential. The reintegration of former combatants into their communities with productive employment is one of the major challenges facing both UNAMSIL and the government.[21] The dearth of qualified Sierra Leoneans to assume ownership and responsibility for the management of the country also remains a serious constraint. I have proposed elsewhere the creation of a national peace corps for Sierra Leone, which would enable qualified Sierra Leoneans living in the diaspora to return home for limited periods of time on a rotating basis.[22]

In sum, by late 2003 Sierra Leone remains at a crossroad, seeking to deal with the devastation of the recent past while lacking the capacity to move beyond emergency and humanitarian operations to full recovery. International, regional, and domestic actors need to work closely together on a broad security, reconstruction, and development agenda. The Security Council, having come so far, needs to find the energy and political will to remain engaged for at least the next five years.

Notes

1. Ivo Daalder, "Knowing When to Say No: The Development of U.S. Policy for Peacekeeping," in William J. Durch, ed., *UN Peacekeeping, American Policy, and the Uncivil Wars of the 1990s* (New York: St. Martin's, 1996), pp. 35–67.

2. Adekeye Adebajo, *Building Peace in West Africa, Liberia, Sierra Leone, and Guinea Bissau*, International Peace Academy Occasional Paper (Boulder: Lynne Rienner, 2002), pp. 43–78.

3. A detailed account of the ECOMOG intervention and its background can be found in Eric G. Berman and Katie E. Sams, *Peacekeeping in Africa: Capabilities and Culpabilities* (Geneva: United Nations Institute for Disarmament Research, 2000), pp. 111–128.

4. John L. Hirsch, *Sierra Leone: Diamonds and the Struggle for Democracy*, International Peace Academy Occasional Paper (Boulder: Lynne Rienner, 2001), pp. 60–61.

5. Resolution 1132, October 8, 1997.

6. See Adebajo, *Building Peace in West Africa*, pp. 89, 93; and Hirsch, *Sierra Leone*, pp. 65–66.

7. Resolution 1306, July 5, 2000.

8. See Abdul Tejan Cole, "U.S., Britain, and Sierra Leone," *West Africa*, June 24–30, 2002, pp. 21–22.

9. Resolution 1270, October 22, 1999.

10. *Tenth Report of the Secretary-General on the United Nations Mission in Sierra Leone*, S/2001/627, June 25, 2001.

11. Interview with Brigadier-General Ahmed Shaja Pasha, Koidu, Sierra Leone, August 16, 2002.

12. Resolution 1315, August 14, 2000.

13. Adebajo, *Building Peace in West Africa*, pp. 72–73.

14. Resolution 1343, March 7, 2001; and Resolution 1408, May 6, 2002.

15. *Report of the Secretary-General on the Establishment of a Special Court for Sierra Leone*, S/2000/915, October 4, 2000.

16. See David Crane's remarks, July 17, 2002, at http://www.sierra-leone.org/slnews0702.html.

17. Interview with Yasmin Jussu Sherif, TRC executive secretary, Freetown, August 20, 2002.

18. Resolution 1436, September 24, 2002, endorses the Secretary-General's recommendations for a phased drawdown of UNAMSIL forces to 5,000 troops by late 2004. *Fifteenth Report of the Secretary-General on the United Nations Mission in Sierra Leone*, S/2002/987, September 5, 2002.

19. Nineteenth report of the Secretary-General on the United Nations Mission in Sierra Leone, September 5, 2003, S/2003/863.

20. United Nations Security Council Resolution 1509, September 19, 2003.

21. Lotta Hagman, "Security and Development in Sierra Leone," IPA workshop report, June 10–11, 2002.

22. John L. Hirsch, "War in Sierra Leone," *Survival* 43, no. 3 (Autumn 2001): 149–173.

34

Kosovo

Paul Heinbecker

The most striking and significant feature of Security Council decisionmaking on Kosovo was its absence, at least in the crucial winter and spring months of 1999. Having set the stage for action over a period of months, indeed years, of informal consultations, presidential statements, and repeated warnings to the Yugoslav government, when the time came to act the Council was silent, effectively condoning military intervention by not condemning it when asked to do so and by endorsing the outcome when presented with it. The Security Council sat out the Kosovo conflict. The North Atlantic Treaty Organization (NATO), under U.S. leadership, prosecuted the war, and the Group of Eight (G8),[1] under German chairmanship, negotiated the peace.

The convergence of the military power of NATO and the political preeminence of the G8, welcomed by some and feared by many, turned out to be a onetime pragmatic means to a widely desired political end. No new template of international management was created out of Kosovo, no new paradigm of international behavior established, as seemed possible at the time. NATO did not become Globocop, and the G8 did not become the Super Security Council. NATO is still wrestling with the out-of-area-or-out-of-business dilemma, made more acute by its nonroles in the Afghan war and the Iraq war after the Kosovo experience soured the Pentagon on NATO's war-making by consensus. The G8 is back doing what it does best, its diplomatic coordination and ginger-group functions. All G8 members returned, some with more alacrity than others, to the comfortable legitimacy of the Charter and the familiar confines of Council diplomacy.

The Security Council to which the parties returned after Kosovo was not the same place it had been pre-Kosovo. Many lessons were learned in the spring of 1999, perhaps the most profound of which was that conscience married with necessity and capability had become a powerful force in international relations. As Czech president Vaclav Havel argued at the time, in an address to the Canadian parliament, "Decent people cannot sit back and watch systematic, state directed massacres of other people. Decent people simply cannot tolerate this, and cannot fail to come to the rescue, if a rescue action is within their power." Perhaps the most practical lesson learned by the United Nations from the Kosovo experience was that if the Security Council proves to be an obstacle to action that the international community at large or a powerful segment of it wants, the Council can and will be bypassed. On this point, "right intention" matters, as do other intervention criteria, but Kosovo did illustrate both the feasibility of protecting the vulnerable and the limits of the veto.[2]

Europe has too much history, it has been famously said, and nowhere has that history been more abundant and more present than in the Balkans. There, the battle of Kosovo Polje has lived on in the recesses of the Balkan mind and has often been evoked to explain the inexplicable to the all-too-often uncomprehending outside world. The stage was set, ominously, for the most recent chapter of the Balkans' troubled history at Kosovo Polje in 1987, when Slobodan Milosevic made himself the face of Serbian nationalism in assuring Kosovar Serbs gathered there that "never again will anyone defeat [them]."[3] He returned to Kosovo Polje two years later, on the 600th anniversary of the battle, and effectively launched the repression that truncated Kosovar rights, fueled Kosovar resentment, and stimulated Serb nationalism. He was to do more harm, arguably, to Serbia and Serbs than any outside power had achieved in the six intervening centuries.

The antecedents of the Kosovo conflict can and inevitably will continue to be debated. What was important, however, was that in 1992, U.S. president George H. W. Bush issued his extraordinary warning to Belgrade that Bosnian-style ethnic cleansing would not be tolerated in Kosovo.[4] It was at once a marked departure from diplomacy as it had been practiced vis-à-vis the Balkans and a first straw in the wind of hyperpower politics. Although there were several false starts and although the course of history rarely seems inevitable to those who have lived it, it is clear now that the scene was set not only for the Kosovo conflict but also for the emergence of preeminent U.S. power.

The United Nations and Kosovo

The first relevant Security Council resolution on Kosovo came in August 1993, when the Council asked the former Federal Republic of Yugoslavia (FRY; Serbia and Montenegro) to reconsider its refusal to permit the Conference on Security and Cooperation in Europe to continue its monitoring activities in, among other places, Kosovo.[5] In the fall of 1994, the General Assembly, acting on a report of the special rapporteur of the Commission on Human Rights, condemned the violations of human rights of the ethnic Albanian Kosovars by the Serbs and demanded that such repression end.[6] Hard on the heels of the Dayton Accords and of the Council's decision in November 1995 to end the arms embargo on the FRY, the General Assembly passed its second resolution on Kosovo, this time "strongly" condemning continued Serbian repression and demanding it be stopped.[7] Nonetheless, Secretary-General Boutros Boutros-Ghali, optimistic that the Dayton Accords presaged an end to the fighting elsewhere in the FRY, saw their signature as portending "a time of hope."[8]

For Kosovars, Dayton seemed an end to hope. When Dayton did not restore their autonomy and it became clear that President Milosevic was not going to keep the promise he made to Richard Holbrooke to restore Kosovar rights,[9] the way was opened for the rise of the Kosovo Liberation Army (KLA).[10] The downward spiral began. Provocation was met with overreaction.

By early 1998, the Bosnia Contact Group (the United States, the United Kingdom, Germany, France, Russia, and Italy) was condemning "the excessive use of force by Serbian police against civilians,"[11] imposing limited sanctions, and urging the Security Council to consider another comprehensive arms embargo against the FRY. On March 31, 1998, Resolution 1160 imposed a new weapons embargo on the FRY and emphasized that "failure to make constructive progress toward the peaceful resolution of the situation in Kosovo [would] lead to the consideration of additional measures."

On the ground in Kosovo, matters progressively worsened, with KLA gunmen killing Serbian policemen, and the Milosevic regime striking back savagely, and in doing so reinforcing support among the Kosovars for the KLA, a pattern that repeated itself throughout 1998. In June, G8 heads of government meeting in Birmingham, United Kingdom, discussed Kosovo for the first time, warning Belgrade that "if a genuine political process [did] not get underway, its isolation [would] deepen."[12] Meanwhile, NATO defense ministers tasked NATO's military planners to develop military options. Secretary-General Kofi Annan added his own warning, subsequently much quoted, that "all our professions of regret; all our expressions of determination to never permit another Bosnia . . . will be cruelly mocked if we allow Kosovo to become another killing field."[13]

The hard men on the ground were not listening. The KLA launched a major offensive, initially seizing 40 percent of Kosovo, only to be pushed back brutally by the Yugoslav army and Serb paramilitary forces, who shelled, looted, and burned entire Kosovar villages, displacing hundreds of thousands of people. In September, expressing alarm "at the impending humanitarian catastrophe" and its "grave concern at the excessive and indiscriminate use of force by the Serbian security forces and Yugoslav Army which [had] resulted, according to the estimate of the Secretary-

General, in the displacement of over 230,000 persons from their homes," the Security Council demanded under Chapter VII, inter alia, that the FRY "cease all action by the security forces affecting the civilian population and order the withdrawal of security units used for civilian repression." The resolution also threatened again to take "further action and additional measures to maintain or restore peace and stability in the region."[14] At the same time, the Russian permanent representative, Sergey Lavrov, insisted that "there [was] nothing in this resolution which authorize[d] the use of force."[15] Peace and stability were not restored.

The Contact Group convened again on October 1, 1998, in London. At that meeting, Foreign Minister Igor Ivanov made it clear repeatedly that Russia would veto any UN Security Council resolution seeking to authorize the use of force in Kosovo. Other Contact Group members apparently drew the conclusion, rightly or wrongly, that Russia would oppose the use of force if the Security Council were asked to mandate it but could accept the Council's being bypassed.[16] (This was the same approach that Jean-David Levitte, former French UN permanent representative and current French ambassador to Washington, was apparently to commend to the U.S. administration in March 2003 on Iraq—that is, save the Council from itself by bypassing it.)[17]

Opportunity Missed

On October 13, 1998, the NATO Council authorized activation orders to prepare for air strikes against the FRY. Armed with the leverage of this enormous military power, the special presidential envoy, Richard Holbrooke, flanked by the chairman of NATO's Military Committee, German general Klaus Nauman, and the U.S. Supreme Allied Commander, Europe, General Wesley Clark, persuaded President Milosevic to cooperate. Limits were agreed on the number of Serbian forces that could be present in Kosovo and on the scope of their operations. The Organization for Security and Cooperation in Europe (OSCE) would establish the Kosovo Verification Mission (KVM) to observe compliance on the ground and NATO would establish an aerial surveillance mission. Negotiations on a framework for a political settlement would be completed by the beginning of November.[18] A few days later the Security Council endorsed the agreements reached and demanded under Chapter VII that the FRY comply fully and swiftly with Resolutions 1160 and 1199.[19] Russia and China abstained.

In his report to the Council of November 12, the Secretary-General reported substantial compliance by the FRY and general adherence to the cease-fire, with only sporadic violations by both sides.[20] But just one month later, he was again reporting to the Council "alarming signs of potential deterioration" of the situation in Kosovo, with fifty killings in two

weeks and no progress in the political dialogue.[21] Two hundred thousand
people remained displaced inside Kosovo, with winter deepening. Annan
urged all concerned "to find a negotiated settlement in early 1999, before it
is too late."

Too Late for Peace

Just three weeks later, forty-five Albanians were murdered at Racak. In a
series of tightly coordinated responses, the U.S. and Russian foreign ministers demanded that the FRY comply fully with Security Council resolutions
and that the KLA cease provocations,[22] the Contact Group countries sum-
moned FRY/Serbian and Kosovar representatives to begin negotiations,
Dayton-style, in Rambouillet,[23] the Security Council offered its support (it
was to be the last discernible engagement of the Council on this issue
before war broke out),[24] and NATO agreed to the use of air strikes in
Kosovo if required.[25]

Through the first three weeks of February 1999, diplomatic action centered on Rambouillet as the Contact Group sought to negotiate an agreement that, inter alia, confirmed Yugoslav Serb sovereignty, provided greater
autonomy for Kosovo, and introduced an international military presence
into the province to ensure security. For all but Russia and
Yugoslavia/Serbia, the force would be NATO-led. Rambouillet ended without an agreement and the protagonists went home to consult. In New York,
in the meantime, China vetoed the extension of the UN Preventive
Deployment in Macedonia, "an unfortunate and inappropriate use of the
veto" in Canadian and other eyes,[26] which added to the uncertainty about
how the Council would deal with a mandate for military intervention in
Kosovo. By mid-March the Secretary-General was reporting "terror tactics
by government forces, ethnically motivated violence, arbitrary treatment,
targeted killings, abductions and bomb attacks" that rendered the October
cease-fire agreement "almost meaningless." "The number of Yugoslav
troops deployed in the field [exceeded] the agreed level by a factor of
five."[27] Reconvened on March 18 in Paris after two weeks of consultations,
the Kosovar delegation signed the draft agreement and the FRY/Serbian
delegation did not. The next day, the OSCE chairman in office, Knut
Vollebaek, foreign minister of Norway, reported that FRY military operations affecting the civilian population had intensified and that the KVM's
ability to function had ended; he withdrew the mission.[28] On March 22 the
Secretary-General reported that there were 269,000 Kosovar refugees outside Kosovo and 235,000 displaced people inside, including 25,000 who
had fled their homes since March 20.[29] Three days later, NATO Secretary-
General Javier Solana wrote to his UN counterpart that following the withdrawal of the OSCE's Kosovo Verification Mission "the FRY [had]

increased its military activities and [was] using excessive and wholly disproportionate force, thereby creating a further humanitarian catastrophe."[30]
On March 24, NATO commenced air strikes, which were to continue for
seventy-seven days. Throughout, division prevented effective Security
Council action.

Speaking before the Council on the day the war started, the UK permanent representative characterized the NATO action as "legal . . . justified as
an exceptional measure to prevent an overwhelming [imminent] humanitarian catastrophe. . . . Every means short of force has been tried. . . . The
force now proposed is directed exclusively to averting a humanitarian
catastrophe."[31] The Canadian permanent representative, Robert Fowler,
added, "We simply cannot stand by while innocents are murdered, [and] an
entire population is displaced . . . because the people concerned do not
belong to the 'right' ethnic group."[32]

Two days later, Russia tabled a resolution in the Security Council calling for an end to NATO's action in Kosovo. The resolution was defeated,
with twelve voting against, and three, Russia, China, and Namibia, voting
in favor. This was a major moral victory for the proponents of military
action, the Security Council thereby effectively condoning the NATO
action by not condemning it when invited to do so. The resounding defeat
of the resolution left no doubt where the sympathies of the majority of the
Council, and in all probability those of the majority of the entire UN membership, lay. The Secretary-General expressed his outrage at the ethnic
cleansing perpetrated by Serb forces in Kosovo and called the attacks on
civilians a "flagrant violation of established humanitarian law." He
remained silent on the NATO intervention.[33] His was to be the only significant UN response to the issue for weeks.

Canada and Explicit UN Authorization for NATO Action

Canada, elected to the Security Council in the autumn of 1998, assumed the
presidency of the Council on February 1, 1999. Skeptical of the efficacy of
the monopoly on Balkan diplomacy of the Contact Group, Canadian officials deliberated on what could and should be done to put the Council and
the United Nations back at the forefront of the effort to end the ethnic
cleansing and to reach a peaceful, negotiated solution. More than once, as
war loomed, Foreign Minister Lloyd Axworthy and Ambassador Robert
Fowler polled colleagues on the Council about the advisability and practi-
cability of seeking explicit Council authorization for intervention. Each
time they were dissuaded. The Russians continued to signal to Contact
Group colleagues and others that they would veto such a resolution.[34] The
Chinese veto of the UN Preventive Deployment Force (UNPREDEP) was
evidence they might oppose as well. In the latter part of February, Fowler

convened the NATO members on the Council to consider again the possibility of a resolution if Rambouillet failed. All indicated that they would prefer a specific authorizing resolution, but none believed one was attainable. They argued that if Milosevic saw an opening with which to divide the Council and NATO, he could be counted on to exploit it, with the result that the ethnic cleansing of Kosovo would continue.

In March in Ottawa, Canada urged Russia, via the latter's ambassador, Vitaly Churkin, not to try to block military action in response to an unfolding humanitarian catastrophe. Canada also warned Russia that it would be futile to veto because some NATO members felt that they already had a satisfactory legal basis on which to act, created by successive Council resolutions under Chapter VII, and all NATO members felt they had a moral responsibility to stop the appalling destruction of the Kosovar minority.

The Canadian government also briefly contemplated a Uniting for Peace resolution in the General Assembly and, again, thought better of it. (The Uniting for Peace process dates from the Korean War and permits the General Assembly to engage if there appears to be a threat to peace and if the Security Council fails to exercise its primary responsibility to respond. The Assembly can recommend collective measures, including the use of armed force.) The Canadian government was unsure how much residual political capital the FRY had with the vast nonaligned movement, which Yugoslavia had helped to build. (The movement's subsequent approach to the Council on April 9 was hardly encouraging.)[35] Although the Canadians were confident of support of the Arab Group and of Islamic countries, they decided nonetheless against risking entanglement, delay, and diversion in the political undercurrents and riptides of the General Assembly at a time when people were dying and Kosovo was being depopulated as brutally as in Bosnia. They also did not want to put NATO's unity at risk, which a delayed and watered-down resolution might have done, and thereby fail the Kosovar people. Ultimately, the Canadians concluded that the Council vote of March 26, with twelve votes against a resolution to end NATO action, was a clear enough reflection of broader membership views.

Comparing the Security Council and the G8

In early April 1999, the Russians signaled that they were prepared to use the G8 forum to try to negotiate an end to the Kosovo war. The other G8 members acquiesced, some with more enthusiasm than others. The United States, at least, preferred a bilateral negotiation. There were several possible rationales for this Russian decision. Perhaps it was because they believed that the division among the permanent five (P-5) was too deep and that the consequences of that division were too significant for the Council to surmount. Perhaps it was because the Contact Group and some of its leading negotiators were too associated with the failure of Rambouillet. Perhaps it was because the G8 schedule presented a clear, ready-made road map culminating in a summit in which harmony would be a premium. Perhaps, even, it was only because the Russian G8 political director, Georgi Mamedov, was a seasoned negotiator and a risk-taker. Whatever the Russians' reasons, the German presidency of the G8, in the persons of Foreign Minister Joschka Fischer and G8 political director Gunter Pleuger, now UN permanent representative, seized the opportunity.

The G8 offered advantages as a forum for negotiations that the Security Council did not. In the first place, in 1999, G8 political directors met in Dresden and Bonn, Germany, far from the eyes of the media. As the negotiations on the "second resolution" to authorize an attack on Iraq approached their climax in New York in early spring 2003, fully 2,000 journalists patrolled the hallways of the UN. The major television and radio networks carried open Security Council sessions live and filled airtime with countless interviews of the leaders and permanent representatives of Security Council countries. In contrast, there was no press whatever at Dresden in early April 1999, when the principles underpinning the peace agreement were first negotiated, and none staking out G8 meeting rooms later in Bonn and Cologne. On Iraq, in New York every advance and setback in the negotiations were recorded. In Germany, discretion and confidentiality were the hallmarks of the negotiations on Kosovo.

The G8 group was by definition smaller than the Council but larger than the Contact Group, bringing fewer voices to the table than the former but also bringing a new dynamic. Where the Security Council with its written records was formal, the G8 was informal and ad hoc. In the G8 there was no voting, no veto, and although one party was clearly more equal than others, no formal negotiating hierarchy. Further, the Russians found the G8 consensus format helpful both in influencing the other seven and also in persuading the recalcitrant back in Moscow. It was manifestly in the interests of a Russia seeking to consolidate its membership in the G8 club not to have such a divisive issue on the agenda for the summit in Cologne in June, where President Boris Yeltsin would have been distinctly the odd man out.

Perhaps the clearest difference between the G8 and the Security Council was the extent and manner of engagement of the respective foreign ministers. With political directors setting the stage at each decision point, the ministers participated directly and intensively in the negotiations. Unlike the ministerial-level Security Council meetings prior to the Iraq war, the G8 ministerial meetings were held exclusively in camera, albeit with press conferences at the end. There was no pitching to the gallery or to hometown audiences during meetings, and not much afterward. Nor did ministers deliver previously written set speeches that would have stiffened positions precisely when flexibility was necessary, as they did in the case of the Iraq ministerial sessions of the Council. Freed from the klieg lights and from their respective publics and cabinet colleagues, the ministers were able to work together with greater frankness, creativity, and mutual accommodation than was in evidence in New York in the Iraq negotiations.

All of this is not to say the G8 process went smoothly, even at the level of political director. It was painful for all concerned, especially for the Russians, who were seriously divided internally. Two months of stop-and-start diplomacy kept a successful outcome in doubt until literally the final hours.

Toward Agreement

NATO foreign ministers made it clear in mid-April 1999 that they wanted the violence and repression stopped, the Yugoslav forces withdrawn from Kosovo, an international military presence to replace them, the unconditional and safe return of the refugees, and credible undertaking by Milosevic to negotiate on the basis of the abortive Rambouillet Accords.[36] These points were subsequently endorsed by the NATO summit in Washington on April 23.[37]

At Dresden in early April, G8 political directors had already begun to develop a set of principles that paralleled the emerging NATO ideas but that, importantly, also provided for the reengagement of the United Nations. The G8 political directors met again in early May to develop those principles for discussion and agreement at a G8 ministerial meeting on May 6 exclusively on Kosovo. The point was that, as and when these ideas were agreed, a Security council resolution would be more readily negotiable. The principles provided, inter alia, for international civil and security presences to be deployed, "endorsed," and "adopted" by the Council (i.e., not "authorized"; the United States would not countenance the idea of NATO subservience), the withdrawal of military and paramilitary forces, an end to the violence, the safe return of refugees and displaced people, and the establishment of an interim administration for Kosovo by the Council.[38] After intensive debate, G8 foreign ministers agreed on the principles and asked the political directors to begin drafting a resolution for a political solution.

Back in New York, meanwhile, the Security Council had taken its first concrete step since defeating the Russian resolution on March 26. In Resolution 1239 of May 14, it encouraged humanitarian assistance in Kosovo and neighboring countries and endorsed the G8 principles as a basis for a political solution to the crisis.

The indispensable diplomatic task of getting Milosevic to yes was carried out in parallel to the G8 negotiations by a troika of Martti Ahtisaari of Finland, Strobe Talbott of the United States, and Viktor Chernomyrdin of

Russia. Meanwhile, G8 political directors were in almost constant session from early May until mid-June, with lengthy meetings in particular in the privacy of the German government's guest house in Petersberg, across the Rhine from Bonn. The negotiations were a snakes-and-ladders game of encouraging advances and dizzying retreats, the latter for the most part a product of continuing deep divisions in Moscow. In one marathon eleven-hour session, one Russian negotiator, Georgy Mamedov, rejected the Dresden principles altogether and repudiated the undertakings of his Russian counterpart who had negotiated them. He even excoriated the troi-ka's efforts and argued at one point that Chernomyrdin spoke without Russian government authority.

There were several major stumbling blocks at the May political direc-tor talks. One was the nature of an "international security presence." As at Rambouillet, the Russians would not accept any reference to an internation-al military force. In order to accommodate them, NATO members of the G8 retreated from "NATO-led" to "NATO-core" to an "international military presence" to an "international security presence" (without, however, con-ceding NATO command and control). Further, the Russians argued, futilely, that any interim administration of Kosovo be appointed by Milosevic and therefore be national, not international, in character. They also tried without success to have the resolution adopted under Chapter VI of the Charter. For the Russians, with their continuing travails in Chechnya, it all came down to national sovereignty. At times, Moscow seemed more intractable than Belgrade.

It was not certain until he arrived for what turned out to be the last G8 ministerial meeting on Kosovo that Foreign Minister Igor Ivanov would attend. The negotiations proceeded despite the absence of a common under-standing on what the substance of the resolution was to be and on the sequencing of the war's conclusion. By extensively reworking a Russian draft, agreement was reached on a text. Ministers also agreed to the near simultaneous finalization of the resolution, transmission of it to the UN and NATO, signature of a military-technical agreement by the Serbs and NATO, Serb withdrawal, verification of their withdrawal, suspension of the NATO air campaign, and the entry into Kosovo mainly from Macedonia of coalition ground forces. When the G8 ministers signed off on the lengthy draft resolution, it was forwarded to New York with clear instructions that the permanent representatives of G8 countries were not to alter a word of the text, lest it unravel. Notwithstanding the fact that the Council had previ-ously sidelined itself, some members contemplated asserting New York's prerogatives but ultimately thought better of it. The Chinese insisted on one minor amendment, making the point that the Council was not subservient.[39]

The direct, active, and lengthy participation of G8 ministers in the negotiations was indispensable to their success. There were countless times when only the intellectual agility inherent in political leadership and the decisionmaking authority vested in ministerial rank could have overcome the profound differences and sold the outcome at home. It seems very unlikely that the Security Council could have solved the many knotty problems in the same time frame, particularly with nonaligned representatives at the table with their historic preoccupation with sovereignty. It is possible that the air war alone would have produced a satisfactory outcome. But it is also possible that NATO would have had to begin a ground campaign, an increasingly clear prospect as the spring campaign approached summer. In any case, the looming G8 summit meeting in Cologne focused the minds of G8 political directors, ministers, and heads of government alike. Without such an action-forcing event, the war would probably have continued, with untold consequences for the Kosovars and the Serbs, for the UN, for NATO, and for regional stability. In the end, however, the G8 did succeed in drafting the complex resolution and was pleased to send the issue back to New York and to reengage the United Nations in the management of the aftermath.

To be sure, there have been problems with the implementation of Resolution 1244. Less than full confidence in the UN's ability to handle a postwar Kosovo had been evident on the part of G8 ministers who foresaw considerable micromanagement by the G8 (which, in the event, scarcely materialized). For its part, the UN Secretariat was dismayed by the enormous size of the task thrust upon it without consultation or input and by the paucity of resources allocated for the job. It was painfully obvious, as it had been in Bosnia before, and would be in Iraq subsequently, that much more urgent effort had gone into planning the war than into planning the peace, and that vastly more money was available for war-making than for peacebuilding. As in Iraq, the UN Mission in Kosovo (UNMIK), which required time inevitably to set itself up, was hampered in its mission by a predictable, indeed predicted, security vacuum and by the inadequacy of the police infrastructure, the judicial process, and the prison system. Despite the deployment of 50,000 troops, it proved impossible to prevent both reprisals by the returning Kosovar refugees and retaliatory, albeit less complete, ethnic cleansing of the minority Serb population. Resolution 1244, which made Kosovo a de facto UN-NATO protectorate, spoke both of "substantial autonomy" and of FRY sovereignty and left it to the parties to work out the final status. Nonetheless, the many problems notwithstanding, the ethnic cleansing was stopped, the refugees and internally displaced did return, the economy was restarted, and the basis for a better future for the Kosovars was laid. The solution had the endorsement of the United Nations; therefore the parties on the ground did not challenge its legitimacy.

Comparing the Council on Iraq and Kosovo

There were important similarities but at least equally important differences in the way the Security Council handled Kosovo in 1999 and Iraq in 2003. In both cases, proponents of action were relying on complex legal positions, drawing legal color and authority from prior resolutions under Chapter VII of the Charter. In both cases, the veto power ultimately prevented the Council from expressing itself in a vote. In both cases, the decision was made by the proponents of military action not to vote lest the existing legal authority be diminished or jeopardized. The similarities end there.

In 1999 the motivation for intervention was singular, constant, and primarily humanitarian, although there were also some concerns about internal conflict spilling over Kosovo's exterior borders. In 2003 the arguments for military intervention were numerous and shifting and included regime change, disarming Iraq of weapons of mass destruction, rescuing the population from repression, implanting democracy in the region, and enforcing UN resolutions.

In 1999 there was, regrettably, only a limited Council debate. An examination of various available proxies, however, indicates that a majority, perhaps a great majority, of the Council and of the General Assembly would have supported an intervention to stop the crimes that the Serb regular and paramilitary forces were perpetrating in Kosovo. In 2003, successive open Council debates revealed modest support for and, unlike in 1999, substantial opposition to military action in Iraq. The proponents of the "second resolution" on Iraq could not reliably muster the nine affirmative votes, with no vetoes, necessary for the Council to endorse the war plan; they left the draft resolution effectively "to die on the order paper."

Conclusion

Kofi Annan spoke for the vulnerable everywhere in his Nobel Prize acceptance speech when he said that "the sovereignty of States must no longer be used as a shield for gross violations of human rights."[40] Kosovo has shown the world that it can do better if it wants to.

Kosovo spawned an entire literature of prevention and protection, including *The Responsibility to Protect*, the seminal work of the International Commission on Intervention and State Sovereignty, which promotes the responsibility, not just privileges, of sovereigns and puts the onus for action on the community of sovereigns and on the Council itself.[41] The attachment to state sovereignty is still very strong among the general UN membership, who find it difficult to reconcile their colonial anxieties about too much intervention, if it prospectively could involve them, with the depressing reality of too little intervention, when it actually involves others. If there is a consensus on this issue, it is "intervention if necessary, but not necessarily intervention." Although some wish it were otherwise, for understandable reasons a new norm of protection is nonetheless emerging, and Kosovo has given it a significant boost. The responsibility to protect the weak has been placed squarely on the UN's agenda, even if the UN had been largely absent on Kosovo. Meanwhile, Resolution 1244 established a new form of undeclared trusteeship, one with no exit strategy attached. Noncolonial intervention remains a work in progress.

Kosovo demonstrated the limits of the veto power as a barrier to action, albeit only if the United States is one of those willing to breach the barrier. It seems likely that the other veto-holders would, only in cases of supreme national interests, risk diminishing their own ultimate diplomatic tools by overriding someone else's veto. The P-5 remains the most exclusive club in the world. The Kosovo experience also stimulated a reconsideration of the balance of power and principle in the conduct of international relations, a discussion likely to accelerate in the wake of the Iraq war. Further, it provoked a reexamination of the centrality of the UN Charter and of the character of international law itself, a debate also made much more urgent by Iraq. Kosovo demonstrated that the United Nations can endure and continue to serve its members, including on important security issues such as terrorism, peacemaking, and peacekeeping, even if on some major security issues it remains on the sidelines. The UN is a multipurpose but not an all-purpose tool.

Once the dust settles after major events, the changes wrought by history are not always as expected. The G8 and NATO did not create a new paradigm of international relations in the spring of 1999. In fact, one unexpected consequence of the Kosovo experience was that many in an ascendant United States persuaded themselves of the military limits of values-based alliances and the military merits of mission-based coalitions. Further, the marginalization of the UN in the Kosovo war did not preclude its helping to pick up the pieces afterward nor disqualify it from intervening militarily in the next major humanitarian crisis, East Timor.

The UN has proven to be a resilient albeit, like its members, very flawed institution and will likely remain so as long as its member countries value its broad range and integrative capacity and the legitimacy it derives from universal membership. One of the most useful lessons learned from the Kosovo experience has been that it is wise not to draw lessons learned too quickly, especially if those lessons purport to write the obituary of the United Nations.

Notes

1. The G8 comprises Canada, France, Germany, Italy, Japan, Russia, the United Kingdom, and the United States. Beginning in Rambouillet in the 1970s as an economic grouping involving France, Germany, Italy, Japan, the United Kingdom, and the United States, it expanded to include Canada and, as the Cold War ended, Russia.

2. For a succinct treatment of the principles of intervention, see International Commission on Intervention and State Sovereignty, *The Responsibility to Protect* (Ottawa: International Development Research Center, 2001), pp. xi–xiii.

3. Robert D. Kaplan, *Balkan Ghosts* (New York: St. Martin's, 1993), p. 39.

4. *Austin American Statesman*, December 28, 1992.

5. Resolution 855, August 9, 1993.

6. Resolution 49/204, December 23, 1994.

7. Resolution 50/190, December 22, 1995.

8. *UN Chronicle* 33, no. 1 (1996).

9. Richard Holbrooke, *To End a War* (New York: Random House, 1998), p. 357.

10. Samantha Power, *"A Problem from Hell": America and the Age of Genocide* (New York: Basic Books, 2002), p. 445.

11. Statement on Kosovo by the Bosnia Contact Group, London, March 9, 1998.

12. G8 communiqué, Birmingham, UK, June 1998.

13. SG/SM/6598, June 15, 1998.

14. Resolution 1199 (1998).

15. Agence France Presse, September 23, 1998.

16. Conversation with Richard Holbrooke, former U.S. permanent representative and special presidential envoy to the UN, New York, April 2, 2003.

17. Council on Foreign Relations transcript, March 25, 2003.

18. S/1998/991, October 23, 1998.

19. Resolution 1203, October 24, 1998.

20. S/1198/1068, November 12, 1998.

21. S/1198/1221, December 24, 1998.

22. S/1999/77, January 27, 1999.

23. S/1999/96, January 29, 1999.

24. S/PRST/1999/5, January 29, 1999.

25. NATO press statement, January 30, 1999.

26. Statement by Ambassador Robert Fowler to the Security Council, New York, February 25, 1999.

27. S/1999/293, March 17, 1999.

28. S/1999/315, March 23, 1999.

29. SG/SM/6936, March 22, 1999.

30. S/1999/338, March 25, 1999.

31. Statement by UK permanent representative Jeremy Greenstock to the Security Council, New York, March 24, 1999.

32. Statement by permanent representative Robert Fowler to the Security Council, New York, March 24, 1999.

33. SG/SM/G942, March 30,1999.

34. Conversation with Richard Holbrooke, April 2, 2003.

35. S/1999/451, April 21, 1999.

36. NATO update for the week of April 7–13, 1999.

37. Statement on Kosovo by NATO Heads of State and Government, Washington, D.C., April 23, 1999.

38. See annex to S/1999/516, May 6, 1999.

39. Resolution 1244, June 10, 1999.

40. SG/SM/8071, December 10, 2001.

41. International Commission on Intervention and State Sovereignty, *The Responsibility to Protect.*

35

East Timor

STEWART ELDON

On September 27, 2002, Timor Leste joined the United Nations. At a gathering the day before, Foreign Minister Jose Ramos Horta, speaking on President Xanana Gusmão's behalf, acknowledged the enormous contribution of the United Nations and the Security Council in bringing East Timor to independence. The UN's contribution had involved the organization of a referendum on autonomy or independence (the "popular consultation"), dispatch of the International Force for East Timor (INTERFET), and establishment of the UN Transitional Administration in East Timor (UNTAET), including a UN peacekeeping force, to prepare the territory for statehood.

For the Security Council, the management of the Timor dossier went some way toward healing the wounds of the disputed intervention in Kosovo and provided reassurance against the background of the teetering UN operation in Sierra Leone. Some of the lessons learned have been applied to other UN operations. Others, such as on the organization of effective Groups of Friends, have not yet been fully documented. This chapter is designed in part to put that right, so that the impetus given by East Timor is not lost in dealing with future trouble spots. It focuses on activity in New York and is not intended as a comprehensive history of the dispute.

The May 5 Agreements

The endgame for East Timor began with the agreements of May 5, 1999, between Indonesia, the occupying power, and Portugal, the former colonial power. These were made possible by Indonesia's decision earlier that year to offer the East Timorese a choice by referendum between autonomy and independence. The diplomacy leading to the conclusion of the agreements is outside the scope of this chapter, but they launched the popular consultation that would lead eventually to independence.[1]

No one could have pretended that the agreements were perfect. The key points of difficulty were the tight timetable and the exclusive responsibility for security assigned to Indonesia during the consultation and its aftermath. The Indonesians stuck hard on both during the negotiation of the texts and after. They resisted efforts to clarify or share their security-related responsibilities, agreeing only to consider a memorandum on security presented to them by the Secretary-General on May 6. The substance of the memorandum was included in the Secretary-General's subsequent report to the Security Council but was not acted on by Indonesia.

On May 7, the Security Council adopted Resolution 1236, welcoming the agreements and the Secretary-General's intention to establish a UN presence. Indonesia and Portugal both lobbied heavily as the resolution was negotiated. It stressed the Indonesian government's responsibility for maintaining peace and security in East Timor and to assist the UN in carrying out its tasks. Importantly, at Brazilian/Portuguese suggestion, the resolution requested the Secretary-General to inform the Council before the start of voter registration whether the necessary security conditions existed for the peaceful implementation of the consultation.

Resolution 1236 reestablished East Timor as an important issue on the Council's agenda and showed political support for the Secretary-General as he moved to implement the May 5 Agreements. Their deficiencies, particularly relating to security, had been discussed in the Core Group of interested member states that had come into being on East Timor. Essentially the Council was faced with the choice of whether, despite the risk of inadequate Indonesian compliance, to take the opportunity the agreements offered to settle the future of East Timor. It, and the Core Group, accepted the deal on offer while signposting clearly where responsibility for security lay. At that stage, and until the outcome of the consultation was announced, any attempt to modify the security arrangements described in the agreements would almost certainly have led to the collapse of the process.

The Core Group

Resolution 1236 was the first public manifestation of the Core Group's role in orchestrating work on East Timor. The group was composed of Australia, Japan, New Zealand, the United Kingdom, and the United States. It came into being following contacts initiated by the Secretariat in late 1998–early 1999 but was largely self-generating and self-selecting. In the early stages meetings were chaired by one of the five delegations, with UN officials not always present. But from the summer of 1999 meetings were convened and chaired by representatives of the Secretariat, either on their own account or at the request of any member of the group.

As with earlier Groups of Friends,[2] part of the Core Group's purpose was to strengthen the hand of the Secretary-General, including by taking national diplomatic action in support of the UN. But in its case the traffic was not all one-way. The group provided a forum to discuss the handling of Security Council business with key non-Council delegations to sort out policy differences among its members and—particularly in the later stages—to engage the Secretariat on planning, justice, and development issues.[3] Portugal joined in mid-2000, once UNTAET was clearly in nation-building mode. But up to that point there was a consensus in the group that it would operate more effectively without Indonesia or Portugal present. Playing to its drafting strengths, the UK took on responsibility for steering the great majority of business through the Security Council. The Core Group did not usually engage in line-by-line drafting, but its members were kept carefully informed of developments in the Council and consulted on drafts before they were tabled.

The group was unusual in that its existence was not acknowledged until early 2000.[4] This was partly to maintain confidentiality and operational flexibility and partly to avoid pressure from those outside to join. A larger Support Group under the chairmanship of the Department of Political Affairs was established in early May 1999 to provide a vehicle for briefing interested member states and soliciting financial and material support.[5] This two-pronged arrangement proved effective. Those who needed to know—including Indonesia, Portugal, and the majority of Security Council members—were well aware of the Core Group's existence. But none chose to contest its role.

The Consultation Process

The establishment of a UN trust fund allowed the Secretariat to accelerate preparations for organizing and conducting the consultation. Advance personnel began to deploy in early May. Ian Martin was appointed UN Special Representative in the middle of that month. By June 9, 1999, there were seventy UN staff in East Timor, a major achievement in the time scale in view of serious personnel and equipment shortages. Resolution 1246, authorizing the establishment of the UN Mission in East Timor (UNAMET), with political, electoral, and information components, was adopted two days later.[6]

An interdepartmental UN scoping mission in late May identified the pro-integration militias as the major threat to the consultation and assessed that only the Indonesian army was capable of dealing with them. The mission accordingly recommended the deployment of a number of military observers to UNAMET, in addition to the planned civilian police element.[7] Although content to see the deployment of civilian police, Indonesia at first flatly refused to accept military observers on the grounds that they were not foreseen in the May 5 Agreements. Eventually, following lobbying by Australia, other Core Group governments, and the UN, the Indonesians accepted up to 280 civilian police and fifty military liaison officers to maintain contact with the Indonesian armed forces. Despite the deteriorating security situation, there were growing Indonesian complaints, which were taken up by Indonesia's nonaligned friends on the Council, that UNAMET was not maintaining its impartiality. This limited the Council's ability to bolster the UN on security issues, though Core Group delegations could, and did, lobby in its support.

By the middle of June, security around Dili and Baucau had improved. But following months of militia violence and intimidation throughout the territory, UNAMET was reporting that the necessary security conditions had not begun to exist. UNAMET was also facing considerable logistical difficulties in beginning registration as planned on June 22. It was becoming increasingly clear that registration, and therefore the date of the ballot, would have to be delayed. But a stark postponement would have risked damaging the basis for the popular consultation and, if justified only on logistic grounds, the UN's credibility.

The Core Group discussed how to reconcile these logistic and security concerns with the May 5 timetable. The Secretariat was attracted by a joint idea of the United States, the UK, and Australia for using a delay in the report required under Resolution 1236 on whether adequate security conditions existed for the consultation to finesse the presentational pitfalls and provide the extra time needed. Jamsheed Marker, the Secretary-General's personal representative for East Timor, briefed the Security Council on June 16 before going to Jakarta and Dili. At the UK's suggestion, the president of the Council spoke privately to the Indonesian permanent representative to express strong concern over security and issued a press statement noting that much work remained to be done to allow a credible and fair consultation.

Following Marker's discussions in Jakarta, the Secretary-General decided to postpone his determination on security by three weeks, to July 13, and the ballot date by two weeks. He noted that conditions did not yet exist to begin the operational phases of the consultation process, given the security situation and the absence of a "level playing field." The Council responded with a Core Group–inspired presidential statement expressing serious concern at the high level of violence and intimidation and calling for utmost restraint.[8] An attack on the UNAMET office in Maliana had underlined the security deficiencies, and the Council demanded a thorough investigation. But the attack presaged an intensification of the Indonesian campaign questioning UNAMET's impartiality. Because of this political pressure, there was no realistic prospect of the Council imposing additional security requirements on Indonesia without agreement from Jakarta.

This brief account illustrates how the Core Group and Secretariat operated to build pressure on Indonesia to fulfill its obligations. Eventually, and since further delay would have played into the hands of those opposed to the ballot, the Secretary-General decided to start registration on July 16 (rather than July 13), on the condition that meaningful improvements in the security situation would be observed.[9] A further assessment would be made at the midpoint of the registration process. The first stages of registration went well. On July 26 the Secretary-General told the Security Council the process would continue on the understanding that the Indonesian authorities would work with UNAMET to achieve improved security.

Attention in New York turned to the postballot phase. In Core Group discussion the Secretariat was urged to reach an early understanding with the Indonesians on arrangements after the ballot. Core Group governments impressed on the Indonesians the importance of getting clarity on this question before the rush of voting.

A clear understanding emerged that a postballot UN presence would be necessary pending the decisions required by the Indonesian parliament in light of the result under the May 5 Agreements and during the subsequent implementation phase. The period leading up to the parliament's decision was dubbed Phase II, and implementation of the result Phase III.

On August 27 the Council extended UNAMET's mandate until November 30, modifying some of its functions in light of this understanding.[10] Negotiations were not easy, partly because continuing Indonesian efforts to portray UNAMET as biased in favor of independence resonated with some nonaligned Council members, and partly because of feelings in the same quarter that the Council was according too high a priority to East Timor at the expense of other crises. There was concern that the Council was not devoting enough attention to Africa; privately, comparisons were made between the Council's reaction to the plight of Muslims in Palestine and Christians in East Timor.

The campaign for the ballot was launched on August 14. Both sides had agreed to a UNAMET-brokered code of conduct. But violence and intimidation by the militias persisted. Six days later the independent electoral commission appointed by the UN wrote to Ian Martin expressing serious concern that without remedial action by Indonesia the poll might be perverted in favor of the pro-autonomy camp.

Sir Kieran Prendergast, Undersecretary-General for political affairs, briefed the Council frankly on August 24 to the effect that the conditions for a free and fair ballot were not yet in place. Nevertheless, the Secretariat remained committed to proceeding with the vote on August 30, because a delay would only encourage those opposed to the ballot. Prendergast suggested the Council send a mission to East Timor—reviving a practice not used in about half a decade—to be present for the vote and the count and for the announcement of the result.

All Council members expressed serious concern at this turn of events. A significant minority, including on this occasion Russia and China, emphasized the need to take a balanced view without blaming Indonesia alone. But it was agreed that the president of the Council should issue a press statement expressing strong concern at the continuing intimidation and violence, recalling Indonesia's responsibility for ensuring a secure environment and supporting the Secretary-General's intention to proceed with the ballot.

At a second briefing on August 26, Prendergast reverted to the idea of a Council mission. Sentiment among Council members was that the dispatch of a mission on this time scale was impracticable. It was unclear exactly what it would achieve. Apart from worries in the Council about the considerable logistical challenge for UNAMET in receiving a mission while the ballot was in full swing, there were concerns that its presence would add to the security problem, as it could easily have become a target for the militias. Nevertheless, as tension mounted, Core Group governments made it clear to the Indonesians nationally and jointly that there would be serious international consequences if further violence occurred.

The Ballot and Its Immediate Aftermath

The exceptionally high turnout and smooth conduct of the vote and count were considerable achievements for UNAMET. In a presidential statement on September 3, 1999, marking the overwhelming vote (78.5 percent) in favor of independence, the Council reiterated that it was for Indonesia to take steps to prevent further violence and guarantee the security of UNAMET personnel and premises.[11]

The violence following the announcement of the result presented the international community with its most serious challenge. The widespread killings by the militia shocked the world. Eighty-five percent of East Timor's buildings and virtually all its schools, businesses, and infrastructure were destroyed, taken to West Timor, or systematically rendered useless. It was probably at this point that the doubters in the Council accepted that some augmentation of security would be required, albeit with the caveat that Indonesian consent would be necessary for whatever was done.

The Core Group—and most Council members—agreed that the immediate priority should be to persuade Indonesia to take action to implement its obligations under the May 5 Agreements. But there was growing recognition that an outside military deployment would be necessary if it proved unwilling or unable to restore order. In a discussion with the Secretariat on

September 3, representatives of Australia, New Zealand, the UK, and the United States agreed to discreet contacts about an international security presence while making it clear that there could be no presumption that an urgent peacekeeping deployment would be necessary. The two key requirements would be Indonesian consent—not least in order to make the operation militarily feasible—and subsequently a clear Security Council mandate, without which potential troop contributors were unlikely to come forward.

The confinement of UNAMET to its compound in Dili, coupled with systematic forced displacements of up to 250,000 East Timorese to West Timor, threw matters into even sharper focus. But in a conversation with the Secretary-General on September 5, Indonesian president B. J. Habibie remained firmly opposed to the deployment of an international force. He acknowledged that the situation was serious and therefore intended to declare martial law in East Timor the following day. If that failed, he would be willing to go to the UN to ask for assistance. The problem for the UN became how to persuade Indonesia to make such a request.

That same day the Security Council, now under the presidency of the Netherlands, agreed to send a mission to Jakarta and, if circumstances permitted, Dili. The Secretariat, supported by Portugal, had lobbied again for the dispatch of a mission over the preceding weekend. With the vote counted and violence escalating, opinion in the Council changed. The mission's terms of reference reflected the Council's concern and its determination to see the May 5 Agreements implemented fully. The terms of reference noted that the Indonesian government's efforts so far had not been able to prevent an intensification of violence.

The mission left New York on September 6. Its leader was the permanent representative of Namibia, Martin Andjaba, who had been president of the Council in August. He was accompanied by the permanent representatives of the UK (because of its leading Council role on East Timor), Slovenia (an expert in international law), and Malaysia (because of its close ties with Indonesia), and the deputy permanent representative of the Netherlands (representing the Security Council presidency). The Secretariat was unable to provide a press officer, so the UK placed its own at the mission's disposal and paid his travel costs. In the event, media handling in Dili proved important in persuading the Indonesians to accept a multinational force; subsequent Security Council missions have all had UN press officers attached.

As the mission flew across the Pacific, many actors were mobilizing in support of an international security presence. The Australians indicated that they would be ready to deploy up to 2,000 troops if other countries contributed to a UN-authorized force. Following the Indonesian announcement of martial law that day, the Secretary-General said publicly that further measures would have to be considered if the situation did not improve within forty-eight hours.

The Security Council mission's initial contacts with the Indonesian government, including President Habibie himself, were not encouraging. Individual members of the mission were able to take advantage of bilateral contacts to hammer home the desirability of international involvement. Core Group governments, notably President Bill Clinton for the United States, made several high-level approaches to the Indonesians, delivering the message that in the absence of firm action, international or otherwise, to restore law and order in Timor, international support for economic reform in Indonesia would be increasingly difficult to sustain. But Habibie and Foreign Minister Ali Alatas stuck firmly to the position that martial law must be given a chance to work. Within the mission pessimism grew, reflected in a series of telephone conversations between the Secretary-General and mission members.

East Timor was discussed at meetings of the Asia Pacific Economic Cooperation forum (APEC) in Auckland beginning on September 9. These meetings provided an important vehicle for discussion and coordination at the highest level, which helped step up pressure on Indonesia. The United States, now fully convinced of the need for military intervention while remaining anxious to safeguard the reform process in Indonesia, played a leading role, as did Australia. Although the UK was not an APEC member, British foreign secretary Robin Cook joined the discussion of Timor with a European Union mandate.

On September 9 the Core Group, which was meeting at the ambassadorial level in Jakarta as well as in New York, received indications that Habibie was moving toward accepting a multilateral force, but that he had not yet convinced other members of his government. Then came the militia attack on the UNTAET compound on September 10. The news arrived while the Security Council mission was meeting Defense Minister Wiranto, flanked by his chiefs of staff. Ambassador Martin Andjaba delivered a stinging warning of the international reaction if the militia were not immediately controlled, and the mission demanded cover from the ministry of defense for a visit to Dili the next day. Wiranto acceded to this. In New York, the Secretary-General said publicly that if Indonesia did not accept international offers of help, it could not escape responsibility for what might amount to crimes against humanity. He announced that Australia, Malaysia, New Zealand, and the Philippines had indicated readiness to participate in an international force.[12]

The first signs of accelerating change in the Indonesian attitude came during the mission's visit to Dili on September 11. Wiranto, who had arranged an air force plane for the mission but himself arrived separately, was visibly shocked by what he saw and angry with his local commander.

No media were present in his party, but television crews coordinated by the mission's press officer were able to broadcast Wiranto's reaction, both his dressing down of the local commander and a subsequent press conference at the airport in which the first explicit indication that the game was up was prized out of him.

In New York the Security Council was receiving daily private briefings. The Portuguese had been pressing for an open Council meeting since September 3. Though sympathetic, some members felt a debate should be delayed until it was clear it would not disrupt UNAMET's withdrawal,[13] and until the mission's return. A further consideration was the need to ensure a strong and united message to Indonesia on accepting an international military force. But concern among the wider UN membership was growing, and the president of the Council decided to hold the debate late on September 11, after the mission had left Dili and against its advice.[14] The debate proved a serious and significant occasion. Opening the proceedings, the Secretary-General urged Indonesia to agree to the deployment of an international force without delay.

Subsequently no less than fifty delegations spoke. The sense of outrage was palpable. Only a handful of Islamic countries, Cuba, and Laos offered any comfort to Indonesia. Russia, China, India, and some of Indonesia's neighbors underlined the need for Indonesian consent and Security Council authorization for outside intervention. But none questioned the need for it, and some offered to take part.

On September 12, Habibie kept the Security Council mission waiting in its hotel while he prepared his decision. Before receiving the mission for the last time, he announced publicly that he had telephoned the Secretary-General to request UN assistance. Alatas would fly to New York the next day to finalize the arrangements.[15]

The mission returned to New York on September 13. After Core Group discussion, the resolution authorizing the establishment of a multinational force (INTERFET) was tabled by the UK in the Security Council on September 14 and adopted fifteen hours later as Resolution 1264. On arrival at the UN, Alatas told the president of the Council that he had come with no conditions, but with hopes and preferences. In fact, the Indonesians had a number of hesitations—including over Australian leadership of the force and the modalities of cooperation with the Indonesian armed forces. The Secretary-General and Core Group representatives overcame these through careful diplomacy.

With Indonesian consent to a multinational force obtained in principle, the key points of the discussion in the Council were the scope of the determination that the situation in East Timor represented a threat to peace and security; how strongly the Council should make clear its determination that INTERFET should be replaced as soon as possible by a UN peacekeeping operation; and continuing Indonesian concerns about criticism of their armed forces and the visibility of Australian participation. Some Council members would have preferred a blue-helmet operation; Canada in particular needed convincing that a multinational force was the only realistic option. But the Secretary-General was clear that the UN did not have the capacity to mount a blue-helmet operation, either in terms of getting troops on the ground quickly enough or of having the necessary resources placed at its disposal to do the job. That all these points were settled within a day was testimony to the momentum that the UN process had established.

The Transition to UNTAET

INTERFET began to deploy to East Timor on September 20, 1999, under Australian leadership. Relations with the Indonesian armed forces were generally smooth. On October 19 the Indonesian National Assembly decided that the integration of East Timor with Indonesia no longer applied. On October 30 the last Indonesian officials left the territory.

With INTERFET deployment under way, attention in the Core Group and Council moved to the humanitarian situation (in West as well as East Timor), human rights (spurred on by the decision of the Commission on Human Rights to request the Secretary-General to establish an international commission of inquiry), the early return of UNAMET, and Phase III (on which Resolution 1264 had invited the Secretary-General to prepare for a UN transitional administration, including a UN peacekeeping operation).

Because of the peacekeeping dimension, lead responsibility for East Timor passed from the Department of Political Affairs (DPA) to the Department of Peacekeeping Operations (DPKO). Core Group members urged the Secretariat to ensure that this did not hamper the smooth running of the UN operation, as well as to integrate the transitional administration with other key actors, notably the UN Development Programme, the Office for the Coordination of Humanitarian Affairs, and the Bretton Woods institutions. The humanitarian and peacekeeping/police elements of the transitional administration had some precedent. But putting the civil administration in place in an infrastructural vacuum was much more difficult. Helpfully, the Indonesians agreed that UNAMET's Phase II activities could be stretched toward a transitional administration, providing that their de jure responsibility for civil administration was maintained pending the National Assembly's formal decision on East Timor's future.

The preparation of the Secretary-General's recommendations to the Council was a considerable task.[16] An early decision was taken to recommend a unitary structure to give the special representative full ownership and avoid the coordination problems experienced with the multipillar UN Interim Administration in Kosovo.[17] The United States in particular was hesitant about passing responsibility for security to a blue-helmet force too soon. And there was debate within the Core Group on the desirability of Council action before the Indonesian National Assembly had rescinded the integration of East Timor. In the end, events including the U.S. requirement for congressional notification delayed adoption of Resolution 1272, establishing UNTAET until October 15, after the National Assembly had acted.

UNTAET and the Second Security Council Mission

After taking over from INTERFET, the peacekeeping element of UNTAET did a remarkable job in containing militia infiltration and ensuring security. The major headaches for the special representative and transitional administrator Sergio Vieira de Mello, who replaced Ian Martin, included humanitarian, resource, and recovery issues, as well as the creation of a functioning civil administration. Many donors, including the UK's Department for International Development, pitched in with short-term recovery assistance. In New York, the DPKO was willing to consider innovative ideas such as giving individual donors planning responsibility for specific sectors such as health. The Secretariat devoted considerable effort to agreeing with the World Bank a joint prospectus for the Tokyo pledging conference in December 1999, though donor—and Timorese—frustrations mounted at the subsequent delay in disbursing money from the UN trust fund managed by the World Bank.

Vieira de Mello also had to manage Timorese frustrations at what they saw as the slow pace of transition.[18] In July 2000, UNTAET was reorganized to strengthen direct local involvement and participation in the administration. The Security Council encouraged this process, as well as the subsequent creation of an East Timorese "cabinet," wholeheartedly. This in practice took much of the responsibility for day-to-day running of the administration—even though formally its role was only advisory. The special representative has since acknowledged that with hindsight measures of this sort ought to have been taken earlier to build UNTAET's legitimacy with the Timorese.[19]

In mid-2000 tensions increased with the murder of Nepalese and New Zealand peacekeepers as a result of militia infiltration from West Timor, and with persistent intimidation in the refugee camps in the West. UNTAET quietly toughened its rules of engagement to allow its military component to deal successfully with militia activity in the East. But on September 6, three UNHCR personnel were brutally murdered by a militia-led mob in Atambua, West Timor.

In November 2000, following an invitation from Vieira de Mello, the Council sent a second mission to East Timor and Indonesia. Like the first, it was led by Ambassador Andjaba of Namibia.[20] But its mandate was very different: to take stock of UNTAET's progress, and to assess the refugee situation in West Timor with a view to getting international relief agencies back into the province and encouraging the return of refugees to East Timor. The Indonesians were initially reluctant to receive the mission, but in the end they proved generous hosts. Some 1,400 Indonesian police and troops were drafted into West Timor to ensure the safety of the seven-member mission during its visit.

In East Timor, the mission found that UNTAET had made real progress. But it was concerned that Timorese expectations were not being met, critical of the lack of progress in the investigation of serious crimes, and worried about the lack of resources and underpinning in the judicial sector. The mission was unanimous that a strong international commitment would be required after independence.

In West Timor intimidation obviously continued. Though formally disbanded, the militias remained active. The human suffering was palpable. In Jakarta the mission's attempts to negotiate a joint statement with the Indonesians failed. But Indonesia did agree to an early meeting of the Joint Border Commission (an important deliverable for UNTAET) and to begin discussions with the UN about a security assessment visit to West Timor (the first step in getting international relief agencies back).

From UNTAET to UNMISET

During 2001 the Council continued to monitor developments through regular briefings (many in public). The elections for the Timorese Constituent Assembly in August 2001 and for the country's first president in April 2002 went well. The underlying theme in both Council and Core Group was to ensure smooth preparations for independence. There was some debate, which at times became quite heated, on the merits (or otherwise) of assessed financing of the postindependence UN presence, whose functions would be essentially developmental and nation-building, and therefore on a strict interpretation of UN rules met from voluntary rather than assessed contributions. But no one wanted to leave East Timor in the lurch; it was agreed that up to 100 core posts should be financed from the UN regular budget, with others funded voluntarily. There was also agreement that UN military and civilian police components would be necessary until the East Timorese police and defense forces were ready to act themselves.

The Council and Core Group were anxious that planning for the successor operation should involve the UN system as a whole and be consistent with the recommendations of the Brahimi Report. The DPKO and UNTAET boxed and coxed over elements of the planning process. A former deputy special representative of the Secretary-General in Bosnia was brought in to provide additional expertise, spending time in both Dili and New York. Following discussion in the Core Group, the Integrated Mission Task Force was established in New York to bring the threads together, though views on its effectiveness were mixed.

In October 2001 the Secretary-General submitted an initial report on the shape of the postindependence presence, which the Council approved in a presidential statement.[21] The UN Mission of Support in East Timor (UNMISET) was established for a period of two years by Resolution 1410, adopted three days before independence. The Secretary-General appointed Ambassador Kamalesh Sharma of India to succeed Vieira de Mello as special representative.

Conclusion

Some authors have pointed to the effect of the disputed Kosovo intervention on the Security Council's handling of East Timor.[22] The Council, and the UN membership generally, were certainly in no mood for another Kosovo, this time in a part of the world where the West could not be allowed to claim the prime responsibility. The Chinese and Russians were unquestionably anxious to avoid a second intervention without a Council mandate to prevent further damage to the authority of the Council and its permanent members.

Enormous international pressure would have resulted had Indonesia refused to accept INTERFET. But there can be no guarantee that China and Russia would have given way if forced to repeat their stand of principle against intervention in Kosovo. Fortunately they did not have to face this choice. Despite Indonesian lobbying, there was no fundamental disagreement in the Council over the substance (as opposed sometimes to the tactics) of what needed to be done. The key requirement was met—to bring Indonesia to accept the action it took.

Why, unlike in Kosovo, did this requirement not become a contentious issue? Australian willingness to lead a multinational force resulted both from its regional interests and a feeling that it was simply the right thing to do. Australian leadership (and the responsible and generous role it played generally) had a wide measure of domestic support. But it was predicated on Indonesian agreement to INTERFET. With martial law declared and large numbers of Indonesian military personnel in East Timor (not to mention those deployable from outside), no other course of action would have been militarily feasible. Without the means to back it up, it would have been pointless for the Council to threaten an imposed Chapter VII operation. So its efforts during the crucial weeks of September 1999 were focused on how to obtain Indonesian consent rather than how to force an intervention come what may. The accent was on persuasion and on underscoring the realities to a government that ultimately had no choice if it was to preserve its international standing and channels of economic assistance.

The smooth interaction between the Council on the one hand and the Secretary-General and Secretariat on the other assisted greatly in securing a successful outcome. No one can say whether the Council would have sent a mission to Jakarta if the Secretariat, having failed twice, had not persisted with the suggestion. But once the decision was taken, the tactical articulation between the Secretary-General's diplomacy and that of the Council in New York and its mission in the region went extremely well. The experience confirmed missions as a useful instrument in the Council's armory, and they have been deployed on a number of occasions since, though not always to such good effect. The messages sent by the United States and other governments (not least in the context of the Auckland APEC meetings), the Secretary-General, the mission, and the open debate in New York on September 11, 1999, must all have contributed to Habibie's decision to ask for UN help. Generally, this was one of the best examples of coordinated action seen at the UN in recent years.

The Core Group acted as an essential bridge between the Council and Secretariat and governments with particular interest in managing the crisis. It was the only proactive Groups of Friends chaired by the Secretariat. And at the peak of its activity it was the only one not formally avowed. It worked partly because its members were not seen to have national axes to grind (though of course the basic unity in the Council helped), and partly because care was taken to handle drafting and other negotiations in a Council framework, rather than presenting faits accomplis. Its dialogue with the Secretariat was more focused, operational, and two-way than in other recent Groups of Friends. In all these respects, it may provide a model for the support of other complex UN operations in the future.

The Secretariat took into account lessons learned both during UNAMET and elsewhere when designing successive Timor operations. The UN's performance was not perfect, particularly in the justice sector and in managing Timorese aspirations. But overall the fault lay as much with the substance of the May 5 Agreements as with their execution, as well as with the inevitable political divisions within East Timorese society. The difficulties in deploying UNAMET and UNTAET added grist to the mill of the Brahimi Report. Many of the Brahimi recommendations were applied to planning for UNMISET, and lessons from East Timor factored into planning for other UN operations.

It is not yet clear how well UNMISET will succeed in helping the independent Timor Leste move successfully from the special mechanisms of postconflict recovery to more normal international development assistance frameworks. As the Security Council's involvement quite properly diminishes, it will be for the rest of the UN system to take up the challenge. But the handling of Timor has demonstrated that the UN can successfully see through a complex and multifaceted intervention, and it has given the organization more confidence and a better sense of its own capacities.

Notes

1. An account of the negotiations can be found in Jamsheed Marker, *East Timor: A Memoir of the Negotiations for Independence* (Jefferson, NC: McFarland, 2003).

2. Jochen Prantl and Jean Krasno, *Informal Ad Hoc Groupings of States and the Workings of the United Nations,* ACUNS Occasional Papers no. 3 (New Haven, Conn.: ACUNS, 2002), contains one survey of UN Groups of Friends.

3. The Core Group was sensitive to the views of the East Timorese, which were fed in either by the Secretariat or through national reporting. Members of the East Timorese "cabinet," once formed, also met the group when in New York.

4. By Ambassador Penny Wensley in her speech "East Timor and the United Nations," Sydney, February 23, 2000.

5. The Support Group comprised about twenty-five member states, including potential major donors and regional players.

6. Ian Martin, *Self-Determination in East Timor: The United Nations, the Ballot, and International Intervention,* International Peace Academy Occasional Paper (Boulder: Lynne Rienner, 2001), gives a full account of events surrounding the popular consultation.

7. The civilian police element of UNAMET did not have executive policing responsibilities.

8. S/PRST/1999/20, June 19, 1999.

9. July 16 was the last date that would allow a ballot before the end of August—a possible deal-breaker for the Indonesians.

10. S/RES/1262, August 27, 1999.

11. S/PRST/1999/27, September 3, 1999.

12. The Secretary-General had been active in support of efforts led by Australia to put together a possible multinational force.

13. On September 8 the Secretary-General had taken a decision in principle to evacuate UNAMET.

14. Ambassador Peter van Walsum has given his own account of these events in "The East Timor Crisis and the Doctrine of Humanitarian Intervention," presentation to the Mials-Asialink Seminar, Melbourne, February 7, 2002, www.asialink. unimelb.edu.au/cpp/transcripts/vanwalsum200202.html.

15. This account of the mission's activities in Jakarta and Dili reflects private contacts with some of its members.

16. S/1999/1024, October 4, 1999.

17. Three current and former special representatives of the Secretary-General spoke at length about the difficulties inherent in a multipillar structure at a conference on "Transitional Administration, State Building, and the United Nations" organized by the International Peace Academy (IPA), New York, October 18–19, 2002.

18. See, for example, Jarat Chopra, "The UN's Kingdom of East Timor," *Survival* 42, no. 3 (Autumn 2000): 27–39; and Jarat Chopra, "Building State Failure in East Timor," *Development and Change* 33, no. 5 (2002): 27–39.

19. At the IPA conference on "Transitional Administration."

20. In addition to Andjaba, the mission comprised the permanent representative of Malaysia and the deputy permanent representatives of Argentina, Tunisia, the UK, Ukraine, and the United States.

21. S/2001/983 and Corr.1, October 18 and 22, 2001; S/PRST/2001/32, October 31, 2001.

22. See Martin, *Self-Determination in East Timor,* and van Walsum, "The East Timor Crisis."

A Field Perspective

IAN MARTIN

The direct encounters between the Security Council and those who serve in the peace operations that it mandates are limited. Periodically the special representative of the Secretary-General (SRSG) will come to brief the Council in New York, usually received in an orgy of slightly guilty congratulation on success in pursuing an impossible mandate; only rarely will the country of the SRSG's responsibility still be high among the Council's current preoccupations. Still more rarely will a Security Council mission visit the operation in the field, a practice that was revived by the Council's mission to Indonesia and East Timor in September 1999. The Council's performance may therefore look somewhat different from the perspectives of New York and of the field.

In many ways, the Security Council has performed well through the multiple stages of the United Nations operations in East Timor, which began when the agreements between Indonesia, Portugal, and the UN of May 5, 1999, mandated a referendum, or "popular consultation," and which are yet to pass off its agenda. Most notably, whether looking back from Council divisions over Iraq or forward from Council divisions over Kosovo, the speed with which the Council reached unanimity in inducing Indonesia's acquiescence and mandating military intervention in response to the violence that followed the vote for independence was impressive. And in contrast to Kosovo or Iraq, that unanimity laid a solid foundation for subsequent international cooperation in supporting the transition to a self-governing, independent Timor Leste.

Yet it is worth asking what is to be learned about the limitations of the Council from the failures within what are generally regarded as the overall successes of the operations. This chapter is not intended to be either a balanced assessment or a comprehensive critique of those operations, which in each phase faced daunting challenges that were in many ways unprecedented. It focuses on difficult issues within the scope of proper Council responsibility or oversight.

The Council's engagement with East Timor resumed only after the negotiation of the May 5 Agreements, whose most unsatisfactory aspect was the reliance on Indonesia to provide security during and immediately after the popular consultation. I have set out elsewhere my own agreement with those who argue that there was no political possibility of negotiating Indonesian acceptance of an international security presence before the ballot, and that the negotiators were right to take the risk of proceeding through the window of opportunity that President B. J. Habibie had opened.[1] If so, the Council was also right to endorse the agreements and to mandate their implementation through the UN Mission in East Timor (UNAMET). But the awareness of Council members that the unsatisfactory security arrangements involved a substantial element of risk, for the East Timorese and for UN personnel, placed upon the Council an obligation to maximize its own influence to ensure that Indonesia fulfilled the security obligation that it had insisted on retaining.

It is hard to conclude that the Council entirely fulfilled that obligation. In response to the immediate and growing evidence that Indonesia was not creating the security conditions defined as essential for the popular consultation, the Council did express repeated concern in presidential statements and on several occasions when the president of the Council called in the permanent representative of Indonesia. But the Council never expressed itself in terms as strong as some of its members—especially those with access to intelligence regarding the extent to which the militias in East Timor were created and directed by the Indonesian army—knew was warranted. Expressions of concern drafted by the UK for the Core Group were watered down in the Council. Indonesia was able to count on the defense of friends on the Council, notably Bahrain and Malaysia, and on Group of 77 solidarity, insisting that it be praised for its cooperation and calling into question the impartiality of UNAMET. Yet in retrospect it is undeniable that UNAMET's analysis of the failure of the government of Indonesia to remain neutral, and its analysis of the security situation, at least as it reached the Council, are open to criticism more for understatement than for exaggeration.

The moment of maximum danger was well known to be the immediate aftermath of the ballot. It is not clear that the Council undertook all the preventive action that it could or should have.[2] Two forms of action needed to be maximized: the strengthening of the UN presence on the ground, and the warnings to Jakarta of the consequences of postballot revenge. UNAMET was promising the East Timorese that the UN would stay on after the ballot whatever its outcome yet was well aware that its electoral staff—the most numerous presence—would be immediately withdrawn. It therefore argued for the maximum increase in the uniformed components—civilian police and military liaison officers—and for these to be in place before the ballot. In fact it was only three days before the August 30, 1999, ballot that the Council mandated increases, which could thus not be in place when they were most needed. The pace at which the Indonesians could be brought to negotiate the stages beyond the ballot and the Secretariat's planning limitations bear much of the responsibility for this. But they do not entirely exculpate the Council's own tardiness, exacerbated by the particular requirement for the U.S. government to consult Congress.

It was the Secretariat that put forward a proposal for preventive action by the Council, when it relayed UNAMET's prediction of violence during or after the ballot—a prediction that, grave as it was, proved to be a considerable underestimation. On August 26, Undersecretary-General Kieran Prendergast suggested that the Council should send a mission of Council members prior to the announcement of the result to demonstrate the seriousness of its concerns regarding future violence. Council members were not ready to act then, or when the proposal was discussed further at the urging of Portugal on September 1. Only when Prendergast pressed it again on September 5, after the violence had broken out and appeared likely to exceed the worst predictions, did the Council act upon it, and then with commendable speed. It is impossible to say to what extent an earlier Council presence might have mitigated the violence or speeded the international response, but it would have been the right thing for a body committed to preventive action to have attempted.

The full-scale scorched-earth operation of the Indonesian army and its militia was signaled by the announcement of the result of the ballot on September 4. The worst-case scenario had become the reality, and it was one for which there had been little contingency planning. The Brahimi Report has since declared that "the Secretariat must not apply best-case planning assumptions to situations where the actors have historically exhibited worst-case behavior."[3] In the case of East Timor, the UN's formal planning was undertaken on the basis of a best-case scenario, which it was hoped could be realized with a high degree of international attention and pressure but which was never realistic. It assumed—as Indonesia was indeed promising in the negotiations—that in the event of a vote for independence, Indonesia would maintain security, administration, and budgetary support to East Timor, not only until its People's Consultative Assembly had voted to implement the outcome but also until some date perhaps months beyond that, when the UN would be ready with a transitional administration and a peacekeeping force. Worst-case planning should be a standard Secretariat responsibility, but member states, including the Security Council, are a constraint upon it.[4] In the case of Indonesia and East Timor, it would have been hard for the Secretariat to be known to be planning for the possibility that an important member state would violate the solemn undertakings it had given even while its friends in the Security Council were insisting on praising it for its cooperation.

Despite the absence of contingency planning, once the scale of the violence became clear, the momentum toward military intervention was rapid. Within eight days of the announcement of the result, President Habibie conceded to pressure to invite international assistance to restore order; three days later, on September 15, the Council mandated a multinational force, the International Force for East Timor (INTERFET); and on September 20 the first elements of INTERFET landed in East Timor. This almost unprecedented speed of international action, combined with consensus decisionmaking, was made possible by a combination of factors. The Security Council mission and the open Council meeting of September 11 were certainly significant among them, although perhaps overemphasized in New York. Alongside the role of the Council must be set the personal diplomacy of Secretary-General Kofi Annan and Prime Minister John Howard of Australia; the willingness of nearby Australia, a country with a robust military capability, to take the lead, as well as the contingency planning it had done, albeit not for peace enforcement; the fortuitous timing and use made of a meeting of leaders of the Asia Pacific Economic Cooperation forum (APEC); the strong warnings of international financial institutions and of key member states, eventually including the United States; and intense media coverage and the mobilization of a strong constituency of concern. But in this phase the Council without doubt performed extremely well.[5]

The inevitable difficulty of the next phase, that of the UN Transitional Administration in East Timor (UNTAET), was exacerbated by late and poor planning. The factors that explain the absence of contingency planning for a military intervention in no way excuse the inadequacy of planning for transitional administration. All informed observers regarded a vote for independence as virtually certain, and thus from May 1999 onward the UN was expecting to oversee such a transition, yet almost no planning toward this was done by the UN or its agencies, until the postballot violence made clear that the UN would have to fill an immediate administrative vacuum.

The deficiencies in the planning and conception of UNTAET, and the consequences for its early performance, have been analyzed by Astri Suhrke. She concludes that "the mission suffered throughout from an underlying contradiction between its structure—based on classic peacekeeping tools—and its mandate, which was to prepare the Timorese for independence."[6] In particular, the failure to include participatory mechanisms from the outset put UNTAET on a difficult course vis-à-vis the local population. The East Timorese resistance movement was expected to keep a low profile in the governing structures, with the UN itself the administrative agent. This reflected a peacekeeping culture of impartiality and neutrality in relation to contending parties and the influence of recent experience in Kosovo. Although these factors operated strongly in the Department of Peacekeeping Operations, which had assumed the Secretariat responsibility with no prior experience in East Timor, its institutional culture of peacekeeping cannot be separated from that of the Security Council, from which it also took the message of deference to Indonesian sensibilities. Suhrke concludes that "given the typical characteristics of 'nation-building' or 'governance' missions—long-term, messy, bottom-up and democratic—the most logical solution appears to be to split the mission with one structure for relief and peacekeeping, and another for governance."[7]

Suhrke notes that the main concern in the Security Council was to avoid another crisis in East Timor, and that when that did not happen other issues elicited little interest. To this author, the Council's consideration of East Timor during the period of transitional administration appeared overeager to proclaim East Timor as a success story and to move on as rapidly as possible to downsize the UN presence, and also lacking appreciation for deficiencies in laying a sound basis for independent self-governance. This is borne out by the most thorough assessment of the period of transitional administration, conducted as part of a multidonor study by King's College London.[8]

The study confirms criticisms of the process of planning UNTAET, in particular the exclusion of the East Timorese from the process. It analyzes the serious consequences of the ambiguity of UNTAET's mandate in relation to the creation of a defense framework for East Timor and the delay in deciding on the future of the pro-independence guerrillas, Falintil. It concludes that UNTAET did not establish effective civilian oversight of the East Timorese security sector and attributes the failure to develop oversight and support structures for the police to the blurred responsibilities between UNTAET as a UN mission and UNTAET as a transitional administration. This confusion regarding UNTAET's dual role also compounded the difficult task of institution-building, of which too much was expected in too short a time. Noting that the record in building an East Timorese public administration was mixed, it cites the uneven quality of international staff and attributes the variation between sectors to the extent to which internationals and East Timorese collaborated in devising capacity-building strategies, which was not systematically encouraged: thus at the end of UNTAET the infrastructure of a functioning civil service was not in place. The absence of a coordinated comprehensive strategy for the administration of justice had a profound effect in all areas of the justice sector and beyond.

The study notes the absence of a clear road map defining the path to independence; in the absence of this, the envisaged time scale of two or three years "could be seen as having been as much driven by what the Secretariat judged major country contributors' budgets and the Security Council's limited patience with nation-building would bear, as by the practicalities of implementing the transitional administration's mandate."9 It cites many of those interviewed in 2002 as suggesting that the brief timetable for political transition and the manner of its implementation inevitably meant that the level of institutional development achieved would be modest and the attachment to democratic values superficial; the shape that governance has taken in the immediate postindependence period has put in doubt the long-term viability of the political foundations established during UNTAET. "Judged by the criterion of bringing East Timor to independence and its own mission to an end, UNTAET can be said to have succeeded. In so far as the political transition was a more ambitious exercise . . . including creating the basis for governance, developing mechanisms for dialogue, and creating non-discriminatory and impartial institutions, UNTAET's record is more patchy."10

If this assessment is substantially correct—and even if it is not—the extent to which the Security Council is an appropriate supervisory and accountability body for the governance functions of a transitional administration must be questioned, along with the parallel issue of whether the Department of Peacekeeping Operations is the appropriate place to develop the expertise in governance required if the UN is to undertake elsewhere the kind of responsibilities it assumed in Kosovo and East Timor. The only detailed scrutiny takes place in the Advisory Committee on Administrative and Budgetary Questions, and there issues of substance inevitably tend to be reduced to their financial implications.

The Council is understandably a source of constant pressure for the early downsizing of expensive peacekeeping operations. While the large numbers of UNTAET civilian staff were progressively reduced toward the agreed date of independence, it was clear that an independent East Timor would require substantial numbers of international personnel, both to fill key gaps in the administration and to undertake continuing capacity-building. Considerable reluctance on the Council—notably from France and the United States—had to be overcome before it was agreed to continue to fund some of these posts from assessed contributions, rather than to regard them as a matter for development budgets. In the event, a suspiciously round number of 100 posts was agreed to, with an additional 200 identified for funding through bilateral development assistance. The latter were only slowly and partially forthcoming, so the new government of Timor Leste found itself well short of its recognized needs. Moreover, the King's College study observes that the initial focus of planning was on the transition to a post-UNTAET peace operation, and less attention was paid to the transition from UNTAET to an independent East Timorese administration: "as a result, the transfer of some residual functions of government from UNTAET to the independent East Timorese administration and the establishment of several new government functions were not achieved."[11] Although the responsibility for transition planning was with UNTAET and the Secretariat, the Council's priorities must have contributed to the emphasis on UN mission planning rather than on the needs of the new government. The late mandating of the UN Mission of Support in East Timor, despite the long foreknowledge of the handover date, and the designation of its head too late for his involvement in the planning (as recommended by the Brahimi Report), were also negative factors in the objective of a seamless transition.[12]

In its initial outrage at the postballot violence, the Council had demanded that those responsible be brought to justice. The International Commission of Inquiry on East Timor, established by the Secretary-General at the request of the Commission on Human Rights, noted in its January 2000 report that in the case of East Timor the UN had an interest beyond its general concern for accountability for crimes against humanity: "The UN, as an organization, has a vested interest in participating in the entire process of investigation, establishing responsibility and punishing those responsible and in promoting reconciliation. Effectively dealing with this issue will be important for ensuring that future Security Council decisions are respected."[13] Moreover, the victims of the crimes in East Timor included murdered UN staff. The international commission recommended the establishment of an international tribunal, but in forwarding its report to the Council the Secretary-General conveyed a commitment from the Indonesian government to bring those responsible to justice through Indonesia's national judicial system. The president of the Council replied that its members encouraged Indonesia to institute "a swift, comprehensive, effective and transparent legal process, in conformity with international standards of justice and due process of law."[14] Meanwhile UNTAET acted under its authority from the Council to establish a unit to address serious crimes and special panels within the district court in Dili to investigate and try those responsible for the serious crimes committed in 1999.

This is not the place for an assessment of the parallel investigations and prosecutions in Jakarta and Dili, which three years after the Council encouraged swift processes have yet to promise effective accountability for major perpetrators.[15] The issue of relevance here is the extent to which the Council has remained or will remain true to its declarations of the importance of accountability. A second Security Council mission to East Timor in November 2000, when UNTAET's Serious Crimes Unit was in disarray, rightly emphasized the issue. But as the first trials in Jakarta conclude in

July 2003, and the Indonesian army command of 1999 stands indicted in East Timor but beyond the reach of its courts, this challenge to the seriousness of the Council still lies ahead.

Notes

1. Ian Martin, *Self-Determination in East Timor: The United Nations, the Ballot, and International Intervention,* International Peace Academy Occasional Paper (Boulder: Lynne Rienner, 2001), pp. 29–34, 121–122.

2. See Tamrat Samuel, "East Timor: The Path to Self-Determination," in Chandra Lekha Sriram and Karin Wermester, eds., *From Promise to Practice: Strengthening UN Capacities for the Prevention of Violent Conflict* (Boulder: Lynne Rienner, 2003), esp. p. 226.

3. *Report of the Panel on United Nations Peace Operations,* A/55/305-S/2000/809, August 21, 2000, para. 9.

4. The recent study by King's College London describes positions within the Core Group (Australia, Japan, New Zealand, the UK, and the United States) as constraining preballot planning. See Conflict, Security, and Development Group, International Policy Institute, King's College London, *A Review of Peace Operations: A Case for Change* (London: King's College, 2003), http://ipi.sspp.kcl.ac.uk/peaceoperationsreview, pp. 224–225.

5. Martin, *Self-Determination in East Timor,* pp. 103–114.

6. Astri Suhrke, "Peace-Keepers as Nation-Builders: Dilemmas of the UN in East Timor," *International Peacekeeping* 8, no. 4 (2001): 1. On the planning of UNTAET, see also Conflict, Security, and Development Group, *A Review of Peace Operations,* pp. 222–228.

7. Ibid., p. 18.

8. Conflict, Security, and Development Group, *A Review of Peace Operations,* pp. 215–291.

9. Ibid., p. 228.

10. Ibid., p. 281.

11. Ibid., p. 285.

12. Ibid.

13. *Report of the International Commission of Inquiry on East Timor,* A/54/726-S/2000/59, January 31, 2000, para. 147.

14. S/2000/137. Letter dated February 18, 2000, from the president of the Security Council to the Secretary-General.

15. See David Cohen, *Intended to Fail: The Trials Before the Ad Hoc Human Rights Court in Jakarta* (International Center for Transitional Justice, 2003), at www.ictj.org/downloads/IntendedtoFailwithAnnexes—FINAL.pdf.

36

Ethiopia/Eritrea

Adekeye Adebajo

To many distant observers, the bloody brothers' war that was waged on the Horn of Africa by Ethiopia and Eritrea between 1998 and 2000 over barren, disputed border territories was like two bald men fighting over a comb. Members of a United Nations Security Council mission that visited the region in May 2000 described the conflict as a "senseless war."[1] The territory being fought over had neither rich resources nor vital strategic value to either side. Many Ethiopians and Eritreans share a common language, culture, religion, and history, and they have coexisted largely peacefully for centuries. The leaders of both countries had waged a successful thirty-year war against the dictatorship of Soviet-backed Mengistu Haile Mariam, and Ethiopia's leader had strongly supported Eritrea's independence in 1993. So, what went wrong?

This chapter seeks to provide a brief background of the origins of the Ethiopia-Eritrea conflict, focusing particularly on military and ideological divisions between the Eritrean People's Liberation Front (EPLF) and the Tigray People's Liberation Front (TPLF), and on the souring of relations between Addis Ababa and Asmara after Eritrea's independence in 1993. I then assess mediation efforts after the outbreak of the conflict between 1998 and 2000, focusing on the role of the Organization of African Unity (OAU) and the United States. The role of the UN Security Council was peripheral during this early period, and the Council mainly issued statements in support of the OAU's mediation efforts, though it imposed an arms embargo on both sides in May 2000.

I next analyze the implementation of the OAU-negotiated Algiers Accords of June and December 2000. I focus on the political and military role of the UN in Ethiopia-Eritrea as directed by the Security Council and highlight the two Security Council missions to the region in 2000 and 2002. I also assess the April 2002 decision of the Boundary Commission in delimiting the common border between Ethiopia and Eritrea, as well as the effect of this decision to date on the implementation of the Algiers Accords. I conclude the chapter by offering some policy lessons for the UN Security Council in undertaking future peacekeeping missions in Africa based on the Ethiopia-Eritrea case.

The Roots of a Border Conflict

The border between the ancient empire of Ethiopia and the new nation-state of Eritrea became a metaphor for other divisions: personal divisions between former warlords in a friendship forged in the crucible of a guerrilla struggle; monetary and trade divisions between two former allies; and political divisions between Tigrinya-speaking kinsmen in Ethiopia and Eritrea. After Italy's occupation of Eritrea by 1890, Ethiopia and Italy largely demarcated the border between the two territories. Benito Mussolini invaded Ethiopia in 1935 and ruled over both territories until Italy's defeat in World War II in 1941. Ethiopia regained its independence, and Eritrea came under British rule. After a decision by the UN, Eritrea was granted autonomous status under a federation with Ethiopia in 1952. Emperor Haile Selassie unilaterally incorporated the region into Ethiopia in 1962.

The EPLF was created in 1971 as a secessionist movement to win independence from Ethiopia. The TPLF was created in 1975 and at first had similar secessionist intentions to create a Tigrayan homeland in order to break the dominance of Ethiopia's Amhara ruling elite. The TPFL eventually decided on a policy of fighting for power for the disadvantaged, impoverished Tigray province in a system of ethnic "nationalities" (kilil) in which each region would be granted the explicit right to self-determination. The EPLF and TPLF collaborated militarily against the central government in Addis Ababa for much of their struggle, though there were shifting alliances involving other rebel movements. The two movements also had ideological differences, with the EPLF favoring a Maoist-style system, whereas the TPLF modeled itself on the Albanian socialist system and was more critical than the EPLF of Soviet foreign policy. The EPLF's decision to block humanitarian assistance to famine-afflicted populations in Tigray in 1985 strained relations between the two groups and resulted in the TPLF supporting several Eritrean opposition groups. The two rebel groups resumed their military cooperation only in 1988, and they worked together until the defeat of Mengistu's dictatorship in 1991.[2]

Despite these military and ideological differences, the TPLF's Meles Zenawi kept his promise to EPLF leader Isaias Afwerki, and following a referendum in 1993 Eritrea became Africa's first territory to secede from a postcolonial state. This was seen at the time as a "velvet divorce." But Meles, himself a Tigrinya-speaker like Afwerki, was widely regarded by Ethiopians as being too close to Eritrea and was often accused of being subservient to his former brother in arms. In the early years of Eritrea's independence, Addis and Asmara continued their wartime alliance. Rendered landlocked as a result of Eritrea's independence, Ethiopia was granted access to the key Eritrean ports of Assab and Massawa. Both countries were also united in opposing Sudan's Islamist government, and both were staunch allies of the United States.

But relations started to sour from early 1997, when Ethiopia and Eritrea accused each other of blocking the free flow of trade and investment. The development needs of Meles's home province of Tigray had been neglected by past regimes in Addis. A major goal of the TPLF struggle was to redress this situation. Tigray's development, however, was felt to require the curtailing of Eritrean exports to Ethiopia, since Eritrean textiles, beverages, and finished products could also be produced locally in Tigray. Tensions came to a head after Eritrea, which had been using the Ethiopian birr as its national currency, introduced the nakfa in November 1997. Addis Ababa introduced new currency notes and insisted that bilateral trade be conducted in hard currency. The nakfa fell sharply against the birr, with a devastating impact on Eritrea's economy. Eritrea retaliated by increasing duties on goods destined for Ethiopia through Assab.[3] Though there were other sources of division, Ethiopia's refusal to guarantee the nakfa's value provided the principal casus belli for the border war that erupted shortly after this currency dispute.[4]

A Bloody War on the Horn of Africa, May 1998–December 2000

Before full-scale war erupted between Ethiopia and Eritrea, both countries had experienced border clashes that were regarded at the time as insignificant local disputes. On May 6, 1998, Eritrean troops attacked and took over Ethiopian-administered Badme. After overwhelming Ethiopian forces, Eritrean troops launched attacks on several fronts to retake what Asmara described as its territories, which were under Ethiopian control. Ethiopia mobilized 450,000 soldiers to fight a 350,000-strong Eritrean army. Ethiopia lost its vital access to the port of Assab—its gateway to the world—and Ethiopian trade had to be diverted to Djibouti. About 350,000 Ethiopians were expelled from Eritrea, and 250,000 Eritreans were expelled from Ethiopia. Addis Ababa and Asmara launched a poisonous, vituperative propaganda war against each other and supported rebels from each other's countries. Regional alliances were hastily reshuffled, as Djibouti and Khartoum moved closer to Addis Ababa, and Asmara scrambled to avoid diplomatic isolation by settling a border dispute with Yemen and supporting warlords in Somalia (Ethiopia also backed rival Somali factions).[5]

Military and diplomatic stalemate ensued after Meles refused to negotiate until Eritrea withdrew its troops, and Afwerki refused to withdraw his
troops until Ethiopia negotiated over disputed territories. Both sides used
different legal arguments to buttress their claims. Eritrea based its claims
on the three treaties signed between colonial Rome and imperial Addis
Ababa between 1900 and 1908 and called for the territory to be demarcated
based on these maps. Ethiopia argued for the principle of *uti possidetis*, or
"effective occupation," noting that the disputed areas were under its peaceful occupation before March 1998.

In an arrogant fit of *folie de grandeur,* Afwerki had become convinced of his military invincibility, having battled a Soviet-backed
Ethiopian army during the EPLF's liberation struggle. Eritrea's early foreign policy was aggressive, and there was a sense that, having built up a
strong army, it could settle disputes through the use of force. Before its
border war with Ethiopia, Eritrea had clashed militarily with Djibouti and
Yemen. With the forcible annexation of Badme, Lilliputian Eritrea, with a
population of about 4 million, was challenging the regional Gulliver with
a population fifteen times larger. Afwerki's action, probably designed to
force international arbitration, turned out to be a disastrous error of judgment. He had concluded that, having demobilized 500,000 soldiers inherited from the Mengistu regime, Ethiopia would be too weak to fight.
Meles, who had often been depicted by non-Tigrayan Ethiopians as an
Eritrean stooge and harshly criticized for backing Eritrea's independence,
was provided with an opportunity to ride on a backlash of Ethiopian
nationalism against Eritrea. Ethiopia's premier felt personally betrayed by
Afwerki, having supported Eritrean independence at great political cost to
himself at home.

Susan Rice, the U.S. assistant secretary of state for African affairs,
launched a peace initiative on May 16, 1998, as part of a U.S.-Rwanda
mediation effort. She offered a plan that called for the settlement of the dispute through border demarcation based on colonial treaties and international law; the withdrawal of Eritrean troops from Badme, followed by the
deployment of a small observer force and resumption of Ethiopian administration; and the demilitarization of the common border. Whereas Meles
accepted the plan, Afwerki rejected it, criticizing the U.S. team for exceeding its mandate of facilitation of contacts to engage in actual mediation and
for trying to pressure Eritrea to make concessions based on Meles's apparently weak political position at home. The OAU thereafter took over leadership of international mediation efforts.

After maintaining a low profile in the conflict, the UN Security
Council roused from its deep slumber to pass several resolutions supporting
the OAU's mediation efforts from June 1998. With the UN involved in
other areas like the Balkans and East Timor, which were considered of

more strategic value to the Western powers, the Council was content to leave peacemaking largely to the Africans. The Council, however, endorsed UN Secretary-General Kofi Annan's decision to send Mohammed Sahnoun, a veteran Algerian troubleshooter who had served as the UN's special representative in Somalia, to the region in 1999. Sahnoun expressed his frustration at the low priority accorded to this conflict by the Council: "the United Nations should be given more means to address such issues and . . . the international community should be more involved. It was not enough to pass a resolution and forget about the issue."[6] Many have often ridiculed the Council's quaint expression of "remaining seized of the matter" as a code for avoiding any practical action.

Following the lethargy of the UN and the failure of the U.S. initiative to end the conflict, the OAU sent a high-level delegation to Addis Ababa and Asmara in June 1998. The delegation met again with Meles and Afwerki in Burkina Faso in November 1998 and devised a peace plan that came to be known as the Framework Agreement. The accord called for the withdrawal of Eritrean troops from Badme; the deployment of military observers by the OAU, with the support of the UN; the redeployment of Ethiopian and Eritrean troops from all contested areas; the delimitation and demarcation of the border with UN assistance; and the establishment of an OAU follow-up committee, with UN assistance, to implement the peace plan, which would be guaranteed by both organizations. The fact that the agreement kept invoking UN assistance was a clear recognition that this was an *international* and not just an *African* problem, but it also reflected the OAU's financial and logistical constraints in implementing the accords.

In the largest military engagement in Africa since World War II, Ethiopia broke through Eritrean defenses at Badme in February 1999, forcing a hasty Eritrean retreat. Afwerki immediately accepted the OAU peace agreement he had spent the last year deriding as biased. But Eritrea rejected Ethiopia's demands to withdraw from other disputed areas like Zalambessa and Alitena. Fighting continued in March and April 1999, before resuming in June. The military balance shifted in Ethiopia's favor, and Addis would eventually use its overwhelming manpower to remove Eritrean troops from most of the disputed territories. At the OAU summit in Algiers in July 1999, African leaders endorsed the "Modalities for the Implementation of the OAU Framework Agreement," calling for a cease-fire, the withdrawal of both sides from disputed territory, and the deployment of military observers to supervise the withdrawals.

After the Algiers summit, representatives from the OAU, the UN, Algeria, and the United States—led by Anthony Lake, the former U.S. national security adviser—met and hammered out the technical details for implementing the accord, which included the deployment of a UN peacekeeping force. The Security Council, acting under Chapter VII of the UN

Charter, imposed an arms embargo on both parties in May 2000. During a trip to Africa two years earlier, U.S. president Bill Clinton had brashly named Meles and Afwerki as belonging to a group of Africa's "new leaders." U.S. frustration at its failure to restrain two of its key African allies was clearly evident in the fact that Washington sponsored the UN resolution calling for the arms embargo on both countries.

In May 2000 a UN Security Council mission that was traveling to the Great Lakes region was diverted to the Horn of Africa. The mission was composed of the principals of three permanent members of the Security Council, the United States, France, and the United Kingdom; all three African members of the Council, Mali, Namibia, and Tunisia; and the country that would provide the force commander and largest contingent for the initial UN force to Ethiopia-Eritrea, the Netherlands. During May 9–10, the plenipotentiaries shuttled between Addis and Asmara, meeting Meles and Afwerki. The Council ended its mission by calling for a resumption of proximity talks without preconditions under the OAU's leadership. Though the Council mission demonstrated well-intentioned concern, according to John Prendergast, a special adviser to the U.S. State Department at the time, the mission contributed negatively to ongoing peace efforts by presenting an unhelpful ultimatum to Ethiopia without coordinating its efforts with other international mediators.[7] Shortly after the Council mission, Ethiopia launched a devastating attack into Eritrean territory, threatening the capital of Asmara.

As fighting continued, Algerian president and OAU chairman Abdelaziz Bouteflika sent his special envoy, Ahmed Ouyahia, on a diplomatic shuttle between Addis and Asmara. Proximity talks finally resumed in Algiers on May 30, 2000, with Anthony Lake and, to a lesser extent, European Union special envoy Rino Serri actively involved in the negotiations. These talks culminated in the signing of the Algiers Accords on June 18, 2000, under which both parties called on the UN to establish a peacekeeping force, in cooperation with the OAU, to implement the Framework Agreement. On July 31 the UN Security Council authorized deployment of the UN Mission in Ethiopia and Eritrea (UNMEE).[8] Kofi Annan attended the signing of another agreement on December 12 in Algiers that committed the parties to implementing the OAU Framework Agreement, to release prisoners of war, to allow an independent investigation into the origins of the conflict, and most significant, to agree to a neutral boundary commission to demarcate their common border, as well as another commission to decide on claims for damages. The Boundary Commission would aim to make its decision six months after its first meeting.

The UN force, established at an annual cost of about U.S.$200 million, was mandated to monitor and verify the withdrawal of troops from both sides to prewar positions, monitor a zone of separation known as the Temporary Security Zone (TSZ), and assist in clearing landmines. Created under a Chapter VI mandate, the peacekeepers could use force in self-defense and to protect international civilians. The agreement also called for the establishment of the UN-chaired Military Coordination Commission (MCC) to resolve problems in implementing the accord. The MCC was to be composed of the UN, the OAU, and representatives of both parties. Botswana's long-serving permanent representative in New York, Legwaila Joseph Legwaila, was appointed special representative of the Secretary-General to lead UNMEE. He is currently assisted by two deputies in Addis and Asmara. Dutch general Patrick Cammaert was appointed as UNMEE's first force commander. The 4,200-strong UN peacekeeping force, including 220 military observers, was to be withdrawn after the demarcation of the border between both countries.

UNMEE's largest contingents were initially from the Netherlands, Jordan, Kenya, Canada, and Denmark. Four of the permanent members of the Security Council—China, France, Russia, and the United States—contributed small military units to the mission. For the first time in its history, the UN's Standby High Readiness Brigade (SHIRBRIG) arrangement was used and contributed to a quicker deployment of UN peacekeepers to the field. The Western countries that initially contributed the largest contingents as part of the SHIRBRIG arrangement gradually reduced their presence in UNMEE, leaving India, Jordan, and Kenya as the largest contingents. The OAU Liaison Mission in Ethiopia/Eritrea (OLMEE), with forty-three military and civilian officials from Algeria, Ghana, Kenya, Nigeria, Tunisia, and South Africa, deployed alongside UN peacekeepers by December 2000 to undertake monitoring tasks similar to those of UNMEE.[9] A war that had resulted in 70,000–100,000 deaths, displaced more than 1.2 million people, and put 10 million people at risk of famine finally seemed to be over.

The early invisibility of the UN and the credibility of the OAU were questioned in the course of this dispute. Eritrea had always had a strained relationship with the OAU, an organization that had treated secession as taboo and strongly supported the inviolability of colonial borders for the first three decades of its existence. Afwerki had described the OAU in 1993 as "a complete failure for thirty years,"[10] and he regarded the Addis-based organization as pro-Ethiopia. During peace talks in Algiers, Ethiopia had insisted on a central monitoring role for the OAU. After disagreements erupted on the implementation of the Algiers Accords in December 2000, Meles appealed to the OAU, while Afwerki appealed to the UN. It was clear that the participation of both the UN and the OAU would be essential to implementing the Algiers Accords.

Implementing the Algiers
Accords, January 2001–March 2002

By April 2001, UNMEE had verified the redeployment of Ethiopian and Eritrean troops. The TSZ was established by April 2001, and the UN presented the final map of the zone to both sides two months later. Even though the military battle had ended, however, both sides refused formally to recognize the TSZ and created obstacles to the full implementation of the Algiers Accords. Eritrea particularly restricted the freedom of movement of UN peacekeepers in the fifteen-kilometer areas adjacent to the TSZ. The parties denied the UN permission to establish a direct high-altitude flight route between Asmara and Addis. Both sides questioned the boundaries of the TSZ. Eritrea failed to provide information on its inflated militia and police presence in the TSZ, and it refused to sign a status-of-forces agreement with the UN.

The MCC tried to resolve differences on the ground between the parties with decidedly mixed results. By February 2002 it had held eleven meetings in Nairobi, Djibouti, and the Mareb River Bridge, a frontier between Ethiopia and Eritrea. The meetings discussed issues like ensuring freedom of movement for UNMEE soldiers; monitoring militia and police in the TSZ; establishing joint investigation teams for military incidents; providing mine information to the UN; overseeing the return of internally displaced persons; and repatriating the remains of soldiers from both sides. Despite the obstacles created by the two parties to resolving these issues, the cease-fire largely held, and Ethiopia and Eritrea respected the TSZ in practice if not always in principle.

An important innovation in this mission and a lesson learned from previous UN peacekeeping efforts was the provision of U.S.$700,000 to undertake quick impact projects in the areas of health, water, sanitation, education, and training during the first year of UNMEE's presence. The idea was to "win hearts and minds" by giving local populations a stake in the peace process through providing tangible signs of socioeconomic progress as a result of the presence of UN peacebuilders. To support its work after the initial funds had been disbursed during the first year of the mission, the UN Security Council established a special trust fund for the peace process in Ethiopia and Eritrea in July 2001.

The Boundary Commission and Claims Commission were established by March 2001. Both parties submitted their claims to the commissions at The Hague. The Boundary Commission, chaired by distinguished jurist Elihu Lauterpacht, heard arguments from both sides in December 2001. Its decision on the demarcation of the border, scheduled for February 2002, was postponed for two months due to logistical difficulties. One of the important observations that a Boundary Commission reconnaissance team made was that, since many border areas between Ethiopia and Eritrea are heavily mined, the demarcation of the boundary would necessarily be a slow and laborious process. These dangers were clearly demonstrated, with twenty civilians being killed and fifty-six being injured by mines and unexploded ordnance between December 2001 and February 2003. The Boundary Commission has been funded by both parties, as well as through a UN trust fund for the delimitation and demarcation of the border, which by February 2003 had collected or been pledged U.S.$10.4 million in voluntary contributions.

In anticipation of the Boundary Commission's decision on the demarcation of the border, a UN Security Council team visited the region from February 21 to February 25, 2001. The team was led by Norway's ambassador to the UN, Ole Peter Kolby, and was composed of representatives from all fifteen Security Council members. This team was less high-powered than the Richard Holbrooke–led Security Council mission to the region in May 2000, and none of the principals of the five permanent members of the Security Council went on the mission. And whereas the earlier May 2000 mission had attempted to bridge differences between the two warring sides, this mission sought to put pressure on both sides to honor their commitments to the Boundary Commission's forthcoming decision.

During the visit to the region in February 2001, the Security Council mission suggested the establishment of sector-level MCC committees, as well as a mechanism to resolve difficulties related to the implementation of the Boundary Commission's decision, with all the guarantors, witnesses, and facilitators of the Algiers Accords playing a role in such a mechanism. The Council team also visited the TSZ, allowing its members a firsthand glimpse of the complexities of implementing UNMEE's mandate on the ground. The mission met with Ethiopian and Eritrean religious leaders who had been trying to bridge the differences between both parties, part of a growing trend of civil society participation in conflict management efforts in Africa.

The Boundary Commission Decision
and Its Aftermath, April 2002–April 2003

The Boundary Commission issued its decision on the delimitation of the Ethiopia-Eritrea border on April 13, 2002.[11] Both parties immediately accepted this "April Decision," which they had agreed beforehand would be binding. But soon after, Ethiopia, in particular, obstructed the implementation of the peace plan. Between April 16 and May 6, Addis refused to allow UNMEE and Boundary Commission staff to cross from Eritrea into Ethiopia. The Ethiopians also questioned the neutrality of the commission and refused to deal with the UNMEE force commander, General Cammaert, holding him personally responsible for authorizing a flight by two international journalists to Badme from Asmara. As a result, the MCC did not meet for seven months. After completing his tour of duty, Cammaert was replaced by British general Robert Gordon in October 2002.

In early 2003, the UN reported that Meles had threatened to reject the decision of the Boundary Commission if Ethiopia's concerns were not properly addressed. In response to a commission request for technical comments on its map for demarcating the border, Ethiopia submitted a 141-page report outlining its views of the measures needed to be taken to complete the demarcation process. In unusually strong language, the commission described Ethiopia's comments as "an attempt to reopen the substance of the April Decision . . . and to undermine not only the April Decision but also the peace process as a whole."[12] The commission further noted that it did not have the power to vary the boundary in ways that would avoid dividing local communities and transferring populations, but that it would be prepared to consider such boundary variations at the request, and with the agreement, of both parties.

Ethiopia and Eritrea finally released their remaining prisoners of war and civilian detainees by November 2002. A glimmer of hope lay in the fact that both sides had stopped shooting at each other for three years and were now waging war through other means. But amid the difficulties of implementing the Algiers Accords, the humanitarian situations in both Ethiopia and Eritrea remain dire. Drought and the failure of the rains have led to massive crop failure and the death of livestock in both countries. Cereal production has also been decimated in regions that were previously self-sufficient. The UN predicted that 14 million drought-afflicted Ethiopians and 1.4 million Eritreans could be in need of food aid in 2003. Even the vengeful rain gods seemed to be expressing their rage at the man-made disaster wrought by two strong-headed guerrilla leaders.

A final resolution of the Ethiopia-Eritrea conflict could be complicated by the domestic political challenges that both Meles and Afwerki currently face. A split in the TPLF in 2001 culminated in the arrest of senior party cadres after they had openly challenged Meles's leadership. Ethiopian security forces killed several students in 2001 and other protesters in 2002. The town of Badme has become a lightning rod for the Ethiopian public. Their opposition to the Boundary Commission's apparent decision to award Eritrea sovereignty over this area has been one of raw, deep-felt anger, and much of this rage has been directed at Meles. Having sacrificed so much in the conflict to recover a territory invaded by Eritrea, many Ethiopians have questioned why they mobilized to fight for territory only to surrender it to the "aggressor." Meles is in danger of losing face among his own people in a struggle that could be as much about his political as his personal survival. Following his decision to agree to a neutral arbitration panel, old accusations of being an Eritrean Trojan horse in Addis have been resurrected.[13] In

Eritrea, Afwerki has clamped down harshly on dissent and muzzled the independent media. In 2001, politicians, party cadres, and journalists were jailed for criticizing government policies. National elections were indefinitely postponed in December 2001. The government has also shut down several churches and banned some religious denominations.

Bilateral relations between Addis and Asmara are unlikely to improve in the short term. Ethiopia hosted a meeting of exiled Eritrean groups in October 2002, and Meles met with the leaders of Sudan and Yemen during the same month in a bid to isolate Eritrea diplomatically. Eritrea subsequently dubbed the trio the "axis of belligerence." The Ethiopian ambassador to Eritrea was withdrawn in December 2002, and Ethiopia's embassy in Asmara closed down. Addis's rejection of Asmara's offer to open Assab and Massawa ports to food aid in November 2002 provided more proof of how profound the resentment and distrust remains between both sides.

The role of the United States, a traditional ally of both Ethiopia and Eritrea, could be vital in achieving a peaceful settlement of this dispute. The U.S.-led "war on terrorism" has now massively increased the strategic value of the Horn of Africa. The establishment of a U.S. base in Djibouti to track suspected terrorists in Somalia and Yemen has been followed by U.S. negotiations for the establishment of a military base in Eritrea. Washington is also hoping to maintain close ties to Ethiopia, the preeminent military power on the Horn, in order to benefit from Addis's experience and intelligence in fighting Islamist networks in the region. In March 2003, Ethiopia granted the United States overflight and basing rights to assist its invasion of Iraq.

Learning Lessons

For many observers, the UN Security Council's lethargic reaction to the Ethiopia-Eritrea conflict was another example of the neglect of African conflicts by the Council after debacles in Somalia and Rwanda in the 1990s. The dispatch of peacekeepers to Ethiopia and Eritrea, however, provided an opportunity for the UN to reengage with Africa. This was a classical peacekeeping mission in which both sides had agreed to stop fighting and to work with an interpositional force. Western armies that had abandoned Africa during its greatest hour of need now took their first tentative steps back into the continent.

Although Western armies from the Netherlands, Canada, Denmark, and Italy did contribute peacekeepers to UNMEE after years of retrenchment, the difficult experience of regional peacekeepers like the Economic Community of West African States Cease-Fire Monitoring Group (ECO-MOG), the Southern African Development Community (SADC), and the OAU in Liberia, Lesotho, Burundi, and Comoros, as well as the near collapse of the ill-equipped UN Mission in Sierra Leone (UNAMSIL), are all clear signs of the need for better-equipped and richer Western peacekeepers to continue to contribute to efforts to maintain peace and security in Africa. It is important that the UN Security Council not turn peacekeeping in Africa into an apartheid system in which the Africans do most of the dying and the West pays some of the bills. The Council's support for "African solutions to African problems" often appears to Africans as a cynical attempt to convert a Cold War battle cry to rid the continent of foreign meddlers into an excuse to abandon the UN's proper peacekeeping responsibilities in Africa.

Despite the UN Security Council's constant talk of strengthening regional organizations, as laid out most prominently by UN Secretary-General Boutros Boutros-Ghali in *An Agenda for Peace* (1992), not much has been done by the Council to strengthen the capacity of regional peacekeepers and to collaborate effectively with them in the field. The August 2000 Brahimi Report on reforming UN peacekeeping was curiously and disappointingly short of details on the subject of establishing an effective division of labor between the UN and Africa's regional organizations. And though the war between Ethiopia and Eritrea signified to many the neglect of Africa by the Security Council, this case also provides an example of the potential of cooperation between the UN and Africa's regional organizations. The UN and OAU eventually cooperated in the deployment of peacekeepers to the Horn of Africa after the OAU had mediated an accord that the UN was asked to implement. In Ethiopia-Eritrea, as in Western Sahara and Rwanda, despite the OAU being the principal early mediator, when it came to deploying peacekeepers on the ground the UN was called upon due to the OAU's lack of logistical and financial capacity. After difficult experiences with ECOMOG in Liberia (1993–1997) and Sierra Leone (1997–1999), there is still great unease within the UN Security Council about working alongside regional peacekeepers. The UN's peacekeeping efforts in Ethiopia-Eritrea and the crucial support of the United States and European Union for the Algiers Accords, however, demonstrate the importance of external actors to peace processes in Africa. Regional actors still lack the financial, diplomatic, and logistical muscle of outsiders, and in this case the main regional mediator—the OAU (now the African Union)—was distrusted by one side.

Finally, a potentially useful mechanism that was employed in this case consisted of the two visits to the Horn of Africa by UN Security Council members in 2000 and 2002. These trips allowed the Council's ambassadors to gain firsthand experience of the situation on the ground and to assess the views and personalities of the leaders of Ethiopia and Eritrea. These missions provided Council members with insights that were useful for making decisions in New York. The two visits to the Horn of Africa, and others to the Great Lakes region, West Africa, and Western Sahara, represent an important diplomatic tool in the Council's conflict management armory. Such high-level field missions can bring home to parties in dispute the Council's seriousness to understand and address conflicts. They can also bring hope to the populations of conflict-ridden areas that they have not been abandoned by the international community.

Notes

I would like to thank Solomon Gomes, Alem Habtu, John Hirsch, Ruth Iyob, Dominique Jacquin-Berdal, David Malone, Ian Martin, and Aida Mengistu for extremely useful comments on an earlier version of this chapter that greatly strengthened the work and helped to avoid several errors of fact and judgment.

1. UN Security Council special mission visit to Eritrea and Ethiopia, May 9–10, 2000, S/2000/413, p. 2.

2. See David Pool, "The Eritrean People's Liberation Front," in Christopher Clapham, ed. *African Guerrillas* (Bloomington: Indiana University Press, 1998), pp. 19–35; Tekeste Negash and Kjetil Tronvoll, *Brothers at War: Making Sense of the Eritrean-Ethiopian War* (Oxford: James Currey, 2000), pp. 12–21; Peter Woodward, *The Horn of Africa: Politics and International Relations* (London: I. B. Tauris, 2003); and John Young, "The Tigray People's Liberation Front," in Clapham, *African Guerrillas,* pp. 36–52.

3. Dominique Jacquin-Berdal and Aida Mengistu, "Nationalism and Identity in the Horn of Africa," in Ruth Iyob and Josephine Odera, eds., *Eastern Africa's Security Challenges* (Boulder: Lynne Rienner, forthcoming).

4. See Christopher Clapham, "The Ethiopia-Eritrea Conflict," *South African Yearbook of International Affairs 1999/2000* (Johannesburg: South African Institute of International Affairs, 1999), pp. 351–356; and Aida Mengistu, "Uneasy Peace," *World Today,* May 2001, pp. 9–10.

5. See Christopher Clapham, "The Ethiopia-Eritrea Conflict (continued)," *South African Yearbook of International Affairs 2000/2001* (Johannesburg: South African Institute of International Affairs, 2000), p. 298; Ruth Iyob, "The Foreign Policies of the Horn: The Clash Between the Old and the New," in Gilbert Khadiagala and Terrence Lyons, eds., *African Foreign Policies* (Boulder: Lynne Rienner, 2001), pp. 107–129; and Terrence Lyons, "The International Context of Internal War: Ethiopia/Eritrea," in Edmond J. Keller and Donald Rothchild, eds., *Africa in the New International Order* (Boulder: Lynne Rienner, 1996), pp. 85–99.

6. Quoted in Negash and Tronvoll, *Brothers at War,* p. 82.

7. John Prendergast, *U.S. Leadership in Resolving African Conflict: The Case of Ethiopia/Eritrea,* U.S. Institute of Peace Special Report, September 7, 2001, p. 4.

8. See Resolution 1312, July 31, 2000.

9. See Festus Aboagye, "Towards New Peacekeeping Partnerships in Africa? The OAU Liaison Mission in Ethiopia/Eritrea," *African Security Review* 10, no. 2 (2001): 19–33.

10. Quoted in Clapham "The Ethiopia-Eritrea Conflict," p. 354.

11. For details, see *Eritrea/Ethiopia Boundary Commission Decision Regarding Delimitation of the Border Between the State of Eritrea and the Federal Democratic Republic of Ethiopia* (The Hague: Eritrea/Ethiopia Boundary Commission, April 13, 2002).

12. *Eighth Report on the Work of the Eritrea/Ethiopia Boundary Commission,* annex 1, *Report of the UN Secretary-General on Eritrea and Ethiopia,* S/2003/257, March 6, 2003, pp. 10–11.

13. I am grateful to professor Alem Habtu for raising these points during a lecture at Columbia University, New York, in April 2003.

PART 5

Implications

37

The Security Council and International Law

STEVEN R. RATNER

The chapters in this volume paint a picture of the Security Council as an organ alternatively robust and paralyzed, playing at best a limited role in international peace and security in the UN's first forty-five years and a more significant part ever since, at least until the 2003 Iraq crisis. There can be little question that the Council's members, with the prodding or acquiescence of other key actors in the United Nations, have used that organ in ways barely if at all contemplated by the Big Three (the United States, the United Kingdom, and the Soviet Union) or the others that joined them in San Francisco. Diplomats and political scientists studying this practice can help discern useful patterns and lessons regarding the Council's effectiveness in addressing the myriad new issues that states bring to the United Nations.

International lawyers, however, seek to transcend description by focusing on whether and how the Council's actions have contributed to the development of a set of legitimate and effective norms to govern state behavior. This inquiry has two core elements pointing in different directions. The first focuses on law as an *output* of the Council's work—how the Council's decisions themselves advance the role for international law by offering important prescriptions, interpretations, endorsements, or enforcements of international law. A second concern is on law as an *input* into the Council's decisions, in which we ask whether the Council itself has been constrained or affected by extant norms of international law. These questions are intertwined, in that the Council's willingness to advance international law is very much a function of its views on the state of the law.

With these two issues in mind, this chapter begins with a brief overview of the Charter's vision for the Council's connection to the law of nations and then examines four aspects of the Council's relationships to the international legal process: declarations of legal rules as well as of their applicability to a particular situation; interpretation of international law, in particular the Charter; promotion of international law as a set of principles to guide the peaceful settlement of disputes; and enforcement of international law. I then offer some conclusions about the two main questions above and the current state of the relationship between the Council and the law.

The Charter's Starting Point

Those seeking to understand the contribution of the Council to international law may have some difficulty in finding direct textual grounds for such a role in the Charter. The Council is not the UN's judicial organ—only the International Court of Justice (ICJ) is required to "decide in accordance with international law such disputes as are submitted to it."[1] And the General Assembly is entrusted in Article 13 with the task of making recommendations for "encouraging the progressive development of international law and its codification."

Nevertheless, the Council's role in the promotion of international law is recognized in three important ways in the text or context of the Charter. First, Article 1, in its first paragraph, states that a core purpose of the UN is to "bring about by peaceful means, and in conformity with the principles of justice and international law," the settlement of international disputes. To the extent the Security Council is involved in that process, as spelled out in Chapter VI, the Council must act according to international law. It is equally significant that the other, indeed the first-listed, core UN function—to prevent and remove threats to the peace and to respond to acts of aggression and breaches of the peace—does not include the proviso requiring conformity with international law. The rejection of such a provision stemmed from concerns by the United States and others that when the Council acts under Chapter VII to respond to threats to the peace, it need not feel constrained by existing law.[2]

Second, the Charter's requirement that all states comply with the decisions of the Council, notwithstanding any contrary obligations under other treaties,[3] means that the Council has the authority to make legally binding decisions with which states must comply *in all circumstances*. This extraordinary power, unique among executive bodies of any international organization, gives the Council the ability to alter the international legal landscape instantaneously.

Third, even though, strictly speaking, the Council is not constrained by international law when acting in response to a threat to or breach of the peace, the Council's actions are meant to advance the goals of the Charter, including the idea that states must observe certain basic norms (most important, Article 2[4]). Moreover, Article 24(2) states that the Council "shall act in accordance with the Purposes and Principles of the United Nations" and spells out the places in the Charter where the Council's specific powers are enumerated.[4] The Council thus acts in order to implement, and to the extent consistent with, the constitutive instrument that created it.

Notwithstanding these provisions in the Charter, most nonlawyers will continue to see the Council as a political organ in terms of its membership, the ways it makes decisions, and the outcomes of most of the decisions. Yet as international lawyers have long recognized, these purportedly political actors repeatedly consider, invoke, influence, and apply international law. Rosalyn Higgins was the first to treat the Council's role systematically in this regard in her 1963 classic text.[5] With respect to invocation, member states routinely make arguments in legal terms (especially to the law of the Charter) in front of the Council, not only as a way of defending their national interests in terms of higher principles but also to influence those states that may be open to deciding their positions based on such principled arguments.

As for the product of those deliberations, when a body as politically significant as the Security Council—one in which the most (or most of the most) powerful states must agree in order for it to decide a matter—addresses, even indirectly, the legal issues underlying many international disputes, it cannot but influence how states regard the contours of the relevant norms. Or in terms of legal doctrine, the Council's lawmaking function under Chapter VII (and, indeed, other chapters)—to alter legal obligations by fiat—is only part, probably the smaller part, of the Council's legal role. Its more significant place is in the formation of customary international law, the law that emerges from the practice of states when those states are acting out of a sense of legal obligation. It is thus through an exploration of the practice of the Security Council that we witness the extent to which it has advanced, retarded, or altered the prospects for a world where international law matters.[6]

The Declarative Function:
The Utterance of Legal Principles and Findings
During the course of considering the hundreds of disputes submitted to the Council, its members have passed resolutions to declare whether a party to a dispute had particular legal obligations and, at times, to declare that that party was violating them. A handful of examples demonstrate this declarative function:

- Resolution 216 (1965), wherein the Council labeled the government of newly independent Rhodesia an "illegal racist minority regime."
- Resolution 276 (1970), wherein the Council declared that South Africa's continued occupation of Namibia was "illegal" and that all its acts there were "illegal and invalid."

- Resolution 598 (1987), wherein the Council, speaking of the Iran-Iraq War, "deplor[ed] the violation of international humanitarian law and other laws of armed conflict, and, in particular, the use of chemical weapons contrary to obligations under the 1925 Geneva Protocol."
- Resolution 687 (1991), wherein the Council declared that Iraq "is liable under international law for any direct loss, damage . . . or injury" to any foreign states or nationals as a result of its invasion of Kuwait.
- Resolution 794 (1992), wherein the Council, in authorizing a U.S.-led force to provide humanitarian relief to Somalia, stated that those committing violations of international humanitarian law in this internal conflict would be held "individually responsible for them."
- Resolution 835 (1993), wherein the Council "endorse[d]" the declaration of the Secretary-General's special representative for Cambodia that that state's recent elections had been "free and fair."

In each of these cases and others, the Council is offering a legal characterization of certain events before it. What is special about these declarations is that they do not constitute interpretations of the Charter (an issue discussed below). Rather, the Council is stating legal conclusions about areas of law not directly part of the Charter, although part of its overall architecture to be sure.

The Council can do so in a number of ways. First, it can overtly identify law violators, as with Rhodesia and South Africa. Second, it can indirectly identify law violators, as Resolution 598 does regarding Iraq and Iran. Third, it can approve of conduct as legal when there may be some doubt as to its characterization, for example regarding Cambodia and the notion of "free and fair" elections. Fourth, it can characterize the legal consequences of a particular law violation, as Resolution 687 does regarding Iraq's violation of Article 2(4). Last, it can endorse a rule of international law without accusing one or more states of violating it. This is commonly done when the Council reiterates states' obligations under the Charter to settle disputes by peaceful means. But in the case of Resolution 794, the Council endorsed a new spin on international humanitarian law. By asserting that individuals should be held liable for violations of the law of war even in a demonstrably internal conflict such as that in Somalia, the Council was effectively declaring, or at least advocating, the existence of a new corpus of war crimes that some states were reluctant to acknowledge—war crimes in civil wars.

The effect of these declaratory resolutions can be highly significant, and those Council members who seek to insert these sorts of clauses know this. Elites around the world often take note of these determinations and use them to their advantage. They can be used to embarrass law violators through the mobilization of shame; they can make their way into peace negotiations as the violations of particular states need to be addressed; and they can be invoked in other, unrelated situations as evidence of where the law is going. Thus, for example, the International Criminal Tribunal for the Former Yugoslavia (ICTY) cited the 1992 Somalia resolution as evidence of changing international attitudes on the scope of war crimes law.[7]

With these legal declarations put to different uses by a variety of different audiences, two issues of importance to doctrinal international lawyers effectively drop out of the picture for most of those audiences. The first is the Council's status as a political as opposed to a legal body. The Council's centrality to international peace and the many bars to passage of its resolutions (mainly the veto power of the P-5) mean that when the Council does speak on international law, many actors will listen. Indeed, it seems safe to say that the legal declarations of the Council almost certainly have a greater impact on international actors than do those of the ICJ. Second, whether these resolutions are taken under Chapter VI, Chapter VII, or elsewhere proves of second-order importance at best. Even the ICTY, a true court, did not seem to care, when it cited the 1992 Somalia resolution for the proposition that international law recognized war crimes in civil wars, whether the Council adopted it under Chapter VI or Chapter VII.

The Interpretive Function: Giving
Meaning to the Charter's Open-Textured Provisions

The Council's chief interpretive function as an international legal actor derives from its role as the lead UN organ concerning the Charter's provisions on international peace and security. The members of the Council have engaged in myriad interpretive discussions and decisions, including over the definition of a "dispute" for purposes of Chapter VI; the meaning of Article 12's requirement that the Assembly refrain from acting while the Council is acting; and important procedural issues such as the meaning of the "concurring votes" of the permanent members in Article 27. These issues fill many legal treatises. Two interpretive issues worth highlighting show the extent to which the Council's members have adopted an overtly teleological interpretation of the Charter to respond to contemporary crises.

The first concerns the decision of the Council in the UN's early years to deploy UN personnel to monitor cease-fires, with the consent of the parties. The Council's first two forays were the UN Truce Supervision Organization, deployed in 1948 under Resolution 50, and the UN Military Observer Group in India and Pakistan, deployed in 1949 originally under the terms of Resolution 47 (1948). Although the generally accepted birth of interpositional peacekeeping took place in 1956, when the General

Assembly deployed the UN Emergency Force in the Sinai, the deployment of observers began with the Council's decisions, and the Assembly has authorized only one other mission with a military component since then.[8] Most notable, the Council approved the significant expansion of consent-based peacekeeping—from monitoring cease-fires to implementing peace agreements—that began in the late 1980s. That process commenced with the UN Transitional Assistance Group in Namibia and assumed its most expansive forms in the UN Transitional Authority in Cambodia in 1992–1993 and then in the missions in which the UN assumed governmental functions at the end of the 1990s—the UN Mission in Kosovo and the UN Transitional Administration in East Timor.

In retrospect, the most remarkable legal achievement of the Security Council may well be that its members did not succumb to a paralytic textualism. (The influence of the politically and legally sophisticated Dag Hammarskjöld was critical.) As a textual matter, Chapter VI reads like a cookbook of obvious diplomatic moves—from encouraging the parties to solve their problem in Articles 33 and 35, to suggesting a settlement to them in Articles 37 and 38. It does not contemplate the deployment of UN personnel in an operational manner (except perhaps as a part of investigating a dispute under Article 34). This type of deployment is mentioned only in Article 42, once the Council has taken the major step of declaring a situation a threat to or breach of the peace. One could have imagined serious objection to the deployment of observers, and later troops, as something the Council could only do under Chapter VII.

Yet most UN peacekeeping operations have been approved without serious consideration of such arguments. The closest thing to a challenge to the authority of the Council were concerns raised by France and the Soviet Union about the lawfulness of the actions and financing of the UN Operation in the Congo (ONUC, 1960–1964), but even those states either voted in favor of or abstained on the key resolutions setting up ONUC; they did not argue that the Council had no authority to set up the operation in the first place. The ICJ, for its part, dismissed in one short paragraph any argument that the Council could deploy peacekeepers only under Chapter VII.[9]

The Council's interpretive breakthrough was in overcoming—or, more accurately, in agreeing with the views of key member states and UN Secretariat officials to break down—two sets of artificial barriers within the Charter. First, it broke down the barriers *among articles*. Sensing that consent-based peacekeeping did not quite come under the investigative power of Article 34 or the recommendatory powers of Article 36 and 38, the Council's members were willing to create operations without recourse to specific textual authority. This blurring of articles in the Charter would later occur during the 1990–1991 Gulf War, where the Council never specified whether the authorization to use force in Resolution 678 was Council "action" under Article 42, endorsement of self-defense under Article 51, or both.

Second, and more significant, it broke down the barriers *between two chapters* of the Charter that many had seen as dealing with different situations. The Council's members discovered, very early in the UN's history, that world crises do not come categorized as either "likely to endanger the maintenance of international peace and security" (Chapter VI), on the one hand, or a "threat to the peace, breach of the peace, or act of aggression" (Chapter VII) on the other. Seeking to develop new strategies without having to make legal conclusions that might come back to haunt them later, the Council accepted Hammarskjöld's argument that consent-based peacekeeping belonged to "Chapter VI-1/2" of the Charter, refusing to invoke either Chapter VI or Chapter VII in consent-based operations.[10] Indeed, perhaps as early as ONUC's later phases, and certainly in the case of the UN Protection Force in the former Yugoslavia (UNPROFOR), the Council combined consent-based mandates and coercive mandates in the same mission (usually with disastrous consequences).

The second great interpretive revolution concerns not breaking down categories but filling them in—in particular, giving meaning to the critical phrase quoted above that triggers action under Chapter VII. The key developments whereby the Council characterized (either in preambular paragraphs or in formal determinations) certain situations as "threats to international peace and security" include:

- Resolution 161 (1961), with respect to the assassination of Patrice Lumumba and the civil war in the Congo.[11]
- Resolution 217 (1965), with respect to the independence of Rhodesia.
- Resolution 418 (1977), regarding the acquisition of arms by South Africa in light of that government's "policies and acts," including "apartheid and racial discrimination."
- Resolution 688 (1991), on repression of Iraqi Kurds leading to refugee flows and cross-border incursions (although the resolution itself did not invoke Chapter VII or take action under it).
- Resolution 748 (1992), on Libya's failure to demonstrate by concrete actions its renunciation of terrorism.
- Resolution 841 (1993), on the continued presence of the illegal regime in Haiti and its effects on the refugee issue.

The Rhodesia resolution, the Council's first formal, operative determination of a threat to the peace outside the context of classic aggression (i.e., Korea),[12] took the organization twenty years. Like many major steps by international organizations, it was in many ways sui generis, in this case in light of Britain's attitude toward the Ian Smith government. One might make the same claim about the apartheid resolutions, but member states truly believed that apartheid itself was inflaming the situation in southern Africa. By the 1990s the trend had snowballed, as internal repression—by selected targets—came to be seen as threat to the peace; nevertheless, the resolutions included the usual transborder link to refugees or arms flows to placate states like China that feared a prodemocratization push under the guise of ending threats to the peace.

These episodes represented important interpretations of a key Charter provision (Article 39), most obviously because they made possible the use of enforcement measures—sanctions and force—against states regarding matters that many states historically considered internal. Yet it would be unfair to give the Council's members the sole credit for this interpretive step. Since 1946 the General Assembly had been dealing with human rights issues and passing resolutions on these matters. Some states invoked Article 2(7) to oppose these resolutions—such as the 1952 General Assembly Resolution 616B on South Africa—but this was ultimately a losing proposition. As long as the General Assembly's members saw human rights as part of the UN's agenda—as was textually mandated—they would continue to narrow Article 2(7) and, as a result, broaden the meaning of an international dispute. It was thus not a leap—though it was significant—for the Council's members to see this trend of internationalizing the domestic and do the same, albeit in fits and starts, in Chapter VII.

In that sense, the Council's expansive interpretations of the term "threat to the peace" may, after all, be about breaking down barriers in the Charter as well—not among articles or Chapters but *among functions.* Ultimately, the Council's members came to recognize that it was not possible always to draw neat lines between "international peace" and "human rights." They still do so in many senses, in refraining from condemning most repressive regimes (let alone imposing sanctions on them or authorizing force); but when the political winds are blowing against a particular target state, its human rights practices have trickled over to the ambit of threats to the peace.

The Promotion Function:
Encouraging States to Deploy International Law

The Council has also taken important steps during the UN's history to promote the application of the law of nations to resolve international disputes. The Charter provides specific textual authority for this function but in a rather narrow way that the Council has clearly transcended. The textual mandates appear in Article 33, which authorizes the Council to call upon the parties to a dispute to settle it through a variety of peaceful means, including arbitration and judicial settlement; and Article 36(3), which advises the Council that "legal disputes should as a general rule be referred by the parties to the International Court of Justice." The Council has, indeed, at times made recommendations that states settle a dispute by judicial settlement through the ICJ or other bodies. For instance, in 1947 the Council in Resolution 22 urged the United Kingdom and Albania to send their dispute over the passage of British warships through the Corfu Channel to the ICJ (which they did). On the whole, however, this sort of promotion of international law in terms of advocating strict judicial settlement is quite rare.

Nonetheless, the Council has promoted international law beyond the strictures of Articles 33 and 36. First, on two fairly recent occasions the Council not only called for the utilization of international courts but also created them. The UN criminal tribunals for the former Yugoslavia and for Rwanda, and the Council's endorsement of the mixed tribunal for Sierra Leone, represent a sort of apogee for the judicialization of Security Council action. In Resolutions 827 (1993) and 955 (1994), the Council approved the statutes of the two UN courts, making them subsidiary organs of the Council and also defining a set of international crimes in the process.

This promotion of international law is of a wholly different nature from that contemplated in Articles 33 and 36 in two senses. First, the tribunals were created under Chapter VII, as part of a strategy—a very belated one—to restore international peace to the former Yugoslavia and Rwanda. They are not suggestions to the warring sides, but new institutions with which all affected parties must cooperate. Second, and more significant, the tribunals are not venues in which the states engaged in the particular dispute argue and obtain a resolution of the matter; indeed, in the case of Rwanda the tribunal responded to a predominantly internal conflict. Rather, they seek to shift accountability from states, or peoples, to individuals, in the hope that identification and punishment of such individuals will pave the way for reconciliation within and among states. The Council's members created the courts not only because they believed diplomacy could not resolve the dispute but also because the nature of the offenses made diplomatic solutions in a sense objectionable. Radovan Karadzic or Jean Kambanda, in a word, needed to be punished, not merely convinced to surrender.

At the same time, however deep—in the sense of genuinely judicial—these tribunals are, their reach is quite narrow in that they address only a handful of conflicts. The Council's second strategy is not as deep, but it is far broader. It entails recommending or demanding that parties overtly consider international legal principles in the solution to their conflict. In these cases, the Council is signaling to the parties that the law might be helpful in resolving the disputes, or that the settlement should respect principles of international law and not merely represent the powerful state strong-arming the weak one.

This sort of promotion of the role—as opposed to the rule—of law in settling disputes is common. Obviously, the Council includes in many resolutions boilerplate language that urges parties to solve the dispute in accordance with the principles of the Charter. But the Council has been more specific on numerous occasions. A few examples paint the picture.

- Resolution 242 (1967), on the Middle East, wherein the Council affirmed "the necessity for guaranteeing freedom of navigation through international waterways in the area," using a principle of customary international law to signal to the Arab states that any peace treaty with Israel would have to include passage through the Strait of Tiran.
- Resolution 598 (1987), on the Iran-Iraq War, which urged the repatriation of prisoners of war after the end of hostilities with a specific reference to the third Geneva Convention, to which both Iran and Iraq had been a party for thirty years and which provides detailed obligations for such repatriation.
- Resolution 1209 (1998), on illicit arms flows in Africa, which urged African states to enact legislation and implement effective enforcement mechanisms and also to consider a regional legal regime for registering arms.
- Resolution 1373 (2001), wherein the Council called upon states to become parties as soon as possible to various antiterrorism conventions, in particular the UN's 1999 Convention for the Suppression of Financing of Terrorism.[13]

For those international lawyers and scholars who see the law's contribution to the settlement of disputes taking place principally outside international courts—through its invocation and use in diplomatic discussions—this promotion function is among the most important roles for the Council. The Council's members recognize that treaties and custom can provide specific rules to help resolve some conflicts or set up regimes and institutions that can address matters of international peace and security. Yet the Council's members are supremely realistic about the promises and limits of the law. They do not expect the parties to turn over their fate on major issues to a court; nor do they probably expect the law to mandate a particular outcome to a dispute (although the freedom of navigation through international straits shows that it can). And they understand that, for some disputes, the law might be limited to general principles of little practical use, or that both sides can come up with facts to show that they are legally in the right.

Nonetheless, legal arguments can shape the outcome of negotiations. They can serve to take extreme options off the table—to serve as a set of bookends within which a constructive solution might lie.[14] The Council's members know this because they—certainly the permanent five—have their own lawyers, who play a critical role in the drafting of resolutions. Just as legal argumentation can affect the outcome of Security Council debates, so too can it affect, through indirect and often untraceable paths, the outcome of political talks.

The Enforcement Function:
Chapter VII as a Means to Compel Compliance with Law

Last, the Council is an enforcement body. Typically, this characterization means that the Council has the unique authority under the Charter to order states to take measures that will result in compliance with its decisions. Those underlying decisions are legally binding themselves under Article 25—they need not have any other grounding in international law—and the decisions to enforce are equally binding. So the enforcement process is very much about using the law, and using the law to enforce the law.

But enforcement is about more than securing compliance with decisions of the Council that are binding only by virtue of Article 25; it is also about securing compliance with international law that is binding independent of Article 25. The Charter does not charge the Council with enforcing extra-Charter law, but the Council's members have done so on numerous occasions. Thus, when the Council directed states in Resolution 276 to cease all actions that constituted acceptance of South Africa's control over Namibia, not only were they enforcing their own determination in Resolution 276 that the occupation was illegal, but they were also enforcing human rights norms against discrimination, norms in favor of decolonization based on the wishes of the people, and even in a somewhat attenuated way the original League of Nations mandate, which South Africa had so long flouted. The resolutions creating the ad hoc criminal tribunals are clearly designed to enforce international humanitarian law found in treaties and custom. Resolution 687 and its successors partly enforce earlier Council resolutions, but they also enforce the 1963 treaty between Iraq and Kuwait that set their border and liability principles in international environmental law (through the garnishment of Iraqi oil income). Resolution 940 (1994), authorizing the restoration of President Jean-Bertrand Aristide to office, was an enforcement of the right of the Haitian people to be governed by the person whom they elected under UN auspices in 1990.

Council action to enforce international law can at times seem to run afoul of the law itself. In Resolution 792, which ordered an arms and air embargo on Libya, the Council was enforcing earlier resolutions that directed Libya to hand over the Pan Am 103 suspects, but it was also enforcing the 1971 Montreal Convention, which prohibits aircraft sabotage. Yet its enforcement message to Libya ended up overriding (or subverting) the very text of the treaty—which gives states a clear choice of extraditing or prosecuting suspected saboteurs—leading Libya to sue the United States and the United Kingdom in the ICJ. In September 2003, Libya dropped the case after the Security Council lifted the embargo as part of a financial compensation deal with the families of Pan Am 103 victims and their governments.

Conclusion

The Council's history offers evidence that international law can serve as both a factor influencing the decisions of the Council and a product or byproduct of the Council's decisions. It rejects any notion that the Council's status as a political organ relegates it to a subsidiary status in the formation and application of international law. Instead, it is a central player by virtue of its capacity to make legal declarations, interpret the Charter's text, promote the relevance of legal norms in resolving disputes, and require states to follow legal rules, even those outside the Charter. To those mapping the legal landscape and gauging how expectations of states change over time, the resolutions and practice of the Council are critical evidence.

But they can also be more: by virtue of the power behind the Council's resolutions—or at least the potential power behind them—they stand a greater chance of influencing state decisionmaking than do many other pronouncements of international law. The UN's history demonstrates amply that such enforcement is never a sure thing; and the Council has been frequently ignored. But a Council pronouncement on a legal issue signals that powerful states are endorsing the legal claims embodied in the resolution. When those states choose to take measures to make the resolution really stick, the Council's legal pronouncements are not merely law on the books but law on the ground.

Yet the categorization and analysis above leaves two major issues hanging in the air. First, to demonstrate the role of law as an *input* into the Council's decisionmaking, one must attempt to trace the causal pathways from the law, to those invoking it, to the outcomes of the Council. International law and international relations theorists are increasingly occupied with the question of whether and how international law really matters—to what extent it exerts an independent influence on state behavior. The influence of law on the recent decisions of the Council—as opposed to the reverse—remains unaddressed. Participants at the January 2003 International Peace Academy (IPA) meeting called to plan this book offered various anecdotes describing situations where legal opinions from the UN Legal Counsel very much affected delegations' decisionmaking, and permanent representatives repeatedly remarked on the frequency with which various international norms are invoked in both public and closed sessions. But they also confessed that such invocation need not lead to action (as, for instance, repeated reference to the Genocide Convention did not provoke a serious attempt by the Council to prevent or stop the 1994 Rwandan genocide), and that states often make their policy decisions first and consider the legal ramifications later.

Second, with respect to *outputs,* the Council's contributions, however significant, stand under a normative shadow. International law, as Michael Reisman has written, is a process of communication—about claim and counterclaim.[15] If the intended recipient does not regard the pronouncement as authoritative or legitimate, its influence will be minimal. This shadow has at least three aspects. One, a favorite of many legal academics but considered rather irrelevant by governmental officials and political scientists, is the concern that the Council might act either beyond its powers in the Charter or in violation of other norms of international law.[16] This was the central question in the ICJ Lockerbie litigation, and that litigation venue accounted for both the fascination of the lawyers and the disinterest of the political scientists and diplomats. This fear reached its zenith in the heady days after the Cold War when the Council seemed forever unified; today that era seems but a distant memory.

The second aspect is the perpetual refusal by the Council's members to solve the membership problem. Despite Article 25's obligation on states to comply with Council decisions, the receptivity of members to the views of the Council will erode if reform remains perpetually stalled. The Council does not need to, and should not, replicate the representativeness of the General Assembly—indeed, it is that very representativeness, including the absence of the veto, that caused the Charter's framers to deny that organ the ability to promulgate binding resolutions other than on the UN's internal issues. But a Council stuck in the world of 1965 (or 1971, when China replaced Taiwan) and fundamentally out of touch with modern power realities risks the prospect that its pronouncements on legal issues will not be authoritative. At the same time, an increase in the size of the Council, with the resultant new hurdles to passage of resolutions, may prompt the United States—as well as other states—to circumvent that body as they did in earlier years, making the Iraq episode simply a prelude to marginalization of the Council on matters of peace and security.

Whether reform means enlargement or something else is, of course, an enormous question, so big that the UN's members seem incapable of addressing it. The attitude of nonpermanent members in the months following Resolution 1441 (2002) may well have undercut much of the logic of reform. When the nonpermanent members suddenly found the permanent five divided, and their long-awaited moment to influence outcomes at hand, most retreated to a position of urging the permanent five to agree and assuring that they would go along with the result. When that failed, they found their position as the target of intense political pressure by France and Russia, on the one hand, and the United States and Great Britain on the other, most uncomfortable.[17] If the nonpermanent members seek to dilute the power of the permanent five, they need to offer a realistic alternative.

Last, the Council is doomed to be inconsistent with its practice. What of the myriad other disputes involving the same norms where the Council does not act—does not condemn, does not extend the application of the Charter, does not promote the law as a solution, and does not enforce? The claim of selectivity or bias is, in one sense, the guilty party's first process-based defense, and criminal courts routinely reject it. But the global arena is not a court; such arguments carry much weight among those who see the Council as failing to act on their behalf. Thus, when the United States and Britain urged the Council to fulfill its "responsibilities" and authorize force against Iraq in 2002–2003, many states asked why the Council was not pushing implementation of various UN resolutions on the Arab-Israeli conflict (though none asked why the Council was not carrying through on, for instance, its 1948 call for a plebiscite in Kashmir). Membership reform might ameliorate the problem somewhat, as more states bring more issues to the Council, but it might mean that the Council simply acts less on all issues as its members disagree more, prompting more actions like that of the United States vis-à-vis Iraq. But the Council will always be a political body, the veto will survive reform attempts, and the Council will pick its targets with politics and not law in mind. International lawyers can no more tell the Council to be consistent than can diplomats.

Inconsistency is not necessarily crippling. As one permanent representative stated at the January 2003 IPA meeting, the Council continues to enjoy significant legitimacy despite the membership problems and the inconsistent and unprincipled way in which it often acts. In practical terms, it might simply mean that the Council's resolutions addressing international law, passed in the context of situation X, will have to be invoked by others—not the Council—in the context of situation Y. This pattern of shifting arenas for invocation of norms is common in international law. But if those in situation X succeed in ignoring the Council, claiming selectivity, those in situation Y may have little incentive to comply as well.

Unless the 2003 Iraq war presages a permanent, significant diminution of the Council's role in responding to global and regional tensions (which I somewhat doubt), the Council will remain at the core of the international legal process. But because the Council is a political organ, the normative implications of resolutions beyond the immediate dispute may get short shrift in the debates over whether and how it should act. The ability of states to take the longer-term normative view depends on the issues under discussion and the composition of the Council itself. The permanent five and states that rotate into the Council with greater frequency thus have a special responsibility in this regard. The Council's place in the legal process ultimately depends upon whether all its members can fully appreciate the full range of their responsibilities as prescribers, interpreters, and enforcers of the law of nations.

Notes

1. *ICJ Statute*, art. 38(1).
2. Bruno Simma et al., eds., *The Charter of the United Nations: A Commentary* (Oxford: Oxford University Press, 1994), p. 52.
3. UN Charter, arts. 25, 103.
4. Compare Legal Consequences for States of the Continued Presence of South Africa in Namibia (South West Africa) Notwithstanding Security Council Resolution 276 (1970), 1970 International Court of Justice (ICJ) 16, 52–53 (June 21).
5. Rosalyn Higgins, *The Development of International Law Through the Political Organs of the United Nations* (Oxford, Oxford University Press, 1963).
6. I focus here on the Council resolutions, though its practice includes presidential statements, debates, and resolutions that do not pass.
7. *Prosecutor v. Tadic, Interlocutory Appeal* (1995), para. 133.
8. That was the military component of the 1962–1963 West Irian operation (the UN Temporary Executive Authority).
9. Certain Expenses of the United Nations, 1962 ICJ 151, 177 (July 20).
10. See Steven R. Ratner, *The New UN Peacekeeping: Building Peace in Lands of Conflict After the Cold War* (New York: St. Martin's, 1995), pp. 56–59, 268, n. 7.
11. See Thomas M. Franck, "The Security Council and "Threats to the Peace": Some Remarks on Remarkable Recent Events," in René-Jean Dupuy, ed., *The Development of the Role of the Security Council: Peacekeeping and Peacebuilding* (Boston: M. Nijhoff, 1993), pp. 83, 91–95.
12. The finding in Resolution 161 concerning the Congo was in a preambular paragraph expressing "deep concern."
13. See Paul Szasz, "The Security Council Starts Legislating," *American Journal of International Law* 96, no. 4 (2002): 901.
14. See Steven R. Ratner, "Does International Law Matter in Preventing Ethnic Conflict?" *New York University Journal of International Law and Politics* 32, no. 3 (2000): 591, 627–628.
15. W. Michael Reisman, "International Lawmaking: A Process of Communication," *American Society of International Law Proceedings* 75 (1981): 101, 105.
16. See, for example, Mohammed Bedjaoui, *The New World Order and the Security Council: Testing the Legality of Its Acts* (Boston: M. Nijhoff, 1994).
17. Maggie Farley and Robin Wright, "U.S., Britain to Set Deadlines for U.N., Iraq," *Los Angeles Times,* February 20, 2003.

38

The Security Council in the Twenty-First Century

CAMERON R. HUME

Interstate relations are changing so rapidly that many scholars are asking how states will meet the challenges of a new century. These changes are certain to have a direct impact on the role of the Security Council.

From the founding of the United Nations in 1945 until the end of the Cold War more than four decades later, most of the Security Council's work involved conflicts that accompanied the process of decolonization. Thus conflicts in the Middle East, including four Arab-Israeli wars and the struggle over the Palestinians' right of self-determination, were constant items on the Council's agenda. Other conflicts before the Council were often the consequence of postcolonial strife, for example the situations in the Congo and Cyprus. The permanent members, in particular the United States and the Soviet Union, used the Security Council as a venue where they managed differences on issues outside the European theater. The era of decolonization was concurrent with the Cold War.

The end of the Cold War launched a different period for the work of the Security Council. In 1987 the permanent members collaborated over the Iran-Iraq War, sponsoring a Chapter VII resolution demanding a cease-fire, establishing a process by which to settle outstanding issues, and threatening the use of sanctions against either party if it did not comply with the cease-fire demand. Iraq's invasion of Kuwait in August 1990 pushed the Council's work to a new level. Despite Iraq's claim that Kuwait was legally part of Iraq and thus that occupation resolved a conflict of decolonization, other UN members responded that the invasion was an act of aggression. In rapid succession the Council condemned Iraq's aggression, demanded its withdrawal, established a comprehensive economic embargo, and then approved the use of "all necessary means" to secure implementation of these decisions.

Collaboration soon extended to other conflicts that had been clogging the Council's agenda: for example, securing Namibia's independence, ending the war in Angola, and administering elections that would give legitimacy and recognition to the Cambodian government. Often the permanent members had supported one side or the other in such conflicts, and by resolving differences among themselves they could give a real boost to settling conflicts involving their clients. The Security Council was making real progress in resolving conflicts, and these decisions represented a new high-water mark for cooperation among the permanent members.

Meanwhile another type of conflict was brewing. Following decolonization some newly independent states had prospered and laid a basis for sustained development; others had not. Leaders in states that were failing the development challenge, such as Siad Barre in Somalia, had often been able to manipulate Cold War rivalries in order to secure external support for their governments. With the end of the Cold War this support had dried up. "Failed states" would give rise to heightened risk of internal conflicts, conflicts that in turn could threaten regional peace. Somalia became the archetypal failed state.

The Decade Just Past

In the 1990s the work of the Security Council expanded dramatically, and the Council shifted more attention toward conflicts in Europe and Africa. At the start of the decade, in 1990, the Council held eighty consultations of the whole and sixty-nine formal meetings, adopting thirty-seven resolutions and fourteen presidential statements. Twenty-five meetings concerned the Arab-Israeli conflict, and nineteen involved Iraq and its invasion of Kuwait. Only one meeting was held on an African issue, the situation in Western Sahara. As in many previous years, almost two-thirds of the Council's work concerned the Middle East.

In the next years the work expanded rapidly. In 1995 the Council held 251 consultations of the whole and 130 formal meetings, adopting sixty-six resolutions and sixty-three presidential statements. Now more than 40 percent of the Council's meetings concerned conflicts in Europe. On the Middle East, other than periodic renewals of peacekeeping mandates, the Council met once on Iraq and three times on the question of Palestine. The number of meetings on African issues jumped to thirty-nine, covering conflicts in Angola, Burundi, Liberia, Mozambique, Rwanda, Sierra Leone, Somalia, and Western Sahara. Although these conflicts in African states affected the interests of other states, they were essentially internal.

In 2000 the pace of activity was comparable. The number of consultations of the whole had dropped to 210, but the number of formal meetings had increased to 167. The Council adopted fifty resolutions and forty-one presidential statements. The shift to African issues continued. Angola, Burundi, the Central African Republic, the Democratic Republic of Congo,

Guinea, Guinea-Bissau, Rwanda, Sierra Leone, and Somalia accounted for almost 40 percent of all meetings. The Council met thirty times on European issues, twenty times on the Middle East, and twenty-three times on Asian issues. Many of the discussions of the Council and peacekeeping operations again concerned conflicts primarily within the domestic jurisdiction of a state, albeit most often with an impact on other states.

The workload, in a striking departure from past practice, now included a large number of thematic issues rather than specific disputes or threats to the peace. The Council met on AIDS in Africa, on children in armed conflict, on the International Criminal Tribunal for the Former Yugoslavia, on international peace and security, on not withdrawing without an exit strategy, on the role of the Security Council regarding armed conflict, on sanctions, on the UN high commissioner for refugees, and on women and conflict resolution. This expansion of the agenda reflected the fact that the Council was confronting new transnational issues and struggling to create effective responses.

Three significant trends were changing the character of the Council's work. First, many situations being discussed arose not from classic disputes pitting one state against another or from struggles for self-determination, but rather from failures of established states to provide competent administration or to meet their obligations to other states. Peacekeeping operations—from Haiti to Bosnia to Sierra Leone—now included in their mandates requirements that they improve the conditions of governance provided by the state rather than monitor a separation of two states' armies. The new electoral assistance unit in the Secretariat had as its primary function helping a state to manage its own elections, certainly an activity that falls within the domestic jurisdiction of any state. From Central America to Mozambique and East Timor this unit helped to conduct elections that established democratic governments.

Some states were failing to maintain internal order, but the international community found it far more difficult to assist in the police function. In Somalia, U.S. forces suffered a serious setback when they attempted to arrest certain individuals. In Rwanda, UN forces stood aside when genocide was perpetrated, and in Bosnia local militias humiliated UN forces who would not take arms to protect civilians. UN police monitors might accompany local police on their rounds, but it would be the local police who retained authority to arrest perpetrators. The United Nations was unable to use force in place of a state that was failing to protect its population.

The second significant trend was that regional initiatives to resolve conflicts, replacing initiatives by the permanent members, became more frequent. The European Union claimed a lead in resolving the conflicts that arose from the dissolution of Yugoslavia. The Organization of American

States was active in dealing with the problems of Haiti. The Economic Community of West African States (ECOWAS) dispatched peacekeepers to Liberia. The Organization of African Unity took initiatives to resolve the conflicts in the Congo and to end the war between Ethiopia and Eritrea. The lesson here was consistent. In regions where self-determination and the process of decolonization had run their course, organizations of states from the region would often claim primacy in conflict resolution

The third significant trend was that Council members began to give specific attention to transnational issues. These are issues that may appear to be within the domestic jurisdiction of states yet soon have consequences for other states. Some members resisted this innovation because they did not want the Security Council, where the permanent members have a special role, to take over an issue from the Economic and Social Council, where developing countries had a preponderant influence. Nevertheless, in part because AIDS has had such a direct impact on the capacity of African states, this reluctance was overcome.

The events of September 11, 2001, engaged the Council at the center of the campaign against terrorism. Once again two of the above-mentioned trends—the attention to transnational issues and the phenomenon of state weakness—were in evidence. The Taliban regime in Afghanistan had failed in its fundamental obligation to govern and to conduct its relations with other states by allowing Al-Qaida cells on its territory to plan and launch terrorist attacks. Terrorism itself was surely a transnational threat to peace and security.

Mounting Pressures on States' Capacities

The years ahead will test the capacity of a significant number of states to govern and to conduct their relations with other states. Population pressures, resource constraints, and uneven economic growth will all present real challenges to the ability of the international system to preserve peace and security.

According to the UN's prospective data for world population as revised in 2000, twenty-two countries will have populations of more than 60 million by 2015. These twenty-two countries include all five permanent members of the Security Council. Except for the United States, the populations of the large, wealthier states are not growing (average rates of population growth for all developed countries will decline from 0.2 to 0.1 percent). Populations are growing in a number of large developing countries, often in regions where the number and frequency of conflicts have been on the rise (average rates of population growth for all developing countries will decrease from 1.5 to 1.1 percent). Most growth will occur in Asia and Africa. These shifts in population will stress the capacity of individual states, making instability both within individual states and among states in those regions more likely. Moreover, the need for wealthier states to support regional efforts at conflict resolution with political, material, and military resources will be even more acute than it is already.

As the recent World Summit on Sustainable Development acknowledged, the world's ecosystem is already under stress because of the pressures exerted by the growth of population, production, and consumption. By 2015, more than 3 billion people (mostly in Africa, the Middle East, southern Asia, and northern China) will live in "water-stressed" areas with less than 1,700 cubic meters of water per capita. Although global grain production has risen consistently from the launch of the green revolution in the 1970s (by almost 60 percent in thirty years), per capita grain availability reached a peak in 1980 and is now declining to the level of thirty years ago.[1] Today's worst famines are in southern and eastern Africa.

Unfortunately, the world cannot count on shifting economic fortunes to counter these trends. One recent study (the Central Intelligence Agency's long-term growth model) predicted that most economic growth will take place in Asia, North America, and Europe and that growth will be slowest in sub-Saharan Africa. Surely it must be a goal of the international community to improve these prospects, but it would be unwise to assume success.

Given these circumstances, the problems posed by states that fail in some significant way, either in providing government or in conducting their relations with other states, are sure to grow. The Security Council will have to confront the problems of failing states and of transnational threats.

The Views of One Member State

One year after the events of September 11, 2001, President George W. Bush issued the new *National Security Strategy*, a document revised and published every four years. The 2002 *Strategy* provided important insights into how the U.S. government perceived the challenges of the new century, as well as explanations of policy. "Now, networks of individuals can bring great chaos and suffering to our shores for less than it costs to purchase a single tank. Terrorists are organized to penetrate open societies to turn the power of modern technologies against us." In other words, it is becoming more difficult for states to protect their own citizens and to prevent their territory from being used as a base for attack against another state.

This shift in focus in the 2002 *National Security Strategy* parallels the growing attention the Security Council accords to the problems of failing states and transnational threats. "America is now threatened less by conquering states than we are by failing ones. We are menaced less by fleets and armies than by catastrophic technologies in the hands of the embittered few." Terrorism and the events of September 11 may provide the foremost example of this focus, but earlier interventions by U.S. and UN forces in Somalia, Bosnia, Haiti, and elsewhere confronted elements of both state failure and transnational threats (such as refugees, famine, arms trafficking, narcotics smuggling, and terrorist sanctuaries).

Two sections of the 2002 *National Security Strategy* relate directly to the work of the Security Council. The section on working with others to defuse regional conflicts affirms the need to remain engaged "in critical regional disputes to avoid explosive escalation and to minimize human suffering," but it also acknowledges that no doctrine could anticipate all of the circumstances that might warrant U.S. action. Moreover, it conforms to the UN experience that more can be done when acting with others than when acting alone, but that without the consent and cooperation of the parties the international community may have little role to play. It affirms that "the United States should invest time and resources into building international relationships and institutions that can help manage local crises when they emerge; the United States should be realistic about its ability to help those who are unwilling or unready to help themselves. Where and when people are ready to do their part, we will be willing to move decisively." This approach promises an active role by the United States in working with others to address conflicts.

The 2002 *National Security Strategy* also gives Africa special notice. The United States will work with others for an African continent that "lives in liberty, peace, and growing prosperity." With regard to the problems caused by individual states that are struggling against the risk of failure, the document cites the need to strengthen fragile states, to reinforce capacity to secure borders, and to build antiterrorist capacity. The strategy recognizes that problems within individual states can spread to create regional war zones. The Security Council has been wrestling with this danger in West Africa and in the Great Lakes region since the end of the Cold War. Washington's preferred approaches to this problem, however, will be through bilateral engagement and coalitions of the willing. These options can be more flexible and at times less costly than UN operations.

The section on preventing threats from the use of weapons of mass destruction addresses the problem of rogue states. Such states, the strategy explains, brutalize their own people, have no regard for international law, seek to acquire weapons of mass destruction, sponsor terrorism, and reject basic human values. "We must be prepared to stop rogue states and their terrorist clients before they are able to threaten or use weapons of mass destruction against the United States and our allies and friends." The document specifically recalls the recognition in international law that "nations need not suffer an attack before they can lawfully take action to defend themselves against forces that present an imminent danger of attack." Although the United States reserves this right in international law, the recent prolonged negotiations that led to the adoption of Resolution 1441, directed at securing Iraq's compliance with its disarmament obligations arising from the conclusion of the Gulf War after more than a decade of noncompliance, demonstrated great persistence in pursuing the multilateral option.

New Departures?

Debates have begun over the evolution of rights and obligations of states under international law. The principle of inviolability, as stated in Article 2(7), is no longer understood as defending absolute conceptions of state sovereignty, as was demonstrated repeatedly by Security Council action on Somalia (1993), Haiti (1994), Albania (1997), and East Timor (1999). At the same time, modern communications and transportation have effectively reduced the distances separating states, increasing the obligations of governments to protect the environment, to provide health services, and to respect human rights. This evolution of rights and obligations of states will have a strong impact on the work of the Security Council.

The two related challenges of dealing with the problems of failing states and with transnational threats have dominated the work of the Security Council decades since the early 1990s and strongly influenced the recent statements in the 2002 *National Security Strategy*. Both trends are likely to continue through the next decade. First, a growing number of states risk "failing" in the sense that they are unable or unwilling to meet the minimum obligations of statehood to govern their population and territory and to conduct relations with other states according to international standards. Second, and in part as a consequence of this failure, there is an expanding list of transnational threats, including terrorism and the spread of weapons of mass destruction, that are often asymmetrical and involve nonstate actors. The traditional tools of diplomacy, as cited in the Charter language of 1945, and the innovations of third-party intervention by the Secretary-General, peacekeeping forces, and coalitions of the willing, have not been adequate to deal with these challenges.

Eventual solutions may come in many forms. The work of the Council suggests at least four, but no doubt others will develop. First, in dealing with transnational threats, such as terrorism or the spread of weapons of mass destruction, the Council must demonstrate the capacity to make new rules and to make operational their implementation. The most urgent threats to international peace and security are not identical to those of greatest concern when the Charter was written sixty years ago. Moreover, the Council must put in place mechanisms for international action. The Council's struggle, retroactively, to confront genocide and war crimes in Yugoslavia and in Rwanda by setting up international courts must be seen in this context, as must the inclusion of arms control provisions in the cease-fire resolution at the end of the Gulf War. Failure of the Council to deal with such issues would represent a diminished international capacity to deal with the peace and security issues of this era.

Second, the Council must lead the way to improved coordination on such problems as refugees, famines, and plagues. After the end of the era of decolonization and the Cold War, it is a fact of international life that neighbors to a conflict often insist that their region take the lead in conflict resolution, even when this effort requires outside support. The track record here is poor. Coordination among UN agencies in the field has required exceptional leadership, as shown in Mozambique, Haiti, East Timor, and Afghanistan. More often leadership is not exceptional. Even more inadequate, however, have been the attempts to secure cooperation among intergovernmental bodies, such as the Security Council and the Economic and Social Council. No combined operation that is responsible to separate competing boards of directors is likely to work well. To answer the Charter's call to save succeeding generations from the scourges of war, the Security Council must concentrate the authority needed to coordinate the work of international agencies.

Third, the Security Council must work with regional organizations and coalitions of the willing. Regional organizations, such as the African Union, can bring an additional element of legitimacy or a more acceptable diplomatic approach in addressing the problems of the failing state. For example, the Lusaka Agreement provided a diplomatic framework for dealing with the conflict in the Democratic Republic of Congo, and the United Nations provided the operational capacity for peacekeeping. ECOWAS has undertaken important conflict resolution and peacekeeping roles in Liberia, Sierra Leone, and Côte d'Ivoire. More recently a coalition of the willing, constituted by states in the region, has intervened in the Central African Republic. If there is a need to establish internal order for the protection of the civilian population, such a coalition may be more able to use force if needed than would a traditional UN peacekeeping operation. Therefore working with a regional organization can add both legitimacy and effectiveness in confronting the problems of a failing state.

Fourth, the Security Council, working most often through the Secretariat, must expand its capacity to deal with nonstate actors. When failing states need help to administer the population and territory, often the most capable agencies will be nonstate actors. On some issues, such as refugee assistance, cooperation is well established; on others, such as bolstering local police forces, progress has been made. But whenever it comes to matters that are essentially within the domestic jurisdiction of a state, such as displaced persons, the mechanisms for international action remain inadequate. Nonstate actors are inherently more able than states or international organizations to finesse the tension between international humanitarian standards and respect for state sovereignty that is embedded in Article 2(7) of the Charter.

Conclusion
The territorial national state is likely to remain the juridical building block of the international system for the foreseeable future. At any time some of these units, however, are likely to be failing in their duty either to provide government or to conduct relations with other states according to international norms. Such failures will be the breeding ground for threats to international peace and security, including terrorism, narcotics trafficking, infectious diseases, the spread of weapons of mass destruction, and other transnational problems. If the Security Council is to play its role in the maintenance of international peace and security, its members will have to display extra measures of flexibility and realism regarding the dangers of the new century.

Notes
I am the ambassador of the United States to the Republic of South Africa. The views expressed in this chapter are my own and do not necessarily represent those of the U.S. Department of State.

1. U.S. National Intelligence Council, *Global Trends 2015: A Dialogue About the Future with Nongovernment Experts* (Washington, D.C.: U.S. National Intelligence Council, December 2000), pp. 19–31.

39

Conclusion

David M. Malone

Significant changes in Security Council objectives, decisions, and working methods should not surprise after nearly sixty years of history. The Cold War confrontation between two dangerously armed blocs has yielded to a unipolar world in which threats derive mostly from "rogue" states and nonstate actors. Nuclear proliferation, long contained during the Cold War, is a disturbing phenomenon today. Enabled and empowered by the new, generally cooperative relationship among the P-5, a number of characteristics mark the Council's record since the mid-1980s.

The Council's usefulness to the community of nations in promoting a degree of international order, in attempting to meet new challenges, and in codifying through its decisions evolving values underpinning international relations emerges from the chapters in this volume. So do the Council's shortcomings, of commission, and importantly in Rwanda and some other crises, of omission. Double standards abound. Order does not necessarily equate to fairness. In the Council the powerful impose what they can, the weak endure what they must.

In the post–Cold War world the key issue for the Council is whether it can engage the United States, modulate its exercise of power, and restrain its impulses. French-led efforts to do so on Iraq in early 2003 proved unsuccessful, and possibly counterproductive, although they were strongly supported by public opinion in many countries. For the United States, the key issue on the Council is the extent to which it can serve as an instrument for the promotion of U.S. interests. (This is, of course, true for other members as well.) While the United States might enjoy the freedom of action provided by solo operations, the company the Council can provide helps in sharing political and other risks and often heavy burdens, including financial ones. A willingness to pursue some policy priorities through the Council has provided an occasional multilateralist tinge to George W. Bush's administration with its undoubted unilateral instincts, but the deadlock in the Council in March 2003 over Iraq could discourage further U.S. engagement.[1] U.S. military power today is so overwhelming relative to that of its principal partners that nothing can be taken for granted in the future, and Washington's patience with the tedium of multilateral bargaining will continue to wear thin when crises appear acute to it. A clear risk for the Council is that Washington will conceive its role mainly, at best, as one of long-term peacebuilding following short and sharp U.S.-led military interventions (the latter whether mandated by the Council or not), as was apparent in President Bush's address to the UN General Assembly on September 22, 2003, at a time when the U.S. military occupation of Iraq was experiencing serious distress.[2]

The chapters in this book have identified key changes in the pattern of the Council's decisions in the post–Cold War period. These include the essentially internal nature of many conflicts on its agenda, its greater tendency to resort to the provisions of Chapter VII, leading to a significant increase in sanctions regimes and in the authorization of force, and a significant role in its decisions for regional organizations. All of these trends have profound implications for the practice of peacekeeping and have introduced shifts in the thinking of many Council members. The Council's disposition to mandate varying forms of transitional administration and support to governments emerging from conflict may also prove increasingly important, conceivably for both Iraq and the Palestinian territories.

The chapters in this book have also suggested that a number of new concerns today contribute to driving decisionmaking in the Council, including the humanitarian impulse, human rights, democratization, and terrorism. Some conclusions relative to these factors are offered next. I have argued that the institutional changes affecting the Council are nearly as important as (and are often related to) doctrinal changes. I offer further below some concluding thoughts, not least on prospects for Security Council reform, on the role of international law, and on conceptions of legitimacy that I hope may be pertinent to the Council today. I then discuss two major challenges facing the Council today and doubtless in years to come: the role of the United States within the Council, and the Council's task in crafting a proactive and realistic response to Africa's multiple security crises.

In the conclusion, I seek to offer an interpretation and an integration of the points we have raised, rather than a comprehensive review of our many interesting findings.

The Nature of the Conflicts Addressed
by the Council, and the Nature of Its Decisions

Internal Conflicts Lead to "New Generation" Peacekeeping
The Council's willingness to involve itself in a broad range of internal conflicts, encompassing intercommunal strife, crises of democracy, fighting marked by a fierce struggle for control over national resources and wealth, and several other precipitating causes or incentives for continuation of war, forced it to confront hostilities of a much more complex nature than the interstate disputes with which it had greater experience. International efforts to mitigate and resolve these conflicts required complex mandates significantly more ambitious than the modalities of "classic" peacekeeping were designed to meet.[3] The most striking features of "new generation" peacekeeping operations (PKOs) launched by the Council in the 1990s were not so much the large numbers of military personnel involved—several earlier PKOs, for example in the Sinai, Congo, and even Cyprus, had featured large deployments of blue helmets—but rather the important role and substantive diversity of their civilian and police components.[4] Civilian functions discharged by PKOs or otherwise mandated by the Council included civil administration; the conduct and monitoring of elections; humanitarian assistance; human rights monitoring and training; police and judicial support, training, and reform; and even a degree of leadership on economic revival and development. Civilian leadership of recent large UN peacekeeping operations was initiated with great success in Namibia in 1989–1990 by Martti Ahtisaari, later president of Finland. The ambitious objectives served by these activities proved significantly more difficult to attain in many circumstances than the Council anticipated. Council-mandated military activities encountered significant resistance by frequently shadowy belligerents, leading to incidents involving heavy loss of life of peacekeepers (in Rwanda, Somalia, and the former Yugoslavia).

The UN Security Council's inability to induce compliance with its decisions fueled two apparently contradictory but all too frequently complementary responses: on the one hand, it moved to enforce decisions that had failed to generate consent in the field, notably in the former Yugoslavia,[5] Somalia,[6] and Haiti,[7] and on the other hand, in the face of significant casualties, it cut and ran, as in Somalia and at the outset of genocide in Rwanda.[8] These developments responded to shifts in thinking and in priorities in key capitals, notably Washington and Moscow. Beijing proved remarkably accommodating to them.

Although its civilian functions have expanded much more rapidly in the post–Cold War era than its military functions, peacekeeping is still primarily thought of as a military pursuit. The cases discussed in this volume suggest that even though no template for successful "new generation" peacekeeping exists, the need for a united Council, a clear mandate, and a good relationship between the Council and the Secretary-General (and his team on the ground) is vital. The desirability of a sound peace agreement and leadership by a regional power or a P-5 member is also clear.

One area in which the Council has fared poorly has been in its design, oversight, and international sponsorship of postconflict peacebuilding strategies, as documented in Chapter 31, on Haiti. The Council has a short attention span, is unable to command significant assessed financial resources not narrowly tied to military operations, and does not feature significant expertise on the developmental, rule of law, and governance aspects of postconflict management. The UK, the Netherlands, and Italy have worked hard and commendably, as of 2001, to create a new role for the UN's enervated Economic and Social Council (ECOSOC) in the oversight of UN peacebuilding efforts, once the Council is ready to hand off, but these have resulted to date only in a modestly conceived joint Security Council–ECOSOC working group on Guinea-Bissau. More and better is needed.

Greater Resort to Chapter VII

Resort to the provisions of Chapter VII of the UN Charter and to enforcement of Council decisions was not new: Council decisions were enforced in Korea and to a much lesser extent in the Congo during the UN's early years. Nevertheless, the extent to which the Council adopted decisions under Chapter VII since 1990 has been wholly unprecedented. At first, it was hoped that the UN would prove capable of launching and managing enforcement operations. In the face of disappointing, occasionally catastrophic results in the former Yugoslavia and Somalia, it became clear to member states—as many within the Secretariat, notably then–Undersecretary-General Marrack Goulding, had argued all along—that transition from peacekeeping to peace enforcement represented more than "mission creep." The two types of operations were, in fact, fundamentally different, one requiring consent and impartiality, the other requiring international personnel to confront one or several belligerent groups, even if in defense of a Council mandate conceived as neutral relative to the parties to the conflict. Nevertheless, as Goulding himself points out, a useful "halfway house" did emerge between peacekeeping and enforcement action, not least when peacekeepers were invited to use force, when necessary, to protect civilians, where possible, for example in Sierra Leone.[9]

Secretary-General Boutros Boutros-Ghali concluded by 1994 that the UN should not itself seek to conduct large-scale enforcement activities. Consequently, the Security Council increasingly resorted for enforcement of its decisions to "coalitions of the willing," such as Operation Uphold Democracy in Haiti in 1994–1995, IFOR and then SFOR in Bosnia since 1995, MISAB in the Central African Republic in 1997, INTERFET in East Timor in 1999, and ISAF in Afghanistan in early 2002.[10] It also alternately both worried about and supported in qualified terms enforcement activities by regional bodies, notably ECOMOG, the military arm of the West African economic cooperation arrangement ECOWAS, in Liberia and Sierra Leone. One enforcement technique, employed only once previously by the Council, against Rhodesia, was the resort to naval blockades to control access of prohibited goods to regions of conflict. Such blockades were mandated and occurred with varying success against Iraq in the Persian Gulf and the Gulf of Aqaba, against various parties in the former Yugoslavia on the Danube and in the Adriatic Sea, and against Haiti.[11]

More common than military enforcement decisions by the Council was the resort to mandatory economic (and, increasingly, diplomatic) sanctions under Chapter VII of the Charter.[12] While arms embargoes remained in vogue, imposition of comprehensive trade and other economic sanctions, seen as more gentle than the resort to force, faded noticeably once the humanitarian costs of sanctions regimes against Haiti and Iraq became widely known. The ability of government leaders in countries struck by sanctions to enrich themselves by controlling black markets in prohibited products also took some time to sink in. By then, more targeted sanctions, such as the ban on air flights to and from Libya aimed at inducing Libyan cooperation with Council efforts to address several terrorist aircraft bombings, and diplomatic sanctions, such as the reduction in the level of diplomatic representation mandated by the Council against the Sudan further to an assassination attempt in Addis Ababa against Egyptian president Hosni Mubarak, were more in favor.[13] Another example of targeted sanctions (addressing financial transactions and air links) went into effect on November 14, 1999, against the Taliban in Afghanistan over the protection it had provided to Osama bin Laden.[14] Some advantages—but also the difficulty—of designing and implementing effective financial sanctions were brought to light by a useful research and dialogue initiative, the Interlaken process, sponsored by the Swiss government in 1998–1999. The German government launched a similar project on arms embargoes and other forms of targeted sanctions in 1999,[15] and Canada that same year focused attention within the Security Council more broadly on the need for more effective and efficient sanctions regimes.[16] (Canada also provided creative and energetic leadership to the Council's Angola sanctions committee, sponsoring a committee of experts who broke ground in engaging for the first time in "naming and shaming" third countries as "sanctions-busters.")[17] In 2002–2003, Sweden followed with a project on strengthening the implementation of targeted sanctions.[18] Before and after sanctions on UNITA, sanctions were imposed by the Council against other nonstate actors such as the Khmer Rouge, the Interahamwe in eastern Congo, and the RUF in Sierra Leone.

The attention devoted to sanctions enforcement and reform encouraged greater Council openness to considering the economic factors at play in many of the wars on its agenda, highlighted in the reports of its committee of experts on the looting of the Congo under cover of its civil war, into which a number of plundering neighboring countries spilled across borders.[19]

The Council and Regional Organizations

The Council during the post–Cold War era increasingly confronted, shaped, and adapted to the role of regional organizations in seeking to prevent and resolve conflict. The UN initially did not seek a lead role on crises in the Western Hemisphere, such as those of Central America and Haiti, constrained by U.S. policy preferences to leave the Organization of American States in the driver's seat. Some tension developed between the UN and OAS staffs addressing the Nicaragua conflict. Nevertheless, in circumstances in which the OAS proved incapable of achieving a negotiated settlement alone or in which parties to conflict and affected regional powers displayed greater confidence in the United Nations, the Council, sometimes reluctantly, did move to center stage, generally continuing to reserve a place for the OAS in its strategies and, in the case of Haiti, largely handing this orphan issue back to the OAS in 2001.

The Organization of African Unity experienced a disappointing middle-age, brought to a conclusion by the creation of the African Union in 2002 (which was somewhat undermined by the simultaneous launch of the ambitious New Partnership for Africa's Development [NEPAD]). The OAU had sometimes claimed the lead role in addressing the many conflicts bedeviling the continent but proved unable to deliver any major successes until Algeria's energetic diplomacy, supported by the United States and other key players, yielded a settlement to the senseless Ethiopia-Eritrea conflict of the late 1990s.[20] The weakness of the organization was not due so much to the OAU secretariat, led by the widely respected Salim Salim, but rather to the difficulty its member states had in agreeing on political strategies to favor conflict resolution, in spite of the mid-decade creation of an OAU conflict prevention "mechanism."[21] Its relations with the UN were characterized by resentment over its own lack of resources and political support from member states and by justifiable demands that the world body not slough off responsibility for some of the worst conflicts of the age onto an underresourced and divided regional body. It is also true that the UN did not always deal sensitively with the OAU, as argued in Chapter 32, on Rwanda.

It remains to be seen whether the African Union will perform better. Many experts believe that subregional organizations such as ECOWAS, the SADC, and IGAD hold out more hope for Africa in the security field. They are seen as potentially more cohesive and effective, sometimes benefiting from the leadership of a regional hegemon such as Nigeria within ECOWAS.[22]

In a rather different vein, the Council and UN staff found themselves contending with an array of regional actors in the former Yugoslavia, including European Community monitors, European Union civil administrators in Mostar, OSCE negotiators, and NATO enforcement units in the skies and subsequently on the ground. The UN, with Council support and jointly with the European Community, led negotiations with various parties to the conflicts in the former Yugoslavia (most memorably in the Vance-Owen and then the Owen-Stoltenberg configurations), but these efforts failed repeatedly. It took strong leadership from the United States at Dayton to impose a settlement on the parties. In other conflicts, such as those in Georgia[23] and several in West Africa,[24] UN missions mandated by the Council monitored the activities of regional organizations purportedly keeping or promoting the peace. This proved particularly delicate in Georgia, where peacekeeping forces of the Commonwealth of Independent States were seen by a number of Western powers as neither markedly impartial nor as deserving treatment that might imply or confer recognition on the CIS as a respectable regional organization.

In the mid-1990s, with the Council stymied by several conflicts and disunited in facing major international challenges, regional organizations came to be seen by some as a possible if not particularly desirable substitute for the UN. However, with the exception of NATO, regional bodies generally commanded even scarcer resources and offered even more limited capacities than the UN. Furthermore, a system of international security founded on regional organizations begged the question of who would arbitrate differences between them and how this would be done. Finally, a number of countries in crisis, notably Afghanistan, turned out not to be members of viable regional organizations. Indeed, for peacekeeping purposes, it was largely NATO members that provided the bulk of ISAF in that country as of early 2002.

Doctrinal Shifts

The shifts in the nature and scope of Council decisions, many setting precedents even where the Council asserted that they did not, arose from evolving interpretations of the Charter and deeply affected understanding of sovereignty at the international level, both shaped by, and influencing, the Council. And whereas states remain highly attached to their own sovereignty, they have become less respectful of that of others where massive human rights violations, genocide, ethnic cleansing, and other hideous manifestations of human behavior, sadly much on display in the post–Cold War period, increasingly commanded consensus (including among the P-5, who might otherwise veto action) that international response is legitimate, indeed necessary. This represents a fundamental shift in international relations, albeit a slow-moving one.

In this period, the Council addressed not only specific country or regional crises but also crosscutting thematic issues, such as the plight of civilians in war, concerns over children and armed conflict, the need for greater efforts to achieve conflict prevention, and the economics of contemporary warfare (and peace). These debates were often interesting but seemed to lead to few concrete improvements within potential or actual theaters of war, although they did contribute to longer, more complex Council resolutions. Early in the following decade, a degree of thematic fatigue set in, with some delegates referring gleefully to those pressing thematic debates as devotees of "theme parks." The P-5, mostly reserved about the usefulness of thematic approaches, nodded approvingly.

Nevertheless, the Council did address a number of newer security challenges at least somewhat convincingly, including, as we have seen, terrorism. AIDS was strongly promoted as a critical security threat in Africa by the U.S. permanent representative, Richard Holbrooke, in early 2000. This brought corridor complaints from many delegations that the Security Council was overreaching itself by poaching the General Assembly's agenda, but such is the torpor affecting the latter that nothing effective was done to discourage the media-savvy, energetic, and effective Holbrooke. Humanitarian intervention was the more controversial face of debates on the plight of civilians in war. Publication of the report of the International Commission on Intervention and State Sovereignty in late 2001, discussed during a Security Council retreat in early 2002, helped educate this particular debate, but it has achieved more impact in the world of ideas (no mean accomplishment) than in the decisions of the Council to date.

The Council's ability to deal effectively with some other critical new issues remains in doubt. Although the United States has trumpeted the risks to be anticipated from "failed states," its most notable response thereto has been military, and often short-lived (as in Somalia), failing to enthuse the publics of many of its closest allies. The importance of "peacebuilding" or, more negatively in Washington-speak, "nation-building" is widely accepted, but its implementation is expensive and complex. It is being tested today in Afghanistan and Iraq after years of determined efforts in East Timor, Kosovo, and Bosnia yielded both a measure of success and of disappointment. Council efforts to address threats arising from the proliferation of weapons of mass destruction might enjoy more resonance if the P-5 did not account for 85 percent of the world's exports of conventional weapons, which kill many more individuals around the world.[25] The Council has accepted the obvious regional nature of several conflicts, notably those of West and Central Africa, but discussion during a Council retreat in August 2001 made clear that several permanent members dislike regional approaches to conflict, one arguing that it undermines the sanctity of state sovereignty and another that conflicts are complex enough when addressed nationally and become impossible to resolve when viewed primarily through a regional prism.[26]

Somewhat surprisingly in the postcolonial era, the UN has found itself, further to Council decisions, overseeing aspects of governance in such places as Namibia, Cambodia, East Timor, and Kosovo. This has raised for some issues of legitimacy, although there appears to be no alternative body that might fulfill a comparable function. Kosovo and Iraq raise for others the specter that such postconflict UN involvement can be designed retroactively to legitimize an illegal use of force. Suffice it to note here that the Council is more attracted to the use of peacebuilding in restoring Council unity than it is over debates on the legitimacy of its decisions.

The Council has not developed an explicit doctrine with respect to the theory of its role and decisions. This points to the continuing salience of questions relating to the Council's identity. Does it operate primarily as a unitary institution or as a political instrument for various member states? The answer varies from question to question, from day to day.

Elements of Continuity

The Council's agenda remains heavily influenced by geopolitical and regional realities and preferences. This explains one element of continuity in its modus operandi—a selective approach to its agenda and differentiated means of addressing those crises it does take on.

Colombia remained off the Council's active agenda (although it was much discussed in the corridors, and the Secretary-General fielded several high-quality special envoys on this violent and complex nexus of conflict) because Latin American countries generally support Colombia's reluctance to see its internal problems "internationalized." Burma (also addressed by the Secretary-General through the widely admired Razzali Ismail in his role as Annan's special envoy) has never made it to the Council's agenda due to a preference by Asian states for noninterference in internal affairs and fears that the Council might become the cockpit for ugly international clashes over the future of Burma between India and China, both of which have strong historical and other ties to the country. India has vigorously opposed a role for the Security Council on the Kashmir problem. Such factors explain the "selectivity" of the Council's agenda, something that is much denounced in the General Assembly.

Some conflicts have remained active on the Council's agenda for many years, defying resolution often for geostrategic reasons, sometimes involving great power interests. The Israeli-Palestinian conflict and Western Sahara come to mind.

Considerations Driving Council Decisionmaking

The Humanitarian Impulse

An innovative feature of the Council's decisions on a number of crises was its concern over the humanitarian plight of civilian victims of conflicts, particularly refugees. Refugees were hardly a new topic of concern for the Council.[27] The miserable fate of Palestinian refugees proved a spur (at least nominally) to the Arab-Israeli dispute following Israel's war of independence in 1947–1948, leading also to the creation of a UN agency, UNRWA, dedicated to their welfare. Those displaced by war, particularly where mass outflows of the population occurred, had long been seen as deserving the care of the international community and were among the prime "clients" of both the Red Cross system (the ICRC and the International Federation of Red Cross and Red Crescent Societies) and the UN High Commissioner for Refugees. Nevertheless, in the 1990s as never before, the Security Council invoked the plight of refugees and their implied destabilizing effect on neighboring states as grounds for its own involvement in conflict. Early Council resolutions on the former Yugoslavia[28] and on Somalia[29] illustrate this development. Any threat that the Haitian crisis of democracy in 1991–1994 may actually have posed to international peace and security could only have arisen from the outflow of Haitian boat-going refugees, which might have threatened to engulf a number of Caribbean countries had the shores of Florida not been their preferred destination. The widespread acceptance that refugee flows could be a major catalyst to conflict, rather than merely an outcome of it, was new. Refugee flows were a convenient prism through which to view often essentially internal crises because they satisfied the transborder-effect requirement for a threat to international peace and security—until this was no longer controversial by the mid-1990s.

Furthermore, the intense if highly selective media scrutiny (the so-called CNN effect) of horrendous conditions endured by victims of war impelled populations worldwide to press their governments to alleviate extreme suffering arising from a variety of conflicts. Several factors conspired to focus attention on the UN to act on behalf of the international community: the limited impact of most bilateral assistance in these dramatic circumstances; the existence of several UN specialized agencies with the skills and "critical mass" required; and the possibility for the UN to deploy peace missions of various types and sizes with mandates focused on humanitarian objectives or at least including them. The most important consideration for many governments was that in delegating to the United Nations the responsibility to act, mostly in situations where few vital national interests were at stake, the costs and risks of response nationally were usefully curtailed. At the peak of media and public fervor for humanitarian initiatives, in the early 1990s, a lively debate unfolded over not only the international right to intervene in the internal affairs of countries to save civilian lives but also a purported duty to do so.[30] By the bleaker end of the decade, with many suffering untold horrors unassisted, mainly in Africa, this debate rang hollow in the absence of any actual desire to intervene on the part of those governments with the capacities to do so. Indeed, efforts by the UN to administer Kosovo (alongside the NATO-dominated military deployment of KFOR) have proved once again how difficult the fallout of ambitious humanitarian action can be. Today, the humanitarian impulse within the Council seems somewhat in check, requiring overlap with other interests to drive Council decisionmaking. This may explain the Council's reluctance to respond meaningfully to the crisis in southern Sudan, preferring to leave the lead UN role to its humanitarian agencies.

Human Rights

Human rights as an issue was long cloistered within intergovernmental machinery and Secretariat bureaucracy—designed in part to keep the topic at a safe distance from those responsible for international peace and security. In the 1990s, however, human rights burst onto the Security Council's agenda with the realization that civil strife was not amenable to negotiated solutions as long as human rights continued to be massively violated. For this reason, UN peacemaking in El Salvador, Guatemala, and Haiti led to the deployment by the Security Council or the General Assembly of human rights monitoring missions, and elsewhere—most notably in postgenocide Rwanda—human rights monitors were fielded under the new mandate of the high commissioner for human rights.[31] The Security Council increasingly overcame its reluctance to embrace human rights and came to see the protection, promotion, and monitoring of human rights as an important part of the mandates of peacekeeping operations.

This tendency to address human rights objectives in Security Council debates and decisions was reinforced by the appointment of a UN high commissioner for human rights as of 1994. Although the first incumbent, an Ecuadorian politician and diplomat, proved lackluster in this role, his successor, Mary Robinson, former president of Ireland, adopted a more assertive approach to her responsibilities, putting pressure on the Council (even while her performance underscored a frequent lack of coordination and identity of view within the UN system). The late Sergio Vieira de Mello, the talented former special representative in Kosovo and East Timor, appointed to this position in mid-2002 and killed in the bombing of the UN complex in August 2003, seemed to be adopting less confrontational strategies and new approaches in pursuit of human rights.[32]

The Council included references to human rights in fully a third of its resolutions in 2000, but, probably in deference to countries such as China, it has not developed a systematic approach to human rights in its work. The quandaries faced by the Council in factoring human rights considerations into its decisions were highlighted when the parties to Sierra Leone's civil war reached a peace agreement in mid-1999 including sweeping amnesty provisions against which Robinson sharply protested (and over which the UN Secretary-General's representative at the peace pact's signing ceremony had registered a formal reservation). On the one hand, Sierra Leone's population was clearly eager for peace on virtually any terms; on the other, the agreement's amnesty provisions patently ran against long-standing and emerging human rights norms. The creation of a special court involving international and Sierra Leonean personnel to address massive human rights violations and war crimes in that country holds out some promise of justice for the victims of these crimes. A truth commission agreed some time earlier may contribute to national reconciliation.

The Council's ability to discuss sensibly the nexus between human rights and security (including with the high commissioner) definitely represents progress, but it remains unclear whether human rights are in the main a driver of Council decisions today or just one of a number of instrumental factors with which the Council juggles rather than a principled commitment.

Democratization

The Council also appeared to be increasingly engaged in the promotion of democracy, inter alia by mandating the organization and monitoring of elections, a trend that a Cold War observer might have regarded as no more probable than the Council's activism on humanitarian and human rights issues. Nevertheless, the Council favored electoral processes less as an end in themselves than as a means of effecting a "new deal" in countries emerging from civil war in which power could, in some cases, be shared with former combatants in rough proportion to electoral results. Such elections proved an unreliable indicator of the extent to which genuinely democratic cultures would take root. The stilted, power-driven, and unstable coalition arrangements resulting from Cambodia's UN-conducted elections of 1993 and 1998 contrast with the more natural, relaxed electoral rhythms apparently achieved in El Salvador, where an alternation of power between rival parties seems more likely in the long run, rooted as it is in a long tradition of multiparty electoral politics.

The UN's mushrooming electoral activities, very much driven by demand rather than supply of the personnel and other resources required for effectiveness in this field, presented multiple risks for the organization.[33] Many of the elections observed by UN teams were conducted in adverse circumstances, often contributing to results that could barely be described as having been attained freely and fairly. Short of massive fraud, UN electoral missions were loath to risk igniting or reigniting civil strife by contesting the results of polling, and consequently they were seen as willing to compromise on principle and to be less than the impartial arbiters local parties had a right to expect. Losers were rarely gracious, and the UN was little thanked for its prominent role in such electoral process, frequently alongside regional organizations and nongovernmental teams of eminent persons such as those associated with former U.S. president Jimmy Carter.[34] And as shown by the case of East Timor, where the outcome of a UN-implemented referendum over independence led to a murderous rampage by militias in 1999, the UN should not promote elections in the absence of adequate measures to protect the civilian population against the wrath of those who end up with the short end of the stick.[35]

Democratization, particularly since the events of September 11, 2001, has been advanced as a foundation of U.S. foreign policy, for example on Iraq, but can simultaneously be downgraded in practice when Washington is faced with other priorities. U.S. support for Pakistan's president, Pervez Musharraf (represented in the Council since January 2003), is an example of the inconsistencies in U.S. policy (and the policies of certain other Western democracies) in this regard. As several permanent members are not unduly motivated by the promotion of democracy in their foreign policies, this can but have an effect on the role democratization plays in at least some Council strategies.

Terrorism

The Council was much more active in addressing terrorism prior to the attacks on the World Trade Center and the Pentagon in September 2001 than is widely believed. At the conclusion of their summit meeting on January 31, 1992, Security Council leaders "expressed their deep concern over acts of international terrorism and emphasized the need for the international community to deal effectively with all such acts."[36] Soon thereafter, the Council adopted sanctions against Libya over its noncooperation with investigation of two airline-bombing incidents; against Sudan, following the assassination attempt against President Mubarak discussed above;

and against the Taliban regime. After the attacks against U.S. targets on September 11, 2001, the Council moved into a new phase of combating the financial networks supporting terrorism and safe havens for terrorists under the terms of Resolution 1373 of September 28, 2001. It created the Counter-Terrorism Committee of all Council members to monitor compliance of all states with its decisions. The committee got off to a brisk start under the energetic leadership of the UK's Jeremy Greenstock, supported by his Russian colleague, Sergey Lavrov. By publishing the extensive correspondence between the committee and member states on this sensitive topic on its website, the committee has blazed new trails in terms of transparency for the Council. Its purpose, beyond encouraging implementation of Resolution 1373, has been to focus on the capacity-building of member states and to create a network of all counterterrorism institutions worldwide relevant to activity by member states.[37] It initially resisted any suggestion that its agenda should include human rights issues relevant to terrorism, but some of its members came to recognize over time that massive human rights violations can generate acts of terrorism in response. Nevertheless, the committee remains regrettably squeamish on this score. It has been critiqued by some as more a "process" response to events than as substantively meaningful, but this may underestimate its impact over time.

Institutional Developments

Working Methods

Under intense pressure from member states not serving on the Council, particularly the troop-contributing countries (TCCs), which provided personnel and matériel to the UN for peacekeeping operations and which were intensely irritated by the Council's working methods, the Council, quite reluctantly, allowed some light to shine on its autocratic and opaque proceedings. Council members, the P-5 in particular, had always needed to consult privately. However, with active cooperation among the permanent members increasingly the norm by 1990, the P-5 saw little value in continuing to conduct much of the Council's business in open, public meetings. "Informal consultations," or "informals," closed to all non-Council members and most Secretariat staff and leaving no formal record, became the norm. Nonmembers were in the dark and had to scramble for information, feeding off scraps in antechambers, a thoroughly humiliating experience. By 1992, leading non-Council TCCs were arguing that if the Council expected them to provide national assets in support of Council decisions, often in risky circumstances, at a minimum consultations were required. As a result, a number of measures were adopted to introduce greater clarity in the Council's program of work and to schedule meetings between the Council and TCCs (long resisted by the P-5, which preferred TCCs to deal principally with the Secretariat).[38]

The current working methods, as all representatives of nonpermanent members confirm, very much favor the P-5 and their continued stranglehold on the Council's business. In this, their silent partner is the Secretariat, whose permanent status also translates into a certain control over procedure. Elected members have trouble mastering procedure, all the more so as Council rules are still "provisional" and often hard to pin down. The importance of procedure in anchoring the dominance of the P-5 is too often overlooked. However, continuity, depth of experience, and the talent of their delegations provide the P-5 with the decisive edge.

A somewhat related development was the emergence of Groups of Friends, composed of countries influential in a given crisis. They not only advised the Secretary-General and Council on strategies to promote settlement of the conflict and implementation of a peace agreement but also, at their best, served as a potent lobby group vis-à-vis parties to the conflict, regional actors, and the General Assembly (from which decisions relating to Council strategies were sometimes required in such areas as human rights monitoring and always on the financing of its initiatives). Often, representatives in the field of such groups, or of Security Council members, helped support locally the efforts of the Secretary-General's special representatives, as was the case in Cambodia, Mozambique, and Haiti. Complaints were sometimes heard that such groups usurped the role of the full Council, and the Secretariat occasionally voiced concern that the Secretary-General was sometimes unhelpfully constrained by them, but given the increased pressure of work within the Council, most members saw Groups of Friends as a useful clearinghouse for developing options open to the Council.

People

The relationship of the three Secretary-Generals of the post–Cold War era to date with the Council has varied. Javier Pérez de Cuéllar of Peru completed his distinguished, quietly creative stewardship in 1991. He had done much to encourage the Council to play a more active role and was highly regarded by most of its members. Boutros Boutros-Ghali, of Egypt, who next took office, proved himself a passionate and well-reasoned advocate of a stronger UN role in conflict resolution and postconflict peacebuilding, launching his seminal work *An Agenda for Peace* in mid-1992. However, he was damaged by the UN's reverses in the former Yugoslavia and Somalia and its ghastly failure in Rwanda. He also disastrously chose to isolate himself from the Council. His brittle personality and tone-deafness relative to the U.S. domestic political scene brought him into conflict with Washington. The latter vetoed his reelection and favored his succession by Kofi Annan of Ghana in late 1996. Annan, the first career UN official to hold the position, staked out new ground in championing human rights and concern for civilians in war as key themes.[39] In spite of occasional clashes with the United States over Iraq, Annan remains persona grata in Washington, including in Congress. In 2001 he was awarded the millennial Nobel Peace Prize and was reelected Secretary-General.[40]

The performance of these three individuals, each with his own strengths and weaknesses, reminds us of the importance of individuals in nearly all of the stories this volume lays out. Would the UN's missions in Mozambique have been as successful (or indeed successful at all) without Aldo Ajello in charge on the ground? Possibly, but highly unlikely. The name of Lakhdar Brahimi recurs as often as it does because he has provided the international community with sterling service and unvarnished advice of the highest order in many tough assignments, from Haiti to the Congo, from Côte d'Ivoire to South Africa, and from Afghanistan to the shoals of peacekeeping reform. Legwaila Joseph Legwaila has performed commendably in Ethiopia and Eritrea, as have a number of his colleagues elsewhere in Africa and beyond. All are not so meritorious. Jacques Roger Booh-Booh, special representative to Rwanda at the time of genocide, contributed little of positive value to the UN's role in this disaster (unlike his force commander, General Romeo Dallaire). A number of other undistinguished appointments have undermined UN effectiveness. Again and again, the importance of the Secretary-General's function as appointer to crucial positions, for good and ill, has been clear in recent years. The success of Rolf Ekeus and of Hans Blix, both steady but determined, as chief UN weapons inspectors stands in contrast to that of others, often for reasons of temperament rather than intellect. Given that the UN bureaucracy can be described (like most) as fueled largely by the efforts of 20–30 percent of its staff, while actively impeded by another 20–30 percent, those falling in each of these categories assume considerable importance.

Representatives within the Council vary strikingly in quality too. The permanent five are normally superbly represented. In recent years, Jeremy Greenstock of the UK, Jean-David Levitte of France, and Wang Yingfan of China have stood out. Russia fields talented envoys, at their best more knowledgeable than others, but they have not found it easy to serve an increasingly erratic, sometimes disabused Russian foreign policy. However, Sergey Lavrov since 1994 has proved as powerful an advocate as any for his government's views. Washington's envoys, so close to their capital, are at the mercy of its legendarily cutthroat defense and foreign policy infighting, although Thomas Pickering's much-admired tenure as U.S. ambassador during the 1990–1991 Iraq crisis stands out. Other countries might be expected to field their best, but quite often this does not happen due to political and bureaucratic maneuvers at home. Small countries can matter within the Council when they send heavyweights to New York, as have Singapore, Botswana, Cape Verde, and New Zealand in recent years. But others see their elected terms mainly as automatically boosting national prestige and fail to mount a focused effort. When countries register strongly on the Council's Richter scale, as did Mexico, Nigeria, and Colombia in their recent terms, their success rests heavily on the personal efforts of a small number within their delegations.

International Law and Notions of Legitimacy

As Steven Ratner has reminded us in Chapter 37, international law, and the Council's role therein, extend well beyond criminal matters. However, the Council in the years covered by this volume may be remembered in part for its contribution to radical innovation in international criminal law, notably through its creation of ad hoc international criminal tribunals for the former Yugoslavia in 1993 and Rwanda in 1994 to bring to justice those responsible for war crimes, crimes against humanity, and genocide. The foremost champion of these tribunals was the United States (in part because of frustration over its own inability at the time to influence the course of events on the ground in the former Yugoslavia due to sharp policy differences with European allies and guilt over its refusal to confront genocide in Rwanda). The creation of the tribunals greatly intensified pressures for a permanent International Criminal Court with universal jurisdiction, but when a statute for the ICC was adopted in Rome in 1998, the United States, along with six other countries of varying respectability, voted against the text out of concern over its potential implications for U.S. citizens, particularly U.S. troops serving abroad. Although President Bill Clinton signed the statute on the last day of 2000, the administration of George W. Bush has since combated the ICC tooth and nail, precipitating an ugly confrontation with its supporters in the Council in mid-2002 and casting a cloud over the ICC's launch in 2003.

The creation of institutions such as the international criminal tribunals and the quasi-legislative provisions of Resolution 1373 suggest that the Council is expanding its powers to make and apply law. This and the Council's expanding role in the early 1990s, and both the number and the sweeping scope of its resolutions, gave rise to growing calls for judicial review of its decisions by the World Court.[41] Libya contested the Council's decisions targeting it, taking its case to the World Court, which accepted jurisdiction in 1998—much to the annoyance of some of the P-5. But the World Court seemed to wait out a diplomatic solution to the impasse without addressing the merits of the case.[42] Pressure for judicial review, as well as for access to advisory opinions from the World Court on peace and security issues by the Secretary-General (a proposal advanced by Boutros Boutros-Ghali in *An Agenda for Peace*), was resisted by the P-5, but a sense of inevitability developed over growing involvement of the World Court in the Council's institutional life. Nevertheless, eminent French legal scholar Jean-Pierre Cot, speaking of decisions adopted by the Council under Chapter VII of the Charter, recognizes that judicial review might doom Council effectiveness: "It is essential for the Security Council, in our unstable world, to act swiftly and decisively. . . . It is important to . . . allow it, unhampered, to discharge its functions related to the maintenance of peace and security. The danger of irrelevance of the Council and Organization, as we know, is not insignificant."[43]

There continues to be significant disagreement in the literature over the extent to which member states actually comply with Council decisions, whether or not adopted under Chapter VII. Mostly, states wish to be seen as complying, at least formally, as is clear from the excellent response to the reporting demands of the Counter-Terrorism Committee since 2001. Nevertheless, widespread sanctions-busting relating to Iraq and a number of other theaters of Council concern, as well as energetic looting of the Congo by a number of occupying armies in recent years, belie the substance of compliance as opposed to the process of it. An assessment may remain very much in the eye of the beholder, but compliance remains the preference of the vast majority of member states.

Questions of law lead on to questions of "legitimacy"—a term not beloved among some international lawyers due to its vagueness. Legitimacy may be considered in two areas:

Principles. The Council's reluctance to be bound to principle is well-established. The assertion that many controversial situations are "unique" and therefore not precedent-setting for the future has led some to argue that the Council is unprincipled. The Council's focus on issues of the day to the exclusion of systemic questions and principles inspires caution in some.

Representativity. As one diplomat has described it, in practice the Council can be either responsible or collective. When the fifteen representatives are acting responsibly, this means they are acting out of their separate national interests as ambassadors for their countries. When the fifteen men and women on the Council attempt to act collectively, however, they are responsible only to themselves. To some degree, this suggests that choice is possible in this matter, where mostly it is not. Ideally, they can be responsible and collective when they work together to advance national interests jointly, and this is the case much of the time. But when it is not, the problem of the representativity of the Council becomes salient.

When the contributors to this volume met in New York, a spirited debate took place on the extent to which the Council makes international law. That its decisions create important precedents (anchored in state acquiescence) that cumulatively shape perceptions and interpretations of law was not doubted. Likewise, it was widely accepted that Council authorization of international action increased legitimacy for a variety of undertakings, hence the intensity of the unsuccessful effort to achieve a Council mandate for military action against Kosovo in 1999 and Iraq in 2003.

The notion of legitimacy itself proves problematic in a Council context. European practitioners and scholars seem more drawn to the legitimacy derived from agreed process, whereas those of the United States remain more impressed by and committed to results. Such differences may be relevant to the transatlantic disagreements over Iraq in 2002–2003, many of which found expression in the cockpit of the Council. Legitimacy is increasingly tied, for the U.S. public (and possibly some others), to the achievement of foreign participation in its military ventures. If this participation can be generated by Council decisions, all well and good, but if it needs to be acquired by other means, if necessary without Council involvement, so be it.

Institutional Issues: Nongovernmental Organizations
Interaction of nongovernmental organizations (NGOs) with the Security Council both grew significantly and evolved in nature during the 1990s. Beyond their humanitarian elements, conflicts, particularly of an internal nature, were increasingly seen as featuring economic and social causes as well as effects. For this reason, inter alia, relevant NGOs clamored for access to the Council—for which the Charter and the Council's long-established working methods made no provision. The role of NGOs as major partners for the UN in humanitarian operations, the success of many NGO programs in the field, the mandate of the Secretariat's Department of Humanitarian Affairs to offer coordination services to NGOs as well as official agencies, the mediagenic nature of some NGO activity, and a rapidly spreading fad late in the 1990s in favor of "civil society" (a term never satisfactorily defined at the UN) all conspired to encourage the Council to display greater openness to NGO views and more generous recognition of NGO achievements.

Within the Council, a number of governments advocated greater access for NGOs (and the Secretary-General lavishly praised them). This was achieved in two ways: In a breakthrough of sorts, the Council met informally with a small group of NGOs in 1998 and since then has been meeting frequently if informally and on an ad hoc basis with NGO representatives under the so-called Arria Formula; and, as detailed in James Paul's chapter, less visibly, Council members increasingly met with NGOs on their own and in groups not only to brief them on recent developments and upcoming debates in the informals but also to seek their input for Council decision-making. And though the sincerity of some Council members in engaging in these exchanges might be questioned, the achievement of genuine access, and the growing recognition of NGOs as significant and mostly constructive contributors to international peace and security, marked a new departure for the Council in its relations with the "outside" world.

The Path Ahead: Washington's Role
The major challenge facing the Council was the parlous state of relations within it between the United States and several other members, threatening the marginalization of the Council or, even worse in the view of some, its co-optation by the United States. It is hardly surprising that Washington's view of its own interests at times diverges from that of its partners. It is in the interests of smaller countries and lesser powers to enmesh stronger ones in institutions and norms, and while the Council was seen by some other permanent members as a forum in which to contain and manage American power, the United States at times resisted such efforts strongly.

The interests of the other permanent members coincided in the Council to the extent that they all wished to regulate U.S. power to varying degrees, in part because they feared that the uninhibited pursuit of U.S. interests could clash with their own and in part in order to leverage in terms of international influence their own seats and vetoes. The latter was particularly true of France and Great Britain, neither of which any longer fit the bill of a "major" power, and both of which claimed (disingenuously at times, given their public squabbling over Iraq and other issues) to be engaged in the construction of a common European Union foreign and defense policy.

The status of France and the UK in the Security Council presents a greater challenge to European foreign and defense policy construction than do their occasional differences of substantive view, however sharp. (On the latter they often tend to cancel each other out, but in their permanent member–induced exceptionalism within the EU they are mutually reinforcing.) When they cohere on Council business, as they often do on African issues, they are hard to oppose, even by the United States. When they oppose each other strongly (and when other EU members of the Council do likewise, as on Iraq in March 2003), the results are usually dreadful for the Council and for EU credibility.

On balance, Washington is likely to endure the P-5 structure as it stands while assessing if and whether to channel its foreign policy through the Council on a case-by-case basis. An instrumental approach of the

United States to the Council need not be disturbing: a Council that is not an instrument of U.S. foreign policy would probably be as ineffective as the League of Nations. But this will make the effort of containing the United States through Council discussions and decisions all the more difficult.

As to elected members, many of them face the challenge, in the words of one ambassador, of establishing whether they have "the courage to disagree with the USA when it is wrong and the maturity to agree with it when it is right."[44] Adolfo Aguilar Zinser, halfway through his term as Mexican ambassador to the UN, in early 2003 argued that it should be possible to dissent with the United States without antagonism and agree without loss of self-esteem.[45] But for many countries, this high-wire act seems stressful and risky. (The reassignment in 2003 of Chile's admired ambassador at the UN, Juan Gabriel Valdés, after complaints from Washington to Santiago about his stance in the Council on Iraq, stoked a sense among Council members that their careers were on the line at all times and that Washington readily engaged in hardball tactics designed to intimidate.)[46]

By the early twenty-first century the emergence of the United States not only as the sole remaining superpower, but also as a singularly dominant international actor, was clear to all. The United States was no longer a permanent member *comme les autres*. Augmenting the status of the United States is the absence of any meaningful opposition, even in a political sense, to U.S. power. Splits within the nonaligned movement have also contributed to changes in the architecture of global order. Only China is widely perceived today as a possible future rival to the United States, and within the Council a newly attentive and respectful relationship seemed to be developing between the U.S. and Chinese delegations. The domestic and foreign policy of the United States is today the dominant driving factor in Council action.

In the absence of a global competitor, the United States today spends as much on defense as the next dozen or more countries combined. And though such "hard" U.S. military power may discourage it from using internationally more attractive "soft" political power, benevolent U.S. hegemonic power may be preferable to a war of all against all, or the rise of a suzerain. Its military might enables the United States to address major contingencies with the consent of the Council, such as enforcing Iraq's withdrawal from Kuwait in 1991. That such action was driven by U.S. self-interest need neither surprise nor shock: like other powers, the United States rarely acts solely out of altruism. Nor does it generally act out of institutional loyalty—in this it may be contrasted to some European actors that privilege institutions and process above what the United States regards as substantive outcomes. Transatlantic differences became more acute after 1998 over whether the mission should define the coalition or the other way around.

The UN in general, and the Security Council in particular, needs the United States, but to what extent does the United States today need the Security Council? Unlike the other permanent members (with the possible exception of China), the United States derives none of its great power status from its permanent seat on the Council. The United States has shown itself willing to use the Council where helpful, but in military engagements the United States does not need (and in Afghanistan did not want) the operational involvement of most other states. Nevertheless, in spite of disagreements over Iraq, the United States (like the other P-5 members), in an age of unconventional and frightening security threats, may continue to value the Council as a "safety net" that encourages company in cases where it embarks on risky endeavors.

Clashes between the United States and others at the UN are not new. The Clinton administration's instinctive penchant for UN-bashing whenever in a tight spot from which blame might be delegated, first on view following the Mogadishu fiasco of October 4, 1993, was displayed again repeatedly in subsequent years. This was most tellingly the case when leaks from Washington in early 1999 suggested that the United States had used the UN expert body charged with overseeing and monitoring Iraq's compliance with Security Council decisions on its weapons programs, UNSCOM, as a cover to spy on Iraq for its own, rather than UN, purposes.[47] Seeming to decide that the best defense was a strong offense, the administration roundly attacked Kofi Annan through the U.S. media for purported "appeasement" of the Iraqi regime.[48] In 2000, most of the U.S. quarrels with the UN over funding were resolved and many of its arrears were repaid in 2001, following the events of September 11, but the relationship remained uncertain at best.

Did the events of September 11, 2001, change the Council much? They certainly had a considerable impact on the Council by changing U.S. threat perceptions. The terrorist attacks instilled in the United States a new feeling of vulnerability, epitomized in the 2002 *National Security Strategy*, which referred to the greatest dangers to the United States coming from failing states rather than from conquering ones. This led to greater suspicion in Washington of attempts at the UN and elsewhere to constrain U.S. power.

The United States failed to gain support of most UN members for its policy of bombing (with the UK) of Iraq in December 1998, which appeared to some as unattractively punitive. Its insistence on maintaining in place a sanctions regime to encourage Iraqi compliance with UN efforts to prevent further development of weapons of mass destruction enjoyed decreasing support at the UN. UK efforts to broker compromises led to a pyrrhic modification of the sanctions regime in 1999 and again in 2002, when the Council eased restrictions on civilian goods.[49] In the wake of successful U.S. military action against the Taliban regime in Afghanistan, U.S.

efforts to reenergize the Council's approach to Iraq in late 2002 initially produced a degree of consensus reflected in Resolution 1441, but the tectonic transatlantic collisions of early 2003 provoked stark discomfort, with consequences for the future of the Council still hard to predict as we go to press, particularly with events on the ground in Iraq deteriorating throughout mid-2003 and the continuing disagreement evident among Western allies over Iraq during the General Assembly session of September 2003.

When in 2002 Washington decided to focus international attention on Baghdad's noncompliance with Security Council resolutions, its rhetoric was fierce and it initially threatened unilateral action. But instead, President George W. Bush on September 12, 2002, exhorted the Security Council to address proactively this challenge. Why the dual track in U.S. rhetoric (and action)? The truth is probably complex.[50] At root, the U.S. public was nervous over the prospect of U.S. military action against Baghdad undertaken on its own or with very few allies. Americans wanted company in this risky undertaking. U.S. allies, including the UK, in turn made clear that as much Security Council cover as possible would be a prerequisite for their participation in a military operation in Iraq. And though the current administration in Washington does not seem much concerned about international perceptions of legitimacy relative to its military ventures, legitimacy can be a valuable commodity, and it would have greatly helped secure international participation in the management of Iraq following the defeat of Saddam Hussein's regime at the hands of the United States and the UK in April 2003. While the UN has no capacity for large-scale use of force, it does have a unique capacity for conferring legitimacy. As Washington bumps up against international opinion in years to come, and experiences self-inflicted difficulties in peacebuilding in Iraq, it may come to see the UN in a more positive light.

The Bush administration's new security doctrine raises prominently the issue of preemptive self-defense in matters of weapons of mass destruction, not as a matter of exception in extreme circumstances but of U.S. policy preference. Predictably, this assertion by the White House has outraged some international commentators and worried others. However, there has been little serious response as to how such threats would best be met in the future, particularly given the fact that international law and multilateral treaties tend to lag developments rather than anticipate them. The Security Council has shown little appetite for a sensible debate on this topic and on evolving conceptions of "security" internationally.

Another Major Challenge: Africa

The Council, which in earlier decades tackled the apartheid regimes of Southern Rhodesia and South Africa (with a transition in the latter to

majority rule in 1994, one of its greatest sources of satisfaction) as well as
the Congolese civil war of the early 1960s, has been much engaged on
African issues in the post–Cold War era. One of its early accomplishments
covered here was the UN's preindependence role in Namibia, during which
it largely oversaw the territory. Its involvement in Mozambique was a rare
and notable success. Less happy were its various interventions in Angola
until the late 1990s. (Its last failing peacekeeping operation there was withdrawn in February 1999.)[51] Its two botched peacekeeping operations in
Somalia (UNOSOM I and II, with the U.S.-led coalition operation UNITAF
sandwiched between), during which member states let the organization
down badly, have left a very bitter taste and produced negative fallout for
UN peacekeeping ever since. Above all, the Council's catastrophic performance on Rwanda in 1994 has yet to be fully digested by the Council, in
particular by the countries most involved. Council action on Western
Sahara, the Central African Republic, and Liberia was more window dressing than deeply substantive, but its efforts to address security crises in
Sierra Leone, on the Ethiopian-Eritrean border, and in the Great Lakes area,
centered on the eastern tracts of the Democratic Republic of Congo, have
been ambitious and at times quite risky.[52]

Africa remains a challenge on the Council's agenda. The Council did
little to solve the acute problems of tiny Guinea-Bissau. The conflict in
Eastern Congo, which for several years drew in numerous neighboring
countries, remains unresolved and dangerous, not least for the UN's
exposed peacekeepers within MONUC. This conflict split the SADC, the
subregional organization of southern Africa, with Zimbabwe and South
Africa, its two most powerful members, at loggerheads. The situation in
Sierra Leone was improving as of mid-2003, with the UN peacekeeping
operation there, having suffered a catastrophic start with 500 of its members held hostage by rebel forces, stabilized by the parallel deployment of
UK troops.

In spite of efforts by France, the UK, and the United States to equip
and train a number of African armed forces to lead regional peacekeeping
efforts, the UN's active involvement continued to be sought by the
Africans. Response from the countries of the North was at best ambivalent.
The UN's peacekeeping operation in the Congo, for example, attracted no
sizable Western participation, in spite of the fact that this conflict has cost
an estimated 3.5 million lives since 1998.[53] This pattern raises major ethical and operational questions.[54] The industrialized countries need to think
hard about their attitudes toward Africa and offer more assistance in conflict prevention, peace implementation, and postwar reconstruction in years
ahead. For their part, African leaders and societies need to provide stronger
support to the African Union and subregional organizations and move from
rhetoric to action on improved governance, as Nigeria has been trying to

do, and as the New Economic Partnership for Africa's Development promises. Otherwise, African resentment of international neglect is bound to
grow in tandem with unreflective criticism of African failings elsewhere in
the world.

The Council spends the majority of its time on African issues, but frequently with little success.[55] It has addressed the AIDS pandemic as a security threat to the continent, but with limited operational effect. Cameron
Hume's thoughtful analysis in Chapter 38 suggests that, in the future, the
Council's agenda may be dominated even more by African conflicts than it
is today. The question arises as to why the Council has not been able to
replicate the early successes of its interventions in Namibia and
Mozambique. Africans, expressing the continent's frustration and disillusionment with the Security Council's role in Africa, sometimes attribute
this to the cynical foreign policies of some P-5 members. However, the
diminished bilateral relationships between several P-5 members and
African countries may be at least as relevant. Whatever the sources of its
very mixed (at best) track record in Africa, unless the Council can do better
in years to come, it will clearly be failing the globe's most challenged continent and the intent of the Charter.

Reform?

Reform of the Council remains a live issue in UN corridors, but one
exhibiting little energy. The hermetic nature of its working methods excited
greater attention at a time when its decisions were proving genuinely
important. In an era marked by a P-5 tendency to impose decisions on the
remainder of the Council, growing resentment among the nonpermanent
members focused largely on the permanent members' possession of the
veto, even though the veto was little used after 1990 (although its threat
was often invoked).

Under intense pressure from TCCs, the Council's working methods
became more transparent and the Council itself somewhat more accessible
to nonmember states (and NGOs), but its reliance on informal consultations
rather than open meetings as the locus for decisionmaking remains
marked.[56] Discussion of the veto among member states revealed broad
understanding of why it had been necessary during the Cold War, as well as
confirmation that it is widely seen by most delegations now as undesirable.
But the existing P-5 members will not give up their vetoes lightly and cannot be compelled to do so under Charter provisions. For this reason, debate
has focused more on whether any new permanent members should be
granted vetoes rather than on veto suppression. Voluntary agreement among
permanent members to use the veto only in relation to decisions under
Chapter VII of the Charter (which would, for example, eliminate vetoes on

the selection of the UN Secretary-General) seems one of the few realistic initiatives mooted to date.

Expansion of the Security Council has proved a difficult element of the package. Germany and Japan early on signaled their wish to be allocated permanent seats. They alternately demanded and waffled on their wish for a veto, emphasizing at times that the Council should not feature "second-class" permanent members. Developing countries made clear that any expansion of the permanent membership would have to include the allocation of several new permanent seats to the developing world, notionally a new seat each for developing countries in Asia, Africa, and Latin America (possibly two for Africa). However, there is little agreement among them on which countries should be granted these permanent seats. While Brazil seemed an obvious candidate for Latin America, the issue generated a squall in Brazilian bilateral relations with Argentina mid-decade. In Africa, neither Egypt (more Arab than African) nor South Africa (under new and very busy management) nor Nigeria (oppressed by a highly reprehensible military regime for most of the 1990s) seemed entirely satisfactory candidates. In Asia, the obvious contender, India, was opposed by Pakistan and more quietly by some others. Meanwhile, a range of "middle powers" strongly opposed any allocation of new permanent seats, instead proposing a variety of schemes including the rotation of several countries through new nonpermanent seats. At times, the only likely outcome seemed a limited expansion of the Council's nonpermanent seats, weighted to accommodate the developing countries so clearly underrepresented in existing arrangements of seat distribution.[57] And yet the disappointing performance of elected members in discussions on Iraq in February and March 2003, when they seemed to freeze under the diplomatic pressure and failed to articulate serious alternative approaches to those favored by various P-5 members, suggests likely limited "value added" from such an outcome.

Nearly ten years after serious discussion of Council reform was last initiated, no progress has been registered, except for limited gains in transparency in the Council's modus operandi. Short of geopolitical shocks, change does not seem nigh.

Envoi

This volume has attempted to address major trends within the Security Council during a very active immediate post–Cold War period, mostly that bracketed by two crises over Iraq, in 1990–1991 and 2002–2003. We may be entering a new period in international relations, one marked by the exercise of U.S. military power unconstrained by the Security Council or other multilateral actors. If so, the period discussed here will be seen as a very active transitional one between the Cold War, when the Council played a useful but limited role, and one in which the Council will again be some-what marginalized.

The early 1990s showed the Council at its most optimistic and activist, leading to some notable successes, as in El Salvador and Mozambique. Wishful thinking on resources, increasing risk, poor planning, the dilution of responsibility inevitable in committee decisionmaking, and the absence of a powerful and consistently engaged leader among its members all contributed to the Council's subsequent decline into recrimination, risk-aversion, and flight from reality. Its pretense of busyness, underscored by myriad resolutions and presidential statements of barely passing interest, failed to disguise a sense of disorientation late in the 1990s.

Nevertheless, often *faute de mieux,* particularly given the limited capacities of most regional organizations, the UN was again called upon in 1999 to deploy large peace operations in Kosovo, East Timor, and Sierra Leone. Two more large operations were deployed subsequently (to the Congo and in Ethiopia and Eritrea), as was an ambitious UN civilian mission in Afghanistan. After several years during which U.S. domestic political factors seriously constrained its capacity to act, the role of the Security Council not only in conferring legitimacy on certain forms of international intervention but also in providing a mechanism for sharing the burden of expenses and risk, in an era averse to both, once again proved attractive. At the height of war fever in Washington in September 2002, the U.S. administration engaged with the Council in the hope of being able to elicit a degree of UN support for its objectives on Iraq. But the outcome of these efforts leaves a cloud of uncertainty hanging over the Council's future role.

National interests, which very much drive Council decisionmaking, vary. While the U.S. approach to the Council is likely to remain instrumental (policy advanced through the Council if possible, but around it where necessary), strengthening the role of the Council is very much in the national interests of the other permanent members. As underscored by Adolfo Aguilar Zinser, for middle powers the rule of law as enshrined in the post–World War II treaty system anchored in the UN and through the promotion of collective security is at the core of their national interests.[58]

Jean-David Levitte, France's outstanding permanent representative to the UN during 1999–2002, believes that the institution's relevance emerged, if anything, reinforced from the intensive diplomacy over Iraq in 2002 and early 2003, with publics the world over (including in the United States) focused on the ebb and flow of these difficult discussions in which basic principles of international relations were at stake. Further, he argues that issues of proliferation (nuclear and otherwise), of critical importance today, can be addressed successfully only with wide and active international support, best mobilized through Council discussion and action. He believes the Council will, at the very least, remain seized of the "orphan" conflicts of the post–Cold War era, those in which the interests of the great powers are only marginally engaged, as in East Timor, the Congo, and Sierra Leone in recent years.[59] Indeed, the Council's willingness in May 2003, in spite of strained relations between France and the United States over Iraq, to agree on a small observer mission for Côte d'Ivoire and a French-led intervention in the northeast of the Democratic Republic of Congo suggests that this custodial role of the Council in addressing geostrategically secondary (even though often intensely murderous) conflicts will remain unimpaired.[60]

Perceptions of the Council tend to be overly complacent among its participants. Minor triumphs are blown up to epic proportions by those involved, whereas nearly unspeakable failures such as Rwanda and Srebrenica are swept under the carpet. Who in the Israeli-Arab theater (on both sides) considers the Council's record on this conflict distinguished or even fair? TCCs, donors, and NGOs all would offer a more jaundiced view of the Council's track record than do some of the Council members. Furthermore, differences over Iraq in the Council in 2003 raise the question, in Jeremy Greenstock's words, of "whether the Council can be effective on the hardest issues."[61] It is hard to be optimistic in this regard, and avoidance in the Council of the hardest issues calls into question the policy of countries relying mostly or entirely on multilateral diplomacy.

Following the Council's inability to agree on Iraq in early 2003, Michael W. Doyle, the distinguished scholar who witnessed these events from within Kofi Annan's office at the UN, where he was serving as Assistant Secretary-General, commented:

> The Council's performance on Iraq in March 2003, was both—and in about equal measure—a massive disappointment and a surprising relief. It disappointed all hopes that this essential international forum for multilateral policy could achieve a viable common policy. At the same time, it demonstrated to the surprise of many that it would not let itself be bullied or bribed by any power, permanent or even hyper. The so far unanswered question is: Can it meet the challenge of keeping intact its integrity while improving its effectiveness?[62]

Arguably the most important, although one of the least noticed, of the consequences of Council decisions in recent years, taken as a whole, has been the erosion and shift at the international level of the understanding of national sovereignty. By 1999 it was widely although not universally accepted that tyrants could no longer seek refuge behind the walls of sovereignty to shield themselves from international concern and even action over massive human rights violations and humanitarian catastrophes. The Council, by intervening repeatedly to address the humanitarian consequences of mostly civil wars, sometimes authorizing coercive measures and, by designing increasingly complex and intrusive mandates for international actors within member countries, sometimes without their consent, has not so much overridden Article 2(7) of the Charter (which exempts Chapter VII decisions from its nonintervention provisions) but rather sharply redefined in practice our conception of what can constitute a threat to international peace and security and a proper topic for international intervention. The degree of intrusiveness the Council was prepared to mandate throughout the 1990s was striking, even though its own members were not always helpful in implementing decisions involving risks to their nationals, for example in the arrest of those indicted by the international criminal tribunals.

Even in its darkest hours mid-decade, no alternative international institution was mooted to supplant the Council—the puzzling advocacy in 2003 by Boutros Boutros-Ghali of a UN of democracies notwithstanding.[63] Indeed, the degree of consensus that would be required to create a different multilateral structure to promote collective security is inconceivable in the absence of a global cataclysm. Thus the Council is fated to muster on. Stronger, more sympathetic U.S. leadership in the Council is urgently required. While all is not for the best in the best of all possible Councils, its permanent members are stuck with each other, and the rest of the member states with them. In years ahead, through decisions taken on a case-by-case basis, they will continue to chart the course of international relations on such sensitive and important issues as humanitarian intervention.

The UN Charter, for all of the failures of UN member states to live up to it, continues to serve as a beacon from this perspective, and its authority, even though sometimes ignored, continues to be invoked even by the United States. Whether it can adapt to changing circumstances and to unipolar U.S. power more often unilaterally exercised remains to be seen. Brian Urquhart, present at the creation of the UN, observed recently:

> When the Security Council's members, especially its permanent members, are united, it can do a great deal. When they are divided, it is often reduced to being a useful scapegoat for governmental intransigence, and an excuse for powerful governments to go it alone. *Quis custodiet ipsos custodes?* But even in its unreformed, and perhaps unreformable, state, the Security Council is the keystone of the concept of international security that came out of World War II. So far, it is the best keystone we have, and the occasional failure of its major members to agree does not make it irrelevant. As the French statesman Joseph Paul Boncour said in 1946: "The strength and weakness . . . of the new institution is that it depends on agreement between the five permanent [members]." How right he was.[64]

Notes

1. See David M. Malone, "A Decade of U.S. Unilateralism?" in David M. Malone and Yuen Foong Khong, *Unilateralism and U.S. Foreign Policy: International Perspectives,* Center on International Cooperation Studies in Multilateralism (Boulder: Lynne Rienner, 2003), pp. 19–40.

2. President Bush's speech available at www.state.gov/p/io/rls/rm/2003/24321.htm.

3. For discussion of the evolution of peacekeeping, see in particular Thomas G. Weiss, David P. Forsythe, and Roger A. Coate, *The United Nations in a Changing World,* 2nd ed. (Boulder: Westview, 1997).

4. See Michael C. Williams, *Civil-Military Relations and Peacekeeping* (London: Oxford University Press, 1998).

5. See Adam Roberts, "Communal Conflict as a Challenge to International Organization: The Case of Former Yugoslavia," *Review of International Studies* 21 (1995): 389–410.

6. See John L. Hirsch and Robert Oakley, *Somalia and Operation Restore Hope: Reflections on Peacemaking and Peacekeeping* (Washington, D.C: U.S. Institute of Peace, 1995); and more recently, Mark Bowden, *Black Hawk Down: A Story of Modern War* (New York: Atlantic Monthly, 1999).

7. See James F. Dobbins, *Haiti: A Case Study in Post–Cold War Peacekeeping,* ISD Reports no. 2.1 (Washington, D.C.: Institute for the Study of Diplomacy, Georgetown University, October 1995); and David Bentley and Robert Oakley, *Peace Operations: A Comparison of Somalia and Haiti,* Strategic Forum no. 30 (Washington D.C.: Institute for National Strategic Studies, National Defense University, May 1995).

8. Beyond the writing cited in the Rwanda-related chapters of this volume, see Gérard Prunier, *The Rwanda Crisis: History of a Genocide* (New York: Columbia University Press, 1995); Michael Barnett, "The UN Security Council, Indifference, and Genocide in Rwanda," *Cultural Anthropology,* 12, no. 4 (November 1997): 551; and J. Matthew Vaccaro, "The Politics of Genocide: Peacekeeping and Disaster Relief in Rwanda," in William J. Durch, ed., *The UN, Peacekeeping, American Policy, and the Uncivil Wars of the 1990s* (New York: St. Martin's, 1996), pp. 367–408.

9. Interview with Marrack Goulding, New York, March 26, 2003.

10. See Oliver Ramsbotham and Tom Woodhouse, *Encyclopedia of International Peacekeeping Operations* (Santa Barbara, Calif.: ABC-CLIO, 1999).

11. United Nations Department of Political Affairs, "A Brief Overview of Security Council Applied Sanctions," informal background paper, *Interlaken 2,* 1998.

12. See David Cortright and George Lopez, eds., *The Sanctions Decade: Assessing UN Strategies in the 1990s* (Boulder: Lynne Rienner, 2000); and David Cortright and George Lopez, *Sanctions and the Search for Security: Challenges to UN Action* (Boulder: Lynne Rienner, 2002).

13. See Daniel W. Drezner, *The Sanctions Paradox: Economic Statecraft and International Relations* (Cambridge: Cambridge University Press, 1999).

14. Resolution 1267, October 15, 1999.

15. See the German Permanent Mission to the UN website for details on this: www.undp.org/missions/germany/state.htm.

16. See "Canada on the UN Security Council 1999–2000," www.un.int/canada/english.html.

17. *Final Report of the UN Panel of Experts on Violations of Security Council Sanctions Against UNITA,* S/2000/203, March 10, 2000.

18. Peter Wallensteen, Carina Staibano, and Mikael Eriksson, eds., *Making Targeted Sanctions Effective: Guidelines for the Implementation of UN Policy Options* (Uppsala, Sweden: Uppsala University, Department of Peace and Conflict Research, 2003).

19. See Mats Berdal and David M. Malone, eds., *Greed and Grievance: Economic Agendas in Civil Wars* (Boulder: Lynne Rienner, 1999). This volume picked up on pioneering work by scholars such as David Keene and Paul Collier, who deserve much credit for opening up to policymakers what had been a typically recondite backwater of academic research.

20. The OAU cooperated well with UNTAG in Namibia, although the Frontline States were the more relevant partners, but it proved sticky on the issue of Western Sahara, which had become highly politicized within the OAU. Formally, the process was initiated as a joint endeavor between the UN Secretary-General and the OAU chairman in office, but no substantive role for the OAU materialized.

21. See Salim Ahmed Salim, "The OAU Role in Conflict Management," in Olara A. Otunnu and Michael W. Doyle, eds., *Peacemaking and Peacekeeping for the New Century* (Lanham, Md.: Rowman & Littlefield, 1998), pp. 245–253. See also Ali A. Mazrui, "The Failed State and Political Collapse in Africa," in ibid., pp. 233–243.

22. See Mwesiga Baregu and Christopher Landsberg, eds., *From Cape to Congo: Southern Africa's Evolving Security Challenges* (Boulder: Lynne Rienner, 2002); Adekeye Adebajo and Ismail Rashid, eds., *West Africa's Security Challenges: Building Peace in a Troubled Region* (Boulder: Lynne Rienner, 2004); and Josephine Odera and Paul Omach, eds., *Eastern Africa's Security Challenges* (Boulder: Lynne Rienner, forthcoming). While Nigeria's leadership of ECOMOG has been key, its political decisions—for example, ultimately to back Charles Taylor in Liberia—have not always been happy ones.

23. The UN Observer Mission in Georgia was established by Resolution 853 in 1993 with the task of observing the operation of the peacekeeping force of the Commonwealth of Independent States, among others.

24. The UN Observer Mission in Liberia was established in September 1993 under Resolution 866. Its mandate was to exercise its "good offices" to support efforts of ECOWAS and the Liberian transitional government.

25. Data for period 1995–1997. See U.S. Department of State, *World Military Expenditures and Arms Transfers* (Washington, D.C.: U.S. Department of State, 1998).

26. *Regional Approaches to Conflict Management in Africa,* IPA Seminar Report no. 8, August 2001, www.ipacademy.org/pdf_reports/reg_appr.pdf.

27. See Francis Kofi Abiew, *The Evolution of the Doctrine and Practice of Humanitarian Intervention* (The Hague: Kluwer, 1999); and Stephen A. Garrett, *Doing Good and Doing Well: An Examination of Humanitarian Intervention* (Westport, Conn.: Praeger, 1999).

28. See the Secretary-General's report (S/23069, 1991) and Resolution 713 (1991), which declare that the "rapid loss of human life and widespread material damage" were a threat to international peace and security, largely due to the spillover of refugees into neighboring countries.

29. See the Secretary-General's report requesting the Security Council to take up the case of Somalia (S/23445, 1991) and Resolution 733 (1992), similarly con-

cerned by the spillover of refugees on the safety and security of bordering countries.

30. For a good collection of works broaching this debate, see Jonathan Moore, ed., *Hard Choices: Moral Dilemmas in Humanitarian Intervention* (Lanham, Md.: Rowman & Littlefield, 1998).

31. On El Salvador, see in particular Michael W. Doyle, Ian Johnstone, and Robert C. Orr, eds., *Keeping the Peace: Multidimensional UN Operations in Cambodia and El Salvador* (Cambridge: Cambridge University Press, 1997).

32. This temporary appointment as SRSG in Iraq in May 2003 threatened to interrupt the reorientation of the high commissioner's office he seemed to be engineering up to that point.

33. Most UN electoral activities, often relating to electoral assistance, have nothing to do with the Security Council.

34. See Krishna Kumar, ed., *Postconflict Elections, Democratization, and International Assistance* (Boulder: Lynne Rienner, 1998).

35. Self-determination involves more than democratization and elections. On this, see Ian Martin, *Self-Determination in East Timor: The United Nations, the Ballot, and International Intervention,* International Peace Academy Occasional Paper (Boulder: Lynne Rienner, 2001). Jamsheed Marker, in his book *East Timor: A Memoir of the Negotiations for Independence* (Jefferson: McFarland, 2003), takes a slightly different view of the referendum.

36. S/23500, January 31, 1992.

37. The United Kingdom sponsored and hosted in New York in March 2003 a conference bringing together regional organizations and others to compare notes and galvanize interaction in this regard.

38. See S/PRST/1994/22, May 3, 1994; S/PRST/1994/62, November 4, 1994; and S/PRST/1996/13, March 28, 1996.

39. Pérez de Cuéllar had also previously worked for the UN, inter alia as a senior envoy in Cyprus, but he had followed a diversified career also involving considerable time in the service of Peru, his native country.

40. Annan's willingness to accept personal responsibility for his role (while Undersecretary-General for peacekeeping operations) in the slaughter of civilians at Srebrenica in 1995 and in the UN's hideously inadequate response to genocide in Rwanda in 1994, in the wake of detailed reports issued on the UN's lamentable performance on these two occasions, enhanced his standing with some observers while undermining it with others. See Barbara Crossette, "Kofi Annan Unsettles People, as He Believes He Should," *New York Times,* December 31, 1999.

41. See Dapo Akande, "The International Court of Justice and the Security Council: Is There Room for Judicial Control of Decisions of the Political Organs of the United Nations?" *International and Comparative Law Quarterly* 46, no. 2 (April 1997): 309; and Mohammed Bedjaoui, *Nouvel order mondial et contrôle de la légalité des actes du Conseil de Sécurité* (Brussels: Bruylant, 1994).

42. See "Libya, the ICJ, and the Security Council," *Middle East International* no. 50 (1998): 18.

43. Remarks before the American Society of International Law, Washington, D.C., April 5, 2003. Permission to quote obtained from Mr. Cot.

44. Confidential interview, January 26, 2003.

45. Interview with Adolfo Aguilar Zinser, New York, January 25, 2003.

46. See Nora Boustany, "With Trade Pact Pending, Chile Replaces UN Envoy Who Angered U.S. over Iraq," *Washington Post,* May 14, 2003.

47. See Philip Shenon, "Ex-Inspector Cites Early Role of CIA on UN Arms

Team," *New York Times,* February 23, 1999. See also, David M. Malone, "Goodbye UNSCOM: A Tale in UN-U.S. Relations," *Security Dialogue* 30, no. 4 (December 1999): 393–411.

48. See Philip Shenon, "Former Arms Inspector Is Criticized by State Department," *New York Times,* February 24,1999.

49. See Resolution 1284, December 17, 1999, which created a new UN monitoring operation, UNMOVIC, to replace a discredited and paralyzed UNSCOM.

50. Edward Luck offers interesting speculations in this regard in "Bush, Iraq, and the UN," in Meg Crahan, John Goering, and Thomas Weiss, eds., *Unilateralism vs. Multilateralism in U.S. Foreign Policy,* forthcoming.

51. See Resolution 1229, February 26, 1999.

52. It can be argued that the Council's action to implement a "peace settlement" on Western Sahara was undertaken in good faith. However, the flaws inherent in that settlement have undermined UN credibility on this question.

53. International Rescue Committee, *Mortality in the Democratic Republic of Congo: Results from a Nationwide Survey,* reported April 2003, http://intranet. theirc.org/docs/drc_mortality_iii_report.pdf. Belated action by Western powers to buttress the UN's weak peacekeeping operation in the DRC in May 2003 only underscores their studied indifference of these countries to the UN's need for their active help in the Congo all along.

54. See *Report of the Panel on United Nations Peace Operations* ("Brahimi Report"), A/55/305-S2000/809, August 21, 2000, paras. 102–116.

55. Frequent Council missions to Africa, intended to gain on-the-ground knowledge and to exert influence over often recalcitrant local actors, are praised by many. However, they have sometimes exposed to local actors significant divisions between Council members over strategy, and several of them have proved financially costly. The Council, ultimately, is judged on the quality of its decisions. If over time these missions prove to have been helpful, the pattern is likely to take hold lastingly. If, however, Council decisions on Africa do not improve, these missions may be seen as diplo-tourism and a flight from responsibility in New York from the hard decisions that needed to be made.

56. It is obvious that detailed negotiation of texts is best carried out in smaller groups and in private, but the critical substantive arguments are also mostly carried forward in private, and therein lies the source of much resentment by other member states.

57. For an eclectic discussion of reform and issues facing the UN today, see James P. Muldoon, ed., *Multilateral Diplomacy and the UN Today* (Boulder: Westview, 1999).

58. Interview with Adolfo Aguilar Zinser, New York, January 25, 2003.

59. Interview with Jean-David Levitte, Washington, D.C., April 3, 2003.

60. On May 13, 2003, in Resolution 1476, the Security Council authorized a UN mission including up to seventy-six military personnel to play a monitoring and diplomatic facilitation role in Côte d'Ivoire.

61. Interview with Jeremy Greenstock, New York, January 25, 2003.

62. Interview with Michael W. Doyle, New York, May 16, 2003.

63. Boutros-Ghali made this suggestion in "War of Liberation for Human Rights—Do We Need New International Law?" "Kontraste," German First Television, ARD, on May 8, 2003.

64. Interview with Brian Urquhart, New York, March 20, 2003.

APPENDIXES

Appendix I UN Security Council–Mandated Peace Operations, 1945–2003

Name (original mandating SCRs)	Location	Time	Mandate	Maximum Troops/ Military Observers/ Civilian Police[a]	Chapter VII?
			1945–1987		
UNTSO (SCR 50)	Middle East	Since June 1948	Originally established to assist in supervising the observance of the truce in Palestine. Since then, UNTSO has performed various tasks including the supervision of the General Armistice Agreements of 1949 and the observation of the cease-fire in the Suez Canal area and the Golan Heights following the Arab-Israeli war of June 1967. At present, UNTSO assists and cooperates with UNDOF on the Golan Heights in the Israel-Syria sector, and UNIFIL in the Israel-Lebanon sector. UNTSO is also present in the Egypt-Israel sector in the Sinai.	— / 572 / —	
UNMOGIP (SCRs 47, 91)	India/Pakistan	Since Jan. 1949	Supervise, in the state of Jammu and Kashmir, the cease-fire between India and Pakistan.	— / 102 / —	
UNOGIL (SCR 128)	Lebanese-Syrian border areas	June–Dec. 1958	Ensure that there was no illegal infiltration of personnel or supply of arms or other matériel across the Lebanese borders. After the conflict had been settled, tensions eased and UNOGIL was withdrawn.	— / 591 / —	
ONUC (SCR 143)	Republic of Congo (now Democratic Republic of Congo)	July 1960– June 1964	Ensure the withdrawal of Belgian forces, to assist the government in maintaining law and order and to provide technical assistance. The function of ONUC was subsequently modified to include maintaining the territorial integrity and political independence of the Congo, preventing the occurrence of civil war, and securing the removal of all foreign military, paramilitary, and advisory personnel not under the United Nations command, and all mercenaries.	19,828 / — / —	
UNYOM (SCR 179)	Yemen	July 1963– Sept. 1964	Observe and certify the implementation of the disengagement agreement between Saudi Arabia and the United Arab Republic.	— / 1895 / —	

continues

Appendix I   continued

Name (original mandating SCRs)	Location	Time	Mandate	Maximum Troops/ Military Observers/ Civilian Police[a]	Chapter VII?
			1945–1987 (continued)		
UNFICYP (SCR 186)	Cyprus	Since Mar. 1964	Originally established to prevent a recurrence of fighting between the Greek Cypriot and Turkish Cypriot communities and to contribute to the maintenance and restoration of law and order and a return to normal conditions. Following the hostilities of 1974, the Security Council adopted a number of resolutions expanding the mandate of UNFICYP to include supervising a de facto cease-fire, which came into effect on August 16, 1974, and maintaining a buffer zone between the lines of the Cyprus National Guard and of the Turkish and Turkish Cypriot forces.	6,411 / — / 35	
DOMREP (SCR 203)	Dominican Republic	May 1965– Oct. 1966	Observe the situation and report on breaches of the cease-fire between the two de facto authorities in the Dominican Republic. Following the agreement on a new government, DOMREP was withdrawn.	— / 2 / —	
UNIPOM (SCR 211)	Along the India-Pakistan border between Kashmir and the Arabian Sea	Sept. 1965– Mar. 1966	Supervise the cease-fire along the India-Pakistan border except in the state of Jammu and Kashmir, where UNMOGIP operated, and the withdrawal of all armed personnel to the positions held by them before August 5, 1965. After the withdrawal of the troops by India and Pakistan had been completed on schedule, UNIPOM was terminated.	— / 96 / —	
UNEF II[b] (SCR 340)	Suez Canal sector and later the Sinai peninsula	Oct. 1973– July 1979	Supervise the cease-fire between Egyptian and Israeli forces and, following the conclusion of the agreements of January 18, 1974, and September 4, 1975, supervise the redeployment of Egyptian and Israeli forces and man and control the buffer zones established under those agreements.	6,973 / — / —	
UNDOF (SCR 350)	Syrian Golan Heights	Since June 1974	Maintain the cease-fire between Israel and Syria, supervise the disengagement of Israeli and Syrian forces, and supervise the areas of separation and limitation, as provided in the disengagement agreement. The mandate of UNDOF has since been renewed every six months.	1,450 / — / —	

Operation	Location	Dates	Mandate	Strength	
UNIFIL (SCRs 425, 426)	Lebanon	Since Mar. 1978	Confirm the withdrawal of Israeli forces from southern Lebanon, restore international peace and security, and assist the government of Lebanon in ensuring the return of its effective authority in the area.	7,000 / — / —	
1987					
UNGOMAP (SCR 622)	Afghanistan/ Pakistan	May 1988– Mar. 1990	Assist in ensuring the implementation of the settlement agreements related to Afghanistan and in this context to monitor (1) the noninterference and nonintervention by the parties in each other's affairs; (2) the withdrawal of Soviet troops from Afghanistan; and (3) the voluntary return of refugees.	50 / — / —	
UNIIMOG (SCR 619)	Iran/Iraq	Aug. 1988– Feb. 1991	Verify, confirm, and supervise the cease-fire and the withdrawal of all forces to the internationally recognized boundaries, pending a comprehensive settlement.	— / 400 / —	
UNAVEM I (SCR 626)	Angola	Dec. 1988– May 1991	Verify withdrawal of Cuban troops.	— / 70 / —	
1989					
UNTAG (SCR 632)	Namibia	Apr. 1989– Mar. 1990	Assist the SRSG to ensure the early independence of Namibia through free and fair elections under the supervision and control of the United Nations.	4,493 / — / 1,500	
ONUCA (SCR 644)	Central America	Nov. 1989– Jan. 1992	Verify compliance by the governments of Costa Rica, El Salvador, Guatemala, Honduras, and Nicaragua with their undertakings to cease aid to irregular forces and insurrectionist movements in the region and to not allow their territory to be used for attacks on other states.	800 / 260 / —	
1991					
UNIKOM (SCRs 689, 806)	Iraq/Kuwait	Since Apr. 1991	Monitor a demilitarized zone along the boundary between Iraq and Kuwait and the Khawr 'Abd Allah waterway, deter violations of the boundary, and observe any hostile action mounted from the territory of one state against the other. In February 1993 the mandate was extended to include the capacity to take physical action to prevent violations of the DMZ and of the newly demarcated boundary between Iraq and Kuwait.	933 / 254 / —	YES

continues

Appendix 1 continued

Name (original mandating SCRs)	Location	Time	Mandate	Maximum Troops/ Military Observers/ Civilian Police[a]	Chapter VII?
			1991 (continued)		
MINURSO (SCR 690)	Western Sahara	Since Apr. 1991	Following the agreement between the government of Morocco and the Frente POLISARIO, MINURSO was deployed to monitor the cease-fire and to organize and conduct a referendum that would allow the people of Western Sahara to decide the territory's future status.	183 / 202 / 26	
UNAVEM II (SCR 696)	Angola	May 1991– Feb. 1995	Verify the peace agreement by UNITA and the government of Angola, monitor the cease-fire and the Angolan police, and observe and verify elections.	— / 171 / 122	
ONUSAL (SCRs 693, 729)	El Salvador	July 1991– Apr. 1995	Verify implementation of all agreements between the government of El Salvador and the FMLN. The agreements involved a cease-fire and related measures, reform and reduction of the armed forces, creation of a new police force, reform of the judicial and electoral systems, human rights, land tenure, and other economic and social issues.	— / 368 / 315	
UNAMIC (SCR 717)	Cambodia	Oct. 1991– Mar. 1992	Assist the four Cambodian parties to maintain their cease-fire during the period prior to the establishment and deployment of UNTAC, and initiate mine-awareness training of civilian populations. Later the mandate was enlarged to include a major training program for Cambodians in mine detection and mine clearance in regard to repatriation routes, reception centers, and resettlement areas.	1,090 / — / —	
			1992		
UNPROFOR (SCRs 743, 776, 795, 982)	Former Yugoslavia	Feb. 1992– Mar. 1995	Initially established in Croatia to ensure demilitarization of designated areas. The mandate was later extended to Bosnia and Herzegovina to support the delivery of humanitarian relief and to monitor "no fly zones" and "safe areas." Subsequently the mandate was again extended to the former Yugoslav Republic of Macedonia for preventive monitoring in border areas.	38,332 / 684 / 803	YES

Mission (SCR)	Country	Dates	Mandate	Troops/Military Observers/Civilian Police	Ongoing
UNTAC (SCR 745)	Cambodia	Mar. 1992–Sept. 1993	Ensure implementation of the Paris Peace Accords, including human rights monitoring, organization of elections, maintenance of law and order, repatriation and resettlement of refugees and internally displaced persons, and rehabilitation of Cambodian infrastructure.	15,991 / — / 3,359	
UNOSOM I (SCR 751)	Somalia	Apr. 1992–Mar. 1993	Monitor the cease-fire in Mogadishu and escort deliveries of humanitarian supplies to distribution centers in the city. The mission's mandate and strength were later enlarged to enable it to protect humanitarian convoys and distribution centers throughout Somalia. It later worked with UNITAF in the effort to establish a safe environment for the delivery of humanitarian assistance.	893 / 54 / —	
ONUMOZ (SCRs 797, 898)	Mozambique	Dec. 1992–Dec. 1994	Help implement the general peace agreement, monitor the cease-fire and the withdrawal of foreign troops and provide security in transport corridors, provide technical assistance, and monitor the entire electoral process.	6,576 / — / 1,087	

1993

Mission (SCR)	Country	Dates	Mandate	Troops/Military Observers/Civilian Police	Ongoing
UNOSOM II (SCR 814)	Somalia	Mar. 1993–Mar. 1995	Establish throughout Somalia a secure environment for humanitarian assistance. To that end, UNOSOM II was to complete, through disarmament and reconciliation, the task begun by UNITAF for the restoration of peace, stability, and law and order.	25,747 / — / —	YES
UNOMUR (SCR 846)	Rwanda/Uganda	June 1993–Sept. 1994	Monitor the border between Uganda and Rwanda and verify that no military assistance was provided across it.	— / 80 / —	
UNOMIG (SCRs 849, 858)	Georgia	Since Aug. 1993	Established to verify compliance with the ceasefire agreement between the government of Georgia and the Abkhaz authorities in Georgia. UNOMIG's mandate was expanded following the signing by the parties of the 1994 agreement on a ceasefire and separation of forces.	— / 134 / —	
UNOMIL (SCR 866)	Liberia	Sept. 1993–Sept. 1997	Exercise good offices in support of ECOWAS efforts to implement the peace agreement, investigate alleged cease-fire violations, assist in demobilization of combatants, support humanitarian assistance, and investigate human rights violations.	65 / 260 / —	

continues

Appendix I continued

Name (original mandating SCRs)	Location	Time	Mandate	Maximum Troops/ Military Observers/ Civilian Police[a]	Chapter VII?
			1993 (continued)		
UNMIH (SCR 867)	Haiti	Sept. 1993– June 1996	Help implement provisions of the Governor's Island Agreement of July 3, 1993. The mandate was later revised to enable the mission to assist the democratic government to sustain a stable environment, professionalize the armed forces and create a separate police force, and establish an environment conducive to free and fair elections.	6,000 / — / 850	
UNAMIR (SCR 872)	Rwanda	Oct. 1993– Mar. 1996	Originally established to help implement the peace agreement signed by the Rwandese parties at Arusha on August 4, 1993. UNAMIR's mandate and strength were adjusted on a number of occasions in the face of the tragic events of the genocide and the changing situation in the country.	5,147 / 295 / 80	
			1994		
UNASOG (SCR 915)	Aouzou Strip, Republic of Chad	May–June 1994	Verify the withdrawal of Libyan administration and forces from the Aouzou Strip in accordance with the ICJ decision.	— / 9 / —	
UNMOT (SCRs 968, 1138)	India/Pakistan	Dec. 1994– May 2000	Monitor the cease-fire agreement between the government of Tajikistan and the United Tajik Opposition. Following the signing by the parties of the 1997 general peace agreement, UNMOT's mandate was expanded to help monitor its implementation.	— / 40 / 3	
			1995		
UNAVEM III (SCR 976)	Angola	Feb. 1995– June 1997	Assist the government of Angola and UNITA in restoring peace and achieving national reconciliation on the basis of the 1991 peace accords and the 1994 Lusaka Protocol.	6,017 / 345 / 246	

Mission (SCR)	Location	Dates	Mandate	Strength	
UNCRO (SCR 981)	Croatia	Mar. 1995–Jan. 1996	Replacing UNPROFOR in Croatia, UNCRO's task was to perform the functions envisaged in the cease-fire agreement of March 29, 1994, facilitate implementation of the economic agreement of December 2, 1994, monitor the crossing of military equipment and personnel over specified international borders, facilitate humanitarian assistance to Bosnia and Herzegovina through the territory of Croatia, and monitor the demilitarization of the Prevlaka Peninsula.	6,581 / 290 / 296	YES
UNPREDEP (SCR 983)	Former Yugoslav Republic of Macedonia	Mar. 1995–Feb. 1999	Monitor and report any developments in the border areas that could undermine confidence and stability in the former Yugoslav Republic of Macedonia and threaten its territory.	1,120 / 35 / 26	
UNMIBH (SCR 1035)	Bosnia and Herzegovina	Dec. 1995–Dec. 2002	Exercise of a wide range of functions related to the law enforcement activities and police reform in Bosnia and Herzegovina, and coordinate other UN activities in the country related to humanitarian relief and refugees, demining, human rights, elections, and economic reconstruction.	3 / — / 2,047	

1996

Mission (SCR)	Location	Dates	Mandate	Strength	
UNTAES (SCR 1037)	Eastern Slavonia, Croatia	Jan. 1996–Jan. 1998	Supervise and facilitate demilitarization, monitor return of refugees, contribute to the maintenance of peace and security, establish a temporary police force, undertake tasks related to civil administration and public services, and organize elections.	4,791 / 100 / 453	YES
UNMOP (SCR 1038)	Prevlaca Peninsula, southern border between Croatia and the FRY	Feb. 1996–Dec. 2002	Taking over from UNCRO, its task was to monitor the demilitarization of the Prevlaka Peninsula.	— / 28 / —	
UNSMIH (SCR 1063)	Haiti	July 1996–July 1997	Assist the government of Haiti in the professionalization of the police and the maintenance of a secure and stable environment.	1,287 / — / 267	

1997

Mission (SCR)	Location	Dates	Mandate	Strength	
MINUGUA (SCR 1094)	Guatemala	Jan. 1997–May 1997	Verify the agreement on the definitive cease-fire between the government of Guatemala and the URNG, signed in Oslo on December 4, 1996. Verification functions included observation of a formal cessation of hostilities, the separation of forces, and the demobilization of URNG combatants.	— / 132 / —	

continues

Appendix 1   continued

Name (original mandating SCRs)	Location	Time	Mandate	Maximum Troops/ Military Observers/ Civilian Police[a]	Chapter VII?
			1997 (continued)		
MONUA (SCR 1118)	Angola	June 1997– Feb. 1999	Assist the Angolan parties in consolidating peace and national reconciliation, enhancing confidence-building, and creating an environment conducive to long-term stability, democratic development, and rehabilitation of the country.	3,026 / 253 / 361	
UNTMIH (SCR 1123)	Haiti	Aug. 1997– Nov. 1997	Assist the government of Haiti by supporting and contributing to the professionalization of the Haitian National Police.	— / — / 156	
MIPONUH (SCR 1141)	Haiti	Dec. 1997– Mar. 2000	Assist the government of Haiti in the professionalization of the Haitian National Police.	— / — / 284	
			1998		
UNPSG (SCR 1145)	Croatia	Jan. 1998– Oct. 1998	Taking over from UNTAES, UNPSG's mandate was to continue monitoring the performance of the Croatian police in the Danube region, particularly with respect to the return of displaced persons for a single nine-month period.	— / — / 114	
MINURCA (SCR 1159)	Central African Republic	Apr. 1998– Feb. 2000	Assist with maintaining and enhancing security and stability in Bangui and vicinity; disarmament; capacity-building of national police; electoral assistance.	1,347 / — / 22	
UNOMSIL (SCR 1181)	Sierra Leone	July 1998– Oct. 1999	Monitor the military and security situation in Sierra Leone, as well as the disarmament and demobilization of former combatants; assist in monitoring respect for international humanitarian law.	— / 192 / —	

1999

Mission	Location	Dates	Mandate	Personnel	Authorized
UNMIK (SCR 1244)	Kosovo	Since June 1999	Authorized the Secretary-General to establish an interim civilian administration led by the UN under which its people could progressively enjoy substantial autonomy. The mission performs the whole spectrum of essential administrative functions and services, covering such areas as health and education, banking and finance, postal services and telecommunications, and law and order.	— / 37 / 4,519	YES
UNAMET (SCR 1246)	East Timor	June–Sept. 1999	Organize and conduct referendum on East Timorese independence.	— / 50 / 271	
UNAMSIL (SCRs 1270, 1289)	Sierra Leone	Since Oct. 1999	Originally established to cooperate with the government of Sierra Leone and the other parties to the Lomé Agreement in its implementation, *including assistance in* disarmament, demobilization, and reintegration. In 2000 the mandate was revised to include the following tasks: to provide security at key locations and government buildings, to facilitate the free flow of people, goods, and humanitarian assistance along specified thoroughfares, to provide security in and at all sites of the disarmament, demobilization, and reintegration program, to coordinate with and assist the Sierra Leone law enforcement authorities in the discharge of their responsibilities, and to guard and destroy collected armaments	17,105 / 261 / 54	YES (since Feb. 2000)
UNTAET (SCR 1272)	East Timor	Oct. 1999– May 2002	Administer the territory and exercise legislative and executive authority and support capacity-building for self-government during the transition period toward independence, for which the people of East Timor voted on August 30, 1999.	8,950 / 200 / 1,640	YES
MONUC (SCR 1279)	Congo	Since Nov. 1999	Monitor implementation of the cease-fire agreement, investigate violations of the agreement, work with the parties to obtain the release of all prisoners of war and military captives, supervise and verify the disengagement and redeployment of the parties' forces, monitor compliance with the provision of the cease-fire agreement on the supply of war-related matériel to the field, facilitate humanitarian assistance and human rights monitoring, with particular attention to vulnerable groups, and demining.	7,431 / 554 / 61	YES

continues

Appendix 1   continued

Name (original mandating SCRs)	Location	Time	Mandate	Maximum Troops/ Military Observers/ Civilian Police[a]	Chapter VII?
2000					
UNMEE (SCRs 1312, 1430)	Ethiopia/Eritrea	Since July 2000	Maintain liaison with the parties and establish a mechanism for verifying the June 2000 ceasefire between Eritrea and Ethiopia. The mandate was later extended to include the deployment within UNMEE of up to 4,300 military personnel to monitor the cessation of hostilities and to help ensure the observance of security commitments.	3,854 / 219 / —	
2002					
UNAMA (SCR 1401)	Afghanistan	Since March 2002	Lend support to the Afghan transition process. Promoting national reconciliation; fulfilling the tasks and responsibilities entrusted to the United Nations in the Bonn Agreement; and managing all UN humanitarian, relief, recovery and reconstruction activities in Afghanistan in coordination with the Afghan administration.	— / 8 / 3 (intl. civilian staff: 211)	
UNMISET (SCR 1410)	East Timor	Since May 2002	Provide assistance to core administrative structures critical to the viability and political stability of East Timor, provide interim law enforcement and public security and to assist in the development of a new law enforcement agency in East Timor, and contribute to the maintenance of the external and internal security of East Timor.	3,742 / 111 / 730	

2003

MINUCI (SCR 1479)	Côte d'Ivoire	Since May 2003	Facilitate the implementation by the Ivorian parties of the Linas-Marcoussis Agreement and including a military component complementing the operations of the French and ECOWAS forces. The Council approved the establishment of a small staff to support the special representative of the Secretary-General on political, legal, and civil affairs, civilian police, elections, media and public relations, humanitarian and human rights issues, and the establishment of a military liaison group.	— / 25 / —
UNMIL (SCR 1509)	Liberia	Since Sept. 2003	Support the implementation of the ceasefire agreement and the peace process; protect UN staff, facilities and civilians; support humanitarian and human rights activities; assist in national security reform, including national police training and formation of a new, restructured military.	14,750 / 250 / 1,115 YES

Notes: Table updated as of September 2003. Parentheses indicate original mandating Security Council resolutions (SCRs).

a. These numbers refer only to actual deployed personnel at the moment of maximum troop/observer/civilian police strength and do not indicate the strength of the international presence as authorized in the respective Security Council resolutions.

b. UNEF II's predecessor force, UNEF I, was mandated by the General Assembly under its 1956 Uniting for Peace resolution.

Sources: For mandates, UN Department of Peacekeeping Operations website, www.un.org/depts/dpko.

For maximum troop/observer/civilian police strength, www.un.org and SIPRI Yearbooks 1994–2002 (Oxford: Oxford University Press, 1994–2002).

Appendix 2 Multinational Operations Tasked and Authorized by the UN, 1945–2003

Name (original mandating SCR)	Location	Time	Mandate	Maximum Troops/ Military Observers/ Civilian Police[a]	Chapter VII?
Gulf War Coalition (SCR 678)	Iraq	Nov. 1990	Evict Iraqi forces from Kuwait and restore international peace and security in the area.[b]	580,000 / — / —	YES
UNITAF (SCR 794)	Somalia	Dec. 1992	Establish a safe environment for the delivery of humanitarian assistance. Secure, in coordination with UNOSOM I, major population centers and ensure that humanitarian assistance is delivered and distributed.	37,000 / — / —	YES
Operation Turquoise (SCR 929)	Rwanda	June–Aug. 1994	Contribute, in an impartial way, to the security and protection of displaced persons, refugees, and civilians at risk in Rwanda.[c]	3,060 / — / —	YES
Multinational Force (MNF)/ Operation Uphold Democracy (SCR 940)	Haiti	Sept. 1994– March 1995	Neutralize armed opposition and create a secure environment for restoration of the legitimate government of Haiti; restore and preserve civil order; and be prepared to pass responsibility for military operations in Haiti to the UNMIH.	7,412 / — / 717	YES
IFOR (SCR 1031)	Bosnia and Herzegovina	Dec. 1995– Dec. 1996	Oversee implementation of the military aspects of the Dayton Peace Accords, bringing about and maintaining an end to hostilities; separating the armed forces of Bosnia's two newly created entities, the Federation of Bosnia and Herzegovina and the Republika Srpska; transferring territory between the two entities according to the peace agreement; and moving the parties' forces and heavy weapons into approved storage sites.[d]	60,000 / — / —	YES
SFOR (SCR 1088)	Bosnia and Herzegovina	Since Dec. 1996	Deter hostilities and stabilize the peace, contribute to a secure environment by providing a continued military presence in the Area of Responsibility (AOR), target and coordinate SFOR support to key areas including primary civil implementation organizations, and progress toward a lasting consolidation of peace.[e]	36,300 / — / —	YES

continues

Appendix 2 continued

Name (original mandating SCR)	Location	Time	Mandate	Maximum Troops/ Military Observers/ Civilian Police[a]	Chapter VII?
MISAB (SCR 1125)	Central African Republic	Feb. 1997– April 1998	Restore peace and security in the Central African Republic by monitoring the implementation of the Bangui Agreements and conducting operations to disarm the former rebels, the militia, and all other unlawfully armed individuals.[f]	800 / — / —	YES
Multinational Protection Force (MPF) (SCR 1101)	Albania	Apr.–Aug. 1997	Ensure safe delivery and distribution of humanitarian aid, take control of the Adriatic ports from which refugees and other would-be immigrants were leaving for Italy, and stabilize the internal situation so as to allow elections to take place in June 1997.[g]	6,294 / — / —	YES
XFOR (SCR 1203)	Former Yugoslav Republic of Macedonia	Dec. 1998– March 1999	Extract OSCE verifiers or other designated persons from Kosovo should all other measures be unsuccessful and at OSCE request.	2,300 / — / —	YES
KFOR (SCR 1244)	Kosovo	Since June 1999	Establish and maintain a secure environment in Kosovo, including public safety and order; to monitor, verify, and when necessary, enforce compliance with the agreements that ended the conflict; and to provide assistance to the UN Mission in Kosovo (UNMIK).[h]	42,700 / — / —	YES
INTERFET (SCR 1264)	East Timor	Sept. 1999– Feb. 2000	Restore peace and security to East Timor, protect and support UNAMET, and facilitate humanitarian assistance operations; Australia appointed lead nation.	11,285 / — / —	YES
Task Force Fox (TFF) (SCR 1371)	Former Yugoslav Republic of Macedonia	Sept. 2001– Dec. 2002	Follow-on force to NATO Task Force Harvest, which operated without UN mandate. Its task was to contribute to the protection of international monitors who would oversee the peace plan in the former Republic of Macedonia.	1,011 / — / —	YES
ISAF (SCR 1386)	Afghanistan	Since Dec. 2001	Assist the Afghan Transitional Authority (ATA) in maintaining security within the ISAF Area of Responsibility so that the ATA as well as the personnel of the United Nations can operate in a secure environment in order to enable the ATA the build up of security structures in Afghanistan in accordance with the Bonn Agreement and as agreed in the Military Technical Agreement (MTA).[i]	4,988 / — / —	YES

Operation Unicorn/ MICECI (SCR 1464)	Côte d'Ivoire	Since February 2003	Authorizes member states participating in the ECOWAS forces together with the French forces supporting them to take the necessary steps to guarantee the security and freedom of movement of their personnel and to ensure the protection of civilians immediately threatened with physical violence within their zones of operation.	5,300 / — / —	YES
Operation Artemis (SCR 1484)	Democratic Republic of Congo	May–Sept. 2003	Authorizes the deployment of an interim emergency multinational force formed by the European Union. The force was mandated to contribute, in close coordination with MONUC, to the stabilization of the security conditions and the improvement of the humanitarian situation in Bunia.	1,850 / — / —	YES

Notes: a. These numbers refer only to actual deployed personnel at the moment of maximum troop strength and do not indicate the strength of the international presence authorized in the respective Security Council resolutions.

b. Security Council Resolutions 660 and 678.

c. Security Council Resolution 929.

d. http://www.nato.int/docu/facts/2000/role-bih.htm.

e. See SFOR Homepage at http://www.nato.int/sfor/organisation/mission.htm.

f. http://www.reliefweb.int/w/rwb.nsf/0/ad813ef76087cd74852565fd0069c4f3?OpenDocument.

g. http://www.assembly-weu.org/en/documents/sessions_ordinaires/reports/1650.html.

h. See KFOR Homepage at www.nato.int/kfor/kfor/about.htm.

i. See ISAF Homepage: www.isafkabul.org/.

Sources: www.un.org and SIPRI Yearbooks 1994–2002 (Oxford: Oxford University Press, 1994–2002).

Appendix 3   Security Council-Mandated Sanctions Regimes

SCR	Date	Measure
		Southern Rhodesia
232	December 16, 1966	Imposed sanctions on commodities in addition to oil.
253	May 29, 1968	Set up a sanctions committee.
460	December 21, 1979	Lifted all sanctions against Southern Rhodesia.
		South Africa
1418	November 4, 1977	Imposed an arms embargo
421	December 9, 1977	Set up a Security Council sanctions committee.
919	May 25, 1994	Terminated the arms embargo and other restrictions imposed on South Africa.
		Iraq
661	August 6, 1990	Imposed comprehensive, mandatory sanctions; created sanctions committee; banned all trade; imposed oil embargo and arms embargo; suspended international flights; froze Iraqi government financial assets/ prohibited financial transactions.
687	April 3, 1991	Established a set of eight specific conditions for the lifting of sanctions.
706	August 15, 1991	Authorized oil-for-food program; permitted sale of up to $1.6 billion in Iraqi oil over six-month period; directed that proceeds be deposited in UN escrow account to finance humanitarian imports and war reparations.
712	September 19, 1991	Established basic structure for oil-for-food program implementation [Iraq rejected SCRs 706 and 712].
778	October 2, 1992	Called upon member states to transfer Iraqi oil funds from pre–Gulf crisis to UN escrow account.
986	April 14, 1995	Established new formula for oil-for-food program; permitted sale of up to $1 billion in Iraqi oil every three months; gave Baghdad primary responsibility for distribution of humanitarian goods [came into force December 1996].
1111	June 4, 1997	Extended oil-for-food program [Baghdad withheld distribution plans and oil sales].
1153	February 20, 1998	Extended oil-for-food program again; raised oil sales to $5.25 billion every six months; permitted revenues to finance urgent development needs.
1284	December 17, 1999	Declared Council's intention to suspend sanctions for renewable 120-day periods if Iraq cooperated with UNMOVIC and IAEA weapons inspectors.

continues

Appendix 3 continued

SCR	Date	Measure
		Iraq (continued)
1409	May 14, 2002	Adopted a revised Goods Review List of military-related goods or commodities, which was to enter into effect on May 30, 2002. From that date onward, states are authorized to sell or supply any commodities not included on the Goods Review List, while the Council would regularly conduct thorough reviews of the Goods Review List.
1472	March 28, 2003	Made technical and temporary adjustments to the oil-for-food program on an interim and exceptional basis, so as to ensure the implementation of approved contracts concluded by the government of Iraq for the relief of the Iraqi people.
1483	May 22, 2003	Ended all sanctions, except those related to the sale or supply to Iraq of arms and related matériel; requested the Secretary-General to terminate the oil-for-food program after a period of six months.
		Former Yugoslavia
713	September 25, 1991	Imposed arms embargo on Yugoslavia.
724	December 15, 1991	Created sanctions committee.
757	May 30, 1992	Banned all international trade with Yugoslavia; prohibited air travel; blocked financial transactions; banned sports and cultural exchanges; suspended scientific and technical cooperation; allowed transshipment of goods through Yugoslavia; exempted humanitarian goods.
787	November 15, 1992	Prohibited transshipment of strategic goods through Yugoslavia; halted all maritime shipping on Danube River.
820	April 17, 1993	Froze Yugoslav government financial assets; prohibited the transit through any country of vessels owned by or registered in Yugoslavia; further limited the transshipment of goods through Yugoslavia.
942	September 23, 1994	Extended full range of sanctions to Bosnian-Serb–controlled territory.
943	September 23, 194	Eased some restrictions on Serbia; suspended sanctions on air and ferry service between Montenegro and Italy; suspended ban on sporting and cultural events.
1160	March 31, 1998	Imposed arms embargo on Yugoslavia; established new sanctions committee to monitor membership compliance.

Somalia

733	January 23, 1992	Imposed arms embargo.
751	April 24, 1992	Created sanctions committee.
954	November 4, 1994	Requested the Somalia sanctions committee to fulfill its mandate (due to poor monitoring).
1407	May 3, 2002	Requested the Secretary-General to establish a team of experts that could provide the Council's sanctions committee on Somalia with an action plan to improve the enforcement of the arms embargo.

Libya

748	March 31, 1992	Imposed aviation sanctions; banned the supply of weapons; required reductions in personnel at Libyan diplomatic/consular missions abroad; restricted travel of Libyan nationals suspected of terrorist activity; created sanctions committee.
883	November 11, 1993	Froze Libyan government assets abroad; tightened the aviation sanctions; banned the import of some oil-transporting equipment.
1192	August 27, 1998	Decided that sanctions shall be suspended immediately if the Secretary-General reports to the Council that the two Lockerbie accused have arrived in the Netherlands for trial.
S/PRST/1999/10	April 8, 1999	Noted that the conditions for suspending the wide range of aerial, arms, and diplomatic measures against Libya had been fulfilled.
1506	September 12, 2003	Lifted sanctions against Libya and terminated the mandate of the sanctions committee.

Cambodia

766	July 21, 1992	Specified that international financial assistance for reconstruction would go only to factions supporting the Paris Accords.
783	October 13, 1992	Demanded compliance with the Paris Accords (again); confirmed that elections would proceed regardless of PDK obstruction.
792	November 30, 1992	Imposed sanctions on PDK-controlled areas of Cambodia; imposed oil embargo; supported moratorium on log exports, previously adopted by Cambodia's Supreme National Council (SNC), to go into effect 1 January 1993; urged the SNC to embargo the export of minerals and gems.

continues

Appendix 3   continued

SCR	Date	Measure
		Liberia
788	November 19, 1992	Imposed limited arms embargo (exempted ECOMOG forces).
985	April 13, 1995	Created sanctions committee.
1071	August 30, 1996	Welcomed proposed ECOWAS punitive measures (including travel and voting restrictions) but did not threaten additional UN sanctions.
1343	March 7, 2001	Reimposed the arms embargo; imposed additional sanctions, which included a ban on trade with rough diamonds and a travel ban against senior members of the government of Liberia or their spouses, as well as of any other individuals providing financial and military support to armed rebel groups in countries neighboring Liberia.
1478	May 6, 2003	Extended the existing sanctions measures until May 7, 2004 and decided that all states shall take the necessary measures to prevent, for a period of ten months, the import into their territories of all round logs and timber products originating in Liberia.
		Haiti
841	June 16, 1993	Imposed fuel and arms embargo; established sanctions committee.
873	October 13, 1993	Reimposed the fuel and arms embargo.
875	October 16, 1993	Called on member states to enforce the fuel and arms embargo with a naval blockade.
917	May 6, 1994	Imposed comprehensive sanctions; imposed flight ban; froze the assets of the military junta and their supporters and families.
944	September 29, 1994	Moved to terminate sanctions upon Aristide's return to power.
		Angola
864	September 15, 1993	Imposed arms embargo on UNITA; imposed petroleum embargo except through ports of entry designated by the Angolan government; created sanctions committee.
1127	August 28, 1997	Imposed travel sanctions banning travel of senior UNITA officials and prohibiting flights to and from UNITA-held territory; imposed diplomatic sanctions closing UNITA diplomatic offices; suspended the sanctions twice, hoping UNITA would document its disarmament efforts; finally imposed the stronger sanctions in October 1997.

Resolution	Date	Description
1173	June 12, 1998	Froze UNITA financial assets; banned all financial transactions with UNITA; imposed an embargo on diamond imports not certified by the Angolan government; banned any form of travel to UNITA-controlled territory.
1202 and 1203	October 15, 1998	Requested the Secretary-General to submit recommendations regarding means for improving the implementation of the measures imposed on UNITA.
1237	May 7, 1999	Established expert panels to undertake studies to trace violations in arms trafficking, oil supplies, and the diamond trade, as well as the movement of UNITA funds.
1295	April 18, 2000	Established a monitoring mechanism for a period of six months in order to collect information concerning violations of the Council's previous sanctions resolutions against UNITA.
1412	May 17, 2002	Suspended the travel ban on senior UNITA officials for a period of ninety days and stated the Council would decide before the end of that period whether to extend that suspension.

Rwanda

Resolution	Date	Description
918	May 17, 1994	Imposed arms embargo; created sanctions committee.
997	June 9, 1995	Specified that the arms embargo applied to groups in other countries operating against Rwanda.
1011	August 16, 1995	Suspended the arms embargo on the Rwandan government; maintained the sanctions on the rebel Hutu groups in eastern Zaire.
1013	September 6, 1995	Established the UN International Commission of Inquiry (UNICOI) to investigate and report arms embargo violations.

Sudan

Resolution	Date	Description
1054	April 26, 1996	Imposed diplomatic sanctions; called on member states to reduce the number of staff at diplomatic missions and consular posts and restrict the movements of those that remained; restricted entry into their territory of Sudanese government officials and military personnel; required international institutions and regional organizations to refrain from convening any conferences in Sudan.
1070	August 16, 1996	Imposed travel sanctions requiring all states to deny Sudanese aircraft permission to take off from, land in, or overfly their territories; called for a separate Security Council decision within ninety days to determine a date for entry into force [aviation ban never went into effect].
1372	September 28, 2001	Lifted the sanctions detailed in Resolution 1054.

continues

Appendix 3 continued

SCR	Date	Measure
		Sierra Leone
1132	October 8, 1997	Imposed an oil embargo and an arms embargo; imposed travel sanctions on members of the AFRC junta and their families; conditioned the lifting of sanctions on the junta relinquishing power; created sanctions committee.
1156	March 16, 1998	Lifted the oil embargo.
1171	June 5, 1998	Confirmed the removal of sanctions on the government; reimposed the arms embargo and travel ban on the RUF and members of the former military junta.
1306	July 5, 2000	Imposed diamond embargo and requested the government of Sierra Leone to establish an effective certificate of origin regime for trade in diamonds.
		Afghanistan
1267	October 15, 1999	Created sanctions committee; imposed aviation and financial sanctions against Taliban regime.
1333	December 19, 2000	Imposed an arms embargo on territory of Afghanistan under Taliban control; imposed financial sanctions against Osama bin Laden and individuals and entities associated with him.
1363	July 30, 2001	Requests the Secretary-General to establish within thirty days a monitoring group to monitor the implementation of the sanctions.
1388	January 15, 2002	Terminated the sanctions measures that applied to Ariana Afghan Airlines.
1390	January 16, 2002	Maintained all sanctions measures in Resolution 1267 except the flight embargo for a period of twelve months.
1455	January 17, 2003	Renewed sanctions; declared the Council's intention to improve those measures within the next twelve months and requested the monitoring group for the sanctions to report on further improvements.
		Ethiopia and Eritrea
1298	May 17, 2000	Imposed an arms embargo against Eritrea and Ethiopia; established a committee consisting of all the members of the Council.
S/PRST/2001/14	May 15, 2001	Noted that the sanctions would expire on May 16, 2001.

Source: David Cortright and George Lopez. *The Sanctions Decade*. Boulder: Lynne Rienner, 2000; United Nations sanctions homepage at http://www.un.org/News/ossg/sanction.htm.

Acronyms

ACABQ	Advisory Committee on Administrative and Budgetary Questions
AFL	Armed Forces of Liberia
AFRC	Armed Forces Revolutionary Council
AIDS	acquired immune deficiency syndrome
ANC	African National Congress
ANSA	armed nonstate actor
APEC	Asia Pacific Economic Cooperation
ASEAN	Association of Southeast Asian Nations
CCA	Common Country Assessment
CHR	Commission on Human Rights (UN)
CINCSOUTH	Commander in Chief, Allied Forces Southern Europe
CIS	Commonwealth of Independent States
CRS	Catholic Relief Services
CSCE	Conference on Security and Cooperation in Europe
CTC	Counter-Terrorism Committee (UN)
DHA	Department of Humanitarian Affairs (UN)
DPA	Department of Political Affairs (UN)
DPKO	Department of Peacekeeping Operations (UN)
DRC	Democratic Republic of Congo
E-10	elected ten (UN Security Council)
EC	European Community
ECOMOG	ECOWAS Cease-Fire Monitoring Group
ECOSOC	Economic and Social Council (UN)
ECOWAS	Economic Community of West African States
EO	Executive Outcomes
EPLF	Eritrean People's Liberation Front
EU	European Union
FAR	Forces Armées Rwandaises

675

FDD	Forces for Democracy and Development (Burundi)
FMLN	Farabundo Martí National Liberation Front
FNL	National Liberation Forces (Burundi)
Frelimo	Front for the Liberation of Mozambique
FRY	former Republic of Yugoslavia
G7	Group of Seven
G8	Group of Eight
G-77	Group of 77
GDP	gross domestic product
IAEA	International Atomic Energy Agency
IBRD	International Bank for Reconstruction and Development
ICAO	International Civil Aviation Organization
ICC	International Criminal Court
ICG	International Crisis Group
ICISS	International Commission on Intervention and State Sovereignty
ICJ	International Court of Justice
ICRC	International Committee of the Red Cross
ICTR	International Criminal Tribunal for Rwanda
ICTY	International Criminal Tribunal for the Former Yugoslavia
IDMA	International Diamond Manufacturers Association
IFOR	Implementation Force
IGAD	Intergovernmental Authority on Development
IMF	International Monetary Fund
INTERFET	International Force for East Timor
Interpol	International Police Organization
IPA	International Peace Academy
IRC	International Rescue Committee
ISAF	International Security Assistance Force
KLA	Kosovo Liberation Army
KVM	Kosovo Verification Mission
LURD	Liberians United for Reconciliation and Democracy
MCC	Military Coordination Commission
MFO Sinai	Multinational Forces and Observers in Sinai
MICAH	International Support Mission in Haiti
MICIVIH	International Civilian Mission in Haiti
MINURCA	UN Verification Mission in the Central African Republic
MINURSO	UN Mission for the Referendum in Western Sahara
MINUSAL	Mission of the United Nations in El Salvador
MIPONUH	UN Civilian Police Mission in Haiti
MISAB	Inter-African Mission to Monitor the Bangui Accords
MNF	multinational force
MONUC	UN Organization Mission in the Democratic Republic of Congo

MSF	Médécins sans Frontières
NATO	North Atlantic Treaty Organization
NEPAD	New Partnership for Africa's Development
NGO	nongovernmental organization
NMOG	Neutral Military Observer Group (OAU)
OAS	Organization of American States
OAU	Organization of African Unity
OCHA	Office for the Coordination of Humanitarian Affairs (UN)
OEWG	Open-Ended Working Group (UN Security Council)
OLMEE	OAU Liaison Mission in Ethiopia/Eritrea
OMV	ongoing monitoring and verification
ONUC	UN Operation in the Congo
ONUCA	UN Observer Group in Central America
ONUMOZ	UN Operation in Mozambique
ONUSAL	UN Observer Mission in El Salvador
OSCE	Organization for Security and Cooperation in Europe
P-5	permanent five (UN Security Council)
PDD	Presidential Decision Directive
PKO	peacekeeping operation
PLAN	People's Liberation Army of Namibia
PLO	Palestine Liberation Organization
PNA	Palestinian National Authority
PRD	Presidential Review Directive
RCD	Rassemblement Congolais pour la Démocratie (Democratic Republic of Congo)
Renamo	Mozambique National Resistance
RPE	Rules of Procedure and Evidence (ICC)
RPF	Rwandan Patriotic Front
RUF	Revolutionary United Front (Sierra Leone)
SADC	Southern African Development Community
SFOR	Stabilization Force
SHIRBRIG	Standby High Readiness Brigade
SRSG	Special Representative of the Secretary-General
SWAPO	South West Africa People's Organization
SWAPOL	South West African Police
TCC	troop-contributing country
TNC	Transitional National Council (Somalia)
TPLF	Tigray People's Liberation Front
TRC	Truth and Reconciliation Commission
TSZ	Temporary Security Zone
UK	United Kingdom
UN	United Nations
UNAMA	UN Assistance Mission in Afghanistan
UNAMET	UN Mission in East Timor

UNAMIC	United Nations Advance Mission in Cambodia
UNAMIR	UN Assistance Mission in Rwanda
UNAMSIL	UN Mission in Sierra Leone
UNAVEM	UN Angola Verification Mission
UNCRO	UN Confidence Restoration Operation in Croatia
UNDAF	UN Development Assistance Framework
UNDOF	UN Disengagement Observer Force
UNDP	UN Development Programme
UNEF	UN Emergency Force
UNFICYP	United Nations Peacekeeping Force in Cyprus
UNGOMAP	United Nations Good Offices Mission in Afghanistan and Pakistan
UNHCR	UN high commissioner for refugees
UNICEF	UN Children's Fund
UNICOI	UN Independent Commission of Inquiry
UNIFIL	UN Interim Force in Lebanon
UNIIMOG	United Nations Iran-Iraq Military Observer Group
UNIKOM	UN Iraq-Kuwait Observation Mission
UNITA	União Nacional para a Independência Total de Angola (National Union for the Total Independence of Angola)
UNITAF	Unified Task Force
UNITAR	United Nations Institute for Training and Research
UNMEE	UN Mission in Ethiopia and Eritrea
UNMIBH	UN Mission in Bosnia and Herzegovina
UNMIH	UN Mission in Haiti
UNMIK	UN Mission in Kosovo
UNMISET	UN Mission of Support in East Timor
UNMOGIP	UN Military Observer Group in India and Pakistan
UNMOT	UN Mission of Observers in Tajikistan
UNMOVIC	UN Monitoring, Verification, and Inspection Commission
UNOGIL	UN Observer Group in Lebanon
UNOMIG	UN Observer Mission in Georgia
UNOMIL	UN Observer Mission in Liberia
UNOMSIL	UN Observer Mission in Sierra Leone
UNOMUR	UN Mission for Uganda-Rwanda
UNOSOM	UN Operation in Somalia
UNPREDEP	UN Preventive Deployment Force
UNPROFOR	UN Protection Force
UNRWA	UN Relief and Works Agency
UNSC	UN Security Council
UNSCOM	UN Special Commission
UNSMIH	UN Support Mission in Haiti
UNTAC	UN Transitional Authority in Cambodia

UNTAES	UN Transitional Administration for Eastern Slavonia, Baranja, and Western Sirmium
UNTAET	UN Transitional Administration in East Timor
UNTAG	UN Transition Assistance Group
UNTEA	UN Temporary Executive Authority
UNTMIH	UN Transition Mission in Haiti
UNTSO	UN Truce Supervision Organization
URNG	Unidad Revolucionaria Nacional Guatemalteca (Guatemalan National Revolutionary Army)
WFDB	World Federation of Diamond Bourses
WMD	weapons of mass destruction

BIBLIOGRAPHY

Key United Nations Documents

United Nations Department of Peacekeeping Operations. *Comprehensive Report on Lessons Learned from United Nations Assistance Mission for Rwanda (UNAMIR)*. New York: United Nations, 1996.

United Nations General Assembly. *Report of the Preparatory Committee on the Establishment of an International Criminal Court*. 2 vols. Official Records of the General Assembly, 51st sess., supps. 22, 22A. A/51/22. New York: United Nations, 1996.

————. *Report of the Secretary-General Pursuant to General Assembly Resolution 53/35: The Fall of Srebrenica*. A/54/549, November 15, 1999.

United Nations General Assembly and Security Council. *Report of the Panel on United Nations Peace Operations*. A/55/305-S/2000/809, August 21, 2000.

United Nations Secretary-General. *An Agenda for Democratization*. A/51/761, December 20, 1996.

————. *An Agenda for Peace: Preventive Diplomacy, Peacemaking, and Peacekeeping (Report of the Secretary-General Pursuant to the Statement Adopted by the Summit Meeting of the Security Council on 31 January 1992)*. A/47/277-S/24111, June 17, 1992.

————. *Supplement to An Agenda for Peace: Position Paper of the Secretary-General on the Occasion of the Fiftieth Anniversary of the United Nations*. A/50/60-S/1995/1, January 3, 1995.

United Nations Security Council. *Final Report of the Monitoring Mechanism on Angola Sanctions*. S/2000/1225, December 21, 2000.

————. *Report of the Panel of Experts on Violations of Security Council Sanctions Against UNITA*. S/2000/203, March 10, 2000.

Other Sources

Abiew, Francis Kofi. *The Evolution of the Doctrine and Practice of Humanitarian Intervention*. The Hague: Kluwer, 1999.

Aboagye, Festus. "Towards New Peacekeeping Partnerships in Africa? The OAU Liaison Mission in Ethiopia/Eritrea." *African Security Review* 10, no. 2 (2001): 19–33.

Académie du Droit International. *Colloque 1992: Le développement du rôle du Conseil de Sécurité.* Dordrecht: Martinus Nijhoff, 1993.

Adebajo, Adekeye. *Building Peace in West Africa, Liberia, Sierra Leone, and Guinea-Bissau.* International Peace Academy Occasional Paper. Boulder: Lynne Rienner, 2002.

Adebajo, Adekeye, and Ismail Rashid, eds. *West Africa's Security Challenges: Building Peace in a Troubled Region.* Boulder: Lynne Rienner, 2004.

Adelman, Howard, and Astri Suhrke. *Early Warning and Conflict Management in Rwanda: Study II of the Joint Evaluation of Emergency Assistance in Rwanda.* Copenhagen: DANIDA, 1996.

Adelman, Howard, and Astri Suhrke, eds. *The Path of a Genocide: The Rwandan Crisis from Uganda to Zaire.* New Brunswick, N.J.: Transaction Books, 1999.

Advisory Council on International Affairs and Advisory Committee on Issues of Public International Law. *Humanitarian Intervention.* The Hague: AIV and CAVV, 2000.

Afoaku, Osita G., and Okechukwu Ukaga. "United Nations Security Council Reform: A Critical Analysis of Enlargement Options." *Journal of Third World Studies* 18, no. 2 (Fall 2001): 149–170.

Akande, Dapo. "The International Court of Justice and the Security Council: Is There Room for Judicial Control of Decisions of the Political Organs of the United Nations?" *International and Comparative Law Quarterly* 46, no. 2 (April 1997): 309–343.

Akashi, Yasushi. "The Limits of UN Diplomacy and the Future of Conflict Mediation." *Survival* 37, no. 4 (Winter 1995–1996): 83–98.

Alger, Chadwick F. "Thinking About the Future of the UN System." *Global Governance* 2, no. 3 (September–December 1996): 335–360.

Allin, Dana H. *NATO's Balkan Interventions.* Adelphi Paper no. 347. Oxford: Oxford University Press, 2002.

Alnasrawi, Abbas. "Iraq: Economic Sanctions and Consequences, 1990–2000." *Third World Quarterly* 22, no. 2 (April 2001): 205–218.

al-Nauimi, N., and R. Meese, eds. *International Legal Issues Arising Under the United Nations Decade of International Law.* The Hague: Kluwer, 1995.

Alvarez, José E. "Judging the Security Council." *American Journal of International Law* 90, no. 1 (January 1996): 1–39.

———. "The Once and Future Security Council." *Washington Quarterly* 18, no. 2 (Spring 1995): 5–20.

———. "What's the Security Council For?" *Michigan Journal of International Law* 17, no. 2 (Winter 1996): 221–228.

American Society of International Law. "The Security Council: Its Authority and Legitimacy." Proceedings of the 87th annual meeting of the American Society of International Law, Washington D.C., March 31–April 3, 1993.

Amuzegar, Jahangir. "Adjusting to Sanctions." *Foreign Affairs* 76, no. 3 (May–June 1997): 31–41.

Angelet, Nicolas. "Criminal Liability for the Violation of UN Economic Sanctions." *European Journal of Crime, Criminal Law, and Criminal Justice* 7, no. 2 (1999): 89–102.

Annan, Kofi A. "Democracy as an International Issue." *Global Governance* 8, no. 2 (2002): 135–143.

———. *Peace Operations and the United Nations: Preparing for the Next Century.* New York: United Nations DPKO, 1996.

———. *The Question of Intervention.* New York: United Nations, 1999.

Anyidoho, Kwami. *Guns over Kigali: The Rwandese Civil War, 1994.* Accra: Woeli, 1997.

Axworthy, Lloyd. "Human Security and Global Governance: Putting People First." *Global Governance* 7, no. 1 (2001): 19–23.

Ayoob, Mohammed. "Humanitarian Intervention and State Sovereignty." *International Journal of Human Rights* 6, no. 1 (Spring 2002): 81–202.

———. "The New-Old Disorder in the Third World." *Global Governance* 1, no. 1 (Winter 1995): 59–77.

Baehr, Peter R., and Leon Gordenker. *The United Nations in the 1990s.* 2nd ed. Basingstoke: Macmillan, 1994.

Bailey, Sydney D. "New Light on Abstentions in the UN Security Council." *International Affairs* 50, no. 4 (October 1974): 554–574.

———. *The UN Security Council and Human Rights.* New York: St. Martin's, 1994.

———. "The UN Security Council and Terrorism." *International Relations* 11, no. 6 (December 1993): 533–553.

Bailey, Sydney D., and Sam Daws. *The Procedure of the UN Security Council.* 3rd ed. Oxford: Clarendon, 1998.

———. *The United Nations: A Concise Political Guide.* 3rd ed. London: Macmillan, 1995.

Baranyi, S., and L. North. *Stretching the Limits of the Possible: United Nations Peacekeeping in Central America.* Aurora Paper no. 15. Ottawa: Canadian Center for Global Security, 1992.

Baregu, Mwesiga, and Christopher Landsberg, eds. *From Cape to Congo: Southern Africa's Evolving Security Challenges.* Boulder: Lynne Rienner, 2002.

Barnett, Michael N. *Eyewitness to a Genocide: The United Nations and Rwanda.* Ithaca: Cornell University Press, 2002.

———. "The New United Nations Politics of Peace: From Juridical Sovereignty to Empirical Sovereignty." *Global Governance* 1, no. 1 (Winter 1995): 79–97.

———. "Partners in Peace? The UN, Regional Organizations, and Peacekeeping." *Review of International Studies* no. 21 (1995): 411–433.

———. "The UN Security Council, Indifference, and Genocide in Rwanda." *Cultural Anthropology* 12, no. 4 (November 1997): 551–578.

Bassiouni, M. Cherif. *International Terrorism: Multilateral Conventions (1937–2001).* Ardsley, N.Y.: Transnational, 2001.

Bedjaoui, Mohammed. *The New World Order and the Security Council: Testing the Legality of Its Acts.* Boston: Martinus Nijhoff, 1994.

———. *Nouvel order mondial et contrôle de la légalité des actes du Conseil de Sécurité.* Brussels: Bruylant, 1994.

Beigbeder, Yves. *Le contrôle international des élections.* Brussels: Bruylant, 1994.

Belgium Senate. *Commission d'enquête parlementaire concernant les événements du Rwanda.* Brussels: Government of Belgium, 1997.

Bentley, David, and Robert Oakley. *Peace Operations: A Comparison of Somalia and Haiti.* Strategic Forum no. 30. Washington, D.C.: Institute for National Strategic Studies, National Defense University, May 1995.

Berberian, Nubar G. *Le Conseil de Sécurité: Ses différences fondamentales avec le Conseil de S.D.N.* Paris: University of Paris, 1947.

Berdal, Mats. *Disarmament and Demobilization After Civil Wars.* Adelphi Paper no. 303. London: International Institute of Strategic Studies and Oxford University Press, 1996.

———. "Fateful Encounter: The United States and UN Peacekeeping." *Survival* 36, no. 3 (Autumn 1994): 121–148.

—. *Wither UN Peacekeeping?* Adelphi Paper no. 281. London: Brassey's for the International Institute of Strategic Studies, 1993.

Berdal, Mats, and David M. Malone, eds. *Greed and Grievance: Economic Agendas in Civil Wars.* Boulder: Lynne Rienner, 1999.

Berman, Eric. "The Security Council's Increasing Reliance on Burden-Sharing: Collaboration or Abrogation?" *International Peacekeeping* 4, no. 1 (Spring 1998): 1–21.

Berman, Eric G., and Katie E. Sams. *Peacekeeping in Africa: Capabilities and Culpabilities.* Geneva: United Nations Institute for Disarmament Research, 2000.

Bertrand, Maurice. "A propos de la reforme du Conseil de Securité." *Études Internationales* 30, no. 2 (June 1999): 413–422.

Bethlehem, D., and Marc Weller, eds. *The "Yugoslav" Crisis in International Law: General Issues.* Pt. 1. Cambridge: Cambridge University Press, 1997.

Bettati, Mario. *Le droit d'ingérence: Mutation de l'ordre international.* Paris: Odile Jacob, 1996.

Bettati, Mario, and Bernard Kouchner. *Le devoir d'ingérence.* Paris: Denoël, 1987.

Betts, Richard K. "The Delusion of Impartial Intervention." *Foreign Affairs* 73, no. 6 (November–December 1994): 20–23.

Bloomfield, Lincoln P., et al. *Collective Security in a Changing World.* Watson Institute Occasional Paper no. 10. Providence, R.I.: Watson Institute, 1993.

Boothby, Derek. *The United Nations and Disarmament.* International Relations Studies and the United Nations Occasional Paper no. 1. New Haven, Conn.: Yale University Press, 2002.

Boudreau, Thomas Eugene. *Sheathing the Sword: The U.N. Secretary-General and the Prevention of International Conflict.* Westport, Conn.: Greenwood, 1991.

Boulden, Jane, and Thomas G. Weiss, eds. *The UN and Terrorism: Problems and Prospects.* Forthcoming.

Bourantonis, Dimitris. "Reform of the UN Security Council and the Non-Aligned States." *International Peacekeeping* 5, no. 1 (Spring 1998): 89–109.

Bourantonis, Dimitris, and Georgios Kostakos. "Diplomacy at the United Nations: The Dual Agenda of the 1992 Security Council Summit." *Diplomacy and Statecraft* 11, no. 3 (November 2000): 212–226.

Bourantonis, Dimitris, and Jarrod Wiener. *The United Nations in the New World Order: The World Oganization at Fifty.* Houndmills, Basingstoke: Macmillan, 1995.

Bourloyannis, Christine. "The Security Council of the United Nations and the Implementation of International Humanitarian Law." *Denver Journal of International Law and Policy* 20, no. 3 (1993): 43.

Boutros-Ghali, Boutros. "Empowering the United Nations." *Foreign Affairs* 71, no. 5 (Winter 1992–1993): 89–102.

—. "Le Sécretaire-Général des Nations Unies: Entre l'urgence et la durée." *Politique Étrangère* no. 2 (Summer 1996): 407–414.

—. *Les Nations Unis et Haiti, 1990–96.* New York: United Nations Blue Book, 1996.

—. "L'ONU et les nouveaux conflits internationaux." *Relations Internationales et Stratégiques, no. 20* (Winter 1995): 15–22.

—. *The United Nations and the Iraq-Kuwait Conflict, 1990–1996.* New York: United Nations, 1996.

—. *The United Nations and Somalia.* New York: United Nations, 1996.

—. *Unvanquished.* New York: I. B. Tauris, 1999.

—, ed. *The United Nations in Mozambique, 1992-1995.* New York: United Nations Blue Book, 1995.

Bowden, Mark. *Black Hawk Down: A Story of Modern War.* New York: Atlantic Monthly, 1999.

Boyd, Andrew. *Fifteen Men on a Powder Keg: A History of the UN Security Council.* New York: Stein and Day, 1971.

Brady, Christopher, and Sam Daws. "UN Operations: The Political-Military Interface." *International Peacekeeping* 1, no. 1 (Spring 1994): 59-79.

Brzoska, Michael, ed. *Design and Implementation of the Arms Embargoes and Travel and Aviation Related Sanctions: Results of the "Bonn-Berlin Process."* Bonn: Bonn International Center for Conversion, 2001.

Bull, Hedley. *The Anarchical Society: A Study of Order in World Politics.* 3rd ed. New York: Columbia University Press, 2002.

Burkhalter, Holly J. "The Question of Genocide: The Clinton Administration and Rwanda." *World Policy Journal* 11, no. 4 (1994): 44–54.

Bustelo, Mara R., and Philip Alston, eds. *Whose New World Order: What Role for the United Nations?* Annandale, NSW, Australia: Federation, 1991.

Butler, Richard. "Bewitched, Bothered, and Bewildered: Rebuilding the Security Council." *Foreign Affairs* 78, no. 5 (September 1999): 9–12.

Buzan, Barry. "New Patterns of International Security in the Twenty-First Century." *International Affairs* 67, no. 3 (1991): 431–452.

Byers, Michael. "Custom, Power, and the Power of Rules." *Michigan Journal of International Law* 17, no. 109 (Autumn 1995): 109–180.

———, ed. *The Role of Law in International Politics: Essays in International Relations and International Law.* Oxford: Oxford University Press, 2000.

Cameron, Iain. *Report to the Swedish Foreign Office on Legal Safeguards and Targeted Sanctions.* Uppsala, Sweden: Uppsala University, Faculty of Law, 2002. www.jur.uu.se/sii/index.html.

Caplan, Richard. *A New Trusteeship? The International Administration of War-Torn Territories.* Adelphi Paper no. 341. Oxford: Oxford University Press, 2002.

Carlsson, Ingvar, Han Sung-Joo, and Rufus M. Kupolati. *Report of the Independent Inquiry into the Actions of the UN During the 1994 Genocide in Rwanda.* New York: United Nations, 1999.

Caron, David. "The Legitimacy of the Collective Authority of the Security Council." *American Journal of International Law* 87, no. 4 (October 1993): 522–558.

Cervetti, Marie, and Emmanuelle Ott. *Des bleus sans casque: Chronique d'une mission civile de l'ONU en Haïti.* Paris: Editions Austral, 1994.

Chesterman, Simon. *Just War or Just Peace? Humanitarian Intervention and International Law.* Oxford Monographs in International Law. Oxford: Oxford University Press, 2001.

———. "Legality Versus Legitimacy: Humanitarian Intervention, the Security Council, and the Rule of Law." *Security Dialogue* 33, no. 3 (September 2002): 293–308.

Chesterman, Simon, Michael Ignatieff, and Ramesh Thakur, eds. *The Failure and the Crisis of Governance: Making States Work.* Forthcoming.

Childers, Erskine, and Brian Urquhart. "Renewing the United Nations System." Uppsala, Sweden: Dag Hammarskjöld Foundation, 1994.

Chopra, Jarat. "Building State Failure in East Timor." *Development and Change* 33, no. 5 (2002): 979–1000.

———. "The UN's Kingdom of East Timor." *Survival* 42, no. 3 (Autumn 2000): 27–39.

———, ed. *The Politics of Peace-Maintenance.* Boulder: Lynne Rienner, 1998.

Chopra, Jarat, and Thomas G. Weiss. "Sovereignty Is No Longer Sacrosanct: Codifying Humanitarian Intervention." *Ethics and International Affairs* 6 (1992): 95–117.

Christakis, Théodore. *L'ONU, le Chapitre VII et la crise yougoslave.* Paris: Montchrestien, 1996.

Ciechanski, Jerzy. "Restructuring of the UN Security Council." *International Peacekeeping* 1, no. 4 (Winter 1994): 413–439.

Clark, Walter S., and Jeffrey Herbst. "Somalia and the Future of Humanitarian Intervention." *Foreign Affairs* 75, no. 2 (March–April 1996): 70–85.

———, eds. *Learning from Somalia: The Lessons of Armed Humanitarian Intervention.* Boulder: Westview, 1997.

Clark Arend, Anthony, and Robert J. Beck. *International Law and the Use of Force: Beyond the UN Charter Paradigm.* London: Routledge, 1993.

Claude, Inis L. "Collective Legitimation as a Political Function of the United Nations." *International Organization* 20 (1966): 367–379.

———. "Peace and Security: Prospective Roles for the Two United Nations." *Global Governance* 2, no. 3 (September–December 1996): 289–298.

———. *States and the Global System: Politics, Law, and Organization.* New York: St. Martin's, 1988.

———. *Swords into Plowshares: The Problems and Progress of International Organization.* 2nd ed. New York: Random House, 1963.

Clements, Kevin, and Christine Wilson. *UN Peacekeeping at the Crossroads.* Canberra: Australian National University Press, 1994.

Cohen, Ben, and George Stamkowski, eds. *With No Peace to Keep: United Nations Peacekeeping and the War in the Former Yugoslavia.* London: Grainpress, 1995.

Coicaud, Jean Marc, and Veijo Heiskanen, eds. *The Legitimacy of International Organizations.* Tokyo: United Nations University Press, 2001.

Collins, Cindy, and Thomas G. Weiss. *An Overview and Assessment of 1989–1996 Peace Operations Publications.* Watson Institute Occasional Paper no. 28. Providence, R.I.: Watson Institute, 1997.

Conflict, Security, and Development Group, International Policy Institute, King's College London. *A Review of Peace Operations: A Case for Change.* London: King's College, 2003. http://ipi.sspp.kcl.ac.uk/peaceoperationsreview.

Cortright, David, and George A. Lopez. *Sanctions and the Search for Security: Challenges to UN Action.* Boulder: Lynne Rienner, 2002.

———, eds. *The Sanctions Decade: Assessing UN Strategies in the 1990s.* Boulder: Lynne Rienner, 2000.

Cot, Jean-Pierre, and Alain Pellet, eds. *La Charte des Nations Unies: Commentaire article par article.* Paris: Éditions Economica, 1991.

Cox, David. *Exploring an Agenda for Peace: Issues Arising from the Report of the Secretary-General.* Aurora Paper no. 20. Ottawa: Canadian Center for Global Security, 1993.

———. "Peace Enforcement: The Case for a United Nations Standby Force." *Canadian Foreign Policy* 1, no. 2 (Spring 1993): 29–38.

Cox, David, and Albert Legault, eds. *UN Rapid Reaction Capabilities: Requirements and Prospects.* Clementsport, NS: Canadian Peacekeeping, 1995.

Crenshaw, Martha. "Current Research on Terrorism: The Academic Perspective." *Studies in Conflict and Terrorism* 15, no. 1 (January–March 1992): 1–11.

Crocker, Chester. *High Noon in South Africa: Making Peace in a Rough Neighborhood.* New York: W. W. Norton, 1992.

Crocker, Chester A., and Fen Osler Hampson. "Making Peace Settlements Work." *Foreign Policy* no. 104 (Fall 1996): 54–71.

Crocker, Chester, Fen Osler Hampson, and Pamela Aall, eds. *Herding Cats: Multiparty Mediation in a Complex World.* Washington, D.C.: U.S. Institute of Peace, 1999.

———. *Turbulent Peace: The Challenges of Managing International Conflict.* Washington, D.C.: U.S. Institute of Peace, 2001.

Clapham, Christopher. *African Guerrillas.* Bloomington: Indiana University Press, 1998.

———. "The Ethiopia-Eritrea Conflict." *South African Yearbook of International Affairs 1999/2000.* Johannesburg: South African Institute of International Affairs, 1999.

———. "The Ethiopia-Eritrea Conflict (continued)." *South African Yearbook of International Affairs 2000/2001.* Johannesburg: South African Institute of International Affairs, 2000.

Daalder, Ivo H. *Getting to Dayton: The Making of America's Bosnia Policy.* Washington, D.C.: Brookings Institution, 2000.

Dahmane, Farid Wahid. "Les mesures prises par le Conseil de Sécurité contre les - entités non-étatiques." *African Journal of International and Comparative Law* 11, no. 2 (June 1999): 227–244.

Damrosch, Lori. *Enforcing Restraint: Collective Intervention in International Conflicts.* New York: Council of Foreign Relations, 1993.

Daniel, C. F., and Brad C. Hayes. "Securing Observance of UN Mandates Through the Employment of Military Force." *International Peacekeeping* 13, no. 4 (Winter 1996): 105–125.

Danish Institute of International Affairs. *Humanitarian Intervention: Legal and Political Aspects.* Copenhagen: Danish Institute of International Affairs, 1999.

David, Charles-Phillipe, and Charles Trottier. *White Helmets/Casques Blancs.* Ottawa: Canadian Center for Foreign Policy Development, 1997.

David, Marcella. "Rubber Helmets: The Certain Pitfalls of Marshaling Security Council Resources to Combat AIDS in Africa." *Human Rights Quarterly* 23, no. 3 (August 2001): 560–582.

Davis, Jane M., ed. *Security Issues in the Post–Cold War World.* Cheltenham: Edward Elgar, 1996.

de Jonge Oudraat, Chantal. "Making Economic Sanctions Work." *Survival* 42, no. 3 (Autumn 2000): 105–128.

de Soto, Alvaro, and Graciana del Castillo. "Implementation of Comprehensive Peace Agreements: Staying the Course in El Salvador." *Global Governance* 1, no. 2 (May–August 1995): 189–203.

———. "Obstacles to Peacebuilding." *Foreign Policy* no. 94 (Spring 1994): 69–83.

de Waal, Alex. *Famine Crimes: Politics and the Disaster Relief Industry in Africa.* Oxford: James Currey, 1997.

de Waal, Alex, and Rakiya Omar. "Genocide in Rwanda and the International Response." *Current History* 94, no. 591 (April 1995): 156–161.

Deldique, Pierre-Edouard. *Le mythe des Nations Unies: L'ONU après la Guerre Froide.* Paris: Hachètte, 1994.

Delon, Francis. "La concertation entre les membres permanents du Conseil de Sécurité." *Annuaire Français de Droit International* 39 (1993) 53–64.

Deng, Francis M. "Frontiers of Sovereignty." *Leiden Journal of International Law* 8, no. 2 (1995): 249–286.

Deng, Francis M., et al. *Sovereignty as Responsibility.* Washington, D.C.: Brookings Institution, 1995.

des Forges, Alison L. *"Leave None to Tell the Story": Genocide in Rwanda.* New York: Human Rights Watch, 1999.

Diehl, Paul F. *International Peacekeeping.* Baltimore: Johns Hopkins University Press, 1993.

Dobbins, James F. *Haiti: A Case Study in Post–Cold War Peacekeeping.* ISD Reports no. 2.1. Washington, D.C.: Institute for the Study of Diplomacy, Georgetown University, October 1995.

Doggett, Martha. *Death Foretold: The Jesuit Murders in El Salvador.* Washington, D.C.: Georgetown University Press, 1993.

Dominicé, Christian, "Le Conseil de Sécurité et l'accès aux pouvoirs qu'il reçoit du Chapitre VII de la Charte des Nations Unies." *Revue Suisse de Droit International et de Droit Européen* 5, no. 4 (1995): 417–439.

Doxey, Margaret. "United Nations Sanctions: Lessons of Experience." *Diplomacy and Statecraft* 11, no. 1 (March 2000): 1–18.

Doyle, Michael. *Peacebuilding in Cambodia.* IPA Policy Briefing Paper. New York: International Peace Academy, 1996.

———. *Ways of War and Peace: Realism, Liberalism, and Socialism.* New York: W. W. Norton, 1997.

Doyle, Michael W., Ian Johnstone, and Robert C. Orr, eds. *Keeping the Peace: Multidimensional UN Operations in Cambodia and El Salvador.* Cambridge: Cambridge University Press, 1997.

———, eds. *Multidimensional Peacekeeping: Lessons from Cambodia and El Salvador.* New York: International Peace Academy, 1995.

Drezner, Daniel W. *The Sanctions Paradox: Economic Statecraft and International Relations.* Cambridge: Cambridge University Press, 1999.

Dupuy, René-Jean, ed. *The Development of the Role of the Security Council: Peacekeeping and Peacebuilding.* Boston: Martinus Nijhoff, 1993.

Durch, William J. *The Evolution of UN Peacekeeping: Case Studies and Comparative Analysis.* London: St. Martin's, 1993.

———, ed. *Peacekeeping, American Policy, and the Uncivil Wars of the 1990s.* New York: St. Martin's, 1996.

Durch, W. J., and B. M. Blechman. *Keeping the Peace: The United Nations in the Emerging World Order.* Washington, D.C.: Henry L. Stimson Center, March 1992.

Eban, Abba. "The U.N. Idea Revisited." *Foreign Affairs* 74, no. 5 (September–October 1995): 39–55.

Egan, Patrick T. "The Kosovo Intervention and Collective Self-Defence." *International Peacekeeping* 8, no. 3 (Autumn 2001): 39–58.

Elsen, T. J. H. *Litispendence Between the International Court of Justice and the Security Council.* The Hague: T. M. Asser Instituut, 1986.

Emmanuelli, Claude. *Les actions militaires de l'ONU et le droit international humanitaire.* Ottawa: Wilson & Lafleur Ltée, 1995.

Enders, Walter, and Todd Sandler. "Transnational Terrorism in the Post–Cold War Era." *International Studies Quarterly* 43, no. 1 (1999): 145–167.

Evans, Gareth J. *Cooperating for Peace: The Global Agenda for the 1990's and Beyond.* St. Leonards, NSW, Australia: Allen & Unwin, 1993.

Evans, Gareth, and Mohamed Sahnoun. "The Responsibility to Protect." *Foreign Affairs* 81, no. 6 (November–December 2002): 99–110.

Fafo Forum for SRSGs. *Command from the Saddle: Managing United Nations Peace-Building Missions.* Fafo Report no. 226. Oslo: Fafo Institute of Applied Science, 1999.

Falk, Richard A., Samuel S. Kim, and Saul H. Mendlovitz, eds. *The United Nations and a Just World Order.* Boulder: Westview, 1991.

Farer, Tom. *Collectively Defending Democracy in a World of Sovereign States: The Western Hemisphere's Prospect.* Montreal: International Center for Human Rights and Democratic Development, 1993.

Fassbender, Bardo. "The Gordian Knot of Security Council Reform." *German Comments* no. 45 (January 1997): 55–61.

———. "Quis judicabit? The Security Council, Its Powers, and Its Legal Control" (review essay). *European Journal of International Law* 11 (2000): 219–232.

———. "Reforming the United Nations." *Contemporary Review* no. 272 (1998): 281–290.

———. *UN Security Council Reform and the Right of Veto: A Constitutional Perspective.* The Hague: Kluwer, 1998.

———. "Uncertain Steps into a Post–Cold War World: The Role and Functioning of the UN Security Council After a Decade of Measures Against Iraq." *European Journal of International Law* 13 (2002): 273–303.

———. "The United Nations Charter as Constitution of the International Community." *Columbia Journal of Transnational Law* 36 (1998): 529–619.

Fearon, James, and David Laitin. "International Institutions and Civil War." Draft report, Stanford University, Department of Political Science, 2001.

Feil, Scott R. *Preventing Genocide: How the Early Use of Force Might Have Succeeded in Rwanda.* Report to the Carnegie Commission on Preventing Deadly Conflict. New York: Carnegie Corporation, 1998.

Ferencz, Benjamin B. *Global Survival: Security Through the General Assembly.* Dobbs Ferry, N.Y.: Oceana, 1994.

———. *New Legal Foundations for Global Survival: Security Through the Security Council.* Dobbs Ferry, N.Y.: Oceana, 1994.

Ferris, E. G., ed. *The Challenge to Intervene: A New Role for the United Nations?* Conference Report no. 2. Uppsala, Sweden: Life and Peace Institute, 1992.

Feuerle, Loie. "Informal Consultations: A Mechanism in Security Council Decision-Making." *New York University Journal of International Law and Politics* 18, no. 1 (Autumn 1985): 267–285.

Fidler, David. P. "Caught Between the Traditions: The Security Council in Philosophical Conundrum." *Michigan Journal of International Law* 17, no. 2 (Winter 1996): 411–453.

Findlay, Trevor. *Cambodia: The Lessons and Legacies of UNTAC.* Stockholm International Peace Research Institute Report no. 9. Oxford: Oxford University Press, 1995.

———, ed. *Challenges for the New Peacekeepers.* Oxford: Oxford University Press, 1996.

Fisas Armangol, Vicenç. *Blue Geopolitics: The United Nations Reform and the Future of the Blue Helmets.* Transnational Institute Series. London: Pluto and Transnational Institute, 1995.

Forsythe, David P. *Human Rights and Peace: International and National Dimensions.* Lincoln: University of Nebraska Press, 1993.

Fortna, Virginia Page. *Regional Organizations and Peacekeeping.* Occasional Paper no. 11. Washington, D.C.: Henry L. Stimson Center, June 1993.

Fox, Gregory H. "International Law and the Entitlement to Democracy After War." *Global Governance* 9, no. 2 (2003).

———. "Strengthening the State." *Indiana Journal of Global Legal Studies* 7, no. 1 (1999).

Fox, Gregory H., and Brad R. Roth. "Democracy and International Law." *Review of International Studies* 27, no. 3 (2001): 327–352.

———, eds. *Democratic Governance and International Law*. Cambridge: Cambridge University Press, 2000.

Franck, Thomas M. *Nation Against Nation: What Happened to the UN Dream and What the U.S. Can Do About It*. New York: Oxford University Press, 1985.

———. *The Power of Legitimacy Among Nations*. New York: Oxford University Press, 1990.

———. *Recourse to Force*. Cambridge: Cambridge University Press, 2002.

———. "Soviet Initiatives, U.S. Responses: New Opportunities for Reviving the United Nations System." *American Journal of International Law* 83 (July 1989): 599–604.

Freudenschuss, Helmut. *Article 39 of the UN Charter Revisited: Threats to the Peace and the Recent Practice of the UN Security Council*. Vienna: Springer-Verlag, 1993.

———. "Between Unilateralism and Collective Security: Authorizations of the Use of Force by the UN Security Council." *European Journal of Public and International Law* 5 no. 4 (1994): 492–531.

Fromuth, Peter. "The Making of a Security Community: The United Nations After the Cold War." *Journal of International Affairs* 46, no. 2 (Winter 1993): 341–366.

Frye, Alton, ed. *Humanitarian Intervention: Crafting a Workable Doctrine*. New York: Council on Foreign Relations, 2000.

Furley, Oliver, and Roy May, eds. *Peacekeeping in Africa*. London: Ashgate, 1998.

Gaja, Giorgio. "Reflexions sur le rôle du Conseil de Sécurité dans le nouvel ordre mondial." *Revue Générale de Droit International Public* 97, no. 2 (1993): 297–320.

Gardam, Judith G. "Legal Restraints on Security Council Military Enforcement Action." *Michigan Journal of International Law* 17, no. 2 (Winter 1996): 285–332.

Garfield, Richard. *The Impact of Economic Sanctions on Health and Well Being*. Relief and Rehabilitation Network Paper no. 31. London: Overseas Development Institute, November 1999.

Garner, Larry. *A New Era of Peacemaking: The United Nations and Elections Monitoring*. Ottawa: Elections Canada, 1993.

Garrett, Stephen A. *Doing Good and Doing Well: An Examination of Humanitarian Intervention*. Westport, Conn.: Praeger, 1999.

Gill, T. D. "Legal and Some Political Limitations on the Power of the UN Security Council to Exercise Its Enforcement Powers Under Chapter VII of the Charter." *Netherlands Yearbook of International Law, 1995*. The Hague: Kluwer, 1995, pp. 33–138.

Ginifer, Jeremy, ed. *Beyond Emergency: Development Within UN Peace Operations*. London: Frank Cass, 1997.

Glass, David S. "The UN Security Council: Perceptions of Bias." *The World Today* 46, no. 12 (December 1994): 217–218.

Glennon, Michael. "Why the Security Council Failed." *Foreign Affairs* 82, no. 3 (May–June 2003): 16–35.

Global Issues Research Group. Foreign and Commonwealth Office. *Research Analysts Memorandum: Table of Vetoed Draft Resolutions in the United Nations Security Council, 1946–1998*. London: Global Issues Research Group, September 1999.

Global Policy Forum. "1994 Conference on Reforming the Security Council." www.globalpolicy.org/security/sonf94/index.htm.

Goldstein, Gordon M. *Leadership, Multilateral Security, and Coercive Cooperation: The Role of the UN Security Council in the Persian Gulf War.* New York: G. M. Goldstein, 1998.

Goodpaster, Andrew J. *When Diplomacy Is Not Enough: Managing Multinational Military Interventions.* Report to the Carnegie Commission on Preventing Deadly Conflict. New York: Carnegie Corporation, 1996.

Goodrich, Leland M. "The U.N. Security Council." *International Organization* 12, no. 3 (Summer 1958).

Goodrich, Leland M., Edvard Hambro, and Anne Patricia Simons. *Charter of the United Nations: Commentary and Documents.* 3rd ed. New York: Columbia University Press, 1969.

Goodrich, Leland Matthew, and Anne P. Simons. *The United Nations and the Maintenance of International Peace and Security.* Washington, D.C.: Brookings Institution, 1955.

Gordenker, Leon. *Thinking About the United Nations System.* John W. Holmes Memorial Lecture Reports and Papers no. 4. Hanover, N.H.: Academic Council on the United Nations System, 1990.

Goulding, Marrack. "The Evolution of UN Peacekeeping." *International Affairs* 69, no. 3 (July 1993): 451–464.

———. *Peacemonger.* London: John Murray, 2002.

———. "The Use of Force by the United Nations." Mountbatten-Tata memorial lecture, University of Southampton, November 23, 1995.

Gow, James, and Christopher Dandecker. "Peace-Support Operations: The Problem of Legitimation." *The World Today* 51, nos. 8–9 (August–September 1995): 48–62.

Gowlland Debbas, Vera. *Collective Responses to Illegal Acts in International Law: UN Action in the Question of Southern Rhodesia.* Dordrecht: Martinus Nijoff, 1990.

———. "The Relationship Between the International Court of Justice and the Security Council in the Light of the Lockerbie Case." *American Journal of International Law* 88, no. 4 (October 1994): 643–677.

———. "Security Council Enforcement Action and Issues of State Responsibility." *International and Comparative Law Quarterly* 43, no. 1 (January 1994): 55–98.

Gray, Christine. *International Law and the Use of Force.* Oxford: Oxford University Press, 2000.

———. "The U.S. *National Security Strategy* and the New 'Bush Doctrine' on Preemptive Self-Defense." *Chinese Journal of International Law* (Boulder) 1, no. 2 (2002): 437–448.

Greenberg, Melanie, John Barton, and Margaret McGuiness. *Word over War: Mediation and Arbitration to Prevent Deadly Conflict.* Lanham, Md.: Rowman & Littlefield, 2000.

Greenstock, Jeremy. *Report to Security Council of Counter-Terrorism Committee.* October 4, 2002.

Greenwood, Christopher. *Humanitarian Intervention: Law and Policy.* Oxford: Oxford University Press, 2001.

———. "Is There a Right to Humanitarian Intervention?" *The World Today* 49, no. 2 (February 1993): 34–40.

Gregg, Robert W. *About Face? The United States and the United Nations.* Boulder: Lynne Rienner, 1993.

Greig, D. W. "Self-Defence and the Security Council: What Does Article 51 Require?" *International and Comparative Law Quarterly* 40, no. 2 (April 1991): 366–402.

Griffin, Michele. "Retrenchment, Reform, and Regionalization: Trends in UN Peace Support Operations." *International Peacekeeping* 6, no. 1 (Spring 1999): 1–31.

Griffin, Michele, and Bruce Jones. "Building Peace Through Transitional Authority: New Directions, Major Challenges." *International Peacekeeping* 7, no. 4 (Winter 2000): 75–90.

Guicherd, Catherine. "International Law and the War in Kosovo." *Survival* 41, no. 2 (Summer 1999): 19–34.

Guillaume, Gilbert. "L'introduction et l'execution dans les ordres juridiques des etats des résolutions du Conseil de Sécurité des Nations Unies prises en vertu du Chapitre VII de la Charte." *Revue Internationale de Droit Comparé* 50, no. 2 (April 1998): 539–550.

Haas, Richard N. "Sanctioning Madness." *Foreign Affairs* 76, no. 2 (November–December 1997): 74–85.

Haberl-Zemljic, Claus Heje, Edward Moxon-Browne, and Arno Truger. *The Training and Preparation of Military and Civilian Peacekeepers.* London: Initiative on Conflict Resolution and Ethnicity, University of Ulster, 1996.

Hagman, Lotta. *Lessons Learned: Peacebuilding in Haiti.* Report of the International Peace Academy, January 23–24, 2002.

Halderman, John W. *The United Nations and the Rule of Law: Charter Development Through the Handling of International Disputes and Situations.* Dobbs Ferry, N.Y.: Oceana, 1966.

Hamburg, David A. *No More Killing Fields.* Lanham, Md.: Rowman & Littlefield, 2003.

Hampson, Fen Osler. *Nurturing Peace: Why Peace Settlements Succeed or Fail.* Washington, D.C.: U.S. Institute of Peace, 1996.

Hannay, David. "The UN's Role in Bosnia Assessed." *Oxford International Review* 7, no. 2 (Spring 1996): 4–11.

Harper, Keith. "Does the United Nations Security Council Have the Competence to Act as Court and Legislature?" *New York University Journal of International Law and Politics* 27, no. 1 (Fall 1994): 103–158.

Hay, Robin. *Civilian Aspects of Peacekeeping: A Summary of Workshop Proceedings.* Ottawa: Canadian Institute for International Peace and Security, 1991.

Heinl, Robert Debs Jr., Nancy Gordon Heinl, and Michael Heinl. *Written in Blood.* Boston: University Press of America, 1996.

Held, David. *Democracy and the New International Order.* London: Institute for Public Policy Research, 1993.

Heldt, Birger, and Peter Wallensteen. "Peacekeeping Operations by the UN and Non-UN Actors, 1948–2000: Two Separate Processes?" Paper presented to the International Studies Association annual convention, Portland, Oreg., February 25–March 1, 2003.

Helms, Jesse. "Saving the UN." *Foreign Affairs* 75, no. 5 (September–October 1996): 1–8.

Henkin, Alice. *Honoring Human Rights and Keeping the Peace: Lessons from Cambodia, El Salvador, and Haiti.* New York: Aspen Institute, 1995.

Herndl, K. *Reflections on the Role, Functions, and Procedures of the Security Council of the United Nations.* Dordrecht: Martinus Nijhoff, 1987.

Higgins, Rosalyn. *The Development of International Law Through the Political Organs of the United Nations.*(Oxford: Oxford University Press, 1963).

Hill, Stephen M. *Peacekeeping and the United Nations.* Aldershot: Dartmouth, 1996.

Hirsch, John L. *Sierra Leone: Diamonds and the Struggle for Democracy.* International Peace Academy Occasional Paper. Boulder: Lynne Rienner, 2001.

———. "War in Sierra Leone." *Survival* 43, no. 3 (Autumn 2001): 149–173.

Hirsch, John L., and Robert Oakley. *Somalia and Operation Restore Hope: Reflections on Peacemaking and Peacekeeping.* Washington, D.C: U.S. Institute of Peace, 1995.

Hiscocks, Richard. *The Security Council: A Study in Adolescence.* London: Longman, 1973.

Hof, Frederic. "A Practical Line: The Line of Withdrawal from Lebanon and Its Potential Applicability to the Golan Heights." *Middle East Journal* 55, no. 1 (Winter 2001): 35–42.

Hoffman, Stanley. "The Politics and Ethics of Military Intervention." *Survival* 37, no. 4 (Winter 1995–1996): 29–51.

Hoffmann, Walter. *United Nations Security Council Reform and Restructuring.* Livingston, N.J.: Center for UN Reform Education, 1994.

Holbrooke, Richard. *To End a War.* New York: Random House, 1998.

Holmes, Kim. "New World Disorder: A Critique of the United Nations." *Journal of International Affairs* 46, no. 2 (Winter 1993): 323–346.

Holzgrefe, J. L., and Robert O. Keohane, eds. *Humanitarian Intervention: Ethical, Legal, and Political Dilemmas.* Cambridge: Cambridge University Press, 2003.

Homonylo, Christina. *Les opérations de maintien de la paix.* Ottawa: Association Canadienne pour les Nations Unies, 1984.

Hopkinson, Nicholas. *Humanitarian Intervention?* Wilton Park Working Paper no. 11. London: HMSO, 1995.

Howard, Lise Morje. "UN Peace Implementation in Namibia: The Causes of Success." *International Peacekeeping* 9, no. 1 (Spring 2002): 99–132.

Howe, Herbert. "Lessons of Liberia: ECOMOG and Regional Peacekeeping." *International Security* 21, no. 3 (Winter 1996): 145–176.

Howe, Jonathan. "The United States and the United Nations in Somalia: The Limits of Involvement." *Washington Quarterly* 18, no. 3 (Summer 1995): 49–62.

Human Rights Watch. *All Our Hopes Are Crushed: Violence and Repression in Western Afghanistan.* New York: Human Rights Watch, 2002.

———. *The Lost Agenda: Human Rights and UN Field Operations.* New York: Human Rights Watch, 1993.

Hume, Cameron. *Ending Mozambique's War.* Washington, D.C.: U.S. Institute of Peace, 1994.

———. *Negotiation Before Peacekeeping.* International Peace Academy Occasional Paper no. 5. New York: International Peace Academy, 1991.

———. "The Secretary-General's Representatives." *SAIS Review* 15, no. 2 (Summer–Autumn 1995): 75–90.

———. *The United Nations, Iran, and Iraq: How Peacemaking Changed.* Bloomington: University of Indiana Press, 1994.

Huntington, Samuel. *The Third Wave: Democratization in the Late Twentieth Century.* Norman: University of Oklahoma Press, 1991.

Hurd, Ian. "Legitimacy, Power, and the Symbolic Life of the UN Security Council." *Global Governance* 8, no. 1 (January 2002): 35–52.

Ignatieff, Michael. *Blood and Belonging.* New York: Penguin Books, 1993.

———. "Human Rights, the Laws of War and Terrorism." Dankwart Rustow memorial lecture, University of New York Graduate Center, October 10, 2002.

———. "Intervention and State Failure." *Dissent* (Winter 2002), p. 115–130.

Ikenberry, John. *After Victory: Institutions, Strategic Restraint, and the Rebuilding of Order After Major Wars.* Princeton: Princeton University Press, 2001.

Independent International Commission on Kosovo. *Kosovo Report.* Oxford: Oxford University Press, 2000.

Independent Working Group on the Future of the United Nations. *The United Nations in Its Second Half-Century.* New Haven, Conn.: Yale University Press, 1995.

International Commission on Intervention and State Sovereignty. *The Responsibility to Protect.* Ottawa: International Development Research Center, 2001.

Jackson, Robert. *The Global Covenant: Human Conduct in a World of States.* Oxford: Oxford University Press, 2000.

Jensen, Erik. "The United Nations Security Council: Action and Inaction." *Cambridge Review of International Affairs* 8, no. 1 (Spring 1994): 8–22.

Jentleson, Bruce W., ed. *Opportunities Missed and Opportunities Seized: Preventive Diplomacy in the Post–Cold War World.* Lanham, Md.: Rowman & Littlefield, 2000.

Jhabak, Kasturchand M. *The Emerging Role of Security Council as an Instrument of International Peace.* Hyderabad, India: Osmania University Press, 1982.

Johansen, Robert C. "The Future of United Nations Peacekeeping and Enforcement: A Framework for Policymaking." *Global Governance* 2, no. 3 (September–December 1996): 299–333.

———. "The United Nations After the Gulf War: Lessons for Collective Security." *World Policy Journal* 8, no. 3 (Summer 1991): 561–574.

Jonah, James O. C. *Differing State Perspective on the United Nations in the Post–Cold War World.* John W. Holmes Memorial Lecture Reports and Papers no. 4. Providence, R.I.: Academic Council on the United Nations System, 1993.

Jones, Bruce D. *Peacemaking in Rwanda: The Dynamics of Failure.* Boulder: Lynne Rienner, 2001.

Kahng, Tae Jin. *Law, Politics, and the Security Council: An Inquiry into the Handling of Legal Questions Involved in International Disputes and Situations.* 2nd ed. The Hague: Martinus Nijhoff, 1969.

Kaplan, Robert D. *Balkan Ghosts.* New York: St. Martin's, 1993.

Karaosmanoglu, Ali L. *Les actions militaires coercitives et non coercitives des Nations Unies.* Geneva: Librairie Droz, 1970.

Karp, Candace. *U.S. Policy Towards Jerusalem and the Occupied Arab Territories, 1948 and 1967.* Jerusalem: PASSIA, 2001.

Katjavivi, Peter. *A History of Resistance in Namibia.* London: Currey, 1988.

Kaufman, Chaim. "Intervention in Ethnic and Ideological Civil Wars." *Security Studies* 6, no. 1 (1996): 62–104.

Kaufmann, Johan, Dick Leurdijk, and Nico Schrijver. *The World in Turmoil: Testing the UN's Capacity.* Hanover, N.H.: Academic Council on the United Nations System, 1991.

Kavanagh, John J. "U.S. War Powers and the UN Security Council." *Boston College International and Comparative Law Review* 20, no. 1 (Winter 1997): 159–187.

Keller, Edmond J., and Donald Rothchild, eds. *Africa in the New International Order.* Boulder: Lynne Rienner, 1996.

Keller, Gabriel. "La France et le Conseil de Sécurité." *Trimestre du Monde* no. 20 (4th Quarter 1992): 41–51.

Kennedy, Paul, and Bruce Russett. "Reforming the United Nations." *Foreign Affairs* 74, no. 5 (September–October 1995): 56–71.

Khadiagala, Gilbert, and Terrence Lyons, eds. *African Foreign Policies*. Boulder: Lynne Rienner, 2001.

Khan, Shaharyar. *The Shallow Graves of Rwanda*. London: I. B. Tauris, 2000.

Khor, Martain, and Chin Oy Sim. *Security Council Reform and Democratization: An Overview*. Geneva: International NGO Network on Global Governance and Democratization of International Relations, 1994.

Kirgis, Frederic L. "Security Council Governance of Postconflict Societies: A Plea for Good Faith and Informed Decision Making." *American Journal of International Law* 95, no. 3 (July 2001): 579–582.

———. "The Security Council's First Fifty Years." *American Journal of International Law* 89, no. 3 (July 1995): 506–539.

Kirsch, Philippe. *The Changing Role of the Security Council*. New York: Ralph Bunche Institute on the United Nations, 1990.

Kissinger, Henry. *Does America Need a Foreign Policy? Toward a Diplomacy for the Twenty-First Century*. New York: Simon & Schuster, 2001.

Klare, Michael, and Yogesh Chandrani, eds. *World Security: Challenges for a New Century*. 3rd ed. New York: St. Martin's, 1998.

Klare, Michael T., and Daniel C. Thomas. *World Security: Challenges for a New Century*. New York: St. Martin's, 1994.

Klinghofer, Arthur Jay. *The International Dimension of Genocide in Rwanda*. New York: New York University Press, 1998.

Knight, W. Andy, and Keith Krause, eds. *State, Society, and the UN System: Changing Perspectives on Multilateralism*. Tokyo: United Nations University Press, 1995.

Köchler, Hans. *The Voting Procedure in the United Nations Security Council: Examining a Normative Contradiction in the UN Charter and Its Consequences on International Relations*. Vienna: International Progress Organization, 1991.

Korn, David A. *The Making of United Nations Security Council Resolution 242: Centerpiece of Arab-Israeli Negotiations*. Wahington, D.C.: Georgetown University, Institute for the Study of Diplomacy, 1992.

Krasner, Stephen D. *Sovereignty: Organized Hypocrisy*. Princeton: Princeton University Press, 1999.

Kühne, Winrich. "The Security Council and the G8 in the New Millennium: Who Is in Charge of International Peace and Security?" Stiftung Wissenschaft und Politik 5th international workshop, Berlin, June 30–July 1, 2000.

———, ed. *Winning the Peace: Concept and Lessons Learned of Post-Conflict Peacebuilding*. Ebenhausen: Stiftung Wissenschaft und Politik, 1996.

Kumar, Krishna, ed. *Postconflict Elections, Democratization, and International Assistance*. Boulder: Lynne Rienner, 1998.

Kuperman, Alan J. *The Limits of Humanitarian Intervention*. Washington, D.C.: Brookings Institution, 2001.

———. "Rwanda in Retrospect." *Foreign Affairs* 79, no. 1 (January–February 2000): 94–118.

La crise d'Haïti, 1991–1996/Sous la direction d'Yves Daudet. Paris: Montchrestien, 1996.

Lall, Arthur S. *The Security Council in a Universal United Nations*. Occasional Paper no. 11. New York: Carnegie Endowment for International Peace, 1971.

———. *The UN and the Middle East Crisis, 1967*. New York: Columbia University Press, 1968.

Landsberg, Chris. "Another Debate on Order? Restructuring the United Nations

Security Council" *ISSUP Bulletin,* March 1995. Pretoria: Universiteit van Pretoria, Institute for Strategic Studies, 1995.

Laurenti, Jeffrey. *Reforming the Security Council: What American Interests?* New York: UNA-USA, 1997.

Lauterpacht, Eli. "Sovereignty: Myth or Reality?" *International Affairs* 73, no. 1 (January 1997): 137–139.

le Peillet, Pierre. *Les bérets bleus de l'ONU: À travers 40 ans de conflit israélo-arabe.* Paris: Éditions France-Empire, 1988.

Leclercq, Claude. *L'ONU et l'affaire du Congo.* Paris: Payot, 1964.

Lee, John M., Robert von Pagenhardt, and Timothy W. Stanley. *To Unite Our Strength: Enhancing the United Nations Peace and Security System.* Lanham, Md.: University Press of America, 1992.

Legault, Albert, Craig N. Murphy, and W. B. Ofuatey-Kodjoe. *The State of the United Nations, 1992.* Providence, R.I.: Academic Council on the United Nations System, 1992.

Lelièvre, Michel. *Sur le chemin de la paix: Avec l'ONU au Salvador.* Paris: Desclée de Brouwer, 1995.

Leprette, J. "Le Conseil de Sécurité comme organe de sécurité collective." *Relations Internationales* no. 86 (Summer 1996): 109–118.

Lesser, Ian O., Bruce Hoffman, John Arquilla, David F. Ronfeldt, Michele Zanini, and Brian Michael Jenkins. *Countering the New Terrorism.* Santa Monica, Calif.: RAND, 1999.

"Libya, the ICJ, and the Security Council." *Middle East International* no. 50 (1998): 18.

Lindenberg, Marc, and Coralie Bryant. *Going Global: Transforming Relief and Development NGOs.* Bloomfield, Conn.: Kumarian, 2001.

Litwak, Robert S. "The New Calculus of Pre-emption." *Survival* 44, no. 4 (Winter 2002–2003): 53–79.

Liu, F. T. *United Nations Peacekeeping and the Non-Use of Force.* Boulder: Lynne Rienner, 1992.

Lobel, Jules, and Ratner, Michael. "Bypassing the Security Council: Ambiguous Authorizations to Use Force, Cease-Fires, and the Iraqi Inspection Regime." *American Journal of International Law* 93, no. 1 (January 1999): 124–154.

Lombardo, Caroline E. "The Making of an Agenda for Democratization." *Chicago Journal of International Law* 2 (2001): 253.

Luck, Edward C. *Mixed Messages: American Politics and International Organization, 1919–1999.* Washington, D.C.: Brookings Institution, 1999.

———. "Security Council Reform: From the Bottom Up." Paper delivered at the conference on "The United Nations Reform at Fifty: A Trilateral Perspective," Fukuoka University, November 11–12, 1995.

Luck, Edward C., and T. T. Gatti. "Whose Collective Security?" *Washington Quarterly* 15, no. 2 (Spring 1992): 43–56.

Luck, Edward C., Jean Krasno, and Roseann Iacomacci, eds. *Reforming the United Nations: Lessons from a History in Progress.* International Relations Studies. New York: Academic Council on the United Nations System, 2003.

Luttwak, Edward. "Kofi's Rule: Humanitarian Intervention and Neocolonialism." *The National Interest* no. 58 (Winter 1999–2000): 60.

Lyons, Gene M., and James Mayall, ed. *International Human Rights in the Twenty-First Century.* Lanham, Md.: Rowman & Littlefield, 2003.

MacFarlane, Neil S. *Intervention in Contemporary World Politics.* Adelphi Paper no. 350. Oxford: Oxford University Press, 2002.

MacFarlane, Neil S., and Thomas G. Weiss. "Regional Organizations and Regional Security." *Security Studies* 2, no. 1 (Autumn 1992): 6–37.

MacKinlay, John. *Globalisation and Insurgency.* Adelphi Paper no. 352. Oxford: Oxford University Press, 2002.

MacKinlay, John, and Jarat Chopra. "Second Generation Multinational Operations." *Washington Quarterly* 15, no. 3 (Summer 1992): 113–134.

MacKinnon, Michael G. *The Evolution of U.S. Peacekeeping Policy Under Clinton: A Fairweather Friend?* London: Frank Cass, 2000.

Macrae, Joanna, ed. *The New Humanitarianisms: A Review of Trends in Global Humanitarian Action.* HPG Report no. 11. London: Overseas Development Institute, 2002.

Makinda, Samuel M. "Sovereignty and International Security: Challenges for the United Nations." *Global Governance* 2, no. 2 (May–August 1996): 149–168.

Malone, David M. *Decision-Making in the UN Security Council: The Case of Haiti, 1990–1997.* Oxford: Clarendon, 1998.

———. "Eyes on the Prize: The Quest for Non-Permanent Seats on the UN Security Council." *Global Governance* 6, no. 1 (January–March 2000): 3–24.

———. "Goodbye UNSCOM: A Sorry Tale in U.S.-UN Relations." *Security Dialogue* 30, no. 4 (December 1999): 393–412.

———. "Le Conseil de Sécurité dans les années 90: Essor et recession?" *Politique Étrangère* 65, no. 2 (Summer 2000): 403–422.

———. "Review Essay: The Greatest Threat: Iraq, Weapons of Mass Destruction, and the Crisis of Global Security" (by Richard Butler). *American Journal of International Law* 95, no. 1 (January 2001): 235–245.

———. "The Security Council and the Future of UN Peacekeeping." *Oxford International Review* 7, no. 2 (Spring 1996): 23–29.

———. "The UN Security Council in the Post–Cold War World: 1987–97." *Security Dialogue* 28, no. 4 (December 1997): 393–408.

Malone, David M., and Yuen Foong Khong. *Unilateralism and U.S. Foreign Policy: International Perspectives.* Center on International Cooperation Studies in Multilateralism. Boulder: Lynne Rienner, 2003.

Malone, David M., and Ramesh Thakur. "UN Peacekeeping: Lessons Learned?" *Global Governance* 7, no. 1 (Spring 2001): 11–17.

Mamdani, Mahmood. *When Victims Become Killers: Colonialism, Nativism, and the Genocide in Rwanda.* Princeton: Princeton University Press, 2001.

Marker, Jamsheed. *Quiet Diplomacy: A Personal Memoir of the East Timor Negotiations.* Forthcoming.

Martin, Ian. *Self-Determination in East Timor: The United Nations, the Ballot, and International Intervention.* International Peace Academy Occasional Paper. Boulder: Lynne Rienner, 2001.

Martin, Lawrence. "Peacekeeping as a Growth Industry." *The National Interest* no. 32 (Summer 1993): 3–11.

Marton, Kati. *A Death in Jerusalem: The Assassination by Extremists of the First Middle East Peacemaker.* New York: Pantheon, 1994.

Matanle, Emma. *The UN Security Council: Prospects for Reform.* London: Royal Institute of International Affairs, 1995.

Mayall, James, ed. *The New Interventionism, 1991–94.* Cambridge: Cambridge University Press, 1996.

Mays, Terry M. *Historical Dictionary of Multinational Peacekeeping.* International Organizations Series no. 9. Lanham, Md.: Scarecrow, 1996.

McCarthy, Patrick A. "Positionality, Tension, and Instability in the UN Security Council." *Global Governance* 3, no. 2 (May–August 1997): 147–170.

McDermott, Anthony. *United Nations Financing Problems and the New Generation of Peacekeeping and Peace Enforcement.* Watson Insitute Occasional Paper no. 16. Providence, R.I.: Watson Insitute, January 1994.

McRae, Rob, and Don Hubert, eds. *Human Security and the New Diplomacy.* Montreal: McGill-Queen's University Press, 2001.

Mearsheimer, John J. "The False Promise of International Institutions." *International Security* 19, no. 3 (Winter 1994–1995): 5–49.

Melvern, Linda R. *A People Betrayed: The Role of the West in Rwanda's Genocide.* London: Zed Books, 2000.

———. "Security Council: Behind Closed Doors." *The World Today* 56, no. 8 (August–September 2000): 9–11.

———. "The Security Council: Behind the Scenes." *International Affairs* (London) 77, no. 1 (January 2001): 101–111.

Mfume, Kwesi. *No Free Ride: From the Mean Streets to the Mainstream.* New York: One World–Balantine Books, 1996.

Mills, Nicolaus, and Kira Brunner, eds. *The New Killing Fields: Massacre and the Politics of Intervention.* New York: Basic Books, 2002.

Minear, Larry. *The Humanitarian Enterprise: Dilemmas and Discoveries.* Bloomfield, Conn.: Kumarian, 2002.

Minear, Larry, and Thomas G. Weiss. *Humanitarian Action in Times of War: A Handbook for Practitioners.* Boulder: Lynne Rienner, 1993.

Minear, Larry, et al. *Toward More Humane and Effective Sanctions Management: Enhancing the Capacity of the United Nations System.* Occasional Paper no. 31. Providence, R.I.: Thomas J. Watson Jr. Institute for International Studies, Brown University, 1998.

Mingst, Karen, and Margaret P. Karns, *The United Nations in the Post–Cold War Era.* 2nd ed. Boulder: Westview, 2000.

———. eds. *The United States and Multilateral Institutions: Patterns of Changing Instrumentality and Influence.* Boston: Unwin Hyman, 1990.

Moore, Jonathan, ed. *Hard Choices: Moral Dilemmas in Humanitarian Intervention.* Lanham, Md.: Rowman & Littlefield, 1998.

Morikawa, Koichi, and Ryo Yamamoto. "National Implementation of United Nations Security Council Resolutions (1990–1998)." *Japanese Annual of International Law* no. 42 (1999): 66–89.

Morillon, Philippe. *Croire et oser: Chronique de Sarajevo.* Paris: B. Grasset, 1993.

Morphet, Sally. "China as a Permanent Member of the Security Council: October 1971–December 1999." *Security Dialogue* 31, no. 1 (June 2000): 151–166.

———. "Resolutions and Vetos in the UN Security Council: Their Relevance and Significance." *Review of International Studies* 16, no. 4 (October 1990): 341–359.

Morris, Justin. "Democracy, Intervention, and the Legitimacy of the Use of Force." Draft paper presented to the British International Studies Association annual conference, Durham, December 1996.

———. "UN Security Council Reform: A Counsel for the Twenty-First Century." *Security Dialogue* 31, no. 3 (September 2000): 265–278.

Morris, Justin, and Hilaire McCoubrey. "Regional Peacekeeping in the Post–Cold War Era." *International Peacekeeping* 6, no. 2 (Summer 1999):129–151.

Moss, Glen, and Ingrid Obery, eds. *South Africa Contemporary Analysis.* London: Hans Zell, 1989.

Mouterde, Pierre, and Christophe Wargny. *Apre Bal, Tambou Lou.* Paris: Austral, 1996.

Muldoon, James P., ed. *Multilateral Diplomacy and the UN Today.* Boulder: Westview, 1999.

Murphy, George J. *International Quick Response Forces.* Newport, R.I.: Naval War College, 1994.

Murphy, Sean D. "The Security Council, Legitimacy and the Concept of Collective Security After the Cold War." *Columbia Journal of Transnational Law* 32, no. 2 (1994): 252–269.

Murthy, C. S. R. "Change and Continuity in the Functioning of the Security Council Since the End of the Cold War." *International Studies* 32, no. 4 (October–December 1995): 423–440.

———. "Reforming the UN Security Council: An Asian View." *South Asian Survey* 5, no. 1 (January–June 1998): 113–124.

Naidu, Mumulla Venkat Rao. *Collective Security and the United Nations: A Definition of the UN Security System.* New York: St. Martin's, 1975.

National Democratic Institute for International Affairs. *Nation-Building: The UN and Namibia.* Washington, D.C.: National Democratic Institute for International Affairs, 1990.

National Security Strategy of the United States. Ref. UA U492. Washington, D.C.: U.S. Government Printing Office, January 1993.

Negash, Tekeste, and Kjetil Tronvoll. *Brothers at War: Making Sense of the Eritrean-Ethiopian War.* Oxford: James Currey, 2000.

Nelson, C. G. "Revisionism and the Security Council Veto." *International Organization* 28, no. 3 (March 1974): 539–555.

Nelson, Richard W. "Multinational Peacekeeping in the Middle East and the United Nations Model." *International Affairs* 6, no. 1 (Winter 1984–1985): 67–89.

Neuhaus, M. F. K. "The United Nations' Security Role at Fifty: The Need for Realism." *Australian Journal of International Affairs* 49, no. 2 (November 1995): 267–282.

Nicol, Davidson. "The Gulf Crisis Politics and Policy Making at the UN Security Council." *Cambridge Review of International Affairs* 8, no. 1 (Spring 1994): 23–39.

———. "Post–Cold War Diplomacy at the United Nations Security Council." *Cambridge Review of International Affairs* 5, no. 1 (Spring 1991): 11–20.

———. *The Security Council and Its Presidency.* New York: Pergamon, 1981.

Nolte, Georg. "Combined Peacekeeping: ECOMOG and UNOMIL." *International Peacekeeping* 1, no. 2 (March–May 1994): 42–45.

Novosseloff, Alexandra. *Le Conseil de Sécurité de l'ONU et la maîtrise de la force armée: Dialectique du politique et du militaire en matière de paix et de sécurité internationale.* Paris: Éditions Bruylant, 2003.

Nye, Joseph S. Jr. *The Paradox of American Power: Why the World's Only Superpower Can't Go It Alone.* Oxford: Oxford University Press, 2002.

———. "Redefining the National Interest." *Foreign Affairs* 78, no. 4 (July–August 1999): 23-35.

Oakley, Robert, and David Bentley. "Peace Operations: A Comparison of Somalia and Haiti." *Strategic Forum* no. 30 (May 1995): 443–446.

O'Brien, Terence. *The United Nations: Legacy and Reform.* Center for Strategic Studies Working Paper no. 6/97. Wellington, New Zealand: Center for Strategic Studies, 1997.

Odera, Josephine, and Paul Omach, eds. *Eastern Africa's Security Challenges.* Boulder: Lynne Rienner, forthcoming.

Off, Carol. *The Iron, the Fox, and the Eagle.* Toronto: Random House Canada, 2000.

Olonisakin, Funmi. "UN Co-operation with Regional Organizations in Peacekeeping." *International Peacekeeping* 3, no. 3 (Autumn 1996): 33–51.

Olsson, Louise. *Gendering UN Peacekeeping: Mainstreaming a Gender Perspective in Multidimensional Peacekeeping.* Uppsala, Sweden: Uppsala University, Department of Peace and Conflict Research, 1999.

O'Neill, Barry. "Power and Satisfaction in the UN Security Council." *Journal of Conflict Resolution* 40, no. 2 (June 1996): 219–237.

O'Neill, William G. *Kosovo: An Unfinished Peace.* Boulder: Lynne Rienner, 2002.

Orbach, William W. *To Keep the Peace: The United Nations Condemnatory Resolution.* Lexington: Kentucky University Press, 1977.

Organization of African Unity (OAU). International Panel of Eminent Personalities to Investigate the 1994 Genocide in Rwanda and the Surrounding Events. *Rwanda: The Preventable Failure.* Addis Ababa, Ethiopia: OAU, 2000.

Organski, A. *The Veto as Viewed by the United States and the Soviet Union.* New York: New York University Press, 1951.

O'Shea, Brendan. *Crisis at Bihac: Bosnia's Bloody Battlefield.* Gloucestershire: Sutton, 1998.

Osterdahl, Inger. *Threat to the Peace: The Interpretation by the Security Council of Article 39 of the UN Charter.* Studies in International Law, vol. 13. Uppsala, Sweden: Iustus Forlag, 1998.

Otunnu, Olara. "Préserver la légitimité de l'action des Nations Unies." *Politique Étrangère* no. 3 (Autumn 1993): 597–619.

Otunnu, Olara, and Michael Doyle, eds. *Peacemaking and Peacekeeping for the New Century.* Lanham, Md.: Rowman & Littlefield, 1998.

Padelford, N. J. "Politics and Change in the Security Council." *International Organization* 14, no. 1 (Summer 1960): 381–401.

Palin, Roger H. *Multinational Forces: Problems and Prospects.* Adelphi Paper no. 294. London: International Institute for Strategic Studies, 1995.

Paquin, Lyonel. *Révélations: Le rôle de l'ONU dans les éléctions de 1990 en Haïti.* Miami, Fla.: Libreri Mapou, 1992.

Paris, Roland. "Blue Helmets Blues: The End of the UN as a Security Organization?" *Washington Quarterly* 20, no. 1 (Winter 1997): 191–206.

Parry, Matthew S. "Pyrrhic Victories and the Collapse of Humanitarian Principles." *Journal of Humanitarian Assistance* (October 2002), www.jha.ac/articles/a094.htm, p. 4.

Parsons, Anthony. *From Cold War to Hot Peace: UN Interventions 1947–1994.* London: Penguin, 1994.

———. *The Security Council: An Uncertain Future.* London: David Davies Memorial Institute, 1994.

Pastor, Robert A. "The Clinton Administration and the Americas: The Postwar Rhythm and Blues." *Journal of Interamerican Studies and World Affairs* 38, no. 4 (Winter 1996): 99–128.

Patil, Anjali V. *The Veto: A Historical Necessity, 1946–2001—A Comprehensive Record of the Use of the Veto in the UN Security Council.* New York: A. V. Patil, 2001.

Patrick, Stewart, and Shepard Forman, eds. *Multilateralism and U.S. Foreign Policy: Ambivalent Engagement.* Boulder: Lynne Rienner, 2002.

Paul, James A. *The Arria Formula.* New York: Global Policy Forum, 2001. www.globalpolicy.org/security/mtgsetc/arria.htm.

Paul, James A. *Security Council Reform: Arguments About the Future of the United Nations System.* New York: Global Policy Forum, 1995.

Peck, Connie. *The United Nations as a Dispute Settlement System: Improving Mechanisms for the Prevention and Resolution of Conflict.* The Hague: Kluwer, 1996.

Pérez de Cuéllar, Javier. *Pilgrimage for Peace.* New York: St Martin's, 1997.

————. "Reflecting on the Past and Contemplating the Future." *Global Governance* 1, no. 2 (May–August 1995): 149–170.

Perry, Michael J. *The Idea of Human Rights: Four Inquiries.* New York: Oxford University Press, 1998.

Picco, Giandomenico. "New Entente After September 11th? U.S., Russia, China, and India." *Global Governance* 9, no. 1 (January–March 2003).

————. "The UN and the Use of Force: Leaving the Secretary-General Out of It." *Foreign Affairs* 72, no. 5 (September–October 1994): 14–18.

Pienaar, Sara. *South Africa and International Relations Between the Two World Wars.* Johannesburg: Witwatersrand University Press, 1987.

Pitt, William Rivers, and Scott Ritter. *War on Iraq.* New York: Context Books, 2002.

Pogany, I. S. *The Security Council and the Arab-Israeli Conflict.* Aldershot: Gower, 1984.

Powell, Colin. *My American Journey.* New York: Random House, 1995.

Power, Samantha. *"A Problem from Hell": America and the Age of Genocide.* New York: Basic Books, 2002.

Prantl, Jochen, and Jean Krasno. *Informal Ad Hoc Groupings of States and the Workings of the United Nations.* ACUNS Occasional Papers no 3. New Haven, Conn.: ACUNS, 2002.

Prins, Gwyn. *The Applicability of the "NATO Model" to UN Peace Support Operations Under the Security Council.* New York: UNA-USA, 1996.

————. "Global Security and Military Intervention." *Security Dialogue* 27, no. 1 (Spring 1996): 77–89.

————, ed. *Understanding Unilateralism in American Foreign Relations.* London: Royal Institute for International Affairs, 2000.

Prunier, Gérard. *The Rwanda Crisis: History of a Genocide.* New York: Columbia University Press, 1995.

Pugh, Michael, ed. *The UN, Peace, and Force.* London: Frank Cass, 1997.

Quandt, William. "Clinton and the Arab-Israeli Conflict: The Limits of Incrementalism." *Journal of Palestine Studies* 30, no. 2 (Winter 2001): 26–40.

————. *Peace Process: American Diplomacy and the Arab-Israeli Conflict Since 1967.* Rev. ed. Washington, D.C. Brookings Institution, 2001.

Queneudec, Jean Pierre. "A propos de la composition du Conseil de Sécurité." *Revue Générale de Droit International Public* 99, no. 4 (1995): 955–960.

Quigley, John. "The 'Privatization' of Security Council Enforcement Action: A Threat to Multilateralism." *Michigan Journal of International Law* 17, no. 2 (Winter 1996): 249–284.

————. "The United Nations Security Council: Promethean Protector or Helpless Hostage?" *Texas International Law Journal* 35 (Spring 2000): 129–172.

Ramcharan, Bertrand G. *The Security Council and the Protection of Human Rights.* International Studies in Human Rights vol. 75. The Hague: Kluwer, 2002.

Ramsbotham, Oliver. "Reflections on UN Post-Settlement Peacebuilding." *International Peacekeeping* 7, no. 1 (Spring 2000): 169–189.

Ramsbotham, Oliver, and Tom Woodhouse. *Encyclopedia of International Peacekeeping Operations.* Santa Barbara, Calif.: ABC-CLIO, 1999.

Ratner, Steven R. "Does International Law Matter in Preventing Ethnic Conflict?" *New York University Journal of International Law and Politics* 32 (2000): 591–698.

———. *The New UN Peacekeeping: Building Peace in Lands of Conflict After the Cold War.* New York: St. Martin's, 1995.

Reichberg, Gregory, and Henrik Syse. "Humanitarian Intervention: A Case of Offensive Force?" *Security Dialogue* 33, no. 3 (September 2002): 309–322.

Reindorp, Nicola, and Peter Wiles. *Humanitarian Coordination: Lessons from Recent Experience.* London: Overseas Development Institute, 2001.

Reinisch, August. "Developing Human Rights and Humanitarian Law Accountability of the Security Council for the Imposition of Economic Sanctions." *American Journal of International Law* 95, no. 4 (October 2001): 851–872.

Reisman, W. Michael. "Assessing Claims to Revise the Laws of War." *American Journal of International Law* 97, no. 1 (January 2003): 82–91.

———. "International Lawmaking: A Process of Communication." *American Society of International Law Proceedings* 75 (1981).

Renner, Michael. *Remaking U.N. Peacekeeping: U.S. Policy and Real Reform.* Washington, D.C.: National Commission for Economic Conversion and Disarmament, 1995.

Renwick, Robin. *Economic Sanctions.* Cambridge, Mass.: Center for International Affairs, 1981.

Rieff, David. *A Bed for the Night: Humanitarianism in Crisis.* New York: Simon & Schuster, 2002.

Rigby, Vincent. *Elections Observer Teams: International Sponsors.* Ottawa: Library of Parliament Research Branch, 1992.

Righter, Rosemary. *Utopia Lost: The United Nations and World Order.* New York: Twentieth Century Fund, 1995.

Risse, Thomas, Stephen C. Ropp, and Kathryn Sikkink, eds. *The Power of Human Rights: International Norms and Domestic Change.* Cambridge: Cambridge University Press, 1999.

Rittberger, Volker, Franz Knipping, and Hans von Mangoldt, eds. *The United Nations System and Its Predecessors: Statutes and Legal Acts/Das System der Vereinten Nationen und seine Vorläufer: Satzungen und Rechtsakte.* 2 vols. Munich: C. H. Beck 1995/1996.

Rittberger, Volker, Martin Mogler, and Bernhard Zangl. *Vereinte Nationen und Weltordnung: Zivilisierung der internationalen Politik?* Opladen: Leske & Budrich, 1997.

Rivlin, Benjamin. "Regional Arrangements for Collective Security and Conflict Resolution: A New Road Ahead?" *International Relations* 11, no. 2 (August 1992): 95–110.

———. *UN Reform from the Standpoint of the United States: A Presentation Made at the United Nations University on 25 September 1995, Tokyo, Japan.* UN University Lectures no. 11. Tokyo: United Nations University Press, 1996.

Rivlin, Benjamin, and Leon Gordenker, eds. *The Challenging Role of the UN Secretary-General: Making "the Most Impossible Job in the World" Possible.* Westport, Conn.: Praeger, 1993.

Roberts, Adam. "Communal Conflict as a Challenge to International Organization: The Case of Former Yugoslavia." *Review of International Studies* 21, no. 4 (1995): 389–410.

———. "From San Francisco to Sarajevo: The UN and the Use of Force." *Survival* 37, no. 4 (Winter 1995–1996): 7–28.

———. *Humanitarian Action in War.* Adelphi Paper no. 305. London: Brassey's for the International Institute of Strategic Studies, 1996.

———. "Humanitarian War: Military Intervention and Human Rights." *International Affairs* 69, no. 3 (July 1993): 429–449.

———. "Law and the Use of Force After Iraq." *Survival* 45, no. 2 (Summer 2003).

———. "The Role of Humanitarian Issues in International Politics in the 1990s." *International Review of the Red Cross 81* no. 833 (March 1999): 19–43.

———. "The United Nations and International Security." *Survival* 35, no. 2 (Summer 1993): 3–30.

Roberts, Adam, and Benedict Kingsbury. *Presiding over a Divided World: Changing UN Roles, 1945–1993.* International Peace Academy Occasional Paper. Boulder: Lynne Rienner, 1994.

———, eds. *United Nations, Divided World: The UN's Roles in International Relations.* 2nd ed. Oxford: Clarendon, 1993.

Roberts, Ken. "Second-Guessing the Security Council: The International Court of Justice and Its Powers of Judicial Review." *Pace International Law Review* 7, no. 2 (Spring 1995): 285–327.

Rochester, J. Martin. *Waiting for the Millennium: The United Nations and the Future of World Order.* Studies in International Relations. Columbia: University of South Carolina Press, 1993.

Ronayne, Peter, and Joel H. Rosenthal. *Never Again? The United States and the Prevention and Punishment of Genocide Since the Holocaust.* Lanham, Md.: Rowman & Littlefield, 2001.

Roper, J., M. Nishihara, O. Otunnu, and E. Schoettle, eds. *Keeping the Peace in the Post–Cold War Era: Strengthening Multilateral Peacekeeping.* New York: Trilateral Commission, 1993.

Rosenau, James N. *The United Nations in a Turbulent World.* International Peace Academy Occasional Paper. Boulder: Lynne Rienner, 1992.

Rossman, James E. "Article 43: Arming the United Nations Security Council." *New York University Journal of International Law and Politics* 27, no. 1 (Fall 1994): 227–264.

Rotberg, Robert I. "Failed States in a World of Terror." *Foreign Affairs* 81, no. 4 (July–August 2002): 127–140.

———, ed. *State Failure and State Weakness in a Time of Terror.* Washington, D.C.: Brookings Institution, 2003.

Rotfeld, Adam Daniel. *"Armaments, Disarmament and International Security." Stockholm International Peace Research Institute Yearbook, 2001.* Oxford: Oxford University Press, 2001.

Ruggie, John G. "Peacekeeping and U.S. Interests." *Washington Quarterly* 17, no. 4 (Autumn, 1994): 161–173.

———. *The United Nations and the Collective Use of Force: Wither or Whether?* New York: UNA-USA, 1996.

———. *Winning the Peace: America and World Order in the New Era.* New York: Columbia University Press, 1996.

Russett, Bruce M., ed. *The Once and Future Security Council.* New York: St. Martin's, 1997.

Russett, Bruce M., Barry O'Neill, and James Sutterlin. "Breaking the Security Council Restructuring Logjam." *Global Governance* 2, no. 1 (January–April 1996): 65–80.

Russett, Bruce M., and James Sutterlin. "The UN in a New World Order." *Foreign Affairs* 70, no. 2 (1991): 69–83.

Saksena, Krishan Prasad. *Reforming the United Nations: The Challenge of Relevance.* Newbury Park, Calif.: Sage, 1993.

———. *The United Nations and Collective Security, 1945–1964: A Historical Analysis.* New York: New York University Press, 1971.

Sarooshi, Danesh. *The United Nations and the Development of Collective Security: The Delegation by the UN Security Council of Its Chapter VII Powers.* Oxford: Clarendon, 2000.

Schachter, Oscar. "United Nations Law in the Gulf Conflict." *American Journal of International Law* 85, no. 3 (1991): 452–473.

Schachter, Oscar, and Christopher C. Joiner, eds. *United Nations Legal Order.* 2 vols. Cambridge: Cambridge University Press, 1995.

Schmidt, Peter. "A Complex Puzzle: The EU's Security Policy and UN Reform." *International Spectator* 29, no. 3 (July 1994): 53–66.

Schoenberg, Harris O. *War No More! A Concrete Action Plan to Revitalize the United Nations Security Council.* New York: Center for Public Policy, 1995.

Schulz, Donald E., and Marcella Gabriel. *Reconciling the Irreconcilable: The Troubled Outlook for U.S. Policy Toward Haiti.* Washington, D.C.: Strategic Studies Institute, U.S. Army War College, 1994.

Schulze, Kirsten. 2001. "Camp David and the Al-Aqsa Intifada: An Assessment of the State of the Israeli-Palestinian Peace Process, July–December 2001." *Studies in Conflict and Terrorism* 24, no. 3 (May–June 2001): 215–233.

Schwebel, Stephen M. "The Roles of the Security Council and the International Court of Justice in the Application of International Humanitarian Law." *New York University Journal of International Law and Politics* 27, no. 4 (Summer 1995): 731–760.

Schweigman, David. *The Authority of the Security Council Under Chapter VII of the UN Charter: Legal Limits and the Role of the International Court of Justice.* London: Kluwer, 2001.

Seara-Vazquez, Modesto. "The UN Security Council at Fifty: Midlife Crisis or Terminal Illness?" *Global Governance* 1, no. 3 (September–December 1995): 285–296.

Shawcross, William. *Deliver Us from Evil: Peacekeepers, Warlords, and a World of Endless Conflict.* New York: Simon & Schuster, 2000.

Shustov, V. "Can the UN Fight a War?" *International Affairs* (Moscow) 47, no. 1 (2001): 7–17.

Simma, Bruno, et al., eds. *The Charter of the United Nations: A Commentary.* 2nd ed., 2 vols. Oxford: Oxford University Press, 2002.

Smith, Charles D. *Palestine and the Arab-Israeli Conflict.* 4th ed. Boston: Bedford/St.Martin's, 2001.

Snow, Donald M. *Peacekeeping, Peacemaking, and Peace-Enforcement: The U.S. Role in the New International Order.* Carlisle Barracks, Pa.: U.S. Army War College, 1993.

Snyder, Jack. *From Voting to Violence.* New York: Norton, 2000.

———, ed. *Civil Wars, Insecurity, and Intervention.* New York: Columbia University Press, 1999.

Société Française du Droit International. *Le Chapitre VII de la Charte des Nations Unies.* Paris: Éditions A. Pédone, 1995.

Soggot, David. *Namibia: The Violent Heritage.* London: Collins, 1986.

Solingen, Etel. "The New Multilateralism and Nonproliferation: Bringing in

Domestic Politics." *Global Governance* 1, no. 2 (May–August 1995): 205–227.

Somavia, Juan. "The Humanitarian Responsibilities of the United Nations Security Council: Ensuring the Security of the People." *Development in Practice* 7, no. 4 (November 1997): 353–362.

Sriram, Chandra Lekha, and Karin Wermester, eds. *From Promise to Practice: Strengthening UN Capacities for the Prevention of Violent Conflict.* Boulder: Lynne Rienner, 2003.

Stanley Foundation. "Getting Down to Cases: Enforcing Security Council Resolutions." Presentation to the 33rd "United Nations of the Next Decade" conference, Muscatine, Iowa, June 7–12, 1998.

———. "The Role and Composition of the Security Council." Report of a vantage conference sponsored by the Stanley Foundation and the International Peace Academy, Harrison Conference Center, Glen Cove, New York, November 12–14, 1993.

Stedman, Stephen John. "Alchemy for a New World Order." *Foreign Affairs* 74, no. 3 (May–June 1995): 14-20.

———. "The New Interventionists." *Foreign Affairs* 72, no. 1 (Winter 1992–1993): 1–16.

Stedman, Stephen John, Donald Rothchild, and Elizabeth M. Cousens, eds. *Ending Civil Wars: The Implementation of Peace Agreements.* Boulder: Lynne Rienner, 2002.

Suhrke, Astri. "Peace-Keepers as Nation-Builders: Dilemmas of the UN in East Timor." *International Peacekeeping* 8, no. 4 (2001): 1–20.

Sutterlin, James S. *Military Force in the Service of Peace.* Aurora Paper no. 18. Ottawa: Canadian Center for Global Security, 1993.

———. *The United Nations and the Maintenance of International Security: A Challenge to Be Met.* Westport, Conn.: Praeger, 1995.

Swiss Confederation, UN Secretariat, and Watson Institute for International Studies at Brown University. *Targeted Financial Sanctions: A Manual for Design and Implementation—Contributions from the Interlaken Process.* Providence, R.I.: Thomas J. Watson Jr. Institute for International Studies, 2001.

Szasz, Paul. "The Security Council Starts Legislating." *American Journal of International Law* 96, no. 4 (2002): 901–904.

Taylor, Paul. *The United Nations and the Gulf War, 1990–1991: Back to the Future?* London: Royal Institute of International Affairs, 1992.

Taylor, Paul, Sam Daws, and Ute Adamczick-Gerteis, eds. *Documents on Reform of the United Nations.* Aldershot: Dartmouth, 1997.

Teixeira, Pascal. *Le Conseil de Sécurité à l'aube du XXIème siècle.* Geneva: UNIDIR, 2002.

Teng, Catherine G., and Kay L. Hancock, eds. *Synopses of United Nations Cases in the Field of Peace and Security, 1946–1965.* New York: CEIP, 1966.

Teson, Fernando R. *Humanitarian Intervention: An Inquiry into Law and Morality.* Dobbs Ferry, N.Y.: Transnational, 1997.

Thakur, Ramesh. "The United Nations in a Changing World." *Security Dialogue* 24, no. 1 (March 1993): 7–20.

Thakur, Ramesh, and Albrecht Schnabel, eds. *United Nations Peacekeeping Operations: Ad Hoc Missions, Permanent Engagement.* Tokyo: United Nations University Press, 2001.

Thakur, Ramesh, and Carlyle A. Thayer, eds. *A Crisis of Expectations: UN Peacekeeping in the 1990s.* Boulder: Westview, 1995.

Thant, U. *View from the UN.* Garden City, N.Y.: Doubleday, 1978.

Tharoor, Shashi. "Should UN Peacekeeping Go 'Back to Basics'?" *Survival* 37, no. 4 (Winter 1995–1996): 52–64.

———. "United Nations Peacekeeping in Europe." *Survival* 37, no. 2 (Summer 1995): 121–134.

Thornberry, Cedric. *The People Must First Lose Their Fear.* Forthcoming from Gamsberg-Macmillan.

Todd, James Edward. *The United Nations Security Council.* Iowa City: University of Iowa Press, 1966.

Touval, Saadia. "Why the UN Fails." *Foreign Affairs* 73, no. 5 (1994): 44–57.

Tsakaloyannis, Panos, and Dimitris Bourantonis. "The European Union's Common Foreign and Security Policy and the Reform of the Security Council." *European Foreign Affairs Review* 2, no. 2 (Summer 1997): 197–209.

Türk, Danilo. "The Role of the UN Security Council in Preventing Internal Conflicts." *International Journal on Minority and Group Rights* 8, no. 1 (2001): 71–73.

Urquhart, Brian. *A Life in Peace and War.* London: Weidenfeld and Nicolson, 1987.

———. *Hammarskjöld.* New York: Alfred A Knopf, 1972.

———. *Ralph Bunche: An American Life.* New York: W. W. Norton, 1993.

———. "The United Nations in the Middle East: A Fifty-Year Retrospective." *Middle East Journal* 49, no. 4 (Autumn 1995): 572–581.

U.S. Army Peacekeeping Institute. *Success in Peacekeeping: United Nations Mission in Haiti—The Military Perspective.* Carlisle Barracks, Pa.: U.S. Army Peacekeeping Institute, 1996.

U.S. Department of State. *World Military Expenditures and Arms Transfers.* Washington, D.C.: U.S. Department of State, 1998.

———. Office of the Coordinator for Counterterrorism. *Patterns of Global Terrorism, 1992, 1995, and 2001.* Washington, D.C.: U.S. Government Printing Office.

U.S. National Intelligence Council. *Global Trends 2015: A Dialogue About the Future with Nongovernment Experts.* Washington, D.C.: U.S. National Intelligence Council, December 2000.

van Baarda, Th. A. "The Involvement of the Security Council in Maintaining International Law." *Netherlands Quarterly of Human Rights* 12, no. 1 (1994): 140.

van Langenhove, Fernand. *Le rôle proéminent du Secrétaire-Général dans l'opération des Nations Unies au Congo.* Bruxelles: Institut Royal des Relations Internationales, 1964.

Väyrynen, Raimo. *The Age of Humanitarian Emergencies.* Research for Action no. 25. Helsinki: World Institute for Development Economics Research, 1996.

Vines, Alex. *Renamo: From Terrorism to Democracy in Mozambique?* London: James Currey, 1996.

Voeten, Erik. "Outside Options and the Logic of Security Council Action." *American Political Science Review* 95, no. 4 (December 2001): 845–858.

Volger, Helmut, ed. *A Concise Encyclopedia of the United Nations.* The Hague: Kluwer, 2002.

von Braunmühl, Claudia, and Manfred Kulessa. *The Impact of UN Sanctions on Humanitarian Assistance Activities.* Report commissioned by the United Nations Department of Humanitarian Affairs (DHA). Berlin: United Nations DHA, December 1995.

von Einsiedel, Sebastian. *You the People: Transitional Administration, State-*

Building, and the United Nations. Report of the International Peace Academy, New York, October 18–19, 2002.

von Einsiedel, Sebastian, and Simon Chesterman. "Doppelte Eindämmung in Sicherheitsrat: Die USA, und Irak im Diplomatischen Vorfeld des Kriegs." *Vereinte Nationen* 2 (April 2003): 47–55.

von Siemens, Christina. "Russia's Policy Towards the War in Bosnia-Herzegovina (1992–1995)." M.Phil. diss., University of Oxford, April 2001.

Wallensteen, Peter. "Representing the World: a Security Council for the Twenty-First Century." *Security Dialogue* 25, no. 1 (March 1994): 63–76.

———. *Understanding Conflict Resolution: War, Peace, and the Global System*. London: Sage, 2002.

Wallensteen, Peter, Carina Staibano, and Mikael Eriksson, eds. *Making Targeted Sanctions Effective: Guidelines for the Implementation of UN Policy Options*. Uppsala, Sweden: Uppsala University, Department of Peace and Conflict Research, 2003.

Weckel, P. *Le Chapitre VII de la Charte et son application par le Conseil de Sécurité*. Paris: Annuaire Français de Droit International, 1991.

Wedgwood, Ruth. "The Enforcement of Security Council Resolution 687: The Threat of Force Against Iraq's Weapons of Mass Destruction." *American Journal of International Law* 92, no. 4 (October 1998): 724–728.

Weiland, Heribert, and Matthew Braham, eds. *The Namibian Peace Process: Implications and Lessons for the Future*. Freiburg: Arnold Bergstraesser Institut/International Peace Academy, 1994.

Weiss, Thomas G. "Humanitarian Shell Games: Whither UN Reform?" *Security Dialogue* 29, no. 1 (March 1998): 9–24.

———. "New Challenges for UN Military Operations: Implementing an Agenda for Peace." *Washington Quarterly* 16, no. 1 (Winter 1993): 51–66.

———. "Overcoming the Somalia Syndrome: 'Operation Rekindle Hope'?" *Global Governance* 1, no. 2 (May–August 1995): 171–187.

———. "The UN's Prevention Pipe-Dream." *Berkeley Journal of International Law* 14, no. 2 (1997): 501–515.

———, ed. *Beyond UN Subcontracting: Task-Sharing with Regional Security Arrangements and Service-Providing NGOs*. London: Macmillan, 1998.

Weiss, Thomas G., David Cortright, George A. Lopez, and Larry Minear. *Political Gain and Civilian Pain: Humanitarian Impacts of Economic Sanctions*. Lanham, Md.: Rowman & Littlefield, 1997.

Weiss, Thomas G., David P. Forsythe, and Roger A. Coate. *The United Nations and Changing World Politics*. 2nd ed. Boulder: Westview, 1994.

———. *The United Nations and Changing World Politics*, 3rd ed. Boulder: Westview, 2001.

Weiss, Thomas G., and Don Hubert. *The Responsibility to Protect: Research, Bibliography, and Background*. Supplementary volume of the International Commission on Intervention and State Sovereignty. Ottawa: International Development Research Center, 2001, www.iciss-ciise.gc.ca.

Wellens, Karel, ed. *Resolutions and Statements of the United Nations Security Council, 1946–2000: A Thematic Guide*. Nijhoff Law Specials vol. 50. The Hague: Kluwer, 2001.

Weller, Marc. "Undoing the Global Constitution: UN Security Council Action on the International Criminal Court." *International Affairs* (London) 78, no. 4 (October 2002): 693–712.

———. "The U.S., Iraq, and the Use of Force in a Unipolar World." *Survival* 41, no. 4 (Winter 1999): 81–100.

Weston, Burns H. "Security Council Resolution 678 and Persian Gulf Decision Making: Precarious Legitimacy." *American Journal of International Law* 85, no. 3 (July 1991): 516–535.

Wheeler, Nicholas J. *Saving Strangers: Humanitarian Intervention in International Society.* Oxford: Oxford University Press, 2000.

Wheeler, Nicholas J., and Tim Dunne. "Good International Citizenship: A Third Way for British Foreign Policy." *International Affairs* 74, no. 4 (1998): 847–870.

White, Nigel D. *Keeping the Peace: The United Nations and the Maintenance of International Peace and Security.* 2nd ed. Manchester: Manchester University Press, 1997.

White, Nigel D., and O. Uelgen. "The Security Council and the Decentralised Military Option: Constitutionality and Function." *Netherlands International Law Review* 44, no. 3 (1997): 378–413.

Whiteman, Marjorie, ed. *Digest of International Law.* Vol. 12. Washington, D.C.: U.S. Department of State, 1971.

Whitfield, Teresa. *Staying the Course in El Salvador, Honoring Human Rights: From Peace to Justice.* Washington, Aspen Institute, 1998.

Whitman, Jim, and Ian Bartholomew. *The Chapter VII Committee—A Policy Proposal: Military Means for Political Ends: Effective Control of UN Military Enforcement.* Cambridge: Global Security Programme, University of Cambridge, 1993.

Williams, Abiodun, José Alvarez, Ruth Gordon, and W. Andy Knight. *Article 2(7) Revisited.* Providence, R.I.: Academic Council on the United Nations System, 1994.

Williams, John. "The Ethical Basis of Humanitarian Intervention: The Security Council and Yugoslavia." *International Peacekeeping* 6, no. 2 (September 1999): 1–23.

Williams, Michael C. *Civil-Military Relations and Peacekeeping.* London: Oxford University Press, 1998.

Williamson, Richard. *Seeking Firm Footing: America in the World in the New Century.* Chicago: Prairie Institute, 2001.

Willum, Bjorn. "Legitimizing Inaction Towards Genocide in Rwanda: A Matter of Misperception." *International Peacekeeping* 6, no. 3 (Autumn 1999): 11–30.

Winkelmann, Ingo. "Bringing the Security Council into a New Era: Recent Developments in the Discussion on the Reform of the Security Council." *Max Planck Yearbook of United Nations Law* 1 (1997): 35–90.

Wolfrun, Rudiger. *United Nations: Law, Policies, and Practice.* Dordrecht: Martinus Nijhoff, 1995.

Wood, A., R. Apthorpe, and J. Borton, eds. *Evaluating International Humanitarian Action: Reflections from Practitioners.* London: Zed Books, 2001.

Wood, Michael C. "Security Council Working Methods and Procedure: Recent Developments." *International and Comparative Law Quarterly* 45, no. 1 (January 1996): 150–161.

Woodward, Peter. *The Horn of Africa: Politics and International Relations.* London: I. B. Tauris, 2003.

World Bank Group. *Haiti: The Challenges of Poverty Reduction.* Washington, D.C.: World Bank, August 1998.

Yamaguchi, Masakuni. *Diplomacy of Sanctions: The United Nations Security Council Sanctions and South Africa.* Ann Arbor, Mich.: UMI, Dissertation Information Service, 1997.

Yannis, Alexandros. "The International Presence in Kosovo and Regional Security: The Deep Winter of UN Security Council Resolution 1244." *Journal of Southeast European and Black Sea Studies* 2, no. 1 (January 2002): 173–190.

Zacarias, Agostinho. *The United Nations and International Peacekeeping.* London: I. B. Tauris, 1996.

Zartman, I. William. *Ripe for Resolution: Conflict and Intervention in Africa.* 2nd ed. New York: Oxford University Press, 1989.

Zedalis, R. J. "The Quiet, Continuing Air War Against Iraq: An Interpretive Analysis of the Controlling Security Council Resolutions." *Zeitschrift fuer Oeffentliches Recht* 55, no. 2 (2000): 181–210.

Zunes, Stephen. "The U.S. and the Breakdown of the Israeli-Palestinian Peace Process." *Middle East Policy* 8, no. 4 (December 2001): 66–85.

THE CONTRIBUTORS

Adekeye Adebajo, director of the Africa Program at the International Peace Academy in New York and adjunct professor at Columbia University's School of International and Public Affairs, has served on UN missions in South Africa, Western Sahara, and Iraq. He is author of *Building Peace in West Africa: Liberia, Sierra Leone, and Guinea-Bissau* and *Liberia's Civil War: Nigeria, ECOMOG, and Regional Security in West Africa* and coeditor (with Chandra Sriram) of *Managing Armed Conflicts in the Twenty-First Century*.

Howard Adelman has been a professor of philosophy at York University, Toronto, since 1966. He founded the university's Centre for Refugee Studies, serving as director until 1993. In addition to numerous writings on refugees, he has published extensively on the Middle East, humanitarian intervention, membership rights, ethics, early warning, and conflict management. In 1999 he and Astri Suhrke coedited *The Path of a Genocide: The Rwanda Crisis from Uganda to Zaire*. His latest volume is *Humanitarian Intervention in Zaire*.

Aldo Ajello has been EU special representative to the Great Lakes region since 1996. From 1992 to 1995 he served as special representative of the Secretary-General for the UN Operation in Mozambique. Before that he worked for almost ten years at the UNDP, first as director of the European Office in Geneva, later as director of the Bureau for Special Activities in New York. With a career in Italian politics, Ajello served for four years as a senate legislator (1976–1979) and for four years as a member of the Foreign Affairs Commission in the chamber of deputies (1979–1983).

David J. R. Angell served as adviser in 1999–2000 to Ambassadors Bob Fowler and Paul Heinbecker as successive chairmen of the Security Council's Angola sanctions committee. He is deputy to the personal representative of Canada's prime minister for Africa and director of the Eastern and Southern Africa Division at the Department of Foreign Affairs and International Trade. He served previously as alternate representative of Canada on the Security Council, head of the political section at Canada's UN permanent mission in New York, and a member of the senior staff of the Northern Ireland peace process.

Blanca Antonini was first officer in the Executive Office of the UN Secretary-General, participating in the 1990–1992 UN-mediated negotiations that led to the signing of the peace accord between the government of El Salvador and the Farabundo Martí National Liberation Front. She served in the UN Observer Mission in El Salvador as senior political adviser until 1995. Before she was appointed head of the Belgrade office of the UN Mission in Kosovo (UNMIK) in 2001 she served as head of the Department of Local Administration in UNMIK and was a member of the joint working group that negotiated the constitutional framework for the provisional institutions of self-government in Kosovo. Antonini is currently deputy director of the Americas and Europe Division of the UN Department of Political Affairs.

Mats Berdal is professor of security and development in the Department of War Studies at King's College, London. In 1999–2003 he was director of studies at the International Institute for Strategic Studies; before that he was a research fellow of St. Anthony's College, Oxford University. His publications include *Whither UN Peacekeeping?* and *Disarmament and Demobilization After Civil Wars*. With David Malone he coedited *Greed and Grievance: Economic Agendas in Civil Wars*.

Frank Berman practices law in London and is visiting professor of international law at Oxford and at the University of Cape Town and King's College, London. He served as legal adviser to the British mission to the UN in the 1980s and was legal adviser to the Foreign and Commonwealth Office between 1991 and 1999, when he led the UK delegation to the Conference on the International Criminal Court. He was recently appointed judge ad hoc on the International Court of Justice.

Simon Chesterman is senior associate at the International Peace Academy (IPA), where he directs its Transitional Administrations Program. Prior to joining the IPA, he worked at the International Criminal Tribunal for Rwanda and with the Office for the Coordination of Humanitarian Affairs in the Federal Republic of Yugoslavia. He is author of *Just War or Just Peace? Humanitarian Intervention and International Law* (2001) and editor of *Civilians in War*.

David Cortright is a research fellow at the Joan B. Kroc Institute for International Peace Studies at the University of Notre Dame and president of the Fourth Freedom Forum in Goshen, Indiana. He also teaches in the Peace, Justice, and Conflict Studies Department at Goshen College. He has authored and edited eleven books, including *The Sanctions Decade:*

Assessing UN Strategies in the 1990s, Smart Sanctions: Targeting Economic Statecraft, and *Sanctions and the Search for Security: Challenges to UN Action.* He is a leading authority on UN policy in Iraq and has completed several scholarly reports on the subject, including *Winning Without War: Sensible Security Options for Dealing with Iraq.* Cortright has served as consultant or adviser for various UN agencies, the Carnegie Commission on Preventing Deadly Conflict, the International Peace Academy, the John D. and Catherine T. MacArthur Foundation, and the governments of Sweden, Norway, and Switzerland.

Elizabeth M. Cousens is director of the Conflict Prevention and Peace Forum at the Social Science Research Council. Before that she served in the office of the UN special coordinator for the Middle East peace process, based in Gaza. Prior to working at the UN, she was based at the International Peace Academy, where she directed its Research Program. Her own research included publications on Dayton implementation in Bosnia and a major, multiauthor study of third-party implementation of peace agreements after civil wars. From 1990 to 1994 she was a visiting fellow at Stanford University while conducting doctoral research on the international right to self-defense.

Sebastian von Einsiedel is senior program officer at the International Peace Academy. Before coming to the United States, he worked as a research assistant at the NATO Parliamentary Assembly in Brussels (1999) and as a member of the Social Democratic Party's security policy advisory staff in the German parliament (2000).

Stewart Eldon is Britain's ambassador to Ireland. He served as the UK's deputy permanent representative to the UN (1998–2002), with previous postings at the UN (1976–1977, 1986–1990) as the UK mission's expert on Africa and Asia. Eldon served as the Foreign and Commonwealth Office's deputy crisis manager for the Gulf War in 1990–1991, followed by two years in the European secretariat of the cabinet office in London dealing with European Union issues (including a British EU presidency) in the aftermath of the Maastricht Treaty. From 1994 to 1997 he was political counselor to the UK delegations to NATO and the Western European Union with responsibility for NATO-Russia relations and European defense, among other issues

Bardo Fassbender is assistant professor of law at Humboldt University in Berlin and a lecturer at the University of St. Gallen, Switzerland, specializing in public international law and constitutional law. He was a Ford Foundation senior fellow in public international law at Yale University and a Jean Monnet fellow at the European University Institute in Florence. His publications include *UN Security Council Reform and the Right of Veto: A Constitutional Perspective*, "The United Nations Charter as Constitution of the International Community," and "Uncertain Steps into a Post–Cold War World: The Role and Functioning of the UN Security Council After a Decade of Measures Against Iraq."

Shepard Forman is founder and director of the Center on International Cooperation at New York University. He has conducted field research in Brazil and East Timor, authored two books on Brazil, and published extensively on humanitarian assistance and postconflict reconstruction assistance. He is coeditor with Stewart Patrick of *Good Intentions: Pledges of Aid to Countries Emerging from Conflict* and *Multilateralism and U.S. Foreign Policy: Ambivalent Engagement.*

Gregory H. Fox is associate professor of law at Wayne State University. He is coeditor with Brad Roth of *Democratic Governance and International Law* and author of numerous articles on international legal subjects. He has taught at Chapman University and New York University law schools and held fellowships at Yale Law School, the Max Planck Institute for Comparative Public Law and Public International Law, and the MacArthur Foundation Social Science Research Council. He served as counsel to the state of Eritrea in the Eritrea–Yemen Hanish Islands arbitration.

Andrés Franco became UNICEF representative in Peru in 2003. From 2001 to 2002 he served as deputy representative and political coordinator in the Security Council after Colombia's election as a nonpermanent member. He is editor of *Financing for Development in Latin America and the Caribbean* and has authored various academic articles and books on Colombia's international relations and politics.

Ibrahim A. Gambari is Undersecretary-General and special adviser on Africa at the UN Secretariat in New York. He recently was special representative of the Secretary-General to Angola. Prior to joining the UN in 1999, he was Nigeria's permanent representative to the UN, minister of foreign affairs, and director-general of the Nigerian Institute of International Affairs. He is widely published in international scholarly journals and has written several books on Nigerian foreign policy. He is currently working on two books: *Africa's Security Questions at the End of the Twentieth Century into the New Millennium* and *The United Nations in a Changing World Order: An African Perspective.*

Marrack Goulding served in Britain's diplomatic service from 1959 to 1985, learning Arabic in Lebanon and subsequently serving in Kuwait, Libya, Egypt, Portugal, the British UN mission in New York, and Angola (ambassador). In 1986 he succeeded Brian Urquhart in the UN Secretariat as head of the Department of Peacekeeping Operations. In 1993 he became Undersecretary-General for political affairs in charge of the UN's preventive and peacemaking efforts worldwide. In 1997 he retired and became warden of St. Antony's College at Oxford University.

Andrew Grene serves as a political affairs officer in the Asia and

Middle East Division of the UN Department of Peacekeeping Operations. Previous service included peacekeeping policy adviser at the DPKO, secretary of the General Assembly's special committee on peacekeeping operations, and speechwriter and assistant in the executive office under Secretary-General Boutros Boutros-Ghali.

Paul Heinbecker was appointed Canada's ambassador and permanent representative to the UN in 2000. He joined the Department of External Affairs in 1965, serving abroad in Ankara, Stockholm, and Paris with the permanent delegation of Canada to the Organization for Economic Cooperation and Development. From 1992 to 1996 he was ambassador to Germany and since has served in the Department of Foreign Affairs and International Trade as assistant deputy minister of global and security policy and as political director.

John Hirsch is adjunct professor of diplomacy and world affairs at Occidental College, directing its UN program in New York. Before joining the International Peace Academy in 1998 he served as U.S. ambassador to Sierra Leone (1995–1998). His extensive African experience has included assignments in Somalia (1984–1986) and Johannesburg (1990–1993). His earlier assignments in Israel at the start of the Middle East peace process in the mid-1970s, and subsequently at the U.S. mission to the UN and in Pakistan, dealt with major issues of multilateral diplomacy and UN peacekeeping. His publications include *Sierra Leone: Diamonds and the Struggle for Democracy* and *Somalia and Operation Restore Hope: Reflections on Peacemaking and Peacekeeping* (coauthor, with Robert Oakley).

John T. Holmes is director of the Human Rights and Economic Law Division of the UN Department of Foreign Affairs and International Trade. He served at Canadian diplomatic missions in Bridgetown, Barbados (1983–1987), Accra, Ghana (1991–1993), and New York (1996–2000). He was a member of the extended Bureau of the Committee of the Whole at the 1998 Rome Diplomatic Conference of the International Criminal Court (ICC) and a member of the Bureau of the ICC Preparatory Commission (1999–2002). He has written numerous chapters and articles on the ICC and has participated at a number of conferences on the Court.

Susan C. Hulton, a public international lawyer, is a senior political affairs officer in the Security Council Affairs Division of the UN Department of Political Affairs. In the 1990s she served as a legal adviser in the Foreign and Commonwealth Office of the United Kingdom. She formerly served as director of Interights at the International Centre for the Legal Protection of Human Rights, London, and was a lecturer in international law at University College, London.

Cameron R. Hume is U.S. ambassador to South Africa, serving previously as U.S. ambassador to Algeria. He has extensive experience in diplomacy at the United Nations, in Africa, and in the Middle East. He has written numerous articles on diplomacy and has published two books, *The United Nations, Iran, and Iraq: How Peacemaking Changed* and *Ending Mozambique's War.*

Patrik Johansson is master of peace and conflict research at Uppsala University, Sweden. His main research interests are the Middle East and humanitarian disasters and conflict. He has written on these subjects for Sweden's Ministry for Foreign Affairs and the Swedish International Development Cooperation Agency.

Mora Johnson has worked in the executive and legislative branches of the Canadian government. She served as legislative assistant to Lloyd Axworthy, minister of foreign affairs, also assisting with the implementation of the Rome Statute and other treaties. She served as legislative assistant to Pierre Pettigrew, minister of international trade, and as executive assistant to Bill Graham, chair of the Standing Committee on Foreign Affairs and International Trade. She is currently studying law at the University of Toronto.

Bruce D. Jones is deputy director at New York University's Center on International Cooperation, where he works on the Transitions in Security Arrangements Project. From 2000 to 2002 he served as chief of staff to the UN's special coordinator for the Middle East peace process. He previously worked in the UN Office for the Coordination of Humanitarian Affairs and was a member of the UN's advance mission in Kosovo and of the DPKO's planning team for the UN Transitional Administration in East Timor. Before joining the UN, he worked for nongovernmental organizations in conflict response, particularly in Central Africa. He is the author of *Peacemaking in Rwanda: The Dynamics of Failure* and *The UN and Post-Crisis Aid.*

Colin Keating is a partner in the New Zealand law firm Chen Palmer and Partners and specializes in public and international law. He has served as New Zealand's UN ambassador and as its ambassador on the Security Council (1993–1994). He has also served as New Zealand's secretary for justice, as legal adviser to the Ministry of Foreign Affairs and Trade, and in various senior positions in the diplomatic service. In 2002 he was invited to sit on the Secretary-General's External Review Committee to advise on the UN reform process.

Philippe Kirsch is Canada's ambassador to Sweden, serving concurrently as ambassador and agent for Canada in the "Legality of Use of Force" case *(Yugoslavia v. Canada)* before the International Court of Justice. Kirsch has represented Canada in many legal organs and conferences, starting with the Sixth (Legal) Committee of the UN General Assembly, of which he was chairman in 1982, and has subsequently presided over a number of international negotiations in the field of international law. Between 1997 and 1999 he chaired the UN legal committee that concluded conventions against terrorist bombings and the financing of terrorism. He also chaired the Committee of the Whole of the Rome Conference, which adopted the Statute of the International Criminal Court in 1998, as well as the Preparatory Commission for the establishment of the Court from 1999 to 2002. He works with and advises the Red Cross and Red Crescent movement. Kirsch is the author of numerous articles and papers on international law and the United Nations.

George A. Lopez is senior fellow and director of policy studies at the Joan B. Kroc Institute for International Peace Studies at the University of Notre Dame. His research focuses on the problems of state violence and coercion, especially economic sanctions, and gross violations of human rights. Working with David Cortright since 1992, he has written more than twenty articles and book chapters, as well as five books, on economic sanctions. They include *Economic Sanctions: Panacea or Peacebuilding in the Post–Cold War World?* and *The Sanctions Decade: Assessing UN Strategies in the 1990s.* He has also advised a number of foundations and organizations involved in human rights, international affairs education, and peace research.

Edward C. Luck is director of the Center on International Organization and professor of practice in international and public affairs at Columbia University. Since 2001, he has served as a member of the UN Secretary-General's Policy Working Group on the United Nations and Terrorism. Previously, he served as one of the architects of the UN reform efforts from 1995 to 1997 and as president and CEO of the United Nations Association of the USA. His most recent book is *Mixed Messages: American Politics and International Organization, 1919–1999.*

Kishore Mahbubani has served as a career diplomat for thirty years, with postings in Cambodia, Malaysia, Washington, D.C., and New York. Currently serving in New York as Singapore's UN ambassador, he presided over the UN Security Council in January 2001 and May 2002. Before coming to New York, he was permanent secretary of the foreign ministry and dean of the Civil Service College in Singapore. His writings have been published in a volume titled *Can Asians Think?*

David M. Malone is president of the International Peace Academy. Currently on leave from Canada's foreign service, he served as director-general of the Policy, International Organizations, and Global Issues bureaus of the Canadian Department of Foreign Affairs and International Trade (1994–1998) and as Canada's ambassador and deputy permanent representative to the UN (1992–1994). He is the author of *Decisionmaking in the UN Security Council: The Case of Haiti.*

Ian Martin is vice president of the International Center for Transitional Justice. He was special representative of the UN Secretary-

General for the East Timor Popular Consultation, head of the UN mission in East Timor in 1999, and deputy special representative of the Secretary-General in Ethiopia and Eritrea (2000–2001). He has held senior human rights field posts in Bosnia and Herzegovina, Rwanda, and Haiti, and served as special adviser to the UN high commissioner for human rights. Martin was secretary-general of Amnesty International from 1986 to 1992 and is the author of *Self-Determination in East Timor: The United Nations, the Ballot, and International Intervention.*

Nathan Miller was junior fellow at the Center for International Studies and an intern with the UN's International Law Commission. He spent a year at the Project on International Courts and Tribunals. Since then he has written and published on development of the international judicial function and relationships among international courts and tribunals. He is currently in Africa studying working models for bringing to justice those accused of participating in the Rwandan genocide.

James A. Paul has served as executive director of Global Policy Forum since 1993. He was founding chair of the NGO Working Group on the UN Security Council (1995–2002) and currently serves as secretary. From 1977 to 1989 he was a staff member of the Middle East Research and Information Project, serving as executive director in 1986–1989. He has written two books and nearly 200 articles and was an editor of the *Oxford Companion to Politics of the World.*

Connie Peck is founder and principal coordinator of the Programme for Peacemaking and Preventive Diplomacy of the UN Institute for Training and Research in Geneva, Switzerland. She is currently directing a project to provide a more systematic briefing and debriefing for special representatives of the UN Secretary-General. She is the author of eight books and numerous articles and chapters, including *Sustainable Peace: The Role of the United Nations and Regional Organizations in Preventing Conflict* and *The United Nations as a Dispute Settlement System: Improving Mechanisms for the Prevention and Resolution of Conflict.* With Roy Lee she is the coeditor of *Increasing the Effectiveness of the International Court of Justice.*

Steven R. Ratner is Albert Sidney Burleson Professor in Law at the University of Texas School of Law. Prior to joining the Texas faculty in 1993, he was an attorney-adviser in the Office of the Legal Adviser at the U.S. State Department. A member of the board of editors of the *American Journal of International Law*, his research focuses on new challenges facing emerging democracies and international institutions after the Cold War. His publications include *The New UN Peacekeeping: Building Peace in Lands of Conflict After the Cold War, Accountability for Human Rights Atrocities in International Law: Beyond the Nuremberg Legacy* (coauthor), and *International Law: Norms, Actors, Process* (coauthor). He was a Fulbright Scholar at The Hague during 1998–1999, where he worked in and studied the office of the OSCE's High Commissioner on National Minorities.

Frederick Rawski is a litigation associate at the New York law firm Stroock and Stroock and Lavan LLP. In the past, Rawski worked as human rights officer with the UN Transitional Administration in East Timor and law clerk with the International Criminal Tribunal for Rwanda. He has published articles on topics including immunity and accountability in UN peacekeeping operations, truth and reconciliation in East Timor, and Indonesian and Malaysian politics and history.

Adam Roberts is Montague Burton Professor of International Relations at Oxford University and a fellow of Balliol College. He is also a fellow of the British Academy and a member of the Council of the International Institute for Strategic Studies, London. His books include *United Nations, Divided World: The UN's Roles in International Relations* (2nd ed., coedited with Benedict Kingsbury) and *Documents on the Laws of War* (3rd ed., coedited with Richard Guelff).

Astri Suhrke is senior research fellow at the Chr. Michelsen Institute in Norway. She has written widely on the politics of humanitarian policies and the role of the UN in the humanitarian sector. She coedited with Howard Adelman *The Path of a Genocide: The Rwanda Conflict from Uganda to Zaire.* Her latest book is *Eroding Local Capacity: International Humanitarian Action in Africa.*

Pascal Teixeira da Silva is a French career diplomat and currently serves as deputy director of the UN and international organizations department in France's foreign affairs ministry. In 1997–2001 he was political counselor of the French delegation to the UN Security Council. He recently published *Le Conseil de Sécurité à l'aube du XXIème siècle: Quelle volonté et quelle capacité a-t-il de maintenir la paix et la sécurité internationales?.*

Cedric Thornberry is a former UN Assistant Secretary-General and served in UN peacekeeping operations in Cyprus, the Middle East, Namibia, Somalia, and the former Yugoslavia, where for two years he was head of civil affairs and deputy chief of mission. He has been visiting professor at the universities of Ulster and London and taught international law at Cambridge and London School of Economics, where he is an honorary fellow. An occasional consultant to NATO and the U.S. National Democratic Institute, he was director of the Special Representative's Office in Namibia. His book on the UNTAG operation, *The People Must First Lose Their Fear,* will be published in 2004.

Peter Wallensteen has held the Dag Hammarskjöld Chair in Peace and Conflict Research at Uppsala University, Sweden, since 1985 and leads the Uppsala Conflict Data Project. He coordinates the Stockholm Process on the Implementation of Targeted Sanctions and was head of the Department of Peace and Conflict Research, Uppsala University, in 1972–1999. His most recent books include *Making Targeted Sanctions Effective: Guidelines* *for the Implementation of UN Policy Options* (coedited with Carina Staibano and Mikael Eriksson) and *Understanding Conflict Resolution: War, Peace, and the Global System.*

Peter van Walsum joined the Dutch foreign service in 1965 and served with his country's permanent missions to NATO, the European Union, and the United Nations. He was ambassador to Thailand (1985–1989), then political director (until 1993) and ambassador to Germany (until 1998). In 1999 and 2000 he was permanent representative to the United Nations. He is now retired.

Thomas G. Weiss is presidential professor at the CUNY Graduate Center and director of the Ralph Bunche Institute for International Studies, where he is codirector of the UN Intellectual History Project and editor of *Global Governance.* He also has been a research professor at Brown University's Watson Institute for International Studies, executive director of the Academic Council on the UN System and of the International Peace Academy, member of the UN Secretariat, and consultant to several public and private agencies. He has written and edited extensively on multilateral approaches to international peace and security, humanitarian action, and sustainable development.

Joanna Weschler has been the UN representative for Human Rights Watch (HRW) since 1994. Prior to coming to the United States from Poland in 1982, she was a reporter for the Solidarity Union press agency, in charge of covering most meetings between union president Lech Walesa and the communist government and meetings of the executive leadership of the union. Prior to her current position, she was the Poland researcher for Helsinki Watch, Brazil researcher for Americas Watch, as well as director of HRW's Prison Project. She has conducted human rights investigations on five continents and has written numerous reports and articles on human rights.

Teresa Whitfield is a visiting fellow at the Center on International Cooperation of New York University, where she is researching her book *Friends Indeed: The United Nations, "Groups of Friends," and the Resolution of Conflict.* In 1995–2000 she served in the UN Department of Political Affairs and in 2001–2002 as acting director of the Conflict Prevention and Peace Forum. She is the author of *Paying the Price: Ignacio Ellacuría and the Murdered Jesuits of El Salvador.*

Patrick Wittmann is a foreign service officer in Canada's Department of Foreign Affairs and International Trade, where he has worked extensively on multilateral issues. In 1993–1995 Wittmann served with the UN Peacekeeping Operation in Mozambique; he also worked for the UNDP in that country. Wittmann has undertaken assignments with the Canadian international aid agency CIDA and the Canadian Council for International Cooperation.

INDEX

Abdullah, Abdullah, 230
Abidjan Agreement (1996), 524, 531
Adeniji, Oluyemi, 528, 529
Ad hoc tribunals, 284–286
Ad Hoc Working Group on Conflict
  Prevention and Resolution in Africa,
  314, 321, 330
Afghanistan: armed nonstate actors in,
  123*tab;* Bonn Agreement and, 63;
  humanitarian impact studies in, 168;
  humanitarian operations/interven-
  tions in, 42; human rights issues, 63;
  International Security Assistance
  Force in, 138, 151*n8,* 164*n35,* 228,
  229, 621; Loya Jirga in, 229, 230;
  Northern Alliance in, 42; Operation
  Enduring Freedom in, 42; Resolution
  1267, 63; Resolution 1333, 63, 176;
  Resolution 1363, 173; Resolution
  1386, 162*n11;* Resolution 1390, 173;
  Sanctions Enforcement Support
  Team, 173; sanctions on, 29, 94,
  170, 176, 674; Soviet Union in,
  18–20; Special Representatives of
  the Secretary-General in, 32*n5;* as
  "strategic orphan," 260; Taliban in,
  29, 63, 95, 96, 125, 129*n4,* 138, 169,
  173, 228, 260, 610, 621; and terrorism, 29, 94; UN missions in, 5, 63,
  227, 228–231; U.S. intervention in,
  41–42, 50, 92, 95, 138
African Union (AU), 622, 623; peacekeeping missions by, 28; rights of
  intervention in, 44; support for additional Security Council seats, 348.

See also Organization for African
  Unity
Africa Watch, 62
Afwerki, Isaias, 576, 578, 580, 584, 585
Agam, Hasmy, 189
Agenda for Peace, An (Boutros-Ghali),
  6, 46, 63, 73, 94, 103, 219, 270, 272,
  360, 463, 586, 634
Aggression, 291; defining, 134
Aguilar Zinser, Adolfo, 637, 643
Ahtisaari, Martti, 271, 410, 412, 413,
  416, 417, 419, 421, 545, 619
Ahtisaari Report, 182
AIDS, 45, 609, 624, 641; African pan-
  demic, 14*n21;* resolutions on, 29
Akashi, Yasushi, 313, 462
Al-Aqsa intifada, 397
Alatas, Ali, 558, 559
Albania: humanitarian operations/inter-
  ventions in, 39; Italy in, 136; resolu-
  tions on, 82*n3,* 162*n11*
Albright, Madeleine, 2, 278, 360, 456
Algeirs Accords (2000), 580–584
Algeria: conflicts in, 22; resolutions on
  terrorism, 88; unaddressed conflicts
  in, 114
Algiers Accords (2000), 575
Al-Qaida, 42, 96, 118, 119, 128, 129*n4,*
  130*n7,* 167, 169, 173, 229, 400
American Convention on Human
  Rights, 83*n7*
Amin, Idi, 89
Amnesty International, 377, 380, 381,
  383, 386*n7*
Amorim, Celso, 212

terrorism and, 86; UN Observer Group in, 5
Chad, 43; conflicts in, 23
Chapultepec Accord, 430
Chechnya: terrorism and, 86; unaddressed conflicts in, 115
Chernomyrdin, Viktor, 545, 546
China: anti-intervention stance of, 44; criticism of Iraq sanctions regime, 190–191; human rights issues, 58, 64; opposition to humanitarian operations/interventions doctrine, 146; opposition to intervention in Iraq, 141; policy toward Bosnia, 457–459; terrorism and, 97; on UN sanctions committee, 200; vetoes by, 14n16, 32n3, 87, 238
Chissano, Joaquim, 443, 444, 447
Chowdhury, Anwarul, 175, 176
CHR. *See* UN Commission on Human Rights
Chrétien, Raymond, 109
Churkin, Vitaly, 458, 543
Clark, Wesley, 540
Claude, Inis, 254, 255, 262, 263
Clinton, Bill, 92, 93, 181, 257, 342, 345, 359, 364, 366, 370n4, 456, 457, 471, 472, 476, 490, 519, 558, 580, 633, 638
Coalitions of the willing, 46, 358–359
Coercive protection, 47, 48
Cold War: change in geopolitical setting, 2; conflict prevention after, 103–105; conflict prevention during, 102–103; frequent use of veto during, 102–103; and Security Council, 17, 357–358
Colombia: conflicts in, 22; in Contadora Group, 424; in Groups of Friends, 315, 423; terrorism and, 86, 90; unaddressed conflicts in, 115
Colonialism, 222, 231, 467
Commission on Global Governance, 44
Commission on Human Security, 43
Conference on Security and Cooperation in Europe, 538
Conflict prevention, 28, 101–115; coercive tools, 112; and the Cold War, 102–105; cooperation in, 103; dependence on regional hegemon in, 113; direct negotiation of outcomes, 109; early, 105, 106; evolution as

term of art, 101–105; fact-finding missions and, 109; failures of, 19, 102–104, 107, 114, 257, 451–464; forms of, 105–108; instruments for, 108–111; in international community's interests, 104; North/South tensions and, 105; political limitations, 113–114; presidential statements and, 108; as prevalent concept, 101; prevention of escalation in, 106; prevention of humanitarian crises in, 107; prevention of recurrence, 107–108; promoted/contested, 105; special envoys and, 109; tools of, 108–111; troop deployment and, 111; uncontested status in UN, 105; use of media in, 108
Conflict(s): Arab-Israeli, 391–404; armed, 27, 104; armed nonstate actors in, 117–129; boundaries of legitimate behavior in, 108; children in, 29; civilian victims of, 37–51; civil war, 70; in context of decolonization, 102; debate over appropriate responses to, 101; domestic governance and, 70; in East Timor, 24; Ethiopia-Eritrea, 575–587; ethnic, 30, 59, 72; from failure to provide competent administration, 609; geographical dimension in agenda choices, 24, 25; as impetus for Security Council actions, 79; intensity levels, 22, 22fig; internal, 619–620; internal political dynamics and, 74; international, 18; international ramifications and, 121, 122, 122tab; interstate, 9, 72, 103; intrastate, 72, 118, 121, 122, 122tab, 296; of liberation, 17; longest, 23; management within borders, 101, 105; not attended to by Security Council, 22; for regime change, 139; regional, 4, 23, 103; regional solutions to, 609–610; regional stability and, 79–80; religious, 72; resolution of, 26fig, 72–74; role of women in, 29; root causes of, 29; selectivity by Security Council on addressing, 22; in Sierra Leone, 9; UN actions and, 26fig
Congo, 607; Resolution 161, 597; UN missions to, 102; UN Operation in, 107
Contadora Group, 316, 424
Convergencia Democrática, 428
Cook, Robin, 529, 558
Coordination and Drafting Group for

divisive politics of, 97; intifada in, 397; mandate-era Palestine, 392; marginalization of UN in, 395; peace process in, 391–404; proliferation of peacekeepers in, 392–395; Resolution 242, 393, 600; Resolution 338, 394; Resolution 1373, 238; Resolution 1397, 238; Resolution 1402, 250n4; resolutions on, 401tab; Special Representatives of the Secretary-General in, 395–396; terrorism and, 86, 88–93; UN Disengagement Observer Force in, 393; UN Emergency Force in, 394; UN in post–Cold War, 395–400; U.S. vetoes on, 393

Military Coordination Commission, 581, 582, 584

Military interventions, 2, 133–150; in Afghanistan, 41–42; by grouping of member states, 159; humanitarian operations and, 45–48; in Kosovo, 537–549; lack of support for, 105; preemptive, 144–146; reasons for use of, 135; responsibility for, 40, 41; for terrorism, 92; threats to peace and, 135

Military Staff Committee, 159

Milosevic, Slobodan, 39, 286, 461, 538–540, 543, 545, 546

MINURCA. See UN Verification Mission in the Central African Republic

Miranda, João Bernardo de, 203

Mission of the United Nations in El Salvador (MINUSAL), 434

Mladic, Ratko, 463

MNF. See Multinational forces

Mobutu Sese Seko, 107

Mollander, Anders, 200

Money laundering, 173

Monroe Doctrine, 135

Monteiro, António, 378–380

Morocco: France and, 124; Frente Polisario and, 120; Friends of the Secretary-General in, 318; relations with Western Sahara, 124, 225

Morris, Nicholas, 456

Mount Etjo Agreement, 417, 418

Mount Igman Demilitarized Zone Agreement (1993), 456

Mouvement pour Latin America

Libération du Congo, 124

Mozambique: conflicts in, 9, 103; demobilization in, 444–445; elections in, 80, 84n40, 446–447; Friends of the Secretary-General in, 313; Front for the Liberation of Mozambique in, 443; Frontline States in, 447; General Peace Agreement in, 438–440; lessons from Angola, 448; Mozambique National Resistance in, 438–441, 443, 445–447, 450n6; multiparty democracy in, 73; observers in, 84n40; peacekeeping operations in, 437–449; Portugal in, 438–440; reintegration of soldiers into, 444–445; Resolution 797, 438; Saint Egidio community in, 438–440, 448, 449; Security Council engagement in, 440–444; Special Representatives of the Secretary-General in, 437, 439–447; Supervision and Monitoring Commission in, 439, 442, 443, 445, 448; support of third countries in, 446; training new armed forces in, 446; transitional administration in, 223; UN missions in, 84n40; UN Operation in, 14n12, 437, 439–441, 446, 448, 449; UN trust fund in, 445

Mozambique National Resistance, 438–441, 443, 445–447, 450n6

MSF. See Médecins sans Frontières

Mubarak, Hosni, 95, 621

Mugabe, Robert, 447

Multilateralism, 93, 149

Multinational forces (MNF), 306, 665–667; in Central African Republic, 301; in Democratic Republic of Congo, 300; development of, 295; in Eastern Slavonia, 300; in East Timor, 301; in Ethiopia, 301; in Gulf War, 298; in Haiti, 47, 298, 473, 476, 480n38; in Somalia, 298; in Zaire, 300

Multinational Forces and Observers in Sinai, 394

Museveni, Yoweri, 485

Mwanawasa, Levy, 203

Namibia: conflicts in, 103; delay in independence for, 412–414; elec-

About the Book

The nature and scope of UN Security Council decisions—significantly changed in the post–Cold War era—have enormous implications for foreign policy. *The UN Security Council* offers a comprehensive view of the Council both internally and as a key player in world politics.

Focusing on the evolution of the Council's treatment of key issues, the authors discuss new concerns that must be accommodated in the decision-making process, the challenges of enforcement, and shifting personal and institutional factors. Case studies complement the rich thematic chapters. The book sheds much-needed light on the central events and trends of the past decade and their critical importance for the future role of the Council and the UN in the sphere of international security.

David M. Malone is president of the International Peace Academy. Currently on leave from the Canadian Foreign Service, he has served as director general of the Policy, International, and Global Issues bureaus in the Canadian Department of Foreign Affairs and International Trade (1994–1998) and as Canada's ambassador to the United Nations (1992–1994). Among his recent publications are *From Reaction to Conflict Prevention: Opportunities for the UN System* (coedited with Fen Osler Hampson) and *Decisionmaking in the UN Security Council: The Case of Haiti.*

The UN
Security Council

 *A project of the International Peace Academy*